Feathered Gods
and Fishhooks

Feathered Gods and Fishhooks

The Archaeology of Ancient Hawai'i, Revised Edition

Patrick Vinton Kirch with Mark D. McCoy

University of Hawai'i Press | Honolulu

© 2023 University of Hawaiʻi Press
All rights reserved
Printed in the United States of America

First printed, 2023

Library of Congress Cataloging-in-Publication Data

Names: Kirch, Patrick Vinton, author. | McCoy, Mark D., author.
Title: Feathered gods and fishhooks : the archaeology of ancient Hawaiʻi / Patrick Vinton Kirch with Mark D. McCoy.
Description: Revised edition. | Honolulu : University of Hawaiʻi Press, [2023] | Includes bibliographical references and index.
Identifiers: LCCN 2022056037 (print) | LCCN 2022056038 (ebook) | ISBN 9780824894498 (paperback) | ISBN 9780824894467 (pdf) | ISBN 9780824894474 (epub) | ISBN 9780824894481 (kindle edition)
Subjects: LCSH: Hawaii—Antiquities.
Classification: LCC DU624.65 .K57 2023 (print) | LCC DU624.65 (ebook) | DDC 996.9/02--dc23/eng/20221206
LC record available at https://lccn.loc.gov/2022056037
LC ebook record available at https://lccn.loc.gov/2022056038

Cover art: The reconstructed funerary temple of Hale o Keawe at Hōnaunau, Hawaiʻi. Photograph by Therese Babineau.

University of Hawaiʻi Press books are printed on acid-free paper and meet the guidelines for permanence and durability of the Council on Library Resources.

Designed by Nord Compo

To *Ka Poʻe Kahiko*
The People of Old

CONTENTS

Figures, Plates, and Tables   xiii
Preface to the Revised Edition   xxiii
Preface to the First Edition   xxv
Note on Hawaiian Words and Place Names   xxvii

Prologue   An Island Civilization   1
  Hawai'i at First Contact   2

Chapter 1   Unearthing the Hawaiian Past: The History of Archaeology in Hawai'i   7
  The Beginnings of Hawaiian Archaeology   8
  The Search for Polynesian Origins   10
  Stratigraphic Archaeology and Artifact Sequences   12
  New Directions: Settlement Patterns and Ecology   15
  From Ivory Tower to For-Profit Consulting   19
  Troubles in the Trenches   21
  New Horizons in Research and Community-Based Archaeology   23

Chapter 2   An Island World   27
  Hawaiian Landforms   29
  The Hawaiian Biota   33
  The Marine Environment   36
  Resources, Constraints, and Hazards   37
  From *Wao Akua* to *Wao Kānaka*: Transformed Landscapes   40

Chapter 3   The Evidence of the Past   46
  The Hawaiian Archaeological Landscape   46
  Seeking the Past: Archaeological Methods   51
  The Temporal Framework: Dating and Chronology   58

CHAPTER 4   **Origins** 63
    The Settlement of Oceania 64
    The Emergence of Ancestral Polynesian Culture 71
    The Great Polynesian Diaspora 73
    Dating Polynesian Arrival in Hawai'i 78
    Where Was the Homeland of the First Settlers to Hawai'i? 81

CHAPTER 5   **Hawaiian Culture History: An Overview** 85
    Integrating Archaeology with Hawaiian Oral Traditions 88
    The Foundation Period, AD 1000–1200 89
    The Late Voyaging Period, AD 1200–1400 92
    The Expansion Period, AD 1400–1600 95
    The Archaic States Period, AD 1600–1795 102
    Traditional History of the Archaic States Period 104
    Explaining Change: Process and Agency in Hawaiian History 110

CHAPTER 6   **History Sedimented in the Earth: Six Stratified Sites** 116
    Kuli'ou'ou Rockshelter (Site O1), O'ahu Island 116
    Pu'u Ali'i (Site H1), Ka Lae, Hawai'i Island 120
    Wai'ahukini Rockshelter (Site H8), Hawai'i Island 124
    Nu'alolo Rockshelter (Sites K3–K5), Kaua'i Island 127
    Bellows Dune Site (Site O18), Waimānalo, O'ahu Island 130
    Hālawa Dune Site (Site Mo-A1-3), Moloka'i Island 134

CHAPTER 7   **The Wet and the Dry: Hawaiian Agriculture, Aquaculture, and the Staple Economy** 141
    The Archaeology of Ancient Agriculture 144
    The Wet and the Dry: Contrastive Agroecosystems 145
    Valley Agroecosystems 147
    Intensive Dryland Field Systems 156
    Arboriculture 168
    Animal Husbandry 170
    Fishponds and Aquaculture 171
    Production, Surplus, and the Staple Economy 174

CHAPTER 8   "Like Shoals of Fish": Population in Ancient Hawai'i   177
    The Population of Hawai'i at Contact   178
    Demographic Characteristics of Precontact Hawaiians   179
    The Demographic History of Ancient Hawai'i   181
    Population, Land, and Intensification   184

CHAPTER 9   Technology, Craft Specialization, and the Wealth Economy   188
    Approaches to the Study of Hawaiian Material Culture   189
    Tools   190
    Fishing Gear   201
    Domestic Implements   208
    Volcanic Glass   211
    Ornaments and Decoration   213
    Other Artifacts   215
    The Wealth Economy: Craft Specialization, Social Status, and Gendered Roles   216

CHAPTER 10   The Archaeology of Everyday Life   220
    Kauhale: The Domestic Unit   220
    Resource Use and Domestic Consumption: The Contributions of Zooarchaeology and Archaeobotany   233
    Networks of Communication: Trails   239
    Inscribing the Land: Petroglyphs   242

CHAPTER 11   The Archaeology of Ritual, Power, and Death   246
    Heiau: Places of Prayer, Sacrifice, and Observation   246
    Heiau Form, Classification, and Size   255
    Heiau Chronology   260
    Heiau Orientations   263
    Landscapes of Power: The Royal Centers   266
    Hōlua Slides   269
    Fortifications and *Pu'uhonua*   270
    The Archaeology of Death: Burial Practices in Ancient Hawai'i   272

CHAPTER 12   From *Uka* to *Kai*: Five Settlement Landscapes   281
    Mākaha Valley, O'ahu   281
    Hālawa Valley, Moloka'i   286

Kawela and Makakupaiʻa Iki, Molokaʻi 290
Kahikinui, Maui 295
Lapakahi, Hawaiʻi 300

Chapter 13 Transformations: The Archaeology of Culture Contact and Colonialism 306
From Stone to Steel: Changes in Material Culture 307
The Transformation of Rural Landscapes 309
The Archaeology of Colonialism 315

Chapter 14 The Archaeology of Hawaiʻi Island 319
East Hawaiʻi: Hāmākua and Hilo 319
South Hawaiʻi: Puna and Kaʻū 323
West Hawaiʻi: Kona and Kohala 333

Chapter 15 The Archaeology of Maui, Lānaʻi, and Kahoʻolawe Islands 353
West Maui 354
East Maui 357
Lānaʻi Island 365
Kahoʻolawe Island 370

Chapter 16 The Archaeology of Molokaʻi Island 374
Kona District 376
Koʻolau District 378
Kaluakoʻi 383

Chapter 17 The Archaeology of Oʻahu Island 386
Koʻolaupoko District 388
Koʻolauloa District 394
Waialua District 396
Waiʻanae District 398
ʻEwa District 400
Kona District 403

Chapter 18 The Archaeology of Kauaʻi and Niʻihau Islands 406
Nāpali District 407
Haleleʻa District 408
Koʻolau and Puna Districts 410

Kona and Mana Districts   412
Ni'ihau Island and the Islets of Lehua and Ka'ula   413

CHAPTER 19   The Archaeology of Nihoa and Mokumanamana Islands   415

Geography and Natural Resources   415
Archaeological Sites   417
Artifacts   421
Chronology   422
External versus Internal Explanations   422

Epilogue   424

Glossary of Hawaiian Words   427
References   431
Index   485

FIGURES, PLATES, AND TABLES

Figures

P.1 The village of Makakupa in Ka'ū District, Hawai'i Island.
P.2 Diagrammatic map of a typical *ahupua'a* land division.
P.3 Hawaiian society at the time of European contact was hierarchically organized.
P.4 Detail of a Hawaiian chief wearing a feathered helmet and feathered cape.
1.1 The Bernice Pauahi Bishop Museum in Honolulu.
1.2 William T. Brigham and his staff at Bishop Museum.
1.3 Kenneth P. Emory excavating a burial cairn in Haleakalā Crater, Maui.
1.4 Kenneth P. Emory and Yosihiko Sinoto at the Pu'u Ali'i dune site, Hawai'i Island.
1.5 Excavations in progress at the Nu'alolo rockshelter, Kaua'i Island.
1.6 Excavation in progress at the Hālawa Valley dune site, Moloka'i Island.
1.7 Excavation of a postcontact house site in the Anahulu Valley, O'ahu Island.
1.8 Bishop Museum staff members visiting the Kawela project on Moloka'i Island.
2.1 Map of the main islands of the Hawaiian archipelago.
2.2 View of the geologically youthful slopes of southeast Maui.
2.3 The sea cliffs of windward Moloka'i are among the highest in the world.
2.4 The deeply incised heads of valleys on the geologically older islands form amphitheater-like basins.
2.5 The endemic *wiliwili* tree.
2.6 Sea cliffs are typical of the geologically younger islands.
2.7 The pollen diagram from Ordy Pond, O'ahu Island.
2.8 Makauwahi Cave, a sinkhole in Pleistocene sandstone deposits on Kaua'i Island.
2.9 Charcoal frequency diagram from Kaupikiawa rockshelter, Kalaupapa, Moloka'i Island.
3.1 Pavement of waterworn cobbles and gravel (*'ili'ili*) incorporating a *papamū* for playing the *kōnane* game.
3.2 Lava-tube shelters at Kalāhuipua'a on Hawai'i Island.
3.3 Sand dune site at Kawela, Moloka'i Island.
3.4 A settlement landscape consists of multiple, hierarchically clustered components.
3.5 The plane table with telescopic alidade is used by archaeologists to make plan maps of Hawaiian stone architecture.

3.6 Excavation of a habitation terrace at Kahikinui, Maui Island (site KIP-752).
3.7 Completed excavation of a house site in the Anahulu Valley, Oʻahu Island.
3.8 Carbonized remains of sweet potato tubers from habitation sites in Kahikinui, Maui Island.
3.9 A branch coral head exposed by collapse of a *heiau* wall in Kahikinui, Maui Island.
4.1 Map of the Pacific, showing the Polynesian triangle.
4.2 Chart showing the diversification of the main branches of the Austronesian languages from Proto Austronesian.
4.3 Lapita pottery is characterized by dentate-stamped decoration.
4.4 Artifacts from the Ancestral Polynesian site of Toʻaga, Ofu Island, American Samoa.
4.5 The replicated voyaging canoe *Hōkūleʻa*.
4.6 Bayesian calibration of radiocarbon dates from the Bellows dune site (O18) at Waimānalo, Oʻahu Island.
4.7 Early Eastern Polynesian artifacts from the Marquesas Islands.
4.8 Chart showing the diversification of the Polynesian languages from the ancestral Proto Polynesian language.
5.1 Waipiʻo Valley was the ancestral seat of the ruling chiefs of Hawaiʻi Island.
5.2 The birthing stones at Kūkaniloko on central Oʻahu.
5.3 The cinder cone of Kaʻuiki at Hāna, Maui Island, a natural defensive position.
5.4 The Hale o Keawe sepulchral temple at Hōnaunau, Hawaiʻi Island.
5.5 The massive temple platform of Piʻilanihale at Hāna, Maui Island.
5.6 The war canoes of Kalaniʻōpuʻu, king of Hawaiʻi Island, greeted Captain James Cook at Kealakekua Bay.
6.1 View of Kuliʻouʻou rockshelter.
6.2 Kenneth P. Emory of Bishop Museum excavating in Kuliʻouʻou rockshelter (site O1) in 1950.
6.3 The Puʻu Aliʻi sand dune site (H1) at the beginning of excavations in 1953.
6.4 Excavations in progress at the Puʻu Aliʻi sand dune site (H1) site in 1954.
6.5 Bayesian calibration of radiocarbon dates from the Puʻu Aliʻi dune site (H1), Hawaiʻi Island.
6.6 Artifacts from the Puʻu Aliʻi sand dune site (H1).
6.7 Frequencies of notched and knobbed two-piece fishhooks from sites in the South Point region, Hawaiʻi Island.
6.8 Stone-faced habitation terraces at Nuʻalolo Kai, Kauaʻi Island.
6.9 Excavations in progress at the deeply stratified Nuʻalolo rockshelter site.
6.10 Bayesian calibration of radiocarbon dates from the Nuʻalolo rockshelter site, Kauaʻi Island.
6.11 Artifacts from the Nuʻalolo rockshelter site, Kauaʻi Island.
6.12 View of stratification in the Bellows dune site (O18), Oʻahu Island
6.13 Excavations in progress in the Bellows dune site (O18), Oʻahu Island.
6.14 Fishing gear from the Bellows dune site (O18), Oʻahu Island.
6.15 Coconut grater from the Bellows dune site (O18), Oʻahu Island.

6.16 Basalt artifacts from the Bellows dune site (O18), Oʻahu Island.
6.17 View of Hālawa Bay, Molokaʻi Island.
6.18 Bayesian calibration of radiocarbon dates from the Hālawa dune site (Mo-A1-3), Molokaʻi Island.
6.19 Round-ended house foundation at the Hālawa dune site, Molokaʻi Island.
6.20 Plan of the upper sector in Mound B of the Hālawa dune site, Molokaʻi Island.
6.21 Conjectural reconstruction of a round-ended house at the Hālawa dune site, Molokaʻi Island.
6.22 Basalt adzes from the Hālawa dune site, Molokaʻi Island.
7.1 Hanalei Valley, in the Haleleʻa District of Kauaʻi Island.
7.2 Stone-faced terraces in Nuʻalolo ʻĀina Valley, Kauaʻi Island.
7.3 The façade of a pondfield terrace in Hālawa Valley, Molokaʻi Island.
7.4 Map of the lower portion of Hālawa Valley, Molokaʻi Island.
7.5 Map of a taro irrigation system at ʻIli Kapuahilua in the Anahulu Valley, Oʻahu Island.
7.6 Map of a system of taro pondfields in Hālawa Valley, Molokaʻi Island.
7.7 Diagrammatic sketch of four types of irrigated pondfield systems.
7.8 Stratigraphic section through a pondfield terrace at Waikolu Valley, Molokaʻi Island.
7.9 Stratigraphic section through pondfields in Hālawa Valley, in Kohala District of Hawaiʻi Island.
7.10 Low stone and earthen embankments define the borders of dryland fields in Kaiholena *ahupuaʻa,* Hawaiʻi Island.
7.11 A partially carbonized sweet potato tuber excavated from a habitation shelter in the uplands of Lapakahi.
7.12 Schematic map of a portion of the Lapakahi field system.
7.13 LiDAR image of a portion of the leeward Kohala Field System in Kaiholena *ahupuaʻa,* Hawaiʻi Island.
7.14 A soil-sampling transect across the leeward Kohala Field System.
7.15 A *kuaiwi* wall in the Amy Greenwell Ethnobotanical Garden, part of the Kona field system.
7.16 Stratigraphic section through a *kuaiwi* wall in the Amy Greenwell Ethnobotanical Garden, Hawaiʻi Island.
7.17 Map of Kaupō, Maui, showing dryland field system walls.
7.18 The wall of a *loko kuapā* fishpond along the south coast of Molokaʻi Island.
8.1 Curves for coastal and inland population on Hawaiʻi Island.
8.2 Radiocarbon date frequency curves for four islands.
8.3 Numbers of radiocarbon-dated habitation complexes in Kahikinui District of Maui Island.
8.4 Simulated population growth curves for hypothetical *ahupuaʻa* in the Kohala region of Hawaiʻi Island.
8.5 Simulated curves of food availability with two hypothetical *ahupuaʻa* in the Kohala region of Hawaiʻi Island.

9.1   Typical Hawaiian basalt adzes with quadrangular cross sections and pronounced tangs, from Kuliʻouʻou rockshelter on Oʻahu Island.
9.2   A workshop area outside a rockshelter at the Mauna Kea adze quarry.
9.3   An adze-grinding boulder in Hālawa Valley, Molokaʻi.
9.4   Five adze preforms with triangular cross-sections, from Hāʻiku, Maui Island.
9.5   Basalt chisel, chisel fragment, and chisel preform from Oʻahu rockshelter sites.
9.6   Large debitage pile of flakes and discarded adze blanks at the Mauna Kea adze quarry site.
9.7   Coral abraders from the Hālawa dune site, Molokaʻi Island.
9.8   Large abraders of scoriaceous lava from Kalāhuipuaʻa, Hawaiʻi Island.
9.9   Abraders of slate-pencil sea urchin spines from the Hālawa dune site, Molokaʻi Island.
9.10 Hammerstone with pecked finger grips, from Lānaʻi Island.
9.11 Stone awls from Oʻahu rockshelter sites.
9.12 Large wooden hooks found in a cache at Kalāhuipuaʻa, Hawaiʻi Island.
9.13 Terminology and classification of Hawaiian fishhooks.
9.14 Large two-piece fishhooks of human bone.
9.15 Bone and pearl-shell fishhooks from Kauaʻi Island sites.
9.16 Bottom and top views of a cowrie-shell octopus lure.
9.17 Bone fishhooks from the Kawākiu Bay site, Molokaʻi Island.
9.18 Persistence and change in Hawaiian fishing gear.
9.19 Two-piece fishhooks of bone from the Hālawa dune site, Molokaʻi Island.
9.20 Relative changes in fishhook head types at sites at South Point, Hawaiʻi Island.
9.21 Stirrup and ring pounders from Kauaʻi Island.
9.22 Awls and picks of bone from Oʻahu rockshelter sites.
9.23 Scrapers of bone, shell, and stone, from Oʻahu rockshelter sites.
9.24 Flakes of volcanic glass from the Waimea-Kawaihae area, Hawaiʻi Island.
9.25 Drilled dog canine teeth from the Hālawa dune site, Molokaʻi Island.
9.26 Fragments of *lei niho palaoa* neck ornaments from Kauaʻi Island.
9.27 Tattooing combs from Oʻahu rockshelter sites.
9.28 Stone tripping club from a habitation site in Hālawa Valley, Molokaʻi Island.
9.29 Sea-urchin-spine images from the Kamohiʻo rockshelter, Kahoʻolawe Island.
9.30 Feathered image of the war-god Kū.
10.1 "An Inland View in Atooi" by John Webber, artist on Captain James Cook's third voyage.
10.2 Plan of a C-shaped shelter at Waikoloa, Hawaiʻi Island.
10.3 A small C-shaped shelter in the Mākaha Valley, Oʻahu Island.
10.4 A stone-outlined hearth in the lower Mākaha Valley, Oʻahu Island.
10.5 A cupboard feature in a shelter at Kawela, Molokaʻi Island.
10.6 Keae rockshelter (site Oa-D6-52) in the Anahulu Valley, Oʻahu Island.
10.7 Plan of site Mo-A1-765 in Hālawa Valley, Molokaʻi Island.
10.8 Plan of site MKI-56 at Makiloa, Hawaiʻi Island.
10.9 Plan of site KIP-117, a priest's dwelling house in Kahikinui, Maui Island.

10.10 View of site KIP-752 in the Kīpapa area of Kahikinui, Maui Island.
10.11 Frequencies of vertebrate faunal remains in household sites in Kahikinui, Maui Island.
10.12 A stepping-stone trail of waterworn cobbles.
10.13 A trail of Apple's "Type B" at ʻAnaehoʻomalu, Hawaiʻi Island.
10.14 A portion of the petroglyph field at Puakō, Hawaiʻi Island.
10.15 Petroglyphs pecked on a group of boulders at Kawela, Molokaʻi Island.
10.16 Petroglyphs continued to be made after the introduction of writing and the Hawaiian alphabet in the early 1820s.
10.17 Examples of petroglyph groups in Kahikinui, Maui Island.
11.1 Interior of a *heiau* near Waimea, on Kauaʻi Island, as drawn by John Webber, artist on Captain James Cook's third voyage in 1778.
11.2 An upright, waterworn stone (*pōhaku o Kāne*) surrounded by offerings of branch coral heads.
11.3 The interior of site AUW-11, a *koʻa* enclosure at Auwahi, Maui Island.
11.4 Plan of a *hale o Lono* temple site at Kawela, Molokaʻi Island.
11.5 Layout of a *luakini* temple, based on ethnohistoric accounts.
11.6 Āleʻaleʻa temple platform at Hōnaunau, Hawaiʻi Island.
11.7 Plan of Kāneʻaki Heiau, a *luakini* temple in Mākaha Valley, Oʻahu Island.
11.8 Stages of construction of Kāneʻaki Heiau in Mākaha Valley, Oʻahu Island.
11.9 View of site ALE-140, a notched enclosure *heiau* in Kahikinui, Maui Island.
11.10 Aerial photo of site KIP-1, an elongated double-court *heiau,* in Kīpapa, Kahikinui, Maui Island.
11.11 View of site NAK-30, a platform type *heiau* in Kahikinui, Maui Island.
11.12 The rank-size distribution of *heiau* in Kahikinui and Kaupō Districts of Maui Island.
11.13 Oxcal plot of AMS radiocarbon dates from *heiau* sites in Kahikinui and Kaupō, Maui Island.
11.14 Temporal distribution of ^{230}Th dates on branch corals from *heiau* sites in Kahikinui and Kaupō, Maui Island.
11.15 The eastern horizon as viewed from site WF-AUW-403, a notched *heiau* in Auwahi, Maui Island.
11.16 Map of Kamehameha's royal center at Honolulu.
11.17 Map of the royal center at Hōnaunau, Hawaiʻi Island.
11.18 A cache of slingstones on a defensive terrace at Kawela, Molokaʻi Island.
11.19 Plan of site 900, a refuge cave inland of Kīholo, Hawaiʻi Island.
11.20 Plan of Forbes Cave, Kawaihae, Hawaiʻi Island.
11.21 The Hale o Keawe at Hōnaunau, Hawaiʻi Island.
12.1 Map of Mākaha Valley, Oʻahu Island.
12.2 Map of a portion of the lower Mākaha Valley, Oʻahu Island.
12.3 Kāneʻaki Heiau in Mākaha Valley, Oʻahu Island.
12.4 Hālawa Valley, at the eastern end of Molokaʻi Island.
12.5 Map of the *ʻili* of Kapana in Hālawa Valley, Molokaʻi Island.

12.6 Stone-faced terraces in Kapana, Hālawa Valley.
12.7 Kawela Gulch, in leeward Moloka'i Island.
12.8 The settlement pattern of Kawela and Makakupai'a *ahupua'a* in south central Moloka'i Island.
12.9 Map of residential complex G at Kawela, Moloka'i Island.
12.10 Map of residential complex H at Kawela, Moloka'i Island.
12.11 An alignment of upright slabs at residential complex H at Kawela, Moloka'i Island.
12.12 A high-status residential complex at Kawela, Moloka'i Island.
12.13 View of Kahikinui District on southeastern Maui Island.
12.14 Map of Kahikinui District on Maui Island.
12.15 Map of site KIP-1400, a large swale used for dryland farming in upland Kahikinui, Maui Island.
12.16 Aerial view of site KIP-1010 in the uplands of Kahikini, Maui Island.
12.17 Map of the *heiau* complex in upland Naka'ohu, Kahiknui, Maui Island.
12.18 View of a portion of Koai'e village site at Lapakahi, Hawai'i Island.
12.19 Map of a portion of the upland field system in Lapakahi *ahupua'a*, Hawai'i Island.
12.20 Plan showing three phases in the use of a field shelter in the uplands of Lapakahi, Hawai'i Island.
13.1 Map of the middle portion of the Anahulu Valley, O'ahu Island.
13.2 The foundations of Kalua's house site in the Anahulu Valley, O'ahu Island.
13.3 Aerial view of the small hamlet of Uliuli in Kahikinui, Maui.
13.4 A portion of the interior wall of Fort Elizabeth at Waimea, Kaua'i Island.
14.1 Map of Hawai'i Island, showing sites and major places mentioned in the text.
14.2 A simple shrine of upright slabs near the Mauna Kea adze quarry.
14.3 Plan of Ahu o 'Umi, a temple situated on the interior plateau of Hawai'i Island.
14.4 Waha'ula Heiau in Puna District, Hawai'i Island.
14.5 Petroglyphs at Pu'uloa, Hawai'i Island.
14.6 A cache of barkcloth (*kapa*) beaters in a shelter cave at Hilina Pali, Hawai'i Island.
14.7 Human footprints in volcanic ash near Kilauea volcano, Hawai'i Island.
14.8 Artificial hole at Ka Lae, Hawai'i, used to moor fishing canoes.
14.9 Artifacts excavated from sites at Wai'ahukini, Hawai'i Island.
14.10 Map of a chiefly residential complex at Wai'ahukini, Hawai'i Island.
14.11 Map of the *pu'uhonua* and *heiau* complex at Hōnaunau, Hawai'i Island.
14.12 The "Great Wall" at Hōnaunau.
14.13 The Hale o Keawe mortuary temple at Hōnaunau.
14.14 Stone-lined fishpond at Hōnaunau, Hawai'i Island.
14.15 The war canoes of Hawai'i Island king Kalani'ōpu'u at Kealakekua Bay, Hawai'i Island.
14.16 Ahu'ena Heiau at Kamakahonu, Hawai'i Island
14.17 Maka'ōpio Heiau at Honōkahau, Hawai'i Island.

14.18 Petroglyhs on *pāhoehoe* lava at ʻAnaehoʻomalu, Hawaiʻi Island.
14.19 A lava-tube rockshelter at Kalāhuipuaʻa, Hawaiʻi Island.
14.20 A cache of wooden fishhooks found in a rockshelter at Kalāhuipuaʻa, Hawaiʻi Island.
14.21 Basin-shaped depressions in scoriaceous lava inland of ʻAnaehoʻomalu, Hawaiʻi Island.
14.22 Puʻukoholā Heiau at Kawaihae, Hawaiʻi Island.
14.23 Map of Kohala peninsula, Hawaiʻi Island.
14.24 Large boulder at Kukuipahu Heiau, Hawaiʻi Island, with raised relief carvings of human figures and turtles.
14.25 Interior of Moʻokini Heiau near ʻUpolu Point, Hawaiʻi Island.
15.1 Map of Maui Island, showing sites and major places mentioned in the text.
15.2 Petroglyphs at Olowalu, Maui Island.
15.3 The main terrace of Halekiʻi Heiau, Maui Island.
15.4 Map of Piʻilanihale Heiau, Maui Island.
15.5 The main façade of Piʻilanihale Heiau, Maui Island.
15.6 The *pānānā* at Hanamauloa, Kahikinui, Maui Island.
15.7 Wooden handle for a shark-tooth knife from a fishing shrine at Palauea, Maui Island.
15.8 Map of Lānaʻi Island, showing sites and major places mentioned in the text.
15.9 Perspective sketch of a Lānaʻi house site with interior fireplace.
15.10 Halulu Heiau at Kaunolū, Lānaʻi Island.
15.11 Map of the site complex at Kaunolū, Lānaʻi Island.
15.12 Bird-men petroglyphs near Halulu Heiau at Kaunolū, Lānaʻi Island.
15.13 Bone trolling-lure points excavated from Lānaʻi sites.
15.14 Map of Kahoʻolawe Island, showing sites and major places mentioned in the text.
15.15 Preforms, reject cores, and flakes litter the surface at the Puʻu Moiwi adze quarry, Kahoʻolawe Island.
16.1 Map of Molokaʻi Island, showing sites and major places mentioned in the text.
16.2 Kanoa fishpond at Kawela, along the southern Molokaʻi Island coastline.
16.3 The eastern facade of Kaluakapiʻioho Heiau.
16.4 A terraced platform shrine at Kawela, Molokaʻi Island.
16.5 Plan of site NI-6 at Nihoa, Molokaʻi Island.
16.6 Ka Ule o Nānāhoa at Palaʻau, Molokaʻi Island.
16.7 Na Imu Kalua ʻUa at Naʻiwa, Molokaʻi Island.
16.8 Rockshelter site Mo. 1 at Kawaʻaloa Bay, Molokaʻi Island.
16.9 Bone fishhooks from site Mo. 1 at Kawaʻaloa Bay, Molokaʻi.
17.1 Map of Oʻahu Island, showing sites and major places mentioned in the text.
17.2 Paleogeographic map of the Kawainui and Kaelepulu area, Oʻahu Island.
17.3 Ulupō Heiau consists of a massive stone platform overlooking adjacent Kawainui Marsh.
17.4 Heʻeia fishpond in Kāneʻohe Bay, Oʻahu Island.
17.5 Pig burial and earth oven at Kualoa, Oʻahu Island.

17.6 Excavation in progress at the Kahana Valley sand dune site, Oʻahu Island.
17.7 View of the middle sector of the Anahulu Valley, Oʻahu Island.
17.8 A large rockshelter in the Anahulu Valley, Oʻahu Island.
17.9 View over the upper court of Puʻuomahuka Heiau, Oʻahu Island.
17.10 A stone-walled *heiau* enclosure in the Hālawa Valley, Oʻahu Island.
17.11 Artificial fosses cut into a ridge at Nuʻuanu Pali.
17.12 A boulder with rare raised-relief carvings, originally from Moanalua Valley, Oʻahu Island.
18.1 Map of Kauaʻi Island, showing sites and major places mentioned in the text.
18.2 The *kahua* or platform for *hula* performance at Keʻe, Hāʻena, Kauaʻi Island.
18.3 View of a portion of the main court of Poliʻahu Heiau at Wailua, Kauaʻi Island.
18.4 A portion of Kīkīaola, showing the cut-and-dressed stonework.
19.1 Map of Nihoa Island, showing the location of archaeological sites.
19.2 Map of Mokumanamana Island, showing the location of archaeological sites.
19.3 View of Nihoa site 50.
19.4 View of Nihoa site 43, a stone-faced habitation terrace.
19.5 An area of agricultural terracing on Nihoa Island.
19.6 Stone images from Mokumanamana Island.
19.7 Sketch and plan map of Mokumanamana site 13.
19.8 Stone adzes and a sinker collected on Nihoa and Mokumanamana Islands during the Tanager Expedition.

Color Plates *(follows page 260)*

1 The Nāpali coast of Kauaʻi Island.
2 An irrigated pondfield or *loʻi* in the Waipiʻo Valley, Hawaiʻi Island.
3 View of a portion of the leeward Kohala Field System as seen from Puʻu Kehena.
4 Distribution of areas of high potential for irrigated and intensive dryland agroecosystems.
5 Aerial photograph of a portion of the Kaupō field system on Maui Island.
6 Close-up view of the surface of the Nuʻu adze quarry in Kaupō, Maui.
7 A Hawaiian chief, wearing a feathered cloak and helmet, as drawn by Jacques Arago in 1819.
8 Kapana Heiau in Hālawa Valley, Molokaʻi.
9 Stone-faced agricultural terraces in Kapana, Hālawa Valley, Molokaʻi Island.
10 Plan of Kukuipahu Heiau in Kohala, Hawaiʻi Island.
11 The main facade of Piʻilanihale Heiau in Hāna, Maui Island.
12 The *pānānā* at Hanamauloa, Kahikinui, Maui Island.
13 Hōkūkano Heiau commands a view over the south Molokaʻi coastline.
14 ʻIliʻiliʻōpae Heiau at Mapulehu, Molokaʻi Island.
15 The sunrise illuminates the narrow, barren ridgeline of Mokumanamana Island.
16 The steep topography of Nihoa Island is dotted with stone-faced terraces.

Tables

2.1 Geographic characteristics of the main Hawaiian Islands.
2.2 Approximate numbers of endemic and indigenous species of the Hawaiian terrestrial biota (includes extinct species).
3.1 A simplified classification of Hawaiian archaeological sites.
5.1 The Hawaiian cultural sequence.
5.2 Approximate chronology and sequence for some principal rulers of Oʻahu, Maui, and Hawaiʻi islands.
7.1 Polynesian plant introductions to the Hawaiian Islands.
7.2 Estimated areas (km^2) of irrigated and intensive dryland agroecosystems.
9.1 Major adze quarries of the Hawaiian Islands.
11.1 Some major *luakini heiau*.

PREFACE TO THE REVISED EDITION

Four decades ago, while I was a member of Bishop Museum's research staff and engaged with archaeological projects on Oʻahu, Molokaʻi, and Hawaiʻi Islands, I set out to write the first book-length synthesis of Hawaiian archaeology. The opportunity to write the first edition of *Feathered Gods and Fishhooks* arose when I was invited to teach a class in Hawaiian archaeology at the University of Hawaiʻi, Mānoa. Following each lecture, I would sit at the typewriter in my Dean Hall office, endeavoring to put into prose what I had been discussing with the class earlier that morning. My intended audience was not only future university classes but the wider public in Hawaiʻi and beyond whom I knew were curious about what archaeologists had uncovered of the Hawaiian past.

At that time, in the early 1980s, archaeology in Hawaiʻi was in the midst of a transition. What had formerly been a largely academic enterprise carried out by a handful of scholars (primarily at Bishop Museum and the University of Hawaiʻi) was rapidly changing into what we then called "contract archaeology." The term arose from the fact that archaeologists were now contracted by federal and state agencies, and by private developers, to consult on the presence and significance of cultural sites likely to be affected by proposed land developments. (We now call this kind of archaeology "cultural resource management," or CRM for short.) Bishop Museum increasingly took on such projects, while other archaeologists began setting up their for-profit consulting firms. This activity generated a significant amount of new data and reports, which I endeavored to incorporate into my book, together with the results of traditional academic studies.

Over the ensuing decades, the first edition of *Feathered Gods and Fishhooks* has become something of a classic, used as an introduction to the field by several generations of archaeologists in Hawaiʻi. As knowledge of the Hawaiian past increased, and in some respects changed significantly, however, the book also became outdated in several respects. Meanwhile, the literature of Hawaiian archaeology—both published and especially the unpublished reports of the CRM consultants—continued to grow exponentially.

I had, in fact, intended to revise *Feathered Gods and Fishhooks* several times over the past decades; in spite of good intentions something always seemed to get in the way. Eventually, I invited my former student and colleague Mark McCoy to aid me in the daunting task of reviewing the ever-expanding body of CRM reports, to identify the gems within a mass of descriptive detail that would be worth incorporating in a new synthesis. Mark spent many hours in the library of the State Historic Preservation Division scanning reports and making notes; without his efforts this revised edition would not have been possible. Mark also took the lead in drafting chapters 14 through 19.

In 2019, after thirty-five years of living on the West Coast, I returned to my home islands of Hawaiʻi, thanks to an offer from the University of Hawaiʻi to join their faculty. Thus, coming full-circle, I find myself again teaching my course in Hawaiian archaeology, providing the impetus to write this revised edition. Although still based in Dean Hall (some things are constant), I now write on a computer, not a typewriter, a reminder of how much things have changed over four decades. In chapter 1, we review some of the major changes in archaeological practice in Hawaiʻi.

As with the first edition, my goal for this revision remains that of providing a synthesis that avoids unnecessary jargon and is comprehensible to the interested layperson yet is sufficiently detailed to be useful to the professional archaeologist. With Mark McCoy's assistance, I have tried to canvass the now vast literature on Hawaiian archaeology—published and unpublished—incorporating those findings and analyses over the past forty years that have advanced our understanding of the Hawaiian past. Not every report or article could be cited, but we trust that nothing truly significant has been ignored. Now—even more than in the early 1980s—the need for synthesis of hundreds of archaeological surveys and reports is critical.

My career in Hawaiian archaeology has spanned fifty-nine years, beginning with my fledgling and somewhat precocious excavation, in the summer of 1964, of a test pit at the mouth of Molokaʻi's Hālawa Valley. Through the decades at Bishop Museum and then the University of California, Berkeley, and now finally at the University of Hawaiʻi, I have never ceased to explore and investigate the Hawaiian past. I have been privileged to have led this life of intellectual engagement, and to have been able to share my experiences with so many colleagues, students, and friends. I regard this revised edition of *Feathered Gods and Fishhooks* as a part of my *kuleana,* what I owe to the islands of Hawaiʻi Nei and her people.

For reading and providing critical comments on the draft of this revised edition, I thank Steve Athens, Paul Cleghorn, Sara Collins, Peter Mills, and Mara Mulrooney. As always, Masako Ikeda at the University of Hawaiʻi Press has been an enthusiastic and supportive editor.

Patrick Vinton Kirch
Maunawili, Oʻahu, October 2021

PREFACE TO THE FIRST EDITION

Archaeology is not a particularly new approach to studying the Hawaiian past. Excavations were conducted on Kahoʻolawe Island as early as 1913, and the last three decades have witnessed a virtual explosion of archaeological surveys and excavations. The literally hundreds of tested or excavated sites, and the thousands more that have been recorded, are reported in an impressive scholarly and scientific literature that now runs to more than one thousand bibliographic entries. For the most part, this literature exists as articles in scholarly journals and monographs or, all too frequently, as typescript reports issued in limited copies through several "contract archaeology" programs. These sources are often unavailable to the general public, and many of them are difficult even for the professional to access. Given such a lengthy history of intensive archaeological research into the Hawaiian past, it is all the more surprising that not a single general synthesis exists to summarize the field for students and the informed public.

For some time, I have been convinced of the need for an up-to-date review of Hawaiian archaeology and prehistory, in sufficient detail to be of use to students and professionals wishing to gain entrée to the Hawaiian archaeological scene, yet written in nontechnical language so as to be intelligible to the interested nonprofessional. In my experience, a large segment of the Hawaiian public is genuinely fascinated with the discoveries and results of work in Hawaiian archaeology. Furthermore, the Hawaiian people themselves—as part of what is often termed the "Hawaiian Renaissance"—have taken the lead in renewed efforts to preserve and enhance aspects of their cultural heritage. Professional archaeologists, in confining their writing to scholarly journals or reports prepared largely with other archaeologists in mind, do an injustice to this public, who, as taxpayers, bear the brunt for a good deal of the archaeological research funded either through grants or by federal and state contract archaeology projects. Like my colleagues, I have found that the pressures of preparing definitive reports and monographs for the permanent archaeological record leave all too little time for dissemination of research results to a wider audience. Yet this is an obligation that cannot be shirked. I undertook to write the present book, therefore, with the conviction that we professionals owe it to society as a whole to set out the fruits of our investigations.

This volume does not pretend to be a definitive synthesis of Hawaiian archaeology and prehistory, a task that will require a great deal of patient sifting of the volumes of evidence accumulated over the past several decades. My present aim is more modest: to summarize the broad outlines of Hawaiian prehistory as seen through the eyes of a single archaeologist who has spent nearly two decades attempting to understand the Hawaiian past, first as a student, and later as a professional researcher. The result doubtless reflects certain personal interests and biases, but I have tried to cover all important aspects of the field.

In my own quest to learn about the Hawaiian past, I have been especially fortunate to have been associated since the beginning with the Bernice Pauahi Bishop Museum—the leading institution in Hawaiian archaeology for nearly a century—and to have had as my colleagues members of its eminent staff. Without the intimate contact with the museum's collections, records, and especially its staff, this book could not have been attempted in its present form. In particular, I owe a debt to my fellow staff members, Kenneth P. Emory, Yosihiko H. Sinoto, Douglas E. Yen (now of the Australian National University), Roger C. Green (now of the University of Auckland), Patrick C. McCoy, and Marion Kelly. After years of close association, including countless "brainstorming" sessions both in the field and in the laboratory, it is often difficult to know where one's own ideas begin and those of others take off. To all of these colleagues and friends, I owe an immeasurable debt.

Many other scholars and friends have over the years contributed their knowledge, given access to unpublished reports and manuscripts, allowed me to visit their excavations or to study their collections, and have in countless other ways contributed to my understanding of Hawaiian prehistory. I cannot name them all here, but the following are due special acknowledgment: Suzy Allen, Russ Apple, Bill Ayres, Bill Barrera, Dorothy Barrère, Pat Beggerly, Peter Chapman, Carl Christensen, Jeff Clark, Steve Clark, Paul Cleghorn, Ross Cordy, Neal Crozier, Bert Davis, Tom Dye, Tim Earle, P. Bion Griffin, E. S. C. Handy, Violet Hansen, Allan Haun, Gil Hendren, Rob Hommon, Mikk Kaschko, Bill Kikuchi, Ed Ladd, Holly McEldowney, Maury Morgenstein, Buddy Neller, T. Stell Newman, Larry Olson, Storrs Olson, Dick Pearson, Rowland Reeve, Tom Riley, Paul Rosendahl, Marshall Sahlins, Rose Schilt, Ragnar Schousboe, Aki Sinoto, Lloyd Soehren, Elspeth Sterling, Cappy Summers, Margaret Titcomb, Myra Tomonari-Tuggle, Dave Tuggle, Marshall Weisler, and Martha Yent.

I would also like to acknowledge the Department of Anthropology at the University of Hawai'i, and its chairman, Richard Lieban, for twice inviting me to teach Hawaiian archaeology and prehistory at the university. The present book has been a direct outgrowth of the lectures originally developed during those courses. My students in Anthropology 460 are also due credit for encouraging me to expand the lectures into book form.

For assistance during the preparation of this volume, I want to thank Eric Komori for his extraordinary efforts in preparing line illustrations, Peter Gilpin for printing a large number of photographs and for shooting many of the better artifact illustrations, and Irene Takata for typing rough drafts of much of the manuscript. Roger Green, Sara Collins, Rob Hommon, and Marshall Weisler kindly read and commented on the draft manuscript. I am especially grateful to Bonnie Clause for the special care she took in editing the manuscript.

The Department of Anthropology at the B. P. Bishop Museum, and its chairman, Dr. Y. Sinoto, have been especially generous in allowing me to reproduce a large number of photographs and line illustrations from the department's archaeology collection and from departmental publications. This assistance is gratefully acknowledged. Similarly, Bishop Museum Photo Archives also has permitted use of a number of older negatives in its collection. I would also like to thank Jo Lynn Gunness, Roger Green, Paul Cleghorn, Toni Han, Yosihiko Sinoto, Paul Rosendahl, Chris Kraft, Bion Griffin, and Suzy Allen for supplying me with individual negatives and illustrations.

Honolulu, 1983

NOTE ON HAWAIIAN WORDS AND PLACE NAMES

Hawaiian words throughout this book have been rendered according to the spelling in Mary Kawena Pukui and Samuel H. Elbert, *Hawaiian Dictionary,* revised and enlarged edition (Honolulu: University of Hawaiʻi Press, 1986). Hawaiian place names are rendered according to Mary Kawena Pukui, Samuel H. Elbert, and Esther T. Mookini, *Place Names of Hawaii*, revised and expanded edition (Honolulu: University of Hawaiʻi Press, 1974).

PROLOGUE
An Island Civilization

Around the late tenth or early eleventh century AD—the dating could yet be pinned down more precisely—a large double-hulled voyaging canoe, held together with flexible sennit lashings and propelled by woven pandanus mat sails shaped like giant crab claws, set a northerly course from central Eastern Polynesia, perhaps the Marquesas Islands. The crew had loaded taro, coconut, bananas, and other useful plants in the craft's deep hulls, and lashed cages holding dogs, pigs, and fowl to the deck. This Polynesian ark and the few dozen people aboard her were bound on a voyage of discovery and colonization—a voyage such as the world had not before witnessed.

More than 4,000 km of ocean would be crossed before the would-be explorers sighted land again. The voyage probably took nearly a month, with precious supplies dwindling as they scanned the trackless North Pacific, day after day, in search of land. What motives inspired these explorers on such an arduous search into the unknown? Defeat in war? Drought and famine in the homeland? Or simply the desire and courage to seek new lands? We can conjecture, but we will never know for certain. What is clear is that after weeks of dauntlessly forging on into the unknown, this voyaging canoe, her design the legacy of generations of expert canoe builders and seafarers, came upon a remote and extensive group of islands never before seen by humans. The snow-capped heights of Mauna Kea and Mauna Loa—if these were the first landfalls to be sighted—must have evoked strange emotions among these islanders who hailed from tropical climes. The name of the Polynesian navigator who directed this vessel to these shores has been lost in the long night of tradition, but the name bestowed upon the islands, in remembrance of an ancestral homeland, has remained: Hawai'i, a variant of the ancient name Hawaiki. Here in this fertile archipelago, the generations who descended from these first settlers would fashion an island civilization that flourished, unknown to the outside world, for nearly 800 years.

On January 18, 1778, the *Resolution* and the *Discovery* of His Britannic Majesty's Navy, under the command of the already famous Captain James Cook, tacked northward at latitude 21°N en route with orders from the Admiralty to undertake explorations for the fabled Northwest Passage. Under sail 39 days since leaving the Society Islands, a pang of excitement rippled through the *Resolution* when the masthead lookout shouted that two high islands could be seen to the northeast. Suspense mounted throughout the day and night as the ships tacked toward landfalls previously unseen by European eyes. Coasting off the southern shore of the larger island the next morning, several canoes ventured out to inspect the foreign vessels. In the words of Lieutenant King of the *Resolution,* "What all the more surprised us, was, our catching the Sound of Otaheite [Tahitian] words in their speech" (Beaglehole 1967, 264n). Cook immediately knew that they had stumbled upon a northern extension of the vast "Polynesian Nation." The island was Kaua'i; Cook's ships had pierced a shroud of isolation that had separated Hawaiian civilization form the outside world for at least three centuries.

How had these Polynesians, whose speech was so clearly related to that of Tahiti, come to these island shores, and at what time in antiquity? Cook, knowing well the vastness of the Pacific, mused in his journal, "How shall we account for this Nation spreading itself so far over this Vast ocean? We find them from New Zealand to the South, to these islands to the North and from Easter Island to the Hebrides [Vanuatu]" (Beaglehole 1967, 279). This puzzle was to consume the efforts of scholars over the next two centuries. Indeed, the quest to uncover the Hawaiian past—the origins and history of this island civilization—remains one of the most absorbing avenues of Pacific anthropology.

Hawai'i at First Contact

At first contact with Europeans, the Hawaiian Islands supported the largest and most densely settled population of any Polynesian island group. Debates have raged over the exact number of Hawaiians living in 1778 (Stannard 1989), before the ravages of foreign diseases took their toll, but increasingly a figure of at least 500,000, and perhaps more, appears likely (Kirch and Rallu, eds., 2007; David A. Swanson 2019). Dispersed over all the main islands, the Hawaiian population was densely clustered in the "salubrious zones" where conditions favored intensive agriculture and fishing (fig. P.1). The windward valleys of O'ahu and Kaua'i, the southern coastline of Moloka'i, the well-watered slopes of East

FIGURE P.1 The village of Makakupa in Ka'ū District, Hawai'i Island, as seen by members of Vancouver's expedition in 1792–1794. Note the intensively cultivated fields outlined with stone walls. *(Lithograph by Thomas Heddington, from George Vancouver, 1798, Voyage of Discovery to the North Pacific Ocean, London)*

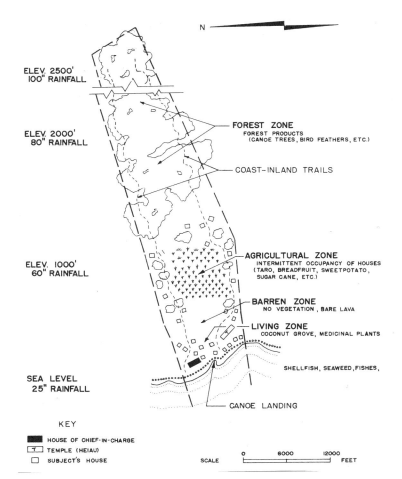

FIGURE P.2
Diagrammatic map of a typical *ahupua'a* land division on the island of Hawai'i, cross-cutting all of the major environmental zones from the coast to the uplands. *(After Apple 1965)*

Maui and the leeward districts of Kohala and Kona on Hawai'i were regions that supported tens of thousands. Drier areas, especially the leeward islands of Lāna'i and Kaho'olawe, were more sparsely populated.

Intensive agriculture and coastal fishponds fueled the Hawaiian economy, with land use linked to a complex, hierarchical system of land divisions. Whole islands constituted independent polities, called *mokupuni,* these being subdivided into *moku* (districts), under the control of major chiefs; the *moku* were yet again subdivided into a large number of land sections, *ahupua'a,* radiating out from the central mountain peaks like slices of a pie. Extending from the forested uplands, across the agricultural lands, and out to the coast and sea, each *ahupua'a* encompassed the full range of island resources (fig. P.2). Each *ahupua'a* was controlled by a chief, who in turn appointed one or more stewards (*konohiki*) to oversee production, organize work parties, collect tribute, and in other ways represent the chief. *Ahupua'a* communities were in theory economically self-sufficient, although differences in the local resource base (agricultural land, water resources, stone for tools, and so on) resulted in differences in the production patterns of individual land sections. Within *ahupua'a* there were yet smaller sections and divisions, especially the *'ili* and *mo'o,* which were held and worked by extended households or groups of commoners.

Hawaiian farmers cultivated a variety of tropical root, tuber, and tree crops, the most important being taro (*kalo, Colocasia esculenta*) and sweet potato (*'uala, Ipomoea batatas*). Taro was grown wherever rainfall was adequate, but produced its highest yields in irrigated, terraced pondfields (*lo'i*) watered by canals (*'auwai*) diverting water from permanent streams. These irrigated valley lands ranked among the most productive agroecosystems anywhere in Oceania. In leeward regions, dryland cultivation of sweet potatoes dominated production; on Hawai'i and Maui Islands, hundreds of square kilometers were cloaked in these intensive field systems. Planting, tending, and harvesting crops tended to be men's work, although on Maui and Hawai'i, women also contributed their labor, as the dryland field systems demanded intensive weeding and crop tending.

For food the Hawaiians raised large numbers of domestic pigs, dogs, and fowl (which had been brought to the islands with the first settlers, along with rats), but the sea yielded the greatest variety and abundance of animal food. Diverse fishing techniques utilizing bone and shell fishhooks, spears, traps, many kinds of net, nooses, sweeps, and weirs enabled the Hawaiians to exploit all ecological zones, from inshore reefs to the deeper benthic waters. Women gathered mollusks, sea urchins, crabs, and seaweed from rocky headlands and bays. No other Polynesians exceeded the Hawaiians in their marine production, for only in Hawai'i was true aquaculture developed, with large fishponds to impound and raise mullet (*Mugil cephalis*) and milkfish (*Chanos chanos*). Such ponds, of which there were several hundred, were under the control of the chiefs and their land managers, the *konohiki*.

The Hawaiian economy also displayed remarkable craft specialization, with expert canoe-makers, adze-makers, bird-catchers, wood-carvers, barkcloth-makers, weavers, and tattooing experts. The most skilled of these specialists worked their crafts under the aegis of the chiefs, whose households were graced by the fine bowls and containers, feather garments, elegant barkcloth and woven mats, and other products of these craftsmen and craftswomen. The workmanship and artistic embellishment displayed in Hawaiian artifacts renders them much sought after by contemporary museums of non-Western art. In particular, the strikingly sculpted wooden temple images, along with the feather capes, cloaks, and helmets that were the insignia of ranking chiefs, represent an apogee of artistic development within Oceania.

The Hawaiians and other Polynesians are usually classified as having a "Neolithic" technology because they lacked metallurgy, yet they also were without pottery, often considered diagnostic of a Neolithic people. Despite such material omissions, the Hawaiians manufactured an extensive range of tools, implements, utensils, garments, ornaments, and other paraphernalia. Among their principal tools were adzes and chisels of dense volcanic andesite and basalt, and files and abraders of stone, pumice, and coral. Agricultural implements included pointed digging sticks, breadfruit pickers, carrying poles, and baskets. Household implements and furnishings included scrapers and pounders for food preparation; bowls, gourds, calabashes, and other containers; stone lamps; and pandanus floor mats. Paper mulberry plants furnished the bark for cloth (*kapa*), used for garments and bed sheets. Hawaiian canoes (*wa'a*) were constructed of large koa logs with separate gunwales and outriggers, and with spritsails of pandanus matting. Large canoes for interisland voyaging and warfare were frequently double-hulled.

The Hawaiians built several kinds of houses for specific functions (dwellings, cook houses, storage sheds, canoe sheds, and so on), all supported by lashed wooden frames with thatched exteriors. Clusters of these functionally discrete houses (*hale*) formed a *kauhale*, or household group. Settlement was mostly dispersed, with some concentrations in favorable areas around sheltered bays and in fertile valleys. Ruling chiefs (*ali'i nui*) occupied "royal centers," in favorable locales such as Waipi'o Valley or Kailua on Hawai'i, or at Waikīkī on O'ahu. At these royal centers, temples (*heiau*) rose upon massive stone platforms evincing the power and authority of ruling chiefs, reminders of the life-ensuring *mana* (supernatural power) bestowed on the community by a pantheon of gods, of whom the most prominent were Kū, Kāne, Lono, and Kanaloa. The common people, the *maka'āinana,* worshipped at smaller agricultural temples (*heiau ho'oulu'ai*) and at family shrines within the men's eating house (*mua*), where daily offerings were presented to the *'aumākua* or collective ancestors.

Hawaiian society was strongly hierarchical (fig. P.3). The *maka'āinana*, also known as *nā kanaka,* farming the valleys and slopes and harvesting the resources of reef and sea, were organized as extended families and households, dispersed over the landscape. Kinship networks facilitated the distribution of economic products, ranging from taro and dried fish to salt and high-quality adze stone. Above the commoner class were the chiefs (*ali'i* or *nāli'i*), elaborately ranked and graded into a pyramidal series capped by the great district chiefs, the *ali'i 'ai moku* (the "district-eating chief"), and ultimately by the paramount ruler himself, the *ali'i nui* ("great chief"). The many *ahupua'a* were apportioned by the paramount to lesser chiefs (*ali'i 'ai ahupua'a*), who in turn appointed *konohiki* or land managers to oversee production and to assure the regular payment of corvée labor and tribute.

Ali'i distinguished themselves from the common people by their access to a variety of high-status goods and insignia, in particular the magnificent feather cloaks, capes, and helmets, and the chiefly neck ornament, the *lei niho palaoa* (fig. P.4). *Ali'i* alone were permitted to lay claim to genealogies (*mo'okū'auhau*) that extended back in time to distant ancestors; indeed, to have a genealogy was to be a chief. The relations between chiefs and commoners were further governed by an elaborate system of sanctions, *kapu*. Commoners, for example, were required to prostrate themselves (*kapu moe*) in the presence

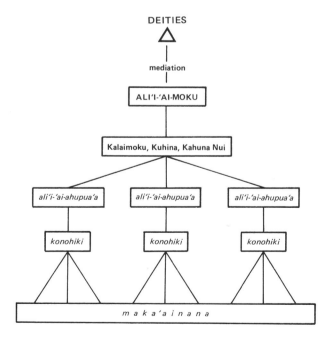

FIGURE P.3 Hawaiian society at the time of European contact was hierarchically organized, with several grades of chiefs (*ali'i*) and land managers (*konohiki*) over the large class of commoners (*maka'āinana*). (After Kirch 1984)

FIGURE P.4 Detail of a Hawaiian chief wearing a feathered helmet and feathered cape, which were symbols of the *ali'i* class. *(Lithograph by John Webber, artist on Captain James Cook's third voyage)*

of the highest chiefs, who often traveled at night so as to avoid disrupting the general populace. The *kapu* system likewise governed the behavior of ordinary men and women in their daily lives, prohibiting women from consuming pork or bananas, and requiring that the food of men and women be cooked in separate earth ovens and eaten apart from one another.

In the decades prior to Cook's arrival, the islands were divided between four to six rival and competing polities centered on the islands of Kaua'i, O'ahu, Maui, and Hawai'i. Moloka'i was at times independent, and at times subject to the ruling chiefs of O'ahu or Maui, who frequently fought over this smaller island. The island of Hawai'i went through a cycle of unifications and subsequent partitions, with a structural rift between the chiefly lines of the windward and leeward districts. The small islands of Kaho'olawe and Lāna'i were generally under the control of Maui.

Religion in contact-period Hawai'i was complex, carried out at a variety of levels. The common people concerned themselves especially with their ancestral deities and spirits (*'aumākua*), to whom daily offerings were made in the men's eating houses. Commoners participated as well in agricultural rituals sponsored by local chiefs and the priests of Lono and of Kāne, the respective deities of dryland and wetland cultivation. An annual harvest cycle of four lunar months' duration sacred to Lono, the Makahiki provided ritual legitimation for the collection of tribute by the *ali'i,* and was also a time for *hula* dance and for competitive games. The largest and most impressive rituals were those dedicated to Kū, god of war, conducted at the imposing *luakini* temples as a prelude to wars of conquest. In addition to the obligatory human sacrifice, spectacular quantities of pigs and other foodstuffs, as well as barkcloth, were required for these *luakini* ceremonies, the offerings furnished by the *maka'āinana* under the supervision of their respective chiefs.

The society encountered by Captain James Cook in Hawai'i in 1778–1779 stands out as one of the most sophisticated and complex among the many hundreds of indigenous societies and cultures dispersed across the Pacific. But Hawaiian culture and society were never static; they evolved and changed over some eight centuries since the first Polynesian voyagers had arrived on the islands' shores. The ancient history of this civilization, its origins and development over many centuries, has gradually emerged through the painstaking research of archaeologists and scholars in allied disciplines of anthropology, ethnohistory, linguistics, ethnobotany, and other fields. This book—the revised version of an effort first produced nearly four decades ago—endeavors to tell this compelling story, a synthesis of our current knowledge concerning the deep history of one of Oceania's most unique and vibrant cultures.

1

UNEARTHING THE HAWAIIAN PAST
The History of Archaeology in Hawai'i

Hawaiians—like other Polynesians—possess a keen interest in their rich history, nourishing a sophisticated oral narrative tradition of accounts (*mo'olelo*) indexed chronologically to the genealogies (*mo'okū'auhau*) of the chiefly lines. The cosmogonic saga of Wākea and Papa tells of the creation of the world out of Pō, the primal, chaotic darkness. Later, in the time of men, the epic voyages of Mo'ikeha, Pā'ao, La'a-mai-Kahiki, and other great ancestors ranged between Hawai'i and Kahiki (Tahiti) and other islands to the south. After these long-distance voyages ceased, the traditions relate in increasing detail the conquests, marriages, intrigues, and other doings of the chiefly families, such as the line of island kings descended from Līloa, including the Hawai'i Island king Kalani'ōpu'u, who greeted Captain Cook at Kealakekua Bay in 1779 (Beckwith 1970; Kamakau 1961). Beginning in the late 1820s, after the Hawaiian language was codified into a standard orthography, indigenous Hawaiian scholars compiled and committed to paper much of this wealth of tradition and lore. In the mid-nineteenth century, Davida Malo (1951), John Papa 'Ī'ī (1959), Kepelino (Beckwith, ed., 1932), and Samuel Kamakau (1961, 1964, 1976) left a priceless legacy in their accounts of old Hawai'i, written from the viewpoint of the first generation born after European contact. Abraham Fornander, a Swedish immigrant who married a Moloka'i chiefess and became fluent in the Hawaiian language, likewise collected and synthesized many important *mo'olelo* (Fornander 1878–1885, 1916–1920).

The indigenous historical traditions (*mo'olelo*), chants (*oli*), and songs (*mele*) offer an "insider" perspective on the Hawaiian past, couched in Kānaka Maoli (Native Hawaiian) terms and cultural concepts. Using a "direct historical approach," archaeologists and culture historians often attempt to project the cultural patterns described by Malo, Kamakau, Kepelino, and others back into the period before the arrival of Europeans. No culture is static, however, and the uncritical projection of early postcontact Hawaiian culture back into the deep past has its limitations. The culture and language of the first Polynesians to settle Hawai'i undoubtedly differed from that of their descendants eight centuries later. Over time, the distinctive cultural patterns of contact-period Hawai'i emerged out of the ancient, ancestral Polynesian culture. Thus, the direct historical approach becomes less useful the further back in time one delves.

Historical sources of the late eighteenth, nineteenth, and even twentieth centuries also offer insights into Hawaiian culture in the period following initial European contact. These include the records and observations of early European explorers, traders, whalers, and missionaries, as well as the extensive archives of the Hawaiian Kingdom. Anthropological studies of the early twentieth century, such as the collaborative work of ethnologist Edward S. C. Handy and Kanaka Maoli scholar Mary Kawena Pukui on traditional agriculture, and on the family system in Ka'ū, Hawai'i Island (Handy and Handy 1972; Handy and Pukui 1958), contribute to this portrait of "traditional" Hawaiian life. For the culture historian, however, these accounts elucidate only the *endpoint* of a lengthy sequence of development, over hundreds of years, during which Hawaiian society and culture evolved from its Polynesian ancestor into something unique and distinctive.

Other clues to the more remote Hawaiian past are provided by the evidence of linguistics, biological anthropology, and ethnobotany. By comparing Polynesian and other Oceanic languages, linguists can determine the position of Hawaiian in the family tree of Oceanic languages. Biological anthropologists can trace the genetic relationships between Hawaiians and other Polynesian peoples. Ethnobotanists, for their part, study the relationship between people and plants—including "canoe plants"—as evidence for the movement into the Pacific of horticultural peoples. All of these approaches to the Hawaiian past contribute to our knowledge regarding the origins and development of Hawaiian society and culture.

Of all the approaches to the Hawaiian past, however, archaeology alone is concerned with the material traces left by ancient peoples, the tangible remains inscribed on the landscape and sedimented in the earth through generations of human activity. From stone adzes and bone fishhooks, to mollusk shells and fishbones discarded from daily meals and ceremonial feasts, to the stone foundations of ancient temples, and even to entire landscapes of once intensively cultivated fields, archaeologists deal with a broad range of material evidence of the past. Studying these remains in their stratigraphic contexts, dating these sites with radiocarbon and other techniques, archaeologists place the material witnesses of the past in a temporal framework, building up a portrait of the past and of cultural change over time.

Archaeology in Hawai'i began with nineteenth-century antiquarianism, advanced in the twentieth century with the development of modern scientific methods, and more recently has been transformed with the rise of "contract archaeology" and cultural resources management (CRM), changes in archaeological practice that have at times led to tensions between archaeologists and Native Hawaiians. Not only have the methods of archaeological research advanced over time, but the fundamental questions that have directed and organized archaeological research in Hawai'i have also changed significantly. Moreover, archaeological work in Hawai'i has been influenced by developments elsewhere in world. In this chapter, we trace these trends and currents in the historical development of archaeology in Hawai'i.

The Beginnings of Hawaiian Archaeology

Scientific archaeology in Hawai'i began with the founding in 1889 of the Bernice Pauahi Bishop Museum of Polynesian Ethnology and Kindred Antiquities (fig. 1.1). Charles Reed Bishop, a prominent Honolulu banker, founded the museum as a memorial to his late

FIGURE 1.1 The Bernice Pauahi Bishop Museum in Honolulu was the leading institution for Polynesian and Hawaiian archaeological research throughout most of the twentieth century. *(Photo by P. V. Kirch)*

wife, Princess Bernice Pauahi, great-granddaughter of King Kamehameha I. Intended to house the rich collection of Hawaiian artifacts of Pauahi, Princess Ruth Keʻelikolani, and Queen Emma, the museum might have remained little more than "the treasure house of Kamehameha" were it not for the appointment of William T. Brigham as its first director, a post he held for 30 years (from 1889 to 1919). Assembling a nucleus of scientists who accumulated the foundation of the museum's superb collections in Hawaiian and Polynesian archaeology, ethnology, and natural history, Brigham strove to make the institution, in his words, more than "a mere dime museum" (Rose 1980).

Brigham authored *Stone Implements and Stone Work of the Ancient Hawaiians* (1902), arguably the first book on Hawaiian archaeology, along with studies on Hawaiian woven mats and baskets, featherwork, the traditional house, barkcloth, and wooden carvings obtained from a burial cave on Hawaiʻi (Brigham 1899, 1903, 1906). Fornander's assertion that a transformation in Hawaiian temple architecture had followed the arrival of the Tahitian priest Pāʻao, who reputedly introduced the worship of Kū and the practice of human sacrifice (Fornander 1878–1885, 2:35–36), fascinated Brigham. According to Fornander, in the ancient period prior to the arrival of Pāʻao, *heiau* or temples were "of the truncated pyramid form," in which the priests and sacrifices were "in plain view of the assembled congregation" (2:59). This temple style was replaced, in Fornander's account, by a walled enclosure form of temple where "the presiding chief, those whom he chose to admit, and the officiating priests, were the only ones who entered the walled enclosure where the high places for the gods and the altars for the sacrifices were erected" (2:59). Wanting to test Fornander's theory with empirical data, Brigham sent the museum's curator of ethnology, John F. G. Stokes, to Hawaiʻi Island in 1906, and to Molokaʻi in 1909, with instructions to obtain plans of all extant *heiau* ruins (Stokes 1909a, 1991).

The first true archaeologist of Hawaiʻi (fig. 1.2), Stokes accurately mapped the locations of *heiau* using an optical transit, preparing detailed site plans (Flexner et al. 2017). Stokes photographed the ruins, not an easy task when the fragile glass plate negatives had to be transported on horseback, or at times via outrigger canoe, and the plates developed in

FIGURE 1.2 William T. Brigham (*fourth from the left*) and his staff at Bishop Museum. John F. G. Stokes, curator of Polynesian ethnology, stands on the right. (*Photo courtesy of Bishop Museum Library and Archives*)

a tent at night. Although Stokes authored important papers on fishponds and petroglyphs, as well as ethnographic studies of netting and the ancient practice of fish poisoning (Stokes 1909b, 1921), he was a perfectionist, reluctant to publish. Stokes' Hawaiʻi *heiau* survey was not published until long after his death (Stokes 1991); his Molokaʻi survey remains in manuscript form (Stokes 1909a).

Stokes was the first archaeologist to excavate at a Hawaiian site, on Kahoʻolawe Island in 1913, at the Kamōhio Bay rockshelter and fishing shrine, a fishermen's camp with stone-faced terraces containing stratified cultural deposits (Mulrooney and Swift 2022). The excavation yielded bone fishhooks in all stages of manufacture as well as the tools used to make them. Regrettably, Stokes' reluctance to finish his reports led Brigham's successor, museum director Herbert Gregory, to relieve Stokes of his curatorial post in 1929, a serious loss to Hawaiian archaeology. When the Kamōhio Bay collection was later published by J. G. McAllister in 1933, the stratigraphic associations so carefully noted by Stokes were ignored; no further digging would be attempted until 37 years later.

Thomas G. Thrum, an amateur archaeologist and publisher of the *Hawaiian Annual*, included accounts of important temple sites in his periodical (Thrum 1906, 1909). Unlike Stokes, Thrum did not map or make detailed recordings of these sites, but as many of these *heiau* have since been destroyed, Thrum's records serve as an invaluable resource today.

The Search for Polynesian Origins

In 1920, Yale geologist Herbert E. Gregory succeeded Brigham as director of Bishop Museum, convening a Pan-Pacific Scientific Conference in Honolulu to assess the major problems requiring scientific study. The conference's "Recommendations for Anthropological Research in Polynesia" laid out an ambitious program of field research:

Since Polynesian archaeology is in most respects a virgin field, the first problem is to make island surveys.... The order of procedure on a particular island might be as follows: location and plotting of village sites, and in relation to these, the water supply, cultivated fields, irrigation ditches, temple sites, fish ponds and weirs, all other evidences of native industries, and burial sites. As a rule, Polynesian temple sites require careful plotting in detail to reveal possible differences in type. Such a survey should not only reveal the content of the archaeology for the island examined but should give hints of time relations and local variations. (Gregory, ed., 1921, 117)

Bishop Museum greatly expanded its scope of research throughout Polynesia through the Bayard Dominick Expeditions, in 1920–1921. Field teams were dispatched to the Marquesas, Tonga, and the Austral Islands, but overshadowed by the excitement of obtaining new data from these remote corners of Polynesia, the Hawaiian Islands took a back seat. The Hawaiian research team was limited to Louis A. Sullivan, a physical anthropologist assigned to conduct a "somatological" study of the Hawaiian people, and Kenneth P. Emory, a recent Dartmouth graduate whom museum director Gregory appointed to the position of assistant ethnologist (fig. 1.3).

Emory's name would become synonymous with Hawaiian archaeology throughout most of the twentieth century, owing to his involvement in the field continuously from 1920 until his death in 1992 (Danielsson 1967; Kirch 1992; Krauss 1988). Having studied botany at Dartmouth, Emory knew almost nothing of ethnology or archaeology when he accepted his Bishop Museum appointment, a defect he soon remedied by taking anthropology courses at Berkeley. Emory's first assignment was to study stone structures in Haleakalā Crater on Maui (Emory 1921). An intensive survey of the island of Lānaʻi soon followed (Emory 1924), then an investigation of archaeological vestiges on remote Nihoa and Mokumanamana (then known as Necker) Islands to the northwest of Kauaʻi (Emory 1928). The unique stone images of Mokumanamana, along with temple platforms akin to those he had found in the Society Islands and Tuamotus (Emory 1933, 1934a), led Emory to theorize about an early period of contact between Hawaiʻi and central Eastern Polynesia.

FIGURE 1.3 Kenneth P. Emory excavating a burial cairn in Haleakalā Crater, Maui, in 1920. *(Photo courtesy of Bishop Museum Library and Archives)*

During the decades between world wars, archaeology was overshadowed by its sister field of ethnology, which drew upon synchronic ethnographic comparisons to reconstruct Polynesian culture history. Te Rangi Hiroa, also known as Peter H. Buck—who in 1936 succeeded to the directorship of Bishop Museum—drew upon detailed analyses of weaving techniques and adze-lashing forms to trace the movement of people across the Pacific (Buck 1938). Hiroa placed the first arrival of Polynesians in Hawai'i at AD 450, based on the Hawaiian genealogies (249). Like Fornander, Hiroa believed that there was a "later influx of people from Tahiti . . . led by chiefs who became distinguished ancestors of the chiefly families of Hawai'i" (249).

Bishop Museum archaeologists from 1920 to 1950 focused almost exclusively on surface surveys of stone ruins (the major exception being excavations of the sand dune burials at Mōkapu on O'ahu by Emory and Bowles; see chapter 11). Several erroneous assumptions underlay their reticence to put spade to earth. First, Polynesian arrival in Oceania was thought to be relatively recent, leaving no time for the accumulation of stratified deposits. Second, it was believed that excavations would yield only the same kinds of stone tools already known from museum collections. Third, the absence of pottery in Polynesia meant that archaeologists would be deprived of their most important tool for relative dating, the seriation of pottery styles (radiocarbon dating was not invented until the late 1940s).

Throughout the 1920s and 1930s, Bishop Museum sponsored islandwide surveys of archaeological sites, focusing on the larger and more impressive *heiau*, mostly ignoring nondescript habitation and agricultural sites. Despite these limitations, the surveys of Wendell C. Bennett (1931) for Kaua'i, J. Gilbert McAllister (1933a, 1933b) for O'ahu and Kaho'olawe, and unpublished manuscript reports for Maui, Hawai'i, and Moloka'i (Hudson 1931; Phelps 1937; Walker 1930) laid important foundations for Hawaiian archaeology.

Stratigraphic Archaeology and Artifact Sequences

World War II brought an abrupt halt to fieldwork in the Pacific, but when hostilities ended, the spotlight that the war had placed on the islands and their inhabitants helped to usher in a new era of scientific research across the region. Professor Edward Gifford of Berkeley, who had led Bishop Museum's Bayard Dominick Expedition to Tonga in 1920, undertook archaeological fieldwork in Fiji in 1947, and in New Caledonia in 1952 (Gifford 1951), overturning long-held assumptions that Pacific archaeological sites lacked stratigraphy, or that the time depth for human occupation in the Pacific islands was shallow. Alex Spoehr's excavations in the Mariana Islands of Micronesia in 1949–1950 likewise demonstrated the potential of stratigraphic excavations on Pacific islands (Spoehr 1957). Spurred on by these promising finds, by the mid-1950s, archaeologists were at work in island groups across Polynesia.

In 1950 Kenneth Emory offered a University of Hawai'i class in archaeological field techniques, choosing as his site a rockshelter in the Kuli'ou'ou Valley (site O1) on O'ahu Island. Never having been formally trained in excavation, Emory drew upon Robert Heizer's field manual for archaeological fieldwork in California (Heizer 1950). Heizer's system was to dig in arbitrary 6-inch levels, rather than by natural strata, thus ignoring the key temporal associations that are revealed when the natural layers are followed. (Emory and Bishop Museum archaeologists would continue to use the method of arbitrary levels well into the 1960s.) Kuliʻouʻou rockshelter's "fertile floor" of fine dusty soil yielded an unanticipated abundance of artifacts, including fishhooks and adzes. More importantly, an opportunity for direct dating of the archaeological materials was at hand. In the late 1940s, chemist Willard Libby of the University of Chicago discovered that the ratio in ancient organic materials of the radioactive ^{14}C isotope relative to its sister ^{12}C and ^{13}C isotopes provided a means for calculating the age of that material. This discovery garnered Libby the Nobel Prize in Chemistry, revolutionizing the field of archaeology. Archaeologists would no longer need to painstakingly analyze stylistic changes in pottery sherds to piece together a relative chronology; they could send a sample of charcoal or bone or shell to a laboratory and receive an assessment of the age of the sample, albeit with a certain error range (the standard deviation or ± factor that follows a given radiocarbon date). Emory lost no time in taking advantage of Libby's remarkable discovery:

> While this [excavation] was in progress, in May of 1950, word came of W. F. Libby's momentous discovery of a method for dating charcoal through measuring radioactivity. A sample of charcoal from a fireplace at the lowest level showing human occupation was submitted to Dr. Libby at the Institute of Nuclear Studies, University of Chicago. The sample gave a reading of 946 years, plus or minus 180 years, . . . revealing that the shelter had been occupied since about A.D. 1004. This was the first radiocarbon date from any island in the Pacific and it opened up undreamed of possibilities for reconstructing the prehistory of the area. (Emory, Bonk, and Sinoto 1959, ix)

Encouraged by the Kuliʻouʻou finds, Emory engaged in an expanded program of fieldwork, with excavations on Kauaʻi, Molokaʻi, and Hawaiʻi. Emory's student William J. Bonk became an active collaborator, writing his master's thesis on the results of excavations at several west Molokaʻi sites (Bonk 1954). They were joined in 1954 by Yosihiko H. Sinoto, a young student from Japan who had studied Jomon period archaeology (Sinoto with Aramata 2016). Sinoto was on his way to Berkeley to study archaeology at the University of California when Emory convinced him to stay and assist in the South Point excavations on Hawaiʻi Island (fig 1.4). Sinoto became Emory's protege, eventually succeeding him as Bishop Museum's senior archaeologist. Under Emory's direction, Bonk and Sinoto were largely responsible for the Hawaiian Archaeological Program (Bonk 1961), during which several important sand dune and rockshelter sites were excavated throughout the 1950s (see chapter 6).

Sinoto realized that Hawaiian fishhooks could be used as a tool for seriation and relative dating, just as pottery was used in other parts of the world: "Many distinctive features of the more elaborate forms can be tied to specific localities and to specific periods of time, which makes them valuable in the tracing of ancient cultural movements and developments. Modern techniques of analysis endow prehistoric fishhooks with the power to draw knowledge from the past, much as the magic hooks of the Polynesian demigods drew islands from the ocean depths" (Emory, Bonk, and Sinoto 1959, 3).

FIGURE 1.4 Kenneth P. Emory and Yosihiko Sinoto at the Puʻu Aliʻi dune site (site H1) at Ka Lae, Hawaiʻi Island, in 1954. *(Photo courtesy Bishop Museum Department of Anthropology)*

The Hawaiian Archaeological Program excavated 32 sites, mostly coastal rockshelters, yielding 4,159 fishhook specimens, reported in the publication *Hawaiian Archaeology: Fishhooks* (Emory, Bonk, and Sinoto 1959). Unfortunately, aside from the fishhooks monograph, only the Oʻahu excavations (Emory and Sinoto 1961) and the work at Waiahukini rockshelter (site H8 on Hawaiʻi; Emory and Sinoto 1969) were ever fully published. Although samples of faunal and floral materials from these sites were usually collected, these too for the most part remained unanalyzed.

A charismatic mentor, Emory gathered around him an enthusiastic cadre of volunteers, among them Catherine Cooke Summers and Elspeth Sterling, who compiled existing sources on the archaeological sites of Oʻahu Island (Sterling and Summers 1978). Sterling then turned to a similar compendium on the sites of Maui (E. P. Sterling 1998), while Summers did the same for Molokaʻi Island (Summers 1971). Dorothy Barrère, another Emory recruit, found her passion in carefully editing the unpublished manuscripts of Samuel Kamakau, based on the translations made by Mary Kawena Pukui, for publication. Henry Kekahuna, a self-taught Kanaka Maoli archaeologist who produced many detailed maps of *heiau* sites, also turned to Emory as a mentor.

In 1961, Emory and Sinoto decided to expand the Bishop Museum's archaeological research to the Society Islands, and soon after, to the Marquesas, where rich archaeological discoveries had been made by Robert Suggs (1961). This shift in geographic focus aligned with Emory's long-held interest in the island cultures of central and southeastern Polynesia. The Bishop Museum's program in Hawaiian archaeology, however, continued under Emory's overall supervision, led by his student Lloyd J. Soehren. In 1964, the museum received a major grant from the National Science Foundation for a three-year program of archaeological research in Hawaiʻi. Soehren oversaw excavations at the deeply stratified Nuʻalolo rockshelter site on Kauaʻi (fig. 1.5), and at sites in the vicinity of South Point, Hawaiʻi (Soehren 1966, n.d.). As before, the primary goal remained the definition of artifact sequences, while stratigraphic control continued to be by means of arbitrary 6-inch levels.

FIGURE 1.5 Excavations in progress at the Nuʻalolo rockshelter, Kauaʻi Island ca. 1963. Among the members of the field team seen here are Lloyd J. Soehren (*with pipe*), Kenneth P. Emory (*holding shovel*), and William J. Bonk (*upper right*). (*Photo courtesy Bishop Museum Department of Anthropology*)

New Directions: Settlement Patterns and Ecology

By the mid-1960s, radiocarbon dating had largely freed archaeologists from the tedious work of constructing chronologies based on detailed studies of pottery or other artifact types. More importantly, a younger generation of archaeologists was questioning the fundamental goals of the discipline. Beginning with Walter Taylor's influential critique (Taylor 1948), continuing with K. C. Chang's call for a "rethinking" of the discipline (Chang

1967), and culminating in Lewis and Sally Binford's proclamation of a "New Archaeology" (Binford and Binford 1968), the field was rife with change. Rather than limiting archaeological research to the construction of artifact-based chronologies, the "New Archaeologists" wanted to investigate the economic, demographic, social, policitical, and religious aspects of ancient cultures, to understand how these had evolved over time. As Lewis Binford famously put it: "Archaeology is anthropology or it is nothing" (Binford 1962).

In 1966, Roger C. Green arrived at Bishop Museum, bringing new ideas about how archaeology in Polynesia should be conducted. Trained at Harvard by the New World archaeologist Gordon Willey, Green had introduced the "settlement-pattern" approach to Polynesia with a comprehensive site survey in the ʻOpunohu Valley on Moʻorea in the Society Islands. Green, along with other Willey students such as K. C. Chang (1967), regarded the settlement-pattern approach as essential to moving archaeology away from its traditional emphasis on building artifact-centered cultural sequences to the scientific study of cultural evolution.

Green included a settlement-pattern survey of the Kahikinui District of Maui in the Bishop Museum's National Science Foundation–funded program in Hawaiian archaeology. The task was assigned to Stanford University graduate student Peter Chapman, who, assisted by museum archaeologist William Kikuchi (and a volunteer team including Kirch), spent the summer of 1966 surveying the arid Kahikinui slopes (see Kirch 2014, 18–26). For the first time in Hawaiʻi, the team attempted an exhaustive survey of all archaeological sites within two traditional *ahupuaʻa,* in order to uncover the settlement pattern of these ancient communities. Global positioning satellite (GPS) technology still being years in the future, this required using a plane table and telescopic alidade to map the location of the several hundred stone structures—enclosures, platforms, terraces, pits, alignments, and walls—that the team discovered in the dense lantana and scrub. Unfortunately, due to illness Chapman never completed his doctoral dissertation on Kahikinui; many years later Kirch would resume work in the district, building upon the results of the 1966 survey (Kirch 2014).

In 1967, Richard Pearson—a recent Yale PhD trained by settlement-pattern archaeologist K. C. Chang—was appointed to the University of Hawaiʻi faculty. Pearson and Roger Green soon obtained National Science Foundation support for an archaeological field school at Lapakahi on Hawaiʻi Island, a project that would continue under the direction of P. Bion Griffin and David Tuggle (Griffin et al. 1971; Tuggle and Griffin 1973). UH graduate student T. Stell Newman, discovering that the remains of an extensive agricultural field system covered the upland slopes of leeward Kohala, used aerial photography to map out the network of field walls and trails (Newman n.d.). Paul Rosendahl more closely mapped the Lapakahi portion of the agricultural fields, and excavated upland residential sites, the first in-depth study of this extensive dryland field system (Rosendahl 1972a, 1994). The field school students also mapped and excavated in the coastal Koaiʻe hamlet, which would become the Lapakahi State Historical Park.

The late 1960s also saw the first contracting by government agencies and private developers for archaeological surveys, and for salvage or rescue excavations. Although Bishop Museum had conducted some work for the National Park Service in the 1960s, the first significant private funding for Hawaiian archaeology began in 1968, in conjunction with a proposed resort development in the Mākaha Valley on Oʻahu. Roger Green organized this three-year effort (Green 1980), which included mapping of dryland agricultural features and associated habitation sites by Robert Hommon (1969a, 1969c, 1970b), and the excavation of the Kāneʻaki temple site by Ed Ladd (1973). The work at Mākaha, like that at Lapakahi, provided new insights to Hawaiian adaptation to island ecology and agricultural systems (Yen et al. 1972), and to precontact social organization.

Roger Green initiated a third settlement pattern–oriented study in 1969 in the windward valley of Hālawa, Molokaʻi, where archaeology students Tom Riley, Gil Hendren, and Kirch investigated a valley once famous for its irrigated taro fields (Kirch and Kelly, eds., 1975). Kirch excavated a stratified sand dune site at the valley's mouth, exposing round-ended house foundations (fig. 1.6), Riley studied the remains of the irrigation systems, while Hendren excavated in inland house sites. The Hālawa team was influenced by the emerging paradigm of the "New Archaeology," represented by the work of the Binfords (1968) and David Clarke (1968).

The Lapakahi, Mākaha, and Hālawa projects (1968–1971) established settlement-pattern archaeology and an ecological approach as a new paradigm in Hawaiian archaeology, superceding the artifact-centered, culture-history approach of Emory, Sinoto, and Soehren. Influenced by the New Archaeology, these and other contemporary projects trained a new cadre of professional archaeologists such as Paul Rosendahl, Rob Hommon, Ross Cordy, and Kirch, who would lead the field of Hawaiian archaeology in coming years. Roger Green, however, left Hawaiʻi in 1970, having become disaffected with director Roland Force's mismanagement of Bishop Museum. Although limited, Green's period of influence had a lasting impact in broadening the horizons of Hawaiian archaeological research.

In the 1970s, the University of Hawaiʻi became increasingly engaged in Hawaiian archaeology, even as Bishop Museum expanded its own program of research and consulting. Dave Tuggle, with funding from the National Science Foundation, expanded the

FIGURE 1.6 Molokaʻi high school students participating in the excavation of the Hālawa Valley dune site (Mo-A1-3) in 1970. *(Photo by P. V. Kirch)*

University's Lapakahi field school into the windward Kohala valleys of Pololū and Honokāne (Tuggle and Tomonari-Tuggle 1980). Bishop Museum's Patrick C. McCoy collaborated with UH professor Richard Gould in investigating the high-altitude basalt quarry of Mauna Kea on Hawai'i Island, one of the largest Neolithic adze-working sites in the world (P. C. McCoy 1976, 1977, 1982). McCoy's work, aided by UH student Paul Cleghorn, redirected archaeological considerations of Hawaiian stone adzes away from typology to questions of production and the exchange and distribution of finished adzes across political boundaries and even between islands (P. L. Cleghorn 1982, 1986). Ross Cordy (1981) drew upon data sets from leeward Hawai'i Island to advance and test a series of hypotheses about demographic and social changes in precontact Hawai'i.

In 1971, anthropologist Marshall Sahlins turned to the rich nineteenth-century archives of the Hawaiian Kingdom to study the historical ethnography of Hawai'i. To augment the archival studies, Sahlins invited archaeology student Tim Earle to map taro irrigation systems in the Halele'a District of Kaua'i (Earle 1978). Sahlins expanded this archaeological collaboration by engaging with Kirch in 1982 on an intensive study of the Anahulu Valley in northwestern O'ahu (fig. 1.7). Here the rich ethnohistoric record could be linked with sites occupied by Hawaiian land claimants during the Māhele of 1848–1854, providing insights into Hawaiian social and economic life during the early turbulent years following Western contact (Kirch and Sahlins 1992).

FIGURE 1.7 Excavation of an early postcontact house site in the Anahulu Valley, O'ahu Island. *(Photo by P. V. Kirch)*

From Ivory Tower to For-Profit Consulting

Throughout the first half of the twentieth century, archaeology in Hawai'i was almost exclusively an academic enterprise, undertaken by a handful of museum or university scholars, and aided by a cadre of students and volunteers. This model of archaeological practice began to change radically after the inclusion of Hawai'i in 1959 as the fiftieth state of the Union. Statehood spurred an influx of investments—initially from the continental United States and later from Japan—in hotels, resorts, golf courses, and residential subdivisions. The state of Hawai'i increasingly funded major infrastructure improvements, including highways, airports, and harbors. Meanwhile, the passage of the National Historic Preservation Act of 1966 mandated archaeological surveys when federal funds were involved or properties were affected, authorizing expanded archaeological and historic preservation work. The Hawai'i state legislature passed a strengthened version of its own historic preservation law (Chapter 6E of the Hawai'i Revised Statutes), while individual counties enacted their own ordinances to protect historic sites. Together, these developments resulted in a ramping up of the pace of archaeological work in the islands, an irreversible shift in the nature of archaeological practice.

The 1968 Mākaha Valley Project was the first to be funded by a commercial developer. Throughout the 1970s, Hawaiian archaeology became increasingly dominated by what was called "contract archaeology" and later came to be known as "cultural resource management," CRM for short. The increased pace of archaeological projects was phenomenal; by the late 1970s annual expenditures for archaeological work in the state approached $500,000, far more than any grant either the museum or the university had ever received for archaeological research. Bishop Museum, with the advantage of its long-established reputation in Hawaiian archaeology, dominated the CRM field into the early 1980s, but was soon competing with a growing number of for-profit consulting firms.

Many of the new consulting archaeologists got their start at Bishop Museum, among them Paul Rosendahl, William Barrera, Steve Athens, Steve Clark, Tom Dye, Robert Hommon, and Paul Cleghorn. Rosendahl founded the firm of Paul H. Rosendahl, Incorporated (PHRI), which by the early 1990s had eclipsed Bishop Museum as the leading archaeological consulting group, bringing in more than $1 million annually, and ultimately conducting more than 2,000 projects. Hal Hammatt, who arrived in Hawai'i in 1982 after earning his doctorate at Washington State University, first partnered with Francis Ching at the Archaeological Research Center Hawai'i, Incorporated. Hammatt then founded Cultural Surveys Hawai'i, Incorporated, which has dominated the CRM field in recent years. As of 2021, there were 29 CRM firms, many with multiple offices, permitted to conduct archaeological work in the state of Hawai'i, as well as a handful of permitted researchers, primarily university-based academics.

By the late 1970s, the increased pace of archaeological work in the islands attracted dozens of lower-level fieldworkers and lab technicians, most of whom came to Hawai'i from the continental United States. Most were young Haole males who, in keeping with the times, sported long hair and beards, prompting Kenneth Emory (then in his early eighties) to famously quip that this was akin to "an invasion of hippies" (Major 1995, 22). Maurice

Major (1995) provides an insightful ethnography of archaeologists and changing archaeological practice during these transition years from academic to CRM archaeology in Hawai'i (see also Griffin 1999).

The National Historic Preservation Act (NHPA) of 1966, and subsequent federal and state legislation, led to direct governmental involvement in archaeology. The NHPA mandated the appointment of a State Historic Preservation Officer, initially housed within the Division of State Parks of the Department of Land and Natural Resources (DLNR) (Kawelu 2015, 30–34). In 1969 the state legislature authorized a statewide inventory of historic and archaeological sites, which was carried out in the early 1970s, largely under contract to Bishop Museum. This inventory became the basis for the Hawai'i Register of Historic Places. In 1990, a separate State Historic Preservation Division (SHPD) was created within DLNR, which today is the agency responsible for enforcing Hawai'i's historic preservation laws, and for reviewing the work of CRM archaeologists.

From the late 1970s into the mid-1980s, Bishop Museum sought to balance research-driven and CRM archaeology (fig. 1.8). On the island of Moloka'i, for example, a survey of a 7.7 km^2 parcel of land including 499 archaeological sites, slated for residential development, allowed for the investigation of leeward settlement patterns (Kirch 2015, 155–159; Weisler and Kirch 1982, 1985). Similarly, two major highway projects on Hawai'i Island, the Waimea-Kawaihae and Kuakini highway corridors, conducted for the State Department of Transportation, provided opportunities to address research questions regarding dryland agriculture and ecological change (Clark and Kirch, eds., 1983; Schilt 1984). Both of these projects were oriented by questions of Hawaiian historical ecology, and included innovative multidisciplinary analyses of charcoal, land snails, pollen, phytoliths, and other indicators of past land use recovered from sites excavated along the highway corridors. Rose Schilt's synthesis of the Kuakini Highway corridor project broke new ground in understanding the importance of the Kona Field System within the political history of Hawai'i Island (Schilt 1984).

The exponential increase in archaeological work driven by the new CRM paradigm was not, however, always matched by concomitant gains in knowledge of the Hawaiian past. In CRM archaeology, the parameters of a project are set by the exigencies of land

FIGURE 1.8 Bishop Museum staff members visiting the Kawela project area on Moloka'i Island in 1980; *left to right:* Patrick C. McCoy, Douglas E. Yen, Carl Christensen, Yosihiko Sinoto, and Patrick V. Kirch. *(Photo by M. I. Weisler)*

development, rather than by fundamental research questions. While raw archaeological data accumulated at an unprecedented rate, little of this new information was synthesized or published. CRM work was typically reported in Xeroxed reports of limited distribution, sometimes referred to as the "gray literature" (and more recently, in digital reports also of limited distribution). Reports can be hard to obtain, or even restricted or suppressed by the contracting agencies (such as the US military), or by developers. Partly to address this problem, and to help set minimal standards for professional work, the Society for Hawaiian Archaeology (SHA) was founded in 1980. SHA quickly became involved in a controversial case at Kawākiu, Molokaʻi, when a group of Native Hawaiians asked SHA to review the work of an archaeological consultant who, they claimed, had failed to record numerous sites. SHA continues to play an important role in Hawaiian archaeology, holding annual conferences and intermittently publishing a journal, *Hawaiian Archaeology*.

Troubles in the Trenches

The heightened pace of archaeological work in the late 1970s and 1980s—spurred on by massive investments in hotel, resort, and housing developments, as well as state and federal infrastructure projects—coninicided with what came to be known as the Hawaiian Cultural Rennaissance. What began initially as a resurgance of interest in music, hula, and language soon expanded into a political movement, with calls for Hawaiian sovereignty (Trask 1993). Many Kānaka Maoli resented the conversion of favored fishing grounds, beaches, and agricultural lands to hotels and golf courses. They saw few benefits flowing to them from these "development" projects. The fact that archaeologists inevitably preceded the bulldozers, combined with the seeming reticence of many CRM archaeologists to consult with Kānaka Maoli or to share their findings, led to increasingly tense relations between archaeologists and Native Hawaiians (Spriggs 1989, 1991). Kathy Kawelu, in *Kuleana and Commitment* (2015), reviews this period of tension and conflict in masterful detail. Here we summarize just two major conflicts that had lasting repercussions for the practice of archaeology in Hawaiʻi.

In 1985, W. Donald Duckworth—an entomologist by training and midlevel bureaucrat at the Smithsonian Institution—was appointed director of Bishop Museum. With no knowledge of Hawaiian archaeology and little interest in supporting research, Duckworth fired 18 of the museum's research staff one year after his arrival, ostensibly for budgetary reasons. These included archaeologist Patrick McCoy and ethnohistorian Marion Kelly. However, the museum had a lucrative contract with the State Department of Transportation for an archaeological survey of the proposed H3 highway that was to traverse the Koʻolau Mountains from Pearl Harbor to Kāneʻohe. Not wishing to give up this source of revenue (including a high "overhead" take), Duckworth reassigned the remaining museum archaeologists to an Applied Research Group whose mission was to maximize revenues from consulting work. Seasoned staff, including Paul Cleghorn and Aki Sinoto, who questioned this approach, were soon fired, replaced by inexperienced workers from the continental United States.

As the archaeological surveys along the route of the H3 highway in North Hālawa and Haʻikū valleys progressed, important findings were suppressed. Eventually, whistleblower

Barry Nakamura, a project historian, leaked word to the press that Bishop Museum was witholding important findings (Kawelu 2015). Nakamura's firing precipitated an uproar. A major site complex in the lower Hālawa Valley, thought to be a *hale o Papa*, or female temple, became the scene of a protest occupation by hundreds of Kānaka Maoli women. In 1993, Native Hawaiian scholar Haunani-Kay Trask called for "an independent investigation into Bishop Museum," citing concerns over "the quality and professional integrity of their contract archaeology, including questions of falsification of reporting on sites and mismanagement of State funds" (Trask 1993, 172–173). In the end, the museum received a staggering $22.3 million for the H3 archaeology work, yet the eventual outcome—after several years of controversy and criticism—would be the loss of the museum's reputation for quality archaeological work, and the demise of its once leading role in Hawaiian archaeology (Sinoto 1999). Tom Dye summed up the toxic effect of CRM archaeology on Bishop Museum: "The cash cow of CRM archaeology was like crack cocaine for a perennially underfunded museum. The combination of Donald Duckworth's complete addiction to it, and the kind of disparagement of research staff that could only come from a failed researcher such as Duckworth, finally killed the Hawaiian archaeology program at the place it was born a century earlier" (Dye 2011b, 130). Today, the museum's small archaeology staff focus their efforts on caring for the legacy collections generated during its decades of research and CRM work, undertaking targeted new research on those collections (e.g., Lundblad et al. 2013; Mulrooney et al. 2014; Wong et al. 2014).

A second case emblematic of the troubled relations between archaeologists and Kānaka Maoli in the 1980s centers on the Honokahua burial site in West Maui (see Kawelu 2015, 54–58, for a detailed account). In 1987, Maui Land and Pineapple Company was in the process of transforming a former pineapple plantation into the sprawling Kapalua Resort complex. The company reached an agreement with the state and two Native Hawaiian organizations allowing for the excavation, documentation, and reburial elsewhere of an unspecified number of burials suspected to be situated within a sand dune at Honokahua Bay, where a 450-room Ritz-Carlton hotel was slated to be built. As predicted, burials soon began to be uncovered, but the actual number was kept a closely guarded secret by the CRM firm of Paul H. Rosendahl, Incorporated, until, after a year of digging, word leaked out that hundreds of *iwi kūpuna* (ancestral bones) were being removed from the dune. When Maui Land and Pineapple and PHRI finally disclosed that the number of exhumed burials had reached 870 (more than 1,000 burials were removed before the project was halted), a public outcry, including protests at Honokahua and at the state Capitol, ultimately forced a halt to the work. Governor John Waiheʻe personally intervened, and a settlement was negotiated whereby the state compensated Maui Land and Pineapple, creating a permanent conservation easement on the site; the *iwi kūpuna* were reburied in the same locations from which they had been exhumed, while the hotel was built on a new site set back from the shoreline.

The Honokahua controversy unfolded at the same time that efforts were proceeding nationally to pass the Native American Graves Protection and Repatriation Act (NAGPRA); congressional hearings had begun in 1986 and the act was passed in 1990, with the backing of Hawaiʻi senator Daniel Inouye. NAGPRA authorized two Native Hawaiian organizations, Hui Mālama I Nā Kūpuna O Hawaiʻi Nei and the Office of Hawaiian Affairs (OHA), to make claims for and repatriate Kānaka Maoli human remains, funerary objects, and objects of cultural patrimony. Hui Mālama and OHA began to advance claims, such as for the extensive sets of skeletal remains excavated in the 1930s and 1940s by Bowles and Emory at Mōkapu, Oʻahu. These claims, however, were often contested by other Native Hawaiian claimants, most famously in the case of objects that had been removed from so-called Forbes Cave at Kawaihae on Hawaiʻi Island, and held in Bishop Museum. The Forbes Cave dispute became one of the most contested in NAGPRA history, leading at one point to the jailing of Hui Malama leader Edward Halealoha Ayau for contempt of federal court orders to reveal the location where Hui Mālama had hidden the Forbes Cave items, after these were inappropriately "loaned" to Hui Mālama by Bishop Museum (see Kawelu 2015, 60–62).

By the late 1990s, archaeological practice in Hawaiʻi was radically different from what it had been just three decades earlier (Cachola-Abad and Ayau 1999; Cordy 1999; Kirch 1999). Bishop Museum was phasing out its archaeology program. The University of Hawaiʻi archaeology faculty, for other reasons, were largely focused on archaeological research elsewhere in Polynesia, or in Southeast Asia. The pace of CRM work, however, had not abated, and the SHPD was struggling to maintain regulatory oversight. Meanwhile, due to NAGPRA and newly passed state laws regarding burials (including the establishment of burial councils on each island), research on human skeletal remains had largely ceased, while existing osteological collections such as that at Bishop Museum were being actively repatriated.

For many Kānaka Maoli, archaeology had become synonymous with development. Kirch recalls a 1993 meeting of the Society for Hawaiian Archaeology on Molokaʻi when young activitists stood in the back of the conference room chanting, "Stop the digging!" As Kawelu (2015) documented through interviews with Kānaka Maoli activitists and community leaders, the perception of archaeologists was that they were "Mainland Haole" who knew little about Hawaiian history and culture (and didn't care to educate themselves about such matters), didn't share the results of their work or engage with the community, and were fundamentally in the business of making money. As one Kānaka Maoli activist summed it up in a conversation with Kawelu, archaeologists "take money from anybody; and service anybody. . . . Archaeologists are pimps. They are whoring for money, and that's why we hate them" (2015, 120).

New Horizons in Research and Community-Based Archaeology

While the late 1990s were a low point in the relations between archaeologists and Kānaka Maoli, the situation has improved considerably since then. To a large degree, the improved climate has been the result of a significant number of Kānaka Maoli entering the field of archaeology, becoming active stakeholders in how archaeology is practiced in Hawaiʻi. Some Native Hawaiians had always worked in archaeology (Henry Kekahuna, Elaine Jourdane, Toni Han, and Charles Keau, to name a few), but their numbers began to increase as the University of Hawaiʻi, at both its flagship Mānoa and its Hilo campuses, actively recruited Kānaka Maoli students into their anthropology programs (Mills 2001). The University of Hawaiʻi at Mānoa established an MA degree program in "applied archaeology" in 2009, training archaeologists who have taken up positions in the CRM field. More recently, the

University of Hawai'i at Hilo began its own MA program in heritage management, with an emphasis on community-based archaeology. Three Kānaka Maoli archaeologists hold doctoral degrees: Kehau Cachola-Abad from UH Mānoa (currently with Kamehameha Schools); Kathy Kawelu from the University of California, Berkeley (now on the faculty at UH Hilo); and Kekuewa Kikiloi from UH Mānoa (now on the faculty of the Hawai'inuiākea School of Hawaiian Knowledge at UH Mānoa). An important force in transforming CRM practice in Hawai'i has been the nonprofit organization Huliauapa'a, and its Wahi Kūpuna internship program (https://www.huliauapaa.org/). The integration of Kānaka Maoli archaeologists into the field has unquestionably changed the practice of archaeology in the islands (Dye 2011b), and will continue to do so, in ways that we have yet to fully appreciate.

Kathy Kawelu, a leading advocate for community-based archaeology, describes the approach this way:

> Community-based archaeology, an application of community-based participatory research, begins with a mind-set situating archaeologists among communities of descendants and other stakeholders who value heritage. By envisioning ourselves among the larger population invested in heritage management, we do not lose our academic freedom but gain legitimacy and relevance in descendant communities. The work of community-based heritage management, which is based on principles of respect for other ways of knowing the past and sharing power, is part of the process to decolonize the discipline. (Kawelu 2015, 137–138)

To be sure, implementing community-based archaeology within the context of the dominant CRM model poses challenges. But if archaeologists and their work are to be accepted and valued by Kānaka Maoli stakeholders, this surely must be the path forward.

Although academically based, research-driven archaeology has become a small fraction of the archaeological work conducted in the islands (perhaps 5 percent in terms of overall money spent on archaeological work), it nonetheless remains critical in advancing the field, especially in terms of method and theory, and in driving the fundamental questions being asked of the past. Strictly regulated by the rules and regulations of the SHPD, and hewing to the necessity of their for-profit firms to attend to "the bottom line," CRM archaeologists cannot on their own be expected to push the field forward into new intellectual terrain. This must be the collective *kuleana* (responsibility) of archaeologists in the universities, museums, or other nonprofit organizations, along with their CRM colleagues.

In 1995, a decade after having left Bishop Museum, Kirch (then at the University of California, Berkeley) initiated a new long-term research program in Kahikinui, Maui, building upon the earlier efforts of Chapman's unfinished 1966 settlement-pattern survey. The project, which would run for nearly two decades and eventually expand into adjacent Kaupō District, collaborated closely with a local Kānaka Maoli organization, Ka 'Ohana o Kahikinui, in an effort at community-based archaeology. Technologies that had been developed in the years following the pioneering 1966 survey were now available to aid the work, among them GPS to map the position of sites and geographic information systems (GIS) to integrate spatial data sets. Other methodological advances included microscale geoarchaeology, household archaeology, and the application of ^{230}Th high-precison dating of corals from *heiau* (Kirch 2014; Kirch and Sharp 2005). Around the same time, Michael Graves of the University of Hawai'i initiated renewed work in the Kohala region of Hawai'i Island where the UH had started its Lapakahi field schools in the late 1960s and 1970s, teaming up with Thegn Ladefoged of the University of Auckland (New Zealand) in a study of the vast upland field system (Ladefoged and Graves 2000, 2007).

In the twenty-first century, archaeologists are increasingly aware that their field has a role to play as a core integrating discipline in the emerging interdisciplinary study of long-term global change, or dynamically coupled human-environment interactions (van der Leeuw and Redman 2002). In 2001, the Berkeley and UH teams joined forces together with Stanford University ecologist Peter Vitousek, and University of California, Santa Barbara, soil scientist Oliver Chadwick, among others, to launch the multidisciplinary Hawai'i Biocomplexity Project (HBP), receiving $1.3 million in support from the National Science Foundation. From 2001 to 2009 the HBP explored the complex interactions among ancient Hawaiian dryland agriculture, soils, climate, and population, using the approach of islands as "model systems" (Kirch, ed., 2011; Vitousek et al. 2004). A second phase of the project involved important household excavations in Kohala sites, directed by Julie Field (Field et al. 2010; Field, Ladefoged, and Kirch 2011; Field, Ladefoged, and Sharp 2011), as well as theoretical modeling of the dynamic interactions between human populations and their food supply (Lee and Tuljapurkar 2010). The HBP demonstrated that research into traditional Hawaiian agriculture and land use has significant implications for understanding sustainability of island systems.

Other researchers have likewise helped to push the boundaries of our knowledge regarding ancient Hawai'i. At UH Hilo beginning in 2004, Peter Mills and his geologist colleague Steven Lundblad have used X-ray fluorescence (XRF) to analyze thousands of basalt adzes and adze flakes, and volcanic-glass flakes, from sites around the islands, enhancing our understanding of how these artifacts were distributed and exchanged (see chapter 9). Jim Bayman at UH Mānoa has not only spearheaded the MA program in applied archaeology but also made contributions to historic-period archaeology in Hawai'i (Bayman 2010). And at the University of Hawai'i–West O'ahu, Ross Cordy has engaged students from the rural Wai'anae District in field school programs, another important community-based effort.

While the early history of archaeology in Hawai'i was shaped by men such as Stokes, Emory, and Green, we cannot overlook the pioneering contributions of women to Hawaiian archaeology and ethnohistory. Mary Kawena Pukui collaborated with Edward Handy (Handy and Pukui 1958), translated the works of Kamakau, and coauthored the Hawaiian dictionary. Elspeth Sterling and Catherine Summers carried out site surveys of O'ahu, Moloka'i, and Maui (E. P. Sterling 1998; Sterling and Summers 1978; Summers 1971). Dorothy Barrère and Marion Kelly made major contributions to Hawaiian ethnohistory (Barrère 1975; Kelly 1975, 1980, 1983), in addition to aiding Marshall Sahlins and Kirch in their Anahulu Valley research. Among the archaeologists who directed high-quality CRM projects in the 1980s and 1990s were Jane Allen (1991, 1992), Rose Schilt (1984), and Melinda Allen (2001). At Bishop Museum, Jennifer Kahn (Kahn et al. 2015), Mara Mulrooney (Mulrooney et al. 2014), and most recently Jillian Swift (Swift et al. 2019) have generated new research projects around the museum's archaeological collections. Presidents of the Society of Hawaiian Archaeology have included Pat Beggerly, Sara Collins, Regina Hilo, and Mara Mulrooney.

A new generation of archaeologists who became active in Hawai'i in the 2000s and 2010s continues to build on existing trends while introducing innovative approaches. Mark McCoy studies the ancient political economy through agricultural intensification, exchange and mobility, religious authority and *kapu,* and the study of royal centers, especially in Kona District on Hawai'i Island, extending the settlement-pattern approach using advances in geospatial archaeology (e.g., M. D. McCoy 2014, 2018, 2020a; M. D. McCoy, Asner, and Graves 2011; M. D. McCoy and Codlin 2016). Julie S. Field has drawn upon Bishop Museum's earlier Nu'alolo Kai excavation materials to address the sustainability and management of natural resources (e.g., Field and Graves, eds., 2015). James Flexner's innovative scholarship on historical artifacts and sites builds on methodological and theoretical advances of the Anahulu project (e.g., Flexner 2011a; Flexner et al. 2018; Flexner and McCoy 2016). And Kekuewa Kikiloi's investigation of Nihoa and Mokumanamana Islands offers new insights into those enigmatic islands (Kikiloi 2012).

When the first edition of this book was published in 1985, this chapter ended with a few predictions of where the field might go (Kirch 1985, 20–21), but no one could have foreseen either the major technological advances that would come (such as the use of GPS and GIS in settlement archaeology, AMS radiocarbon dating and Bayesian modeling, ^{230}Th high-precision dating of corals, stable isotope analysis of faunal remains, or XRF geochemical analysis of stone artifacts), or the upheavals precipitated by the increasing tensions between CRM archaeology and the Kānaka Maoli cultural renaissance. Certainly the demise of Bishop Museum's dominance in Hawaiian archaeology was unanticipated. What path the field will follow over the next few decades is equally unpredictable. It seems likely, however, that Kānaka Maoli archaeologists will increasingly shape that direction, with a community-based approach that seeks to empower multiple stakeholders. Two things, however, are certain. First, that there is still a great deal to learn about the Hawaiian past, especially as we raise new questions and employ new methods and techniques. And second, that the archaeological record is a finite resource, that once destroyed, *wahi kūpuna* (ancestral places) can never be recovered. Too much has already disappeared. Let us all strive to preserve and protect what remains.

2

AN ISLAND WORLD

The most isolated archipelago in the world, the Hawaiian Islands straddle the Tropic of Cancer amid the trackless waters of the North Pacific. Isolation has fundamentally shaped the islands' natural history, the vast oceanic expanse acting as barrier and filter to plants and animals as well as to humans. The coast of North America lies 3,800 km to the east, while Japan is almost 6,200 km to the west. Excepting the low coral islets of the Pacific equatorial region (such as Fanning and Christmas Islands), other Polynesian and Micronesian island groups are similarly distant. Tahiti and the Marquesas—the islands from which the immediate ancestors of the Hawaiians most likely departed—lie 4,410 and 3,862 km to the south, respectively. The history of life in the Hawaiian Islands is one of long-distance dispersal, including the arrival of seafaring Polynesians in their double-hulled canoes.

Although the entire Hawaiian archipelago, consisting of 132 islands, islets, sand cays, and reefs, extends over a distance of 2,450 km, fully 99 percent of the archipelago's land area is encompassed by eight principal high islands at the chain's eastern end (fig. 2.1). The westerly, leeward islands comprise a few tiny volcanic pinnacles and numerous coral reefs and atolls never inhabited by Polynesians. The exceptions are Nihoa and Mokumanamana (Necker Island), rocky vestiges of formerly larger islands, uninhabited at the time of European discovery but exhibiting archaeological testimony to former human occupation (see chapter 19). These eight main islands vary in configuration, land area, and height above sea level (table 2.1). The two smallest islands, Kahoʻolawe and Niʻihau, are arid, with water available only at springs and seeps along the coast; consequently, they played only marginal roles in the social and political life of ancient Hawaiʻi. In order of increasing size, the next islands are Lānaʻi (also relatively dry), Molokaʻi, Kauaʻi, Oʻahu, and Maui. The largest of them all, Hawaiʻi, popularly known as the "Big Island," comprises nearly twice as much land as the other seven islands combined.

Communication between some islands was more difficult than between others. Kauaʻi and Niʻihau are separated from Oʻahu by the 117-km-wide Kauaʻi Channel, with notoriously turbulent seas. The ʻAlenuihāhā Channel separating Maui and Hawaiʻi, although just 46 km wide, has a similar reputation for fierceness. When today we travel by jet between islands in a few minutes, it is easy to overlook the challenges to interisland communication

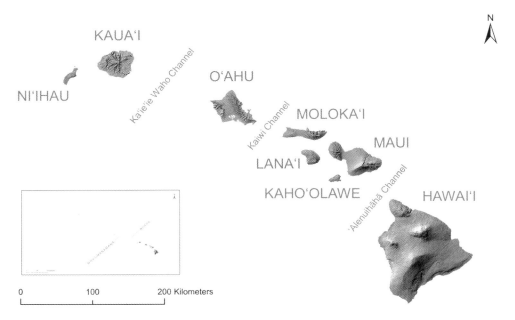

FIGURE 2.1 Map of the main islands of the Hawaiian archipelago; inset shows the main islands along with the northwestern islands, or Papahanaumokuākea, including Nihoa and Mokumanamana Islands. *(Map by Mark McCoy)*

TABLE 2.1. Geographic characteristics of the main Hawaiian Islands

ISLAND	AREA (KM²)	HIGHEST POINT (M)	AGE (MA)
Mokumanamana (Necker)	0.24	84	10.3
Nihoa	0.77	277	7.2
Ni'ihau	189	390	5.5
Kaua'i	1,433	1,598	5.1
O'ahu	1,574	1,232	3.7–2.6
Moloka'i	676	1,515	1.8–1.3
Lāna'i	361	1,027	1.6
Maui	1,887	3,056	1.3–0.7
Kaho'olawe	117	450	1.0
Hawai'i	10,458	4,206	0.6–0

that such distances imposed on the early Hawaiians. The great warrior chief Kamehameha's plans for the conquest of Kaua'i were thwarted in 1796 when a sudden storm sundered his fleet of war canoes in the Kaua'i Channel. Although contact between Kaua'i and O'ahu was sustained throughout the precontact era, this was probably less frequent than between the more closely situated islands of Moloka'i, Maui, Lāna'i, and Kaho'olawe (a group sometimes known as Maui Nui). Certain distinctive Kaua'i Island styles of stone pounders, images, and other artifacts as well as dialect differences reflect this relative isolation.

Hawaiian Landforms

Geologically, the Hawaiian Islands are the exposed tips of a northwest-southeast-trending linear chain of volcanoes resting upon the Pacific Plate, the largest of the tectonic plates making up the Pacific region. The islands have been emerging over millions of years over a fixed "hot spot" or magma plume originating deep in the Earth's mantle. The oldest islands of this age-progressive chain lie at the northwest end, with the youngest, still active, volcanoes in the southeast. Kīlauea on Hawai'i Island and the submarine mountain Lō'ihi currently lie over the active hot spot. The gradual movement of the volcanic masses from southeast to northwest results from the slow drift of the Pacific Plate across the fixed hot spot. Potassium-argon dating of volcanic rocks (Clague and Dalrymple 1987) provides the time frame for the formation of the Hawaiian volcanoes. Rocks obtained from cores drilled deep into Midway Atoll near the northwest end of the chain date to 28.3 million years ago. The last lava flows to have erupted on the island of Kaua'i date to about 5.25 million years old, Moloka'i rocks range from 1.9 to 2.1 million years, and the oldest rocks of the still active Mauna Loa shield on Hawai'i Island are less than 0.5 million years in age. Virtually all of the Kīlauea shield on Hawai'i has been inundated by fresh lava flows within the past few thousand years, many within the time span of Polynesian occupation.

The age of an island determines how extensively it has been weathered, with incised valleys, coastal plains, and fringing reefs all taking hundreds of thousands to a few million years to develop (MacDonald and Abbott 1970; Ziegler 2002). The oldest, northwestern islands (encompassed within the Papahānaumokuākea Marine National Monument) have been almost entirely leveled by erosion, their volcanic bases now submerged and capped by coral reefs. Of the main high islands, Kaua'i and O'ahu are the oldest and most dissected by erosion (color plate 1). The relatively young volcanic shield of Haleakalā, forming East Maui, exhibits some valley incision with the Ko'olau and Kaupō Gaps (fig. 2.2), along with narrow stream valleys on the windward side. The young, towering volcanoes of Mauna Kea and Mauna Loa on Hawai'i Island have only minor stream incision on their windward slopes, while their leeward, dry sides exhibit little erosion and no permanent streams at all.

The Hawaiians recognized this geological age progression in their accounts of island origins (Beckwith 1970). In one myth, the demigod Maui uses his magic fishhook to pull the islands up from beneath the sea, beginning with Kaua'i, and progressing down the island chain to Hawai'i. The same sequence of island emergence is followed in the Pele and Hi'iaka myth cycle, in which the volcano godess Pele dwells at first on Kaua'i, then moves progressively down the island chain to end up in her current home in the fire pit of Halema'uma'u on Kīlauea.

Hawaiian landforms reflect not only their geological age but also the effects of climate. The pattern of northeasterly trade winds creates distinct windward (*ko'olau*) and leeward (*kona*) sides of each island. The Hawaiian words *ko'olau* (windward, northeast) and *kona* (leeward, southwest) derive from the older Proto-Polynesian words *tokerau* and *tonga,* which referenced a north-south axis in the Western Polynesian homeland (Kirch and Green

FIGURE 2.2 View of the geologically youthful slopes of southeast Maui, looking toward Kaupō Gap and the rim of Haleakalā Crater. *(Photo by P. V. Kirch)*

2001, 107). In addition to being general geographical referents, Kona became the proper name of several leeward districts (as on Oʻahu, Molokaʻi, and Hawaiʻi Islands), while Koʻolau became the name of one or more windward districts (as in Koʻolauloa and Koʻolaupoko on Oʻahu, and Koʻolau on Molokaʻi).

Rainfall in Hawaiʻi is controlled largely by the phenomenon of orographic ("mountain-caused") precipitation (Giambelluca and Schroeder 1998). Warm, moisture-laden trade winds overriding the steep mountain ranges rise abruptly, cooling and dropping rain on the windward slopes; rainfall decreases rapidly as the winds flow down toward the leeward regions. Thus each island has a wet windward and a dry leeward side. On Oʻahu, rainfall on the windward coast near Kāneʻohe averages 1,875 mm annually, rises to more than 6,250 mm at the crest of the Koʻolau mountains, then drops to less than 500 mm on the leeward coast at ʻEwa. This windward-leeward rainfall gradient, whose northeast-southwest axis cross-cuts the southeast-northwest geological age progression, is the second major factor in the development of Hawaiian landforms, also strongly influencing vegetation zones. Together these geological and climate axes create a mosaic of old and young, wet and dry environments across the archipelago. The orthogonal nature of these two cross-cutting axes renders the Hawaiian Islands a remarkable "model system" for studying aspects of island ecology as well as human adaptations to this ecological mosaic (Kirch 2007a; Vitousek 2004).

Hawaiian rainfall varies seasonally as well as topographically. Generally, the winter months from October to April are the wettest, while summers are considerably drier. (An exception to this pattern occurs across the Kona District of Hawaiʻi Island, where the peak rainfall months are June and August.) Between October and April there are frequent reversals in wind direction, with periods of southerly winds known in Hawaiian as *kona,* associated with muggy weather and heavy downpours that can turn otherwise dry watercourses into raging torrents. To the ancient Hawaiians, especially those dwelling in leeward areas, this winter rainfall was essential for the scheduling of agricultural activities, especially sweet potato planting.

Rainfall and other aspects of climate have also varied over longer time periods. Diaz et al. (2016) reconstructed winter rainfall patterns in Hawai'i back to AD 1500, showing an overall drying trend, but with significant wetter and drier periods. Periods with greater rainfall around AD 1500 and from about AD 1625 to 1675 may have encouraged expansion of the leeward agricultural field systems that were dependent upon rainfall to grow sweet potato and dryland taro. Unusually dry periods during the mid- and later 1700s, however, may have stressed these same field systems, possibly inducing conflict and warfare between the Hawai'i and Maui kingdoms, as documented in oral traditions of this period (Kamakau 1961). Further refinement of the paleoclimate record for the islands could provide new insights regarding the influence of climate on Hawaiian history.

Variations in landform across the islands offered different opportunities and challenges for settlement and agriculture. Broad valleys with well-developed soils and permanent streams on the older, westerly islands were more attractive to Polynesians than the hot, dry lava landscapes of eastern Maui or Hawai'i Islands. The early Polynesians in Hawai'i had to adapt their agricultural practices and settlement patterns as they moved across this mosaic of differing ages and landforms.

During the Pleistocene, fluctuations in sea level resulted in considerable modification of Hawaiian coastlines and landforms. High sea cliffs were cut in some places at times of higher stands of the sea (fig. 2.3), while during periods of lowered sea level several islands were joined as a single land mass (Moloka'i, Lāna'i, and Maui). The extensive leeward plains of Honolulu and 'Ewa on O'ahu are emerged coral reefs, built by coral polyps during a higher sea level of the Sangamon Interglacial (Stearns 1978).

As the oldest of the main islands, Kaua'i has the greatest extent of deeply eroded valleys and cliffs, with limited remnants of the original volcanic shield surfce. Windward O'ahu

FIGURE 2.3 The sea cliffs of windward Moloka'i are among the highest in the world. *(Photo by P. V. Kirch)*

is likewise heavily sculpted by erosion, as are the windward coasts of Moloka'i and West Maui. Hawaiian valleys begin their development as narrow V-shaped gulches that cut deep into the volcanic slopes. As these gulches widen over many thousands of years, the valley floors become gentler, and stream capture occurs. Eventually, as valley heads migrate inland, an amphitheater-like formation develops (fig. 2.4). A series of such amphitheater-headed valleys frame the Kāne'ohe area on windward O'ahu, once a major center of irrigated taro cultivation.

Upland slope landscapes consist of the original surface of a shield volcano, ranging from undissected slopes with little or no established surface drainage to deeply dissected terrain incised by substantial V-shaped gulches. With increased age and weathering, deeply dissected slopes are gradually transformed into the valley and cliff complex. Undissected or slightly dissected uplands are represented on Mauna Loa and in the Kula area of Maui. The Hāmākua coast of Hawai'i Island typifies dissected uplands, while the leeward side of East Moloka'i exemplifies deeply dissected uplands transitional to cliff and valley complex.

Saddle regions, formed by the coalescence of two volcanoes, include the Schofield Plateau on O'ahu, the Ho'olehua plains on Moloka'i, the Waimea saddle on Hawai'i, and the high plateau between Mauna Kea and Mauna Loa volcanoes on Hawai'i. Such regions are only slightly dissected by stream erosion, if at all.

Each of these major physiographic types was settled or utilized by the ancient Hawaiians in distinctive ways. The valley and cliff complex offered the most favorable locale for taro pondfield irrigation, while undissected uplands favored extensive dryfield cultivation. We explore the adaptation of Hawaiian agriculture to such varied environments in greater detail in chapter 7.

While some natural ponds and small lakes are scattered across the islands, most surface water is carried in streams that are either perennial or intermittent. Perennial streams are found on all of the main islands except for Ni'ihau and Kaho'olawe, which have only intermittently flowing watercourses. Perennial streams are fed primarily by groundwater

FIGURE 2.4 The deeply incised heads of valleys on the geologically older islands form amphitheater-like basins, as in Hālawa Valley, Moloka'i. *(Photo courtesy Bishop Museum Library and Archives)*

perched in high-level aquifers, supplemented in some cases by basal groundwater springs where the streams flow across coastal plains. On Kaua'i, perennial streams are found around most of the island, offering extensive possibilities for taro irrigation. On O'ahu, Moloka'i, Maui, and Hawai'i, perennial streams are mostly limited to the windward regions. Large sections of geologically young Hawai'i Island, including Kona and Ka'ū Districts, have no stream channels at all.

The Hawaiian Biota

The overriding characteristic of Hawaiian terrestrial life is its *endemism:* by far the greater proportion of species of plants, insects, mollusks, and birds inhabiting the islands are found nowhere else in the world, a result of the islands' great isolation. Once a colonizing plant or animal had managed to pass through the "sieves of difficulty of overseas transport" (Zimmerman 1963, 58), it more likely than not found the environment free of competitors. A process of *adaptive radiation* and evolution of new species followed, with descendants of the original ancestor spreading out into a variety of habitats, and diversifying to fill a wide variety of ecological niches (Wagner and Funk, eds., 1995). The Hawaiian honeycreepers (Drepanididae) are an oft-cited case in point; this family of birds evolved through adaptive radiation into no less than 39 species and subspecies across the main islands, over a period of at least six million years (Lerner et al. 2011). Variation in the functional morphology of the honeycreeper bill and in the range of food-getting behavior is truly remarkable (Berger 1972). One consequence of this high degree of endemism for newly arrived Polynesians was that the majority of plants and animals they encountered in their new island home would have been unfamiliar to them. The first people to see Hawai'i's honeycreepers, for example, would come to call them *manu mūkīkī,* literally the bird that sucks. Over time people would need to name and discover the properties and potential uses of all of these species that are unique to Hawai'i.

Isolation restricted terrestrial life to forms adept at long-distance dispersal (though many species subsequently lost such ability in the course of island evolution). The endemic and indigenous biota was thus limited to certain families of plants, insects, terrestrial mollusks, and birds, what biologists call a *disharmonic* biota. The only native land mammals in Hawai'i were two species of bat, one still extant (*Lasiurus cinereus semotus*), and one that went extinct in the precontact period (*Synemporian keana;* Ziegler et al. 2016). No quadruped vertebrates inhabited Hawai'i prior to the Polynesian introduction of pigs, dogs, and rats. However, several species of large, flightless birds had evolved on the main islands. These vulnerable birds became extinct soon after human arrival (Olson and James 1982a, 1982b, 1984). Table 2.2 lists the numbers of endemic as well as indigenous species (that is, native but not found exclusively in Hawai'i) known for the Hawaiian archipelago. With the destruction of so much of the native flora and fauna, especially in the lower altitude zones, the numbers in table 2.2 can be taken only as a conservative estimate of the numbers of species that flourished in Hawai'i prior to the arrival of humans.

Botanists and ecologists have devised several schemes for classifying the major biological zones in Hawai'i (e.g., Carlquist 1970; Hosaka 1937; Ripperton and Hosaka 1942; Rock 1913;

TABLE 2.2. Approximate numbers of endemic and indigenous species of the Hawaiian terrestrial biota (includes extinct species); adapted from Ziegler (2002, table 13.1)

GROUP	ENDEMIC SPECIES	INDIGENOUS SPECIES	TOTAL
Ferns and fern allies	125	53	178
Flowering plants	907	113	1,020
Insects	5,293	84	5,377
Spiders	126	0	126
Snails	762	8	770
Fishes	4	1	5
Birds	98	6	104
Mammals	2	1	3
Total	7,317	260	7,577

Wagner et al. 1990; Ziegler 2002). For our purposes, Sherwin Carlquist's simple classification suffices: (1) the coast; (2) the dry forest; (3) the wet forest; and (4) the alpine zone.

Prior to human arrival in Hawai'i, the immediate foreshore was dominated with such species as the beach morning glory (*Ipomoea pes-caprae*) and *naupaka* (*Scaevola taccada*), with dense stands of *hala* (screwpine, *Pandanus* spp.) directly inland. *Hau* (*Hibiscus tiliaceous*) may have formed thickets in low-lying, swampy areas, both along the coast and in valley bottoms. Ancient pollen recovered from sediment cores on O'ahu shows that there were extensive forests of *loulu* palms (*Pritchardia* spp.), which declined rapidly within one to two centuries after Polynesian arrival (Athens 1997; Athens and Ward 1993; Athens, Ward, and Wickler 1992; Athens, Ward, and Blinn 1995; Athens et al. 2002). The introduction of the small but fast-reproducing Pacific rat (*Rattus exulans*), which may have consumed both seeds and seedlings of native plants, could have contributed to this lowland forest decline (Athens et al. 2002).

Before human arrival, the coastal zone supported large nesting populations of seabirds, providing a ready food source for the settlers. The deeper layers of some stratified sites, such as Nu'alolo rockshelter on Kaua'i, and the Kuli'ou'ou rockshelter on O'ahu, contained significant quantities of seabird bones (Esh 2015; Emory and Sinoto 1961, 17, fig. 13). Evidence for the former existence of several species of flightless ducks and geese (Anatidae), ibises (Threskiornithidae), and rails (Rallidae) has been found in late Pleistocene and Holocene fossil deposits, and in a few cases in archaeological contexts (Olson and James 1982a, 1982b; Ziegler 2002, table 22.1). With just two exceptions, these flightless birds all became extinct prior to European contact, most likely soon after Polynesian arrival in the archipelago. Particularly striking were the large *moa nalo* (*Thambetochen* spp.), with distinct endemic species on O'ahu, Moloka'i, and Maui. As large as turkeys and with no natural predator-avoidance instincts, these birds would have been an attractive food source for early Polynesian settlers. Their extinction, however, may have been more a consequence of the collapse of the lowland dryland forests than a result of direct predation by humans.

The dry forest zone, now nearly replaced with invasive plants (such as *koa haole* and *kiawe*), and the setting for extensive sugarcane and pineapple plantations in the twentieth century, was a major habitat occupied by the early Hawaiians. In most areas, the lower dry forest comprised an open, parkland vegetation, rather than a closed canopy. Dominant trees included the *wiliwili* (*Erythrina sandwicensis,* fig. 2.5), *naio* (*Myoporum sandwicensis*), *lama* (*Diospyros ferra*), *'ohe* (*Reynoldsia sandwicensis*), *'iliahi* (sandalwood, *Santalum freycinetianum*), and *'āla'a* (*Planchonella* spp.). Herbs and grasses were common, including *pili* grass (*Andropogon contortus*), used by the Hawaiians as their principal thatching material. The dry forest provided habitat for many species of endemic land snails, whose diminutive shells have been recovered in archaeological excavations (Christensen 1983; Christensen and Kirch 1986). Certain wet sites with anaerobic conditions, such as the Makauwahi cave complex on Kaua'i, have preserved the remains of endemic insects such as now-extinct beetles (Liebherr and Porch 2015). The lowlands were also home to a great variety of native land birds, most of which have become extinct (James and Olson 1983; Olson and James 1982b). These included the flightless ducks and geese (larger than the *nēnē*), rails, and ibises mentioned above. The *nēnē* (*Branta sandvicensis*), known historically only from Hawai'i Island, has turned up in archaeological deposits on O'ahu, Moloka'i, and Kaho'olawe; it seems to have been widespread and abundant when the first Polynesians arrived.

The upper dry forest, which persists in some regions, is dominated by the endemic *koa* tree (*Acacia koa*). Other native trees found in the upper dry forest, and utilized by the Hawaiians for a variety of purposes, are the *kauila* (*Alphitonia ponderosa*), *koai'a* (*Acacia koaia*), *'ohe* (*Tetraplasandra hawaiiensis*), *olopua* (*Osmanthus sandwicensis*), sandalwood (*Santalum freycinetianum*), *hō'awa* (*Pittosporum terminaloides*), and *māmane* (*Sophora chrysophylla*). Common shrubs are *pūkiawe* (*Styphelia tameiameiae*) and *ko'oko'olau* (*Bidens* spp.).

FIGURE 2.5 The endemic *wiliwili* tree, characteristic of leeward, dryland environments in Hawai'i, is able to grow out of barren lava fields. *(Photo by P. V. Kirch)*

Growing beneath the *koa* are fairly dense *'ie'ie* vines (*Freycinetia arborea*), used for making baskets and traps, and the fragrant *maile* (*Alyxia* spp.) prized for *lei*. As with the lower zone, the upper dry forest had its own unique invertebrate, insect, and bird life.

The wet forests, generally above the areas heavily occupied by the ancient Hawaiians, have survived relatively intact, although they are increasingly threatened by invasive species. The transition from dry to wet forest is marked by a change in the dominant tree from koa to *'ōhi'a* (*Metrosideros polymorpha*). Common in the wet forest are the araliads (*Tetraplasandra* spp.), *'ōlapa* (*Cheirodendron* spp.), *hame* (*Antidesma platyphyllum*), *hō'awa* (*Pittosporum* spp.), *alani* (*Pelea* spp.), and *kōlea* (*Myrsine lessertiana*), with native *loulu* palms (*Pritchardia* spp.) and tree ferns (*Cibotium* spp.) scattered throughout. Among the shrubs of the montane forest are the marvelously speciated lobelias. Epiphytes are frequent, and wet forest trees are hung with cascades of mosses and liverworts. The fauna of the montane forest is equally diverse and included the famous achatinellid tree snails (*Achatinella* spp.), most of which are now sadly extinct or endangered. Among the native birds, the honeycreepers (Drepanididae) were especially prominent in the wet forest.

Persons unfamiliar with Hawai'i are often surprised to hear that alpine environments exist on these subtropical islands, yet they occur on the four highest mountains: Haleakalā, Mauna Kea, Hualālai, and Mauna Loa. Today the depredations of introduced feral sheep and goats have left the alpine vegetation a mere shadow of what it must have been during the late precontact period. Plant materials excavated from shelter caves on Mauna Kea, used by Hawaiians quarrying adze rock (M. S. Allen 1981), indicate something of the former extent of the alpine flora. Among the extant alpine plants are the famous silverswords (*Argyroxiphium* spp.), as well as the *'ōhelo* (*Vaccinium* spp.) with its delicious berries.

The Marine Environment

To the Hawaiians, the sea and its resources rivaled the land in importance. In Hawai'i there are fewer endemic species of marine life than of land flora and fauna. Many of the species of Hawaiian fish and shellfish are also known from tropical parts of the South Pacific, although the Hawaiian marine fauna is less diverse. There are about 450 species of reef and shore fishes in Hawaiian waters, 150 species of crabs, and about 1,000 species of mollusks (Edmonson 1946; Gosline and Brock 1960: Kay 1979; Randall 2010).

The main islands encompass 1.2 million km of coastline, but fully 22 percent of this is made up of sea cliffs with heights greater than 30 m, rendering these coastal areas largely inaccessible (fig. 2.6). The most extensive reef areas are found on the older, westerly islands, especially on Kaua'i and O'ahu, along the south coast of Moloka'i, and to some extent around West Maui. On O'ahu, Kāne'ohe Bay and a former bay in what is now Kawainui Marsh had the most developed reefs in the entire archipelago. The island of Hawai'i is too young to have appreciable reef development; only small patch reefs dot the western coastline (as at Kalāhuipua'a in South Kohala).

The shoreline or "littoral fringe," with its diversity of invertebrates and seaweeds, was an important resource zone for the Hawaiians. Exposed windward coasts are noted for *'opihi* (*Cellana* spp.), while leeward shores are the preferred habitat of *leho* (cowries, *Cypraea*

FIGURE 2.6 Sea cliffs, such as these along the Kahikinui coastline of southeast Maui, are typical of the geologically younger islands. *(Photo by P. V. Kirch)*

spp.), *pūpū'awa* (drupes, *Drupa* and *Thais* spp.), and *pipipi* (nerites, *Nerita* spp.), all gathered and eaten by the Hawaiians. The shore zone is also a source of edible sea urchins, *hā'uke'uke* and *wana* (*Colobocentrotus atratus* and *Echinothrix diadema*) and of seaweeds (*limu*).

Most Hawaiian fishes, as well as octopus and lobster, frequent the inshore reef zone (generally the area with depths of 30 m or less). Hawaiians intensively fished this inshore zone using fishhooks, nets, spears, traps, and other gear. Extending beyond the reef, the benthic zone was less important, though it is the habitat of some important food fish, such as snappers (Lutjanidae). Finally, the open sea, or pelagic zone, is the home of large carnivorous fish such as *mahimahi* (Coryphaenidae), *ahi* and *aku* (tuna, Scombridae), and *a'u* (marlin, Istiophoridae). These fish were prized by the Hawaiians, who used canoes and trolled for them with lures of pearl shell (see chapter 9).

Resources, Constraints, and Hazards

The first Polynesians to beach their canoes on Hawaiian shores encountered pristine, verdant islands, with forests teeming with strange plants and inhabited by abundant birds, and with reefs abounding in fish and shellfish. Among the resources critical to the Polynesians were fresh water (both to drink and for agriculture), soils, the natural vegetation (for wood, cordage, thatching materials, and so on), wild animals and marine life, and stone for tool production. This environmental canvas offered abundant resources for the support of human populations, but also imposed constraints on Polynesian cultural patterns, as well as a few distinct hazards.

For their crops Polynesians required adequate rainfall, usually in excess of 750 mm annually, even for the most drought-tolerant crops, such as sweet potato. One of the two main staple crops, *kalo* (taro, *Colocasia esculenta*), requires annual rainfall of at least 1,500 mm, providing the highest yields when irrigated. Windward valleys offered reliable sources of water, with higher annual rainfall and permanent streams that could be dammed and diverted into stone-lined canals to deliver water to terraced pondfields. The greatest areas of *kalo* irrigation were centered in windward regions such as the Haleleʻa District on Kauaʻi, Koʻolaupoko District on Oʻahu, Koʻolau District on Molokaʻi, and the Nā Wai Ehā region of West Maui. Leeward valleys vary greatly in amount of annual rainfall and in intensity and permanence of streamflow. The more marginal leeward valleys and gulches, in which the intermittent streams flow only after heavy rains, were not suited to taro irrigation. Leeward slopes, especially on the younger islands of Maui and Hawaiʻi Islands, lack flowing surface water; in those regions, extensive rain-fed dryland field systems were developed, primarily for sweet potato (*ʻuala*) cultivation.

The nature of Hawaiian soils—and in particular their fertility—also corresponds with the geological age of each island and with the windward-leeward rainfall gradient (Chorover and Chadwick 2001; Cline 1955; Vitousek 2004). Especially desirable for agriculture were the alluvial and colluvial soils of windward and leeward valleys. While stony, these fertile soils are easily worked by hand tillage with a digging stick. When inundated for extended periods, as in taro irrigation, alluvial soils develop classic gray and rust colored "paddy soil" profiles, with an organically rich anaerobic horizon overlying a zone of oxidation (Kirch 1977). Also significant were latosols on the leeward flow slopes of the younger islands, especially Hawaiʻi and Maui. These younger soils are rich in nutrients, and where the annual rainfall was suitable for nonirrigated cultivation of crops such as sweet potato, yams, and dryland taro, supported extensive field systems (Ladefoged et al. 2009; Vitousek et al. 2004). Areas with this ideal mix of younger soils and adequate (but not too high) rainfall included leeward Kohala, Kona, and Kaʻū Districts on Hawaiʻi Island, leeward East Maui (Hāna through Kaupō, Kahikinui, and Kula Districts), and the Kalaupapa Peninsula on Molokaʻi. These field systems are discussed in greater detail in chapter 7.

The rainfall, streamflow, and soil regimes of the Hawaiian Islands exhibit a complex environmental mosaic. Colonizing Polynesians and their descendants had to discover through trial and error how to adapt agricultural practices originally developed in the tropical central Polynesian homeland. Early settlers from the Marquesas or Society Islands were confronted in Hawaiʻi with the challenge of transferring and adapting tropical Oceanic crops to local conditions. The windward valleys most fully satisfied the climate and soil requirements for successful cultivation of taro, yams, bananas, and other Oceanic crops. Second in importance were the larger, leeward valleys with intermediate rainfall, but with more variable streamflow (such as Mānoa on Oʻahu). Leeward slopes were more challenging due to the lack of permanent streams, and to the frequent occurrence of droughts or insufficient annual rainfall.

The extreme endemism of the native Hawaiian plants and animals also had implications for the colonizing Polynesians arriving from tropical Oceania. The wild plants of their tropical homeland being largely absent in Hawaiʻi, they had to explore and discover which species were suited to house construction, thatching, preparation of cords and rope, medicine, and other purposes. During this process of familiarization, many old Polynesian plant names were transferred to local species. One striking case of name transfer is that of koa. In the South Pacific, the cognate term *toa* is applied to the ironwood tree (*Casuarina equisitifolia*), noted for its excellent hardwood. Ironwood was absent in Hawai'i (though it was later introduced by Europeans), and the term *toa* was transferred to the local *Acacia koa*, a tree similarly suited to construction and carving. (The term *toa/koa* was also used metaphorically throughout Polynesia to refer to a warrior.)

The igneous rocks of the Hawaiian Islands also posed constraints on the raw materials available for making stone tools and implements. Hawaiian rocks consist mostly of successive lava flows, primarily of tholeiitic and alkalic basalts. Glassy phases of basalt (volcanic or basaltic glass) are present, either as surface chills on lava flows, or associated with dikes. One rare eruptive event on Hualālai at Pu'u Wa'awa'a produced trachytic glass, which is richer in silica than basalt, but less siliceous than obsidian; this source of glass was extensively exploited. Hawaiians utilized this volcanic glass, not as rich in silica as true obsidian, for diminutive flake tools. Dense, fine-grained basalt was the main material used for adzes and chisels, while various kinds of bowls, mortars, pestles, sinkers, and so on were manufactured from the vesicular, easier-to-work lavas. The scoriaceous lava of certain kinds of *pāhoehoe* flows was well suited for use as abraders (Kirch 1979a).

Natural materials for tool and artifact production—stone, wood, coral, fibers, and the like—were widely available throughout the island chain. Some materials, however, such as dense basalt suitable for adzes, scoriaceous lava for abraders, and hematite for octopus-lure sinkers, have localized distributions. Due to its younger geological age, Hawai'i Island offers the greatest variety of lithic resources, including the fine-grained Mauna Kea basalt prized for adzes (see chapter 9). Communities with access to a particular resource sometimes specialized in its extraction, and materials were widely exchanged or traded between communities and islands.

While in many respects benign, the Hawaiian environment nonetheless posed some hazards, including floods, tsunamis, drought, and volcanic eruptions. Irrigation dams and canals (*'auwai*) were prone to inundation and destruction by torrential floods. Hawaiian valleys differ in their susceptibility to flooding, depending upon the size of the drainage basin, the stream gradient, and the degree of vegetation cover. Geologically young valleys, such as Waipi'o and Pololū in Kohala District of Hawai'i Island, are especially prone to flash floods, as demonstrated in 1977, when the taro fields of Waipi'o Valley were largely destroyed. A similar disastrous flood is referenced in Hawaiian oral traditions, causing the chiefs Mo'ikeha and Olopana to abandon their taro fields in Waipi'o (Fornander 1878–1885). Clearing of native forest cover on valley slopes for agriculture may have also heightened the local effects of flooding. In the Mākaha Valley of O'ahu, archaeological excavations demonstrated that an irrigation system was inundated by flooding and buried under a landslide, initiated by clearing of the forest on slopes above the irrigated fields (Yen et al. 1972).

Tsunamis can be generated by local Hawaiian earthquakes (as with the 1868 earthquake in Ka'ū, Hawai'i), but are more often caused by earth movements around the Pacific rim. In 1946, an Aleutian quake generated a tsunami that hit Hawai'i about 4.5 hours later, driving water inland to heights as great as 17 m above sea level and flooding the main taro fields in Hālawa Valley on Moloka'i. Historical records indicate that eight major and six minor tsunamis have caused proportionate levels of damage along Hawaiian coastlines since 1820. At an average frequency of about one tsunami every 10 to 11 years, it is likely that

125 to 150 such waves have hit the islands since the initial arrival of Polynesians. Certainly some of these tsunamis must have caused considerable damage and loss of life. At Hāʻena, Kauaʻi, archaeological investigations demonstrated stratigraphic evidence of prehistoric tsunamis in the form of laminated deposits of well-sorted sand with larger coral debris up to 3 m above present sea level (Griffin et al. 1977). Sediment cores extracted from valley bottoms on several islands have revealed marine sand deposits that may be evidence of a major tsunami between 500 and 700 years ago (La Selle et al. 2019).

Drought is a hazard with great potential impact in leeward areas, where agriculture was dependent upon rainfall. Diaz et al. (2016) modeled winter rainfall in the Hawaiian Islands over the past 500 years, finding that there were periods of relatively high rainfall, for example around AD 1500 and again between 1625 and 1675, which may have been favorable to the intensification of the leeward slope field systems. Persistent droughts in the leeward regions might have necessitated local population movements, or temporary abandonment of settlements.

Most spectacular of all potential hazards in Hawaiʻi are volcanic eruptions and associated phenomena, such as faulting and steam explosions. Within the time that humans have occupied the islands, only Maui and Hawaiʻi Islands have seen volcanic activity. On Maui, a flow of *ʻaʻā* lava emanated from the southwest rift of Haleakalā about AD 1790, forming a prominent peninsula, Cape Kīnaʻu, jutting into the sea (MacDonald and Abbott 1970, 50–51). This eruption must have covered Hawaiian settlements, since the coastline in this area is known to have been heavily populated.

The island of Hawaiʻi has been the main center of active vulcanism over the past 1,000 years. Kīlauea volcano and particularly the firepit Halemaʻumaʻu are noted in Hawaiian mythology as the abode of Pele, the fire goddess. Oalalauo and Uwēkahuna were two important temples (*heiau*) situated at Kīlauea, where rituals were performed for the propitiation of Pele. It is not surprising that Pele was held in awe, for volcanic eruptions have been a frequent cause of population dislocations when settlements and agricultural land were buried under lava flows. About 1790, the army of Keōua, chief of Puna and Kaʻū, was decimated on the Kīlauea trail by a violent explosive eruption and ash fall (Brigham 1909, 36–39). Human footprints may still be seen in the area, impressed into the hardened ash by people crossing the Kaʻū desert, perhaps including the survivors from Keōua's army.

From *Wao Akua* to *Wao Kanaka*: Transformed Landscapes

Hawaiian ecosystems evolved in isolation over millions of years prior to the arrival of Polynesians. Noted Pacific botanist Raymond Fosberg observed that "many or most of the older island ecosystems had reached such relative stability that changes were mostly very slow. . . . [The arrival of people] . . . has invariably increased, to some extent, the degree of instability in these systems" (Fosberg 1963, 5). Over time Polynesians wrought extensive changes in the Hawaiian landscape. The impact of these changes was reciprocal, for Hawaiian culture and environment were inseparably linked. Humans modify and manipulate their environment to suit their needs, while nature reciprocally exercises constraints on human activities and aspirations. Thus what were originally entirely natural ecosystems became transformed into *socio-ecosystems* (Barton et al. 2004). By modifying the natural Hawaiian landscape over some eight centuries, people created new environmental challenges and constraints.

The nineteenth-century Native Hawaiian scholar Davida Malo referred to the majestic forests cloaking the islands' higher mountains as the *wao akua,* the "forests of the gods," below which "comes the belt called *wao-kanaka* . . . and here men cultivate the land" (1951, 17). When Polynesians first arrived in Hawai'i, the *wao akua* stretched from the mountains down to the sea shore; everything was primeval wilderness. Over time, as people cleared the land for gardens and houses, population increased, and the reach of human activities expanded into the valleys and onto leeward slopes, *wao kanaka* came to replace *wao akua.*

A substantial body of research, mostly accumulated since the first edition of this book was published, documents the conversion of Native Hawaiian ecosystems—the original *wao akua*—into the mosaic of agroecosystems and otherwise anthropogenically transformed landscapes—the *wao kanaka*—that existed at the time of European contact. These environmental transformations are evidenced by a variety of paleoecological indicators, including pollen, charcoal, phytoliths and other plant remains, land snails, and faunal materials recovered from both archaeological and natural sedimentary contexts (Athens 1997; Athens and Ward 1993; Athens, Ward, and Wickler 1992; Athens et al. 2002; Burney et al. 2001; Christensen and Kirch 1986; James et al. 1987; Kirch 1982; Olson and James 1982a, 1982b, 1984).

Prior to Polynesian arrival in Hawai'i, about 100 species of birds as well as two bat species made up the nonmarine terrestrial vertebrates; the birds included both flightless and volant species. Among the flightless birds were an endemic genus of ibis (*Apteribis* spp.), at least four genera of geese or anatids (*Geochen, Thambetochen, Ptaiochen,* and *Chelychelynechen*), and a number of rails (*Porzana* spp.). The large-bodied anatids doubtless provided ready food sources for colonizing humans. All of the flightless birds disappeared fairly quickly after Polynesian settlement; they rarely appear in archaeological contexts, being known primarily from paleontological deposits predating human arrival (James et al. 1987; Olson and James 1982a, 1984). It likewise appears that formerly extensive populations of nesting or roosting seabirds, such as petrels and shearwaters, were reduced in numbers following human arrival on the main islands.

While direct predation for food was likely a factor in the extinction of the large flightless anatids, indirect factors probably also played a significant role. In their investigations of karstic sinkholes on the 'Ewa Plain, O'ahu Island, Athens et al. (2002) dated the bones of the commensal Pacific rat (*Rattus exulans*) that accompanied Polynesian voyagers. Bones of these rats frequently occur in the sinkholes, with the bones dating as early as AD 850–1289. Athens et al. (2002, 73–75) argue that the rapid decline of native dry forest on the 'Ewa Plain was a consequence of an exploding rat population, which comsumed the vulnerable seedlings and seeds of native plants. "The rats could have produced their damage through seed and fruit predation, consumption of seedlings and new leaf production, and girding of soft-barked trees, as well as consumption of invertebrates critical to plant pollination and the nutrient cycle" (Athens et al. 2002, 74; see also Athens 2008). Additional evidence for such ecological shifts on the 'Ewa Plain is found in the changing frequencies of endemic land snails in the sinkholes (Christensen and Kirch 1986), co-occuring with dense deposits of bird bones in the upper levels. The reductions in populations of both birds and land snails on the ʻEwa Plain is presumably linked to collapse of their shared habitat—the native dryland forest—as a consequence of human introduction of the rat.

The most pervasive impact of land use was alteration of the natural vegetation communities of the lowland and mid-altitude zones (i.e., below about 900 m elevation). On Oʻahu and Kauaʻi, where swamps, bogs, or small lakes have preserved pollen archives in their muddy layers, the transformation of lowland forests over the past 1,000 years has been documented through coring and pollen analysis (Athens 1997; Athens and Ward 1993; Athens, Ward, and Wickler 1992; Burney 2002; Burney and Burney 2003; Burney et al. 2001). The cores exhibit dramatic increases in microscopic charcoal particle influxes beginning after about AD 1000, a signal of human-ignited fires on adjacent landscapes. People lit fires for a variety of purposes, one of which was forest clearance to open up land for gardens, following traditional shifting cultivation practices that had been used for millennia by the Austronesian ancestors of the Polynesians (Yen 1973). On Oʻahu, the cumulative effect of forest clearance was the transformation of *wao akua* into a thoroughly anthropogenic, managed landscape, a mosaic of agroecosystems (fig. 2.7). As Athens puts it, "Pollen diagram after pollen diagram from the coastal lowlands of Oʻahu show the same thing. The native forests of the lowlands disappeared in a matter of centuries. By A.D. 1400 to 1500 there was essentially nothing left of the lowland forest. *Pritchardia* palms had all but disappeared, *Kanaloa* did disappear, and the other native trees and shrubs dwindled to negligible numbers, if not outright rarity" (Athens 1977, 261).

A remarkable archive of botanical and faunal remains spanning more than 8,000 years from the early Holocene up to modern times has been preserved in sediments within the Makauwahi Cave, a large limestone sinkhole at Māhāʻulepū, Kauaʻi (Burney 2010; Burney and Kikuchi 2006; Burney et al. 2001; Liebherr and Porch 2015). Nearly 10 m of waterlogged deposits preserved pollen, land snail shells, bones from birds and other vertebrates, insect remains, and plant macrofossils (seeds and wood), providing a detailed picture of the prehuman ecology of lowland Kauaʻi, and its subsequent transformation after human arrival (fig. 2.8). The first presence of humans is indirectly indicated by a rat bone dated to AD 1039–1241; the sediments above this (stratigraphic Unit VI) date to the Polynesian period, and show the appearance of pigs along with several "canoe plants," including candlenut, the bottle gourd, coconut, and the bitter yam (Burney et al. 2001, 633). "The disappearance of several species of endemic snails in Unit V, and the possible decline of flightless birds about this time, would hint that early human impacts might have occurred" (634).

A similar anthropogenic transformation of a lowland landscape is documented in the Kaupikiawa rockshelter on the Kalaupapa Peninsula of windward Molokaʻi (Kirch et al. 2004). Here, the evidence comes from charcoal in stratified cultural deposits documenting a local record of vegetation change. Human land use adjacent to the Kaupikiawa lava tube shelter began around AD 1300; the shelter cave itself was occupied from about AD 1650 into the early historic period. The charcoal sequence is shown in figure 2.9, and is divided into three analytical zones. Analytical zone 3, at the base of the depositional sequence, represents a period prior to permanent occupation of the shelter, but following human land use on the peninsula. During this initial period, charcoal fragments began to wash into the

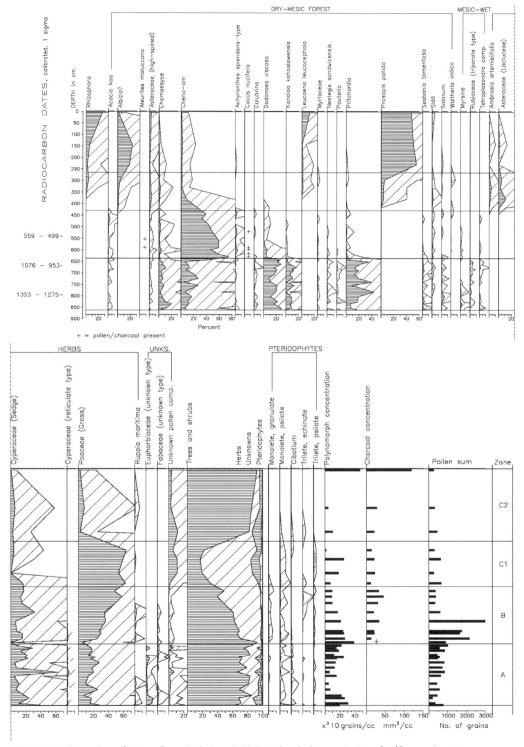

FIGURE 2.7 The pollen diagram from Ordy Pond, Oʻahu Island, demonstrates significant changes in the lowland vegetation following Polynesian arrival, and then again after European contact. Zone A represents the prehuman period, Zone B the period of Polynesian land use, and Zones C1 and C2 the postcontact period. *(Diagram courtesy J. Steve Athens and Gerome Ward)*

FIGURE 2.8 Makauwahi Cave, a large sinkhole in Pleistocene sandstone deposits on Kaua'i Island, has yielded a rich record of ancient lowland biota. *(Photo by Anthony Crider, reproduced under Creative Commons license)*

shelter and were deposited in a matrix of reddish, clayey sediment. The charcoal in zone 3 is dominated by endemic arboreal or woody taxa (*Diospyros, Acacia, Antidesma, Flueggea, Psycotrax, Chenopodium, Osteomeles, Senna,* and *Wikstroemia*), representing a mixed, native lowland dry forest and shrubland community. With analytical zone 2, the rate of deposition increased substantially; the shelter was now being used as a locus of human activity. The charcoal assemblage in zone 2 changes in favor of shrubby taxa, dominated by *Chamaesyce, Chenopodium,* and *Osteomeles;* two Polynesian-introduced trees (candlenut and breadfruit) also make their appearance. This shift in the charcoal diagram reflects the conversion of the Kalaupapa landscape to an intensive dryland agricultural zone, dominated by fire-tolerant shrubs growing in fallow or noncultivated zones. Analytical zone 1 represents the transition to the historic (postcontact) period, with an even more striking reduction in plant diversity. The Kaupikiawa charcoal sequence encapsulates five to six centuries of irreversible transformation of the Kalaupapa landscape from a natural ecosystem dominated by native dryland forest into a fully anthropogenic socio-ecosystem, the *wao kanaka*.

The extent to which eight centuries of land use by the indigenous Polynesian inhabitants of the Hawaiian Islands had modified the natural ecosystem, transforming at least the lowland and to some degree intermediate zones on the main islands to managed landscapes, has yet to be fully determined. Gon, Tom, and Woodside (2018) utilized a geographic information systems (GIS) approach drawing upon spatial data sets derived from historic records and archaeological surveys, producing color-coded maps showing the inferred human "footprint" in AD 1770. They estimate that the "geospatial footprint

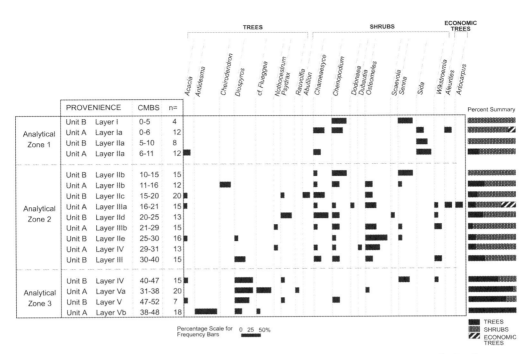

FIGURE 2.9 Charcoal frequency diagram from Kaupikiawa rockshelter, Kalaupapa, Moloka'i Island, showing the transformation of the area's vegetation from native dryland forest to an open, anthropogenic association dominated by shrubs and grasses. *(After Kirch et al. 2004)*

of human-transformed areas across the precontact Hawaiian archipelago comprised less than 15% of total land area" (2018, 1). However, there is reason to believe that their spatial mapping underestimates some kinds of land use, such as colluvial slope agriculture, as well as some forms of forest-resource utilization. A refinement of this GIS model incorporating more recent archaeological data would help to more accurately determine the footprint of human activities at the time of Western contact.

3

THE EVIDENCE OF THE PAST

Each region of the world exhibits its own unique record of indelible marks on and sedimented in the land, inscribed by previous generations. The city-mounds or "tells" of the Near East, the Mousterian rockshelters of southern France, the temple pyramids of central America, and the great shell mounds of San Francisco Bay each typify their regions; each also poses unique challenges of archaeological study and interpretation. How an archaeologist goes about surveying, recording, excavating, analyzing, and interpreting the evidence of the past depends on such local circumstances. To understand the aims and methods of archaeologists in Hawai'i, we must first consider the local archaeological landscape: the kinds of sites present, their frequency and distribution, the variety of material evidence they contain, and the methods available for their analysis.

The Hawaiian Archaeological Landscape

The Hawaiian landscape bears the traces of generations of human occupation and use of the land, manifested in sites and artifacts dispersed across the landscape or buried under its surface. To determine how humans modified their island ecosystems, we can turn to evidence such as pollen or phytolith archives in wetlands and soils, or charcoal and land snails in colluvial deposits, to augment the archaeological record (see chapter 2). Thus, archaeologists often work collaboratively with palynologists, paleontologists, geomorphologists, and other scientists to unravel the long-term history of human activities. However, if asked to name the most typical aspect of the Hawaiian archaeological landscape, most archaeologists would point to the ubiquitous stone structures that are found in a sometimes-bewildering variety of configurations, sizes, and combinations everywhere throughout the islands but are particularly concentrated in the lowland to mid-altitude zones.

Locally available stones, whether stream-rolled cobbles or the coarser ʻaʻā and pāhoehoe lava blocks of volcanic slopes, were piled, heaped, and closely fitted together with remarkable skill (and without mortar) to construct house platforms, walls for thatched houses and shelters, animal enclosures, the facades of taro pondfields and canals, burial

FIGURE 3.1 This pavement of waterworn cobbles and gravel (*'ili'ili*) incorporates a *papamū* or pecked grid for playing the *kōnane* game. In the left foreground is a large salt pan. *(Photo courtesy Bishop Museum Department of Anthropology)*

cairns, agricultural mounds, temple platforms, and a variety of other features. The surfaces of platforms and terraces were often paved with smooth cobbles (fig. 3.1) or with fine water-rolled gravel, known in Hawaiian as *'ili'ili*. Only rarely did Hawaiians cut and dress volcanic stone, as in the facing of the Kīkīaola irrigation canal (sometimes called the "Menehune Ditch") on Kaua'i, or at Kukuipahu Heiau on Hawai'i Island (see chapters 14 and 18).

The majority of precontact Hawaiian sites are found below about 900 m elevation, reflecting both the Hawaiian orientation to the sea and the agricultural productivity of the lowland valleys and slopes. The pattern of settlement in ancient Hawai'i was dispersed, rather than nucleated, with few true villages or centers of population aggregation. A few such concentrations did nonetheless exist, typically in association with the residences of ruling chiefs, which we refer to as "royal centers." Most of the Hawaiian archaeological landscape, however, consists of dispersed stone constructions, with residential, special-purpose, and religious sites distributed among the walls, canals, mounds, trails, and other traces of an agriculturally oriented society. Unfortunately, large expanses of such sites were obliterated by postcontact land alteration, including sugarcane and pineapple plantations, housing tracts, and resort developments.

It is uncommon to find deep, well-stratified occupation deposits in Hawai'i, although some coastal dune environments and rockshelters (fig. 3.2) do contain relatively deep accumulations of occupation layers (fig. 3.3); we discuss six such stratified sites in chapter 6. More frequently, cultural deposits associated with stone structures are about 10 to 40 cm thick, representing at most one or two centuries of habitation and use. This poses a challenge in establishing the chronological relationships among a group of structures, for it cannot be assumed that all features in an area are contemporaneous (Dye, ed., 2010).

The classification of Hawaiian stone structures and sites is a complex issue that engaged archaeologists in the 1960s and 1970s (Hommon 1970a). Thanks to early European accounts of Hawaiian life and to the writings of nineteenth-century Hawaiian scholars, we do know a great deal concerning the *functional* categories of structures in use in the late 1700s and early 1800s. Archaeologists commonly use such functional categories such as "house site," *"heiau,"* "temple," or "canoe shed" in describing Hawaiian stone structures. In some cases, historical documents provide information regarding particular structures, as with the more prominent

FIGURE 3.2 Lava-tube shelters, such as this one at Kalāhuipuaʻa on Hawaiʻi Island (site Ha-E1-342), were frequently used as dwelling sites or temporary camping places. *(Photo by P. V. Kirch)*

FIGURE 3.3 Sand dune sites, such as this one at Kawela, Molokaʻi Island, often exhibit deep deposits with complex stratigraphy. Here multiple occupation episodes can be discerned with the thin layers darkened with charcoal and shellfish midden. *(Photo by P. V. Kirch)*

temple sites. There is a risk, however, in assigning functional categories to archaeological survey data. It can be difficult to determine a priori the function of a stone structure; archaeologists need to avoid uncritically assuming what they should be attempting to determine through survey and excavation. To avoid functional classifications, archaeologists use strictly *formal* classifications, which do not associate a particular architectural form with a specific function (e.g., Hommon 1970a). Given the range of forms and permutations that Hawaiian stone structures take, however, no single formal classification is entirely satisfactory. In practice, Hawaiian archaeologists commonly use ad hoc combinations of functional and formal types in their surveys, applying functional terms to sites whose past use seems relatively unambiguous, and using formal, descriptive terms for sites whose function is not entirely evident.

Table 3.1 presents a simplified classification of the more significant and frequently encountered varieties of Hawaiian archaeological sites. This classification is not exhaustive and is intended simply to introduce the reader to the range of archaeological site types encountered

TABLE 3.1. A simplified classification of Hawaiian archaeological sites.

I. Residential sites
    A. Stone structures
        1. Walled enclosures
        2. Stone-faced terraces and platforms
        3. C- and L-shaped shelters
    B. Rockshelters and lava tubes
    C. Sand dune occupation sites

II. Ceremonial or ritual sites
    A. Upright stones and natural features
    B. Simple enclosures and platforms (shrines)
    C. *Heiau* (major temples and shrines)
        1. *Pōhaku o Kāne*
        2. Household shrines
        3. Fishing shrines
        4. Agricultural temples
        5. *Luakini* (war) temples

III. Agricultural and aquacultural sites
    A. Irrigated field systems
        1. Canals (*ʻauwai*)
        2. Pondfield terraces (*loʻi*)
    B. Dryland field systems
        1. Field borders and embankments (*kuaiwi*)
        2. Mounds, planting circles, and minor agricultural features
    C. Temporary field shelters
    D. Fishponds
        1. *Loko kuapā*
        2. *Loko ʻumeiki*
        3. *Puʻuone*
        4. Other
    E. Animal enclosures, pens, walls

IV. Special-function sites
    A. Petroglyphs and *papamū*
    B. Trails
        1. Stepping-stone type
        2. Curbstone type
    C. *Hōlua* slides
    D. Adze quarries
    E. Abrader manufacturing areas
    F. Fortifications

in the Hawaiian landscape, using terms common in the literature. The major divisions in the table are functional, while formal variations appear at the level of specific categories.

The term "site" has been applied inconsistently by archaeologists in Hawai'i. Often, the term refers to single constructions (such as a platform, or a C-shaped shelter), or to a spatial aggregation or cluster of several structures. (In calling such a spatial aggregation a "site," archaeologists sometimes assume that all of the individual structures in the group are of the same age, which may or may not be true.) Each individual structure may be made up of a number of components, such as wall segments, pavements, hearths, ovens, post molds, or alignments.

In a settlement-pattern study of 495 stone structures at Kawela on Moloka'i Island, Weisler and Kirch (1985) developed a hierarchical system for labeling and analyzing the components of Hawaiian stone structural sites. As shown in figure 3.4, the lowest level—the "building blocks" of the settlement pattern—is composed of individual *architectural components,* which include pavements, facing walls, alignments, freestanding walls, hearths, and so forth. Architectural components may stand alone (as in a simple mound) but more frequently are combined to form *features.* Features typically comprise spatially bounded or delineated areas, such as a platform with earthen fill and pebble paving, or a C-shaped shelter. Two or more features may be combined to form *compound structures.* Larger groupings or aggregations of architectural components, features, and compound structures over the landscape are termed *complexes* (such as all of the features and structures that make up a residential unit, or *kauhale*). In this system, the term "site" is used arbitrarily, as a convenient labeling device at any level.

Until the 1960s, there was no uniform system of numbering or indexing features or sites in Hawai'i. Bishop Museum archaeologists of the 1920s and 1930s simply assigned an Arabic numeral to sites on individual islands (e.g., Bennett 1931; McAllister 1933a, 1933b). When Kenneth Emory began excavating sites in the 1950s, he designated these simply with a letter indicating the island, followed by a number (thus Kuli'ou'ou on O'ahu was site O1, Pu'u Ali'i on Hawai'i was site H1, etc.). In the early 1960s, as settlement-pattern surveys commenced, Bishop Museum developed a more complex site coding system

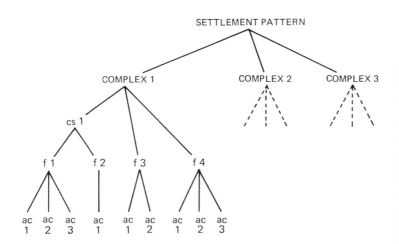

FIGURE 3.4 A settlement landscape may be analytically broken down into multiple, hierarchically clustered components, as indicated in this diagram (*ac:* architectural component; *f:* feature; *cs:* compound structure).
(*Diagram by P. V. Kirch*)

patterned after the Smithsonian Institution's River Basin Surveys (Soehren, in Green, ed., 1969, 26). This system was based on the indigenous, hierarchical Hawaiian land units, with sites designated according to the island, district, and *ahupuaʻa* in which they are located. Thus site 50-Ha-C23-1 refers to Hikiau Heiau, the first site (1) recorded in the *ahupuaʻa* of Kealakekua (23), in South Kona District (C), on the island of Hawaiʻi (Ha), in the State of Hawaii (50). Later, the Hawaiʻi Register of Historic Places, maintained by the State Historic Preservation Division, implemented a site numbering system based on the US Geological Survey 7.5-minute quadrangle maps. In that system Hikiau Heiau is designated 50-10-47-3732. Throughout this book, we use the site number given by the archaeologist who recorded or excavated a particular site, whether in Bishop Museum, state, or other system.

How many archaeological sites are there in Hawaiʻi? The answer depends in part on how a "site" is defined (whether as a single feature, or as an aggregate or cluster of features). And because vast tracts throughout the islands were converted to plantation agriculture or were urbanized long before the advent of systematic archaeological work, tens of thousands of stone structures and other kinds of sites have undoubtedly been destroyed and forever lost to our knowledge. Even for areas with relatively intact landscapes, often only a fraction of the extant sites has been recorded. For example, in 1981 a large segment of the south Molokaʻi slopes centering on the *ahupuaʻa* of Kawela was intensively surveyed by Bishop Museum (Weisler and Kirch 1985). Prior to this survey, only four archaeological sites had been recorded in this area (Summers 1971). The 1981 survey added 495 new features, an increase of 12,000 percent! Likewise, prior to 1976, only 50 sites had been recorded on Kahoʻolawe Island (McAllister 1933b). Intensive surveys of the island between 1976 and 1980 recorded a total of 544 sites, representing 2,337 individual features. A third example is the ancient *moku* (district) of Kahikinui in southeast Maui, where a long-term project added more than 3,000 new features to the archaeological record (Kirch 2014).

From the 1960s through the early 1990s, Bishop Museum's Anthropology Department documented more than 12,800 archaeological sites throughout the islands. As of April 2021, the State Historic Preservation Division reported 31,692 sites in its database. Over half of these (16,769 sites) are located on Hawaiʻi Island, almost 20 percent on Oʻahu (6,468), and 15 percent on Maui (4,712). All other islands combined account for the remaining 3,743 sites, or about 12 percent of the total. Only a small number of these sites are officially listed on the Hawaiʻi Register of Historic Places (1,053 sites) or the National Register of Historic Places (368 sites).

Seeking the Past: Archaeological Methods

Archaeological Survey

The archaeologist's first task is *survey,* the discovery, locating, and recording of the physical evidence of former human occupation or land use. Archaeological survey is not so much a matter of knowing *where* to look—sites can be found in almost any environment—but *what* to look for. Anyone with a basic knowledge of Hawaiian culture can discern the larger stone structures such as house sites and *heiau,* but it takes experience and training to recognize the often subtle but significant clues such as stone flakes or bits of shell midden, or a layer of ancient charcoal exposed in a wave-cut bank.

Archaeologists distinguish between *reconnaissance* and *intensive* survey. In a reconnaissance, the aim is to determine whether sites are present in a particular area, and their approximate frequency and potential significance. In an intensive (or inventory) survey, the objective is to locate every feature within the defined area, plot these on an appropriately scaled base map, and document each feature. Intensive survey may also involve testing for subsurface deposits or within individual structures to determine whether cultural remains are present. Intensive survey is time-consuming, requiring the use of surveying instruments such as GPS, and sometimes a plane table and alidade, for accurate site locating and mapping (fig. 3.5).

Aerial photography, either from fixed-wing aircraft or more recently from drones, can assist in archaeological survey and mapping. In the Lālāmilo area of Hawai'i Island, where the low pasture grasses do not obscure stone structures, aerial photographs were used to map the extensive remains of ancient Hawaiian agricultural fields, clearly visible in false-color infrared aerial photos (J. T. Clark 1981). Aerial photography assisted Lloyd Soehren and Stell Newman in their pioneering identification of ancient field systems at Kealakekua Bay and at Lapakahi, Hawai'i (Newman n.d.; Soehren and Newman 1968).

A major advance in airborne survey came with the development of LiDAR, which stands for "light detection and ranging" and makes use of a laser (see M. D. McCoy 2020a; M. D. McCoy and Ladefoged 2009). A low-flying aircraft or drone with a LiDAR instrument mounted in the fuselage flies over the terrain to be mapped, sweeping back and forth in systematic survey lines, while the LiDAR shoots hundreds of thousands of laser pulses per second toward the ground; these are reflected off the ground, to be registered by the on-board

FIGURE 3.5 The plane table with telescopic alidade is used by archaeologists to make detailed plan maps of Hawaiian stone architecture and settlement patterns. *(Photo by P. V. Kirch)*

detector. The first LiDAR flights for archaeology in Hawai'i were in 2009, flown by ecologist Gregory Asner over Hawai'i Island's Kohala District. The resulting LiDAR imagery produced near-ground survey-quality data over 240 km^2 (Ladefoged et al. 2011; M. D. McCoy, Asner, and Graves 2011), more than twice the land area of Kaho'olawe Island.

Intensive survey requires consistent recording, augmented by scale drawings and photographs; these data are typically integrated along with other spatial information in a geographic information system or GIS. Similar to Google Maps, the GIS programs that archaeologists use integrate maps and satellite images with site survey data, allowing one to search, measure distances and areas, and conduct a variety of geographic analyses, such as working out the shortest route between two points. Just as there is no universal agreement on what constitutes a "site," there is no one way that archaeologists create geospatial data sets (M. D. McCoy 2020b).

Despite decades of fieldwork in Hawaiian archaeology, only a fraction of the state has been covered by intensive survey; many regions have yet to be surveyed even at a reconnaissance level. Kaho'olawe is the only island to have been entirely covered by an archaeological inventory survey (Hommon 1980a, 1980b). Kirch's long-term project in Kahikinui on Maui recorded more than 3,000 sites over about 12 km^2, and some CRM projects have covered fairly extensive areas, for example in the islands' National Parks and in some major highway surveys. The majority of CRM projects have taken place in leeward regions where resort developments have concentrated, leaving large windward regions underresearched. We still know too little, for example, regarding ancient settlement patterns along the extensive windward regions of Maui and Hawai'i Islands.

Excavation

While survey is the essential first stage in any archaeological program, *excavation* is necessary to acquire data on the age and function of ancient sites, and to probe or search for buried sites and cultural deposits not evident on the surface (fig. 3.6). Where one excavates depends to a large degree on the questions being asked. Given limitations in research funds, time, and personnel, it is impossible to excavate all of the sites relevant to a particular problem; even those sites selected are usually only partially excavated. Moreover, because archaeological sites are unique, and because research methods improve over time, it is desirable to leave some parts of a site intact for future study (unless, of course, the site is threatened by imminent destruction). Before digging, the archaeologist must also decide *how* to excavate: what particular areas to dig in, what degree of stratigraphic control to exercise, what sieve meshes to use, what materials to retain for laboratory analysis, and so forth.

Excavation entails *sampling* at several levels. In a given area a sample of sites to be excavated must be selected out of the total range of sites, requiring an assessment of which sites are most likely to yield information relevant to the research problem. Then an excavation strategy needs to be implemented, such as trenching, random or systematic test-pitting, or extensive areal excavation. The mesh size to be used in sieving the excavated earth affects the recovery of artifacts and faunal remains. Prior to the 1980s, archaeologists in Hawai'i often used 1/4-inch mesh screens, resulting in the loss of smaller objects and of the bones of small fish and birds. Use of at least 1/8-inch mesh is now regarded as standard; even finer

FIGURE 3.6 Excavation of a habitation terrace in progress at Kahikinui, Maui Island (site KIP-752). Note the pins denoting the corners of 1-m excavation units; the stadia rod is being used to measure the depth of finds below a fixed datum point. *(Photo by P. V. Kirch)*

mesh may be necessary in some cases. Flotation of sediment in water can help to recover carbonized plant remains (M. S. Allen 1981, 1983, 1989); however, the lack of carbonized seeds in Hawaiian sites renders this method less useful than in other regions of the world.

The kinds of sites selected for excavation have changed along with the evolving research agendas in Hawaiian archaeology. In the 1950s, Emory and his colleagues focused their efforts on rockshelters and sand dune middens, because these sites often yielded large numbers of fishhooks and other artifacts useful for establishing cultural sequences. As archaeologists in Hawai'i broadened their research agendas in the 1970s to include settlement patterns and ecological adaptation, the focus shifted to other kinds of sites, including field shelters, dwelling terraces, stone mounds, and agricultural fields. Such sites do not yield large quantities of artifacts—indeed, sometimes no artifacts at all—but contribute to the overall picture of life in ancient Hawai'i. Charcoal dug out of the soil of an ancient taro terrace may not be as exciting to find as a polished stone adze, but when radiocarbon dated, the charcoal can tell us when the terrace was constructed, important information for understanding the development of ancient economies.

Excavation strategies must be tailored to research objectives and to available time and funds. Often, one begins with small test excavations (generally one-meter squares) to determine the depth and nature of the cultural materials in a site. These test pits may be laid out using randomized or stratified sampling strategies, in order to ensure statistically representative coverage. The construction sequence of a structure, however, may be best interpreted through the use of longer trenches, which expose continuous stratigraphic profiles. It is critical that such excavations abut the surface architecture, integrating the stone structures with the subsurface stratigraphy (Dye 2010b). Areal excavations, large-scale exposures of extensive areas over a site, are required if spatial activity patterns and the configurations of buried structures and features are to be recovered (fig. 3.7). Areal excavations are costly and time-consuming, however, and relatively few have been conducted on Hawaiian sites, limiting our knowledge of ancient household activity patterns.

One promising but as yet little-used approach in Hawaiʻi is the study of sediment micromorphology (Kirch et al. 2004; Vacca 2019). A solidified block of sediment is extracted from a site with its structural features intact, and from this a thin section is cut and prepared. When examined under a microscope, the components and structure of the sediment may reveal information about activity areas or site function that are not evident at the macroscale.

Since the 1970s, most archaeological work in Hawaiʻi has resulted from development projects, mandated by historic preservation laws at federal and state levels, often referred to as "contract archaeology" or cultural resources management (CRM). CRM is a broad category that includes the work of government agency archaeologists as well as museum professionals who curate artifact collections. While site preservation is an ideal goal, trade-offs are typically made, with some sites tested or excavated to "mitigate" or lessen the damage or loss of information when they are then destroyed to make way for a development. If such excavations are going to enhance our knowledge of the past, however, they need to be conducted within the framework of a research design, with appropriate sampling strategy and methods. CRM projects can best contribute to new knowledge

FIGURE 3.7 Completed excavation of an early postcontact house site in the Anahulu Valley, Oʻahu Island (site Oa-D6-38). Note the small circular hearth defined by a ring of stones. *(Photo by P. V. Kirch)*

regarding the Hawaiian past when they are linked to regional research designs, which pose broad-ranging research questions and specify the kinds of data required to generate answers to those questions (Dye, ed., 2010).

ANALYSIS, CURATION, AND PUBLICATION

Survey and excavation, despite being often hot, dusty, and physically trying, are generally viewed as the "glamorous" side of archaeology, yet these are only the first steps. After the scraps of ancient stone, shell, and bone have been exposed, plotted, and photographed in situ, or systematically bagged when found in the sifting screens, they must be cleaned, conserved, catalogued, identified, and analyzed before any interpretations can be advanced. Moreover, the results of field and laboratory work must be written up and published or otherwise made available to scholars and the general public. The materials recovered from an excavation (artifacts, faunal and floral materials, samples of soil and charcoal), along with the associated records (notebooks, photographs, and plan maps), also must be permanently deposited in an institution or facility with the resources to care for and preserve them, to ensure their availability for use by future generations, who can pose new questions and who will be able to employ new and improved analytical methods. The largest archaeological research collection in Hawaiʻi is housed at Bishop Museum, which contains artifacts and specimens from hundreds of sites throughout the islands. Federal agencies with substantial lands to manage, such as the National Parks, maintain their own curatorial facilities and data management systems.

Unfortunately, much of the archaeological material recovered through CRM projects in Hawaiʻi over the past several decades has never been placed in suitable repositories. The State Historic Preservation Division maintains a library of CRM reports, and these are beginning to become available online through the State Historic Preservation Office's HICRIS system (https://dlnr.hawaii.gov/shpd/Hawaiʻi-cultural-resource-information-system/). A partial list of reports, papers, books, and other publications relevant for archaeology in the Hawaiian Islands is also available on the Digital Archaeological Record (tDAR). However, out of the more than 4,000 entries, only a fraction are readily available, posing a barrier to research and synthesis. Indeed, there is a physical and digital curation crisis in Hawaiian archaeology; until steps are taken to remedy this, a great deal of the information generated through hundreds of CRM projects is at risk of being lost.

Artifacts constitute only a small percentage of the material evidence of the past. Visitors to an archaeological laboratory will find technicians sorting and identifying scraps of shellfish, bone, charcoal, seeds, and other faunal and botanical materials. These nondescript remains, often referred to as "midden" (from the old Scandinavian word *mödding,* meaning a kitchen dump heap), provide evidence on ancient diet and environmental conditions. The identification of midden materials requires specialist skills and extensive reference collections. One example of the contributions made through such midden studies is the identification of the bones of the native *nēnē* goose (*Branta sandvicensis*) on Molokaʻi, Kahoʻolawe, and Oʻahu Islands. The *nēnē* was previously believed to have lived only on Hawaiʻi and Maui, but archaeological finds demonstrated that at one time these birds were more widely distributed across the archipelago.

Plant remains are also recovered from some archaeological contexts. Organic materials, including the leaves, flowers, and bark of plants, are often well preserved in rockshelters, whereas open sites in wetter regions may preserve only charcoal. Wood charcoal can be identified to genus and species, through microscopic examination of anatomical features visible when the charcoal is sectioned (Kolb and Murakami 1994; Murakami 1983, 1989; Weisler and Murakami 1991). Identification of charcoal and selection of short-lived taxa prior to radiocarbon dating has largely resolved the problem of "inbuilt age," resulting in significant revision to the chronology of Polynesian arrival in the islands (see chapter 4). Quantitative analysis of charcoal from stratified deposits can reveal vegetation changes in the area around a site (see chapter 2). In addition to charcoal, the carbonized remains of cultivated tuber plants such as sweet potato are sometimes recovered (fig. 3.8).

Other sources of information inform us about the dynamic interactions between human populations and their environment, and aid in the reconstruction of past Hawaiian ecosystems. Subfossil shells of the many endemic Hawaiian species of land and tree snails from archaeological deposits provide valuable clues regarding changes in local environments (Christensen 1983; Christensen and Kirch 1986; Dixon, Soldo, and Christensen 1997; Kirch 1989). Other data on ancient vegetation and plant use comes from microscopic plant remains such as pollen, phytoliths, and starch grains extracted from sediment sampled at archaeological sites (Coil 2003, 2004; Horrocks and Rechtman 2009; Vacca 2019).

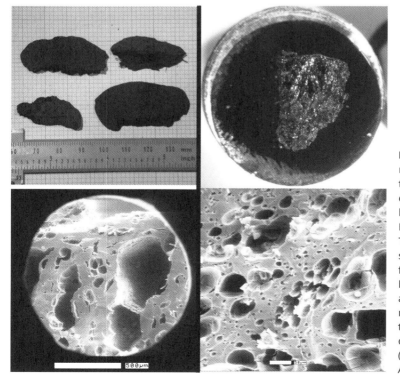

FIGURE 3.8 Carbonized remains of sweet potato tubers (parenchyma) excavated from habitation sites in Kahikinui, Maui Island. The top two photos show carbonized tuber fragments, while the bottom two photos are scanning electron microscope images of the anatomical structure of the parenchyma. *(Photo by J. Coil, Oceanic Archaeology Laboratory)*

The Temporal Framework: Dating and Chronology

Interpreting the past requires a secure chronological framework. In Hawai'i, four techniques for establishing archaeological chronologies have been used: (1) relative dating based on seriation of artifact or architectural styles; (2) radiocarbon dating; (3) hydration-rind dating of volcanic glass; and (4) ^{230}Th dating of corals found in archaeological contexts. By "relative dating," archaeologists refer to an assessment of the age of one site relative to certain other sites. "Absolute dating" (as in the radiocarbon and ^{230}Th methods, among others) refers to the determination of an age range in calendar years. In addition to these techniques, archaeologists commonly use the presence of artifacts made of imported metal, ceramics, or glass in the way that geologists use "index fossils" to date sites and deposits to the postcontact era. A postcontact age may also be indicated by the presence of historically introduced fauna or flora (such as goat or cattle bones, or charcoal from trees such as *kiawe*). This method must be applied with caution since not all postcontact activities involved imported items, especially in the first few decades after Western contact.

SERIATION DATING

Traditionally in world archaeology, the relative dating of sites by means of *seriation* (Michels 1973, 66–82) has focused on pottery, based on gradual stylistic changes in vessel form and in decoration. In Eastern Polynesia, where ceramics are largely absent, it was held for many years that relative dating on the basis of artifact styles was not possible (see chapter 1). When Emory and his colleagues began excavating Hawaiian coastal sites in the early 1950s, however, they found that bone and shell fishhooks, often present in large numbers (up to 1,710 fishhooks in site H1), exhibited distinctive changes over time. Focusing on the large series of fishhooks from the South Point sites, Emory, Bonk, and Sinoto (1959) produced a relative fishhook chronology that they expected would be widely applicable throughout the islands. Suggs (1961) put forth a similar seriation of Marquesan fishhooks, prompting comparison between the archipelagoes (Y. H. Sinoto 1967, 1983, 1996).

Unfortunately, the original promise of relative site dating using fishhooks was not realized. Few sites produced fishhook samples large enough to overcome the problem of statistical error; indeed, most sites in Hawai'i have no fishing gear at all. Moreover, later work has shown that while the South Point fishhook sequence is valid for that region, it may not be applicable to other parts of Hawai'i Island, let alone to other islands. And, because the rate of change in fishhook styles was slow, sites can be assigned with confidence to only one of three broad chronological phases.

More recently, seriation has been extended to stone structures such as house sites and *heiau* (Graves and Cachola-Abad 1996). The idea here is that architectural styles also exhibit temporal trends, coming in and then going out of favor over time. One of the reasons that seriation has been applied to architecture is that, unlike fishhooks, it is possible to record large numbers of architectural components, features, and complexes, across a variety of environments, which together show a remarkable amount of variation. Appreciating this variation requires considering how architectural trends changed over time. For example, among upland *heiau* recorded in the leeward Kohala Field System, styles have been identified based on subtle additions and subtractions of features (M. D. McCoy, Ladefoged, et al. 2011). The earliest features were built combining platforms, upright stones, and terraces. Next, temple architects focused on just platforms, terraces, and courtyards, and then after that added notches to the layout of *heiau* complexes. While architectural seriation appears to work well in some areas, research on *heiau* sites in the Kahikinui area of southeast Maui suggests all of the major architectural styles persisted together over several centuries, so that a seriation of temples in that region has not been possible (Kirch and Ruggles 2019).

Radiocarbon Dating

The most extensively used method of determining the age of Hawaiian archaeological materials is radiocarbon dating, originally developed by Willard Libby in the late 1940s. (Readers who are unfamiliar with the basic principles of radiocarbon dating are referred to c14.arch.ox.ac.uk/calibration.) In theory, any organic material can be dated using the radiocarbon method; in Hawai'i, commonly dated materials include wood charcoal, candlenut (*kukui*) endocarps, bone, shell, sea urchin spines, and noncarbonized wood. Rarely does one encounter a site without some kind of datable organic material, so that radiocarbon dating can be applied to virtually the entire range of Hawaiian archaeological sites. In the decades since Emory obtained the first radiocarbon date from Kuli'ou'ou rockshelter (Emory and Sinoto 1961; see also Kahn et al. 2014), thousands of radiocarbon age assessments have been made on samples from Hawaiian sites. No other Polynesian island group except New Zealand has so extensive a record of radiocarbon dates.

Radiocarbon dating, however, is not without limitations and potential sources of error. The method has undergone major advances over the past few decades, most importantly the development of accelerator mass spectrometry (AMS) radiocarbon dating, allowing very small samples to be dated, with much greater precision. The "date" reported by a radiocarbon laboratory is not a true calendrical date but rather a statistical estimate of the sample's age, expressed in radiocarbon years "before present" (BP, standardized to the year 1950). The statistical error is given by the standard deviation (±), as in the "date" 550 ± 100 years BP. There is a 68 percent probability that the true age of this sample lies within one standard deviation, in this example within the range 450 to 650 BP. Doubling the standard deviation increases to 95 percent the probability of the age falling within the stated range (i.e., 350 to 750 BP). Given the relatively short time scale for the precontact Polynesian occupation of Hawai'i (about 800 years), the statistical error in many radiocarbon dates spans much of the period that people occupied the islands. With the latest AMS dating technology, statistical error ranges have been reduced to ± 20 or even ± 15 years at one standard deviation. Dating a series of samples from the same site or layer greatly helps to narrow down the age range and to determine if one or more dates in a series are aberrant (or "outliers").

A further complication with radiocarbon dating is that *radiocarbon years*, in which laboratory results are expressed, do not correlate one-to-one with *calendar years*, because the amount of radioactive ^{14}C in the earth's atmosphere has varied over time. By calibrating the radiocarbon time scale with precisely dated long-lived trees such as bristlecone pines (independently dated using the dendrochronological technique of counting tree rings), radiocarbon laboratories have developed a calibration curve that allows the conversion of radiocarbon years to a range of calendar years. However, because this calibration curve exhibits numerous humps and troughs, a radiocarbon age may have two or three corresponding calendar age ranges (each with its own statistical probability), generated by the points at which the radiocarbon age intersects with the calibration curve.

A significant advance in radiocarbon dating in Hawai'i came with the ability to identify the dated charcoal to genus and species. Most of the wood charcoal samples dated in the pioneering decades of Hawaiian archaeology, especially those from coastal sites, were not identified in this way. Many of these samples were probably from old wood, including driftwood that was in some cases hundreds of years older than the burning event that was intended to be dated (see Dean 1978). While these dates may accurately date the time when the wood was growing, they do not date the time when that wood was used as fuel in an earth oven or hearth. By identifying wood charcoal prior to dating, archaeologists are able to select only short-lived species, or at least those with only a modest amount of inbuilt age. This has resulted in a shortening of the chronology for Polynesian arrival in the Hawaiian Islands, as discussed further in chapter 4.

Radiocarbon dating has also been aided by the application of Bayesian statistics to the calibration and modeling of radiocarbon dates (Bronk-Ramsey 2009). The Bayesian approach incorporates independent archaeological information, such as the sequence of stratified layers from which a series of dated samples was obtained, to constrain the age calibration. The Bayesian approach to modeling radiocarbon dates has been increasingly applied in recent years (Athens, Rieth, and Dye 2014; Bayman and Dye 2013; Dye 2011a, 2015; Dye and Pantaleo 2010).

Despite its limitations, radiocarbon dating is the most widely used technique for establishing the age of Hawaiian archaeological sites. The chronology used throughout this book is based primarily on the existing corpus of Hawaiian radiocarbon dates. For many sites, the only available dates were run on unidentified wood charcoal samples, so some degree of caution must be applied in their interpretation. We have flagged AMS radiocarbon dates that were processed on identified, short-lived materials with an asterisk (*); these are the most reliable dates available.

Hydration-Rind Dating of Volcanic Glass

In the 1970s and 1980s, a third method of age assessment—the hydration- or alteration-rind dating of volcanic-glass flakes and cores—was widely applied in Hawai'i. Based on a technique for dating obsidian artifacts in other parts of the world the hydration-rind dating of Hawaiian volcanic glass was developed in 1970 by geologist Maury Morgenstein (Barrera and Kirch 1973; Morgenstein and Riley 1974; Morgenstein and Rosendahl 1976). The method is based on the principle that volcanic glass *hydrates* or absorbs water, which chemically alters its composition at a constant rate over time. When a flaked tool or core is produced, a fresh surface of unaltered glass is exposed, initiating the hydration process. By thin-sectioning the volcanic-glass flake and measuring the thickness of the hydration-rind or rim, it is possible in theory to assess the approximate time at which the flake was originally struck.

The hydration-rind method at first promised to be a valuable chronometric tool in Hawaiian archaeology. Volcanic-glass flakes are ubiquitous in many Hawaiian archaeological contexts, providing a ready source of datable material. During the mid- to late 1970s, many archaeologists abandoned the use of radiocarbon dating, relying almost exclusively on the less expensive volcanic-glass dating method, which was being carried out locally at the University of Hawaiʻi and Bishop Museum. Initial claims for the accuracy of the hydration-rind method, however, were premature. Later studies (e.g., Olson 1983; Tuggle and Olson 1978) showed that several factors can substantially influence the thickness of the hydration or alteration rind on volcanic-glass artifacts. Among these are the chemical composition of the glass, which varies throughout the islands, and the temperature at which hydration takes place. Consequently, the hydration-rind dating of volcanic glass largely dropped out of use in Hawaiʻi. Unfortunately, some important sites excavated during the 1970s were dated only with the hydration-rind method; redating of these sites with high-precision AMS radiocarbon dating would be desirable.

Stevenson and Mills (2013) applied infrared photoacoustic spectroscopy and secondary ion mass spectrometry to track the diffusion of water in samples of volcanic glass from Puʻu Waʻawaʻa, and in archaeological samples from a rockshelter at Kahaluʻu, Hawaiʻi. They showed that the rate of water diffusion in trachytic glass is linear with time, and that trachytic-glass artifacts from the Kahalu'u site yielded age estimates in the seventeenth to eighteenth centuries, consistent with radiocarbon dates and artifactual data that bracket the site occupation. However, the glass dates did not correlate well with the site's stratigraphy, again casting doubt on the utility of volcanic-glass dating in Hawaiʻi.

^{230}TH DATING OF CORAL

The most recently developed method of absolute dating is ^{230}Th dating of corals found in Hawaiian archaeological contexts. This method is based on the principle that uranium (U), which occurs in ocean water and is taken up into the hard exoskeletons of corals, gradually decays over time into thorium (Th). By measuring the U/Th ratio in corals, a date can be calculated, one that is more precise than radiocarbon, with a smaller margin of error (frequently just ± 2–3 years at two standard deviations). Of course, to apply this method one must have corals present in an archaeological context, and be reasonably confident that those corals were collected and brought to the site while living. Dead corals collected from a beach context will have an inbuilt age factor, as with old wood.

Coral dating was first applied in Hawaiʻi by Kirch and Sharp (2005), who recognized that *heiau* sites in the Kahikinui District of Maui could be dated with branch corals placed as dedicatory offerings on temple altars, or incorporated in wall fill during temple construction (fig. 3.9). Kirch et al. (2015) expanded their chronology of Kahikinui *heiau* with an increased sample of corals from 26 sites. Coral dates from other sites in the islands have been obtained by Weisler et al. (2006), P. C. McCoy (P. C. McCoy, Weisler, et al. 2009; P. C. McCoy, Nees, et al. 2012), and Kikiloi (2012). More than 100 dates representing the use of coral for offerings in different contexts in Hawaiʻi range from as early as AD 1099 (at Kou Heiau on Maui;

FIGURE 3.9 A branch coral head exposed by partial collapse of a *heiau* wall in Kahikinui, Maui Island. The coral head was incorporated into the wall fill during construction. *(Photo by P. V. Kirch)*

Kirch and Ruggles 2019, 328) through AD 1794. These dates represent activity on six different islands in the main Hawaiian Islands as well as the northwest islands: Maui (52 dates), Moloka'i (14 dates), Hawai'i (7 dates); Lehua, a small islet off of Kaua'i (2 dates), Nihoa (36 dates), and Mokumanamana (1 date). The potential to date other kinds of coral artifacts, such as abraders, has yet to be extensively tested in Hawai'i.

4

ORIGINS

The "problem of Polynesian origins" has captivated and challenged Pacific scholars for more than two centuries (Howard 1967; Thompson 2019). In the late eighteenth century, Captain James Cook and his officers mused about how it was that the Polynesian "Nation" had come to be distributed across the vast triangle from New Zealand to Easter Island to Hawaiʻi. Cook surmised that these peoples had moved into the Pacific from the west, arguing that the Malaysian area was a likely homeland:

> In these Proes or Pahee's as the[y] call [their canoes] . . . these people sail in those seas from Island to Island for several hundred Leagues, the Sun serving them for a compass by day and the Moon and Stars by night. When this comes to be prov'd we Shall be no longer at a loss to know how the Islands lying in those Seas came to be people'd, for . . . it cannot be doubted but that the inhabitants of those western Islands may have been at others as far to westward of them and so we may trace them from Island to Island quite to the East Indies. (James Cook 1769 [in Beaglehole, ed., 1955, 154])

The missionaries, traders, whalers, and naturalists who came after Cook continued to ask the same question; many of them advanced their own theories to account for Polynesian origins, and some became so enthralled with the issue that they devoted a lifetime attempting to resolve it. Some of the nineteenth- and early twentieth-century theories were based on speculations regarding the Lost Tribes of Israel, or spurious comparisons between the Indus Valley script and Polynesian petroglyphs. Others speculated that there had once been a Pacific continent ("Mu") that—like Atlantis—had sunk beneath the waves, leaving the Polynesians stranded on its former mountaintops. Once geological exploration of the Pacific Ocean floor revealed absolutely no evidence of a former continent, this was sent to the graveyard of bad theories.

Many early scholars concerned with Polynesian origins adduced linguistic evidence to support their theories. Indeed, the name "Polynesia" was first proposed by De Brosses

(1756) based on similarities in word lists compiled by early explorers on various islands. Horatio Hale (1846), philologist with the United States Exploring Expedition, advanced a well-reasoned argument based on a close comparison of Pacific languages. He proposed that the Polynesian ancestors had originated in the west, in a homeland called Pulotu (after the Tongan and Fijian name for the traditional homeland). From Pulotu they migrated to Fiji, and from that large archipelago they had settled Samoa and Tonga. Tahiti was next to be settled, and in Hale's view it was from Tahiti that the first voyagers set out to colonize Hawai'i. (Hale's theory was remarkably prescient of the picture that has emerged from modern linguistic and archaeological research.)

In 1920 Bishop Museum's Herbert Gregory declared the "problem of Polynesian origins" to be an urgent priority for Pacific science (see chapter 1). Unfortunately, anthropologists of this period were swayed by a "migration mentality," imagining fleets of canoes rapidly advancing across the ocean. In 1930 Edward S. C. Handy, one of the museum's young ethnologists, opined that the Polynesians were a mixture resulting from two "waves" of migrations, the first with origins in "Indian Brahmanical" culture, the second deriving from "Dynastic Indo-Malaysian" culture with "Buddhistic" overtones (Handy 1930). The *manahune* population of Tahiti, Handy believed, were the descendants of the first migration, who were later conquered by a superior, invading *ari'i* culture. None of this was actually supported by rigorous ethnographic comparisons, let alone archaeological data.

Norwegian adventurer Thor Heyerdahl advocated his own theory of Pacific migrations, arguing that the source region was not Asia but the Americas (Heyerdahl 1952). In 1947, Heyerdahl constructed a balsa raft, the *Kon-Tiki,* and drifted on it for 101 days across the Pacific, crash-landing on the reef of Raroia atoll in the Tuamotu Islands. The raft voyage caught the attention of a war-weary public, making Heyerdahl famous, but from a scientific point of view his adventure proved little.

What was lacking in all of these early attempts to trace Polynesian origins was the direct evidence of archaeology. Throughout the first half of the twentieth century, it was assumed that there was no point in digging in Pacific Island sites. After World War II, when Edward Gifford, Alexander Spoehr, and Kenneth Emory first began to excavate in Fiji, the Marianas, and Hawai'i, they were amazed not only at the richness of their finds but also at the substantial time depth for human occupation in Oceania. Since their pioneering efforts, archaeological investigations throughout Oceania have provided a richly detailed portrait of the human settlement of this vast region (Kirch 2017). In this chapter we summarize the current understanding of the peopling of the Pacific.

The Settlement of Oceania

Near and Remote Oceania

The tripartite division of Oceania into Melanesia, Micronesia, and Polynesia put forward by the French explorer Dumont D'Urville in 1832 has become so entrenched that it is difficult to dispense with, even though the categories were hardly well thought out, not to mention overtly racist in their overtones. Of the three regions, only Polynesia has proven to be a meaningful culture-historical category: all Polynesian populations and languages have been shown to be descendants of a common ancestral culture, comprising branching lineages or "clades" of related cultures (Kirch and Green 2001).

In 1991, Roger Green proposed a new division of the Pacific into *Near Oceania* and *Remote Oceania,* a distinction that more accurately encapsulates the history of human settlement of the Pacific (Green 1991). Near Oceania incorporates New Guinea, the Bismarck Archipelago, and the Solomon Islands as far as Makira and Santa Anna. Remote Oceania includes the rest of the Pacific proper, including the Vanuatu, New Caledonia, and Fiji archipelagoes of Melanesia, and all of Micronesia and Polynesia (fig. 4.1). These divisions are based on the archaeological evidence that Near Oceania was settled significantly earlier than Remote Oceania. The first incursion of humans into Near Oceania occurred during the late Pleistocene around 40,000 years ago, whereas human expansion into Remote Oceania did not begin until around 4,000 BP (in western Micronesia) and was not completed until about eight centuries ago, with the discovery and settlement of New Zealand.

Some of the oldest evidence for humans in Near Oceania comes from the Huon Peninsula on the northern coast of New Guinea, where split-cobble axe-like tools have been dated between 60,000 and 40,000 years BP (Groube, Muke, and Price 1986). The large islands of New Britain and New Ireland in the Bismarck Archipelago were settled by at least 36,000 BP (Jim Allen 1996; O'Connell and Allen 2015). These early people hunted wild marsupial animals, harvested fish and shellfish along the islands' coastlines, and gathered wild tubers and fruits; they did not practice horticulture or have domesticated plants or animals. They must have possessed some form of simple watercraft to move between the intervisible

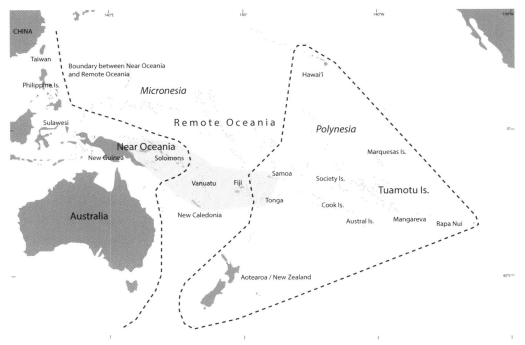

FIGURE 4.1 Map of the Pacific, showing the Polynesian triangle, and the boundary between Near Oceania and Remote Oceania. The shaded zone indicates the area of Lapita site distribution. *(Map by M. D. McCoy)*

islands, but almost certainly lacked sailing canoes. By the early Holocene, however, about 8,000 years ago, there is evidence that some people in Near Oceania were experimenting with plant domestication and horticulture (Denham 2011; Golson 1997). Plants such as taro and bananas, along with tree crops including coconut, *Canarium* almond, Tahitian chestnut, and others, were being grown in Near Oceania by the mid-Holocene, around 4,000 years ago. These and other plants would later be transported to the islands of Remote Oceania, where they formed the basis of island economies.

Over the 30 or more millennia that people lived in Near Oceania, they developed a high degree of linguistic diversity (the so-called Papuan or non-Austronesian languages), as well as a significant range of human biological diversity. This biological diversity is evident not only in the variability in the physical characteristics (phenotypes) of the people occupying New Guinea, the Bismarcks, and the Solomons but also in their genomic diversity, as indicated by recent work on DNA sequencing (Friedlaender, ed., 2007; Hurles et al. 2003).

Austronesian Origins

The settlement of Remote Oceania—and ultimately of Hawaiʻi—was one of the greatest diasporas of human history, the expansion of the Austronesian language speakers. The Austronesian language family (which includes Hawaiian and indeed all of the languages spoken throughout Remote Oceania) includes some 1,200 extant languages, spoken from Madagascar in the west to Rapa Nui (Easter Island) in the east. (The so-called Papuan languages of New Guinea and nearby islands in Near Oceania, however, and the indigenous languages of Australia, are *not* part of the Austronesian language family.)

Austronesian origins have been traced to the large island of Taiwan off the Chinese mainland (Bellwood 2017), around 5,000 BP. On Taiwan, the earliest archaeological evidence of Austronesian culture is the Dabenkeng (or Ta-p'en-k'eng) culture, marked by distinctive cord-marked pottery, along with ground-stone adzes, and fishhooks and ornaments of *Trochus* and other shells. These people were horticulturalists, although more work needs to be done to reconstruct their subsistence economy. Around 4,200 BP, some Austronesians settled in the northern Philippines to the south of Taiwan, evidenced by pottery sites in the Cagayan Valley (e.g., the Lal-lo and Magapit sites) in northern Luzon (Hung and Carson 2014). Soon after, pottery-using peoples expanded southeast to Sulawesi and adjacent islands. At the Uattamdi rockshelter on Kayoa Island west of Halmahera, red-slipped pottery associated with a rich diversity of stone and shell artifacts has been dated to 3300–2800 BP (Bellwood 1996, 2017, 2019; Bellwood et al. 2019). This progression of pottery-using cultures from Taiwan, through the Philippines, and into the equatorial islands of Southeast Asia represents the expansion of the Austronesian speakers (Carson et al. 2013). The archaeological chronology is remarkably consistent with the internal relationships or subgrouping (the "family tree") of the Austronesian languages (fig. 4.2) as worked out through careful linguistic comparisons (Blust 2013; Pawley and Ross 1993).

The early Austronesians were horticulturalists, raised domestic animals (including pigs and chickens), fished the inshore and offshore waters, made red-slipped

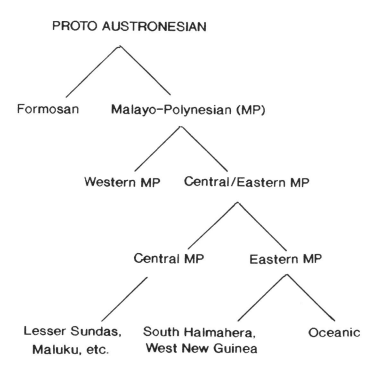

FIGURE 4.2 Chart showing the progressive diversification of the main branches of the Austronesian languages from Proto-Austronesian. The Oceanic branch (*lower right*) includes most of the languages spoken in island Melanesia, Micronesia, and Polynesia.

earthenware pottery, used ground-stone and shell adzes, and possessed a variety of other tools and implements made from shell. Linguistic reconstructions of the Proto-Austronesian and Proto–Malayo-Polynesian vocabularies include words for such important Pacific crops as taro, coconut, banana, and breadfruit, and for the domesticated pig, chicken, and dog (Blust 1976). Most importantly, the Austronesians were canoe builders and navigators. Linguists Andrew and Medina Pawley (1994) have reconstructed early Austronesian terms for canoe parts and for sailing, finding that speakers of these languages had outrigger canoes (Proto-Austronesian *wagka,* from which Hawaiian *waʻa* ultimately derives) with planks, washstrakes, and possibly carved endpieces, and with platforms between hull and outrigger. Based on the reconstructed linguistic terms, these canoes had masts and were propelled by sails, or paddled, and were captained by expert seafarers.

Austronesians first appeared in the islands of the Bismarck Archipelago in Near Oceania in the mid–second millennium BC. Their outrigger canoes must have been a novel sight in Pacific waters. They established stilt-house settlements fringing the beaches of Mussau, New Ireland, and New Britain. Yet they were not the first inhabitants of these islands; on these beaches the newcomers encountered the descendants of the much earlier settlers of Near Oceania, whose ancestors had arrived 30,000 years earlier. In contrast with the seafaring newcomers who spoke a Proto-Oceanic dialect of Austronesian, the indigenous people of Near Oceania spoke not just one language but a plethora of Papuan (or non-Austronesian) languages. Out of these encounters—no doubt tentative and cautious at first—came a cultural synthesis that would change the course of Pacific history.

The Lapita Trail

The sites occupied by these early Austronesians in Near Oceania contain a distinctive kind of dentate-stamped pottery (fig. 4.3), known as *Lapita* (Green 1979; Kirch 1997). The name comes from a site on the Foué Peninsula of New Caledonia, where Professor Edward W. Gifford and his student Richard Shutler, Jr., of the University of California, Berkeley, discovered such pottery in 1952. As seafarers, the Lapita people ventured beyond the inshore waters to move pottery, obsidian, chert, oven stones, and other materials between their communities, frequently over hundreds of kilometers. They used adzes of both stone and shell, flake tools of obsidian and chert, shell scrapers and peeling knives, anvil stones, polishers, slingstones, shell rings of a variety of sizes and shapes, bracelets, arm-rings, beads, discs, needles, awls, tattooing chisels, fishhooks, net sinkers, and other items.

The earliest dates for Lapita in the Bismarck Archipelago range between 3360 and 3240 BP (Denham et al. 2012), and come from the large stilt-house settlement of Talepakemalai (ECA) in the Mussau Islands (Kirch, ed., 2021). Talepakemalai and other Lapita sites in Near Oceania were stilt house villages standing over shallow lagoons or tidal flats. Their pottery assemblages include flat-bottomed dishes, bowls supported on pedestals (ring-feet), cylinder stands, and large carinated jars, often elaborately decorated with dentate-stamped (and less frequently, incised) motifs, many displaying human faces.

Around 3050 BP, some Lapita groups started to voyage past the invisible boundary of Near Oceania (at the southeastern end of the main Solomons chain), which for 30,000 years or more had marked the limits of human existence in the Pacific. Lapita canoes rapidly searched out the islands of the Santa Cruz group, 380 km southeast of Makira, establishing small settlements along the coast of the main island of Nendö and on the small coral islets of the nearby Reef Islands. Other Lapita groups soon pressed south, through the Banks Islands and into the

FIGURE 4.3 Lapita pottery is characterized by dentate-stamped decoration, as seen in his sherd from the Talepakemalai site in the Mussau Islands of the Bismarck Archipelago. *(Photo by P. V. Kirch)*

Vanuatu archipelago, where by 2900 BP they were emplaced on small islets off the coasts of Santo and Malekula (Sand and Bedford, eds., 2010, 122–137). On the large island of Efate, in central Vanuatu, the discovery in 2004 of the Teouma site was especially remarkable, including an intact Lapita cemetery. The complex mortuary practices at Teouma, including the removal of skulls and secondary reburial, sometimes in pots, or in one case with skulls placed across the chest of an adult male whose own cranium had been detached, are suggestive of ancestor worship. Moreover, three of the oldest Lapita skeletons at the Teouma site have had their DNA sequenced (Skoglund et al. 2016), exhibiting a genome almost entirely of East Asian ancestry (only 5% or less of Papuan admixture). The clear genetic links of this population of "First Remote Oceanians" back to Taiwan is further compelling evidence of a Southeast Asian origin of the initial Lapita colonizers of Remote Oceania.

The Lapita diaspora proceeded rapidly down through the Vanuatu archipelago, to the upraised coral or makatea islands of the Loyalty group, and on to discover La Grande Terre of New Caledonia (Sand 2010). Simultaneously with the Lapita expansion through Vanuatu to New Caledonia, other explorers undertook awe-inspiring voyages due east from either the Santa Cruz or northern Vanuatu islands, sailing upwind against the prevailing trades and currents, to cross 850 km of trackless ocean, with no stepping-stone islands in between, arriving in the Fiji archipelago. The earliest radiocarbon dates from Fiji come in between 3020 and 2860 BP (Nunn and Petchey 2013).

From Fiji, there was rapid exploration eastward, via the many small islands of the Lau archipelago and on to the Tongan islands of Tongatapu and 'Eua. The earliest known site on Tongatapu, Nukuleka, has been precisely dated using the ^{230}Thorium method on coral abraders, with an age of 2838 ± 8 years BP (Burley et al. 2010; Burley et al. 2015). Decorated pottery from Nukuleka exhibits similarities with the Western Lapita style of the Santa Cruz Islands. Lapita colonists then expanded northward through the Tongan archipelago, via the Ha'apai group of low coral islands, to Vava'u (around 2800 BP). Isolated Niuatoputapu, with the Lolokoka Lapita site, was probably settled from Vava'u. The Lolokoka site on Niuatoputapu contained not only dentate-stamped pottery but also an array of shell, stone, and sea urchin tools and implements (Kirch 1988). Futuna and 'Uvea, between Fiji and Samoa, were also discovered and settled in roughly this same time period.

The arrival of Lapita voyagers in the large Samoan archipelago is attested at the site of Mulifanua on 'Upolu Island, a submerged deposit under a capping of reef rock, fortuitously discovered by offshore dredging for a ferry berth. Mulifanua, with classic dentate-stamped pottery, is dated to 2880–2750 BP (Petchey 2001). The absence of other Lapita sites in Samoa is probably due to the islands' rapid geological subsidence and likely drowning of other Lapita sites. In the tiny Manu'a Islands, at the far eastern end of the Samoan chain, the To'aga site on Ofu with a thin, fine-ware pottery lacking dentate-stamped decoration dates to around 2700 BP (Petchy and Kirch 2019). Other kinds of artifacts from To'aga, including basalt adzes, abrading tools, shell fishhooks, and ornaments, attest to the range of early Polynesian material culture (fig. 4.4).

The Lapita expansion out of Near Oceania into Remote Oceania—as far south as New Caledonia and as far east as Tonga and Samoa—was accomplished in less than three centuries. These small groups of seafarers explored an ocean realm stretching across 4,500 km

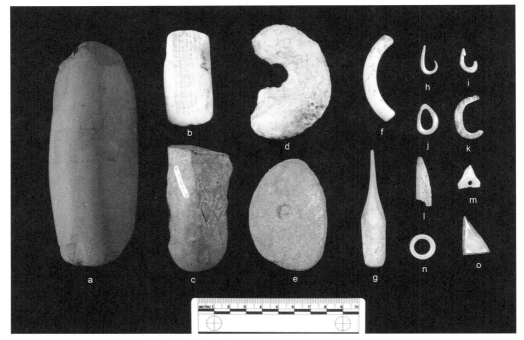

FIGURE 4.4 Artifacts from the Ancestral Polynesian site of Toʻaga, Ofu Island, American Samoa: (a) basalt adze; (b) shell adze; (c) basalt adze; (d) unfinished *Tridacna*-shell ring; (e) abrading stone; (f) cone-shell ring fragment; (g) sea-urchin-spine abrader; (h), (i), and (k) *Turbo*-shell fishhooks; (j) unfinished fishhook; (l) bone chisel fragment; (m) drilled shark's tooth; (n) cone-shell bead; and (o) cut pearl shell. *(Photo by P. V. Kirch)*

during the course of just 10 to 15 successive human generations (taking 20 years as the reproductive length of a generation). These were not merely voyages of discovery by itinerant sailors who came for a brief period and then returned to a homeland in the western Pacific; they were purposeful voyages of discovery and colonization. The earliest Lapita sites are permanent habitations, not temporary camps. The Lapita expansion reflects successive groups of settlers, each in its turn founding a new colony on a previously uninhabited island. Within a generation or two, descendants of the group then repeated the scenario, setting out to find yet another new island.

This sequence of island colonization raises fundamental anthropological questions, both demographic and social. Demographically, this process of expansion—which established new, permanent settlements and yet continued to bud off colonizing daughter populations—required a high net population growth rate, presumably achieved by a combination of a high fertility or birth rate and a low mortality or death rate. Otherwise, there simply would not have been a sufficient demographic "head of steam" to keep the process moving. Even so, colonizing populations were small, resulting in genetic bottlenecks that are evident in genetic variation among Polynesians (Flint et al. 1989; Martinson et al. 1993).

What motives impelled these people to keep exploring southward and eastward into the unknown waters of the Pacific? It could not have been the sometimes-cited "population pressure" of overcrowded islands, for many of the newly discovered lands were vast and uninhabited; it would take centuries before large islands such as Efate or Viti Levu were densely populated. Rather than a "push" factor, we must invoke "pull" factors in trying to understand the Lapita expansion. Initially, one kind of "pull" incentive that brought Austronesian speakers from Southeast Asia into the Bismarck Archipelago might have been a search for new trading opportunities (such as obsidian). However, once the Lapita peoples left Near Oceania and ventured into uninhabited Remote Oceania, trade seems an unlikely explanation.

Lapita social structure may have played a key role in driving the engine of exploration and colonization. Linguistic reconstructions of Proto-Oceanic words for kinship and social statuses reveal that these peoples put much emphasis on birth order. Older and younger siblings were ranked, with the inheritance of house sites, garden lands, and other kinds of property, as well as such intangibles as ritual privileges and esoteric knowledge, passing from parents to firstborn offspring. In such societies, "junior siblings frequently adopt a strategy of seeking new lands to settle where they can found their own 'house' and lineage, assuring their own offspring access to quality resources" (Kirch 1997, 65). Rivalries between older and younger brothers are a frequent theme in the oral traditions of Polynesians, the direct descendants of one branch of the Lapita peoples. Peter Bellwood (1996) has argued that such a "founder-focused ideology" is inherently characteristic of Austronesian-speaking peoples; discovery and settlement of a new island (or later, a new valley or part of an island) served to enhance founder rank. We cannot underestimate as well the importance of new voyaging strategies (such as upwind search-and-return voyages) and of improved watercraft, which provided the technological basis for such expansion (Irwin 1992).

The Emergence of Ancestral Polynesian Culture

With the discovery of Tonga and Samoa, and of the smaller Western Polynesian islands of Niuatoputapu, 'Uvea, and Futuna, the Lapita peoples had crossed the threshold of Oceania proper. Here, the islands are geologically young, consisting of basaltic rocks, or of coral atolls and uplifted limestone (*makatea*) built on volcanic bases. Islands in the eastern Pacific are also generally smaller than in Melanesia. In addition, the biodiversity of the eastern islands is restricted. All of these conditions posed new constraints and challenges to the Lapita colonizers of Western Polynesia. No longer did they have access to a wide range of rock types from which to make stone tools; they had to adapt their technology to the use of the tough and hard-to-work basalts. The lack of edible plants meant that transporting seedling stocks of cultivated plants was critical to the success of founding settlements. And, with the increased distances between islands in the eastern Pacific, they had to sharpen their voyaging and navigational skills if they were to maintain contact between islands.

These were a few of the adaptive changes that transformed the Lapita technology and culture of the early first millennium BC into what is called *Ancestral Polynesian* culture. Change was gradual, over a period of about 1,000 years, in the islands of Tonga, Samoa, Futuna, and 'Uvea, the "homeland" of Polynesian cultures. In archaeological sites of this period we can identify some of the material culture changes that marked this transformation from Lapita to Polynesian. Most striking was the gradual loss of pottery. By about 2450 BP, the ancestral Polynesians no longer decorated their pots with the characteristic dentate-stamped Lapita designs; they abandoned the more complex vessel types, using only simple jars and bowls. By 2000 BP, they were producing only simple, crude earthenware bowls, and by around 1650 BP pottery production ceased entirely. Why they should have given up this useful craft is not known, although it was not for a lack of potting clay. Many of the stone and wooden bowls found in later Polynesian sites seem to carry on the same shapes and some of the same functions as the earlier pottery. Adzes from sites of the first millennium BC also exhibit a gradual change in technology, with the development of distinctly Polynesian types (Green 1971a). These changes were occasioned, in part, by the need to adapt to the restricted raw material, primarily basalt.

While archaeological evidence offers important clues about Ancestral Polynesian culture, especially aspects of its subsistence base and material culture, it is possible to reconstruct some non–material cultural traits using a "triangulation approach." Kirch and Green (2001) laid out the methodology for this approach in detail, using a phylogenetic model of cultural differentiation that integrates linguistic and comparative ethnographic data with archaeological sources.

Based on the application of the triangulation approach, we know that Ancestral Polynesian communities supported themselves with a mixed horticultural-maritime economy inherited from their Lapita ancestors. They cultivated tuber and root crops, including taro and yams, but also tree crops such as coconut, breadfruit, and bananas. The main gardening method was shifting cultivation, in which garden patches in the forest are cleared and burned prior to planting. Households kept pigs, dogs, and chickens, but fish and shellfish provided most of the protein in the Ancestral Polynesian diet, augmented by hunting or catching birds. A wide range of fishing methods is attested by linguistic reconstructions; archaeologically, fishing is indicated by simple shell fishhooks, and by net weights, as well as from faunal remains.

Food was prepared in separate cookhouses that sheltered earth ovens, shallow pits usually about one meter in diameter in which stones were first heated over a fire and, when white-hot, used to steam the food. Food preparation involved scraping and peeling, pounding, mixing, and kneading. Puddings made from combining one or more kinds of staple starch (such as taro) with an emollient, usually coconut cream, were a core part of the cuisine. These, along with combinations of meat, taro leaves, and coconut cream, were parceled in wrappers of banana or *Alocasia* leaves and cooked in earth ovens.

Ancestral Polynesian artifacts included the plainware pottery (largely simple bowls and cups), adzes of *Tridacna* shell or (increasingly over time) of basalt, one-piece fishhooks of *Turbo* shell, beads and rings of *Conus* shell, hammerstones, files or abraders of sea-urchin spine and of coral or pumice, and amorphous scrapers or other ad hoc tools made from flakes of basalt or obsidian (see fig. 4.4). Much of this material culture did not get preserved in the archaeological record, for it was made of wood or vegetable fibers. In Ancestral Polynesian houses one would have seen mats woven from coconut and pandanus leaves, wooden bowls and containers, coconut water bottles, baskets, and clothing (loincloths and skirts) made from the bark of paper mulberry (*Broussonetia papyrifera*) and other plants. Gardeners used digging sticks (which sometimes doubled as coconut-husking poles), and had carrying poles to transport the harvest back to their cookhouses.

Linguistic reconstructions provide important clues regarding Ancestral Polynesian kinship, social organization, and religion (Kirch and Green 2001). The primary social group was the *kaainga* (the asterisk indicates a reconstructed term), a descent or lineage group holding an estate of land as well as other tangible and intangible property and rights. The head of such a *kaainga* group was the *fatu,* in most cases a senior (ranking) male, who served as both secular and ritual leader. There were also special terms for an expert or knowledgeable craftsperson (*tufunga*), sea expert or navigator (*tautai*), and warrior (*toa*). All of these Ancestral Polynesian words carry on into later Hawaiian language and culture.

A more inclusive social group was the *kainanga,* which was also a descent group of some kind, and may have been linked with the term *sau,* a ruler or high-ranking elite. The leader of the *kainanga* was called *qariki,* a term that is ancestral to the word for "chief" in most Polynesian languages (e.g., Hawaiian ali'i and Tahitian ari'i). In these small communities, some degree of ranking based on the hereditary principle of seniority (birth order) seems to have been key, but it may be more reasonable to think of these societies as heterarchical rather than hierarchical. Subtle differences in ranking and access to resources by different *kaainga* or *kainanga* and their leaders would provide the structural basis for the evolution of hierarchy and stratification once large and dense populations had developed on particular islands, and competition for land and resources intensified.

Ancestral Polynesian society possessed the classic Polynesian concepts of *tapu* (sacredness) and *mana* (spiritual power) that were at the core of their belief system. Only the god Tangaloa (the ancestral name for the Hawaiian god Kanaloa) seems to have been known in these early times, and his import is not clear. Ritual activity was conducted in a house (*fare*) much like an ordinary dwelling—perhaps the residence of the *qariki* or ritual elder—and on an open, cleared space (called the *malaqe*) to the seaward side of that house. Key posts within the house, and/or simple upright stones placed around the perimeter of the *malaqe* represented specific ancestors or spirits, to whom prayers and invocations were directed. Deceased ancestors were buried beneath the house floor. Some evidence hints at the presence of an annual ceremonial feast, perhaps a first-fruits ritual. The year was organized according to a lunar calendar of 13 months, which was indexed to the rising and setting of the constellation Pleiades (*Mata-liki*) as well as to the annual spawning of the reproductive segments of a sea worm, the *palolo*. The lunar month names were concerned largely with an annual ecological rhythm, especially the wet-dry seasonality so critical to the timing of the yam crop.

By the early first millennium AD, this distinctive Ancestral Polynesian culture had emerged in the Western Polynesian homeland, an adaptation to new, truly oceanic environmental conditions, the result of gradual and random change. As Roger Green succinctly put it, "Thus there never was a Polynesian migration from elsewhere; becoming Polynesian took place in Polynesia itself as the archaeology of Tonga and Samoa over the last 3,000 years readily attests. One begins with Eastern Lapita, and ends with Polynesians" (Green 1977, 237).

The Great Polynesian Diaspora

Having successfully adapted to truly oceanic conditions, the early Polynesians in the late first millennium BC were poised for the final phase of human expansion into Remote Oceania—the settlement of the most far-flung islands of the eastern Pacific, including

Hawai'i. One technological innovation in the Western Polynesian homeland—the development of the double-hulled, oceangoing canoe—would prove essential to this next phase of exploration and discovery. Accompanied by sophisticated methods of noninstrumental navigation or "wayfinding"—using star paths, wind compasses, observation of ocean swells and refraction patterns, and other natural phenomena—Polynesians launched a remarkable diaspora that took them literally to the eastern edge of the Pacific world and back.

In contrast with earlier views that the settlement of Eastern Polynesia was accomplished merely by random drift (Sharp 1956), it is now certain that these widely dispersed islands were discovered through purposive voyages of exploration enabled by a sophisticated canoe technology and navigational abilities (A. Anderson 2001; Irwin 1992; Finney, 1994, 1996a, 1996b; Finney et al. 1989). In this respect, archaeologists have been aided by the knowledge gained from the experimental voyages of the *Hōkūle'a* and other replicated Polynesian double-hulled voyaging canoes (fig. 4.5). Although there is some debate on this point, it appears that the large oceangoing double-hulled sailing canoe (as opposed to the simpler sailing canoe with outrigger) was invented and perfected in the Western Polynesian homeland during the Ancestral Polynesian period. These canoes, with their vastly expanded range and cargo capacity, enabled the peopling of Eastern Polynesia.

In the 1960s, Kenneth Emory and Yosihiko Sinoto pinpointed the Marquesas Islands as the first archipelago to be settled by voyagers from Western Polynesia. They saw the Marquesas as a "primary dispersal center" in Eastern Polynesia, with successive dispersals extending from the Marquesas to the Society Islands, and subsequently radiating from both of these archipelagoes out to the other Eastern Polynesian islands. Based on available radiocarbon

FIGURE 4.5 The replicated voyaging canoe *Hōkūle'a* has sailed on experimental wayfinding voyages throughout Polynesia. *(Photo courtesy Bishop Museum)*

dates of the time, they put the initial settlement of the Marquesas at AD 300, and the settlement of both the Society Islands and Hawai'i at AD 500 (Emory and Sinoto 1965; Jennings, ed., 1979). This "orthodox scenario" was widely accepted at the time that the first edition of this book was published in 1985. Since then, however, significant refinements in radiocarbon dating, along with the discovery and excavation of new sites throughout Eastern Polynesia, have substantially revised our understanding of the settlement of this vast region.

For some years, a debate regarding Eastern Polynesian settlement revolved around the "long pause," the gap between the arrival of Lapita populations in the Western Polynesian homeland and the later expansion of Polynesians into the islands of Eastern Polynesia. (The "long pause" was in part the basis for the popular Disney film *Moana*.) While Tonga, Samoa, and other Western Polynesian islands were settled by 900–800 BC, it at first seemed that the earliest sites in Eastern Polynesia dated to around 200 BC–AD 300, based on radiocarbon dates from the Marquesas Islands (Y. H. Sinoto 1966; Suggs 1961). This left a "pause" of between six to nine centuries between the settlement of the Polynesian homeland and the later diaspora to Eastern Polynesia.

In 1993 Matthew Spriggs and Atholl Anderson proposed that there had been an even longer pause between the settlement of the Western Polynesian ancestral homeland and the exploration and settlement of Eastern Polynesia (Spriggs and Anderson 1993). Arguing that many of the original radiocarbon dates from Eastern Polynesian sites were inaccurate, Spriggs and Anderson applied "chronometric hygiene" to the radiocarbon dates, eliminating dates that did not meet certain strict criteria. Spriggs and Anderson suggested that initial Marquesan settlement had not occurred until AD 300–600, while the "central, northern, and eastern archipelagoes" were not settled until AD 600–950, with New Zealand being the last to be discovered around AD 1000–1200 (1993, 211). Subsequent redating of key early sites soon began to push those dates even closer to the present.

Why were the initial radiocarbon carbon dates obtained by archaeologists in the 1950s and 1960s inaccurate? Most of the initial dates had large standard errors, a reflection of the crude solid-carbon counting methods used by Willard Libby and other radiocarbon-dating pioneers in the 1950s and 1960s. The later shift to liquid scintillation methods reduced such errors, but the greatest advance came in the 1990s with the development of accelerator mass spectrometry (AMS). AMS dating reduced standard errors to as little as ± 15 years, while also permitting the dating of minute samples. With sample sizes as small as 10 milligrams for carbonized plant materials, short-lived individual seeds or small twig fragments could be directly dated.

A second major advance has been the ability to identify the charcoal selected for dating. In the early years of radiocarbon dating there had been a tendency to select large pieces of wood charcoal, probably biasing samples in favor of old hardwoods. Often, the entire contents of hearths or earth ovens were submitted in bulk. Such samples likely often included old-growth timber, with an "inbuilt" age significantly older than the time at which the wood was gathered and burnt. At coastal sites, driftwood may often have been used for fuel; driftwood logs from North American old-growth trees regularly wash up on Hawaiian beaches. Dating such driftwood could potentially yield dates hundreds of years older than the actual burning event.

By identifying individual charcoal specimens for AMS dating, and selecting only short-lived species such as shrubby plants, or individual seeds, archaeologists eliminated the problem of old wood that was not directly related to the age of human occupation of a site. These methodological advances have revolutionized the radiocarbon chronology for Eastern Polynesia. A new consensus has emerged around a "short chronology" in which the central archipelagoes of Eastern Polynesia were not settled until after AD 900.

It is still not entirely certain which archipelago or island in Eastern Polynesian was the first to see voyaging canoes from Western Polynesia arrive on its shores. The most likely candidates are the Society Islands and the southern Cook Islands. For the Society Islands, Kahn and Sinoto (2017) argue that revised dating of early sites indicates Polynesian arrival around AD 1000–1100. Sediment coring and pollen analysis at Lake Temae on Moʻorea documents initial human presence on the island, including cultivation of *Colocasia* taro, by AD 1000 (Stevenson et al. 2017). In the southern Cook Islands, the Tangatatau rockshelter on Mangaia has been extensively dated using the AMS method on identified, short-lived plant remains and on the bones of the Polynesian-introduced Pacific rat; these dates indicate initial human arrival between AD 906 and 1180 (Kirch, ed., 2017). On Aitutaki Island in the southern Cooks, the base of the Moturaku rockshelter dates to AD 1047–1297 (Allen and Morrison 2013). Most recently, Sear et al. (2020) have dated human presence on Aitu Island at AD 800–1004, based on anthropogenic signals in a swamp core.

The chronology of Marquesan settlement has been similarly shortened. Suggs' original date of 150 BC from Haʻatuatua on Nuku Hiva (Suggs 1961), and Sinoto's date of AD 300–600 from the Hane site on Ua Huka (Y. H. Sinoto 1966) can now be rejected as being due to the "inbuilt age" problem. When Anderson and Sinoto (2002) redated 10 samples from Hane, none was earlier than AD 1000. In 2009, Conte and Molle (2014) reexcavated at Hane, obtaining a new series of AMS dates from the lowest deposits dating to AD 900–1000. This is consistent with Rolett's dates for the earliest levels at Hanamiai on Tahuata Island, bracketed between AD 1025 and 1300 (Rolett 1998, 241, table 4.1).

Recent chronologies for other Eastern Polynesian islands likewise support initial settlement of between AD 900 and 1100. AMS dates from the Onemea site on Taravai Island in the Gambier (Mangareva) Islands indicate Polynesian arrival around AD 950–1050 (Kirch et al. 2010), while Weisler's dates from Henderson Island are no earlier than AD 1050 (Weisler 1995, 389, table 2). Despite some claims that Rapa Nui was not settled until AD 1200, AMS dates from the Anakena dune site (Steadman et al. 1994) suggest colonization of Rapa Nui as early as AD 1000–1100. To sum up, the central and southeastern archipelagoes and islands of Eastern Polynesia now have well-supported radiocarbon chronologies converging on the period from AD 900 to 1100.

In a recent genomic (DNA) study, Alex Ioannidis et al. (2021) proposed a sequence for the settlement of Eastern Polynesia that originates in Samoa and progresses rapidly eastward through the Cook Islands, thence to the Society and Tuamotu Islands, and finally to the widely separated islands of the Marquesas, Raʻivavae, and Rapa Nui. Ioannidis et al.'s analysis draws upon genome-wide data from 430 contemporary individuals representing 21 island populations. This geographic range expansion across the eastern Pacific is marked by a "telescoping" succession of genetic bottlenecks, each resulting from a founder effect as small colonizing populations moved from one island to discover and settle another. (Founder effects arise when a few individuals in a population leave to found a new population that does not encompass the full genetic complement of the parent population.) The "directionality index" resulting from this analysis provides an arrow delineating a parental population from its child. Dates for these parent-child population separations were then estimated by comparing "identical by descent" segments of the genomes. The chronology indicated by this genomic analysis begins in the ninth century with the initial movement out of Samoa to the Cooks, and ends by the mid-fourteenth century with the establishment of settlements across Eastern Polynesia. In general, this chronology accords quite well with the archaeological chronology provided by the most recent series of radiocarbon dates.

The great Polynesian diaspora did not only result in the discovery and settlement of virtually every island in the central Eastern Pacific—it also led to Polynesians reaching the shores of South America. The sweet potato (*Ipomoea batatas*), a plant of undoubted American origins that was widely cultivated in Eastern Polynesia (especially in New Zealand, Hawai'i, and Easter Island) at the time of European contact, has long been noted as likely evidence for Polynesian contact with South America. Based on his extensive study of the plant, Douglas Yen (1974) proposed a "tripartite hypothesis" in which the sweet potato arrived in Eastern Polynesia in pre-European times, with Polynesians as the most likely transferors. Roullier et al. (2013) validated Yen's hypothesis through molecular genetic analysis of historical sweet potato collections. Moreover, the discovery of carbonized sweet potato tubers (parenchyma) in early layers of the Tangatatau rockshelter on Mangaia in the southern Cooks (Hather and Kirch 1991) provides direct evidence of sweet potato transfer into central Polynesia in precontact times. Archaeobotanical samples of sweet potato have now been radiocarbon dated to precontact contexts in both New Zealand and Hawai'i. Given the evidence for rapid Polynesian expansion throughout southeastern Polynesia between ca. AD 950 and 1200, it seems evident that at least one voyaging canoe reached South America to establish contact and return with sweet potato tubers, which then entered the Polynesian horticultural complex. The Proto–Eastern Polynesian name for sweet potato, **kuumara*, is likely a borrowing from a South American dialect in which the term for the crop is *kumar* or similar variants (Yen 1974, appendix; Green 2005). In addition to the sweet potato, the bottle gourd (*Lagenaria siceraria*), a useful plant known to have been present in the Americas by at least 9900 BP, was also carried into Eastern Polynesia. Archaeobotanical remains of bottle gourd (gourd fragments and seeds) have been recovered in precontact contexts in Hawai'i and elsewhere in Eastern Polynesia.

Genetic evidence for contact between Polynesians and indigenous populations in South America was reported by Ioannidis et al. (2020), based on analysis of genome-wide variation in 807 individuals from 17 island populations and 15 Pacific coast Native American groups. They found "conclusive evidence for prehistoric contact of Polynesian individuals with Native American individuals (around AD 1200) contemporaneous with the settlement of remote Oceania" (2020, 1). While Ioannidis et al. (2020) point to the debunked Thor Heyerdahl theory of Native Americans arriving in the Marquesas or another island group of Eastern Polynesia prior to the advent of the Polynesians, given the total absence of archaeological evidence for a pre-Polynesian Native American presence on any of the eastern Pacific islands—or a tradition of long-distance seafaring and colonization by South Americans—the far more plausible explanation is that such genetic introgression occurred as a result of voyaging Polynesians making contact with South American people. The Ioannidis et al. (2020) study establishes that one or more Polynesian voyages extending as far as the coast of South America not only returned with the sweet potato and bottle gourd but with an additional genetic component to their own population as well.

Dating Polynesian Arrival in Hawai'i

Two kinds of evidence can be used to date human arrival on an island or archipelago: (1) direct evidence from settlement sites, and (2) indirect evidence in the form of proxy signals of anthropogenic or "human-caused" disturbance to the environment. This second kind of evidence includes increases in microscopic charcoal content in lake or swamp sediments (indicative of anthropogenic burning), declines in the frequencies of native plant pollen in these sediments (indicative of forest clearance), or the appearance of human-introduced plants and animals. One such introduction was of the small, commensal Pacific rat (*Rattus exulans*), which accompanied Polynesians on their voyages of exploration. With their high reproductive rate (females can give birth to several litters of multiple pups each year), the numbers of rats increased exponentially once they were established on a new island.

Although several coastal sites, including the Pu'u Ali'i (H1) sand dune on Hawai'i Island and the Hālawa Valley dune site (Mo-Al-3) on Moloka'i, were originally thought to date to the early settlement phase, redating of such sites with new AMS methods has failed to replicate the early dates (see chapter 6). The Bellows Dune site (O18) at Waimānalo, O'ahu, however, has yielded new AMS dates that put it within the time span of early Eastern Polynesian expansion. Site O18 was excavated in 1967 by Richard Pearson et al. (1971), who found pearl-shell fishhooks, adzes, and other artifacts with stylistic traits similar to early Eastern Polynesian artifact assemblages in the Marquesas Islands (see chapter 6). Based on four initial radiocarbon dates on unidentified wood charcoal from both cultural layers of the site, Pearson et al. (1971, 230, fig. 14) suggested that the site was occupied between AD 600 and 1100. These dates, however, had large standard errors and displayed some stratigraphic inversions. Tuggle and Spriggs (2000) reported an additional five dates run on curated samples from the 1967 excavations; however, they could only conclude that the earlier Layer III "pre-dates AD 1000," and that Layer II "post-dates AD 1000" (2000, 181).

Dye and Pantaleo (2010; see also Dye 2011a) dated an additional nine samples from O18 recovered during the original 1967 excavations, selecting short-lived materials, and using the AMS radiocarbon method. Four of these samples were worked pieces of pearl shell, while the other five were charcoal from native plants identified to genus and species (Dye and Pantaleo 2010, table 1). Based on Bayesian calibration and modeling of these new dates, Dye and Pantaleo concluded that the O18 site was "established in AD 1040–1219" (2010, 113). They further argued that this was "some 260–459 years after the current estimate of first settlement" of Hawai'i, basing that conclusion on a questionable assumption that the islands had been settled by AD 800 (following Athens [1997]).

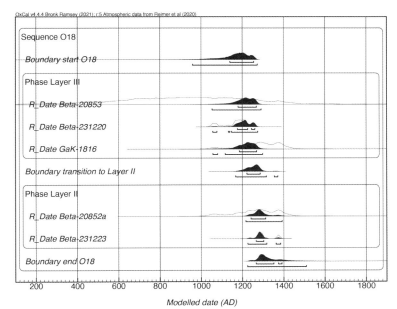

FIGURE 4.6 Bayesian calibration of radiocarbon dates from the Bellows dune site (O18) at Waimānalo, Oʻahu Island. *(Oxcal plot by P. V. Kirch)*

An alternative Bayesian calibration and modeling for the O18 site, which does not assume an initial settlement date for the islands, and which excludes the four dates on pearl shell (because we lack appropriate knowledge regarding the necessary marine reservoir correction for shell) can be put forward. This model also rejects four dates that when incorporated in an initial run using the Oxcal calibration program prove to be in "poor agreement." Figure 4.6 shows the Oxcal plot for three dates from Layer III and two dates from Layer II that model the age of those two strata with a high statistical agreement ($A_{overall}$ index = 116.6). This Bayesian calibration model brackets the age of Layer III between a lower boundary of AD 1121–1250 and an upper boundary of AD 1216–1282 (at one standard deviation).

There is no reason to think that the Bellows Dune or O18 site was the initial or first settlement site in the islands; indeed, that is unlikely. All we can confidently say is that the site exhibits artifacts similar to those in other early sites in central Eastern Polynesia, and that O18 is at present the earliest village site yet to be discovered by archaeologists in Hawaiʻi. To establish when Hawaiʻi was likely settled by Polynesians, however, we can turn to paleoenvironmental or "proxy" evidence.

One indication comes from the O18 site itself, in the form of a nut shell (technically, the endocarp) of the candlenut or *kukui* tree (*Aleurites moluccana*) recovered from Layer II during the 1967 excavation. The *kukui* tree was one of the "canoe plants" transported to the islands by the Polynesians. *Kukui* nuts are hard and durable; they frequently wash down island streams from the interior valleys where the trees flourish, to end up on the island's beaches. The *kukui* nut shell from O18 Layer II is considerably older than the other samples from that stratum, and thus we reject it in the Bayesian modeling of the age for Layer II. But that does not mean that the date on the nut shell itself is not accurate. The nut shell has a calibrated age of AD 840–1159, and as Dye and Pantaleo point out, "It is likely that the *A. moluccana* tree was planted by Hawaiians who lived at some other site in Waimānalo prior to settlement at O18" (2010, 118).

Proxy evidence for early human presence in the islands also comes from lowland swamps or ponds, where anaerobic sediments preserve the pollen from vegetation that formerly surrounded the wetlands. Pollen grains in samples extracted from cores taken through the sediments can be identified to genus and species. The sediments also trap microscopic particles of charcoal that resulted from human-induced burning around the margins of the wetlands, giving an indication of fire frequency. On geologically older islands such as Oʻahu that lack active volcanoes, such fires would almost certainly be due to human activity.

In the early 1990s, Steve Athens and his collaborators began to apply sediment coring and pollen analysis (palynology) to wetland sites on Oʻahu Island, such as ʻUkoʻa Pond and Kawainui Marsh (Athens 1997; Athens and Ward 1993, 1997; Athens, Ward, and Wickler 1992). Analysis of cores showed unmistakable signals of anthropogenic disturbance, with dramatic increases in microscopic charcoal (from near 0 in prehuman levels to 25 mm^2/cc in the upper levels of the cores). The pollen of native plants, especially the endemic *loulu* palm (*Pritchardia* spp.) and a now-extirpated shrub *Kanaloa kahoolawensis,* showed significant declines at the same time that the charcoal counts increased. These data revolutionized our understanding of changes to the Oʻahu landscape following Polynesian settlement. In an influential article, Athens wrote,

> What, then, is the very earliest coring evidence we have for the Polynesian presence in Hawaii? The answer is approximately AD 800, which is from ʻUkoʻa Pond. The securest evidence is in the form of microscopic particulate charcoal, though it is also supported by the pollen evidence. . . . Because particulate charcoal does not occur in sample intervals predating Polynesian occupation in any of our cores on Oʻahu, we feel confident that its presence in the ʻUkoʻa Pond core (and other cores) must be entirely due to anthropogenic causes. (Athens 1997, 266)

Radiocarbon dates from ʻUkoʻa Pond bracketed these dramatic changes between AD 800 and 1200, although the early end of this date range was soon revised as additional dates were obtained. In later work at Ordy Pond on Oʻahu, Athens et al. (1999) reported that the first presence of charcoal is bracketed by two radiocarbon dates between AD 1000 and 1100. And a core in an inland location in Maunawili Valley on windward Oʻahu showed *Pritchardia* palms and other indigenous plant taxa declining after AD 1200 (Athens and Ward 1997). In all, Athens' coring program on Oʻahu makes it clear that by AD 1200 anthropogenic disturbance was widespread on the island. Initial Polynesian settlement must therefore have occurred sometime prior to AD 1200 but is unlikely to have been much before AD 1000.

On Kauaʻi Island, Lida and David Burney (2003) used sediment coring and dating of charcoal influxes to establish the earliest presence of Polynesians on different parts of the island. Their earliest reliable record for anthropogenic charcoal came from Kekupua fishpond on the island's southwestern coast, where charcoal in a 2.2 m deep core first appears at 1.4 m with an associated radiocarbon date of cal AD 1165–1260.

As noted earlier, once Pacific rats arrived on Hawaiian shores in Polynesian canoes, they would have reproduced rapidly. The bones of rats began to be incorporated into sedimentary deposits, such as the Makauwahi limestone sinkhole on Kauaʻi (Burney 2010;

Burney et al. 2001; Burney and Kikuchi 2006). In this remarkable site with a long record of biotic changes, the deepest rat bone is a pelvis radiocarbon dated to AD 1160–1270.

Bones of *Rattus exulans* have also been recovered from limestone sinkholes in the karstic 'Ewa Plain on O'ahu, associated with the bones of extinct or extirpated birds such as the large flightless anatids (*Thambetochen* sp.), and with the shells of extinct endemic land snails (Athens et al. 1999; Athens et al. 2002; Christensen and Kirch 1986). Direct AMS radiocarbon dating of two *R. exulans* bones from 'Ewa yielded a highest-probability calibrated age range of AD 890–1040.

Athens, Rieth, and Dye (2014) drew upon 33 radiocarbon dates from introduced plants, rat bones, and short-lived native plants, selected from a variety of archaeological and paleoenvironmental contexts on O'ahu, Maui, and Hawai'i Islands, to derive a Bayesian statistical model for the settlement of the archipelago. They conclude that "the best estimate of the colonization event" is AD 940–1129 (at 95% confidence), or between AD 1000 and 1100 at a 67 percent confidence level (151). They further note that "scarcely 50 years later in the Ordy Pond record, by AD 993–1176, population expansion on O'ahu is evident in substantially increased charcoal counts and major pollen changes at Ordy Pond" (151).

When the first edition of this book was published three and a half decades ago, the "orthodox scenario" of Eastern Polynesian settlement (Emory and Sinoto 1965; Jennings, ed., 1979) held that the Marquesas had been discovered around AD 300, with Hawai'i settled by voyagers from the Marquesas soon after, around AD 400–500. A great deal of painstaking field and laboratory research, including major improvements in the way that samples are selected and radiocarbon dated, has now significantly revised that chronology. We now know that the Marquesas, Societies, and other islands of central Eastern Polynesia were settled during a period of rapid exploration and expansion out of Western Polynesia, between AD 900 and 1100. Based on the emerging archaeological and paleoenvironmental data from Hawai'i, this northern Pacific archipelago was discovered and settled between AD 1000 and 1100.

Where Was the Homeland of the First Settlers to Hawai'i?

In their formulation of the "orthodox scenario" for Eastern Polynesian settlement, Emory and Sinoto (1965, 102) postulated an initial settlement of Hawai'i from the Marquesas Islands, followed by a secondary "migration" from the Society Islands. This was based on stylistic similarities between material culture, especially fishhooks, but also certain other artifact types, such as adzes and ornaments (fig. 4.7). As Emory and Sinoto explained,

> While studying Suggs' fishhook types [from Nukuhiva in the Marquesas], we noticed a close similarity between early Marquesan fishhooks and early Hawaiian fishhooks. Fishhooks from Hane appear to have an even closer resemblance to early Hawaiian hooks, not only in the types of fishhooks present but also in the materials, in the ratio between the height of the fishhook point to that of the shank, and in the tools used in their manufacture. The late Hawaiian fishhooks are closely related to the late Tahitian fishhooks. The above is evidence for postulating that the earliest migration to Hawaii was most likely from the Marquesas and that contact between Hawaii and the Society Islands came later. (1965, 102)

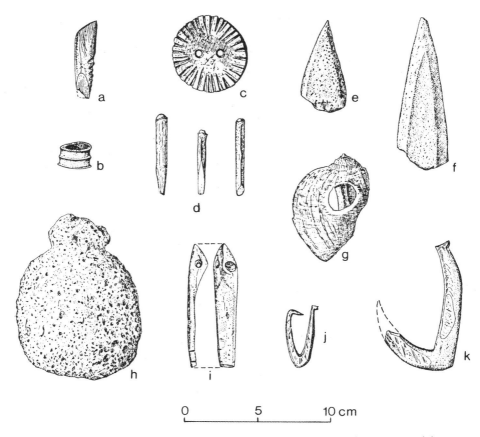

FIGURE 4.7 Early Eastern Polynesian artifacts from the Marquesas Islands: (a) shell chisel; (b) bone reel ornament; (c) pearl-shell ornament; (d) sea-urchin-spine abraders; (e) and (f) coral abraders; (g) vegetable peeler of *Tonna* shell; (h) stone sinker or net weight; (i) shank of pearl-shell trolling lure; and (j) and (k) one-piece fishhooks of pearl shell. *(After Suggs 1961)*

While this argument seemed reasonable, it was influenced by the lack of comparably early artifact assemblages from other central Eastern Polynesian islands. This has now changed; excavations at sites in the Society Islands, the Cook Islands, the Austral Islands, and Mangareva (Kirch 2017, table 7.2) have documented a range of fishhooks, adzes, ornaments, tools, and other artifacts that were widely shared among these early communities. On strictly archaeological criteria, therefore, the argument that the Marquesas Islands must be the exclusive immediate homeland of the first settlers to Hawai'i is no longer as compelling as it once was.

There are, however, a few other lines of evidence that do support a link between Hawai'i and the Marquesas. The first of these is linguistic. In the subgrouping of Eastern Polynesian languages derived from the work of a number of historical linguists (R. Clark 1979; Elbert 1953, 1982; Green 1966), and synthesized by Marck (2000), the Hawaiian and Marquesan languages group together in a "Marquesic" branch that split off from Proto–Eastern Polynesian. This Marquesic branch is distinct from the "Tahitic" branch that includes the Tahitian language of the Society Islands. That Hawaiian and Marquesan languages are closely related would lend support to the idea that the first settlement of Hawai'i was from the Marquesas (fig. 4.8). However, some linguists have questioned this classic subgrouping model; Mary Walworth, for example, argues that Hawaiian, Marquesan, and Tahitian are all part of a single, "rake-like" branch of Eastern Polynesian that developed as part of a dialect network as the Eastern Polynesian islands were rapidly discovered and settled (Walworth 2014, fig. 2). University of Hawai'i, Hilo, linguist Pila Wilson has advanced an alternative hypothesis that the languages of Eastern Polynesia share a common origin with those of

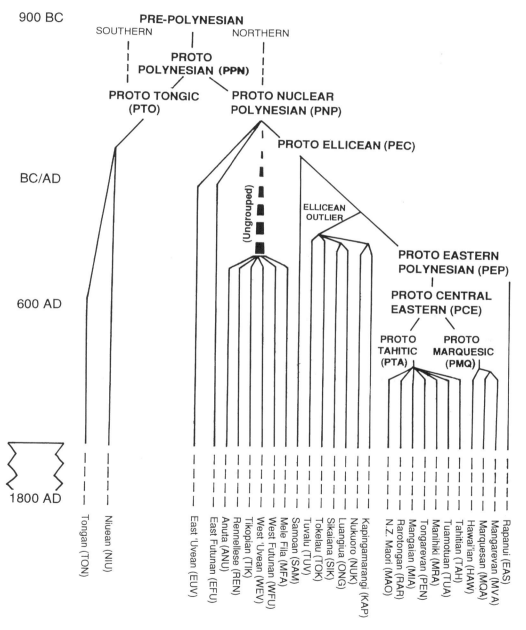

FIGURE 4.8 Chart showing the diversification of the Polynesian languages from the ancestral Proto-Polynesian language. Note that Hawaiian and Marquesan are both situated within the Marquesic branch of Eastern Polynesian languages. *(After Kirch and Green 2001)*

certain Northern Polynesian Outliers, small islands situated north of the Solomon Islands (Wilson 2012, 2021). In Wilson's model, the Hawaiian language groups more closely with Tahitian than with Marquesan. More research is needed to reconcile these competing linguistic hypotheses with the archaeological evidence, and with recent genomic studies.

Bioanthropological studies of human skeletal remains, such as multivariate statistical analysis of metric and nonmetric traits of the skull, have also been used to infer a connection between the populations of Hawai'i and the Marquesas (Pietrusewsky 1970, 1971a, 1997). Michael Pietrusewsky inferred that "the Marquesas may represent the most recent homeland of Hawai'i's indigenous inhabitants" (1997, 1). With recent advances in the genetic sequencing of aDNA extracted from skeletal remains, it would be possible to test this hypothesis more definitively; however, such analysis of human remains is not currently supported by most Native Hawaiians (e.g., Trask 1993).

Some evidence for a direct connection between Hawai'i and the Marquesas comes from the work of Lisa Matisoo-Smith et al. (1998) on the DNA of the Pacific rat. A phylogeny of these rats based on the sequencing of mtDNA reveals a distinct clade or lineage of rats uniquely shared between Hawai'i and the Marquesas, providing "evidence of a directional connection from the Marquesas to Hawaii for the introduction of *R. exulans*" (1998, 15148). Significantly, however, Hawai'i also has representatives of a separate rat lineage that is also shared with the Society Islands and the southern Cook Islands, supporting the idea of a secondary contact between Hawai'i and those island groups.

In sum, an initial voyage of discovery and settlment from the Marquesas Islands to Hawai'i remains likely, although the archaeological evidence is inconclusive (see M. S. Allen 2014 for further discussion on this point). When combined with the indications from linguistics, bioanthropology, and the genetics of the Pacific rat, however, this still remains the most plausible scenario.

5

HAWAIIAN CULTURE HISTORY
An Overview

A long-standing practice in any historical synthesis is to subdivide time into a series of phases or periods. European history breaks time down into such periods as the Dark Ages, the Renaissance, and the Enlightenment. Chinese history divides time according to successive dynasties: Shang, Zhou, Han, and so on. Archaeologists likewise categorize different time periods, sometimes by reference to essential aspects of technology or material culture, as in the classic sequence of Paleolithic, Neolithic, Bronze Age, and Iron Age. Other schema index the progressive rise and fall of great civilizations, as in the Pre-Classic, Classic, and Post-Classic periods of the Maya of Central America. So, too, the approximately eight centuries between initial Polynesian arrival in Hawai'i and the coming of Europeans at the end of the eighteenth century is usefully divided into a series of periods.

Archaeologists sometimes propose *local* sequences of culture change, based on the evidence from a particular area. The South Point fishhook sequence outlined by Emory, Bonk, and Sinoto (1959) was the first local sequence of this kind. A local sequence based on settlement patterns and subsistence trends as well as portable artifacts was proposed by Kirch (1975b) for Hālawa Valley on Moloka'i. Similarly, Tuggle and Griffin (1973) sketched out a local sequence for Lapakahi on Hawai'i, and Green (1980) a sequence for Mākaha Valley on O'ahu. Griffin et al. (1977) outlined a suggested phase sequence for the Ha'ena area on Kaua'i, while Hommon (1980a) delineated a phase sequence for Kaho'olawe Island. Newman (1969) offered a speculative sequence for the island of Hawai'i, based more on theory than on direct archaeological evidence.

Ross Cordy (1974a) synthesized settlement pattern and subsistence data from the late 1960s and early 1970s into an archipelago-wide culture-historical sequence, and later postulated a sequence for the evolution of Hawaiian society through a series of three stages or "societal types" (Cordy 1981). In Cordy's sequence, the earliest stage consisted of a "simple society" with two "rank echelons" (i.e., chiefs and commoners); he speculated that the populations of independent chiefdoms at this time ranged from 500 to 1,500 individuals. The second stage was a "complex society," marked by the addition of a third "rank echelon," and by the growth of chiefdom populations in the range of 2,000 to 8,000 persons. Finally, in the period prior to European contact, this complex society developed further with a fourth "rank echelon," and the growth of island-wide (multidistrict) polities of up to 100,000 individuals (Cordy 1981, table 7).

Robert Hommon (1976a, 1986) proposed an alternative sequence for Hawai'i based on the emergence of "primitive states" prior to European contact. Hommon integrated archaeological data with Hawaiian oral traditions to define four phases of sociopolitical development. However, Hommon based the dating of his phases on the then-available radiocarbon chronology, which indicated Polynesian settlement of Hawai'i at AD 500. Hommon (2013) later revised his three-phase sequence based on more recent radiocarbon dates. Phase I (AD 860–1029 to 1290–1409) saw the arrival of Polynesians with an agricultural economy and an ancestral form of social organization. By the end of Phase I, small communities had been established in various "salubrious cores," defined as ecologically favorable zones. "According to the salubrious cores hypothesis, within one or two centuries of the founding of the original colony, population was expanding not simply by settling new lands adjoining those already occupied but by establishing daughter settlements in nonadjacent 'sweet spots' of abundant marine resources and fertile lands far from the pioneer settlement" (2013, 226). Phase II (AD 1290–1409 to 1640–1729) was associated with agricultural expansion, both of irrigation systems in windward valleys and of shifting cultivation in leeward regions. Hommon's Phase III (AD 1640–1729 to 1790) was then marked by agricultural intensification, with the conversion of shifting cultivation regimes in leeward regions to formal, dryland field systems, such as the leeward Kohala Field System. Phase III also saw the rise of warfare, which Hommon regards as a major factor influencing the rise of political states in Hawai'i:

> In troubled times such as the seventeenth century, increased numbers of chiefs fighting in wars, revolts, and usurpations, together with the positive feedback of status rivalry and cycles of interpolity iterated retaliation, especially between Maui and Hawai'i Island, probably tended to produce more willing, seasoned warriors available for subsequent battles; wars making warriors and warriors making wars. Though in my view the delegation of political power, rather than warfare, is the underlying organizational principle of state formation, the hierarchical structure of bureaucracy may have developed in part from the stratified military command structure that served to organize army units in battle. (Hommon 2013, 255)

In the first edition of *Feathered Gods and Fishhooks,* Kirch outlined a culture-historical sequence that, while differing from Cordy's or Hommon's schema, was also based on the integration of archaeological data on material culture, settlement patterns, subsistence economy, population, and sociopolitical organization. This sequence (Kirch 1985, 298–308, fig. 239) had the following periods and associated dates:

Colonization Period, AD 300–600
Developmental Period, AD 600–1100
Expansion Period, AD 1100–1650
Proto-Historic Period, AD 1650–1795

Revisions in the dating of Polynesian settlement throughout Eastern Polynesia, and in particular of the first arrival of people in Hawai'i (see chapter 4), necessitates revision to this chronology. A younger date for initial settlement of Hawai'i, in particular, requires that the long first two periods originally envisioned for the Hawaiian sequence be compressed. Mark D. McCoy (2005, 2007) and Kirch and McCoy (2007) proposed replacing these Colonization and Developmental Periods with a single *Foundation Period,* starting with Polynesian arrival around AD 1000–1100 and ending at AD 1200. Kirch's original Expansion Period (AD 1100 to 1650) can also be divided into a Late Voyaging Period (AD 1200 to 1400) and an Expansion Period (AD 1400 to 1600). We have renamed the final Proto-Historic Period as the Archaic States Period, in keeping with recent scholarship on the emergence of an archaic state form of sociopolitical organization during the last two centuries prior to European contact (Hommon 2013; Kirch 2010, 2012). The Archaic States Period extends from AD 1600 to 1795. Although first contact with Europeans occurred in AD 1778–1779, with the third voyage of Captain James Cook, we use the date of AD 1795—marking the conquest of O'ahu Island by Kamehameha I—as the end date for the Archaic States Period. This revised Hawaiian cultural sequence is summarized in table 5.1.

The culture-historical schema outlined in table 5.1 is a heuristic device enabling one to analyze and discuss a continuous sequence of historical change in terms of conveniently labeled, discrete blocks of time. It is neither an account nor an explanation of change. Although this sequence divides precontact Hawaiian history into two-century-long

TABLE 5.1. The Hawaiian cultural sequence

TIME SPAN (AD)	PERIOD	SALIENT CHARACTERISTICS
1000–1200	Foundation	Initial discovery and settlement by Polynesians arriving from central Eastern Polynesia. Small founding population; settlements in a few ecologically favorable locations, primarily on O'ahu and Kaua'i Islands.
1200–1400	Late Voyaging	The last period with long-distance voyaging contacts with central Eastern Polynesia. Build up of population in windward valleys and other ecologically favorable areas. Adaptation of technology and subsistence economy to local conditions. Development of significant taro irrigation systems on O'ahu, Kaua'i, and Moloka'i Islands, along with parts of West Maui and Hawai'i.
1400–1600	Expansion	Population continues to grow, leading to expansion of settlements into leeward and marginal zones. Formation of large-scale dryland field systems on Maui and Hawai'i Islands. Considerable investment in monumental architecture begins.
1600–1795	Archaic States	Transition from complex chiefdoms to archaic states with divine kingship. Class stratification and land alienation from commoners. High density but stable (not expanding) population. Settlements across all ecological zones. Secondary intensification of the dryland field systems. Conquest warfare increasing.

blocks of time, the break points between the periods are not entirely arbitrary, and mark critical junctures. Thus, for example, the end of the Late Voyaging Period at AD 1400 signals the approximate time when long-distance voyaging between Hawai'i and islands to the south ceased. Likewise, the transition from the Expansion Period to the Archaic States Period, around AD 1600, is the time when influential rulers such as 'Umi on Hawai'i Island and Kiha-a-Pi'ilani on Maui came to power. Clearly, these dates are not absolute; when we write that the transition from the Expansion to the Archaic States Period occurred around AD 1600, this must be taken as an approximation, with the understanding that change was a continual process, not an event.

Integrating Archaeology with Hawaiian Oral Traditions

While the culture-historical sequence outlined in table 5.1 has been defined based on archaeological criteria and radiocarbon dating, it is possible to link this sequence to the indigenous Hawaiian political history recorded in oral traditions. Hawaiian *ali'i* were profoundly interested in their own political histories; their traditions (*mo'olelo*) and genealogies (*mo'okū'auhau*) were meticulously preserved and transmitted from one generation to the next. Specialists (*kū'auhau*) within the royal courts mastered these genealogies and histories (Malo 1951, 261). Samuel Mānaiakalani Kamakau describes the importance of the genealogists, noting that the *ali'i* "took care of people who knew genealogies—lest they be scorned, *ho'okae 'ia*, or be regarded as 'juniors,' *ho'okaikaina 'ia*; or as the 'youngest,' *ho'opoki'i 'ia*" (1991, 80). In contrast with most other Polynesian societies, however, in Hawai'i at the time of European contact, the possession of a genealogy had become an exclusively chiefly prerogative. According to Kamakau, "To commoners, genealogies were of no value because their parents forbade them to act like chiefs or to have children born in the back country who would trace their ancestry up to the chiefs (*pi'i aku i na li'i*). So the children of the *maka'āinana* were taught only the names of their fathers, mothers, and grandparents" (1991, 80).

Abraham Fornander, the great chronicler of Hawaiian traditions, aptly observed, "Hawaiian chronology counts by generations, not by reigns nor by years" (Fornander 1878–1885, 2:108). The Hawaiian chiefly genealogies provide an internally consistent historical framework extending back at least 23 generations prior to the rulers encountered by early European voyagers at the close of the eighteenth century. These genealogies codify the succession within chiefly lines, as well as the marriages between chiefly houses. Linked to this genealogical framework are specific *mo'olelo* (histories) that chronicle wars and battles, the construction of temples and the offering of human sacrifices, the initiation of administrative structures and the building of famous fishponds and great irrigation works.

Davida Malo and Kamakau were among the Native Hawaiian scholars who collected and assembled the chiefly genealogies and their linked traditions. Kamakau was especially prolific in collecting *mo'olelo*, publishing these in a series of articles in Hawaiian language newspapers, which were later translated by Mary Kawena Pukui and edited by Dorothy Barrère (Kamakau 1961, 1991). Equally important was the work of Abraham Fornander, a Swedish immigrant who arrived in Hawai'i in 1838 and a decade later married 'Ālanakapu, a Hawaiian *ali'i* from Moloka'i Island (Davis 1979). In addition to his *Account of the Polynesian*

Race (Fornander 1878–1885, vol. 2), Fornander's collection of *moʻolelo* was published posthumously in three volumes in dual Hawaiian and English text (Fornander 1916–1920).

The first modern scholar to integrate the genealogically based oral traditions with archaeology was Robert Hommon (1976a) in his doctoral dissertation on Hawaiian "primitive states." Hommon recognized that while the deeper portions of the chiefly genealogies were "cosmogonic in nature," he regarded the last 21 generations of these genealogies as historically accurate. Hommon followed John F. G. Stokes' lead of using 20 years to a generation (Stokes 1933), which would take Hawaiian political history back to approximately AD 1400, a time just after the "voyaging" or "migratory" period. Drawing upon Kamakau (1961) and Fornander (1878–1885, vol. 2), Hommon compiled chronological listings of the ruling *aliʻi* of each of the main islands (Hommon 1976a, appendices A to C; see also Hommon 2013), integrating these into a comprehensive political history. He then incorporated evidence from the archaeological record to outline a model of "state formation" in Hawaiʻi.

Cordy (2000a, 2000b), in an extensive treatment of Hawaiʻi Island and in shorter reviews of Oʻahu and its Waiʻanae District, offered a narrative history linking oral traditions to specific archaeological sites. Cordy's account of Hawaiʻi Island for the "dynastic" period after about AD 1400 is written in terms of the sequence of ruling chiefs and kings. Kehau Cachola-Abad (2000) also used the *moʻolelo* to examine the evolution of Hawaiian sociopolitical complexity.

A key issue in correlating Hawaiian traditional history with the temporal sequence of archaeology is the average length of time to assign to each generation in the chiefly genealogies. Fornander (1878–1885, 2:85) used 30 years, but for various reasons this seems too long. Stokes (1933), in a carefully reasoned assessment that included a consideration of the reproductive ages of the *aliʻi,* came to the conclusion that 20 years was most likely; Hommon (1976a) also used 20 years. We likewise favor a 20-year generational interval, finding that it fits best with the independent archaeological evidence. In table 5.2 we provide estimated AD dates for 23 generations of chiefs, each with a 20-year interval, counting back from chiefs born around AD 1750. Table 5.2 lists some of the principal *aliʻi* of Oʻahu, Maui, and Hawaiʻi Islands who will be mentioned in various chapters of this book, as they relate to specific archaeological sites, such as royal centers and *heiau*.

In the remainder of this chapter, we provide an overview of the four periods of our revised Hawaiian culture-historical sequence, integrating where possible the Hawaiian traditional history with the record provided by archaeology. (The summaries of Hawaiian political traditions in this chapter have been abstracted from the longer treatment provided by Kirch [2010]; see also Kirch [2012].)

The Foundation Period, AD 1000–1200

Current evidence points to the first arrival of Polynesians in the Hawaiian Islands during the eleventh century (see chapter 4). Only a single habitation site has been firmly dated to the Foundation Period, the Bellows Beach (O18) sand dune site at Waimānalo on Oʻahu's windward coast (see chapter 6). However, there is no reason to think that this was the *first* settlement site in the islands. By AD 1200 extensive human activities on Oʻahu Island

TABLE 5.2. Approximate chronology and sequence for some principal rulers of Oʻahu, Maui, and Hawaiʻi Islands (after Kirch 2010)

GENERATION	ESTIMATED AD DATE, 20-YEAR INTERVAL	SOME PRINCIPAL OʻAHU ISLAND RULERS	SOME PRINCIPAL MAUI ISLAND RULERS	SOME PRINCIPAL HAWAIʻI ISLAND RULERS
1	1310	Māweke		
2	1330	Muliʻelealiʻi		Pilikaʻaiʻea
3	1350	Kumuhonua		
4	1370			
5	1390			
6	1410			
7	1430			
8	1450			Kalaunuiohua
9	1470	Haka		
10	1490	Māʻilikūkahi		
11	1510		Kakaʻalaneo	
12	1530			
13	1550		Kawaokaʻōhele	Līloa
14	1570		Piʻilani	Hākau, ʻUmi a Līloa
15	1590		Kiha a Piʻilani	Keawenui a ʻUmi
16	1610	Kākuhihewa	Kamalālāwalu	Lonoikamakahiki
17	1630		Kauhi-a-Kama	
18	1650		Kalanikaumakao-wākea	
19	1670		Lonohonuakea	
20	1690	Kūaliʻi	Kaʻulahea	Keaweikekahialiʻi-okamoku
21	1710	Peleiōhōlani	Kekaulike	Alapaʻinui
22	1730	Kūmahana	Kamehamehanui, Kahekili	Kalaniʻōpuʻu
23	1750	Kahāhana, Kahekili, Kalanikūpule		Kīwalaʻō, Kamehameha

are reflected in the sedimentary records of ʻUkoʻa and Ordy ponds, and on Kauaʻi Island in the Makauwahi sinkhole deposits. Elsewhere in the archipelago, there are indications that small settlements may have been established in other ecologically favorable locales, on eastern Molokaʻi, in the Waiheʻe-Waiehu area of West Maui, and in some of the valleys or gulches of Kohala on Hawaiʻi Island. But vast tracts of Maui and Hawaiʻi, as well as the more arid regions of the all of the islands, remained largely unpopulated.

The first settlers to Hawaiʻi probably numbered no more than a few dozen; by the close of the Foundation Period the population may still have been no more than a few thousand persons. Given the dearth of identified sites for this early period, population estimates are only guesswork. The evidence preserved in the Bellows Dune site (presented in detail in chapter 6) provides a glimpse of life during the formative two centuries of Hawaiian history. The Bellows site occupies an ecologically favorable niche (what Hommon [2013] calls a "salubrious core"), in a windward valley setting next to a permanent stream, with fertile agricultural resources a short distance inland.

More is known about material culture than about other aspects of the Foundation Period. The stone adze kit included reverse-triangular, plano-convex, and quadrangular forms, in keeping with similar adze styles in other early Eastern Polynesian adze assemblages. The later rectangular-sectioned, tanged adze so characteristic of Hawai'i had not yet been developed. One-piece fishhooks were made of both pearl shell and bone, with forms similar to early Marquesan counterparts. An incipient form of the Hawaiian two-piece fishhook was developed during the Foundation Period, judging from an example from Layer III at site O18. Porpoise-tooth and imitation porpoise-tooth pendants are also represented in the Bellows site. Other portable artifacts include coral and sea-urchin-spine abraders, flake tools, and a *Conus*-shell coconut grater.

The house styles of the Foundation Period are not well attested, although the Bellows site contained evidence of pole-and-thatch dwellings, with floors paved with waterworn pebbles and with small fire hearths. Of special interest was the practice of subfloor burial, an ancient Polynesian trait that was to disappear from later Hawaiian burial practices (see chapter 11). Cooking was done in typical Polynesian earth ovens, also present in the Bellows site.

The subsistence economy of the Foundation Period is likewise only partially evidenced. Pigs, dogs, and fowl probably came on the first voyaging canoes (along with rats, which may have been either inadvertent, or perhaps purposeful, introductions). We assume that crop plants were also included in the cargo, and the O18 coconut grater hints that the coconut palm was among these, for the coconut was not present in Hawai'i prior to human arrival. While it seems probable that the first settlers introduced most—if not all—of the crops upon which later Hawaiian agriculture depended, the archaeobotanical record is still scanty. Among the Polynesian canoe plants that have relatively early direct radiocarbon dates are the *kukui* tree (*Aleurites moluccana*), the breadfruit (*Artocarpus altilis*), the *kī* plant (*Cordyline fruticosum*), and the mountain apple (*Syzgium malaccense*) (Athens, Rieth, and Dye 2014, table 2). The early colonists made extensive use of natural food resources, especially native birds, fish, and shellfish.

We can only make educated guesses regarding the social, political, and religious organization and beliefs of the early settlers, based on the evidence of comparative ethnography and linguistic reconstruction (Kirch and Green 2001). This early society was likely structured around the Ancestral Polynesian concept of hereditary chieftainship. The settlers were presumably organized into corporate descent groups or lineages known as *mata-kainanga* in the early Eastern Polynesian dialect (Hommon's "archaic *maka'āinana*"). Residential household groups were called *kainga* (the Proto-Polynesian word that later became Hawaiian *'āina*). Status differences between chiefs and commoners were probably minimal during the Foundation Period, when the small population would still have been closely interrelated by bonds of kinship.

The pan-Polynesian concepts of *mana* and *tapu* (*kapu*) were surely an integral part of the social and ritual lives of these first Hawaiians; from comparative linguistics it is also certain that they worshipped the four widespread Eastern Polynesian gods (*atua*): Tū, Tāne, Rongo, and Tangaloa. But the precise nature of their beliefs and rituals will probably never be known.

We have not mentioned the Native Hawaiian oral traditions in regard to this initial period in our sequence. There are, to be sure, accounts of early arrivals from ancestral lands to the south (lands glossed in Hawaiian as "Kahiki"), including such legendary figures as Pele and Hawai'i-loa (Fornander 1878–1885, vol. 2), but these are difficult to connect directly to the later genealogies. Nānā'ulu and his brother 'Ulu, important founders in the genealogies, may have arrived in Hawai'i during this early time (Cachola-Abad 2000, 266).

The Late Voyaging Period, AD 1200–1400

With the Late Voyaging Period, we can begin to incorporate Hawaiian traditions into the historical sequence, for this period is notable for accounts of long-distance voyaging between Hawai'i and "Kahiki." One important voyaging saga features several generations of the extended family of *ali'i* descended from Māweke, a ruling chief of O'ahu in the Nānā'ulu line at the beginning of the fourteenth century (see table 5.2). Māweke partitioned O'ahu among his three sons: Muli'eleali'i, the firstborn, ruled over the Kona District; Keaunui controlled the leeward districts of 'Ewa, Wai'anae, and Waialua; and Kalehenui received the windward Ko'olau District with its fishponds and irrigated fields. Muli'eleali'i in turn had three sons, Kumuhonua, 'Olopana, and Mo'ikeha. Upon Muli'eleali'i's death the oldest son, Kumuhonua, took control of the primary Kona estates, leaving 'Olopana and Mo'ikeha with only minor landholdings. Unhappy with their lot, the younger brothers 'Olopana and Mo'ikeha plotted against Kumuhonua, attempting a coup. When the plot failed, 'Olopana and Mo'ikeha were forced into exile.

'Olopana and Mo'ikeha left O'ahu for Waipi'o Valley on Hawai'i Island, where they developed the irrigated taro fields (fig. 5.1). 'Olopana took as his wife Lu'ukia, the daughter of the local Kohala chief Hīkapoloa (which suggests that Kohala already had a small population). When floods destroyed the taro fields, 'Olopana and Lu'ukia, along with Mo'ikeha, abandoned the valley, voyaging to their ancestral homeland in Kahiki.

FIGURE 5.1 Waipi'o Valley was the ancestral seat of the ruling chiefs of Hawai'i Island. *(Photo by P. V. Kirch)*

The three *aliʻi* settled in the land of Moa-ʻula-nui-ākea, probably the fertile Punaʻauia District along the southwestern coast of Tahiti in the Society Islands. This district remains the domain of the prominent ʻOropaʻa line of Tahitian chiefs (*ariʻi*), ʻOropaʻa being the Tahitian spelling of ʻOlopana. In the center of Punaʻauia lies the great valley of Punaruʻu, which has its equivalent on Oʻahu (Punaluʻu), as well as a sacred temple Taputapuātea, which is matched by temples of the same name (Kapukapuākea) on northern Oʻahu and on Molokaʻi (Sterling and Summers 1978, 112–113; Summers 1971, 177).

ʻOlopana remained in Moa-ʻula-nui-ākea, but Moʻikeha, after an affair with Luʻukia, returned to Hawaiʻi, guided by his chief navigator Kamahualele. Arriving at Kauaʻi, Moʻikeha married the two daughters of the reigning *aliʻi* Puna, and after Puna's death succeeded to the paramountship of Kauaʻi. Late in life, Moʻikeha asked his son Kila to sail to Kahiki to fetch Moʻikeha's son Laʻa (by another partner in Kahiki) who was left behind as an infant when Moʻikeha departed Moa-ʻula-nui-ākea. Kila made the voyage, returning with Laʻa to see his father Moʻikeha in Kauaʻi. Laʻa henceforth became known as Laʻa-mai-Kahiki (Laʻa-from-Tahiti). After spending time in Hawaiʻi, Laʻa-mai-Kahiki departed again for Kahiki, leaving from the southeastern point of Kahoʻolawe Island, known as Lae-o-Ke-ala-i-Kahiki ("Cape of the Road-to-Tahiti").

Another important voyaging tradition is that of Pāʻao, roughly contemporary with Moʻikeha, also in the fourteenth century. Pāʻao was a priest who the traditions associate with an origin place named Wawau, probably Porapora Island in the Society group, whose ancient name was Vavaʻu. In Wawau, Pāʻao quarreled with his older brother Lonopele, who accused Pāʻao's son of stealing breadfruit. Pāʻao slit his son's stomach open to prove his innocence. He then killed Lonopele's son in retribution, using the child's body as a roller for launching his voyaging canoe. Pāʻao then left Wawau for Hawaiʻi, taking with him the high chief Pilikaʻaiea, a descendant of the ʻUlu branch in the founding Hawaiian genealogies. After arriving at Hawaiʻi Island, Pāʻao built a temple called ʻAhaʻula (later Wahaʻula) in Puna, installing Pilikaʻaiea as the ruling chief of that island. Traveling to Kohala District in the north, Pāʻao also constructed Moʻokini Heiau. One of the most important lineages of Hawaiʻi Island priests trace their descent from Pāʻao down to Hewahewanui at the time of Kamehameha I (Fornander 1878–1885, 2:38).

Both Laʻamaikahiki and Pāʻao are credited with introducing significant changes to the religion and ritual practices of Hawaiʻi. The former brought his idols along with the type of cylindrical temple drum called *pahu* (Buck 1957, 396–401, fig. 298). Drumming of the *pahu* was a key part of *luakini* temple rituals; in the Society Islands *paʻu* drums (with a nearly identical shape) played a similar role in *marae* ceremonies. Pāʻao, for his part, introduced the cult of Kū along with the practice of human sacrifice.

Previous generations of scholars have questioned whether Moʻikeha, Kila, Laʻamaikahiki, Pāʻao, and others of this time period were real historical actors who made the round-trip voyages credited to them by the *moʻolelo* (e.g., Cordy 1974c). Our heightened understanding of Polynesian double-hulled canoe voyaging capabilities, in part due to the experimental voyaging of the *Hōkūleʻa* (Finney 1994), make this more plausible than was thought a few decades ago. Moreover, there is increased evidence for extensive voyaging throughout central Eastern Polynesia during this time frame (Rolett 2002; Weisler 1998). Direct archaeological evidence in support of voyaging from Hawai'i to the South Pacific consists of a stone adze from the Tuamotu Islands that was sourced to basalt from Kaho'olawe Island in Hawai'i (Collerson and Weisler 2007). Our view is that although the voyaging *mo'olelo* may have been embellished by later generations, they have a core of historical truth, indexing a period when the Hawaiian Islands were still linked to ancestral lands in the south, most likely to Tahiti and the other islands of the Society archipelago. What is also clear is that as the fourteenth century came to a close, all long-distance voyaging ceased. One of the last voyages referenced in the *mo'olelo* is of a grandson of Mo'ikeha, Kaha'i-a-Ho'okamali'i, who made a round-trip voyage to Kahiki, returning with the first breadfruit tree to be introduced to Hawai'i. At 20 years per generation, this voyage would have occurred between AD 1310 and 1390. Hawai'i subsequently became a world isolated unto itself.

Returning to the archaeological record, there are more sites dating to the Late Voyaging Period than to the earlier Foundation Period. Some important sites include the lower deposit in rockshelter site H8 at South Point and the sand dune site in Pololū Valley, both on Hawai'i Island (Field and Graves 2008; Mulrooney et al. 2014); the deeper deposits in the Hālawa dune site on Moloka'i (Kirch and McCoy 2007); and the lower deposits in the Nu'alolo rockshelter on Kaua'i Island (Field and Graves, eds., 2015). The geographic locations of these sites suggest that settlements of the Late Voyaging Period continued to be concentrated in the fertile and well-watered windward valleys, although the South Point sites indicate that Hawaiians were aware of the rich fishing grounds in this region. Moreover, early dates from rockshelters in Haleakalā Crater (Carson and Mintmier 2006), and from the Mauna Kea adze quarry (P. C. McCoy 1990), suggest that the early Hawaiians had by this time thoroughly explored their island world, among other things discovering the high-quality stone resources of these mountain regions.

Based on the increased number of settlements, the archipelago's population continued to grow throughout the Late Voyaging Period. With no restrictions on the availability of agricultural land, and with natural resources still plentiful, it is likely that population growth rates continued to be high, with rapid doubling times. In particular, the populations of the "salubrious cores" were becoming dense, as suggested by the rapid expansion of population into increasingly marginal zones beginning in the succeeding Expansion Period.

The Late Voyaging Period saw the development of distinctive forms of Hawaiian material culture. The stone adze kit was standardized with a quadrangular-sectioned, tanged form of adze blade. Fishing gear reflects successful adaptation to local marine environmental conditions and material constraints. Bone had become the dominant fishhook material, with the two-piece hook being elaborated into larger variants, such as those from the South Point sites. A new form of one-piece fishhook appears in coastal sites during this period, marked by a distinctive knobbed line-lashing device (Type HT4; see chapter 9). This hook type, which rapidly came to dominate one-piece fishhook assemblages, is similar to hooks found in sites of the same age in the Society Islands; Emory and Sinoto (1965; Y. H. Sinoto 1962, 1967) argued that the introduction of this style reflects the arrival of immigrants from Tahiti. The bone crescent point (lashed onto large wooden hooks) and the distinctive trolling-lure point with distal limb were present by this time. From specimens of the unique Hawaiian *'ulu maika* bowling stones excavated at the Hālawa dune site, it appears that the *maika* game was invented by this period. Other types of artifacts, which continued more or less unchanged, were coral and sea-urchin files, awls, scrapers, flake tools, dog-tooth ornaments, and others.

From the Hālawa dune site we have evidence of small, round-ended huts with internal, stone-outlined hearths, a house form known in the South Pacific, but not present in Hawai'i at the time of Western contact. Whether other house forms, including rectangular types, were also present is not certain.

The subsistence basis of the Hawaiian economy was firmly established during the Late Voyaging Period. Hawaiians had adapted to local marine conditions and were extensively exploiting marine resources. The faunal remains from Hālawa show an increase in the frequency of dog and pig bone, implying a corresponding expansion of the agricultural system, as pigs and dogs were both fed on agricultural produce. Also in Hālawa, the geomorphic evidence from colluvial slope deposits near the coast (site Mo-A1-4) indicates that by the close of the Late Voyaging Period shifting cultivation on the valley slopes had resulted in episodes of erosion. Other indications of shifting cultivation in windward valleys have been reported from Lumaha'i on Kaua'i and from Kahana Valley on O'ahu.

One of the most significant developments during the Late Voyaging Period was the establishment of irrigated pondfields in suitable valleys on Kaua'i, O'ahu, Moloka'i, and to a lesser extent probably also on West Maui and in Kohala District on Hawai'i. In the Ko'olaupoko District of windward O'ahu, irrigation works were present in the Luluku and Maunawili valleys by AD 1200–1250 (Jane Allen, ed., 1987; J. Allen et al. 2002). On eastern Moloka'i, the initial phase of an irrigation system at the mouth of Waikolu Valley dates to AD 1240–1280 (Kirch, ed., 2002, 46). In the much larger Wailau Valley, McElroy (2007, table 6.2) dated significant irrigation works to AD 1200–1300. In the narrow Hālawa Valley of Kohala, Hawai'i Island, M. D. McCoy, Browne Ribeiro, Graves, et al. (2013) found stratified evidence of pondfield irrigation dating to the thirteenth century.

The Expansion Period, AD 1400–1600

By the close of the Late Voyaging Period a distinctive Hawaiian cultural pattern had arisen. The ecologically favorable zones on all of the major islands were by now well populated, supported by irrigation works wherever permanent streams provided a reliable water supply. Over the next two centuries, the Hawaiian population would burgeon to several hundred thousand persons, expanding out of the "salubrious core zones" into the arid leeward regions that were increasingly marginal and risk-prone for growing traditional Polynesian canoe plants. This would necessitate new ways of growing crops, especially sweet potato and dryland taro. The ancestral forms of social and political organization also began to change, and along with this came new forms of religious belief and ritual.

During the Expansion Period a wide array of new sites and settlements were established, most of these in previously unoccupied leeward regions. On O'ahu, settlement expansion has been documented for leeward Mākaha Valley, the Kalaeloa and 'Ewa plains, and the interior of the Anahulu Valley, among others (Green 1980; Kirch, ed., 1989; Tuggle and Tomonari-Tuggle 1997). On Moloka'i, settlement expanded across the Kalaupapa Peninsula

(Kirch, ed., 2002; M. D. McCoy 2005, 2007), while in the arid tracts of Kaluakoʻi fishing camps were established and adze-quarrying activity commenced (Bonk 1954; M. D. McCoy 2007; Weisler 1989a). On Maui, the vast leeward slopes of Kahikinui and Kaupō began to see permanent occupation and dryland farming during the early decades of the Expansion Period (Kirch 2014). Small settlements sprang up even on marginal Kahoʻolawe Island, and on the leeward coast of West Hawaiʻi small villages or campsites are well attested at such locations as Lapakahi, Kalāhuipuaʻa, and ʻAnaehoʻomalu (Barrera 1971a; Field, Ladefoged, Sharp, and Kirch 2011; Kirch 1979a).

This rapid dispersal of population into leeward valleys and along leeward coasts provides the rationale for the "Expansion" label. The occupation of leeward regions did not occur all at once. Kawela on south Molokaʻi, for example, was not settled until late in the Expansion Period (Weisler and Kirch 1985). The first settlements in many leeward areas were usually situated at favorable spots, such as near the natural fishponds at Kalāhuipuaʻa and ʻAnaehoʻomalu, or around the sheltered Koaiʻe inlet at Lapakahi along the leeward Hawaiʻi Island coast.

As the expansion of settlement sites into so much previously unoccupied territory indicates, this period was marked by exponential population growth, empirically documented by radiocarbon dates and site frequency curves (Carson 2005a; Dye and Komori 1992; Kirch 2007c, 2010). The total population of the archipelago might have reached half a million by the close of the Expansion Period (see chapter 8). This increase in population was arguably a major factor underlying the technological, social, and political changes of the Expansion Period. The settlement of previously unoccupied lands provided both opportunities and challenges for agricultural production, for territorial reorganization, and for intergroup competition.

By the Expansion Period, the Hawaiian material culture inventory had been fully established and would change little until the arrival of Europeans. Hawaiian adzes became standardized as the rectangular-sectioned, tanged form so common in later sites. The large Mauna Kea adze quarry, and several other quarries on Maui, Molokaʻi, Oʻahu, and Kauaʻi, were in full operation, and the standardization of adze forms may reflect the rise of adze-maker specialists.

Whereas during preceding periods settlements tended to be small nucleated clusters of dwellings located in ecologically favorable spots, a pattern of dispersed residence now began to develop. Small household clusters sprang up throughout the interior portions of windward valleys (in areas where settlement had previously concentrated on the coasts), and along leeward coastlines. A large number of rockshelters began to be utilized for occupation (both temporary and permanent) during the Expansion Period (e.g., the southeast Oʻahu sites such as O1 through O4, rockshelters in the Anahulu Valley, and those on west Molokaʻi). Houses with rounded ends may have persisted in limited numbers early into the Expansion Period (as suggested by a site in South Hālawa Valley, Oʻahu), but the dominant style of permanent dwelling was now rectangular. Houses were frequently set upon stone-faced, earth-filled rectangular terraces; the pattern of separate dwellings and cookhouses was well established. Stone shelters in C- and L-shaped configurations became a common architectural style during the Expansion Period, correlated with the development of leeward agricultural field systems (as in the lower Mākaha Valley on Oʻahu, in the Kahikinui region of Maui, and at Lapakahi and other parts of leeward Hawaiʻi Island).

The Expansion Period is characterized by intensification of all aspects of production. Fishing and shellfish gathering continued to supply much of the daily protein intake. As with the adzes, fishing gear was increasingly standardized. Along with the proliferation of fishermen's camps (especially rockshelters in coastal areas), this suggests that fishing may also have become an increasingly specialized economic activity.

In the newly populated leeward regions, this was a time of rapid agricultural expansion and adaptation, as dryland forests and scrub were cleared, initially through shifting cultivation but increasingly through the delineation of formal field boundaries. In these expanding leeward agricultural systems sweet potato became the main staple. Of South American origin, sweet potato arrived in central Eastern Polynesia between about AD 1200–1400, almost certainly by means of a Polynesian voyage to the coast of South America and back (Green 2005; Roullier et al. 2013; Yen 1974). Just when the plant arrived in Hawaiʻi is not certain, but it may have been toward the end of the Late Voyaging Period. A carbonized sweet potato tuber from Kohala has been radiocarbon dated to AD 1290–1430 (Beta-210381; Ladefoged, Graves, and Coil 2005); this is the earliest directly dated example from Hawaiʻi. The plant's ability to grow in relatively dry conditions, and to tolerate colder temperatures, made it well suited to the leeward regions. Indeed, without the sweet potato it is doubtful that Hawaiian farmers could have expanded as successfully as they did into the drier regions.

On the leeward slopes of Kohala, on Hawaiʻi Island, the beginnings of what would become a vast formal dryland field system were established during the Expansion Period (Ladefoged and Graves 2008a). Other field systems were also being laid out in Kona and Kaʻū on Hawaiʻi Island, in the Kaupō District of Maui (Baer 2015; Kirch, Holson, and Baer 2009), and on the Kalaupapa Peninsula on Molokaʻi (M. D. McCoy 2005). At first these systems were relatively low in intensity, probably with fallow periods between sweet potato crops. But as the Expansion Period progressed, formal fields with stone embankments or rows (*kuaiwi*) were increasingly constructed.

The first true fishponds and associated techniques of aquaculture were developed during the Expansion Period, adaptations from earlier fish traps that had been used by ancestral Polynesians. Genealogies associated with a number of ponds indicate that the earliest examples were constructed around the fifteenth century, under the aegis of chiefs who could command the labor necessary to transport the tons of rock and coral used in the enclosing walls. These ponds converted coastal flats into husbandry devices capable of yielding hundreds of pounds of fish per acre annually.

Toward the end of the Expansion Period the social and political organization of Hawaiʻi began to be radically transformed. Artifactual evidence of increasing rank differences include such items as *lei niho palaoa* and various kinds of elaborate pig-tusk ornaments (anklets, pendants, bracelet segments). The expansion of settlement throughout the lowlands, and the establishment of inland field systems and the dispersed residential pattern, laid the groundwork for major territorial and political reorganization. In particular, the establishment of the *ahupuaʻa* system as a formal set of nested, hierarchical units appears to have arisen during the Expansion Period. As open lands suited for agriculture were cultivated, and the amount of available land diminished (Hommon [2013, 228–231] refers to this as the "filled land hypothesis"), the necessity of defining territorial boundaries increased; local conflicts over arable land precipitated intergroup warfare and competition between chiefly lines. Success in warfare provided opportunities for increasingly powerful chiefs to annex conquered lands and to place the control of *ahupuaʻa* in the hands of junior *aliʻi*, a pattern seen also in other Polynesian islands such as Mangaia and Mangareva (Kirch 1984). In this manner, the Ancestral Polynesian *mata-kainanga* (Hommon's "archaic *makaʻāinana*") were gradually broken up and ceased to exist as corporate descent groups holding land in common. They were replaced instead by *ahupuaʻa* territorial units under the control of subchiefs owing allegiance to a district paramount, subject to redistribution in the event of conquest and annexation by a new ruling chief. In time, the ancestral Eastern Polynesian word *mata-kainanga* became the Hawaiian *makaʻāinana*, referring to the common people at large, rather than to a lineage group. These new *makaʻāinana* mostly remained on the land they cultivated, within the same *ahupuaʻa*, but were increasingly socially distanced from the chiefs. By the end of the Expansion Period—to judge from both settlement patterns and oral traditions—this transformed system of sociopolitical organization, with class stratification and territorial rather than kin-based social groupings, was firmly established.

The oral traditions tell us that the origins of the *ahupuaʻa* system can be traced to Māʻilikūkahi, an Oʻahu ruling chief who reigned at the end of the fifteenth century (Kamakau 1991, 76–78). Māʻilikūkahi was born at Kūkaniloko (fig. 5.2), the sacred birthing place of *aliʻi kapu*, sacred chiefs, situated on the interior plateau of Oʻahu (see chapter 17); he was installed as the paramount when he was 29 years old, in a ceremony at the sacred Kapukapuākea temple. Māʻilikūkahi moved his residence to Waikīkī, which thereafter became a royal center of the Oʻahu kings. The *moʻolelo* describe how Māʻilikūkahi organized the island's lands and chiefs:

> When the kingdom passed to Māʻilikūkahi, the land divisions were in a state of confusion; the *ahupuaʻa*, the *kū* [*ʻili kūpono*], the *ʻili ʻāina*, the *moʻo ʻāina*, the *pauku ʻāina*, and the *kīhāpai* were not clearly defined. Therefore Māʻilikūkahi ordered the chiefs, *aliʻi*, the lesser chiefs, *kaukau aliʻi*, and warrior chiefs, *pūʻali aliʻi*, and the overseers, *luna* to divide all of Oʻahu into *moku* and *ahupuaʻa*, *ʻili kūpono*, *ʻili ʻāina*, and *moʻo ʻāina*. There were six districts, *moku*, and six district chiefs, *aliʻi nui ʻai moku*. Chiefs were assigned to the *ahupuaʻa*—if it was a large *ahupuaʻa*, a high chief, an *aliʻi nui*, was assigned to it. Lesser chiefs, *kaukau aliʻi*, were placed over the *kūpono* lands, and warrior chiefs over *ʻili ʻāina*. Lands were given to the *makaʻāinana* all over Oʻahu. (Kamakau 1991, 54–55)

Kamakau emphasizes the "prosperity of the kingdom" under Māʻilikūkahi, how the "land was full of people" (55): "They brought him goods, *waiwai*, and vegetable food, *ʻai*, and pigs, dogs, fowl, and fish." Kamakau stresses that these were brought as "gifts, *hoʻokupu*, not as tribute." Yet in these offerings we begin to see the roots of the tribute extraction system that would, in the succeeding Archaic States Period, come to be closely linked with the land hierarchy; the word used for such tribute, after all, continued to be *hoʻokupu*.

FIGURE 5.2 The birthing stones at Kūkaniloko on central Oʻahu were associated with the most ancient ruling chiefs of the island. *(Photo by Therese Babineau)*

The rich tradition of Māʻilikūkahi provides clues to the religious practices of the Expansion Period. Māʻilikūkahi continued to carry out ancestral Eastern Polynesian ritual traditions, evidenced not only by his investiture at the temple of Kapukapuākea (see Kirch and Sahlins 1992, 1:21) but also by the fact that "he did not sacrifice men in the *heiau* and *luakini*" (Kamakau 1991, 56). This, Kamakau tells us, was the way of the sacred chiefs born at Kūkaniloko, descendants of the Nānāʻulu line.

But the religious system was beginning to undergo important changes, especially toward the end of the Expansion Period, in consort with the social and political changes. The Makahiki ritual cycle, for example, which was so closely tied to the *ahupuaʻa* pattern of territorial organization, became elaborated over the course of the Expansion Period out of earlier and simpler rituals of first fruits and agricultural fertility that trace back to ancestral Polynesia. By the close of the Expansion Period, the Makahiki had become a ritualized system of tribute exaction. Similarly, the rise of intergroup warfare and conflict went hand in hand with the elaboration of the Kū cult, originally introduced to Hawai'i Island by Pā'ao in the Late Voyaging Period.

The closing decades of the Expansion Period were a pivotal era in the evolution of Hawaiian society, marking the transition from what anthropologists call a "chiefdom" stage of sociopolitical development to one of "archaic states." This transition involved structural changes of great consequence, including the emergence of two distinct, endogamous classes: *nā li'i,* the chiefs, and *nā kānaka,* the people. The chiefs held the land while the commoners worked the land and provided tribute to the chiefs. The chiefly class itself became internally ranked with multiple named grades, the highest of whom promoted the ideology that they were divine, *ali'i akua* ("god kings").

At this critical juncture in Hawaiian history the *mo'olelo* offer detailed accounts of several powerful chiefs and their struggles for power, especially on Hawai'i and Maui Islands. On Hawai'i, the key persons are Hākau and his half-brother 'Umi-a-Līloa, who defeated Hākau in a war of succession and seized control of the entire island for the first time. The details of 'Umi's life and rise to power are recounted elsewhere (Fornander 1917, 178–235; Kamakau 1961, 1–21; Kirch 2010, 92–98). 'Umi's father Līloa, who traced his genealogy back to the 'Ulu line of chiefs through Pilika'aiea, resided in Waipi'o Valley, with the largest expanse of irrigated taro lands on Hawai'i Island. 'Umi was conceived when Līloa became enamored of a beautiful young commoner woman, Akahiakuleana, with whom he had an affair. After being raised in the country by Akahiakuleana, 'Umi at puberty went to live with his father, the *ali'i nui,* in Waipi'o. Līloa, however, already had a royal heir, Hākau, offspring of his *pi'o* (incestuous) marriage to Pinea, Līloa's own sister. Some years passed and when Līloa was on his deathbed he proclaimed that the kingdom would be left to Hākau, but that 'Umi be given possession of the feathered war god, Kū-ka'ili-moku (Kamakau 1961, 9). Līloa's bones were enshrined in a wicker casket of anthropomorphic shape (*ka'ai*), and placed in a mausoleum in Waipi'o.

The truce between Hākau and 'Umi did not last long, forcing 'Umi to flee to Hāmākua, taking with him the feathered image of Kū-ka'ili-moku. 'Umi took up residence in the *ahupua'a* of Waipunalei, where assisted by the priest Kaleioku they planted extensive gardens and trained an army of commoners. 'Umi's army arrived at the rim of Waipi'o on the night of Kāne, 27th in the Hawaiian lunar sequence. The following day, the people of Waipi'o went up into the mountains to fetch *'ōhi'a* logs for the annual rededication of the war temple, leaving Hākau unprotected. 'Umi and his warriors descended into Waipi'o; defenseless, Hākau was stoned to death. The body of the deposed king was offered up on the temple altar.

Following his installation as the king of Hawai'i, 'Umi asserted his power by making a division of the lands. Keleioku was made the chief priest and *ali'i-'ai-moku* over Hāmākua District; the other districts were put under the control of his principal adopted sons and loyal supporters. 'Umi's unification of Hawai'i Island was memorialized in a monumental construction, a temple known as the Ahu-a-'Umi, situated at an elevation of 1,585 m near the center of the island, on a high plateau of lava and volcanic cinder (see chapter 14). At the point where all of Hawai'i's six districts come together, its stones are reputed to have been carried from all parts of the island, symbolizing 'Umi's feat of unification.

At approximately the same time, on Maui Island, the *ali'i nui* Pi'ilani, a contemporary of Līloa, integrated the west and east sides of that island for the first time. Pi'ilani also controlled nearby Lāna'i and Kaho'olawe Islands and at least part of Moloka'i. Following his unification of Hawa'i Island, 'Umi married Pi'ilani's daughter Pi'ikea, forming an alliance between the two kingdoms. With Pi'ilani, the lineage of western Maui chiefs for the first time asserted its power over eastern Maui, in particular the independent chiefs of fertile Hāna District. Fornander writes that "the Hana chiefs acknowledged the suzerainty of the Moi [king] of Maui, and Piilani made frequent tours all over his dominions, enforcing order and promoting the industry of the people" (1878–1885, 2:87). He probably constructed the first phase of the massive residential and temple complex in Hāna, Pi'ilanihale ("House of Pi'ilani," see chapter 15).

A struggle for hegemonic control over the unified Maui kingdom followed Pi'ilani's death, in this case a rivalry between the junior and senior sons of the late king (see Beckwith 1970, 387–89; Fornander 1878–1885, 2:85, 2:98, 2:205–206; Fornander 1916–1920, 236–255; Kamakau 1961, 22–33). The two brothers were of equally high rank, differentiated only by birth order, with Lono-a-Pi'ilani the first in line to inherit the title of *ali'i nui* from Pi'ilani. Abused by Lono-a-Pi'ilani and fearing for his life, Kiha fled first to Moloka'i, then into the uplands of Kula, on the leeward slopes of Haleakalā. That Kiha-a-Pi'ilani chose to flee to an area of intensive dryland cultivation, where sweet potatoes were raised in the rain-fed gardens, parallels the saga of 'Umi. Much like the latter, Kiha became proficient at sweet potato cultivation, gaining respect and fame among the *maka'āinana* farmers for his ability to clear and plant large fields. After an unsuccessful attempt to gain the support of the Hāna chief Ho'olaemakua, Kiha-a-Pi'ilani sailed to Hawai'i to enlist the aid of his brother-in-law 'Umi-a-Līloa (married to Kiha's sister Pi'ikea).

After a year of building double-hulled canoes and making war implements, the forces of 'Umi and Kiha-a-Pi'ilani attacked Ho'olaemakua and his warriors in their fortress hill of Ka'uiki, overlooking Hāna Bay (fig. 5.3). Upon discovering a way into the fortress, 'Umi's warriors slaughtered the Maui defenders. Ho'olaemakua escaped but was hunted down at Kapipiwai, tortured, and killed; his hands were brought to Kiha-a-Pi'ilani to confirm his death (Kamakau 1961, 31). Lono-a-Pi'ilani is said to have died of fright at his royal residence in Wailuku (31).

FIGURE 5.3 The cinder cone of Ka'uiki at Hāna, Maui Island, provided a natural defensive position used in several prominent battles between the forces of Maui and Hawai'i Islands. *(Photo by P. V. Kirch)*

The rise to power of ʻUmi on Hawaiʻi and of Kiha-a-Piʻilani on Maui signal a critical juncture in Hawaiian political history. Their personal histories were intertwined through bonds of kinship and mutual assistance. Both were usurping chiefs, who overthrew the legitimate hereditary lords to whom their kingdoms had been entrusted. Both usurpations were considered justifiable, because Hākau and Lono-a-Piʻilani were "evil," oppressive lords who did not display the proper attributes befitting a high chief. But there are other similarities between these two histories of usurpation and political consolidation. One is the association between ʻUmi and Kiha with the farming population and, in particular, with the dryland cultivation of sweet potatoes. This is especially clear in the details that correlate ʻUmi's rise to power with sweet potato cultivation and the god Lono, but the links are also found in Kiha's stay in the Kula District of Maui (a major dryland cultivation zone) and in his demonstration of great skill in sweet potato cultivation. Both *aliʻi* sought political strength not in the more ancient and well-established systems of wetland taro cultivation but in the extensive dryland sectors where growing populations had the potential to radically transform the landscapes into vast productive zones. Both rulers took advantage of these new opportunities. After unification of their respective islands, both kings moved their royal residences away from the old centers of irrigation (Waipiʻo on Hawaiʻi, and Wailuku on Maui) into the core of the dryland sweet potato field systems (Kona on Hawaiʻi, and Hāna and Kaupō on Maui). ʻUmi and Kiha-a-Piʻilani were profound agents of change, but both also took advantage of emerging systems of production that allowed for new opportunities of exploitation and political control.

The Archaic States Period, AD 1600–1795

The close of the sixteenth century and early decades of the seventeenth century mark a major transition in Hawaiian political history. The *aliʻi nui* consolidated power in a form previously unknown, taking charge of dominions that encompassed the largest two islands, and in the case of Maui brought nearby islands under its sway. Lands were redistributed to loyal warrior chiefs. The *ahupuaʻa* system of land territories came into full force, along with a tribute system marked by elaboration of the Makahiki into ritualized tribute collection; *kōʻele* fields were set aside for the production of food to support the chiefly households. The temple system and the priesthood became similarly elaborated, with separate rites of Kū and Lono and distinct priesthoods devoted to each god. The archaeological record marks the ensuing Archaic States Period as a time of peak population, agricultural intensification, and construction of monumental architecture. Significantly, these developments were primarily centered on the large easterly islands of Maui and Hawaiʻi.

By the end of the Expansion Period, Hawaiian culture had been substantially transformed from its Ancestral Polynesian predecessor; the basic technological, social, and political patterns witnessed at European contact had come into existence. This final period prior to the arrival of Europeans was one of elaboration of the existing social order and of further intensification of the means of production. We have chosen the date AD 1795 as the end of this period (rather than the usual date of 1778, the arrival of Captain James Cook) because: (1) 1795 marks Kamehameha's conquest of Oʻahu Island and the end of the old political order with its competing independent chiefdoms; and (2) after this date European ships began to call with regular frequency in the islands, introducing foreign goods and ideas, increasingly making inroads to the traditional culture (see chapter 13).

By the beginning of the Archaic States Period there were few if any significant lowland tracts not already subject to some level of occupation and exploitation. On the marginal plateau land of Kahoʻolawe, a phase of abandonment set in with a retraction of settlement to the island's coastal strip. In many other areas, however, settlements continued to grow, as at Kawela on Molokaʻi, or in the southernmost part of the leeward Kohala Field System (Field, Ladefoged, and Kirch 2011). The settlement pattern remained that of dispersed households (*kauhale*) both along the coastlines and inland, set among the agricultural fields. In certain locales, denser aggregations developed where ruling chiefs established royal centers. In such places the ruling households were surrounded with those of other high *aliʻi*, of retainers, and of craft specialists. On Hawaiʻi, such royal centers were located at Hōnaunau, Kealakekua, and Kailua; on Maui, they could be found at Wailuku, Hāna, and Kaupō. Waikīkī on Oʻahu remained the principal royal center for that island, as did Wailua for the ruling elite of Kauaʻi.

Demographic trends during the Archaic States Period remain uncertain. Radiocarbon dates and site frequency counts—to the extent that these can be taken as proxies for population trends—suggest that the *rate* of population growth was declining. In some areas populations may have been oscillating around a plateau that approximated the carrying capacity of the intensified agricultural systems. These, however, are issues requiring more research (see chapter 8).

The material culture of the common people changed little, if at all, during the Archaic States Period. In the chiefly sphere, however, there were further elaborations and refinements of the featherwork, ornaments, *kapa* (barkcloth), wooden bowls, and other elite status goods that the chiefly class coveted as visual symbols of their elevated status. The production of valued goods, and of a range of utilitarian items, was standardized and controlled by craft specialists, themselves under the auspices of the chiefs. Although there is little direct evidence in the archaeological record, the desire for the feathered cloaks, capes, and helmets that the *aliʻi* used to differentiate among their own graded ranks may have led to increased pressure on the populations of forest birds that provided the brilliant red- and gold-colored plumage. Control over these feathers and over the production and distribution of the prized feathered garments resulted in a "wealth economy" being grafted onto the older "staple economy" of agricultural production. Yet another aspect of the wealth economy was the husbandry of pigs (Dye 2014a), not only an elite food item but essential as offerings at major temple rituals. Pigs by the hundreds were required for the most important *luakini* rites (Malo 1951).

Throughout the Archaic States Period, agriculture and aquaculture continued to be intensified. The largest valley-bottom irrigation systems were expanded in these final centuries prior to European intrusion. In leeward Hawaiʻi, the dryland field systems in Kohala, Kona, and Kaʻū continued to be subdivided into ever smaller field parcels, marked by the insertion of new field embankments and trails demarcating territorial boundaries. Fishponds were constructed along the sheltered bays of Oʻahu, along the south Molokaʻi coast, and elsewhere. The fishponds, especially, were under the direct control of the chiefly class.

Traditional History of the Archaic States Period

The political developments of the Archaic States Period are among its best-known aspects, from the wealth of oral traditions recorded by Kamakau, 'Ī'ī, Malo, and Fornander. Here we briefly summarize some of the main actors and events of this period, as recounted in the *moʻolelo*. More detailed discussions of these traditions and their relationship to archaeological sites are presented by Kirch (2010, 2012).

Hawaiʻi Island in the Archaic States Period

ʻUmi-a-Līloa, who unified Hawaiʻi Island at the end of the Expansion Period, had two male heirs of the highest rank, Keliʻiokaloa-a-ʻUmi (senior) and Keawenui-a-ʻUmi (junior) (Fornander 1878–1885, 2:103; Kamakau 1961, 34). When Keliʻiokaloa was killed in a battle between them, Keawenui-a-ʻUmi became the ruler of a once again unified island. Upon his death, Keawenui-a-ʻUmi's bones were interred in the sepulchral temple at Hōnaunau that bears his name (fig. 5.4). A complex succession occurred, with Kaikilani-Aliʻi-Wahine-o-Puna acting as a kind of regent and simultaneous co-wife (*punalua*) of two of Keawenui's sons, Kanaloakuaʻana and Lonoikamakahiki. Lonoikamakahiki eventually was elevated to the kingship (Beckwith 1970, 292–295; Fornander 1916–1920, 256–363; Kamakau 1961, 47–63).

Following Lonoikamakahiki the island again fragmented politically, with the leeward and windward regions coming under the control of the Mahi and 'Ī lineages of Kohala and Hilo, respectively. A complex series of successions followed, with several female rulers whose power was limited to the leeward regions, during the latter part of the seventeenth century. Around AD 1690, Keawe-ʻikekahi-aliʻi-o-ka-moku was installed as king (Fornander 1878–1885, 2:85, 2:129; Kamakau 1961, 64–65). Keawe established some degree of unity over the island, in part through marriage to Lonomaʻaikanaka, a chiefess of the powerful 'Ī line.

Following the death of Keawe, Alapaʻinui reasserted a strong kingship. At the time of Keawe's death on Hawaiʻi, Alapaʻinui was residing on Maui, in the court of King Kekaulike, who had married Alapaʻinui's half-sister Kekuʻiapoiwanui. Alapaʻinui immediately sailed for Kohala, assembling a force of warriors loyal to the Mahi line. Alapaʻinui's army defeated an opposing force under one of Keawe's sons, Kalanikeʻeaumoku, who had asserted his claim to the Kona and Kohala lands (Fornander 1878–1885, 2:132–133). Alapaʻinui gained control of the leeward districts, but Hawaiʻi was then threatened by the decision of Maui king Kekaulike to invade Hawaiʻi Island. Kekaulike's army was repulsed by Alapaʻinui's forces in a naval battle off Kona. Alapaʻinui counterattacked the Maui forces at Kaupō, Maui, but on landing heard that Kekaulike had died. Alapaʻinui proclaimed Kamehamehanui as the new king of Maui, bringing an end to the interisland hostilities (Fornander 1878–1885, 2:136; Kamakau 1961, 70).

Returning to Hawaiʻi Island, Alapaʻinui took into his court two grandsons of Keaweʻikekahialiʻiokamoku, named Kalaniʻōpuʻu and Kalanikepua Keōua, who were in the patrilineal line of descent of Hawaiʻi kings. According to Kamakau, around AD 1752 Keōua took ill and died; it was rumored that Alapaʻinui was responsible for

FIGURE 5.4 The Hale o Keawe sepulchral temple at Hōnaunau, Hawai'i Island, housed the bones of the island's ruling chiefs. The temple and its images were reconstructed by the National Park Service, based on early nineteenth-century drawings and descriptions. *(Photo by Therese Babineau)*

the death. The death of his half-brother prompted Kalani'ōpu'u to take action against Alapa'inui. Kalani'ōpu'u gained control of Ka'ū and Puna Districts, while Alapa'inui ruled the remainder of the island. Becoming ill, Alapa'inui named his son Keawe'ōpala as his successor.

The reign of Keawe'ōpala, beginning about AD 1754, was short. He deprived a number of the chiefs of their lands in the division of *ahupua'a,* causing the disaffected war leaders to rebel. Kalani'ōpu'u joined forces with Ke'eaumoku, a brother of Alapa'inui (Fornander 1878–1885, 2:85, 2:145) and together they defeated Keawe'ōpala, leaving Kalani'ōpu'u in control of all of Hawai'i Island. Around 1759 Kalani'ōpu'u led an invasion across the 'Aleinuihāhā channel to Hāna, Maui (Fornander 1878–1885, 2:146–147; Kamakau 1961, 79–81). Kalani'ōpu'u took Hāna and Kīpahulu Districts, establishing a fortress on the hill of Ka'uiki overlooking Hāna Bay. When Captain James Cook arrived off the windward coast of Maui in late November of 1778 he was greeted by Kalani'ōpu'u, who was engaged in warfare with Maui king Kahekili, who was attempting to reconquer eastern Maui.

FIGURE 5.5 The massive temple platform of Piʻilanihale at Hāna, Maui Island, also served as the seat of the island's rulers from the time of Kiha-a-Piʻilani. *(Photo by Therese Babineau)*

Maui Island in the Archaic States Period

The succession of Kiha-a-Piʻilani to the Maui paramountship has already been described (Kamakau 1961, 22–33; see also Beckwith 1970, 387–389; Fornander 1878–1885, 2:98, 2:205–206; Fornander 1916–1920, 236–255). Kiha-a-Piʻilani established his seat at the great temple complex of Piʻilanihale in Hāna District (fig. 5.5).

Kiha-a-Piʻilani was succeeded by his son Kamalālāwalu, whose long reign ended in a disastrous war against Hawaiʻi (Fornander 1878–1885, 2:207). Despite warnings from the sorcerer-priest Lanikāula, Kamalālāwalu sailed with his warrior fleet to Puakō on the lee side of Hawaiʻi. Having underestimated the strength of the Hawaiʻi forces, the Maui army was severely routed, Kamalālāwalu killed, and his son Kauhi-a-Kama barely escaped (Fornander 1916–1920, 338–350).

Kauhi-a-Kama's reign ended in an attempted military campaign against Oʻahu, when he was slain at Waikīkī (Fornander 1878–1885, 2:208), an event that might be associated with a mass burial pit uncovered at Fort DeRussy (Carlson, Collins, and Cleghorn 1994; see chapter 11). Kauhi-a-Kama was succeeded by his son Kalanikaumakaowakea; the succession then passed to Lonohonuakini, and then to Kaʻulahea (Fornander 1878–1885, 2:209). Kaʻulahea had two wives, a high-ranking chiefess from Hawaiʻi Island named Kalanikauleleiaiwi, and Papaikaniau. The former bore him a sacred daughter, Kekuʻiapoiwanui, whereas Papaikaniau bore him a son, Kekaulike, who would succeed to the Maui kingship.

Kekaulike engaged in a classic *pi'o* mating with his own half-sister Keku'iapoiwanui (Davenport 1994, 55–56), producing a son, Kamehamehanui, and a sacred daughter, Kalola (who would become one of the wives of Kalani'ōpu'u of Hawai'i). Kekaulike established his royal seat at Mokulau, in Kaupō, where he rededicated the war temple of Lo'alo'a, as well as a vast complex named Pōpō'iwi (Kamakau 1961, 66; E. P. Sterling 1998, 172–174). Toward the end of his reign, Kekaulike determined to attack Hawai'i Island, which was ruled by his sacred wife Keku'iapoiwanui's half-brother Alapa'inui. The raid on Hawai'i was indecisive (Fornander 1878–1885, 2:133); Alapa'inui retaliated with an attack on Maui. Kekaulike died just prior to the Hawai'i army's landing at Mokulau, declaring that his son Kamehamehanui (offspring of his *pi'o* union with his half-sister Keku'iapoiwanui, and hence also the nephew of Alapa'inui) should succeed him. Fornander puts the time of Kekaulike's death between the years 1736 and 1740.

Kamehamehanui ruled Maui until an abrupt invasion by Kalani'ōpu'u, which Fornander (1878–1885, 2:214) attributes to the year 1759, when Kalani'ōpu'u successfully annexed Hāna and Kaupō. Having lost these key lands, the Maui court moved from East Maui to Wailuku (ancestral home of the Pi'ilani line), where Kamehamehanui died about 1765. At the death of Kamehamehanui the kingship passed to Kamehamehanui's younger brother, Kahekili, third-born child to Kekaulike's *pi'o* wife Keku'iapoiwanui.

Kahekili was nearly 50 years old when he became Maui's ruler; Fornander says he was "laborious and persistent, cold, calculating, and cruel" (1878–1885, 2:215). Kahekili would prove a formidable enemy to Kalani'ōpu'u and his successor, Kamehameha I, rulers of Hawai'i in the early postcontact era.

The Western Islands in the Archaic States Period

Unlike the rich traditions concerning the political histories of Hawai'i and Maui Islands in the late precontact period, what we know of the western islands from Moloka'i to Kaua'i is much more limited. It is unclear whether Moloka'i was unified under a single ruling chief during the transition from the Expansion Period to the Archaic States Period. There are some allusions to the involvement of Maui chiefs in local political life. Sometime between AD 1600 and 1620, the Maui chief Pi'ilani ruled over an extensive territory that may have included the southern portion of Moloka'i visible from Lāhaina on Maui (Pukui and Elbert 1957, 74, "*na hono a Pi'ilani*"; Summers 1971, 13).

The line of Moloka'i rulers during the second half of the Archaic States Period, the Kaiakea dynasty (AD 1700–1795), begins with Kalanipehu and ends with the dynasty's namesake in the years after European contact. An island-wide civil war broke out when Ko'olau made a bid for control of the Kona fishing grounds. The Kona chiefs entreated O'ahu chief Kuali'i to invade and help defeat the Ko'olau warriors. After subjugating Ko'olau, Kuali'i considered Moloka'i under his dominion. He made a new division of lands, then returned to O'ahu, from whence he reigned.

Kumuko'a—the heir to the powerful and much-feared Kalaipahoa wooden idols—became *ali'i nui* of Moloka'i around AD 1740–1760, refusing to accept the authority of O'ahu. The son and successor to Kuali'i tried to retake the island by force but was killed at Kawela. In this battle, the Hawai'i Island chief Alapa'inui came to the aid of Kumuko'a but did not annex Molokaʻi after the skirmish (Fornander 1916–1920). Alapaʻinui may, however, have dedicated Mana Heiau in Hālawa Valley at that time (see chapter 16).

Around AD 1760–1780, Peleiʻōhōlani took control of Oʻahu, threatening the Molokaʻi chiefs to submit to his power and "acknowledge him as their sovereign" (Fornander 1878–1885, 2:289). Following the threat, for reasons not fully explained in the traditions, the Oʻahu chief's daughter, who had married a Molokaʻi *aliʻi,* was killed at the hands of the Koʻolau chiefs. Her father traveled to Molokaʻi and exacted harsh retribution; commoners were "brutalized," and chiefs were driven off or killed and "roasted" (Kamakau 1961, 232). Once the island was annexed, the Oʻahu king left a local *aliʻi* named Kaiakea in charge.

Kaiakea's reign (AD 1780–1795) was unusual in several respects. First, he was revered as a skilled religious practitioner and his person was considered a sacred refuge (*puʻuhonua*). Second, he had kinship ties to all four major kingdoms as well as an implied connection to Molokaʻi's earlier Kamauaua line. Lastly, not only had he come to power by annexation, he remained the island's leader even as it was annexed four more times.

Turning to Oʻahu Island, following the reign of the famous Māʻilikūkahi during the Expansion Period there were four successive rulers of Oʻahu until the sacred female *aliʻi* Kalani-maunia, who ruled at the beginning of the Archaic States Period (Cordy 1996; Kamakau 1991, 57–61). Of high rank like her ancestor Māʻilikūkahi, Kalani-maunia encouraged agriculture and the building of fishponds. Upon her death, Kalani-maunia divided the Oʻahu lands between her three sons and one daughter. The firstborn, Kūamanuia, attacked his younger brother Kaʻihikapuamanuia, who with the aid of his brother Haʻo slew Kūamanuia; the rule then passed to Kaʻihikapuamanuia. Kaʻihikapuamanuia and Haʻo then fought with each other, and Oʻahu was not unified again until the death of Haʻo (Kamakau 1991, 61–67).

After Kaʻihikapuamanuia the rule of Oʻahu passed to his son Kākuhihewa, one of the island's most renowned kings (Kamakau 1991, 68–72). Born at Kūkaniloko, he was an *aliʻi akua* or divine king. Kākuhihewa made peace with the son of Haʻo, Nāpūlānahumahiki, bringing all of Oʻahu under unified rule. Kākuhihewa built a large "palace" at Kailua, named Pāmoa (Fornander 1878–1885, 2:274; Kamakau 1991, 69).

Following the reign of Kākuhihewa came a succession of three undistinguished *aliʻi nui,* and the district chiefs began acting independently (Fornander 1878–1885, 2:275–278). All this changed with the rise to power of Kualiʻi, around the close of the seventeenth century. The *moʻolelo* of Kualiʻi has an almost mythic tone about it (Fornander 1916–1920, 364–434; see also Beckwith 1970, 395–400; Fornander 1878–1885, 2:278–288, 2:371–399, appendix V). Fornander offers a reason for the unusual nature of the Kualiʻi tradition:

> The political destruction of the house of *Kualii* by *Kahekili* of Maui, the spoliation of the territorial resources of its scions by the successful conquerors, and perhaps in no inconsiderable degree the idea set afloat by both the Maui and Hawaii victors that the *Kualiis* were a doomed race, all these co-operative causes first rendered the recital of such legends treasonable, next unfashionable, and lastly forgotten. (1878–1885, 2:279)

The Kualiʻi tradition valorizes a king who, although he lived a mere half century prior to European contact, was bestowed with almost superhuman qualities by those who dared to remember him after the devastation of Oʻahu in the late eighteenth century, first by the Maui war king Kahekili and soon after by his Hawaiʻi Island rival Kamehameha I, who conquered Oʻahu in 1795.

To the extent that the deeds attributed to Kualiʻi can be considered historically valid, they include his subjugation of the independent Oʻahu chiefs who had been controlling the ʻEwa and Kona Districts; one or two military raids against the Hilo District of Hawaiʻi Island; a war on Molokaʻi in which Kualiʻi aided the Kona chiefs in their dispute against the windward Koʻolau chiefs; and gaining control over the windward districts of Kauaʻi Island. Fornander (1878–1885, 2:295) speculates that Kualiʻi claimed the Kauaʻi succession through his grandmother Kawelolauhuki. Details of Kualiʻi's genealogy were suppressed after Kahekili's conquest of Oʻahu, but we do know that Kualiʻi fathered a son Peleiʻōhōlani by a chiefess from Kauaʻi, evidently setting Peleiʻōhōlani up to administer his Kauaʻi dominions.

After the death of Kualiʻi, the Oʻahu kingship passed to his son Kapiʻiohookalani, like his brother Peleiʻōhōlani an *aliʻi kapu* of the highest rank. Kapiʻiohookalani led an unsuccessful military campaign against Molokaʻi in which Alapaʻinui of Hawaiʻi came to the aid of the Molokaʻi chiefs, and Kapiʻiohookalani was slain. His infant son Kanahaokalani being too young to assume the rule, Peleiʻōhōlani was brought from Kauaʻi to assume the Oʻahu kingship (Fornander 1878–1885, 2:289). Peleiʻōhōlani expended considerable effort in subjugating the rebellious Molokaʻi chiefs. After some Molokaʻi chiefs killed a daughter of Peleiʻōhōlani's named Keelanilonuaiakama, Peleiʻōhōlani descended upon Molokaʻi with a vengeance, and "the revolted Molokai chiefs, mostly from the Koolau and Manae sides of the island, were either killed and burned or driven out of the island to seek refuge at the courts of Maui and Hawaii" (2:289–290).

Fornander (1878–1885, 2:290) reports that Peleiʻōhōlani died about 1770. It is evident from the accounts of Cook's third voyage, however, that Peleiʻōhōlani still ruled over Oʻahu and Kauaʻi in 1778–1779. In his account of political leaders in the archipelago, written in March 1779, Lieutenant King states, "The two most powerful Chiefs of these Islands are Terreeoboo [Kalaniʻōpuʻu] of Owhyhee [Hawaiʻi], & Perree orannee [Peleiʻōhōlani] of Wo'ahoo [Oʻahu]," and further makes mention of "Atou I [Kauaʻi] with its adjoining Isles being governd by the Grandsons" of Peleiʻōhōlani (Beaglehole, ed., 1967, 614). At the time of the Cook expedition, Peleiʻōhōlani and Kahekili were locked in combat on Molokaʻi, the old Oʻahu king trying to forestall Kahekili's efforts to expand the Maui kingdom by annexing the westerly islands.

The dynastic history of Kauaʻi Island in the Archaic States Period is very incompletely known. In Fornander's words, "The legends are disconnected and the genealogies are few" (1878–1885, 2:291). This is no doubt due to the ascendancy of Kualiʻi and his son Peleiʻōhōlani, to whose genealogists the Oʻahu lineages were far more important; and, following the removal of Kaumualiʻi (last independent king of Kauaʻi) to Oʻahu in 1821, the Hawaiʻi Island ruling lines dominated the political scene. Fornander offers a brief account of the succession of kingship on Kauaʻi, confused as this is (2:291–298). Until the time of Kualiʻi the island retained its status as an independent polity. To be sure, Fornander mentions a number of Kauaʻi *aliʻi* who became allied with various Oʻahu chiefs. In addition, the high-ranking Kauaʻi chiefesses were sought out as spouses by the ruling lines of other islands. For the most part, however, Kauaʻi functioned as a separate entity, the 116 km wide, frequently stormy Kaʻieʻie Waho channel separating Kauaʻi from Oʻahu and serving as a geographic barrier that discouraged frequent interisland communication.

Such then, was the island civilization that greeted the crews of the *Resolution* and *Discovery* in 1778 and 1779 (fig. 5.6); it was a civilization that had evolved over some eight centuries of cultural development, the last four entirely isolated from external contact. But the story does not end with European intrusion, for Hawaiian culture continued to evolve and change through the course of the ensuing decades of increasing engagement with the "World System." This postcontact history, of the rise and fall of the Hawaiian Kingdom, and the subsequent development of a modern multiethnic society, is one to which archaeology also contributes, as we discuss in chapter 13.

Explaining Change: Process and Agency in Hawaiian History

Over the years a number of anthropologists and archaeologists have addressed the question of how Hawaiʻi came to be the most socially and politically complex of all Polynesian groups. The work of five scholars has been especially influential: Irving Goldman, Marshall Sahlins, Timothy Earle, Robert Hommon, and Patrick Kirch. Anthropologists Goldman and Sahlins based their analyses largely on the documentary and ethnographic records. Earle, Hommon, and Kirch have put forward models of the changes in Hawaiian society based on the evidence from their archaeological fieldwork.

Irving Goldman (1970) classified Polynesian societies based on the degree of hierarchy and stratification, with three groups: traditional, open, and stratified (see Kirch 1984,

FIGURE 5.6 The war canoes of Kalaniʻōpuʻu, king of Hawaiʻi Island, greeted Captain James Cook at Kealakekua Bay, Hawaiʻi Island. *(From Cook and King 1784)*

table 2). Only Tonga, the Society Islands (Tahiti), and Hawai'i were included in the "stratified" category. Goldman regarded Hawai'i as being at the apex of this spectrum of political development, especially due to its emphasis on divine kingship: "The power of the chief had become equivalent to the power of a god" (1970, 218). With this power came the new *ahupua'a* system of landholding, accompanied by a transformation of the Polynesian "descent group organization" that now "diverged so strongly from the traditional Polynesian type that at first glance Hawaii seems altogether unrelated in this aspect to Polynesia generally" (233). Social and political change in Polynesia was driven by what Goldman called "status rivalry," and this in turn drove economic change. As the economy came under chiefly control, earlier institutions of "first-fruits" offerings were transformed into compulsory systems of tribute, exemplified by the institution of the Makahiki (511). In this fundamental shift from a segmentary system based on kinship, to one based on territories controlled by chiefs, Goldman saw that Hawai'i had pushed Polynesian cultural evolution to its apogee.

Like Goldman, Marshall Sahlins (1958) drew upon ethnohistoric sources to classify Polynesian societies into four groups based on their degree of stratification. Hawai'i (along with Tonga, Tahiti, and Samoa) was part of his Group I, exhibiting the most elaborate indices of hierarchy. Sahlins argued that there was a strong correlation between productivity and social stratification (1958, table 1). Sahlins realized that the surplus that could be captured and used by chiefs to advance their own economic and political agendas provided the key linkage between productivity and stratification: "The intimate relationship between productivity and stratification is intelligible in Polynesia because of the fact that a redistributive economic system prevailed in these islands" (250). In Hawai'i, chiefs achieved power through effective redistribution of the surplus made possible by a naturally rich environment exploited through efficient technology.

Sahlins later refined and expanded his theory, especially in *Stone Age Economics* (1972), in which he addressed the transformation of a "domestic mode of production" to a larger political economy. Sahlins argued that time and again in the course of human history, "main control over the domestic economy seems to pass from the formal solidarity of the kinship structure to its political aspect. As the structure is politicized, especially as it is centralized in ruling chiefs, the household economy is mobilized in a larger social cause" (130). Over time, the increased demands of the emerging chiefly economy have a tendency to grate against the inherent anti-surplus tendencies of the domestic mode of production, leading to resistance on the part of the people. Junior chiefs pounce on any opportunity to usurp the chiefship. But rather than lessen their demands for surplus, ruling chiefs frequently turn to a strategy of territorial conquest:

> Conscious, it seems, of the logistic burdens they were obliged to impose, the Hawaiian chiefs conceived several means to relieve the pressure, notably including a career of conquest with a view toward enlarging the tributary base. In the successful event, however, with the realm now stretched over distant and lately subdued hinterlands, the bureaucratic costs of rule apparently rose higher than the increases in revenue, so that the victorious chief merely succeeded in adding enemies abroad to a worse unrest at home. The cycles of centralization and exaction are now at their zenith. (145)

While asserting that the Hawaiian chiefs were not kings (1972, 148), Sahlins recognized that the chiefs had broken structurally with the *makaʻāinana*. In an unpublished work, Sahlins (n.d.) noted that the Hawaiians had a distinctly politicized concept of "the people," *nā kānaka,* as standing in opposition to "the chiefs," *nā liʻi*. Thus, Sahlins concludes, if the Hawaiians "did not achieve state formation as such . . . they did develop a genuine political society" (n.d., 23).

In 1971–1972, at the beginning of his career, Timothy Earle mapped the archaeological remains of irrigation systems in Haleleʻa District on Kauaʻi Island, as an adjunct to Sahlins' study of the early Hawaiian kingdom (Earle 1978). Although he did not continue fieldwork in Hawaiʻi, Earle's work on Kauaʻi irrigation strongly influenced his views on the formation and evolution of chiefdom societies. His earlier writings stress the significance of *irrigation* as the principal source of economic surplus and political power, as well as the importance of *redistribution* in the functioning of the Hawaiian political hierarchy (Earle 1977, 1978, 1980).

For Earle, Hawaiʻi represents an archetypical *staple-finance* chiefdom, in which "chiefs created an intensive production system relying on irrigation, dryland terraces, and fishponds" (1997, 210). In his most influential work, Earle (1997) explores three sources of power that chiefs exploited: economic, military, and ideological. His examination of Hawaiian *economic* power (75–89) perpetuates Earle's irrigation-centric perspective: "The Hawaiian case illustrates how irrigation technology served as a source of economic control in the emergence of complex chiefdoms" (75).

Earle argues that the intensification of agricultural production in Hawaiʻi "was not a response to population growth" (1997, 87) but rather that intensification drove population to increase. "An increasing dependence on agriculture supported the spread of population through the islands, and, after AD 1200, rapidly expanding populations *required* sustained agricultural intensification" (41; emphasis added). Seeing the Hawaiian case as a prime example of "staple finance," for Earle the intensified production systems were "the very essence of the ordered political economy" (201). While acknowledging two other main sources of power—military and ideological—used by the Hawaiian chiefs, for Earle the Hawaiian power strategy "came eventually to rest firmly on the intensive agricultural facilities" (202). Conquest warfare "did not seek land primarily, but the improved productive facilities (agricultural fields and fishponds) and commoner labor that produced the 'surplus' that financed the political economy" (132). War was the means of control over the system of staple finance (142).

Earle's consideration of ideology in the Hawaiian political economy builds on his own work on "materialization" (DeMarrais, Castillo, and Earle 1996), the way that abstract values are translated into and reinforced by material objects. Ideology as a power strategy lies in the *public presentation* of the systems of ideas and beliefs, through ceremonies, displays, and other occasions, these being "created and manipulated strategically by . . . the ruling elite, to establish and maintain positions of social power" (Earle 1997, 149). Earle argues that ideology and its materialization in Hawaiian chiefly strategies reinforced the staple economy. The major public ceremonies were the annual rituals of the Lono and Kū cults, the first essential to agriculture and the second to war (the means to capture agricultural resources). Hawaiian chiefs used featherwork as material symbols of their godlike status: "The [feathered] cloak was an ultimate power dress, signifying the sacred and potent persona of its owner" (173). More than anything else, Earle sees Hawaiian ideology as materialized in its cultural landscapes. *Heiau* were one component of these landscapes, providing the stage settings for the chiefs' ritual performances. But Earle regards the most significant materialization of ideology as "the building of the agricultural facilities on which the political economy was based" (179). It was this formalized, socially and politically codified, and materially demarcated agricultural landscape that translated ideology into power: "Property rights became formalized, given permanency, in the constructed, productive facilities—the irrigation systems, the fishponds, and the fenced house lots. . . . The symbolic order was thus grounded and subsumed within the everyday practice of ritual and subsistence labor in the monuments and fields of the chiefs" (183–184).

Robert Hommon's ideas regarding the evolution of Hawaiian society trace back to his unpublished doctoral dissertation (Hommon 1976a), in which he proposed that Hawai'i witnessed the emergence of what he termed "primitive states." These ideas were further developed in a later article (Hommon 1986) but were most fully elaborated in Hommon's book *The Ancient Hawaiian State: Origins of a Political Society* (2013). In this broad-ranging work, Hommon begins with a review of Hawaiian economy, society, and political organization in the early contact era, carefully delineating the multiple criteria upon which contact-era Hawaiian polities should be considered as states, rather than chiefdoms. He then turns to a series of comparative analyses across Polynesia, most notably with Tikopia, the Marquesas, Society Islands, and Tonga where, in the last case, he also finds evidence for the emergence of a state-level society.

The final part of Hommon's 2013 treatise outlines his theory of Hawaiian "state emergence." This begins with a careful consideration of the chronology for political evolution in the archipelago, integrating advances in radiocarbon dating and Bayesian calibration with the genealogical chronology of Hawaiian chiefs (something pioneered in Hommon [1976a]). The actual model of state emergence is laid out in terms of a succession of phases. Phase I (roughly equivalent to our Foundation Period) sees the colonization of the islands with settlement concentrated in the "salubrious cores." Phase II (roughly spanning our Late Voyaging and Expansion Periods), puts an emphasis on an initial period marked by extensive "shifting cultivation," leading gradually to a "filled land" situation, in which all arable land was territorially claimed; by the end of this phase "intensive cultivation had expanded to the limits of land that would reliably produce crops" (2013, 228). Hommon's final Phase III (more or less equivalent to our Archaic States Period) was marked by agricultural intensification and—now in the face of high population density—stress on the socioeconomic system itself:

> I suggest that during Phase III, the array of factors reviewed here—increased labor requirements, the addition of field work to women's traditional tasks, diminished productivity, rapid population growth, reduced soil fertility resulting from shortened fallow, government levies, and finally infrastructure development that reached the limits of cultivable land—probably led to an increased frequency and degree of food stress among the commoners who were dependent on rain-fed systems. (237)

This situation of increased food insecurity (especially on Hawai'i and Maui, which were largely dependent on rain-fed dryland field systems), along with a decreased ability on the part of the chiefs to levy taxes of all kinds, leads to Hommon's "hard times hypothesis," in which "a leader of an autonomous group tends to respond to a perceived extraordinary threat to the group with extraordinary action that can transgress sociopolitical norms" (2013, 241). This resulted in an emergent strategy of conquest warfare, amply attested to in the indigenous Hawaiian traditions. As Hommon writes, "War-making, once pursued for a variety of reasons including revenge and status rivalry[,] was repurposed to expand government power by means of conquest and annexation of lands and their inhabitants' production" (258). Indeed, Hommon provocatively suggests that "the hierarchical structure of bureaucracy [in Hawaiian archaic states] may have developed in part from the stratified military command structure that served to organize army units in battle" (255).

Kirch has long advocated multicausal explanation of cultural change in Polynesian societies, including Hawai'i. In *The Evolution of the Polynesian Chiefdoms,* Kirch (1984) identified several factors that he felt were essential to cultural evolution throughout Polynesia. These included the effects of initial settlement and adaptation to new environments, population growth on islands where land was initially not limiting, the anthropogenic transformation of landscapes and challenges of further adaptation these entailed, the intensification of production systems and control of surplus by chiefly elites, and warfare and competition among chiefly polities, especially following the rise of dense populations.

A quarter century later, Kirch (2010, 2012) returned to the problem of explaining Hawaiian cultural evolution. In these efforts, Kirch's analysis of the transformations of Hawaiian culture and society was significantly aided by the study of Ancestral Polynesian Society that he and Roger Green undertook using a phylogenetic model and a "triangulation approach" that integrates data from archaeology, historical linguistics, and comparative ethnography (Kirch and Green 2001). Having extensively reconstructed the contours of Ancestral Polynesian Society—which preceded the later diversification of the Eastern Polynesian societies including that of Hawai'i—made the later changes in Hawaiian culture and society more evident to Kirch. Such changes stand out through contrastive analysis. This is especially clear, for example, in the transformation of Ancestral Polynesian *kainga* to Hawaiian *'āina,* or of ancient Proto–Eastern Polynesian *mata-kainanga* to Hawaiian *maka'āinana* (see Kirch 2010, 24–27, for a full discussion of these lexical transformations).

Over the past few decades, anthropological archaeologists have debated whether cultural change is best understood as the outcome of large-scale *processes* or of individual *agency.* Kirch regards both process and agency as essential components of any explanatory model—as complementary rather than competing modes of explanation. He argues that "any compelling theory of change must attend to both *ultimate* and *proximate* causations, to long-term context and process, and to short-term dynamism and agency" (2010, 178), taking this distinction from the work of evolutionary biologist Ernst Mayr (1997).

For Kirch, long-term, ultimate causation includes such key processes as the demographic transition from small, density-independent founding populations to large, density-dependent populations; landscape-scale biogeographic and biogeochemical gradients that structured and constrained Hawaiian production systems; and differential wetland and dryland pathways of agricultural intensification. Ultimate causation must also take account of deeply ingrained cultural structures, especially the birth rank ordering and status rivalry that pervade Austronesian and Polynesian societies. Yet a model situating causality exclusively in such ultimate factors will, in Kirch's view, fall short of constituting an adequate theory of change. Proximate causation must also be invoked, situated in individual historical actors engaged with manipulating, constructing, and reconstructing their social and political world. In the Hawaiian case, the rich oral traditions offer a window into this world of agency, of political power, and of proximate causation. Leaders such as 'Umi and Pi'ilani changed the course of Hawaiian history through their actions, but we cannot ignore the fact that their generation occupied a critical time and place that was the outcome of a long-term contingent history of which they were the inheritors (Kirch 2010, 178–179).

6

HISTORY SEDIMENTED IN THE EARTH
Six Stratified Sites

Stacked stone architecture dominates the archaeological record of Hawai'i. Excavations conducted in and around these pavements, platforms, terraces, walls, enclosures, mounds, and alignments typically reveal only shallow cultural deposits, often just 10 to 40 cm deep, lacking in stratified sequences of multiple occupation layers. Yet some Hawaiian sites do exhibit true stratification—deeper deposits where a succession of occupations has resulted in discernable layers or strata one on top of the other. Most of these stratified sites occur in one of two contexts. The first consists of rockshelters or lava tube caves, which offered convenient living spaces for small groups of people; the confined space between natural lava walls resulted in dense and thick accumulations of occupation debris. The second context consists of coastal sand dunes or beach ridges, where successive periods of human activity were sandwiched between episodes of sand accumulation. Not all rockshelters and not all sand dunes in Hawai'i have well stratified archaeological deposits. But in a few cases where these existed, the local archaeological records have been remarkably rich, both in material culture and in associated faunal and botanical remains. Some of these sites also span fairly long time periods.

In this chapter we discuss six sites with unusually good stratification, three sand dunes and three rockshelters, all of which played important roles in the history of Hawaiian archaeology. In addition, these six sites were subject to extensive excavations covering large areas, a strategy typical of the 1950s and 1960s but rarely practiced today. The legacy collections from these excavations have also been revisited in recent years either for redating their chronologies using new AMS radiocarbon dating, or for reanalysis of certain kinds of artifacts or of their faunal assemblages. All six sites have continued potential to yield new insights through further reanalysis of these legacy collections, mostly curated in Bishop Museum. The sites are discussed in the order in which they were excavated.

Kuli'ou'ou Rockshelter (Site O1), O'ahu Island

Kuli'ou'ou rockshelter, designated site O1 by Bishop Museum, holds iconic status as the first site to be excavated during the modern era of Hawaiian archaeology; the shelter yielded the first radiocarbon date from any site in the Pacific (Emory and Sinoto 1961).

Excavations at Kuliʻouʻou were started in 1938 by John R. Porteus, an anthropology student at the University of Hawaiʻi. In the spring of 1950, when Kenneth Emory began to teach a class in archaeological methods at the university, "he decided to have the class take up where Porteus had left off and carry his work to completion" (Emory and Sinoto 1961, 3). Among the students who participated in that course were William J. Bonk, who would soon join Emory in excavations throughout the islands, and William Davenport, who went on to a career in Pacific cultural anthropology. Although Yosihiko Sinoto assisted in the analysis of artifacts from the site, and coauthored the final publication, he did not participate in the excavation (Sinoto did not arrive in Hawaiʻi until 1954).

Kuliʻouʻou rockshelter "is a remnant of a lava tube which forms a spacious natural shelter" (Emory and Sinoto 1961, 4), situated at the end of Ka-lapa-o-Mana ridge, which marks the division between the *ahupuaʻa* of Niu on the west and Kuliʻouʻou on the east (fig. 6.1). The shelter's floor has a maximum length of about 50 feet and depth of 25 feet, while the roof is high enough that people living within could stand upright over most of the area. The shelter commands a view to the coastline a short distance to the south, and over the broad sweep of Maunalua Bay. Two natural ponds, Paikō and Waiha, lie at the base of the ridge.

FIGURE 6.1 View of Kuliʻouʻou rockshelter during Bishop Museum excavation in 1950. *(Photo courtesy Bishop Museum Department of Anthropology)*

The cultural deposit within the rockshelter was stratified into several layers, along with numerous ash and charcoal lenses (fire hearths), pits, and other disturbances. One deep pit cutting through a sequence of ash and charcoal deposits is visible in a photo included in Emory and Sinoto's report (1961, fig. 9). Three main cultural layers were discerned by Emory during the excavation. The uppermost, Layer I, was described as a "yellow-brown, powdery soil" containing postcontact historic artifacts. Layer II was a "gray-brown soil" ranging from 12 to 18 inches thick, "which was impregnated with ash, shells, fish bones and scales, and various animal and vegetable remains," along with traditional Hawaiian artifacts (14). Below this was Layer III, about 12 inches thick, with more gravel and some larger stones, in which "the refuse material and artifacts diminished considerably."

Unfortunately, Emory did not excavate Kuli'ou'ou shelter according to these stratigraphic layers. Instead, following methods developed by Professor Robert Heizer of the University of California, Berkeley (Heizer 1950), Emory laid out a grid of 3-foot squares, then dug within these squares in arbitrary 6-inch levels (fig. 6.2). No attempt was made to follow the main strata; features such as fire hearths or the larger pits that cut through the strata were ignored. These pits and other disturbances had undoubtedly resulted in some mixing in the deposits; with everything dug out by arbitrary 6-inch blocks, stratigraphic integrity was lost. Emory did reserve two of the 3-foot squares, labeled D6 and D7, for more carefully controlled excavation in order to conduct a "detailed analysis of the floor content" (1961, 15). This was the first quantitative midden analysis in Hawaiian archaeology (see chapter 10).

While the excavation was in progress, Leo Fortess, a former graduate student at the university, alerted Emory to the fact that Willard F. Libby—who had recently developed the new method of radiocarbon dating—was requesting samples from various parts of the

FIGURE 6.2 Kenneth P. Emory of Bishop Museum began excavating in Kuli'ou'ou rockshelter (site O1) in 1950. *(Photo courtesy of Bishop Museum Library and Archives)*

world (Emory and Sinoto 1961, 3). Emory promptly sent Libby a sample of charcoal from between 24 and 36 inches below surface (presumably from Layer III) in square D7, next to a large boulder (1961, fig. 11). The resulting date (C550, AD 1004 ± 180) evoked considerable excitement when it was received some months later. As Emory recollected, "It opened up undreamed of possibilities for reconstructing the prehistory of the area" (Emory, Bonk, and Sinoto 1959, ix). A second sample obtained from the same square at a depth of 18–24 inches yielded a much younger date (M564, AD 1739 ± 150), attributed by Emory and Sinoto to "a rapid rate of deposition in the last few centuries" (1961, 15).

In an effort to establish a more precise chronology for Kuliʻouʻou rockshelter, Jennifer Kahn et al. (2014) turned to charcoal samples from the 1950 excavation that had been curated in Bishop Museum. Nothing remained from square D7, but six samples were available from the adjacent square, D6. After botanical identification of the charcoal, short-lived taxa were submitted for AMS radiocarbon dating; one sample returned a "modern" age while the other five samples provided acceptable dates (Kahn et al. 2014, table 2). The oldest date (Beta-306124*, 470 ± 30 BP), with a calibrated age of AD 1409–1457, came from the 18- to 24-inch level in square D6. The other four dates are considerably younger, with age ranges in the sixteenth and seventeenth centuries. These results led Kahn et al. to conclude that Kuliʻouʻou rockshelter "can no longer be considered relevant to the early period of Polynesian colonisation in Hawaiʻi." They stated that "the site is informative for understanding the transition between the Late Expansion (AD 1400–1650) and Proto-Historic (AD 1650–1778) Periods of the Hawaiian cultural sequence" (2014, 87).

There are reasons, however, to question the outright rejection of Libby's original radiocarbon date, along with the idea that the deepest deposits in Kuliʻouʻou shelter date to a time soon after the arrival of Polynesians on Oʻahu. The first reason lies in the presence of abundant seabird bones in the lower part of the cultural deposit. Emory and Sinoto wrote,

> Porteus, who collected bird bones aggregating 113 grams in weight, was impressed with the number he came across as he neared the sterile floor, particularly at its juncture with the fertile floor [i.e., the cultural deposit]. He concluded that this was the start of occupation on this part of the coast, when sea birds would have been most numerous. In squares D6 and D7 we found a sharp increase at the bottom of the cultural layer. . . . None of the bird bones were larger than what would be expected from petrels or shearwaters. (1961, 17)

The presence of significant numbers of bird bones is a likely indicator that the initial use of the shelter occurred at a time prior to extensive human activity in the region. If the shelter was not occupied until the Expansion Period, we would not expect to see such an accumulation of bird bones.

The second line of evidence suggesting use of the shelter during either the Foundation or Late Voyaging Periods lies in the artifact assemblage. While many of the one-piece fishhooks from the site have line-lashing devices of the knobbed form that is typical of the Expansion to Archaic States Periods (see chapter 9), several have incurved shanks with notched heads characteristic of early central Eastern Polynesian fishhook assemblages (e.g.,

Emory and Sinoto 1961, fig. 38, *i, k, m,* and *o*). A partial adze with reverse-triangular cross section (1961, fig. 56, *i*) and a portion of a well-ground chisel (1961, fig. 59, *b*) are also artifact forms known from early contexts.

Returning to the radiocarbon dates for Kuli'ou'ou shelter, we note that the early Libby date from square D7 came from a depth of 24–36 inches, deeper than any of the AMS-dated samples from square D6. This deepest 6-inch level, at the base of the cultural deposit, was also that yielding the abundant seabird bones. Therefore, outright rejection of the Libby date, calibrated to AD 995–1285 (1σ) using a Bayesian model for the site, may not be warranted. It remains possible that the initial use of the shelter—the period when the bird bones were accumulating—was in the Foundation or Late Voyaging Periods. Further reanalysis of the site O1 collections in Bishop Museum may shed new light on this possibility. Of course, the upper strata in the site (Layers II and I) clearly date to the Expansion Period and after.

The main significance of Kuli'ou'ou rockshelter lies in the role that it played in the early days of archaeological research in Hawai'i. Kuli'ou'ou could have revealed much more, could have told other stories about O'ahu's past, had it been more carefully excavated with modern controls. But hindsight is always 20/20. The history of the Kuli'ou'ou excavation, however, does reinforce the fact that every archaeological site is unique; once dug, it can never be reexcavated.

Pu'u Ali'i (Site H1), Ka Lae, Hawai'i Island

One can readily understand why Polynesians arriving in the islands would choose to settle in locations such as Waimānalo, O'ahu, or Hālawa Valley on eastern Moloka'i, with abundant resources, fresh water, and good soils. The South Point (Ka Lae) of Hawai'i Island, in contrast, is an arid leeward region with no permanent streams and limited agricultural potential. Ceaseless winds buffet the dry, grassy, plain at this southernmost tip of Hawai'i, giving one pause to wonder why people were attracted to the area. The answer lies in the adjacent deep-sea fishing grounds. The calm waters in the lee of Ka Lae are famous among island fishermen for their abundance of pelagic fish, including tunas (Scombridae), *mahi-mahi* (Coryphaenidae), and marlin (Istiophoriaae) (Hosaka 1944). These fish were prized by the Polynesians; *aku,* the skipjack tuna, was subject to a yearly *kapu* period and figured in rites of the Makahiki (Malo 1951, 189). It probably did not take inquisitive Polynesians long to explore the waters surrounding the Hawaiian Islands, and to quickly discover the bounty of these Ka Lae fishing grounds.

The Pu'u Ali'i sand dune site (H1) was one of the first to be excavated (fig. 6.3) as part of Emory's Hawaiian Archaeological Program, inspired by the artifact finds and early radiocarbon date from Kuli'ou'ou rockshelter (see chapter 1). Excavations at site H1 were carried out from 1953 to 1955, during which time more than 200 3-foot squares were opened up (fig. 6.4); in excess of 14,000 artifacts were recovered. Most of these objects were related in one way or another to fishing, including 1,710 fishhooks, as well as 12,314 abraders of coral and sea urchin spines, used to manufacture the hooks. The predominance of fishing gear, along with fishhook manufacturing tools and detritus such as cut bone and shell, indicates that Pu'u Ali'i was a fishermen's encampment. Fishermen may have resided for portions of

FIGURE 6.3 The Puʻu Aliʻi sand dune site (H1) at the beginning of excavations in 1953, with William J. Bonk standing at the transit. The early cultural deposit is visible as a dark band at the base of the tripod. *(Photo courtesy Bishop Museum Department of Anthropology)*

FIGURE 6.4 Excavations in progress at the Puʻu Aliʻi sand dune site (H1) site in 1954. *(Photo courtesy Bishop Museum Department of Anthropology)*

the year in the upland regions of Kaʻū where farming was productive, camping here when the weather permitted offshore fishing. Alternatively, this could have been a permanent settlement of fishing specialists who exchanged dried fish for agricultural produce grown by kinsfolk in the uplands (as suggested by Handy and Pukui 1958).

As with Kuliʻouʻou rockshelter, site H1 was dug in arbitrary 6-inch levels rather than by stratigraphic layers. Regrettably, due in part to personality clashes between Emory and his former student William Bonk, a final report on the excavation was never completed, one

SIX STRATIFIED SITES • 121

of the tragedies of the early years of Hawaiian archaeology. Our comments here are based on Kirch's examination of notes, photographs, and artifacts in Bishop Museum, and on discussions with Emory and Sinoto.

Pu'u Ali'i sand dune included three major occupation strata. The uppermost occupation layer consisted of dark brown sand, about 3 inches thick, with a thick charcoal band near the top, possibly representing a burning of the little fishing camp. Underlying this was a thick cultural deposit (Layer II) containing the bulk of the artifacts, with a stone pavement and pebble paving near the base of the stratum. Underlying the pavement was Layer III, about 5 to 8 inches thick, which also contained many artifacts, including several with stylistic traits similar to those found in early central Eastern Polynesian sites. Beneath Layer III was the natural Pahala ash that forms the surface soil in the Ka Lae area. Capping the cultural deposits, and postdating the period when Pu'u Ali'i was used as a fishing camp, is a deposit of sand about one meter thick that contained 97 burials (Underwood 1969). Following the passage of the Native American Graves Protection and Repatriation Act (NAGPRA) in 1990, the Pu'u Ali'i skeletal remains were reinterred in the sand dune.

Dating the Pu'u Ali'i dune site has posed more problems than almost any other site in Polynesia (Dye 1992; Emory and Sinoto 1969; Green 1971b). Based on the fishhook styles present, Emory anticipated that Layer III in H1 should be one of the earliest in the Hawaiian Islands. Thus, when the Groningen Laboratory returned a radiocarbon date of AD 290 ± 60 it seemed a reasonable age estimate for the site's initial occupation (Emory, Bonk, and Sinoto 1959). Later, however, other dates gave younger results, leading to a major program of radiocarbon dating of no less than 27 samples, including not only charcoal but also *Cypraea* shell and sea urchin spines (Emory and Sinoto 1969, table 5). The results were confusing; Emory and Sinoto could only conclude that the Pu'u Ali'i site was abandoned by the mid-thirteenth to early fourteenth century, but remained uncertain of when occupation there had begun. Based on a seriation of fishhook types (see chapter 9), they argued that Layer III in the H1 site predated the H8 rockshelter site at nearby Wai'ahukini (see below).

With some caveats, a Bayesian model of the charcoal radiocarbon dates from Layers II and III at site H1 can be put forward (see Emory and Sinoto 1969, table 5, for the list of available dates). We need to restrict the model to charcoal dates, because the shell and sea urchin dates require a marine reservoir correction (the ΔR factor), for which we lack sufficient information. Additional caution is necessary because the charcoal samples were not identified to botanical taxon; some of the samples may have been from old wood (with inbuilt age). In addition, these dates from the early period of radiocarbon dating were not corrected for $\delta^{13}C$ fractionation. Acknowledging these limitations, a Bayesian calibration for five dates from Layer III and six dates from Layer II yields a chronological model (fig. 6.5) with a high overall agreement ($A_{overall}$ index = 193.2). (Note that this model eliminates four outlier dates that have very low agreement with the majority of the dates.) This model accords reasonably well with the revised chronology for Hawaiian precontact history. It suggests that Layer III was deposited from the late fourteenth into the fifteenth centuries, and that Layer II accumulated soon after, with the fishermen's camp being

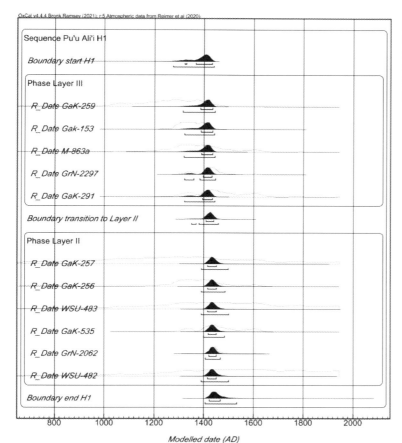

FIGURE 6.5 Bayesian calibration of radiocarbon dates from the Puʻu Aliʻi dune site (H1), Hawaiʻi Island. (Oxcal plot by P. V. Kirch)

abandoned by the end of the fifteenth century. In terms of the cultural sequence outlined in chapter 5, the cultural deposits at H1 thus span the Late Voyaging to early Expansion Periods. After that, as sand began to accumulate over the low hill, Puʻu Aliʻi was used only as a burial place.

As Emory and Sinoto recognized, the artifacts from Layers III and II at Puʻu Aliʻi are similar to artifacts from early sites in central Eastern Polynesia, especially the Marquesas (fig. 6.6). The stone adzes include a reverse triangular adze nearly identical to an adze from the early Bellows (O18) site on Oʻahu, and two adzes with reverse trapezoidal sections, as well as many quadrangular specimens. A porpoise-tooth pendant is another item also found at the Bellows site. Most significant, however, are the fishhooks. Site H1 yielded the only example ever recovered from a Hawaiian site of a double-perforated pearl-shell point from a trolling hook, an early Eastern Polynesian type. The one-piece fishhooks also show similarities with early Marquesan hooks, including examples of double-notched line-lashing attachments, and of strongly incurved shanks.

Unfortunately—lacking a full analysis and report—we remain ignorant of other aspects of the Puʻu Aliʻi site, such as the form of the early structures indicated by the stone pavements and post molds. A future study of the faunal remains from H1 may yet tell us more regarding early Hawaiian fishing practices.

FIGURE 6.6 Artifacts from the Puʻu Aliʻi sand dune site (H1). *Far left:* reverse triangular and trapezoidal basalt adzes. *Upper row, from left to right:* crescent points of bone, notched two-piece fishhook points of bone, and pearl-shell trolling lure points. *Bottom row, left to right:* one-piece fishhooks of bone and shell, and pearl-shell pendant. *(Photo by P. V. Kirch)*

Waiʻahukini Rockshelter (Site H8), Hawaiʻi Island

A short distance north of Ka Lae is the H8 lava tube rockshelter, situated a few hundred meters inland of the canoe landing at Waiʻahukini, in the lee of the Kahuku Pali. The shelter, formed by a lava tube with partial collapses, has two entrances. The main living floor—which remains cool during the day while the lava terrain outside bakes in the sun—has an area of about 50 m², providing a convenient camping spot for fishing parties. Site H8 was excavated by Emory and his colleagues between 1954 and 1958. Like the H1 site, H8 yielded a great number of artifacts, including 1,211 fishhooks and 6,809 coral and sea-urchin-spine abrading tools. Emory, Bonk, and Sinoto (1969) published a summary report on the excavations, while the fishhooks were reported in their earlier volume (Emory, Bonk, and Sinoto 1959).

The rockshelter stratigraphy was complex, with three main strata. The upper two strata (Layers I-1 and I-2) were separated from underlying Layer II by a stone pavement (Emory, Bonk, and Sinoto 1969, fig. 6). The total deposit reached a depth of about 2 feet at the contact with the lava bedrock floor. A number of stone-lined fire hearths were exposed during the excavation.

Emory and Sinoto (1969) attempted to establish the age of the H8 cultural deposits with an extensive series of 25 radiocarbon dates, on cowrie shells, sea urchin spines, and fish scales and fishbones, as well as on charcoal (the charcoal samples were not botanically identified). The results were contradictory, and the standard errors on some samples exceeded 300 years (1969, table 1). Emory and Sinoto concluded that the site was first occupied around AD 750, that the pavement separating Layers I and II was laid down around AD 1250, and that final abandonment was around AD 1850 (1969, 10; see also Dye 1992). This chronology was revised by Mara Mulrooney et al. (2014), who redated the site with charcoal samples from the original excavation. Seven samples from collections at the University of Hawaiʻi, Hilo, were botanically identified to obtain short-lived taxa, and these were dated using the

AMS method (2014, table 1). A Bayesian calibration of these new AMS dates (2014, fig. 8) suggests that the H8 rockshelter was first used around AD 1400, and that most of the Layer II deposit accumulated during the Expansion Period. The pavement was probably laid down at the beginning of the Archaic States Period, during which Layer I continued to accumulate.

The fishhooks from site H8 exhibit a sequence of trends in line-lashing devices ("head" forms) and in the frequency of notched and knobbed two-piece hook points that is similar to those in site H1 (fig. 6.7). Notched line-lashing devices (Sinoto's types HT1a, HT1b, HT2, and HT3) are more frequent in the deeper deposits, while the knobbed form of head (HT4) dominates in Layer I at H8. This fishhook seriation reinforces the interpretation that the occupation at site H1 began before that at site H8, although the main occupations at both sites overlap during the Expansion Period.

Steve Lundblad et al. (2014) applied nondestructive, energy-dispersive X-Ray fluorescence (EDXRF) to the collection of 1,562 flakes of volcanic glass and 295 basalt artifacts recovered from the original H8 excavations in order to determine the geologic sources of these objects. Three different sources of volcanic glass are represented, one of which is the Pu'u Wa'awa'a trachyte cone in North Kona District (30 specimens came from this source). The basalt artifacts originated from at least nine different sources, of which Mauna Kea was the most frequent, with 113 specimens (Lundblad et al. 2014, table 1). Somewhat surprising is the presence of three flakes from the Keāhua I source on Kaua'i Island.

A thorough analysis of fishbones from site H8 has yet to be conducted (but see Goto 1984, 1986). An inspection of some of the material in storage at Bishop Museum suggests that large game fish dominate. A quantitative analysis of faunal remains from square E8 was reported by Emory, Bonk, and Sinoto (1969, table 2), revealing a significant pattern with the bird bones.

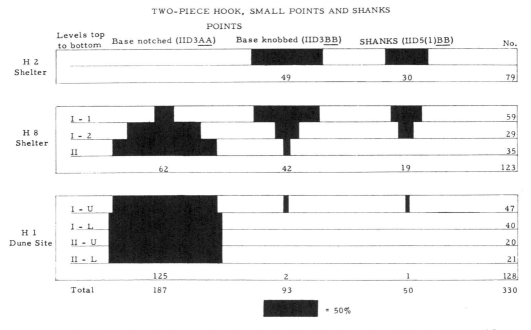

FIGURE 6.7 Diagram showing the frequencies of notched and knobbed two-piece fishhooks recovered from the H1, H8, and H2 sites in the South Point region, Hawai'i Island. *(After Emory, Bonk, and Sinoto 1959)*

FIGURE 6.8 View of the stone-faced habitation terraces at Nuʻalolo Kai (sites K3, K4, and K5), Kauaʻi Island, during Bishop Museum excavations in the early 1960s. *(Photo courtesy Bishop Museum Department of Anthropology)*

Whereas bird bone was frequent at the base of the site (40 grams in the lowest ½ inch of deposit), the quantity rapidly diminished moving up the stratigraphic profile, a pattern one would expect with initial human exploitation of a previously unoccupied area. Before Polynesians arrived in Hawai'i, nesting seabirds were presumably numerous, because there were no ground predators. Once humans began to take the young birds for food, the local bird populations would have declined; introduced rats may also have preyed on some seabird species.

Nu'alolo Rockshelter (Sites K3–K5), Kaua'i Island

In a pioneering survey of Kaua'i Island, Wendell Bennett (1931) identified the isolated Nā Pali valleys as a prime location for intensive archaeological study. In 1958, Kenneth Emory began a major excavation at Nu'alolo Kai, a dry valley where a high overhanging cliff provided natural shelter from the elements. A series of stone-faced house terraces (identified by Emory as sites K3, K4, and K5) had been constructed at the base of the towering cliff (fig. 6.8). Bishop Museum excavations, later under the direction of Emory's student Lloyd Soehren and continuing through 1964, revealed that these terraces had been occupied and rebuilt over a long period. As many as 15 stratigraphic layers with a total depth of about 2 m were in evidence (fig. 6.9). In all, approximately 145 m^3 of earth were excavated and sieved at Nu'alolo, making this one of the largest excavations ever carried out in Hawai'i; an astounding 18,000 artifacts and other specimens were recovered (Field and Graves, eds., 2015, 3).

FIGURE 6.9 Excavations in progress at the deeply stratified Nu'alolo rockshelter (site K3 habitation terrace), where dry conditions resulted in the preservation of normally perishable artifacts. Excavation director Lloyd Soehren is wearing the floppy hat. (*Photo courtesy Bishop Museum Department of Anthropology*)

As with other early Bishop Museum excavations, the Nuʻalolo terraces were excavated according to arbitrary 6-inch levels; stratigraphic disturbances such as pits or fire hearths were not separately distinguished. Although the excavation records indicate that the main strata were horizontally laid down, the arbitrary 6-inch levels do not neatly correspond to the natural layers. Soehren (n.d.) authored a detailed report on the excavations, using the 6-inch levels as the basis for analysis, although this was never published. In part to clarify the site's stratigraphy, a small (1 × 2 m) excavation was carried out by Terry Hunt of the University of Hawaiʻi in 1990, in the K3 terrace (Hunt 2006). Subsequently, Julie Field and Michael Graves, along with a number of University of Hawaiʻi students, reanalyzed selected collections from Nuʻalolo (Field and Graves, eds., 2015; Graves and McElroy 2005).

Field (in Field and Graves, eds., 2015, 26–30) summarizes prior efforts to date the deeply stratified Nuʻalolo cultural deposits. Bishop Museum obtained five radiocarbon dates, all on unidentified wood charcoal, while the University of Hawaiʻi researchers dated an additional four samples on materials originally excavated by the museum (Field and Graves, eds., 2015, table 3.1). Hunt (2006) dated four samples, also of unidentified wood charcoal, from his 1990 excavation. Although there may be unknown issues with old wood and inbuilt age with some of these dated samples, until further redating is conducted, we must base the chronology of Nuʻalolo on these available dates. Using the "analytic zones" outlined by Field and Graves (2015, table 3.2), which correlated Bishop Museum's excavation depths with cultural levels, the available radiocarbon dates for sites K3 and K5 at Nuʻalolo can be modeled with a Bayesian calibration, as shown in figure 6.10. This temporal model utilizes all of the available dates except for one (Beta-37874, rejected as it has poor agreement), and yields a model with high overall agreement ($A_{overall}$ index = 101.2). Based on this Bayesian model, the deepest strata at Nuʻalolo (Analytical Zone 3) were deposited between approximately AD 1300 and 1500, spanning the Late Voyaging to Expansion Periods; the middle strata accumulated between AD 1500 and 1700, from the later Expansion into the Archaic States Periods; and, the uppermost deposits were laid down from 1700 and on into the postcontact era. Analytical Zone 1, the most recent, contains historic-period as well as traditional Hawaiian artifacts.

Not only does the Nuʻalolo rockshelter provide the longest continuous occupation sequence for Kauaʻi Island, the site is unique for the wealth and variety of well-preserved artifacts. Two factors contributed to the unusual preservation of a wide range of wooden and vegetable materials at Nuʻalolo: first, the dry, protected nature of the site (under the overhanging cliff), and second, the heavy sea spray, which permeated the deposits with salt. The salt prevented degradation and decomposition of organic materials, although it also poses conservation challenges for the artifacts recovered through excavation. The Nuʻalolo house terraces yielded large arrays of bone and shell fishhooks, stone adzes, sinkers, and other tools, and an extraordinary variety of well-preserved cordage, matting and plaiting, worked wooden implements and tools of all sorts, gourds, and even *kapa* (fig. 6.11).

The rich artifact assemblage from Nuʻalolo provides a rare opportunity to investigate changes in Hawaiian material culture over a long time span. Soehren (n.d.) noted that most of the stone adzes from the site were of the quadrangular-sectioned, tanged form typical of later Hawaiian adzes. However, he pointed out that the deepest strata in site K3 contained one adze with a plano-convex cross section, similar to one of the adzes from the

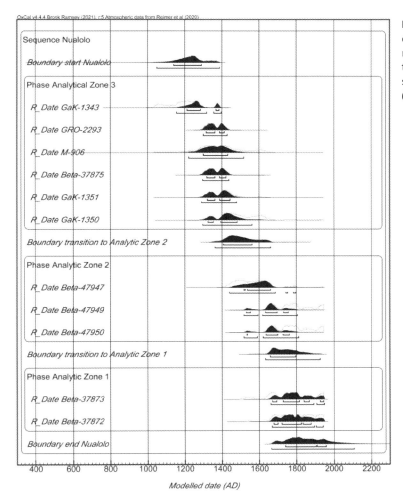

FIGURE 6.10 Bayesian calibration of radiocarbon dates from the Nuʻalolo rockshelter site, Kauaʻi Island. *(Oxcal plot by P. V. Kirch)*

early Bellows (O18) site on Oʻahu, as well as a few adzes with trapezoidal or reverse-triangular sections. These finds add to the evidence that the adze kit of the earliest Polynesians in Hawaiʻi was akin to that of other early Eastern Polynesian islands.

Nearly 900 whole or partial fishhooks were recovered during the Nuʻalolo excavations, providing the basis for an analysis of changes in fishhook style by Graves and McElroy (2005). One significant change was in the use of pearl shell, which declined over time in relation to bone. Another significant temporal trend was in the shape of the line-lashing device (or "head" of the shank) on one-piece angling hooks. Early hooks are dominated by angled heads with notches, while later hooks are dominated by "stepped" heads with protruding knobs (Graves and McElroy 2005, fig. 16). Whether such changes in fishhook form were functional or stylistic is unclear.

The assemblage of 807 basalt artifacts from Nuʻalolo, including adzes, chisels, and two stone mirrors, along with a number of expedient flake tools, were geochemically analyzed using EDXRF by Mills et al. (2010). Eleven distinct geochemical groups are present, all from Kauaʻi Island, except in the case of the two stone mirrors, which derive from an unknown source, possibly outside of the Hawaiian Islands. The Nuʻalolo adzes were primarily from sources elsewhere on Kauaʻi Island, but many of the expedient tools were made from local Nā Pali region stone.

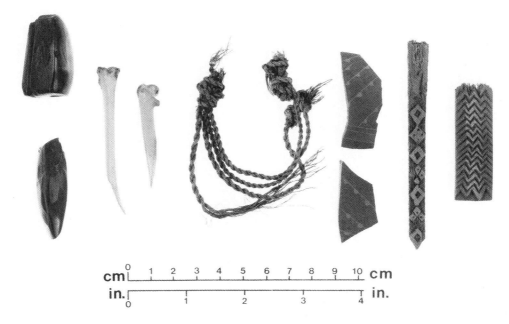

FIGURE 6.11 Artifacts from the Nuʻalolo rockshelter site, Kauaʻi Island. *Upper left,* breadloaf sinker of hematite; *lower left,* basalt chisel. *Left to right:* bird-bone picks, knotted cordage, fragments of decorated gourds, barkcloth stamps of bamboo. *(Photo by P. V. Kirch)*

The legacy collection of faunal remains from Nuʻalolo has provided materials for new analyses of the subsistence practices of the ancient community and their relationship to the Nā Pali environment. Studies of bird and fish bones have been especially informative (Esh 2015; O'Leary 2005). Significantly, the frequency of seabird bones in the Nuʻalolo deposits does not decline over time; seabirds there do not exhibit a pattern of "resource depression" (Esh 2015, 105). Whether this was due to conservation practices, or to the fact that seabirds may have been harvested over a wide area, including the Northwestern Hawaiian Islands, is not clear. The fish-bone assemblage is dominated by inshore, reef species, especially wrasses and parrotfish, a pattern fairly typical in Hawaiian midden sites (O'Leary 2005).

Bellows Dune Site (Site O18), Waimānalo, Oʻahu Island

As is sometimes the case in archaeology, the discovery of the Bellows dune site was accidental. During the winter of 1967, human burials were reported to be eroding from the exposed face of a sand dune on the Bellows Air Force Base at Waimānalo on Oʻahu's windward shore; as was often the case in this pre-NAGPRA era, Bishop Museum was notified. On a site visit Lloyd Soehren observed cultural deposits, visible in the eroded sand bank as dark gray bands indicating a cultural horizon containing midden and artifacts; these darker layers contrasted sharply with the clean white beach sand above and below (fig. 6.12). A test excavation convinced Soehren that the site deserved further attention, but he was preoccupied with the analysis of the Nuʻalolo collections. Richard Pearson, then with the University of Hawaiʻi, agreed to conduct an excavation with students from the Anthropology

FIGURE 6.12 View of stratification in the Bellows dune site (O18), O'ahu Island, during excavations in 1967; P. Kirch is setting up the plane table for mapping. The dark, lowest stratum is Layer III; post molds can be seen extending down into the culturally sterile beach sands. *(Photo by Richard Pearson)*

FIGURE 6.13 Excavations in progress in the Bellows dune site (O18), O'ahu Island, during 1967. *(Photo by Richard Pearson)*

Department's summer archaeological field school (fig. 6.13). In August 1967, 52 m² were excavated (Pearson, Kirch, and Pietrusewsky 1971). Unlike the preceding Bishop Museum excavations in which Heizer's method of arbitrary 6-inch levels had been used (Heizer 1950), Pearson applied stratigraphic excavation methods he had learned from Professor K. C. Chang at Yale. Students in the field course (including Kirch, then a Punahou School student) used Chang's *Rethinking Archaeology* as their textbook (Chang 1967). Some years later, another field school excavation was conducted at the dune site by David Tuggle and Ross Cordy, also of the University of Hawai'i. By that time, however, continued erosion had removed a large part of the ancient habitation deposits; this second excavation yielded relatively little in the way of new data (Cordy and Tuggle 1976; Tuggle, Cordy, and Child 1978).

The O18 sand dune lies on the north bank of Waimānalo Stream, about 50 m inland of the present shoreline. The presence of fresh water and of low-lying marshy terrain suitable for taro cultivation just inland may have been important inducements for the early Polynesians who established their hamlet or village here. The Mokulua Islets offshore are an important seabird nesting ground. The broad sweep of Waimānalo Bay offered good fishing grounds, while the long sandy beach was ideal for landing and launching canoes in virtually any weather. Outcrops of andesitic dike stone in the nearby Keolu Hills provided a source of rock from which to make stone tools.

The stratigraphy at O18 consisted of discrete occupation layers separated by culturally sterile dune sand representing periods when the site was unoccupied. Layer III, the deepest and oldest habitation layer, and two succeeding deposits, Layers IIa and II, yielded most of the features and artifacts. The dating of site O18 has already been discussed in chapter 5. Layer III dates to approximately AD 1150–1250, while Layer II dates to roughly AD 1250–1300. Each occupation may have lasted only a decade or so, as suggested by the relatively thin occupation strata and low density of artifacts and faunal remains.

Excavation of Layer III revealed a cluster of features indicative of pole-and-thatch dwellings, either for permanent habitation or for occupation of a more temporary nature. These features included numerous post molds, two pavements of waterworn pebbles (*'ili'ili*), small hearths, and trash pits with concentrations of fish bones. An elderly female had been buried in a shallow pit beneath one of the pebble pavements, presumably a house floor. The burial of individuals under house floors is an ancient pattern in Polynesia, one that was later abandoned in the Hawaiian Islands (see chapter 11). Artifacts from Layer III include one-piece fishhooks, a coconut grater of cone shell, several stone adzes, abraders, a stone drill, worked bone and shell, and a pendant of imitation porpoise tooth.

After a short interval during which drifting sand covered the initial habitation layer (in two phases, with the ephemeral Layer IIa deposits accumulating in between), a second occupation resulted in the deposition of Layer II. Pole-and-thatch houses were again indicated by post molds and hearths. Several individuals were buried at this time, including a young child (about nine years old), possibly female, who wore an anklet of pig tusks and a neck ornament (*lei niho palaoa*), suggesting that she was of chiefly rank. The sand around this burial was stained red; this young woman may have been wrapped in barkcloth dyed with turmeric or ochre. The other burials were of an elderly female, an adult male, and a small child, one to two years of age. (After the passage of the NAGPRA act, these *iwi kūpuna* were repatriated and reburied.)

Layers III and II at site O18 yielded artifacts indicative of the material culture of this early phase in the Hawaiian cultural sequence. The one-piece fishhooks, mostly of pearl shell (fig. 6.14), are stylistically similar to early hook forms known in the Marquesas Islands, characterized by incurved shanks and notched, or double-notched, line-lashing devices (heads). Two examples of two-piece bone fishhooks are of a simple type that is a forerunner to the larger two-piece hooks seen in later Hawaiian sites. The *Conus*-shell coconut grater (fig. 6.15) is noteworthy, not only because it points to the early presence of the coconut palm in the area but also because it resembles pearl-shell graters from other early central Eastern Polynesian sites. The basalt adzes from O18 (fig. 6.16) are of types not found in later Hawaiian sites, again suggesting close links with the Marquesas and other early Eastern Polynesian assemblages. These include a small tanged adze with a reverse triangular cross section, and an adze with plano-convex cross section. Other manufacturing tools, including abraders of coral and sea urchin spines, rubbing stones, stone drills, and flake "knives," are types that did not change much over time and are found in both early and late sites.

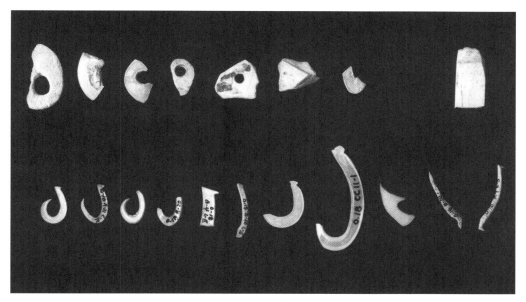

FIGURE 6.14 Fishing gear from the Bellows dune site (O18), Oʻahu Island. *Top row:* unfinished fishhooks of bone and, and fragment of possible cone-shell trolling lure shank. *Bottom row:* one-piece fishhooks (note incurved shanks), and two-piece point and shank (*far right*). (Photo by P. V. Kirch)

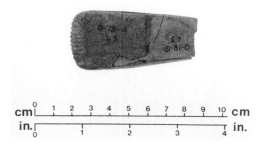

FIGURE 6.15 Coconut grater of *Conus* shell from the Bellows dune site (O18), Oʻahu Island. (Photo by P. V. Kirch)

FIGURE 6.16 Basalt artifacts from the Bellows dune site (O18), Oʻahu Island. *Left to right:* reverse triangular adze, plano-convex adze, two chisel fragments, and awl. *(Photo by P. V. Kirch)*

The few ornaments excavated at the Bellows site are particularly interesting. Pendants of porpoise teeth, real or imitation (such as that from O18), while rare, are another characteristic trait of early Eastern Polynesian sites. The *lei niho palaoa*—made of the rock oyster shell (*Chama iostoma*) rather than of whale ivory, as in later pendants of this type—is the earliest excavated pendant of this type known in Hawaiʻi, suggesting that this symbol of chiefly status had been developed soon after the islands were settled.

Bone and shellfish remains in the Bellows site were not heavily concentrated as in some other coastal dune sites, but those present suggest that the occupants were exploiting a range of marine resources, as well as nesting seabirds. Of particular note are the presence of pig, dog, and the Polynesian rat (*Rattus exulans*).

What emerges from the data recovered at the Bellows dune site is a portrait, while hazy in many details, of a small hamlet of thatched huts situated on the banks of the Waimānalo Stream. The early Polynesians who dwelt there, off and on over a period of perhaps a century and a half, supported themselves by cultivating root crops in the fertile valley inland; by raising pigs, dogs, and fowl; by fishing and shellfish gathering; and by hunting the seabirds on the nearby offshore islets. They had adapted to local conditions and had already invented certain distinctly Hawaiian artifacts, such as the two-piece fishhooks and the *lei niho palaoa*. In other respects, their technology was unlike that seen by Europeans six or seven centuries later. To judge from the material symbols interred with the young woman, they had distinct concepts of social stratification, which presumably led over time to the elaboration of the social hierarchy characteristic of later Hawaiian society.

Hālawa Dune Site (Site Mo-A1-3), Molokaʻi Island

Four great amphitheater-headed valleys breach the precipitous windward coast of Molokaʻi. Hālawa, the most easterly, is the only valley readily accessible by sea throughout the year, offering a protected bay and sandy beach suitable for canoe landings (fig. 6.17). A short distance behind the beach, on a grassy floodplain of the meandering Hālawa Stream, lies the sand dune site designated Mo-A1-3 in Bishop Museum system, also known as the

FIGURE 6.17 View of Hālawa Bay, Molokaʻi Island; the dune site (Mo-A1-3) is situated on the sand spit jutting into the bay, just inland of the boulder rampart. *(Photo by P. V. Kirch)*

Hālawa dune site. The 1946 tsunami, which so heavily damaged parts of all the main islands, swept far into Hālawa Valley, eroding away a large part of the dune site and leaving only two small mounds standing on the floodplain. During a visit to the valley in 1964, Kirch observed cultural material eroding out of the edge of the smaller Mound A, and excavated a test pit. In 1969–1970 Kirch directed a more extensive excavation in the larger Mound B. An area of 55 m² was opened up, although not all of this was taken down to the sterile base (Kirch 1971b; Kirch and Kelly, eds., 1975). As at site O18, the excavation proceeded by following the natural stratigraphy. In 2020, Kirch and Swift excavated a 1 × 2 m test pit in Mound A, which is now endangered by active erosion from Hālawa Stream and from periodic "king tides." The renewed excavations provided an opportunity for more precise and accurate dating of the Mound A cultural deposits.

Hālawa Valley was an ideal locus for establishing a permanent settlement. The wide floodplain and gentle colluvial slopes offer fertile agricultural soils, rainfall is adequate (ca. 500 mm annually at the beach, and increasing steadily inland), and the large stream flows year-round. The marine resources of Hālawa Bay are not as abundant as along the island's southern coast, since the freshwater outflow of Hālawa Stream inhibits coral growth. Nevertheless, the rocky headlands on both sides of the valley are noted among local fishermen for parrotfish, wrasses, and jacks, while the shoreline supports shellfish such as *ʻopihi* (*Cellana* spp.) and *pipipi* (*Nerita* spp.). Shellfish remains excavated from the dune site indicate that when humans first colonized the valley the stream mouth was a habitat for the prized *hīhīwai* (*Theodoxus cariosus*) shellfish, though none are present today.

The site's stratigraphy is relatively simple, with a base of sterile, calcareous dune sand, capped by a thin flood deposit (ca. 12 cm thick) of yellowish alluvial clay underlying the cultural layer. It was upon this alluvium that the first settlers constructed their houses; post molds from the lower cultural deposit penetrated the clay in various places. The cultural deposit in Mound B averaged about 60 cm thick and consisted of dark gray, sandy, midden soil with relatively high concentrations of fish and animal bone, shellfish, charcoal, and artifacts. During the excavation of Mound B, the cultural deposit was divided into upper and lower sectors, with a thin, discontinuous sand lens marking the division between them. It is possible that this sand lens indicates a discontinuity, or period when the deposit was not accumulating (or may even have eroded somewhat). A thin layer of sterile dune sand capped this precontact cultural layer; overlying this was a thin historic-period midden, associated with a frame house that stood on the site prior to the 1946 tsunami.

As with other sites excavated prior to more recent advances in radiocarbon dating, the age of the cultural deposit in the Hālawa dune site has proved to be contentious. An initial set of dates obtained by Kirch (1975a, table 20) led to the interpretation of initial settlement in the valley at around AD 650. This depended primarily on one early date (GaK-2743, 1421 ± 90 BP), which in retrospect likely consisted of old wood with some inbuilt age, perhaps driftwood, which we now must reject as too early.

Kirch and Mark McCoy (2007) dated six additional samples collected during the 1969–1970 excavation; unfortunately, the provenience of these samples could only be designated as from either the lower or upper sectors. More recently, a series of high-precision AMS dates on both *Aleurities* nut shell and on *Cellana* mollusks from a new excavation in the

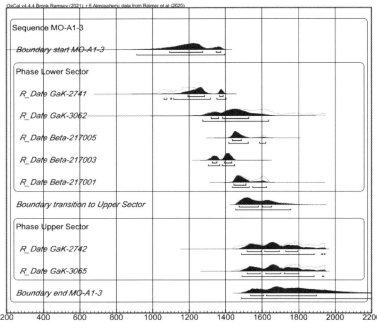

FIGURE 6.18 Bayesian calibration of radiocarbon dates from the Hālawa dune site (Mo-A1-3), Moloka'i Island. *(Oxcal plot by P. V. Kirch)*

smaller Mound A at the dune site indicates that the deposit there began to accumulate by cal AD 1456–1519, the beginning of the Expansion Period. However, the base of Mound B may predate that of Mound A. A Bayesian calibration integrating what we regard as the most reliable of the original and more recent AMS dates from Mound B is shown in figure 6.18. This suggests that the lower sector may span the Late Voyaging to Expansion Periods, while the upper sector is likely to date to the end of the Expansion and into the Archaic States Period. Renewed excavations at the Hālawa dune site will help to resolve the chronology of this important site.

The cultural deposit contained structural remains indicative of permanent settlement. The earliest structures were evidenced by post molds, but, unfortunately, we were not able to expose enough area of this early horizon to determine the form of the structures. Near the top of the lower sector, however, the excavation exposed a series of house outlines, of a type uncommon in Hawai'i. Two of these structures had stone alignments marking their edges (fig. 6.19), while the others were indicated by post molds (fig. 6.20). These were small huts (about 5 m long and 2 m wide) with rounded ends and with stone-slab-lined hearths in the interior. A conjectural reconstruction of one of these houses is shown in figure 6.21. Although such houses were unknown in Hawai'i at the time of European contact, they are known from other parts of central Eastern Polynesia, such as the Tuamotus and Easter Island.

FIGURE 6.19 Round-ended house foundation of waterworn beach cobbles exposed during the excavation of Mound B at the Hālawa dune site (Mo-A1-3), Moloka'i Island, in 1970. *(Photo by P. V. Kirch)*

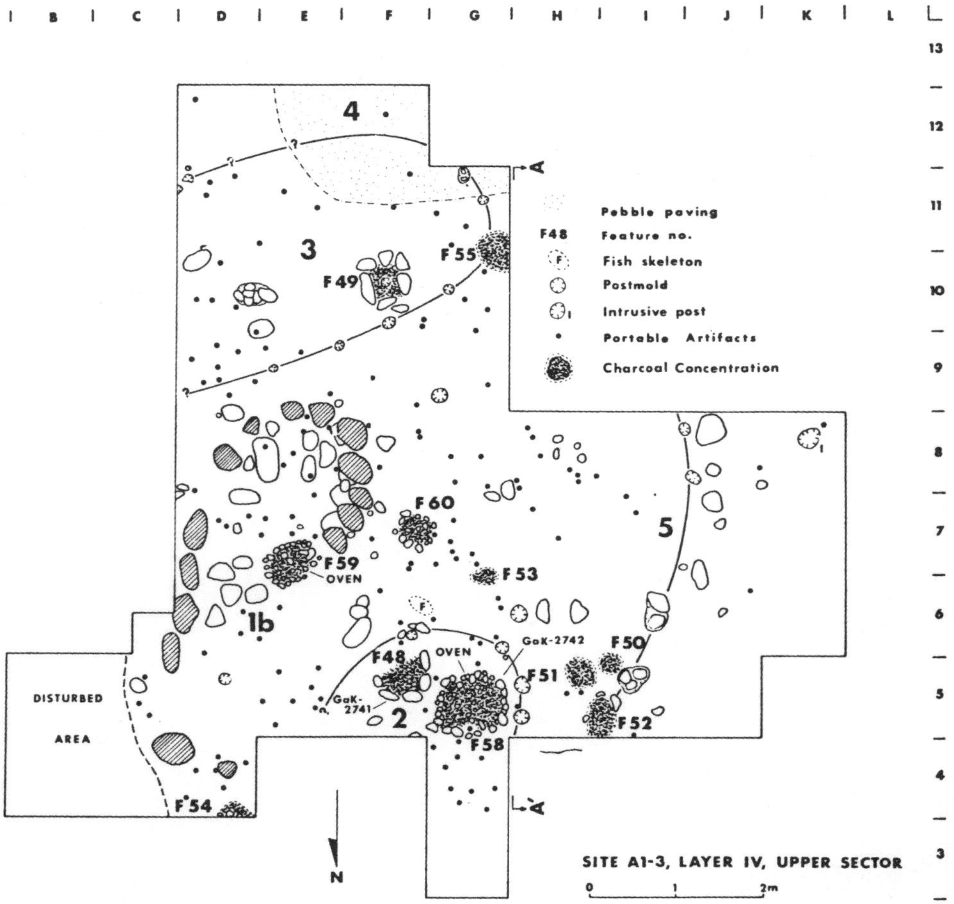

FIGURE 6.20 Plan of the upper sector in Mound B of the Hālawa dune site (Mo-A1-3), Molokaʻi Island, showing the round-ended house foundation of waterworn cobbles, and other traces of round-ended houses indicated by post-mold patterns. *(Plan by P. V. Kirch)*

FIGURE 6.21 Conjectural reconstruction of a round-ended house at the Hālawa dune site (Mo-A1-3), Molokaʻi Island. *(Drawing by P. V. Kirch)*

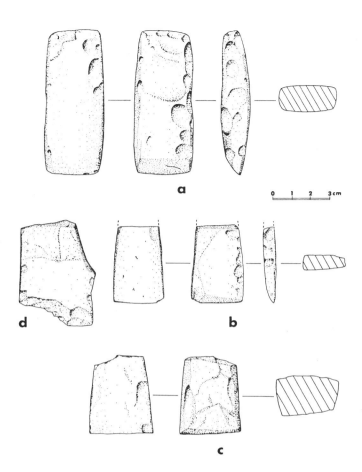

FIGURE 6.22 Basalt adzes from the Hālawa dune site (Mo-A1-3), Molokaʻi Island. The well-polished, untanged adze *a* is similar to adzes from remote Nihoa and Mokumanamana Islands. *(Drawing by P. V. Kirch)*

Portable artifacts recovered from the excavations included adzes and flaked stone (basalt and volcanic glass), fishing gear, manufacturing tools, and ornaments. A well-polished basalt adze (fig. 6.22), quadrangular and untanged, especially well ground and polished overall, came from the base of the cultural deposit. This adze is nearly identical to adzes from the remote islands of Nihoa and Mokumanamana (see chapter 19). The fishhooks are mostly of bone and include many examples of the same early style of two-piece hook found at the Bellows site (O18) on Oʻahu. The few one-piece hooks include two examples with the double-notched head-lashing device. A pearl-shell trolling lure and a netting shuttle of bone, as well as a small line sinker, are also among the fishing gear. Other artifacts from the site include a small *Conus*-shell adze, abraders of coral and sea urchin spines, whetstones, hammerstones, bone awls, dog-tooth ornaments, and gaming stones (*ʻulu maika*). A technological and geochemical analysis of 1,593 basalt flakes from the site by Mills et al. (2018) showed that while eight different geological sources are represented, most of the material derived from East Molokaʻi basalt. Although major adze quarries are known on West Molokaʻi, stone from these sources is present in Hālawa in only minor quantities. In 2020, the discovery of a major adze quarry site in a small valley to the south of Hālawa, Honokoʻi Bay, revealed the likely source of most of the flaked basalt in the Mo-A1-3 site.

The occupants of the Hālawa dune site raised pigs and dogs; the commensal rat was ubiquitous in the small thatched huts. The presence of the domestic dogs and pigs, as well as the permanent nature of the site, suggest that these early settlers were agriculturalists. This interpretation was bolstered by geomorphological investigations at an erosional fan not far from the dune (site Mo-A1-4), where charcoal and land snail shells in deposits derived from eroded hillslopes indicated agricultural clearance (Kirch and Kelly 1975, 54). Recent AMS dating of snails in these deposits indicates that such forest clearance began as early as cal AD 1217–1265 (UCIAMS-233658*, 2σ). The relative frequencies of pig and dog bones in the prehistoric cultural layer at the dune site increased gradually over time, presumably correlating with the intensification of the valley's agricultural production system.

The Hālawa dune site inhabitants also harvested the rocky shore zone and deep bay, and the site contained abundant shellfish remains and fish-bones. Most important among the various shellfish species is *'opihi,* accounting for as much as 50 percent of the total shell weight in the cultural deposit. Among the identified fish bones are parrotfish, groupers, wrasses, sharks, surgeonfish, triggerfish, snappers, and spiny puffers.

The three sand dunes and three rockshelters described in this chapter were all excavated in the first two decades of modern archaeology in Hawai'i, following Emory's realization in 1950 that excavation could open a window on the ancient Hawaiian past. Unlike contemporary excavations, these opened up large areas, sometimes exposing entire house features. In hindsight, the excavation methods were in some cases less than satisfactory, especially the use of arbitrary levels rather than stratigraphic excavation, and the use of coarse ¼-inch mesh for screening. The dating of many of these sites proved contentious, but redating and Bayesian modeling have allowed them to be chronologically repositioned into the revised Hawaiian cultural sequence. Most importantly, the rich artifact and faunal-floral legacy collections from these excavations—for all but one site curated in Bishop Museum—have continued to provide new insights into aspects of ancient Hawaiian life. Indeed, the very fact that these sites were stratified, and that in many cases those strata spanned long periods of the Hawaiian past, makes them especially valuable for the study of cultural change.

7

THE WET AND THE DRY
Hawaiian Agriculture, Aquaculture, and the Staple Economy

Hawaiians were first and foremost cultivators of the land. Their ancestors—voyaging thousands of kilometers across ocean voids—stocked double-hulled canoes with a precious cargo of taro, yams, bananas, sugarcane, and other plants of industrial, ornamental, and medicinal value. Nurturing these plantings in the new landfall, the first Hawaiian colonizers reproduced the basis of their subsistence economy. Over ensuing centuries, as populations grew and settlements expanded over the archipelago's lowlands and into the deeper valleys, farmers adapted their agricultural methods to suit these new landscapes. By the time of European contact, Hawaiian farmers had achieved a level of agricultural production virtually unrivalled elsewhere in Oceania. Much of this was achieved with technology no more complex than the simple wooden digging stick, the 'ō'ō. Captain James Cook understated the case: "What we saw of their agriculture," he remarked, "furnishes sufficient proofs that they are not novices in that art" (in Handy and Handy 1972, 406). Nor did Cook's fellow officer Lieutenant James King hide his own admiration for the Hawaiian cultivator: "The inhabitants far surpass all the neighboring islanders in the management of their plantations. In the low grounds, adjoining to the bay where we lay at anchor [Waimea, Kaua'i], these plantations were divided by deep and regular ditches; the fences were made with a neatness approaching to elegance, and the roads through them were thrown up and finished, in a manner that would have done credit to any European engineer" (406).

A few years later, Nathaniel Portlock expressed similar enthusiasm for the taro cultivations at Waimea, Kaua'i:

> This excursion gave me a fresh opportunity of admiring the amazing ingenuity and industry of the natives in laying out their taro and sugar-cane grounds; the greatest part of which are made upon the banks of the river, with exceeding good causeways made with stone and earth, leading up the valleys to each plantation; the taro-beds are in general a quarter of a mile over, dammed in, and they have a place in one part of the bank, that serves as a gateway [for water]. (Portlock 1789, 191–192)

Hawaiian horticultural skills were not restricted to taro irrigation. Vast stretches of the leeward slopes of Hawai'i Island were laid out in gridiron field systems, with sweet potato and dry taro fields bordered with rows of sugarcane, or of the *kī* plant. John Ledyard of Captain Cook's 1779 expedition described this scene in the uplands above Kealakekua Bay:

> About two miles without the town [the settlement at Kealakekua Bay] the land was level, and continued of one plain of little enclosures separated from each other by low broad walls. . . . Some of these fields were planted, and others by their appearance were left fallow: In some we saw the natives collecting the coarse grass that had grown upon it during the time it had lain unimproved, and burning it in detached heaps. Their sweet potatoes are mostly raised here, and indeed are the principle [*sic*] object of their agriculture, but it requires an infinite deal of toil on account of the quantity of lava that remains on the land notwithstanding what is used about the walls to come at the soil. . . . We saw a few patches of sugar cane interspersed in moist places, which were but small: But the cane was the largest and as sweet as any we had ever seen, we also passed several groups of plantain-trees. (Ledyard 1963, 118–119)

The early Polynesian settlers to Hawai'i brought with them a suite of tropical plants, largely of Southeast Asian and Melanesian origin (see chapter 4); the exceptions were the sweet potato and the bottle gourd, which originated in South America. These "canoe plants" (Whistler 2009) are listed in table 7.1. The dominant staples were taro (*Colocasia esculenta*), a water-loving root crop that thrives under irrigation, and sweet potato (*Ipomoea batatas*), more tolerant of dry conditions and capable of producing high yields even in marginal lands. Also important were many varieties of banana (*Musa* hybrids), breadfruit (*Artocarpus altilis*), sugarcane (*Saccharum officinarum*), yams (*Dioscorea alata, D. pentaphylla, D. bulbifera*), and coconut (*Cocos nucifera*). Other plants extensively cultivated were the paper mulberry (*Broussonetia papyrifera*) to manufacture barkcloth (*kapa*), 'awa (*Piper methysticum*) as a narcotic, bottle gourds (*Lagenaria siceraria*) for containers and musical instruments, *hala* or screwpine (*Pandanus* sp.) for mats, and other useful and medicinal plants.

Hawaiian farmers possessed sophisticated knowledge of their plants; many hundreds of varieties of taro and sweet potato were named and recognized (Handy 1940). The traditional system of agriculture was part of an intricate web of social, religious, and political relationships that tied the farmers to the land, to their chiefs, and to their gods. The deities of agriculture were Kāne, god of flowing waters and thus also of irrigation, to whom taro was sacred; and, Lono, deity of rain, thunder, and the dryland gardens where sweet potato thrived. Lono reigned over the annual Makahiki period of four lunar months' duration.

Agricultural development in Hawai'i, as elsewhere in Polynesia, involved three distinct processes. The first was the *adaptation* of crops and cultivation practices to local conditions. Lying marginally within the humid tropics, Hawai'i was not as conducive to the cultivation of certain crops as the central Eastern Polynesian homeland; the islands'

TABLE 7.1. Polynesian plant introductions to the Hawaiian Islands

HAWAIIAN NAME	ENGLISH NAME	SCIENTIFIC NAME	COMMENTS
ʻape	Elephant ear taro	*Alocasia macrorrhiza*	Pig fodder, famine food
ʻawa	Kava	*Piper methysticum*	Psychoactive drink, used ritually
hoi	Bitter yam	*Dioscorea bulbifera*	Famine food
ipu	Bottle gourd	*Lagenaria siceraria*	Used for containers, rattle; South American origin
kalo	Taro	*Colocasia esculenta*	Staple starch; leaves eaten also
kamani	Alexandrian laurel	*Calophyllum inophyllum*	Hardwood tree, used for carving
kī	Ti	*Cordyline fruticosa*	Starchy root, leaves used in various ways
kō	Sugarcane	*Saccharum officinarum*	Stalk chewed; planted as windbreak in dryland field systems
kukui	Candlenut	*Aleurites moluccana*	Tree with oily seed
maiʻa	Banana	*Musa* hybrids	Fruit eaten raw or in some varieties cooked
niu	Coconut	*Cocos nucifera*	Nut eaten, leaves used for mats
noni	Indian mulberry	*Morinda citrifolia*	Fruit used medicinally
ʻohe	Bamboo	*Schizostachyum glaucifolium*	Used for fishing poles
ʻōhiʻa ʻai	Mountain apple	*Syzygium malaccense*	Edible fruit
ʻolena	Turmeric	*Curcuma longa*	Reddish pigment extracted from tuber, ritually important
pia	Polynesian arrowroot	*Tacca leontopetaloides*	Starchy tuber
ʻuala	Sweet potato	*Ipomoea batatas*	Major starch staple in dryland areas; South American origin
uhi	Greater yam	*Dioscorea alata*	Dryland starch crop
ʻulu	Breadfruit	*Artocarpus altilis*	Large tree with starchy fruit; wood provides useful timber
wauke	Paper mulberry	*Broussonetia papyrifera*	Used for barkcloth

variegated landscapes required many kinds of local adaptation in planting practices. The second process was *expansion,* the pioneering process of transforming a natural landscape into a managed agroecosystem. As populations grew and agricultural fields were expanded, lowland forests were cleared, slopes were terraced, and field plots laid out. Third was the process of *intensification,* in which technological innovations and greater labor inputs were applied to an agricultural system in order to achieve increased yields (Brookfield 1972, 1984). Intensification ranges from the construction of permanent infrastructure, such as irrigation canals and terraces (referred to as *landesque capital* intensification), to the application of labor-intensive practices, such as the use of green manure and mulch. Hawaiian agriculture at the time of European contact was highly intensive; how it developed to this end point has been of particular interest to archaeologists.

The Archaeology of Ancient Agriculture

In the 1930s, Edward S. C. Handy studied Hawaiian agriculture and its cultural matrix, traveling throughout the islands to interview traditional planters in the outlying districts (Handy 1940; Handy and Handy 1972). While valuable, Handy's research came after several generations of wrenching changes in Hawaiian society and economy, too late to record the full range of ancient agricultural practices. The intensive dryland field systems, for example, were already long abandoned by Handy's time. Fortunately, the insights provided by archaeology now give us a more comprehensive picture of Hawaiian production systems prior to European contact.

Early archaeologists, including Wendell Bennett (1931) on Kaua'i and J. Gilbert McAllister (1933a) on O'ahu, made note of stone-walled remains of ancient irrigation systems, but not until the 1960s did archaeologists begin to address how and why Hawaiian agriculture developed its uniquely intensive configurations. Richard Pearson in 1962 made a fledgling attempt to investigate "the extent of precontact cultivation and its location" in the Hanapēpē Valley on Kaua'i (1962, 379).

With the advent of a settlement-pattern approach in the late 1960s (see chapter 1) came a new interest in agricultural features. T. Stell Newman, an airline pilot and archaeology student, observed from his cockpit window the traces of a hitherto unrecorded field system covering the upland slopes of Kohala on Hawai'i, then turned to aerial photographs to map these features in the *ahupua'a* of Lapakahi (Newman, n.d.). Paul Rosendahl (1972a, 1994) mapped the Lapakahi fields in greater detail on the ground using traditional surveying methods, and excavated in field shelters within the upland field complex. In Hālawa Valley, Moloka'i, Tom Riley (1973, 1975) studied the extensive remains of taro pondfields for his doctoral research at the University of Hawai'i.

Douglas Yen tackled the archaeological study of ancient agricultural systems in Hawai'i in 1970 as a part of the Mākaha Valley Historical Project (Yen et al. 1972). Through excavation, Yen's team determined stages of wall construction and rebuilding and, for the first time in Polynesia, radiocarbon dated charcoal contained in buried cultivation soils.

Studies of ancient Hawaiian agriculture soon proliferated, with Timothy Earle's mapping of irrigation works in the Halele'a District of Kaua'i (1978), David and Myra Tuggles' study of the Kohala valleys on Hawai'i (Tuggle and Tomonari-Tuggle 1980), and Patrick Kirch and Matthew Spriggs' investigations of taro irrigation in the Anahulu Valley on O'ahu (Kirch 1979b; Kirch and Sahlins 1992; Spriggs and Kirch 1992). Cultural resource management projects throughout the islands contributed studies of both irrigation and dryland field systems (e.g., Jane Allen 1991, 1992; Athens 1983a; J. T. Clark 1981; Clark and Kirch, eds., 1983; Hommon and Barrera 1971; Schilt 1984). In the mid-1990s, archaeologists from the University of Auckland and the University of Hawai'i recommenced investigations of dryland field systems in leeward Kohala, Hawai'i, building upon the earlier Lapakahi project results (Ladefoged, Graves, and Jennings 1996; Ladefoged, Graves, and McCoy 2003; Ladefoged and Graves 2000; Ladefoged, Lee, and Graves 2008). In 2001, a consortium of archaeologists, ecologists, soil scientists, demographic modelers, and others joined forces as the Hawai'i Biocomplexity Project, launching a decade-long project on the dryland agricultural systems of leeward Hawai'i and Maui Islands (Kirch, ed., 2011; Kirch et al. 2012; Ladefoged et al. 2011; Vitousek 2004). Research on ancient agroecosystems continues to be an active part of archaeology in Hawai'i (e.g., Kurashima, Fortini, and Ticktin 2019; Lincoln 2020; Lincoln, Chadwick, and Vitousek 2014; Lincoln and Ladefoged 2014; M. D. McCoy, Asner, and Graves 2011; M. D. McCoy, Browne, et al. 2013; McCoy and Codlin 2016; Morrison et al. 2022; Quintus and Lincoln 2018; Quintus et al. 2019).

The Wet and the Dry: Contrastive Agroecosystems

Following an ancient dichotomy in oceanic agricultural systems (Barrau 1965; Kirch 1994; Yen 1973, 1991), Hawaiian agroecosystems were of distinct "wet" and "dry" types, a distinction deeply encoded in indigenous Hawaiian concepts of horticulture. Davida Malo wrote,

> In the Hawaiian Islands agriculture was conducted differently on lands where there were streams of water and on dry lands. On lands supplied with running water agriculture was easy and could be carried on at all times, and the only reason for a scarcity of food among the people on such lands was idleness. Sometimes, however, the water supply failed; but the drought did not last long.
>
> On the *kula* [dry] lands, farming was a laborious occupation and called for great patience, being attended with many drawbacks. (1951, 204).

On the older, westerly islands with their deep valleys and permanent streams, agriculture was dominated by the irrigated cultivation of taro (color plate 2). Alluvial and colluvial slopes were terraced, with sometimes extensive arrays of flooded pondfields (*lo'i*), stream water being diverted by dams into irrigation canals (*'auwai*); in some coastal areas such as southeastern Moloka'i, *lo'i* were irrigated by natural springs. The steeper slopes above the irrigation canals constituted the *kula,* or nonirrigated garden lands, devoted to mixed planting of secondary crops with dwelling sites interspersed. We refer to these as "colluvial slope" systems.

On geologically younger landscapes, especially of East Maui and most of Hawai'i, dryland or rain-fed farming systems (also known as *kula* lands) dominated the agrarian landscapes, characterized by reticulate grids of stone and/or earthen walls or bunds, demarcating individual field plots (color plate 3). Extensive dryland field systems on these two islands included the Kohala, Kona, and Ka'ū field systems on Hawai'i, and the Kaupō and Kahikinui field systems on Maui (M. S. Allen, ed., 2001; Coil 2004; Coil and Kirch 2005; Kirch, ed., 2010; Ladefoged, Graves, and Jennings 1996, 2003). Some taro was grown in higher elevation zones within these dryland fields, but sweet potato (*Ipomoea batatas*) was the most important crop, supplemented by yams (*Dioscorea* spp.).

The uneven archipelago-wide distribution of these "wet" and "dry" agroecosystems mirrors the geological age progression and biogeochemical gradients of the Hawaiian Islands (Vitousek et al. 2004; Vitousek et al. 2014). The vast zones of dryland production were confined almost entirely to Hawai'i and East Maui, with one other significant area on the Kalaupapa Peninsula of Moloka'i. Conversely, the main zones of irrigation are found on the older islands of Kaua'i through Moloka'i, with more limited areas in West Maui and Kohala on Hawai'i Island. Research by the Hawai'i Biocomplexity Project showed that "low soil fertility precluded the development of large-scale intensive dryland agricultural systems on stable upland surfaces on the older islands of the archipelago" (Vitousek et al. 2004; Vitousek et al. 2014, 1668; Kirch, ed., 2010). The intensive rain-fed dryland field systems of the younger islands targeted zones of relatively fertile soils (accompanied by adequate precipitation), where leaching had not deprived soils of rock-derived phosphorus and other plant nutrients. On the older islands, volcanic shield surfaces with adequate rainfall for cultivation typically have insufficient soil nutrients to sustain intensive agriculture. Only in valleys where erosion and streamflow tap unweathered rock and release new nutrient sources could intensive agriculture be practiced, both in irrigated pondfields and on the adjacent colluvial slopes.

Using a geographic information systems (GIS) approach, Thegn Ladefoged et al. (2009) modeled the distribution of the irrigated and intensive dryland agroecosystems across the Hawaiian archipelago, estimating the areas amenable to those two systems on each of the main islands (color plate 4). This improved on prior estimates based on ethnohistoric accounts and mid-nineteenth-century land records (Kirch 1994, fig. 101; see also Vitousek et al. 2004, fig. 1). Further GIS modeling by Kurashima, Fortini, and Ticktin (2019; Kurashima and Kirch 2011) added the colluvial slope cultivation zones to these estimates, suggesting that the colluvial slope systems accounted for about 26.5 percent of total agricultural production.

Hawai'i Island has the greatest extent of agricultural land, yet a mere 1.4 percent of this consists of prime irrigation lands (table 7.2). Thus, although Hawai'i Island supported the largest population of any of the contact-era polities, most of its production came from the dryland field systems. These required the highest ratios of labor input to yield and, at the same time, were the most vulnerable to drought. O'ahu had substantial areas in irrigated pondfields and the greatest extent of colluvial slope cultivation. The Maui kingdom (which at contact included Moloka'i and Lāna'i) enjoyed substantial areas of irrigation, due to the many permanent streams and suitable valley topography on West Maui (the Nā Wai Ehā region) and East Moloka'i. Kaua'i, the geologically oldest island, mostly lacked dryland field systems but had extensive areas of pondfield irrigation and colluvial slope cultivations.

TABLE 7.2. Estimated areas (km²) of irrigated and intensive dryland agroecosystems (after Kirch 2010, table 4.3).

ISLAND	IRRIGATED CULTIVATION	INTENSIVE DRYLAND CULTIVATION	TOTAL
Hawaiʻi	14.3	556.6	570.9
Maui	25.7	139.4	165.1
Molokaʻi	8.7	7.5	16.2
Oʻahu	83.3	34.1	117.4
Kauaʻi	57.6	0	57.6

Valley Agroecosystems

Irrigated Pondfield Systems

Small areas of irrigated taro are still cultivated in the islands today, as in Hanalei on Kauaʻi, Waiahole on Oʻahu, Keʻanae on Maui, and Waipiʻo on Hawaiʻi. These, however, are only remnants of the once more extensive complexes of *ʻauwai* and *loʻi* that formed intricate grids across the alluvial bottomlands of most Hawaiian valleys (fig. 7.1), or sets of steeply descending stone-faced terraces as in Nuʻalolo ʻĀina Valley on Kauaʻi (fig. 7.2).

FIGURE 7.1 The Hanalei Valley, in the Haleleʻa District of Kauaʻi Island, is covered in irrigated taro pondfields, many still in use today. *(Photo courtesy Bishop Museum Department of Anthropology)*

FIGURE 7.2 Stone-faced terraces, formerly irrigated, in Nuʻalolo ʻĀina Valley, Kauaʻi Island. Taro and ʻape plants, visible in the foreground, are survivals from former cultivation. *(Photo courtesy Bishop Museum Department of Anthropology)*

Forms of irrigation and water control for taro culture are practiced throughout many parts of Polynesia and Melanesia (Barrau 1965; Yen 1973). There is little evidence, however, that pondfield terracing is an ancient practice in Oceania. Unlike the case with dryland gardening, no Proto-Oceanic vocabulary for irrigation technology can be linguistically reconstructed (Kirch and Lepofsky 1993). The Hawaiian term for an irrigated pondfield, *loʻi*, is, however, cognate with the word *roki* in the southeastern Polynesian language of Rapa Island, suggesting that we may reconstruct a Proto–Eastern Polynesian term for pondfield, **roki* or **loki*.

Water, *wai*, was essential to taro irrigation: ample, endlessly flowing water. The Hawaiian word for "wealth" is *waiwai*, water reduplicated; the word for "law" is *kanawai*, or that pertaining to water. From an agronomic perspective, the importance of water in irrigation was that "irrigation waters brought nutrients from rocks to the windward crops"

(Palmer et al. 2009, 1444). Nutrients in taro pondfields were supplied not only by the colluvial and alluvial soils but also by this continual transport of dissolved nutrients in the live-giving *wai*.

Irrigation systems ranged from small sets of as few as 10 fields situated on streamside terraces in the deeper valley interiors, up to large valley-bottom complexes with hundreds of pondfields. System 22 at Wai'oli, Hanalei, on Kaua'i Island is one of the largest irrigation complexes known, extending over nearly 54 hectares (Earle 1978, 67–69). Most valley-bottom systems covered between 5 and 18 hectares. The longest known *'auwai,* in Halele'a District on Kaua'i, spanned 3.7 km from stream intake to outlet; the shortest canals were a mere 10 to 20 m long. Pondfield terraces were usually constructed with retaining walls of carefully stacked stone cobbles (fig. 7.3).

In spite of being among the largest irrigation systems recorded anywhere in Polynesia, Hawaiian taro systems did not require elaborate management; most could have been constructed and maintained by small social groups (Earle 1978, 1980). Some coordination of labor in the tending of shared canals, and especially in the repair of dams after flooding, was necessary and was managed by the resident *konohiki,* representing the *ahupua'a* chief. Once constructed, irrigation systems produced high yields in relation to labor invested. This advantage was not lost on the Hawaiian chiefs, who seized every opportunity to expand the irrigation systems under their control, rewarding loyal supporters with grants of prime irrigation land.

Representative irrigation systems that have been mapped by archaeologists are illustrated in figures 7.4 through 7.6. The lower alluvial floodplains of Hālawa Valley, Moloka'i,

FIGURE 7.3 The carefully constructed façade of a pondfield terrace in Hālawa Valley, Moloka'i Island. *(Photo by Therese Babineau)*

shown in figure 7.4, has two large irrigation complexes, one on each side of the stream. Each of these extensive complexes was fed by two canals and was cultivated by as many as thirty households, with sections controlled directly by the *konohiki* and cultivated by the commoners on specified days (pondfields supplying taro to the *konohiki* and *ali'i* were called *kō'ele* fields). A smaller irrigation system, situated in the middle of the Anahulu Valley on O'ahu and shown in figure 7.5, was about one-ninth the size of either of the Hālawa Valley complexes, with fields watered by a single canal that split into two branches near the uppermost fields, feeding water to sets of fields worked by three households. A very small irrigation system, at Hipuapua in the interior of Hālawa Valley, Moloka'i (fig. 7.6), was cultivated by a single household.

Boulder-and-cobble dams diverted irrigation water into stone-lined canals. In some areas, however, as at Waialua on O'ahu, or along the southeastern coast of Moloka'i, pondfields were watered by natural springs upwelling along the coastal plain. In other areas, as in the upper Mākaha Valley on O'ahu, streamflow was supplemented by cutting trenches into the hillslope just above the terraces, tapping into the shallow water table (Yen et al. 1972).

Hawaiian irrigation systems can be classified based on topographic setting and the nature of the canal layout, as shown in figure 7.7 (Kirch 1977; Riley 1975). Type I systems consist of simple, stone-faced "barrage" terraces constructed across a narrow stream channel, lacking a canal. These systems, found along the sides of Hālawa Valley on Moloka'i, for example, would have been simple to construct but also susceptible to damage from flooding. Type II systems, typical of inland valley areas, are made up of small sets of fields watered by a single canal that feeds directly into the uppermost field. Water then flows from field to field through small gateways in the embankments. In Type III (the Anahulu system, illustrated in figure 7.5, is an example), the irrigation canal runs along the periphery of the field complex, allowing greater control of water distribution and allocation. The most complex systems, Type IV (illustrated by the Hālawa examples, figure 7.4), have two irrigation canals, with the lower canal acting as both a drainage and an irrigation device.

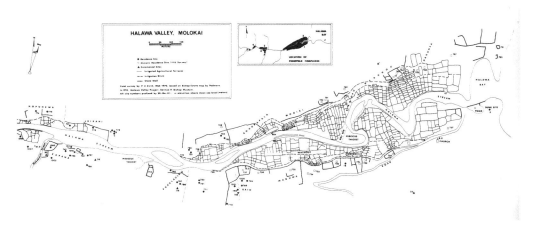

FIGURE 7.4 Map of the lower portion of Hālawa Valley, Moloka'i Island, showing the extensive grid of taro pondfields, irrigated by twin 'auwai on each side of the river. *(After Kirch and Kelly, eds., 1975)*

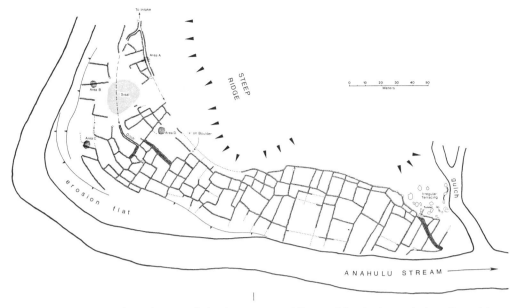

FIGURE 7.5 Map of a medium-sized taro irrigation system at ʻIli Kapuahilua in the Anahulu Valley, Oʻahu Island. *(Map by P. V. Kirch)*

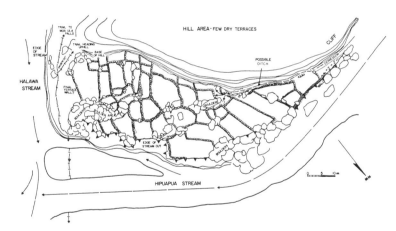

FIGURE 7.6 Map of a small system of taro pondfields in the interior of Hālawa Valley, Molokaʻi Island. *(After Kirch and Kelly, eds., 1975)*

As Malo (1951) pointed out, during periods of drought the flow of even permanent streams declined such that there was insufficient water for all of the fields in a system, necessitating some rotation of watering. At these times water distribution was controlled by the *konohiki* or the *luna wai* (water master), as described by Emma Nakuina (1894). In the Anahulu Valley, Spriggs and Kirch (1992) mapped irrigation systems whose multiple landholders are known from the records of the Māhele (1848–1854). They found that the "hydraulic infrastructure" of canal layout correlated closely with the social relationships of the landholders. In several systems there is a consistent pattern in that landholder A, "who effectively controls the water supply, is usually related to C in some way, with B usually unrelated. A can therefore assure C a water supply independent of field-to-field flow from B" (Spriggs and Kirch 1992, 155).

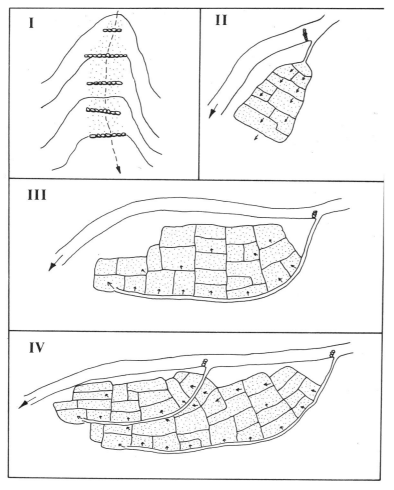

FIGURE 7.7 Diagrammatic sketch of four types of irrigated pondfield systems. *(After Kirch 1977)*

The windward Koʻolaupoko District represents the core region of prime irrigation lands on Oʻahu. Perennial streams flowing down the amphitheater valleys of Waiāhole, Kaʻalaea, Waiheʻe, Heʻeia, and Kāneʻohe, and extending southeast to Kailua and Maunawili, supported thousands of irrigated *loʻi* at the time of European contact (Handy and Handy 1972, 452–460). Jane Allen's (ed., 1987; Allen et al. 2002) study of irrigation systems at Luluku site Oa-G5-85 revealed a complex sequence of pondfield construction, well dated by radiocarbon samples; in Maunawili Valley a number of pondfield complexes were also excavated and dated (Jane Allen et al. 2002, fig. 227). The Luluku dates reveal that irrigation in the interior of Kāneʻohe Valley started by AD 1250; most of the dates for the G5-85 complex "fall between AD 1250 and 1425" (Jane Allen, ed., 1987, 230). Continued rebuilding of the Luluku terraces is reflected in five or possibly six stratified pondfield layers dating later than AD 1400 (249). From the Luluku evidence, Allen argues that "increased political control and integration within a socioeconomic system involving an area larger than the local valley are strongly suggested by the evidence for well-coordinated construction of large numbers of terraces, effective control over landslides and floods, cooperation in terms of water rights and maintenance of patent [sic] irrigation ditches, and cultivation of taro in

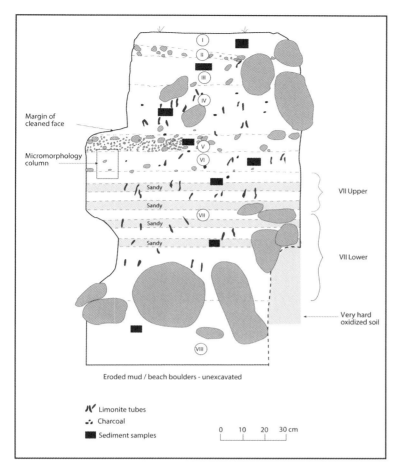

FIGURE 7.8 Stratigraphic section through a pondfield terrace at the mouth of Waikolu Valley, Molokaʻi Island, showing multiple phases of sediment accumulation and pondfield cultivation. *(After Kirch, ed., 2004)*

quantities large enough to suggest production for a consumer group larger than the local population" (250–251).

In Maunawili Valley, pondfield cultivation commenced by AD 1200 (J. Allen et al. 2002, 608). The irrigation works were significantly expanded between AD 1400 and 1650; Kūkapoki Heiau, an important temple, was also built at this time. The Luluku and Maunawili irrigation systems are "impressive in their own right as hydraulic and architectural—perhaps even monumental—features" (Jane Allen 1991, 122). The Luluku and Maunawili sequences confirm the onset of irrigation system construction on windward Oʻahu by AD 1200–1300, with intensification following in the fifteenth and sixteenth centuries. According to Hawaiian traditions, the Oʻahu *aliʻi nui* Māʻilikūkahi, who reigned toward the end of the fifteenth century, is credited with developing the agricultural productivity of Oʻahu (Kamakau 1991, 55).

The four large amphitheater-headed valleys of eastern Molokaʻi (from west to east, Waikolu, Pelekunu, Wailau, and Hālawa) constituted a major region of taro irrigation (Handy 1940, 101–103). Riley (1975) reported stratigraphic evidence from the Hālawa Valley (not radiocarbon dated) for early side-stream irrigation and later expansion of the main-stream watered pondfields. In Waikolu Valley, a stratigraphic section through ancient pondfield deposits at the valley mouth revealed multiple phases of cultivation, flooding, and rebuilding (fig. 7.8). The initial phase of irrigation at the Waikolu Valley mouth was dated to AD 1240–1280 (Kirch, ed., 2002, 46). More extensive evidence comes from Wailau Valley, where Windy McElroy (2007, 2012) mapped, excavated, and dated 19 of the valley's irrigation complexes. With 18 radiocarbon dates from nine complexes, McElroy's data show that the Wailau irrigation works were under construction by AD 1200–1300 (2007, table 6.2). McElroy (145, figure 6.8) divides these dates into three temporal units. The oldest, from about AD 1200–1400, included terrace sets with the best land and water supply, "capable of producing high crop yields" (247). Later intensification efforts (after AD 1400) targeted less desirable tracts of land. As McElroy writes, "Farmers first took advantage of any area capable of supporting a high producing *lo'i* system, regardless of risks of flooding or the amount of effort needed to construct a system or transport products to the coast. After these large, high-yielding complexes were established, smaller *lo'i* systems were built, until every cultivable tract of land was under production" (248–249).

In the narrow Hālawa Gulch of windward North Kohala, Hawai'i, M. D. McCoy, Browne, et al. (2013; see also M. D. McCoy and Graves 2010) excavated across a pondfield embankment, revealing a deep sequence of wall rebuilding and stratified layers of pondfield cultivation (fig. 7.9). The earliest construction phase was associated with a radiocarbon date on breadfruit charcoal of 690 ± 35 BP (OS-72163*), calibrated to AD 1260–1400 (2σ) (NOAMS-0809-26; McCoy, Graves, and Murakami 2010). The pondfields in Hālawa Gulch were repeatedly rebuilt over the centuries as flood events periodically deposited new alluvium, raising the level of the valley floor.

In sum, pondfield irrigation on windward O'ahu and Moloka'i was established by the end of the Foundation Period, and was present in North Kohala on Hawai'i by the early Late Voyaging Period. The chronology for irrigation on Kaua'i needs to be determined but was probably also established early. Irrigation systems were seemingly well developed across all the islands in suitable zones by AD 1400. By the fifteenth to sixteenth centuries, major irrigation complexes covered the valley floors and colluvial slopes of windward valleys on both O'ahu and Moloka'i, and, one presumes, on Kaua'i, West Maui, and the Kohala valleys of Hawai'i as well.

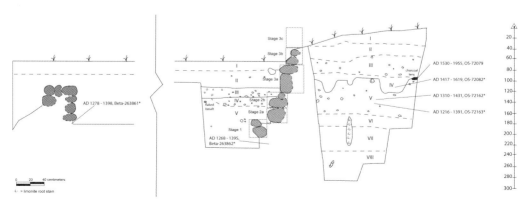

FIGURE 7.9 Stratigraphic section through two adjacent pondfields in Hālawa Valley, in Kohala District of Hawai'i Island. The stone retaining wall between the fields was constructed in several stages, with the earliest phase dating to the thirteenth century and the last phase to the historic period. *(Drawing by M. D. McCoy)*

COLLUVIAL SLOPE CULTIVATION

While taro irrigation on alluvial flats and stream terraces was the most intensive form of cultivation in Hawaiian valleys, a greater proportion of valley land was farmed without the aid of irrigation on valley slopes of up to 30 degrees. Geomorphologically, these colluvial slopes consist of unconsolidated sediments derived from mass wasting of the higher cliffs, from landslides, and from debris flows; clay sediments containing angular gravel are typically interspersed between larger cobbles and boulders. Cline (1955) classified colluvial slope soils as being of the Kawaihapai soil family, well supplied with bases and abundant calcium and potassium, or of the Hanalei family with greater amounts of nitrogen (Kirch 1977, 250). Peter Vitousek et al. (2010), in a study of soil fertility in Pololū (Hawai‘i) and Hālawa (Moloka‘i) valleys, quantified the high fertility of colluvial slopes. In Hālawa, the *base saturation,* a general indicator of nutrients in soils available to plants, of colluvial slopes (61%) is higher than that of the irrigated alluvial land (43%) (2010, table 1). This high soil fertility is due to the continual contribution of mass wasting, in which fresh rock is added to the slope soils (Palmer et al. 2009; Porder et al. 2005).

Kirch (1977) first drew attention to the importance of cultivation on valley colluvial slopes, citing archaeological studies of Hālawa, Moloka‘i, and Mākaha, O‘ahu. He noted that archaeological signs of former cultivation included often ubiquitous stone mounds and dryland terracing, augmented by ethnobotanical evidence of "cultigen survivals," ranging from tree crops such as breadfruit and coconut to feral survivals of taro, *kī,* yams, bananas, and others (1977, table 5). Kurashima and Kirch more formally defined colluvial slope cultivation as a "rain-fed, integrated cropping system that was developed on the fertile lower slopes of the larger valleys," noting that these systems had been "largely overlooked in recent discussions of pre-contact Hawaiian agriculture" (2011, 3664). GIS modeling of colluvial slope cultivation on Moloka‘i Island showed that the area in slope cultivation (1,386 ha) greatly exceeded that in irrigated pondfields (762 ha). On Moloka‘i, colluvial slope cultivation may have been responsible for as much as 37 percent of the island's total agricultural production (Kurashima and Kirch 2011, table 2). Unlike pondfield irrigation, which concentrated on the monocropping of taro (albeit with some secondary crops such as sugarcane or bananas grown on the intervening embankments between *lo‘i* fields), colluvial slope gardens contained a broad mix of crops, including food plants such as dryland taro, yams, sweet potato, bananas, arrowroot, and *kī,* but also paper mulberry for *kapa* and *olonā* for cordage, and ritually important *‘awa.*

The *‘ili* of Kapana in Hālawa Valley, Moloka‘i provides an example of a colluvial slope system in a wet valley setting (Kirch and Kelly 1975). This area of Kawaihapai soils is bisected by Maka‘ele‘ele Stream, a tributary that provided water to a small Type II pondfield system. Most of the colluvial slope land in Kapana was not irrigated but exhibits descending tiers of artificially leveled terraces, defined on the downslope side by low stone facings (ca. 30–50 cm high). These nonirrigated terraces probably served multiple functions, including retarding of soil erosion, water retention after heavy rains, and soil catchment behind the terrace facings. The regular spacing of the terraces suggests that they may have served as individual garden plot boundaries. Habitation and ritual sites (*heiau ho‘oulu‘ai*) are interspersed among these horticultural features.

A second example of modifications for colluvial slope cultivation, in a much drier landscape, is found in "Archaeological Zone 1" in the lower Mākaha Valley, Oʻahu, intensively mapped by Hommon (1969a, 1970b; see also Takayama and Green 1970). A mapped portion of this dryland agricultural zone covering about 1.4 ha included 145 mounds, 14 clearings, six stone enclosures, nine small habitation sites, and several low stone "field borders" (Kirch 1977, 267, fig. 7). Given the lower rainfall in this area (600–900 mm annually), the main crops were probably sweet potatoes and yams.

In a recent study, Alex Morrison et al. (2022) report on archaeological mapping and excavation of colluvial slope agricultural features in the Punaluʻu Valley of Oʻahu. Expansion of the agricultural infrastructure, such as stone walls delineating fields, occurred through the sixteenth and eighteenth centuries. Agricultural *heiau* and associated features integrated into the colluvial slope landscape were built as early as the seventeenth century and later.

Modeling traditional agricultural systems across the entire archipelago, Kurashima, Fortini, and Ticktin (2019, table 1) estimated that colluvial slope systems accounted for approximately 26.5 percent of the total population carrying capacity. The distribution by island, however, is uneven, with Oʻahu having 22,921 ha of colluvial slope land, far greater than that of any other island. Although Oʻahu is much smaller in total land area than Hawaiʻi, large areas of colluvial slope land combined with extensive pondfield systems gave Oʻahu almost as much overall production as Hawaiʻi Island.

Intensive Dryland Field Systems

Whereas taro irrigation continues to be practiced in Hawaiʻi (Handy and Handy 1972; Linnekin 1985), the nonirrigated or dryland systems were largely abandoned during the nineteenth century. Early explorers, including Cook's officers, remarked upon intensive forms of dryland field cultivation on Hawaiʻi Island, but these were mostly ignored in later discussions of Hawaiian agriculture. A major contribution of Hawaiian archaeology has been to bring these remarkable field systems into the story of this island civilization.

The dryland field systems are essentially *intensified* versions of a form of farming known as *shifting cultivation* (also called slash-and-burn cultivation, or swidden farming) in which gardens are rotated sequentially through forest or secondary growth. In many parts of the Pacific, the fallow rotation period for shifting cultivations may be 10 or 20 years, before the same piece of land is cleared again for a new crop (Kirch 1994). As the population on an island with limited land increases, however, the length of fallow time may be reduced to only a few years, leaving only grasses or herbs to regenerate for a year or two before a new crop is planted. An ethnographic case of such short-fallow field rotation is the traditional agricultural system of the Polynesian Outlier of Anuta (Yen and Gordon, eds., 1973).

Such gradual transformation of long-fallow shifting cultivation to short-fallow crop rotation is evidenced in leeward parts of the Hawaiian Islands. Farming in these regions began as pioneering shifting cultivation in areas of dryland forest with sufficient rainfall and adequate soil nutrients. Over time, the cropping cycle became compressed with shortened fallow intervals, with the agricultural landscape taking on aspects of permanent field cultivation, including a physical infrastructure of walls, embankments, and terraces defining garden plots (what Brookfield and Blaikie [1987] call "landesque capital intensification"). The Hawaiian field systems were intensive not only with respect to their shortened fallow time but also in the amount of labor needed for weeding, mulching, and other crop-tending activities.

The most important crop of the dryland systems was sweet potato, *'uala* (*Ipomoea batatas*), although in areas with greater rainfall—usually the higher elevation areas within field systems—taro was also important. The dominance of sweet potato is due to its ability to withstand arid conditions, its high yields, and the fact that it can be propagated from either tubers or cuttings (Yen 1974). In addition, sweet potato tubers as well as leafy growth provide high-quality pig fodder, enabling the maintenance of substantial pig herds (Dye 2014a). Unlike most Polynesian canoe plants, the sweet potato is not of Southeast Asian or Indo-Pacific origin; it was almost certainly transferred into central Eastern Polynesia by Polynesian voyagers who made contact with South America and returned with planting stocks (Green 2005; Roullier et al. 2013; Yen 1974). Carbonized remains of sweet potato tubers in the Tangatatau rockshelter on Mangaia Island in the southern Cook Islands have been dated to the fourteenth century (Hather and Kirch 1991). The earliest directly dated tuber fragment of *'uala* from a Hawaiian archaeological context was recovered by Ladefoged, Graves, and Coil (2005) from Kohala, Hawai'i, with an age of 580 ± 40 BP, calibrated to AD 1290–1430 (Beta-208143*, 2σ). It appears then that the sweet potato was introduced toward the end of the Late Voyaging Period.

While sweet potato was the most important dryland crop, it was by no means the only crop. Dryland taro was prevalent, and sugarcane lined the field embankments. Sugarcane mulch was probably an important source of nitrogen input to these agroecosystems (Lincoln and Vitousek 2015). Other field-system crops included yams, gourds, bananas, *kī*, and paper mulberry, the latter providing the raw material for *kapa* production.

All Hawaiian dryland field systems exhibit a reticulate grid of field walls, terraces, and bunds or linear mounds, along with trails or territorial boundary markers, features that divide the landscape into a rectilinear patchwork of individual garden plots. The orientations of these features, and some of their details, vary from system to system. Interspersed among the fields are residential features (both permanent and temporary), and pens or enclosures, as well as *heiau* and agricultural shrines. Field systems are limited to those regions where the combination of geological substrate age and rainfall resulted in a combination of moisture and soil nutrients adequate to support intensive cropping of sweet potatoes, dryland taro, and other crops (Kirch et al. 2004; Ladefoged et al. 2009; Vitousek et al. 2004). On Hawai'i, field systems covered significant areas along the leeward Kohala mountains, the area around Waimea, the leeward flow slopes of Kona, and in parts of Ka'ū. On Maui, a major zone of field systems and dryland cultivation was from Kaupō through Kahikinui to Honua'ula (Kirch et al. 2004, 2009). Given its young substrates and abundant rainfall, Hāna District presumably supported extensive dryland cultivation, but has not been investigated well archaeologically. On Moloka'i, the geologically young Kalaupapa Peninsula supported an intensive field system (M. D. McCoy 2005, 2006). Small areas with late-stage volcanic rejuvenation on southeast O'ahu also offered spatially discrete possibilities for intensive dryland cultivation, such as Pu'u 'Uala or "Round Top"; we as yet know essentially nothing of these O'ahu areas from archaeology.

THE LEEWARD KOHALA FIELD SYSTEM

The most intensively studied dryland field system is that of leeward Kohala. Archibald Menzies saw the area in 1793, remarking that "it bears every appearance of industrious cultivation by the number of small fields into which it is laid out" (Menzies 1920, 52). Archaeological study in Kohala began in 1968 with the University of Hawai'i field school in Lapakahi *ahupua'a* (Newman n.d.; Rosendahl 1972a, 1994; Tuggle and Griffin, eds., 1973), continued with work in the southern part of the field system (Ladefoged and Graves 2008a; Ladefoged, Graves, and Jennings 1996; Ladefoged, Graves, and McCoy 2003), and later was a main focus of the multidisciplinary Hawai'i Biocomplexity Project (Kirch 2007a; Kirch et al. 2012; Vitousek et al. 2004). Covering approximately 60 km² on the leeward slopes of the Kohala Mountains (see color plate 3), the field system is bounded on its lower and upper edges by annual rainfall isohyets of 750 and 1900 mm, respectively. The fields extend over two distinct geologic substrates, the 400,000-year-old Hawi series in the north, and the 150,000-year-old Pololu series in the south. Thirty-five *ahupua'a* territories crosscut the field system, their boundaries marked by trail systems that run up and down the slopes; other trails define *'ili* boundaries within *ahupua'a*. The stone alignments marking these trails are one of the main archaeological characteristics of the Kohala Field System, a feature not found in other field systems (Cordy and Kaschko 1980; Ladefoged and Graves 2008b). Running between the trails are thousands of low field divisions, often referred to as "walls," but perhaps better described as stone and earth bunds or embankments, typically 1–2 m wide and 0.5–.75 m high (fig. 7.10). These embankments divide the long *mauka-makai* strips between the stone-lined trails into rectangular field plots. Early European accounts describe the embankments as being planted in rows of sugarcane, which served as windbreaks to protect the sweet potato and taro plants from the strong winds that sweep down from the Kohala Mountains; the rows of cane also served as moisture-catching devices.

Rosendahl's map (1972a, 1994) of a section of the Lapakahi uplands noted trail and field embankment joins and matching patterns, as well as a host of minor agricultural features, such as stone mounds, low stone alignments, agricultural windbreaks, planting circles, small

FIGURE 7.10 Low stone and earthen embankments define the borders of dryland fields in Kaiholena *ahupua'a*, within the extensive leeward Kohala Field System, Hawai'i Island. *(Photo by P. V. Kirch)*

clearings, simple terraces, and animal enclosures or pens. Numerous habitation features were also present, especially C- and L-shaped structures of various sizes, nine of which Rosendahl excavated. Plant remains from the excavations included the carbonized remains of sweet potato tubers (Rosendahl and Yen 1971), as shown in figure 7.11. Rosendahl's excavations produced 10 radiocarbon dates (1972a, table 53), suggesting "an overall time estimate of AD 1400–1760 . . . for the upland occupation at Lapakahi" (436). Toward the end of the precontact period, use of the fields intensified, indicated by a shift from temporary to permanent habitation with the upland field zone. Rosendahl (1972a) suggested that the Lapakahi system began in the fifteenth century as a long-fallow shifting cultivation regime, which was later intensified to a field system with permanent plot boundaries, short-fallow crop rotation, and intensive labor practices.

FIGURE 7.11 A partially carbonized sweet potato tuber excavated from a habitation shelter in the uplands of Lapakahi, within the leeward Kohala Field System. *(Photo courtesy Paul Rosendahl)*

Kirch (1984, 185, fig. 60) used Rosendahl's detailed map of the Lapakahi field system to define a temporal sequence of successive divisions of originally large fields into increasingly smaller plots (fig. 7.12). Expanding on this method of relative dating, Ladefoged, Graves, and McCoy (2003) explored similar patterns of spatial intensification in other parts of leeward Kohala. In a similar manner, Ladefoged and Graves (2008a) showed that the *ahupua'a* territories that subdivide the entire Kohala Field System into thirty-five radial segments resulted from the successive subdivision of what were initially just nine

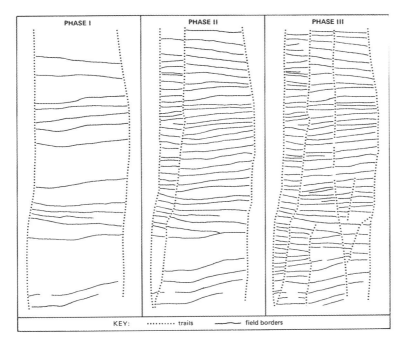

FIGURE 7.12 Schematic map of a portion of the Lapakahi field system, showing the successive subdivision of larger fields into smaller plots over time, along with the insertion of new trails marking land unit boundaries. *(After Kirch 1984)*

AGRICULTURE AND AQUACULTURE • 159

large *ahupuaʻa* territories. The sequential partitioning of both field plots and of larger territorial boundaries documents decreasing garden plot size and decreasing territory size, signifying both agricultural intensification (Brookfield 1972) and a kind of "agricultural involution" (Geertz 1963).

Thirty-three AMS radiocarbon dates, obtained by the Hawaiʻi Biocomplexity Project, refined the chronology of the Kohala Field System (Ladefoged and Graves 2008a). Integrating these radiocarbon results with the relative chronology of field walls and territorial boundaries, Ladefoged and Graves write,

> The first phase of landesque capital improvements, that is, the construction of walls and trails, probably occurred sometime within the range of AD 1410 to 1630. The relative chronology of territorial units would suggest that some territory boundaries, bracketing larger geographic areas, were in place prior to the construction of the initial set of agricultural walls, but it is unclear how much earlier. Most wall and trail construction in this portion of the [leeward Kohala Field System] associated with both agricultural expansion and intensification probably occurred after AD 1650. The relative chronology of agricultural development identified at least four phases of construction after this time. There is no evidence of residential occupation before AD 1640, although our sample size is very small. It is tempting to suggest that ca. AD 1650 marks the point when people shifted from seasonal to permanent occupation of the area, but there is as yet limited evidence to confirm this hypothesis. (Ladefoged and Graves 2008a, 784)

While low-intensity, long-fallow shifting cultivation commenced on the leeward Kohala slopes as early as the late thirteenth or early fourteenth century, the grid of trails and field embankments that characterize the system did not begin to be constructed until after AD 1400. A final phase of intensification, marked by subdivision of larger land units into narrow *ahupuaʻa* and by small individual plots, took place between AD 1650 and the early postcontact period (fig. 7.13). Tom Dye (2011c, 2014b), reanalyzing the radiocarbon dates of Ladefoged and Graves (2008) in a Bayesian model, argues that intensification of the system—and the construction of facilities such as embankments and trails—continued after Cook's arrival in 1779, into the early postcontact period.

The chronology of field construction and intensification has been augmented by extensive dating of residential features associated with the Kohala Field System (Field, Ladefoged, and Kirch 2011; Field, Ladefoged, Sharp, and Kirch 2011). A three-phase temporal sequence is evidenced with 49 AMS radiocarbon dates on short-lived, identified taxa. The first phase, from AD 1400 to 1520, is represented by only five sites, primarily along the coast. In the second phase, from AD 1520 to 1650, there was an increase in residential sites both along the coast and within the field system, indicative of population growth. In the final period, from AD 1650 to 1800, there was a marked increase in residential architecture. "The overall pattern is one of an exponential rate of increase in residential features, with the greatest number of such features existing in temporal period III (AD 1650–1800), just before European contact" (Field, Ladefoged, and Kirch 2011, 7331).

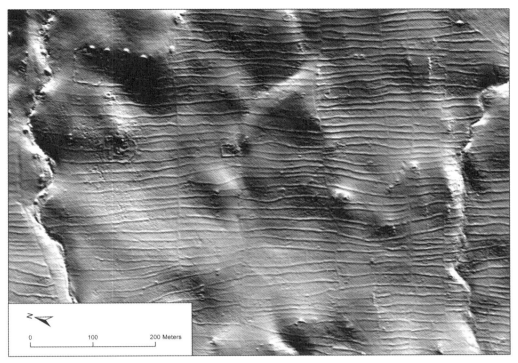

FIGURE 7.13 LiDAR image of a portion of the leeward Kohala Field System in Kaiholena *ahupua'a*, Hawai'i Island. Several trails run up and down slope, while residential enclosures can also be discerned among the grid of field embankments. *(After Field, Ladefoged, and Kirch 2011)*

The Hawai'i Biocomplexity Project studied the biogeochemical gradients and nutrient status of soils associated with the Kohala Field System (Meyer, Ladefoged, and Vitousek 2007; Vitousek et al. 2004). By the time of European contact, the field system incorporated the entire area of the leeward Kohala slope with suitable soil conditions. Figure 7.14 depicts a transect across the field system in relation to available phosphorus (P). At its lower limit, the system was constrained by low P and high aridity, whereas at the inland extent it was low P (and other nutrients) due to leaching from high rainfall that determined the limits to expansion. In short, the Kohala Field System had reached its geographic limits of potential expansion (Kirch 1984, 187–190). More significantly, analyses of total P and the P:Nb ratio from soil samples taken from paired samples under field embankments and from adjacent fields suggest decreased nutrient availability due to continued cropping. Meyer, Ladefoged, and Vitousek

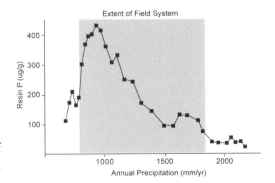

FIGURE 7.14 A soil-sampling transect across the leeward Kohala Field System, made by the Hawai'i Biocomplexity Project, shows how a critical soil component, phosphorus (P), gradually declines with increasing elevation and rainfall, reaching a point where intensive cropping was no longer feasible. *(After Kirch 2010)*

(2007, table 1) demonstrate statistically significant differences in P availability between older soils capped by field embankments and the open, cultivated field soils. They conclude that "over time Hawaiian agriculture decreased levels of P in soils of the Kohala Field System" (352). In sum, the long-term consequences of cropping-cycle intensification in the Kohala Field System were due not only to decreasing field size but also to decreases in nutrient availability, and—one presumes—declining yields.

THE KONA FIELD SYSTEM

An even larger field system, expanding over 139 km², straddles the leeward flanks of Kona District, on relatively young substrates of the Mauna Loa and Hualālai volcanoes (M. S. Allen, ed., 2001, 4). Noa Lincoln, Oliver Chadwick, and Peter Vitousek (2014) describe the "moderate but varying rainfall" and "young substrates" that made the Kona field system somewhat different from other intensive systems on Hawai'i Island. In the Kona system, "areas of high fertility were used in intensive, systematic ways, . . . [and] there existed a range of intensities across the fertility gradients, and that informal techniques were applied in areas in which systematic agriculture was constrained" (13). Like the other dryland field systems, Kona's fell into decline soon after European contact; much of this area was put into commercial coffee production during the twentieth century. In Kona, taro was perhaps of equal significance with sweet potato, while breadfruit trees were also extensively cultivated, unlike in the other two systems (Kelly 1983; Lincoln and Ladefoged 2014).

The Kona field system was first archaeologically recognized by Lloyd Soehren and T. Stell Newman (1968; see also Newman, n.d.), who used aerial photographs to map field walls above Kealakekua Bay. The construction of a 4.9-km-long highway corridor running from Kailua into the Kona uplands provided a transect across the Kona field system, permitting Rose Schilt (1984) to study variation in agricultural and residential features and to obtain a series of radiocarbon dates. Neal Crozier (1971a, 1971b) mapped and excavated features in a small segment of the Kona field system in the land division of Kahalu'u, where several *kuaiwi* walls, minor agricultural features, and residential sites were evident. A section within the main upland field system, on the Amy Greenwell Ethnobotanical Garden (AGEG) property has been intensively studied by several archaeologists (M. S. Allen, ed., 2001; M. D. McCoy, Mulrooney, et al. 2017).

In the Kona field system, the principal agricultural features are parallel stone walls or rows (*kuaiwi*) running up and down rather than across the slope as in Kohala (fig. 7.15). These *kuaiwi,* literally meaning "backbone," may have defined the boundaries of individual garden plots. At the AGEG site, *kuaiwi* range from 2 to 7 m wide, and from 0.2 to 0.8 m high; they are regularly spaced between 16 and 20 m apart (Kirch, in M. S. Allen, ed., 2001, 54). Smaller features between the *kuaiwi* include stone-faced terraces (for soil retention and planting) and numerous stone mounds, as well as residential features. Horrocks and Rechtman analyzed 12 soil samples from a portion of the Kona field system, finding banana phytoliths as well as starch grains and xylem cells of sweet potato tubers, suggesting that both crops were cultivated within the study area (2009, 1115).

Based on 22 radiocarbon dates from the Kuakini Highway transect, Schilt (1984, 276–280) proposed three phases of development of the Kona field system. "Pioneer settlement" from

FIGURE 7.15 A *kuaiwi* wall in the Amy Greenwell Ethnobotanical Garden, part of the Kona field system. *(Photo by Therese Babineau)*

AD 1050 to 1400 was marked by limited archaeological evidence, suggesting low-intensity land use. The second phase, from AD 1400 to 1600/1650, saw the beginnings of the garden complex, while in the third phase, from AD 1600/1650 up to European contact, "gardening and seasonal occupation of *kula* slopes . . . increased dramatically" (278). Intensive horticultural features were developed during this last period in every *ahupua'a* unit crossed by the Kuakini Highway transect. Schilt's temporal sequence is supported by 11 radiocarbon dates from the AGEG site in the upland core of the field system, all but one of these samples dating from after AD 1400 (M. S. Allen, ed., 2001, fig. 11.1). Allen suggests that at AGEG the cross-slope terraces may have been constructed first, with the formalized *kuaiwi* being built after AD 1450, and "quite possibly in the mid-1500s to 1600s" (2001, 140). M. D. McCoy, Mulrooney, et al. (2017) carried out new excavations across the *kuaiwi* at AGEG, obtaining high-precision AMS dates on charcoal from identified, short-lived taxa (fig. 7.16). They found that "infrastructural improvements" were made within the Kona field system by AD 1400, and that there is evidence for "use of all environmental zones by cal AD 1500–1600," with additional infrastructure added in the most optimal zone after AD 1700 (2017, 78). In general, the chronology of the Kona field system parallels that for Kohala, with initial developments beginning around AD 1400, and with a phase of intensification—including formal field divisions—after AD 1600.

Other Field Systems on Hawai'i, Maui, and Moloka'i

A third Hawai'i Island field system lies on the upland plateau in the vicinity of Waimea. Agricultural features including earthen embankments similar to those of Kohala were recorded during archaeological survey of a proposed highway corridor bypassing

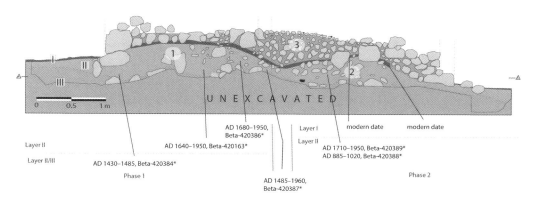

FIGURE 7.16 Stratigraphic section through a *kuaiwi* wall in the Amy Greenwell Ethnobotanical Garden, Hawai'i Island, showing multiple construction stages with associated radiocarbon dates. *(Section by M. D. McCoy)*

Waimea town (Clark and Kirch, eds., 1983). A more formalized system incorporating intermittent irrigation canals was surveyed at Lālāmilo (J. T. Clark 1981). The Lālāmilo system incorporates an extensive network of irrigation canals radiating out from two permanent streams that drain the Kohala slope. The fields are not true pondfields of the type found in the windward valleys but rather are like the fields of Kona and Kohala. Irrigation appears to have been seasonal and supplementary, probably using furrows to direct water across the sloping field surfaces. The capacity of the canals was insufficient to have kept all fields continually watered; some method of water rotation must have been practiced. Burtchard and Tomonari-Tuggle (2004) examined parts of this Waimea field system, obtaining radiocarbon dates suggesting that farming in this area began around AD 1400. The addition of irrigation, however, may be quite late, even early postcontact. It is possible that the Lālāmilo system was intensified in order to supply Kamehameha's army while it was encamped at Kawaihae, during the construction of Pu'ukoholā Heiau (see chapter 14).

A fourth Hawai'i Island field system in Ka'ū District has yet to be thoroughly investigated. The potential of this area for intensive dryland cultivation was indicated in the GIS analysis of Ladefoged et al. (2009); a reticulate field system grid can be detected on aerial photographs, with the embankments oriented in a manner similar to that of the leeward Kohala Field System. Handy (1940, 165–166) noted the importance of sweet potato cultivation throughout this area. Seth Quintus and Noa Lincoln (2018) mapped agricultural features and excavated across linear embankments in a small *kipuka* within the larger Ka'ū field system. Eight AMS radiocarbon dates on identified wood taxa were modeled within a Bayesian model, providing unusually well-constrained age estimates for the construction of this dryland field system infrastructure: between AD 1471 and 1614 for an initial phase, and between AD 1537 and 1637 for a second phase (Quintus and Lincoln 2018, 61, fig. 7).

For Maui Island, high potential for intensive dryland farming exists across four zones: (1) a band across the lower eastern slopes of the west Maui mountains; (2) a strip running inland from Ha'ikū to Makawao in Hamakuapoko District; (3) the area surrounding Hāna; and (4) a

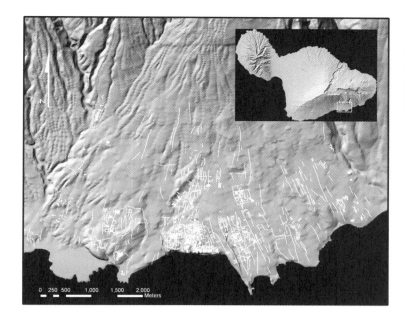

FIGURE 7.17 Map of Kaupō, Maui, showing dryland field system walls visible on aerial photographs. *(After Kirch, Holson, and Baer 2009)*

zone from Kaupō through Kahikinui to Honua'ula (Ladefoged, et al. 2009). Only the Kaupō-Kahikinui-Honua'ula zone, which Handy (1940, 161) called "the greatest continuous dry planting area in the Hawaiian islands," has been thoroughly investigated. Kaupō has a reticulate field system with regularly spaced field terraces running between longer boundary walls oriented *mauka-makai* (much like the Kohala Field System in configuration, but with these being boundary walls rather than trails). The Kaupō system, which was mapped through remote sensing and ground survey (Baer 2015; Baer, Chadwick, and Kirch 2015; Kirch et al. 2009), extends over about 15 km² (fig. 7.17; color plate 5). Kaupō was the seat of Maui *ali'i nui* Kekaulike in the early eighteenth century; the intensive field system was no doubt essential to feeding the large warrior force he had assembled for a planned conquest of Hawai'i Island (Kamakau 1961, 66).

In Kahikinui District, intensive dryland gardening took on a somewhat different character, as the area largely lacks an extensive, reticulate field system grid. Rather, the region's farmers adapted to the youthful *'a'ā* lava flow topography by focusing their efforts on the numerous natural swales or depressions, some of which were terraced or divided with low walls or embankments into formal garden plots, and to farming in *kīpuka* (older lava patches) where the substrate was of ideal age (Dixon et al. 1997a, 1999, 2002; Kirch et al. 2004; Kirch et al. 2005; Kirch et al. 2013). James Coil and Kirch (2005; see also Coil 2004; Holm 2006) discuss the "Ipomoean landscape" of dryland farming in Kahikinui, evidenced by various kinds of field evidence as well as by the presence of carbonized sweet potato tubers in habitation sites. Permanent occupation of the Kahikinui uplands began around AD 1400. Coil and Kirch discerned an early phase of agricultural development from AD 1400 until about 1640, followed by a phase of increased investment in agricultural facilities from AD 1640 to the early contact period.

The Hawai'i Biocomplexity Project mapped the relationships between soil nutrients and evidence for intensive farming on the Kahikinui leeward slopes (Hartshorn et al. 2006; Kirch et al. 2004). As in Kohala, the upland farming zone in Kahikinui corresponds to a "sweet spot" of nutrient availability, defined by aridity in the lower-elevation reaches, and by steeply declining nutrient levels at the upper elevations. Detailed studies of two garden locations where digging stick impressions and other indicators of intensive cultivation were present (Kirch et al. 2005) allowed for quantitative comparison of cultivated soil with uncultivated parent material. Tony Hartshorn et al. (2006) estimated significant reduction in soil nutrients due to intensive cultivation and nutrient uptake from repeated harvesting of sweet potatoes. Given continuous and intensive cropping in the Kahikinui uplands, a phase of declining yields during the late phase of cultivation seems likely.

Due to their age and weathering, the volcanic shield surfaces from West Maui to Kaua'i and Ni'ihau have nutrient-depleted soils and were not suitable for intensive dryland farming. However, limited late stage volcanic rejuvenation on both Moloka'i and O'ahu provided areas where field systems were developed on younger substrates with adequate nutrient supplies. The most significant of these is at Kalaupapa, on windward Moloka'i Island, where much of the peninsula is covered in closely spaced low stone walls defining sweet potato garden plots (Kirch, ed., 2002; M. D. McCoy 2006). Based on 13 radiocarbon dates, McCoy concluded that "widespread burning across the Kalaupapa Peninsula indicative of the initiation of the Kalaupapa Field System does not commence until AD 1450–1550" (2005; 2006, 128). More intensive use began after AD 1650, when residential sites and rockshelters within the field system were permanently occupied (Kirch et al. 2004).

In sum, the Kohala, Kona, Waimea, Kahikinui, and Kalaupapa field systems all exhibit a similar pattern of chronological development. Low-intensity land use is evident in Kohala and Kona prior to AD 1400, reflective of long-fallow shifting cultivation; significant dryland cultivation in all dated systems begins around AD 1400. Following two centuries of initial development, a late phase of intensification, marked by formalized garden plots and territorial boundaries, commenced about AD 1600–1650, continuing into the early postcontact period. The dryland field systems were then rapidly abandoned during the first half of the nineteenth century, as the Hawaiian population declined following European contact.

Risk and Uncertainty in the Dryland Field Systems

All forms of agriculture are inherently risky. Farmers in the windward valleys were periodically challenged by flooding, which could destroy the irrigated taro fields, or by drought that could lower stream flow to a point where there was insufficient water for all the pondfields in a system. But the risk of crop failure and potential famine was unquestionably higher in the dryland farming zones. The Hawaiian sage Davida Malo made this clear when he wrote that dryland farming was "attended with many drawbacks" (1951, 204).

Beginning with the Hawai'i Biocomplexity Project in the early 2000s, substantial effort has been devoted to modeling spatial and temporal variability in the Hawaiian dryland cultivation systems in order to understand how the dynamics of these systems interacted with and influenced sociopolitical evolution in Hawai'i. A well-known simulation model, CENTURY, was adapted to estimate the spatial variation in sweet potato production across the leeward Kohala Field System, as well as stochastic variation in annual rainfall (Kirch et al. 2012; Lee et al. 2006; Lee et al. 2009; Lee and Tuljapurkar 2010). The results showed that yields increase while variability decreases with increasing elevation along every *makai* to *mauka* transect, until the phosphorus-leached soil threshold that defines the upper boundary of the field system was reached

(Lee et al. 2006). In years with good rainfall, it was possible to push production downslope, while in drought years these lower elevations would likely have witnessed crop failure.

Variability across the Kohala Field System is evident not only along elevation transects but on a wider spatial scale from north to south as well. The highest and most stable productivity would have been in several *ahupua'a* (such as Kaiholena and Makeanehu) situated in the central core of the field system (Kirch et al. 2012, fig. 4). To the north of this core productivity becomes more variable, while to the south productivity declines significantly. Testing this model with archaeological data, Field, Ladefoged, and Kirch (2011) showed that while the numbers of residential sites within the core *ahupua'a* stabilized by the end of the Expansion Period, settlement continued to expand into the riskier southern sector during the Archaic States Period.

Ladefoged, Lee, and Graves (2008) showed that the variation in production across the Kohala Field System had demographic consequences for the occupants of different *ahupua'a* territories. The segmentation of the field system into increasingly smaller *ahupua'a* "lowered the life expectancy of residents confined to some of the territories relative to others, but boosted potential surplus production and tempered year-to-year variation in surplus" (108). Thus, "dividing the area into 32 controllable territories and then facilitating either redistribution or relocation amongst the larger politically integrated area reflects a group strategy that enhanced potential sources of new recruits, mechanisms of social control, and promoted the periodic high level of surplus production."

Robert DiNapoli and Alex Morrison extended the analysis of spatial and temporal variation across the Kohala Field System by modeling "paleo-droughts" over the region "during the pre-Contact period using a multivariate proxy reconstruction of ENSO based on sea surface temperature (SST) anomalies for the time period AD 1301–1900" (2017, 112). Their results showed that "a large region of the central core of the [field system] experienced very few droughts, but risk increases along a steep gradient with distance from this central region, suggesting that agricultural risk was very high in certain areas but quite low in others" (113). High-risk areas included lower-elevation zones and the northern and southern portions of the field system. The paleo-climate modeling suggested that "the period from AD 1451–1600 experienced higher than average frequencies of droughts, with the most susceptible locations in the southern areas at low elevations experiencing drought conditions nearly half of the time" (115). The fact that this period of greater risk appears to correlate with "the onset of *heiau* temple construction" in the Kohala Field System possibly signals "community cooperation" as a risk-management strategy (117).

At a broader regional scale, Aurora Kagawa-Viviani et al. (2018) explored how annual cycles of climate constrained seasonal cultivation and crop production across the Kohala, Kona, and Ka'ū field systems on Hawai'i Island. The three systems are distinctive in terms of "climatic variables associated with evaporative water loss and in the timing of the rainy season" (1). Due to its greater cloud frequency, the Kona field system suffers less from evapotranspiration than Kohala or Ka'ū. And while the period of greatest rainfall for the latter two systems is from November to April, in Kona the rainy period extends from June to September. The seasonal complementarity in these systems may have played a role in the rise of archaic states on the island:

Over time, and as the power of individual polities spread throughout the leeward districts and the entire Island of Hawai'i, these systems were integrated through redistribution or coordination to enhance food security and surplus production as populations grew.... The complementary seasonality of production of the three systems ... would indicate that consolidation and increased coordination (through coerced redistribution or cooperative exchange) could create more stable political hierarchies. This characteristic of these systems might have facilitated increased security enabling increased wealth asset investment and the development of both a staple and wealth finance political economy that underpinned the polities on the island. (10)

Arboriculture

A neglected component of traditional Hawaiian production systems is the planting and management of tree crops, referred to as arboriculture or alternatively as agroforestry (Quintus et al. 2019). (We prefer the term "arboriculture," with the connotation of tree propagation and management as a form of horticulture, rather than "agroforestry," which has connotations of industrial-scale tree monocropping.) Such managed trees included not only several of the canoe plants, such as coconut and breadfruit, but also naturally occurring trees that, being useful to the Hawaiians, were selectively planted and tended. The introduction of domesticated tree crops combined with the selective tending and encouragement of useful indigenous trees resulted in the creation of "novel forests" in the low- to mid-altitude zones of the islands. Direct archaeological evidence for arboriculture comes primarily from the identification of wood charcoal in excavated sites (e.g., Kolb and Murakami 1994). Therefore, most of what we know of traditional arboriculture derives from either ethnohistoric sources or ethnobotanical surveys (e.g., Handy 1940).

In precontact Hawai'i, only two varieties of coconut (*Cocos nucifera*) were present, one with a dark green nut (*niu hiwa*) used ceremonially, and one with a reddish nut (*niu lelo*) used secularly (Handy 1940, 190). Both of these varieties were of the type known more generically as "*niu kafa*" (Harries 1978), with a relatively small liquid cavity but possessing long husk fibers that could be twisted to make sennit cordage. Occasionally old trees of the true Hawaiian varieties are encountered, as at a house site deep in O'ahu's Anahulu Valley (Kirch, in Kirch and Sahlins 1992, 2:60, 2:63).

As Handy observed, "In old Hawaii cultivation of the coconut was limited, because these islands are a little too far north for this tropical tree to flourish" (1940, 192). Nonetheless, important coconut groves were planted in coastal areas, often associated with areas of *ali'i* residence. A sacred grove was located at Wailua on Kaua'i; Waikīkī, O'ahu, was likewise notable for its coconut palms. Handy reports that "Puna [on Hawai'i] has probably always had the greatest continuous planting area for coconuts in the Hawaiian islands; today old coconut groves are scattered everywhere along the wet lava-covered coastal plain" (193).

Breadfruit or '*ulu* (*Artocarpus altilis*) was the most important tree crop in terms of its dietary contribution. According to tradition, breadfruit was first brought to Hawai'i by

Kahaʻi, a son of the voyaging chief Moʻikeha, on a voyage from Kahiki (Handy 1940, 186); this would date the introduction of breadfruit to the Late Voyaging Period. According to Handy, in Hawaiʻi (and unlike in the Marquesas or Society Islands) breadfruit bears fruit for only a single season, typically from May into September (189). There were important planting localities throughout the islands, typically in the windward valleys or other areas with sufficient rainfall.

In Kona, Hawaiʻi, a zone of breadfruit trees, the *kaluulu,* was an integral part of the extensive Kona field system (Kelly 1983; Schilt 1984). In this belt, which extended from about 150 up to 300 m elevation above sea level, both sweet potato and paper mulberry plants were cropped under perennial breadfruit groves. Two other tree crops, mountain apple (*Syzygium malaccense*) and candlenut (*Aleurites moluccana*), were also interspersed through the *kaluulu* zone. Lincoln and Ladefoged (2014) calculated that the breadfruit zone in Kona could have yielded 12,570 metric tons of dry weight fruit per hectare per year, a significant addition to the region's total production and carrying capacity. As they state, "Breadfruit was not a favored food, but had the added benefit of low maintenance and greater surplus" (201).

The candlenut tree, *kukui,* was widely disseminated throughout the Pacific by the colonizing Austronesians. The primary use of the oily kernel is for lighting or in torches, making it the most commonly identified plant taxon found in house sites and rockshelters. But the plant also has medicinal uses, and the timber is valuable. *Kukui* trees were planted extensively on colluvial slopes and especially in upland ravines, where their distinctive light-green leaves stand out against the darker green vegetation. Lincoln (2020) has drawn attention to a unique system of shifting cultivation under extensive anthropogenic stands of candlenut, known as the *pākukui,* which covered a large part of the Hāmākua District of Hawaiʻi Island. This system operated on relatively infertile soils, where

> [*kukui*] litterfall was gathered into relatively impermeable pits in the lava and composted in order to create a growing medium. Local organic waste and small amounts of soil that could be excavated nearby was added to these enclosures, or *pā,* to aid in the rotting of composts. . . . The beds would be prepared several months before the rainy season so that when the rains came the new soil would be at an optimal level of development. In such enclosures, sweet potatoes, taro, and sugar cane grew luxuriantly. . . . While a handful of these cultivation pits would commonly be located near households to compost local waste, within novel or native forests "many times 40" of substantial pits would comprise an agricultural field. When candlenut (*kukui*) was the principal component, these *pā* (enclosures) were appropriately referred to as *pākukui.* (Lincoln 2020, 3–4)

Hawaiian arboriculture was not restricted to the introduced "canoe plants" but also encompassed species naturally present in the islands, whose distribution was extended through purposeful tending and planting. Perhaps the most remarkable of these was the domestication of the endemic shrub *Touchardia latifolia,* known to the Hawaiians as *olonā,* the bast fibers of which when processed produced extremely fine and strong cordage (Funk 1982). *Olonā* cordage was used for fishing lines, to make fishing nets, to lash canoes, and for the netting framework upon which feathers were tied to make the highly prized feather capes, cloaks, helmets, and war god images (see chapter 9). *Olonā* prefers wet habitats, such as the interior portions of windward valleys. On Molokaʻi, the dry leeward *ahupuaʻa* of Kawela incorporated a small portion of the interior of windward Pelekunu Valley, specifically to grow *olonā*, essential to produce the fish lines and nets needed by the coastal-dwelling Kawela people.

Animal Husbandry

A triumvirate of three domesticated animals—pig, dog, and jungle fowl—has deep associations with the Austronesian-speaking peoples, carried with them on their long pathways of expansion throughout the Pacific region. In Hawaiʻi, all three were regarded as "sources of wealth" (Malo 1951, 78). Bones of both pig and dog were recovered from the early Bellows (O18) site at Waimānalo, Oʻahu, indicative of early transfer to the islands; the jungle fowl, the same species as chickens, probably also arrived with early voyagers from central Eastern Polynesia. While fowls were eaten and their feathers used in cloaks, *kahili,* and other objects, they roamed free and foraged for themselves. Pigs and dogs, in contrast, were raised in large numbers for food. This required that they be penned and fed, as one component within the larger production system. This was especially important for pigs, which if allowed to roam free would have devastated gardens and fields.

Pigs (*puaʻa*) were culturally more esteemed than dogs. Malo (1951, 37) called pigs the "most important animals" in Hawaiʻi, noting that named varieties were classified according to the colors of their bristles. In the *kapu* system that prevailed at the time of European contact, women were forbidden to eat pork. And while males of any rank could consume pig flesh, in practice this was a delicacy consumed largely by the *aliʻi* class. Correspondence between Paulo Kanoa, secretary to the high chiefess Kīnaʻu, and Gideone Laʻanui, the *konohiki* of Waialua, Oʻahu, during the 1830s documents frequent demands upon the people of that district for hogs to be supplied to the *aliʻi* household in Honolulu (Sahlins, in Kirch and Sahlins 1992, 1:144–145).

Pigs were essential sacrificial offerings at many kinds of religious and ritual events, including the birth of a child, circumcision, and healing of the sick, but most especially at state ceremonies held on the major *luakini* temples (Malo 1951, 87–88, 93–96). Kamakau wrote that pigs selected for offerings in *heiau* rituals "had to be fine ones, fattened until the snout almost disappeared and the neck rolled with fat, the ears drooping, and the mouth standing open" (1976, 139). During the dedication of a *luakini* war temple, as many as 800 hogs were said to be cooked and consumed by the priests, warriors, and other male officiants (172). Pig sacrifice was not restricted to the state temples. The dedication of local agricultural temples (*heiau hoʻouluʻai*) also necessitated the baking and consumption of hogs: "The dedication of these heiaus belonging to the people called for pig eating, and when it was heard that some prominent person had a heiau to dedicate, *hoʻokupu,* and that many pigs had been baked, the *poʻe paʻa mua akua* came from all about to the pig-eating' (Kamakau 1976, 132).

Although pigs had ritual associations with all the major Hawaiian gods, there was a particularly strong association between pigs and Lono, deity of dryland cultivation and the sweet potato (Valeri 1985, 10). One of the *kinolau* or "bodies" of the pig god Kamapuaʻa is the sweet potato; the gnarly *ʻuala* tubers that grew in stony land were likened metaphorically to pig feces. Thomas Maunupau (1998, 152–153) was told by the old *kahuna* Poouwahi of Kaupō, Maui, about the prayers made to Kamapuaʻa upon the planting of sweet potatoes. The pig god was entreated to "root" and "excrete" in the newly planted fields, an abundance of pig "feces" representing an abundant crop of sweet potato tubers. In his study of the sweet potato in Oceania, Yen remarked upon the "singularly important role of conversion of vegetable material into rich sources of protein and fat—animal husbandry—that the sweet potato attains" (1974, 52). Indeed, as Yen argues, it was the unique ability of the sweet potato plant to sustain large herds of pigs that lent Hawaiian production systems their well-earned reputation among early European voyagers of a seemingly boundless source of these animals (312). Captain Cook noted that the Hawaiian Islands were "abounding in hogs and roots" (Beaglehole, ed., 1967, 151). Dye (2014a) argues that pig herds were wealth-assets, "capable of growing in size, theoretically limited only by the high natural growth rate of the pig population" (65). The controlled growth of pig herds, drawing upon surplus production of the intensive field systems, allowed for the conversion of staple starch into highly valued protein "on the hoof" that could be managed and at appropriate times converted into social and political capital.

If pig was the high-status, ritually marked, male-restricted flesh food of ancient Hawaiʻi, dog (*ʻilio*) was its counterpoint, more widely available to commoners and to women; indeed, dog meat was a favorite among Hawaiian *aliʻi wahine* (Titcomb 1969). Captain Cook remarked that dogs were "fed, and left to herd with the hogs" (quoted in Titcomb 1969, 3). Puppies were observed to be suckled by Hawaiian women, as indeed were piglets. William Ellis wrote that "numbers of dogs, of rather a small size, and something like a terrier, are raised every year as an article of food. They are mostly fed on vegetables; and we have sometimes seen them kept in yards, with small houses to sleep in" (quoted in Titcomb 1969, 8). A starchy diet is confirmed by the presence of abundant caries in the dentition of skeletal remains of Hawaiian dogs in Bishop Museum (Svihla 1957). Dogs are frequently depicted in Hawaiian petroglyphs, clearly identifiable with their pointed ears and curled tails (see chapter 10); pigs do not seem to be represented in this way.

In addition to their use for food, the bones of both pigs and dogs, along with pig tusks and dog teeth, were used to make several kinds of artifacts (see chapter 9). The long bones of both animals provided material for fishhook manufacture. Dog canine teeth were drilled and tied to fiber netting to make anklets worn by men in hula dancing (Titcomb 1969, fig. 7). Dog teeth were also used to outline the gaping mouths of feathered god images.

Archaeological evidence for the husbandry of pigs and dogs consists primarily of small, stone-walled enclosures or semisubterranean pits that are presumed to have functioned as pens, and are often found integrated with agricultural features. The consumption of pigs, dogs, and fowl is evidenced by faunal remains of these species in both household and ritual contexts; this is discussed further in chapters 10 and 11.

Fishponds and Aquaculture

Samuel Kamakau wrote that those who had fishponds on their lands "loved the lands where they dwelt. . . . Fishponds were things that beautified the land, and a land with many fishponds was called 'fat'" (1976, 47). The invention of fishponds—as opposed to fish traps and weirs—was a unique achievement of the Hawaiians, for nowhere else in Polynesia was true aquaculture developed. With this fishpond technology the Hawaiians moved beyond simple harvesting of natural populations of fish into the realm of fish production and husbandry. Fishponds constituted a highly productive artificial ecosystem. The development of several hundred fishponds throughout the islands was yet another aspect of intensification of production in ancient Hawai'i. Detailed studies of traditional fishponds were carried out by Stokes (1909b), Cobb (1902), Summers (1964), and Kikuchi (1973, 1976), among others.

Fishponds are found on all of the major islands but were particularly extensive on Kaua'i, O'ahu, Moloka'i, and Hawai'i. William Kikuchi (1973) reports that 449 ponds are known to have been constructed prior to AD 1830, most of these during the precontact era.

The extent and distribution of ponds was dictated by local environmental conditions, especially by the presence of shallow reef flats or embayments where ponds could be constructed in broad semicircular arcs out from the shoreline. Among the most suitable localities were Kāne'ohe Bay and Pearl Harbor on O'ahu, and along the southern coastline of Moloka'i. While Hawai'i Island lacks such coastal environments, it does have many natural ponds in lava basins (known as anchialine ponds) along the shoreline; these were modified by the Hawaiians with walls and gates to render them operational as fishponds.

Ponds varied in construction and form, in methods of operation, and in the species of fish raised. The general Hawaiian term for "pond" is *loko,* or *loko i'a,* derived from the Proto-Polynesian word **roko* meaning "pond" or "lake" (*i'a* means fish). *Loko* were divided into two major categories, *shore ponds* and *inland ponds*.

Of the shore ponds, the most important was the *loko kuapā,* consisting of an arc-shaped wall extending out from the shore onto the reef flat and back again (fig. 7.18). The walls, constructed of basalt and coral blocks, were usually several meters thick and projected about one meter above the highest tide level. They were gapped in one or more places with carefully constructed sluice gates (*mākāhā*), which permitted the flow of seawater into the pond. Gates were blocked with panels made of small wooden slats, which allowed young fry

FIGURE 7.18 The wall of a *loko kuapā* fishpond along the south coast of Moloka'i Island. *(Photo by Therese Babineau)*

to enter from the sea but kept the larger, mature fish from escaping. *Loko kuapā* ranged in area from 1 ha up to 211 ha.

Several score *loko kuapā* ponds are strung out along the southern shoreline of Moloka'i; a few are still operational. Aerial photographs show not only the extant ponds but also the remnants of older *loko kuapā* whose walls have been flattened, and which now lie beneath the sea even at low tide.

Also classed with shore ponds, but actually a kind of sophisticated fish trap, is the *loko 'umeiki*, which in plan resembles a *loko kuapā* but has numerous lanes leading inward from the sea. Nets or traps were placed at the heads of these lanes to catch fish during the incoming tide.

Inland ponds include three major types: (1) *pu'uone* ponds, situated near the sea but separated from it by a ridge of sand, connected to the ocean by a channel or ditch; (2) *loko i'a kalo,* freshwater taro fields that were stocked with fish; and (3) *loko wai,* freshwater ponds. The kinds of fish that could be raised in the latter two categories were obviously limited.

The primary species of fish raised in ponds were *awa* or milkfish (*Chanos chanos*) and *'ama'ama* or mullet (*Mugil cephalis*). Both thrive in slightly brackish water. In the true freshwater ponds were *'o'opu,* an endemic goboid fish, and *'ōpae,* a small shrimp. Cobb (1902), who studied Hawaiian fishponds operating at the turn of the century, estimated that they could yield, on the average, about 166 kilograms of fish per acre. Based on Kikuchi's (1973) estimate of yield, Hawaiian fishponds may have produced more than two million pounds of fish each year. That is nearly equal to the annual volume of fish caught in the near shore today (K. S. McCoy et al. 2018).

Based on chiefly genealogies, the earliest true ponds (as opposed to traps and weirs) may have been built in the fourteenth century; there are many references to ponds constructed in the sixteenth through eighteenth centuries. Hawaiian fishponds were, as Kikuchi (1976, 296) points out, symbols of chiefly status and power. Ponds were usually under the direct control of chiefs or their land managers (*konohiki*); fish harvested from ponds frequently went to feed chiefly households and retainers. Early historic records from the Waialua District of O'ahu indicate that fish harvested from Lokoea and 'Uko'a ponds were regularly sent by boat to the chiefs who resided at Honolulu (Kirch and Sahlins 1992). As Kikuchi wrote, "Fishponds became symbols of the chiefly right to conspicuous consumption and to ownership of the land and its resources. They were manifestations of the chief's political power and his ability to control and tap his resources" (Kikuchi 1976, 299).

Being partly submerged and situated in a dynamic marine environment, fishponds are inherently difficult for archaeologists to study. Based on references to construction of particular fishponds and their association with named chiefs in Hawaiian oral traditions, Kikuchi (1976, 295) concluded that most ponds had been constructed from the fourteenth through the nineteenth centuries. The probable construction dates for several ponds on O'ahu, Kaua'i, and Moloka'i have been established by radiocarbon dating of pond sediments sampled by coring (Athens 2002; Carson 2005a; Denham et al. 1999). When fishponds were constructed, the enclosing walls created sediment traps; the depositional regime within the pond typically changed in a manner that can be detected through physical and biotic changes in the sediment core. Radiocarbon dates from sediments thought to mark the onset of artificial pond conditions are now available from more than 10 ponds (Athens 2002, table 1). These suggest initial efforts at fishpond construction beginning in the fourteenth century, and continuing into the fifteenth to seventeenth centuries, corroborating the testimony of the oral traditions.

Production, Surplus, and the Staple Economy

In this chapter we have canvassed the remarkable variability of indigenous Hawaiian agricultural practices, their adaptation to environments wet and dry, windward and leeward, and their gradual intensification over time. By the time of Captain Cook's arrival in 1778–1779, the lowland and intermediate zones across all the islands were cloaked in a complex mosaic of gardens, fields, managed woodlands, and novel forests, a highly productive and thoroughly anthropogenic landscape. In chapter 8, we explore further the demographic consequences and correlates of this intensive production system. In concluding this overview of ancient Hawaiian production systems, however, we wish to put a spotlight on their capacity to produce surplus, which was critical to the evolution and transformation of Hawaiian society and culture over the long run of history.

Timothy Earle was one of the first archaeologists to explore the importance of agricultural production—and particularly of taro irrigation—for Hawaiian history (Earle 1977, 1978, 1980, 1997). Drawing upon the writings of Karl Wittfogel (1957) on irrigation and "oriental despotism," and inspired by Marshall Sahlins' ethnohistorical research into the socioeconomics of the contact-era Hawaiian kingdoms (Kirch and Sahlins 1992; Sahlins 1972), Earle studied the role of irrigation in the chiefship of Halele'a District, Kaua'i. Although rejecting some of Wittfogel's claims regarding the linkage between irrigation and incipient bureaucracy, Earle recognized that control over the surplus generated by wet taro cultivation held a key to understanding the evolution of the Hawaiian sociopolitical system. With his research program limited to Kaua'i, Earle did not have the benefit of seeing firsthand the field evidence for other forms of intensified production, notably the vast rain-fed dryland field systems of Hawai'i and Maui Islands. More recently, however, Earle poignantly wrote the following regarding intensified production in ancient Hawai'i:

> Although the forms of intensification varied, it invariably involved the engineering of landscapes to increase and stabilize production and created land tenure systems that set rights of use and transfer across generations. The lands of irrigation, dryland farming and fishponds in Hawai'i provide magnificent examples of how engineered landscapes supported pristine state formation. Irrigation and the other facilities were critical, because they provided the productive and sustainable base for surplus extraction that financed complex chiefdoms and eventual states. Highly intensified landscapes of water management created an artificial world that could be controlled by elites to generate the surplus that fuelled political ambitions. The landesque capital helped structure patterns of everyday and long-term activities that made possible the imposition of new hierarchies of property

ownership. Irrigation provided opportunities for control through property rights encoded in ritual practice and the built landscape. That a farming family held subsistence rights in a permanently marked plot effectively tethered that family to the land and made them an easy target for emergent elites in search of reliable incomes. (Earle 2012, 109)

Just how much surplus the Hawaiian taro irrigation systems were capable of producing was demonstrated by Spriggs and Kirch (1992) in their analysis of production in the Anahulu Valley of Oʻahu in the early postcontact era. Comparing the caloric needs of known household numbers (provided by the ethnohistoric records) with the modeled projections of yield from mapped irrigation complexes allowed them to estimate the amount of surplus produced, a value usually impossible to determine on strictly archaeological data. The Anahulu data demonstrate that pondfield irrigation could support fully 50 percent above and beyond the basic subsistence requirements of the cultivator households. In early nineteenth-century Oʻahu, this surplus sustained the large *aliʻi* households of Kinaʻu and others not just with regular quantities of taro and *poi* but also with the fattened hogs that the *aliʻi* were constantly demanding of the common people (Kirch and Sahlins 1992).

The surplus generated by the lower-yielding and more labor-intensive dryland field systems was certainly less than that of the bountiful taro irrigation systems. Yet the ability of even these field systems, based on the cultivation of sweet potato, to support substantial surplus in the form of pig herds, has already been noted (Dye 2014a). Surplus, indeed, was the key to what Earle called a "staple economy" (Earle 1987, 1997), a kind of economic system for which he regarded Hawaiʻi to be a classic instance.

Anthropologists have long recognized the importance of surplus (Dalton 1960; Orans 1966; Polanyi 1944; Polanyi et al., eds. 1957), that portion of production extending beyond what Sahlins (1972) famously called the "domestic mode of production." Surplus finances the larger political economy and the political aspirations of chiefly elites. Surplus is the difference noted by Brookfield (1972), in his analysis of agricultural intensification, between "production for use" and "social production." Sahlins recognized that the domestic mode of production is inherently antisurplus; therefore, the "political pressures that can be mounted on the household economy" expose a key to sociopolitical transformation in hierarchical societies such as that of ancient Hawaiʻi (1972, 82). As the economy is increasingly politicized, household production becomes co-opted in the service of those in control of land and labor, of the means of production. As Sahlins put it so succinctly, "The development of rank and chieftainship becomes, *pari passu,* development of the productive forces" (130, 140).

As output above the household level of minimal subsistence and reproduction, surplus enhances overall household quality of life; alternatively, it can be siphoned off by the nonproducer segment of the population as a tax. In ancient Hawaiʻi, formal taxation during the Makahiki along with other mechanisms of tribute collection allowed the *aliʻi* to sustain their own households and to fund their political aspirations, by supporting craft specialists, warriors, and priests.

The staple economy of ancient Hawai'i, rooted in a remarkable array of surplus-generating agroecosystems, was the foundation upon which the entire society was constructed. But it was not the sole component of the traditional economy. In chapter 9 we consider the *wealth economy* based upon the extraction of resources and manufacture of a diversity of material goods and elite status artifacts that was equally essential to the functioning of the hierarchical sociopolitical system.

8

"LIKE SHOALS OF FISH"
Population in Ancient Hawai'i

The first voyaging canoes to beach on Hawaiian shores around AD 1000 likely carried no more than a few dozen individuals; the original colonists may have numbered no more than 100 persons. Yet when Captain Cook arrived in AD 1778–1779, the islands were inhabited by dense populations residing not only along the coast but extending well up into the valley interiors and on the leeward slopes of Maui and Hawai'i. On entering Kealakekua Bay in January, 1779, Cook wrote that "I have no where in this Sea seen such a number of people assembled at one place" (Beaglehole, ed., 1967, 490).

Human populations are inherently capable of rapid growth and expansion. In a study of historically documented growth on three isolated islands, including tiny Pitcairn of HMS *Bounty* fame, Joseph Birdsell (1957) showed that even small colonizing groups can rapidly achieve large numbers, with a doubling time on the order of one generation. Over the course of eight centuries the Polynesian population of Hawai'i had grown significantly, expanding from a few founders to densely populate the lowlands and mid-elevations of all the major islands. By European contact, the more environmentally favorable and productive areas, the "salubrious cores," had population densities of 500 or more persons per square kilometer. Even marginal and drought-prone lands such as Kahikinui District on Maui had population densities of 50 or 60 persons per square kilometer (Kirch 2007d).

The demographic history of precontact Hawai'i is key to understanding the evolution of Hawaiian society and economy, not because population growth was in and of itself a "prime mover" of change (Cordy 1974b) but because demographic variables are dynamically linked with systems of production and land tenure, and with social and political organization. Before one can assess demographic cause and effect, however, it is necessary to trace the major demographic trends in ancient Hawai'i. Archaeologists have devoted some effort to this problem, as this chapter reviews.

The Population of Hawai'i at Contact

The size of the Hawaiian population at the moment of European contact in 1778–1779 has been a matter of contention and debate. Cook and his officers were impressed with the large numbers of people they encountered, particularly on Hawai'i Island. Lieutenant James King, in a carefully reasoned estimate, opined that the archipelago might hold half a million people (Beaglehole, ed., 1967, 620), but reduced this to 400,000 for the official admiralty account of the voyage. King based his estimate on the average numbers of houses along the shore multiplied by the total length of coastline, assuming an average of six persons per house. King, however, did not factor in the presence of inland settlements.

Actual census taking did not commence until the arrival of the Protestant missionaries, more than five decades after Cook's visit, by which time the Hawaiian population had suffered the devastating effects of Western-introduced diseases. A head-count census in 1832 enumerated 130,393 persons across the main islands (Schmitt 1973). A decline from 400,000 or more in 1778–1779 down to 130,000 five decades later seemed to some twentieth-century historians and demographers to be more drastic than was possible, leading them to suggest that King's figure of 400,000 had been inflated. Robert Schmitt (1971), for example, concluded that the Hawaiian population at contact had numbered no more than 250,000 and possibly only 200,000.

The question was thrown open by David Stannard (1989), who was influenced by arguments for virgin soil epidemics and their catastrophic effects in the New World. Referencing archaeological reports of extensive inland settlements, Stannard argued that Lieutenant King's estimate was, if anything, too low, as it was based only on the coastal population. Stannard suggested that the Hawaiian population might have exceeded 800,000. Historical demographer Jean-Louis Rallu (in Kirch and Rallu, eds., 2007) has shown that the effects of epidemics in Polynesia—where indigenous populations had no prior exposure to diseases such as syphilis, smallpox, measles, dysentery, and respiratory ailments—were indeed often devastating.

Archaeological evidence draws into question Schmitt's (1971) low estimates of contact-era population. Regional-scale estimates for the districts of Kahikinui on Maui and Kohala on Hawai'i, based on settlement densities, are roughly consistent with the population levels estimated by Lieutenant King (Kirch 2007c; Ladefoged and Graves 2007). Furthermore, a GIS-based analysis of irrigated and dryland production capacities across the archipelago (Ladefoged et al. 2009) suggests that nearly a quarter of a million people may have been engaged in agricultural labor, which in turn implies an even larger total population.

Robert Hommon drew upon calculated areas of high-potential agricultural land on the five largest Hawaiian Islands to arrive at an estimate of how many persons might be supported, given certain assumptions regarding the average yield for different kinds of cropping systems, and average caloric intake of the population (2013, table 4.2). This method suggests a minimum population of 520,297 and a theoretical maximum of 1,036,928. While overly precise, Hommon's range of possible population sizes does suggest the potential of the archipelago's agroecosystems to support large populations.

David Swanson, a demographer, has approached the question of the Hawaiian population on the eve of European contact by applying the method of "backcasting," working from known postcontact demographic trends in cohort change ratios (2019). The method is normally used for demographic "forecasting" but can be run in reverse to retrodict the Hawaiian population from known historic parameters. With this approach, Swanson arrived at an estimate of 683,200 Native Hawaiians at the time of Cook's arrival. If accurate, this implies a shocking decline in the Native Hawaiian population of fully 83.8 percent between 1779 and 1840. As Swanson writes, "These declines are consistent with the newly introduced diseases and related factors that affected the Native Hawaiian population from the time of first contact to 1840" (210). It was, as Stannard claimed, a holocaust.

While the debate over the actual number of Native Hawaiians living in 1778–1779 will likely continue, the fact that the Hawaiian population grew over the course of eight centuries to become *the* largest of any Polynesian group is not in question. A founding cohort of a few score colonizers burgeoned into a population of several hundred thousand. The intrinsic rate of increase (r) required for such growth in a simple exponential model would be roughly 0.5 percent (Rallu, in Kirch and Rallu, eds., 2007, 19–20), well below potential human reproductive capacities, and much lower than the historically documented r of 3.7 percent for the *Bounty* mutineers and their Tahitian wives who fled from the British to settle remote Pitcairn Island.

Hawaiian population growth, however, was unlikely to have followed a simple exponential trajectory of constant growth from first settlement up to the time of contact. The conditions affecting fertility and mortality of the initial settlers were undoubtedly not the same as for their descendants centuries later, after drought-prone marginal lands had been occupied, and high-density conditions prevailed across the archipelago. Population growth is likely to have been rapid and exponential in the first few centuries following initial arrival, when there was no scarcity of prime agricultural land. Later on, when agricultural land had become limiting and populations had expanded even into the marginal lands, feedback loops are likely to have had damping effects on the rate of population growth (Kirch 1984, 101–104; Puleston and Tuljapurkar 2008). Moreover, it is likely that population dynamics differed between islands or even between districts with varying production regimes and risk factors. These issues can be addressed by archaeologists and paleodemographers with empirical data.

Demographic Characteristics of Precontact Hawaiians

Since the passage of the Native American Graves Protection and Repatriation Act in 1990, it is no longer considered ethical to excavate and analyze ancient Hawaiian skeletal remains (*iwi kūpuna*). Prior to that time, however, several major burial sites were excavated and studied. Moreover, burial sites continue to be exposed through development and construction activities. The observations of *iwi kūpuna* at these sites provide information on the biological and demographic characteristics of precontact Hawaiians that remains valuable for understanding the health and demographic characteristics of these populations. By examining skeletal remains, physical anthropologists are able to determine for individuals the age at death, sex, stature, some aspects of diet, patterns of physical activity, the general state of health, some specific diseases suffered, sometimes the cause of death, and for adult women even the number of children borne. For entire populations, such as all of those buried in a single sand dune cemetery, these studies can reveal the rate of mortality and life expectancy of the group.

Anthropological analysis of Hawaiian skeletal remains began with Chappel's study of the jaws and teeth of ancient Hawaiians (1927). The most extensive analysis of Hawaiian skeletal material was Snow's (1974) examination of 1,171 burials from the Mōkapu sand dune site on Oʻahu. Other osteological studies of major archaeological burial complexes, all on Hawaiʻi Island, include those of Underwood (1969) for the Puʻu Aliʻi burials at South Point, Pietrusewsky (1971b; Pietrusewsky et al. 1990) for the ʻAnaehoʻomalu cave burials, Kam (1979) for the Kalāhuipuaʻa burials, and Han et al. (1986) for 347 burials at Keōpū, Kona. The large sand dune burial site at Honokahua, Maui, excavated by a CRM project linked to a proposed hotel development (see chapter 1), contained the *iwi kūpuna* of 1,016 individuals, with an analysis of the skeletal remains by Pietrusewsky et al. (1991; see also Donham 1989, 2000). The following comments touch on just a few of the results of these and other studies.

The *average* age at death of early Hawaiians was about 30 years, with a slightly longer average life span for males (32 years) than for females (29 years). Less than 4 percent lived past age 40, and only an even smaller handful of *kūpuna* lived past 50 years of age. As Sara Collins writes, the age distribution evident in the burial populations "meant that, on the whole, two generations were alive at any one time. Put another way, each child's parents were probably living, but his or her grandparents were probably dead" (in Han et al. 1986, 245). While these numbers might seem low, they are actually quite high when compared to life expectancy in other ancient societies around the world. In classical Rome, for example, life expectancy at birth was in the range from 20 to 30 years (Frier 2009). Collins provides life tables giving specific data on life expectancy and survivorship for the Keōpū and Mōkapu populations (in Han et al. 1986, tables 48 and 49; see also Collins, Han, and Armstrong 1993 for a revised life table for the Mōkapu population).

Snow notes that the Hawaiians were a physically homogeneous population; indeed, their phenotype is statistically distinguishable from other Polynesian populations. In height, the average man stood about 5 feet 7 inches, while the average woman was a bit shorter, 5 feet 3 inches. Among the phenotypic characteristics typical of early Hawaiians were their generally large heads and a high frequency of "rocker jaws" and of shovel-shaped incisors. Hawaiians were especially noteworthy for their muscular bodies and narrow hips. As Charles Snow comments, "The limb and hip bones showed an extraordinary muscular development, in women as well as men. Indeed, all of their bones bespeak the vigorous and strenuous outdoor existence of these people" (Snow 1974, 11). Careful observation of wear and stress patterns on bones also reveals some insights regarding the motor habits of pre-contact Hawaiians: "The tilt of the tibial plateau reveals that they habitually kept their knees bent, both when in motion and when standing. Interestingly enough, their carved figurines are represented in this position. . . . All who could . . . squatted with their feet flat on the ground, as do all young children, and thus marked their bones with extra facets (squatting facets) on the hip, knee, and ankle joints" (11).

Precontact Hawaiians generally enjoyed good health, although their skeletal remains exhibit some pathologies. Most common is chronic arthritis (both osteoarthritis and rheumatoid arthritis) and osteophytosis. Other pathologies that have been noted include osteomyelitis, and congenital malformations such as spina bifida. Dental caries and pyorrhea are frequently evident. Rarer diseases or disorders are noted occasionally, such as a large gallstone found in the abdominal region of a middle-aged female in the Kalāhuipua'a burial cave (Kam 1979); the gallstone may have been responsible for her death.

Snow was intrigued by the evidence for artificial deformation or shaping of the head, citing ethnographic descriptions of the practice among historic-period Hawaiians. Snow's conclusions were supported by computer-assisted analyses of cranial morphometrics by Schendel, Walker, and Kamisugi (1980). A second cultural practice frequently seen in skeletal material is the removal of the front teeth (incisors), ethnographically documented as an expression of grief or mourning upon the loss of a close relative or of an *ali'i*.

The Demographic History of Ancient Hawai'i

Archaeologists cannot directly count past populations, so some kind of indirect or "proxy" data representative of population numbers is required. Skeletal series provide information on life expectancy and survivorship, health, and nutrition but cannot inform us about population size or growth rates. Archaeologists in Hawai'i have used two methods to estimate population growth rates. The first involves a kind of paleo–census taking, by counting house sites that have been radiocarbon dated and plotting these per unit interval of time. If an average number of occupants per household is further assumed, such house counts can be transformed into population estimates. The second method is based on the assumption that the production of anthropogenic charcoal correlates with population size (Rick 1987); series of radiocarbon dates provide a proxy for the rate of population growth but do not estimate actual population size. Both methods, of course, are specific to regions where such data have been obtained.

Archaeologists began to study ancient Hawaiian population trends in the 1970s. Drawing upon data from 51 dated habitation sites on the western side of Hawai'i Island, Robert Hommon (1976a, 189–224), generated a set of "site-population growth sequences." These curves suggested a nonlinear rate of population increase, with the west Hawai'i population growing rapidly before AD 1400, then tapering off, and either leveling off or even declining from AD 1600 to contact (fig. 8.1). Hommon argued that a major phase of "inland expansion" had commenced around AD 1400, linked with the development of the dryland field systems.

Ross Cordy attempted to track population growth in North Kona District on Hawai'i Island by counting the archaeological

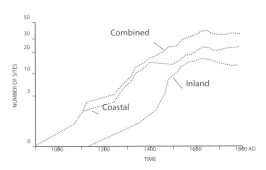

FIGURE 8.1 Robert Hommon developed curves for coastal and inland population on Hawai'i Island, based on a total of 51 dated habitation sites. *(After Kirch 2010)*

remains of "contemporary sleeping houses" and multiplying this number "by 6 [persons] to gain an absolute population estimate" (Cordy 1981, 91). The house sites were dated using the then-prevalent method of volcanic-glass dating (see chapter 3), now regarded as of questionable validity. Data from eight *ahupua'a* in North Kona showed a regional population beginning with 18 persons at AD 1400–1450, rising to a maximum of 240 persons at AD 1650–1700, and falling off slightly to 216 persons at AD 1750–1780 (Cordy 1981, table 58).

Kirch argued that "population dynamics" played an important role in Polynesian and Hawaiian cultural evolution (Kirch 1980, 41–43; 1982; 1984, 104–111; 1985, 286–289), drawing upon the r/K selection theory of island biogeography (MacArthur and Wilson 1967). (The r stands for the intrinsic rate of population growth, and the K for carrying capacity or maximum population that can be supported at a given level of technology.) In this model, colonizing Polynesian populations were characterized by the cultural equivalent of an r-selection pattern—with a high rate of population growth, generalizing and broad-based subsistence practices, and only weakly developed sociopolitical controls on production. Later in time, populations that had reached high density levels transitioned to a K-selection pattern, with conscious regulation of reproduction, economic specialization, well-developed sociopolitical controls on production, and intense competition. Kirch (1984) drew upon two data sets to test a model of *logistic* population growth, in which r is increasingly influenced by K as the population size grows (Hutchinson 1978). Data from west Hawai'i Island showed that "the period from about AD 1250 to 1650 was critical and, in this region at least, may have been a major era of technical, social, and political change in which demography played a significant role" (Kirch 1985, 289). Rapid population growth and the expansion of population into inland and ecologically marginal regions were key characteristics used to define the "Expansion Period" (AD 1100–1650) in Kirch's four-period cultural historical sequence (303–304). For the following Proto-Historic Period (AD 1650–1795) just prior to European contact, the data suggested that "growth rates had declined substantially and that local populations may have been oscillating around a 'plateau'" (307).

Following these pioneering efforts, larger data sets have become available, partly as a result of CRM archaeology. Tom Dye and Eric Komori exploited these expanded data (Dye and Komori 1992; Dye 1994; see also Jane Allen 1992; Spear 1992; Williams 1992), using cumulative probability distributions of radiocarbon dates as a proxy measure of population. Dye and Komori summed the individual probability distributions in a sample of 598 radiocarbon dates into a single cumulative distribution, which they regarded as a proxy for actual population numbers over time. (The assumption here is that if populations were stable, all time periods would be represented by similar numbers of radiocarbon dates. As populations increase, however, more fires are lit and thus more radiocarbon samples were left behind for archaeologists to find and date.) The Dye-Komori growth curve consists of two distinct sectors: a pre–AD 1450 sector with exponential growth, and a post–AD 1450 stable or fluctuating sector, suggesting that something happened around the fifteenth century to result in a dramatic demographic shift.

Mike Carson (2005a) compiled 272 radiocarbon dates for Kaua'i Island, with a curve that exhibits exponential increase beginning around AD 1000 and continuing up to about AD 1500. Mark D. McCoy's (2007) analysis of 137 radiocarbon dates from archaeological contexts on Moloka'i Island showed an exponential rise during the Expansion Period, and a leveling off of growth during the final Proto-Historic Period. Kristen Hara (2008) analyzed

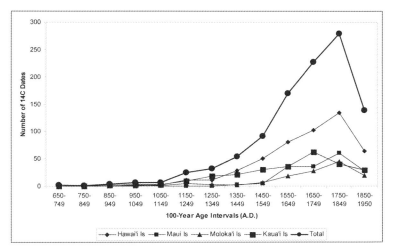

FIGURE 8.2 Radiocarbon date frequency curves for four islands have been used as proxy indicators of population growth. Note that the curve for Kaua'i Island peaks slightly earlier than those for the other three islands. *(After Kirch 2010)*

397 radiocarbon dates from Hawai'i Island, mostly from Kohala and Kona Districts. The frequency distributions of these larger radiocarbon data sets are displayed by 100-year temporal intervals in figure 8.2 (note that "conventional" radiocarbon ages, rather than calibrated ages, are plotted). The cumulative distribution exhibits a distinct exponential growth phase from around the twelfth to sixteenth centuries, followed by a slowing in the rate of increase—but not a cessation of growth—in the seventeenth and eighteenth centuries.

Kirch (2007d) analyzed a paleodemographic data set from Kahikinui District on leeward Maui, with 169 radiocarbon dates. Intensive archaeological survey over about 12 km² of Kahikinui, combined with excavation and dating of 51 residential complexes, allows the calculation of population sizes using a more precise house-count method. Figure 8.3 shows the frequency of these dated house sites by century. Settlement in Kahikinui did not commence until ca. AD 1400, no doubt reflecting the region's aridity and challenges for agricultural production. The number of residential complexes in Kahikinui grew slowly at first, peaked in the eighteenth century, and then declined rapidly after European contact.

Kahikinui—one of the most arid and marginal zones for agriculture—represents the low end of the Hawaiian population density spectrum. At its peak, the ratio of people to land in the zone below 900 m elevation in Kahikinui was between 43 and 57 persons per km² (Kirch 2007d). The Kaupō District to the east of Kahikinui, with higher average annual rainfall, nutrient-rich soils, and a well-developed dryland field system (Kirch, Holson, and Baer 2009), had a density in 1831–1832 of 146 persons per square kilometer, according to the missionary census (Schmitt 1973, 18). This, however, was after decades of contact and depopulation;

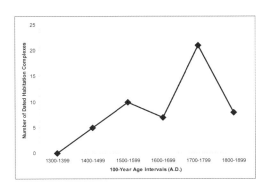

FIGURE 8.3 Numbers of radiocarbon-dated habitation complexes in Kahikinui District of Maui Island suggest continued population increase up until the time of initial European contact. *(After Kirch 2010)*

it seems plausible that precontact population density in Kaupō was considerably higher, perhaps as much as 300 persons per km^2. Based on a study of part of the leeward Kohala Field System on Hawai'i, Ladefoged and Graves (2007, 86) estimated that this zone of intensive dryland agriculture had a density of 139 persons per km^2. These estimates for Kahikinui, Kaupō, and Kohala give a reasonably good indication of density levels for areas that were dependent on intensified dryland cultivation, with sweet potato as the primary crop.

In zones dominated by irrigated taro cultivation, population densities reached even higher levels. Hālawa Valley on windward Moloka'i offers a good example, where the valley floor was covered in about 22 ha of irrigated pondfields, and remained a major center for wet taro production well into the nineteenth century (P-K. Anderson 2001; Kirch and Kelly 1975). The colluvial slopes provided additional fertile land for dryland cropping of aroids, bananas, and tree crops. In 1836, the missionary Harvey R. Hitchcock reported a local population of 506 in Hālawa, which amounted to a population density of 418 persons per km^2. Waialua District on northern O'ahu, with extensive irrigation complexes and fishponds (Kirch and Sahlins 1992), supported an even higher density. In 1831, Waialua's population was 2,640 persons (Schmitt 1973, 19), and with 3.5 km^2 of arable land, the density was 754 people per km^2. These examples reflect the high densities possible in zones with extensive irrigation coupled with large fishponds.

Population, Land, and Intensification

The long-term demographic history of Hawai'i is relevant to larger issues regarding the linkages between human population, agriculture, and food supply. Debate over these issues traces back at least to Thomas Malthus (1798), who observed that whereas human reproduction has the potential to expand exponentially (e.g., 2, 4, 8, 16, . . .), increases in the food supply are typically arithmetic (e.g., 2, 4, 6, 8, . . .). From his work derives the classic notion of "Malthusian" checks on population growth resulting from food shortage, famine, and the like. In the 1960s, economist Ester Boserup (1965) countered Malthus by arguing that technology and innovation are able to head off the inevitable Malthusian crunch; her theory inspired debate among anthropologists over the processes of agricultural "intensification" (Brookfield 1972, 1984; Kirch 1994; Morrison 1994; Spooner, ed., 1972).

The apparent contradiction between Malthus and Boserup can, however, be resolved. Ronald D. Lee (1986) and James Wood (1998) developed models that reconcile conflicts in the theories of Malthus and Boserup. Wood combines these two perspectives in a "Malthus-and-Boserup (MaB) ratchet" where technological advances allow for "a Boserupian escape from the Malthusian trap" (1998, 113); such escapes, however, are only temporary. Shripad Tuljapurkar and his colleagues, working within the Hawai'i Biocomplexity Project, integrated food supply and demographic rates including fertility and mortality into a demographic model of food availability (Lee, Puleston, and Tuljapurkar 2009; Lee and Tuljapurkar 2010; Puleston and Tuljapurkar 2008; Puleston, Tuljapurkar, and Winterhalder 2014).

On an island with limited arable land, the amount of land cultivated is a function of available labor. In the initial settlement period, when the population is small, the cultivated area expands in proportion to the labor supply, as the population grows. As population increases over time, the cultivated area eventually expands to reach the limits of arable land; at this point land—not labor—becomes the limiting factor. Until the limits on the supply of new land have been reached, the rate of population increase can be quite high, essentially exponential.

Human mortality and fertility, however, respond sensitively to food supply. Cedric Puleston and Shripad Tuljapurkar (2008) defined the *food ratio* (E), a key measure of food availability. When E is greater than 1, the population is able to increase, but when E approaches or drops below 1, negative feedback effects impinge on mortality and fertility, causing the population growth rate to decline. The dynamics of this feedback are nonlinear, with the food ratio responding to variation in crop yield as well as to variability in the population structure. Consequently, the population dynamics are stochastic: "Variable climate interacts with the plant–soil dynamics and affects yield, and the population responds to changing yields via changing mortality and fertility" (Kirch et al. 2012, 25).

The Hawai'i Biocomplexity Project developed simulations of population growth and food availability for different areas and levels of agricultural productivity in the leeward dryland field systems of Hawai'i. These growth curves all exhibit an early phase of exponential growth followed by a rapid transition to a stochastic equilibrium as the food ratio E approaches 1 (fig. 8.4). The food ratio, for its part, exhibits a mirror image of the population curve, with at first gradual but then rapid decline to a stochastic equilibrium of E < 1 (fig. 8.5). As Puleston and Tuljapurkar observe, "When E < 1 the population experiences some degree of food deprivation and so we call E the hunger level" (2008, 149). In these simulations, the time between initial colonization and the achievement of a stochastic equilibrium is about 250 years, regardless of differences in territory size or productivity. This insight is significant, given that archaeological dating of the leeward Kohala Field System

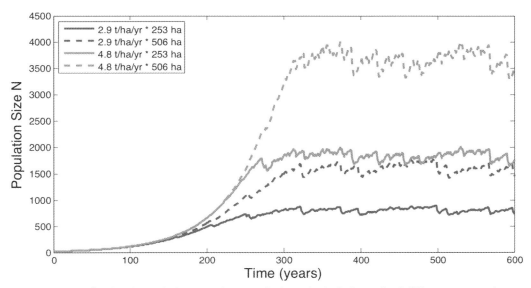

FIGURE 8.4 Four simulated population growth curves for hypothetical *ahupua'a* of different areas and with different levels of soil fertility in the Kohala region of Hawai'i Island. Despite differences in area and soil fertility, all four simulations display a similar pattern, reaching carrying capacity after approximately 250 to 300 years. *(After Kirch, Asner, et al. 2012)*

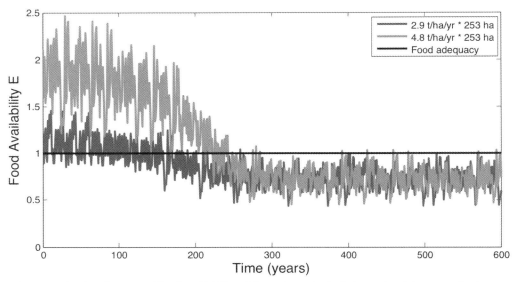

FIGURE 8.5 Simulated curves of food availability with two hypothetical *ahupua'a* of the same size but with differing levels of soil fertility in the Kohala region of Hawai'i Island. In both simulations, food availability declines to less than 1 after 250 to 300 years. *(After Kirch, Asner, et al. 2012)*

indicates that initial settlement and farming in the region began about AD 1400, and that a "full land" situation had been reached by AD 1650, two and a half centuries later.

These models suggest that in any given area within the Hawaiian Islands, initial population growth would have been essentially exponential, fueled by abundant food (E > 1). Labor—the numbers of able-bodied individuals available to clear and work the land—was the limiting factor. As population increased and the limits to arable land were approached, the food ratio would have started to decline, lowering the rate of population growth as periodic food shortages began to have an effect on mortality and fertility. Of course, investments in agricultural infrastructure, such as terracing for pondfield irrigation in valleys, or the development of short-fallow field systems with intensive sugarcane mulching, could have improved the food ratio (the Boserup effect). This is the essence of the MaB rachet.

The paleodemographic evidence accumulated by archaeologists in Hawai'i indicates a phase of exponential population increase from initial settlement up to about AD 1550–1600; during this phase the intrinsic rate of increase (r) is likely to have been in the range of 1.2 to 1.8 percent, with the population doubling every 40 to 60 years, or every two to three generations. Thus, for a period of about five centuries, Hawaiian society was evolving in the context of an expanding, growth economy. But by the mid-sixteenth century—the close of the Expansion Period—the rate of population growth began to decline; in the leeward zones with their dryland field systems, growth may have leveled off. Even where population continued to grow, this would have been at significantly lower rates. A rapid shift in the inflection point of the Hawaiian population curve is thus critical for understanding the political dynamics of the succeeding Archaic States Period. The change in the rate of population growth was likely to have been accompanied by increasing stress on these populations, as the population neared its equilibrium saturation point (Wood 1998, 107).

Periodic food shortages are referenced in the Hawaiian *moʻolelo,* as, for example, a famine in the Kula and Makawao areas of Maui in the time of Kiha-a-Piʻilani, and another in the Kona region of Hawaiʻi during Kalaniʻōpuʻu's reign (Kamakau 1961, 23, 105). Both of these regions were dependent upon rain-fed dryland cultivation. Davida Malo (1951, 22, 43) refers to *pala* and *hapuʻu* ferns and other wild plants as famine food. Further evidence for periodic food stress was noted by Collins in her study of the Keōpū skeletal remains, where several juveniles showed signs of "occasional shortage of food" (in Han et al. 1986, 247).

As Kirch (2010, 195–196) has argued, the MaB ratchet model is critical to explaining the archaeological record of agricultural intensification in Hawaiʻi. On Oʻahu and Molokaʻi the MaB ratchet is evident in the intensification of taro irrigation systems, which had commenced by AD 1200 and resulted in the construction of extensive valley pondfield systems by AD 1400–1500. On Maui and Hawaiʻi Islands, population began expanding out of the limited valley regions (primarily windward Kohala District) by around AD 1400, when cultivation on the leeward slopes first becomes evident in the archaeological record. The sequence of agricultural development in leeward Kohala (Ladefoged and Graves 2008a) begins with an initial stage of intensification from AD 1400 to 1650, followed by a second stage from AD 1650 to contact:

> During this second stage field plot size was significantly reduced and labor inputs presumably reached their maximum with the use of agronomic strategies such as intensive mulching.... Such progressive intensification of the major dryland field systems can be seen as sequential turns of the MaB ratchet. These allowed population size to keep expanding, but after each turn of the ratchet the system once again followed the inevitable progression towards marginal returns and an equilibrium saturation point, requiring further adjustments in agronomic methods and / or labor inputs. (Kirch 2010, 195–196)

In sum, the islands' population first underwent a period of exponential expansion, beginning with initial settlement and continuing to about AD 1550–1600. Population was initially concentrated in those regions most suitable to agricultural development, through irrigation and colluvial slope gardening, then after about AD 1400 with shifting cultivation and increasingly intensive dryland farming in the leeward regions. This initial phase of exponential growth ended around the close of the Expansion Period, followed by a phase of declining population growth rates, but with continued expansion of settlement into the most marginal ecological zones (such as Kahikinui, Maui) where local populations may have continued to grow. From the Foundation Period, through the Late Voyaging Period, and up to the close of the Expansion Period, the population of the islands skyrocketed; doubling times probably spanned one to two human generations. By the late fifteenth century, however, all of the lowland regions had been territorially claimed and demarcated; the "salubrious cores" had extremely high population densities. Quite rapidly, the initial phase of exponential growth shifted to one with markedly lower growth rates, and presumably stabilization of population in some areas. While this demographic history did not directly "cause" the remarkable sociopolitical transformations of the late Expansion and Archaic State Periods, it was a necessary condition underlying those transformations.

9

TECHNOLOGY, CRAFT SPECIALIZATION, AND THE WEALTH ECONOMY

This chapter focuses on *portable artifacts,* the individual objects—such as adzes, fishhooks, or flake tools of volcanic glass—excavated from the floors of house sites, rockshelters, and other archaeological contexts, or sometimes found on the surface of sites. Portable artifacts are only one aspect of technology and material culture, but they form a convenient class for analysis and discussion.

No two artifacts are exactly alike (particularly in the case of nonindustrial, nonstandardized material culture); variation, the differences and similarities between individual artifacts, provides the basis for archaeological analysis. The museum curator often hears such comments as "Why do you need to keep all those hundreds of adzes? Won't one or two do?" But to the archaeologist, an adze is not just "another adze." A particular adze may be large or small, rectangular or triangular in cross section, with or without a tang, of high-quality basalt or lesser-quality stone, fully polished or unfinished, and so on. Each of these variations has the potential to reveal something significant about the culture and society of which the adze was, long ago, a small but vital component.

Just as significant as an object's physical attributes (measurements, weight, or material) is its *context.* To the archaeologist, the most "valuable" artifacts are those that can be assigned not only to a particular location but also to a specific stratigraphic context and, therefore, a place in time. Objects found together in the same site and layer constitute an *artifact assemblage* that was used by people who occupied that particular site during the time that the cultural layer accumulated.

Over time the material culture of any society changes; some objects continue to be made just as they were by the ancestors, while others will be made in new ways, or with new materials, or simply in different shapes and forms. Documenting *sequences* of artifact change has long been a main task of archaeology; this is usually referred to as the culture historical approach. Archaeologists also seek to understand *why* artifacts change over time. Was a change in fishhook or adze forms an adaptive response to environmental conditions, such as the lack of a critical raw material? Or was it a stylistic change, an innovation that "caught on" and became the new vogue? Changes in artifact styles were not uniform across the archipelago, so tracing stylistic differences that arose between island communities is yet another goal of archaeological research.

Approaches to the Study of Hawaiian Material Culture

The classification of artifacts into series of classes, or types (sometimes referred to as typology), is the oldest approach to the study of Hawaiian artifacts. William T. Brigham, who amassed Bishop Museum's collection of artifacts, published monographs on stone implements, barkcloth, and featherwork (Brigham 1899, 1902, 1903). In the 1920s and 1930s, island-wide surveys of Hawaiian archaeology included typological discussions of artifact collections, but these were based almost entirely on surface-collected artifacts lacking temporal context (e.g., Bennett 1931; McAllister 1933a, 1933b). In this early work, little if any attention was placed on artifact context.

The Hawaiian Archaeological Program of the 1950s (see chapter 1) accumulated large assemblages of artifacts from excavated sites. Fishhooks were emphasized (Emory, Bonk, and Sinoto 1959; Y. H. Sinoto 1962), although adzes, ornaments, and other objects were also studied (Emory 1968; Sinoto, n.d.a, n.d.b). Kenneth Emory and Yosihiko Sinoto thought that by comparing artifacts found in early Hawaiian settlement sites with those in the Marquesas Islands, the Society Islands, and elsewhere in Polynesia, they would be able to trace early migration routes (Emory 1968; Emory and Sinoto 1965; Y. H. Sinoto 1967, 1970, 1983, 1996). Descriptive accounts and classifications of Hawaiian artifact assemblages, illustrating a variety of artifacts frequently encountered in Hawaiian sites, include Bonk (1954); Chapman and Kirch (1979); Emory and Sinoto (1961); Kirch (1979a); Kirch and Kelly, eds., (1975); Pearson, Kirch, and Pietrusewsky (1971); Soehren (1966); and Tuohy (1965).

Another approach focuses on artifact manufacture: the raw materials used, tools required, steps or stages in production, and the resulting discard or waste products. Many Hawaiian artifacts are either tools used to make other artifacts (such as files and abraders of coral, stone, and sea urchin spines) or the by-products of manufacture (such as cut fragments of bone and shell). Emory and his colleagues studied processes of fishhook manufacture (Emory, Bonk, and Sinoto 1959). Others have focused on the technology of stone adze production, or on the resharpening and rejuvenation of adzes (e.g., Bayman et al. 2004; Bayman and Moniz-Nakamura 2001; Clarkson et al. 2014, 2015; P. L. Cleghorn 1982, 1986; Dixon et al. 1994; Kahn et al. 2009; P. C. McCoy 1976, 1977; P. C. McCoy and Gould 1977; Olszewski 2007; Weisler 1988, 1990a; Weisler et al. 2013). There is much scope, nonetheless, for additional studies of artifact production.

Darby Filimoehala et al. (2015) focus on a class of artifacts defined by the material from which they were made, in this case *hematite*, a mineral form of iron oxide with a red to reddish-brown color. A surprising range of artifacts were made from hematite, including abraders, adzes, pitching discs, food pounders, bowling discs, and most frequently sinkers for use in the *lūheʻe* octopus lure rig (2015, table 1). While found across all of the main islands, artifacts of hematite are most abundant on Kauaʻi, somewhat less so on Oʻahu and Molokaʻi, and rare on Hawaiʻi. This correlates with the fact that as a weathering product, hematite is naturally more abundant on the geologically older islands.

The functions of many artifacts are often known from ethnographic information (Buck 1957). Adzes, for example, were generally used for working wood. However, which of the many varieties of adze were used for timber felling, which for canoe manufacture, which for image carving, and so on? Were adzes ever used as agricultural implements, for cutting terraces out of hillsides or digging irrigation channels? With stone tools such as adzes and scrapers, techniques have been developed for examining edge wear or edge damage, such as striations, microflakes, or gloss. The basic assumption is that distinctive kinds of use (e.g., cutting, scraping, chopping) produce equally distinctive wear patterns. Relatively few use-wear studies have been carried out on Hawaiian artifacts, although Weisler and Haslam (2005) examined residues on volcanic-glass flakes. Paul Cleghorn (1982) experimented with the edge-holding properties of Mauna Kea adze basalt, while Schousboe, Riford, and Kirch (1983) studied edge-damage patterns on volcanic-glass flakes from the Waimea-Kawaihae Road corridor sites. More research of this kind would be informative.

Controlled experiments can aid in functional research on artifacts. Cleghorn (1982) studied archaeological flakes and preforms for clues about adze manufacture sequences, and replicated adzes using identical raw material and hammerstones. In these experiments, Cleghorn tested hypotheses concerning techniques and steps in adze manufacture, developing interpretations that could not have been derived solely from the observation of archaeological specimens. Clarkson et al. (2015, 71) applied experimental replication to the study of Hawaiian adze production, leading to the view that "some adze makers were undoubtedly specialists."

An exhaustive review of ancient Hawaiian artifacts is beyond the scope of this book, but the most frequently encountered artifact types are reviewed in the following pages. For a detailed ethnographic treatment of Hawaiian material culture, the reader is referred to the classic study of Peter Buck (1957). The nineteenth-century collection of Hawaiian artifacts accumulated by the Rev. J. S. Emerson, described by Catherine Summers (1999), is likewise a valuable source on Hawaiian material culture.

Tools

Adzes and Chisels

Probably the single most important Hawaiian tool, used for a variety of tasks, was the adze (*koʻi*), consisting of a stone head or blade hafted to a wooden handle with sennit lashing. The wooden handle and lashing almost never survives in archaeological contexts, but the stone heads are ubiquitous (fig. 9.1). Although they are only part of a compound tool, archaeologists commonly refer to these stone heads as adzes, and we follow suit here. Adzes range in size from tiny blades, only a few centimeters long, up to a length of 55 cm, the largest known specimen (illustrated in Brigham 1902, pl. LVII). They were manufactured by percussion flaking and reduction of a *blank* of dense basalt or andesite into a *preform*, where the cross section and general shape of the adze is evident, followed by grinding and polishing of the finished adze (fig. 9.2). The fine-grained, dense basalt or andesite was obtained from quarries distributed throughout the islands (see below). Achieving the nearly

FIGURE 9.1 Typical Hawaiian adzes with quadrangular cross sections and pronounced tangs, from Kuli'ou'ou rockshelter on O'ahu Island. *(After Emory and Sinoto 1961)*

90-degree angles seen on most Hawaiian adzes (resulting in square cross sections) required great knapping skill (Clarkson et al. 2014, 2015; P. L. Cleghorn 1982). Grinding was performed on large, stationary boulder grindstones, often situated near streams (fig. 9.3). The front faces and bevels of Hawaiian adzes were typically well ground, while the back and the tang were often left rough, with flake scars remaining, helping to keep the sennit binding from slipping.

Considerable variation in adze form is exhibited across Polynesia, with each island group having distinctive characteristics (Buck et al. 1930; Duff 1959). Emory's analysis of Polynesian adzes suggested that the form of the cross section (quadrangular, triangular, trapezoidal, etc.) was a key variable in such comparative studies (Emory 1968). Roger Green (1971a) found important chronological changes in adze form over time, from early Western Polynesian adzes with plano-convex cross sections to later Eastern Polynesian forms

FIGURE 9.2 A workshop area outside a rockshelter at the Mauna Kea adze quarry, with numerous adze blanks and preforms visible. *(Photo courtesy Bishop Museum Department of Anthropology)*

FIGURE 9.3 A large boulder in Hālawa Valley, Moloka'i, exhibits basin-shaped depressions where adzes were ground and polished. *(Photo by P. V. Kirch)*

dominated by quadrangular cross sections. The presence or absence of a tang is another feature with temporal significance.

Emory noted that "no place exhibits such a steadfast adherence to one form of adz as Hawaii" (1968, 162). Hawaiian adzes are highly standardized, distinguishable from other Polynesian adzes by their rectangular or quadrangular cross sections, with angles of nearly 90 degrees. They usually have a distinct tang, which facilitated lashing of the stone blade to a wooden handle; some of the smaller, thinner adzes, however, lack a tang. While adzes from later Hawaiian sites almost invariably display these characteristics, a few adzes excavated from sites of the Foundation and Late Voyaging Periods (such as the Bellows dune site, the Hālawa dune site, and the Pu'u Ali'i site at South Point) do not fall into this pattern. These early adzes are notable for their plano-convex, trapezoidal, and reverse-triangular cross sections, and lack of a developed tang, traits with parallels in early Eastern Polynesian adzes excavated from the Marquesas, Society Islands, and Cook Islands.

Cleghorn (1992) examined 147 adzes excavated from 21 archaeological sites, analyzing the temporal distribution of several attributes, including cross section and presence/absence of a tang, concluding that "adzes forms were variable throughout the Hawaiian prehistoric sequence" (129). Cleghorn postulated that variation in adze cross section had to do more with different functions than with temporal change. However, Cleghorn's univariate analysis (examining one variable at a time) did not assess whether clusters of variables might be indicative of distinct adze types. In our view, a multivariate reanalysis of Hawaiian adzes from secure stratigraphic contexts would be informative.

Occasionally one finds unusual or anomalous adzes, such as a cache of five specimens from Haʻikū, Maui (Kirch 1972). These five adzes (fig. 9.4), of a grayish andesite, exhibit triangular cross sections with distinctive tangs, of a type otherwise known only from the Marquesas Islands (the *koma* type adze; Suggs 1961, 111, fig. 31b). Since the Haʻikū adzes were surface finds, we do not know their age or associations.

In a study of more than 800 adzes in Bishop Museum, Jennifer Kahn and Tom Dye (2015) identified 11 specimens with symmetrical, double bevels, distinct from the asymmetrical bevel characteristic of adzes. These double-beveled tools can be classified as axes. None of the axes are from a dated archaeological context, so their chronological associations are not known. Double-beveled axes are common in the Mangareva Islands but otherwise rare in Polynesia.

As valuable objects made from stone that often came from distant locales, and that required hours of skilled labor to fashion and polish, adzes were not always discarded when they broke or were damaged during use. There was considerable resharpening of adzes by chipping and regrinding the bevel, and even complete rejuvenation (recycling) of adzes by reworking a once larger adze into a new, smaller one. Deborah Olszewski (2007) found that recycling of adzes was a significant activity at several sites in North Hālawa Valley, Oʻahu.

Aside from adzes, basalt cores were fashioned into narrow-bladed chisels or gouges, with rounded bevels (fig. 9.5). Handheld, or perhaps hafted onto a straight wooden shaft, these chisels would have been useful for hewing out the interiors of smaller bowls.

FIGURE 9.4 Five adze preforms with triangular cross sections, from a cache found at Hāʻiku, Maui Island. *(Photo by P. V. Kirch)*

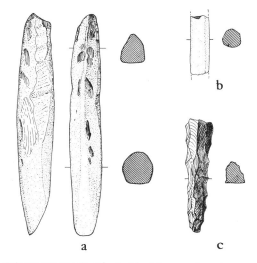

FIGURE 9.5 Basalt chisel, chisel fragment, and chisel preform from Oʻahu rockshelter sites. (*After Emory and Sinoto 1961*)

Adze Quarries

At least 25 quarries where fine-grained basalt (or in a few cases, andesite) was extracted from rock exposures or outcrops have been identified, distributed across all of the main islands except Niʻihau. Only a few of these have been studied in any detail. Other quarries are certainly yet to be discovered. Table 9.1 lists some of the major quarries in the archipelago.

The largest quarry by far—and also the most intensively studied—is situated between 3,355 and 3,780 m elevation on the south slope of Mauna Kea on Hawaiʻi Island. This quarry complex includes extraction areas, workshops (with extensive debitage

TABLE 9.1. Major adze quarries of the Hawaiian Islands

ISLAND	QUARRY	COMMENTS AND REFERENCES
Kauaʻi	Waimea, Mokihana Ridge	Bennett 1931, 56
	Nonou Ridge, Wailua River	Bennett 1931, 56
Oʻahu	Waiahole Valley	Boulders strewn over a slope. Sterling and Summers 1978, 189
	Mokulua Islets	Sterling and Summers 1978, 240
	Kailua, Kawainui	Inland of Kaiwainui Marsh. Sterling and Summers 1978, 229. Destroyed by modern quarrying.
	Nānākuli	Weisler et al. 2013
Molokaʻi	ʻAmikopala	Flanks of Mauna Loa volcano. Phelps 1937, 19–21; Summers 1971, 66–68; Weisler 2011
	Moʻomomi	Weisler 2011
	West Waiakāne	Weisler 2011
	Kāhinawai	Weisler 2011
	Kaʻeo	Weisler 2011
	Kaluakoʻi minor quarries	Eight "minor" quarries dispersed over this large *ahupuaʻa*; Weisler 2011
	Honokoʻi	Kirch et al. (in prep.)
Lānaʻi	Kapohaku	Emory 1924, 76; Weisler 1990a
Kahoʻolawe	Puʻu Mōiwi	McAllister 1933a, 29; McCoy, Makanani, and Sinoto 1993
Maui	Haleakalā	Mintmier 2007
	Nuʻu	Kahn et al. 2009
Hawaiʻi	Mauna Kea	Situated on the south slope of Mauna Kea, the largest quarry in the islands. P. C. McCoy 1977; P. L. Cleghorn 1982
	Pololū	Tuggle and Tomonari-Tuggle 1980

heaps), rockshelters where workers camped, and shrines, covering an estimated 19.4 km² (fig. 9.6). Patrick McCoy and Paul Cleghorn carried out extensive fieldwork at the Mauna Kea quarry complex in 1975–1976 (P. L. Cleghorn 1982; P. C. McCoy 1976, 1977; P. C. McCoy and Gould 1977; P. C. McCoy and Nees 2010, 2013; P. C. McCoy et al. 2009; P. C. McCoy et al. 2012). A flow of extremely fine-grained and dense blue-black basalt, the best single source of adze rock in the archipelago, attracted people to these inhospitable heights. The isotropic quality of this basalt is due to its having been extruded at a time when Mauna Kea summit was capped with glacial ice; rapid cooling of the flow in contact with the ice prevented the formation of a more crystalline structure. According to McCoy et al. (2012), two related sources of fine-grained toolstone were exploited at Mauna Kea:

> The primary source is a series of basalt flows found along and below an escarpment at 3750 m elevation in the vicinity of Puʻu Koʻokoʻolau and at similar elevations in the Pōhakuloa and Waikahalulu gulch drainages. Here are found the largest and most diverse sites in the quarry complex, defined in terms of the number, density and variety of extraction areas, other workshops, habitation rockshelters, shrines, petroglyphs, a basaltic glass source and possible burials. The second raw material source consists of glacial drift deposits of different ages containing lithologically similar sub-angular to sub-rounded boulders and cobbles that occur in both unconsolidated and indurated form. (409)

Twenty-three radiocarbon dates from three excavated rockshelter sites suggest that work at the quarry could have commenced as early as AD 1100, although this may reflect some inbuilt age in the unidentified wood charcoal that was dated. The radiocarbon dates indicate a "period of peak production" from about AD 1400 to 1750 (P. C. McCoy et al.

FIGURE 9.6 Large debitage pile of flakes and discarded adze blanks at the Mauna Kea adze quarry site. *(Photo courtesy Bishop Museum Department of Anthropology)*

TECHNOLOGY, CRAFT, ECONOMY • 195

2009, 445). Branch coral from a rockshelter was ^{230}Th dated to AD 1355 ± 28, while two separate coral offerings associated with shrines yielded calibrated ages of AD 1451 ± 39 and 1441 ± 3 (P. C. McCoy et al. 2009; P. C. McCoy et al. 2012).

Cleghorn's study of adze production at the Mauna Kea workshops indicated the following major manufacturing stages:

> It appears that the basic strategy was to establish and maintain the length of the adze early in the reduction sequence. The primary reduction of the length was done when the bevel was created. Bevels were usually created by the removal of three to five flakes . . . primarily in a direction parallel to the long axis of the adze, using the future cutting edge as the platform. Often, some flakes were also detached perpendicular to the long axis. . . . Preforms were made with parallel sides, with edge widths roughly equaling both midsection and butt widths. Thickness measures almost the same as these three widths. There seems to be little variability in these proportions, and this parallel-sided adze with a relatively equal width-to-thickness ratio appears to be the dominant form at the Quarry. (P. L. Cleghorn 1982, 216–217)

From his analyses, Cleghorn also drew inferences concerning the organization of labor at the Mauna Kea quarry:

> Preform manufacture generally followed a set sequence of manufacturing steps . . . where the basic cross section was formed first, then the bevel was created, and finally the tang was formed. Reasonable explanations for this sequence, stemming from the preform-making experimental program, have been offered (e.g., create the bevel early so as to reduce the risk of end shock). These results point to one fact, that there was a tremendous amount of standardization at the Quarry—standardization in adze form, standardization in size proportions, and standardization in procedure. This high degree of standardization supports the contention that the adze makers were craft specialists.

This study has also provided details on the dynamics of behavior at the quarry. It appears that expert craftsmen worked at the escarpment where there was abundant raw material. Novices or, perhaps more accurately, apprentices foraged for suitable raw material on the outwash plain, where they practiced their skills (P. L. Cleghorn 1982, 343).

Another quarry complex, smaller in scale than Mauna Kea but like the latter including multiple workshop areas as well as several shrines with uprights, is found at Puʻu Mōiwi on Kahoʻolawe Island (P. C. McCoy, Makanani, and Sinoto 1993). A single radiocarbon date on unidentified wood charcoal from a hearth feature at the complex (Beta-7900) yielded a calibrated age of AD 1250–1400 (82). P. C. McCoy, Makanani, and Sinoto (149–150), on the basis of some differences in the adze preforms found in the western and eastern sectors of the complex, speculate that two discrete communities residing at Hakioawa and at Ahupu may have accessed the fine-grained stone resources at Puʻu Mōiwi.

A quarry in the Nānākuli Valley on leeward Oʻahu was reported by Marshall Weisler et al. (2013), who describe the site as a series of small rockshelters with flaking debitage located around a steep gulch where an exposed dike or sill of fine-grained basalt about 2.4 m thick provided the rock source. A piece of branch coral from one of the rockshelters was ^{230}Th dated to AD 1234 ± 6. The basalt source exhibits a natural "jointed" formation, with a scree slope of angular cobbles providing a ready source of material from which to rough out preforms.

The arid western side of Molokaʻi Island was known as Kaluakoʻi, which literally translates as "the adze pit." No less than five major quarries and eight minor quarries or workshops have been documented across this region (Weisler 2011; Weisler et al. 2015). Most of the major quarries are found along the summit area of Mauna Loa volcano (Weisler 2011, fig. 1). Based on radiocarbon and branch coral dating, quarrying activity in Kaluakoʻi began as early as the thirteenth to fourteenth centuries. As at other quarries in the islands, shrines are associated with many of these quarries. At the eastern end of Molokaʻi, a previously unknown quarry and associated workshops were recently discovered in Honokoʻi Valley (Kirch et al. in prep.); Honokoʻi translates as "Adze Bay." Geochemical analysis of the Honokoʻi rock indicates that it was the main source for adze production at the Hālawa dune site.

A small quarry at an elevation of 580 m on the southern slope of Haleakalā, in the *ahupuaʻa* of Nuʻu, Maui, was studied by Jennifer Kahn et al. (2009). The rock source here consists of several outcrops of dense basalt of the Kula volcanic series. Individual cobbles were prized out of the ground and worked into preforms at the site (color plate 6). An analysis of blanks and preforms from the Nuʻu site demonstrates variation in both size and cross section, indicating that "adze production focused on creating the full adze kit needed for the variety of woodworking tasks that would be carried out in this *ahupuaʻa*" (Kahn et al. 2009, 158). On Maui, additional quarrying took place within Haleakalā Crater (Mintmier 2007; Mintmier, Mills, and Lundblad 2012).

On Lānaʻi Island, an adze quarry at Kapohaku on the eastern side of the Palawai Basin was first recorded by Emory (1921), and later studied by Weisler (1990a). The quarry extends over at least two hectares, including both extraction and workshop areas. According to Weisler, "small quadrangular adze blanks and preforms, both broad and thin in transverse section, were the dominant type of artefact" produced at Kapohaku (1990a, 46).

Geochemical Sourcing of Adzes and Basalt Lithics

Archaeologists in Hawaiʻi have long been interested in tracing adzes and adze-making debitage to the quarries where the fine-grained basalt was obtained. In the 1960s, William Kikuchi submitted rock samples from several quarries to University of Hawaiʻi geologist Gordon Macdonald, who provided petrographic descriptions of the quarry rocks based on thin sections. This petrographic approach was extended by Paul Cleghorn et al. (1985), who examined 43 thin sections from eight known quarries, producing a key to identification of the sources based on rock texture and the presence or absence of particular phenocrysts. Barbara Lass also used petrographic analysis to study the distribution of adzes on Hawaiʻi Island (Lass 1994; Withrow 1991). Although the petrographic approach was promising, it was superseded by the development of quantitative geochemical methods, especially energy-dispersive X-ray fluorescence (EDXRF). This nondestructive method produces a quantitative geochemical analysis that avoids the qualitative issues with thin-section petrography. The full potential for adze sourcing research was realized after the University of Hawai'i at Hilo (UHH) acquired an EDXRF spectrometer in 2004. Since then, under the direction of archaeologist Peter Mills and geologist Steve Lundblad, the UHH lab has analyzed more than 21,000 adzes, flakes, and other lithics from numerous sites across the islands (Mills and Lundblad 2014, 32). Some of the key sites whose lithic assemblages have been analyzed by the UHH EDXRF facility include the Nu'alolo rockshelter on Kaua'i (Mills et al. 2010); the Hālawa dune site on Moloka'i (Mills et al. 2018); habitation and ritual sites in Kahikinui District, Maui (Kirch et al. 2012); a stratified rockshelter at Kahalu'u, Hawai'i (Mills et al. 2011); and a series of habitation sites in leeward Kohala, Hawai'i (Mills et al. 2022).

The Nu'alolo assemblage of 807 basalt artifacts, along with 34 adzes in the Kaua'i Museum, revealed that 100 percent of the material came from sources on Kaua'i Island (Mills et al. 2010). There were no representatives of the Mauna Kea quarry, indicating that adzes from this major source were not transported as far as Kaua'i (although about 4% of adze material in O'ahu sites is consistent with the Mauna Kea source [Mills and Lundblad 2014, fig. 1]). Equally significant, much of the Nu'alolo assemblage consists of basalt not found locally in the Nā Pali District. Much of the material came from the Keahua I source in eastern Kaua'i, and was thus carried across the island, or transported by canoe to Nu'alolo. This contradicts the idea that *ahupua'a* communities were entirely self-sufficient.

At the other end of the archipelago, Mills et al. (2011) analyzed 955 flaked stone artifacts from the Kahalu'u Habitation Cave in Kona, on Hawai'i Island. The site lies on the Hualālai volcanic shield, yet less than 7 percent of the basalt debitage in the site matched the local Hualālai geochemistry. These results suggest that

> one of the largest population centers on Hawai'i Island was heavily reliant on non-local sources for their adzes, a condition that would foster interdistrict exchange either through chiefly intervention or commoner networks. Approximately half of the adze debitage at Kahalu'u Habitation Cave is consistent with the Mauna Kea Adze Quarry source and is present throughout the entire stratigraphic sequence. Eleven other geochemical groups were also present. (Mills and Lundblad 2014, 34)

Tim Rieth et al. (2013), analyzing lithics from two assemblages within the Hōnaunau National Historical Park, also found a diversity of sources from different regions of Hawai'i Island represented, again indicative of movement of adzes or adze stone between *ahupua'a* and *moku*.

Interdistrict and interisland movement of adzes and adze rock was demonstrated by the analysis of 328 adzes and basalt debitage from 36 sites in the Kahikinui District of Maui (Kirch et al. 2012). The material in this study came from a variety of both habitation and ritual (*heiau*) site contexts. Seventeen different sources were represented, and while the majority of material (71%) came from Maui Island, 27 percent derives from eight non-Maui sources, including Mauna Kea. Furthermore, the nonlocal source material appeared in higher frequency in elite residential features and in *heiau*. "The disproportionately high frequency of extralocal, fine-grained volcanic rock artifacts in either high-status residence sites or ritual, temple contexts strongly suggests that control over access to and distribution of these stone resources was controlled by elites," including district and *ahupuaʻa* chiefs, and priests (Kirch et al. 2012, 1060). As Kirch et al. remark, the "extra-Maui quarries lie beyond the political boundaries of the late precontact Maui kingdom," and include the separate polities of both Hawaiʻi and Oʻahu (1059), pointing to the significance of a wealth economy based on the control and distribution of high-valued items such as adzes made of superior, fine-grained stone.

Abrading Tools

Abrading tools made of coral (fig. 9.7), scoriaceous lava (fig. 9.8), dense basalt, pumice, and coral conglomerate, as well as from the spines of the slate pencil sea urchin (*Heterocentrotus mammillatus*) (fig. 9.9) are commonly found at Hawaiian sites. Early efforts at classification of abraders, especially those made of *Porites* coral, categorized them into functional types, such as "files," "saws," or "rubbing stones" based on their morphology and analogy with Western metal abrading tools (e.g., Ladd 1967; Emory and Sinoto 1961; Sinoto n.d.b; Soehren, n.d.). With a soft material such as *Porites* coral, however, a single abrading tool rapidly changes form as it is worn down through use. Kirch (1971a, 74, fig. 8) showed

FIGURE 9.7 Coral abraders of varied shapes from the Hālawa dune site, Molokaʻi Island. *(Photo by P. V. Kirch)*

FIGURE 9.8 Large abraders of scoriaceous lava from the Kalāhuipuaʻa area, Hawaiʻi Island. *(Photo by P. V. Kirch)*

FIGURE 9.9 Abraders of slate pencil sea urchin spines from the Hālawa dune site, Molokaʻi Island. *(Photo by P. V. Kirch)*

that a sample of 55 coral abraders from a site at Palauea, Maui, displayed a unimodal size distribution, with most abraders being between 10 and 35 mm in length, with only a few specimens in the 35–60 mm range. Although virtually ubiquitous at coastal sites, abraders are a largely neglected artifact class in Hawaiʻi. One exception is the study of 564 abraders at Nuʻalolo, by Calugay and McElroy (2005), who examined both morphology and wear patterns.

While coral and basalt abraders seem to have been intentionally shaped before use, sea urchin spine files offered a naturally sufficient shape for abrading. Wear analysis revealed that multiple surfaces were utilized for abrasion, and additionally for sea urchin files, multiple wear types were observed, suggesting that coral, basalt, and sea urchin spine files were manipulated in a number of directions and angles and employed for possibly multiple functions (Calugay and McElroy 2005, 233).

It is unusual for an artifact class not already documented ethnographically to be discovered in an archaeological context, but this was the case with diminutive abraders made from the slender spines of the *wana* sea urchin (*Echinothrix diadema*). These unusual abraders turned up during CRM monitoring work on the Bellows Air Force base at Waimānalo, Oʻahu (McElroy, Dye, and Jourdane, et al. 2006; see also Bayman and Dye 2013, fig. 5.6).

Other Tools

Hawaiian craftsmen used a variety of other tools that are sometimes recovered in site surveys and excavations. Hammerstones used to make stone adzes and other flake tools (fig. 9.10) are often round or discoidal in shape, identified by telltale battering around their perimeters. Some hammerstones have pecked finger grips on their sides. Adzes were finished and polished on large grindstones, sometimes found near streambeds where water

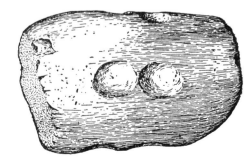

FIGURE 9.10 Hammerstone with pecked finger grips, from Lānaʻi Island. *(After Emory 1924)*

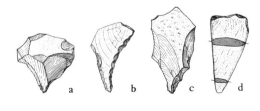

FIGURE 9.11 Stone awls from Oʻahu rockshelter sites. *(After Emory and Sinoto 1961)*

to cool the stones was readily available. Less frequent than stone adzes are small adzes of cone shell. Perforations in wood were made either with stone awls (fig. 9.11) or with pump drills equipped with points of shell (Emory, Bonk, and Sinoto 1959).

Fishing Gear

The Hawaiians utilized a wide array of fishing equipment, including fishhooks of many shapes and sizes, nets, traps, spears, trolling gear, octopus lures, and snares. Much of the equipment used by ancient Hawaiian fishers does not normally survive in archaeological sites and is best known from ethnographic specimens. Nonetheless, dry cave sites sometimes preserve fragments of fishing line, fragments of nets of various sizes and gauges, and even large shark hooks of wood, such as a cache from Kalāhuipuaʻa, Hawaiʻi (fig. 9.12). Fishhooks, however, were usually made of more durable materials, especially bone and shell, and these along with stone sinkers and shell lures have been excavated in large numbers from coastal and occasionally inland sites throughout the islands. The definitive study of Hawaiian fishhooks, by Emory, Bonk, and Sinoto (1959), was based on 4,159 hooks excavated from 33 sites in the 1950s. Since then, many additional specimens have been recovered, in some cases revealing previously unknown geographic styles or temporal variations.

Fishhook Classification

Archaeologists classify Hawaiian fishhooks according to the basic form of the hook, with subtypes representing minor variations in attributes such as barbs and line-attachment devices (fig. 9.13). A detailed classification of Hawaiian fishhooks was presented by Emory, Bonk, and Sinoto (1959), with later refinements by Lloyd Soehren (1966) and Sinoto (1991). *One-piece fishhooks* are divided into *jabbing hooks,* with the point and shank more or less parallel, and *rotating hooks,* in which the point curves in toward the shank. Further variation in one-piece hooks takes into consideration the curvature of the shank, the bend shape, and the type of line-lashing device, as well as the size of the hook.

The two kinds of *two-piece fishhooks* are (1) those in which the shank and point are each a separate piece, lashed together at the bend, and (2) crescent points, usually of bone, lashed onto large wooden hooks. The first type is a Hawaiian innovation, an adaptation to the lack of large pearl shells (found in central Eastern Polynesia) and the need to substitute bone for hooks. Because of its cross-laminated structure, shell is much stronger than bone, which tends to break at weak points (such as the bend of a hook) when stress is applied. By artificially "breaking" the hook into two parts, and replacing the weak section with a strong and flexible lashing of fine cordage, Hawaiian fishhook makers overcame this raw material constraint, and were thus able to manufacture bone two-piece hooks of sizable proportions (fig. 9.14). The form of the bases of both points and shanks is important in the classification of two-piece hooks, with either notches or knobs provided for the lashing. These notched and knobbed styles have chronological significance, at least in the South Point region of Hawaiʻi Island. The crescent type of two-piece hook is relatively rare in Hawaiian sites, although several hundred were excavated at the South Point sites. These large hooks were used primarily for catching pelagic fish and sharks.

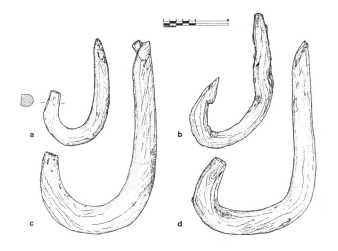

FIGURE 9.12 Large wooden hooks for taking sharks, found in a cache at Kalāhuipuaʻa, Hawaiʻi Island. Hooks *a*, *c*, and *d* were designed to have bone points lashed to the faceted ends. *(After Kirch 1979a)*

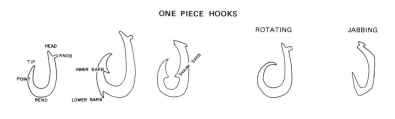

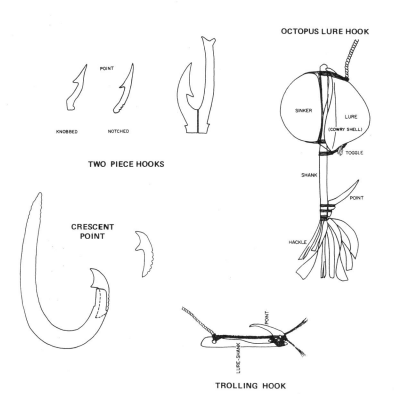

FIGURE 9.13 Terminology and classification of Hawaiian fishhooks. *(After Emory, Bonk, and Sinoto 1959)*

One- and two-piece fishhooks exhibit stylistic variation over the archipelago. Kaua'i sites, for example, yield distinctive one-piece fishhooks with barbs on the inner sides of both point and shank (fig. 9.15). Likewise, the multiple-notched base type of the two-piece fishhook appears to be confined to the South Point region on Hawai'i Island; only a handful of specimens of this style have been excavated from elsewhere in the islands.

Composite fishhooks are of two types: (1) trolling hooks for bonito and tuna; and (2) octopus hooks. The trolling hooks consist of a lure shank, usually of pearl shell, lashed to a point, often of bone. These lures were used from canoes on the open sea to obtain fish such as the skipjack tuna or *aku* (*Katsuwonis pelamis*). The octopus lure is a complex piece of equipment, consisting of a stone weight or sinker, and a lure (fig. 9.16) of cowrie shell (*Cypraea* sp.) lashed opposite each other on a wooden shaft. Below the sinker and lure, at the

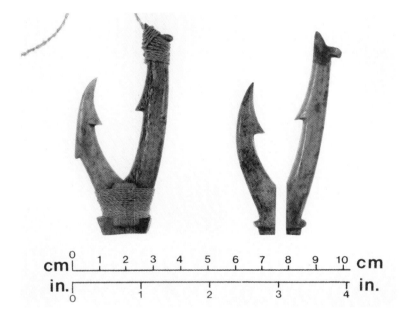

FIGURE 9.14 Large two-piece fishhooks of human bone. *(Photo by P. V. Kirch)*

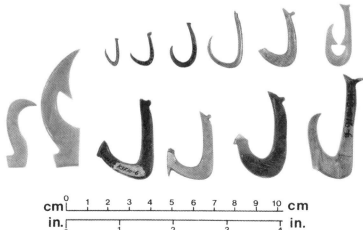

FIGURE 9.15 Bone and pearl-shell fishhooks from Kaua'i Island sites. The hook on the upper right exhibits the distinctive Kaua'i style of double inner barbs. *(Photo by P. V. Kirch)*

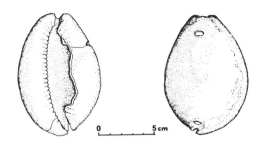

FIGURE 9.16 Bottom and top views of a cowrie shell octopus lure; note the drilled perforations for line attachment. *(Drawing by P. V. Kirch)*

base of the shaft, a bone point was attached. Lowered on a line from a canoe to the ocean floor, the shell lure attracted the octopus. A few local fishermen still use this *lūheʻe* method (Hosaka 1944).

Octopus lure sinkers are of two main types: (1) coffee-bean, and (2) breadloaf, terms that evoke the basic shapes of the sinkers. The coffee-bean type is flat on one surface, and curved on the other (a plano-convex cross section), with a longitudinal groove to aid in lashing the sinker to the shaft. The breadloaf type is narrower and usually more finely manufactured, closely resembling a loaf of bread that has been baked in a narrow, high-sided mold. When available, hematite was a preferred material for making octopus lure sinkers, possibly because its reddish-brown color was attractive to the prey (Filimoehala et al. 2015).

Michael Pfeffer (1995) notes that octopus lures have a wide geographic distribution in Polynesia; the method is therefore probably quite ancient. However, outside of Hawaiʻi and the Marquesas the lures are of an "imitation rat" form, consisting of "several cowrie shell plates tied over a conical, non-grooved or grooved stone sinker" (1995, 48). Lures with a distinctively shaped coffee-bean or breadloaf shape, a whole cowrie shell, and a wooden shaft with bone or wood point are known from Hawaiʻi and the Marquesas, although possibly also from the Society Islands.

Michael Graves and Windy McElroy (2005) proposed an alternative classification based on their analysis of the fishhook assemblage from the Nuʻalolo rockshelter on Kauaʻi. Building upon the work of Melinda S. Allen (1996) on style and function in Polynesian fishhooks, Graves and McElroy developed a paradigmatic classification in which variations in the upper portion of the fishhook shank were classified according to "proximal end modes," "inner edge modes," and "outer edge modes," (2005, fig. 9). The chronological distribution of two major modes, angled proximal ends and stepped proximal ends, shows the former declining over time and the latter increasing over time (2005, fig. 16). This is not surprising, given that Sinoto (1962) had previously demonstrated that Hawaiian fishhook heads were sensitive temporal indicators.

Materials used for fishhooks include animal bone (commonly pig and dog, and also human bone), pearl shell, bird bone, turtle shell, wood, and even dog teeth. Pearl shell was prized for hook manufacture but was not readily available on all islands. Kauaʻi and Oʻahu, with their developed reefs, were the major sources for pearl shell; archaeological sites on these islands yield higher frequencies of pearl-shell hooks. Within the stratified deposits at Nuʻalolo, the use of pearl shell for hooks declined over time as the use of bone increased (Graves and McElroy 2005, fig. 14). On Hawaiʻi Island, pearl-shell hooks are only rarely found. In the South Point region, the large pieces of pearl shell used for trolling lures must have been imported from one of the easterly islands; suitably large pearl shells were probably valuable items of exchange between communities. The largest one-piece and two-piece hooks were made from human long bones, prized not only for their size and strength but also because the *mana* of the deceased would render the hook particularly efficacious. The practice of making hooks from human bone was also used to humiliate enemies defeated in war; chiefs went to considerable lengths to camouflage their burial places so that their bones would not fall into the hands of would-be fishhook makers. The use of human bone for fishhooks increased in the Archaic States Period, and was relatively uncommon in earlier periods.

Tools used in fishhook manufacture and the resulting waste debris are often the most common artifacts excavated at Hawaiian coastal sites. At the Puʻu Aliʻi (H1) dune site, for example, more than 12,000 coral and sea-urchin-spine abraders were recovered (Sinoto n.d.b). The work of preparing a tab or preform of bone or shell was carried out with abraders made from *Porites* sp. block coral; many of these tools have shapes reminiscent of metal files or saws and may have been used with similar actions. Once a hook preform had been prepared, finer finishing work was done with the abrasive spines of the slate pencil sea urchin (*Heterocentrotus mammillatus*). Pump drills tipped with cone-shell points were used to drill out the initial perforation in a hook preform. Manufacturing techniques included simple drilling, double-drilling, and notching-and-filing, as described by Sinoto (1967, 1991).

Fishhooks range in size from diminutive specimens no longer than a fingernail to large shark hooks with shanks as long as 32 cm. Hooks of different sizes were intended for specific kinds of fish. An analysis of hook size may help to determine the fishing strategies used at any particular locality. From rockshelters at Kalāhuipuaʻa and ʻAnaehoʻomalu, where the main fishing strategies focused on smaller inshore fish species, the excavated fishhooks are mostly small jabbing hooks (Kirch 1979a, 1982e). In the South Point region, in contrast, where fishermen set out in canoes to exploit the large pelagic fish that abound in the lee of Hawaiʻi Island, the fishhooks recovered are often large and massive.

Marshall Weisler and Richard Walter (2002) analyzed a fishhook assemblage excavated from a single stone structure at Kawākiu Nui, west Molokaʻi. The "notched" enclosure was probably a combined *koʻa* (fishing shrine) and *mua* (men's house), where fishermen gathered both to make offerings to Kūʻula, and to tend to their fishing gear. The enclosure's interior was partially excavated as part of a CRM project (Hammatt 1979a), yielding 470 artifacts, including 48 whole or fragmentary bone fishhooks (fig. 9.17). One-piece, two-piece, and trolling and/or octopus lure points were all represented. Weisler and Walter observed that in manufacturing these hooks from mammal bone, the hook makers were careful to orient the hook so that the natural grain of the bone ran parallel to the shank, thus minimizing the likelihood of breakage (2002, 53). As a total assemblage, the hooks from the Kawākiu Nui site were

> designed primarily for inshore exploitation with a specialization for targeting benthic fish communities. The one-piece hooks were dominated by rotating forms which may be more suitable for bottom and mid-water feeders, and were almost certainly cast from canoes stationed offshore, probably over a reef or coral rubble surface. The fishhook sizes were in the mid-range for one-piece varieties which suggests that the fishers were targeting medium to large benthic predators such as serranids, carangids, and lutjanids. (57)

CHRONOLOGY OF HAWAIIAN FISHHOOKS

Emory, Bonk, and Sinoto (1959) presented a chronology of fishhook change based on the large collection they obtained from the H1, H8, and H2 sites in the South Point region of Hawai'i Island. Sinoto (Sinoto and Kelly 1975) later analyzed the chronological sequence of fishhook styles in sites at Wai'ahukini, near South Point. The most striking chronological change in the South Point fishhooks occurs between the two forms of two-piece hook points and shanks, those with notched bases and those with knobbed bases. As seen in figure 9.18, the notched base form preceded the appearance of knobbed bases in the early H1 site. In site H8, the relative frequency of the two styles changed steadily over time, with an early emphasis on notched bases gradually giving way to a predominance of knobbed bases. In the late H2 site, there were only two examples of notched base hooks, versus 74 examples of hooks with knobbed bases. This sequence from notched to knobbed two-piece hook styles has also been validated by Sinoto for the Wai'ahukini sites.

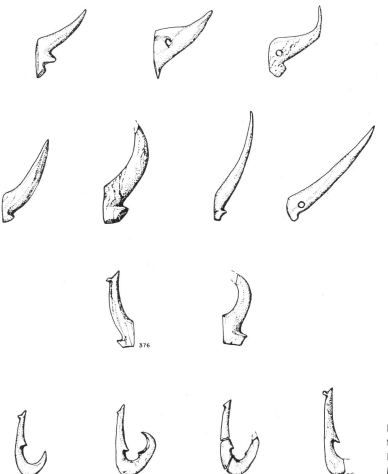

FIGURE 9.17 Bone fishhooks from the Kawākiu Bay site, Moloka'i Island. *(After Hammett 1979a)*

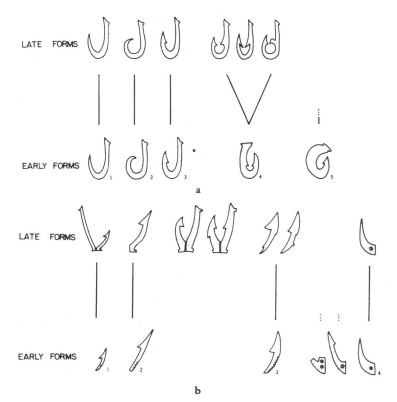

FIGURE 9.18 Persistence and change in Hawaiian fishing gear, from early to later time periods; a: one-piece hooks; b: two-piece hooks. (After Emory, Bonk, and Sinoto 1959)

The notched/knobbed fishhook sequence, however, has not proven to be applicable outside the South Point region, probably because the notched style was a local geographic variant. Only a handful of notched-base hooks have been excavated from other areas (such as one from Kalāhuipuaʻa; Kirch 1979a); these may have been made by the South Point fishhook craftsmen and traded or exchanged with fishermen residing elsewhere.

The fishhook typology devised by Emory, Bonk, and Sinoto (1959) combines several variants of knobbed-base two-piece hooks, including (1) small hooks with the knob made by cutting a shallow notch in the outer base of the point or shank, and (2) hooks, often larger and massive, with the knob more clearly defined and elaborated. Excavations at the Bellows dune site (O18) and the Hālawa dune site (Mo-A1-3) yielded examples of the first variety, which Kirch (1975a) termed an "incipient" style of two-piece fishhook (fig. 9.19). This simple

FIGURE 9.19 Two-piece fishhooks of bone from the Hālawa dune site, Molokaʻi Island. (Photo by P. V. Kirch)

TECHNOLOGY, CRAFT, ECONOMY • 207

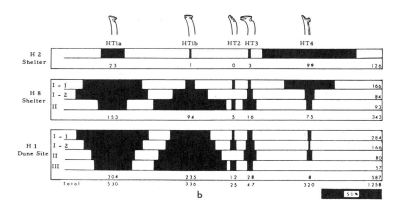

FIGURE 9.20 Relative changes in fishhook head types at sites in the South Point area, Hawai'i Island. *(After Y. H. Sinoto 1962)*

style of two-piece hook appears to be an early form of this unique Hawaiian invention, whereas the more massive type with its well-defined knob developed later.

After the initial study of Hawaiian fishhooks had been completed, Sinoto (1962) realized that variations in the head types or line-lashing devices also showed changes over time that could be used for relative dating. Sinoto defined four major types of head form and plotted their stratigraphic distribution in sites at South Point, and at Nu'alolo rockshelter on Kaua'i (fig. 9.20). Among the chronological changes in head form were the reduced popularity over time of Type 1b and the great increase in the frequency of Type 4. Unlike the chronology of two-piece hook bases, that for fishhook head forms appears to be consistent over the archipelago; later excavations have reinforced the temporal trends pointed out by Sinoto (1962). Nonetheless, it would be useful to have a comprehensive study of change in Hawaiian fishhook head types, based on the expanded collections now available.

Domestic Implements

An iconic Hawaiian artifact is the *pōhaku ku'i 'ai*, or food pounder, often called a *"poi pounder*," used to mash the cooked corms of *kalo*, which when mixed with water while mashing yields *poi*, the glutinous taro paste that was the preferred staple core of Hawaiian cuisine. Three major styles of *poi* pounder exist, two of which are almost exclusively restricted to Kaua'i Island. Most common and found across all of the islands is the conical pounder with flaring base and a knobbed head. Similar conical pounders are known from other parts of central Eastern Polynesia, especially the Marquesas Islands, suggesting that this kind of pounder is of some antiquity.

The ring and stirrup types of pounders (fig. 9.21) are known, with just a few exceptions, only from Kaua'i Island. Whether their limitation to Kaua'i was a consequence of the relative isolation of that island, and hence development of a local style as suggested in the first edition of this book, is a matter that was taken up by McElroy in a methodologically innovative analysis of *poi* pounder stylistic variation (McElroy 2004). McElroy made careful observations on a sample of 94 Kaua'i pounders, applying the method of occurrence seriation to construct a chronology of pounder development. She assumes that the conical form with knobbed head was the last type to be used on Kaua'i, because this form was still in use

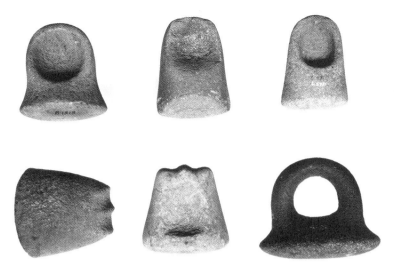

FIGURE 9.21 Stirrup and ring pounders from Kaua'i Island. *(Photo courtesy of Bishop Museum Library and Archives)*

in the historic period. McElroy's seriation suggests that the stirrup and ring forms are older, and gradually developed over time, with the conical form appearing on Kaua'i only late in time (McElroy 2004, fig. 12). She also notes that Sinoto (1970) excavated what appear to be early forms of stirrup pounders at the Hane site on Ua Huka Island in the Marquesas. This supports her contention that the stirrup form of pounder was an early type. However, the absence of stirrup pounders on the other islands of the Hawaiian archipelago suggests to us that conical pounders (perhaps originally made of wood?) were also early, and were transferred into stone at some point on the other islands of Hawai'i.

Habitation sites contain a variety of domestic implements. Among the most common are awls and "picks" of mammal, bird, and fish bone (fig. 9.22). Some of these may have been used to split *hala* (*Pandanus*) leaves into thin strips for mat making, while others are interpreted as picks for extracting shellfish meat. Scrapers and flake "knives" of basalt are not uncommon. Scrapers were also frequently made of shell, including cone shell, limpets, and pearl shell (fig. 9.23). At the Bellows dune site, a cone-shell coconut grater with serrated edges was recovered.

Less frequently found are stone bowls and cups, and stone lamps, probably because such items were prized possessions and were rarely abandoned at sites. In dry sites such as Nu'alolo on Kaua'i and Kalāhuipua'a on Hawai'i, a variety of normally perishable items were preserved, including remnants of *kī*-leaf food parcels, sandals, barkcloth (*kapa*), barkcloth beaters and stamps, wooden ploughs for making fire, coconut cups, cordage, gourds for holding water and food, and carrying poles. In her study of Hawaiian cordage, Catherine Summers (1990) included an analysis of 223 specimens recovered from Nu'alolo, where six different species of plants were utilized: coconut, *'uki'uki* (*Dianella* spp.), *hau* (*Hibiscus tiliaceus*), *'ahu'awa* (*Cyperus javanicus*), *olonā* (*Touchardia* spp.), and *wauke* (*Broussonetia papyrifera*).

A seemingly prosaic yet symbolically potent artifact consists of "both natural, unmodified pebbles and pecked, ground and/or polished stones resembling small pestles and phallic emblems" (P. C. McCoy 2011, 65). Called *'eho*, or *pōhaku 'eho*, some of these are described from ethnographic collections in Bishop Museum as having served as

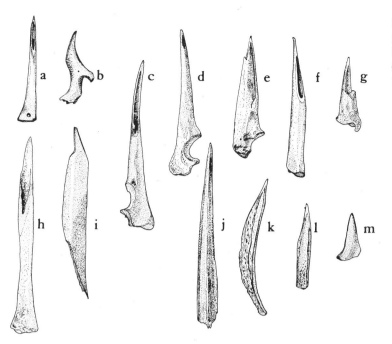

FIGURE 9.22 Awls and picks of bone from Oʻahu rockshelter sites. *(After Emory and Sinoto 1961)*

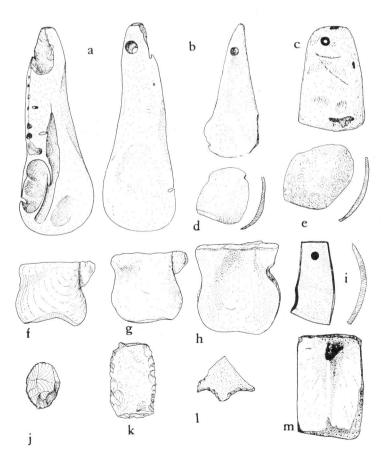

FIGURE 9.23 Scrapers of bone, shell, and stone, from Oʻahu rockshelter sites. *(After Emory and Sinoto 1961)*

"cook stones," inserted after heating into the body cavities of birds such as dark-rumped petrels (Summers 1999, 2–3, figs. 4, 5). Patrick C. McCoy studied an archaeological assemblage of these stones from Puʻu Kalepeamoa on Mauna Kea, arguing that in addition to their practical use in cooking, these phallic-shaped stones were imbued with layers of symbolic meaning:

> I think it is reasonable to suggest that the word ʻeho, which was used for three seemingly very different things—cook stones, boundary markers and god images—but which share in common the phallic shape representing potency, can be viewed as three variations on a common theme of power, food and boundaries—of marking or creating boundaries to mark a social transition, or to protect and thus guarantee the availability of food sources by appealing to the gods for their assistance. (P. C. McCoy 2011, 98)

McCoy believes that the cooking of petrels, which nest in the upland saddle region of Hawaiʻi Island, was part of a series of rituals practiced by the adze makers who ascended and then descended from the heights of the sacred mountain, Mauna Kea, in order to ply their craft in the high-altitude quarries.

Volcanic Glass

Among the most ubiquitous artifacts in Hawaiian archaeology are the small cores and flakes of volcanic (sometimes called "basaltic") glass, which have been found in densities as great as 1,350 pieces per m^3 of cultural deposit (in site Ha-E1-355 at Kalāhuipuaʻa, Hawaiʻi). Barrera and Kirch (1973), who were among the first to consider these artifacts, commented on possible functions: "Basaltic glass holds a fine, sharp edge and the tools make excellent cutting and scraping implements. They may have been used in food preparation, for cutting and scraping plant materials, or for delicate woodworking. . . . The suggestion, then, is that the ubiquitous basaltic-glass flakes functioned as a prehistoric 'pocket knife,'" to use a modern analogy (185–186).

In any collection of volcanic-glass flakes, usually only a limited number of pieces show evidence of actual use (often less than 10 to 20 percent); these are generally among the larger flakes in the entire lot. Schousboe, Riford, and Kirch (1983), studying assemblages from sites in the Waimea-Kawaihae Road corridor on Hawaiʻi Island, concluded that flakes were produced primarily by bipolar flaking, in which a core is placed against an anvil and struck with a hammerstone. Edge-damage patterns (fig. 9.24) suggested that flakes were used for both cutting and scraping actions. Weisler and Haslam (2005) examined residues on 14 volcanic-glass flakes from Molokaʻi, finding cellulose and matted cellulose tissue on two of these, indicative of plant processing. The hypothesis that volcanic-glass flakes were used for plant processing has received support from Roland Reeve (1983, 230–231), who excavated two open sites in the uplands of Waikōloa, Hawaiʻi, consisting of scatters of volcanic-glass flakes. Based on ethnohistoric information, Reeve interpreted these scatters as activity areas where the bark was stripped from paper mulberry (*wauke*) plants as the first stage in barkcloth manufacture. Reeve's work provides an important clue as to one possible use of volcanic-glass flakes, although there certainly could have been multiple uses for these sharp-edged expedient tools.

Volcanic glass occurs in three major geological contexts in Hawai'i: (1) in trachyte cones, such as Pu'u Wa'awa'a on Hawai'i Island; (2) as chilled borders along vertical dikes where these are exposed along cliff faces; and (3) as surface chills on lava flows, this latter largely restricted to younger flows on Hawai'i or East Maui (Weisler 1990b, 17). Marshall Weisler (1990b) used this geological model to predict and search for volcanic-glass sources on west Moloka'i, finding two sources and geochemically characterizing them. M. D. McCoy (2011) used EDXRF to examine the variation within the Pu'u Wa'awa'a trachyte cone, a major source of volcanic glass on Hawai'i Island, while M. D. McCoy, Mills, et al. (2011) analyzed 3,329 glass artifacts from 87 sites throughout the islands to determine geographic distribution of material deriving from the Pu'u Wa'awa'a cone. Their study showed that Pu'u Wa'awa'a glass artifacts were largely restricted to Hawai'i Island (M. D. McCoy, Mills, et al. 2011, table 2), although later studies have noted a very small amount on Moloka'i and O'ahu. A cost-surface analysis showed a remarkably linear relationship between travel time and the frequency of Pu'u Wa'awa'a glass in sites distributed over Hawai'i Island. This led

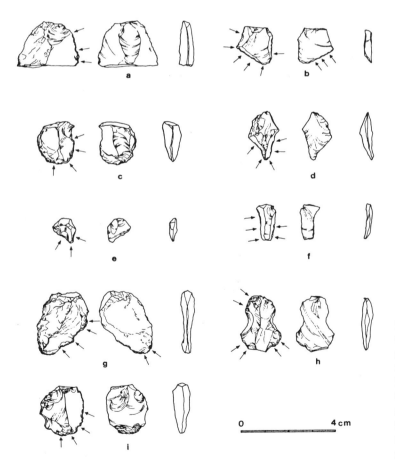

FIGURE 9.24 Flakes of volcanic glass from sites in the Waimea-Kawaihae area, Hawai'i Island. The arrows point to areas with edge damage, due to use of the flakes for cutting or scraping. (After Clark and Kirch, eds., 1983)

them to conclude that "territorial boundaries do not appear to have effectively restricted volcanic-glass quarrying and exchanges between neighboring communities in Hawaiʻi. But, volcanic glass was not commonly involved in activities beyond a single day's walk from sites. Direct access beyond a single day's travel did occur but appears to have been rare" (2559).

Jeff Putzi et al. (2015) suggest an alternative model, in which volcanic glass from Puʻu Waʻawaʻa was carried down to Kahuwai Bay on the coast, and from there distributed by canoe to *ahupuaʻa* communities north and south; this alternative model fits the distance-decay curve for Puʻu Waʻawaʻa glass equally as well as an overland transport model.

Steve Lundblad et al. (2013) analyzed 1,576 volcanic-glass artifacts from sites on the leeward side of Hawaiʻi Island, finding that the geochemical compositions indicated three discrete groups. Group 1 matched the Puʻu Waʻawaʻa trachyte source. Group 2, with the greatest number of artifacts, is consistent with a source on the Mauna Loa volcanic shield. Group 3 appears to match the geochemistry of the Kilauea volcano; the presence of a significant number of Group 3 artifacts at the "royal center" of Hōnaunau may be significant. Subsequent detailed geochemical studies have noted these groups are not exclusive to these Hawaiʻi Island volcanoes.

A recent study of a large collection of 1,258 volcanic-glass artifacts from coastal Kualoa on Oʻahu found a high frequency of Puʻu Kaʻīlio volcanic glass, a source located 32 km away in Waiʻanae (DiVito et al. 2020). The quantity and types of artifacts found suggests people living on the shores of Kāneʻohe Bay had unfettered access to this upland source. The Kualoa volcanic-glass study also gives us a rare example of interisland movement between Hawaiʻi and Oʻahu Islands. Previous research produced a distance-decay model that predicts that Puʻu Waʻawaʻa volcanic-glass artifacts, originating from West Hawaiʻi, would be incredibly rare at Kualoa, just 0.3 percent of an assemblage (M. D. McCoy, Mills, et al. 2011). In studies with fewer than 100 pieces it would therefore be unlikely to be detected, and even out of 1,258 artifacts, one would only expect to find just 4 examples. The study found 3 pieces of Puʻu Waʻawaʻa glass—a surprisingly strong confirmation of the modeled distribution of this material (M. D. McCoy, Mills, et al. 2011). However, this is likely due to large sample size examined rather than reflecting an unusually close connection between these two locations.

Ornaments and Decoration

Among the frequently encountered ornaments in Hawaiian sites are dog's canine teeth, drilled for suspension as pendants or used in dance anklets (fig. 9.25), as well as beads made from several kinds of shell. Less common are bracelet or anklet segments, carefully worked from bone or pig tusk. One such anklet was found on one of the burials in the O18 site at Waimānalo, Oʻahu. An assemblage of shell, bone, and invertebrate ornaments from the Nuʻalolo rockshelter on Kauaʻi was analyzed by Field and McElroy (in Field and Graves, eds., 2015).

The Hawaiians developed stone mirrors, circular disks of finely polished dense basalt that reflect light when wet. Two such mirrors from the Nuʻalolo rockshelter on Kauaʻi are made of dense basalts with geochemistry that is entirely different from the dense basalts used to make adzes at the same site. These anomalous compositions hint at the possibility

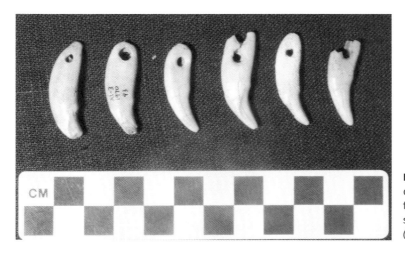

FIGURE 9.25 Drilled dog canine teeth from the Hālawa dune site, Molokaʻi Island. *(Photo by P. V. Kirch)*

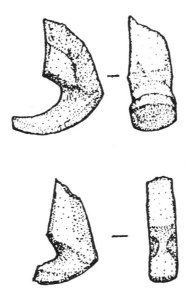

FIGURE 9.26 Fragments of *lei niho palaoa* neck ornaments, made of rock oyster shell, from Kauaʻi Island. *(After Denison and Forman 1971)*

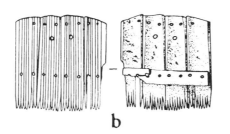

a b

FIGURE 9.27 Tattooing combs from Oʻahu rockshelter sites. *(After Emory and Sinoto 1961)*

that the stones are from distant sources, and possibly even outside the Hawaiian archipelago (Mills et al. 2010).

The most distinctive of all Hawaiian artifacts is the *lei niho palaoa,* the chiefly neck ornament, a tongue-shaped carving suspended on a thick necklace of braided human hair. Most of the ethnographically documented specimens are carved from whale ivory, hence the name *niho palaoa,* "whale tooth." The use of whale ivory appears to be a late phenomenon, however, perhaps postdating European contact, when whaling ships replenished their supplies in the islands. A number of *lei niho palaoa* have been excavated from archaeological sites (fig. 9.26) and none is of whale ivory. Rather, most are made from rock oyster shell (*Chama iostoma*), with a few of coral or wood. Based on the specimen excavated at the O18 dune site, also made of rock oyster shell (see chapter 6), this ornament style has a long history in Hawai'i and may have developed from earlier ornament styles found in central Eastern Polynesia.

Also occasionally recovered in excavations are tattoo needles or combs of several styles. Like other Polynesians, the Hawaiians decorated their bodies with geometric tattoos, the ink being set under the skin with comblike needles; some examples of these (from Makani'olu Shelter on O'ahu) are illustrated in figure 9.27.

Other Artifacts

Aside from the principal artifact classes described above, a variety of miscellaneous objects are encountered in Hawaiian sites. Frequently found are discoidal gaming stones (*'ulu maika*) used in the *maika* game, where they were bowled between two upright pegs. A rare find is the stone quoit, with plano-convex section, used in a pitching game (Emory and Sinoto 1961).

Hawaiian warfare is reflected in a number of artifacts, especially slingstones. These may be naturally rounded river pebbles, carefully selected, as were found in a cache on the

FIGURE 9.28 Stone tripping club from a habitation site in Hālawa Valley, Moloka'i Island. *(Photo by P. V. Kirch)*

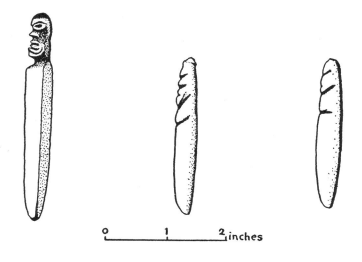

FIGURE 9.29 Sea-urchin-spine images from the Kamohi'o rockshelter site and fishing shrine, Kaho'olawe Island. (After McAllister 1933b)

fortified ridge at Kawela, Moloka'i, or they may be shaped stones, pointed at both ends. Rarely, stone clubs are found, such as the tripping club excavated from an inland house site in Hālawa Valley on Moloka'i (fig. 9.28), or a fragment of a club with a drilled perforation for line attachment found at a site in leeward Kohala (Field et al. 2009, 28, fig. 3.12).

Religious or cult objects are also discovered occasionally. Fragments of wooden images have occasionally turned up in dry sites, as at Nu'alolo rockshelter. More frequently, waterworn elongate stones, set upright on platforms and enclosures, distinguish these sites as fishing shrines, or household shrines. Known only from archaeological contexts are the rare images carved on the spines of slate pencil sea urchins, as from the Kamōhio Bay shrine on Kaho'olawe Island (fig. 9.29).

The Wealth Economy: Craft Specialization, Social Status, and Gendered Roles

Among all of the Polynesian cultures, traditional Hawaiian material culture is arguably the richest in terms of diversity of tools, implements, garments, ornaments, and other kinds of artifacts, and exhibits the greatest degree of sophistication in material arts (Buck 1957). While many objects were made within commoner households, using locally available materials, others were produced by specialists who had access to the best materials. Craft specialization is an aspect of economic and social organization that has become of increasing interest to archaeologists in many regions of the world, including in Hawai'i (Costin 1991; Costin and Wright, eds., 1998). In many ancient societies, increased craft specialization accompanied the rise of social stratification and hierarchy; Hawai'i appears to be no exception.

In chapter 7, we reviewed the intensive agricultural and aquacultural production that underwrote the "staple economy" essential to the social and political system of ancient Hawai'i. The idea of a staple economy—one that depends upon the control of foodstuffs and the extraction of a surplus that can be put to political purposes—derives from the work of scholars such as Marshall Sahlins (1958, 1972). Timothy Earle (1997) argued that this was the basic form of the ancient Hawaiian economy. While it is true that control of agricultural production was fundamental to Hawaiian chiefship, the Hawaiian economy was not exclusively based on a surplus of staple crops. Ethnohistoric sources indicate that during the annual Makahiki collection of *hoʻokupu* or tribute from each *ahupuaʻa,* much emphasis was placed on nonfood items, such as feathers, barkcloth, and cordage (Malo 1951, 145). Davida Malo (76–80) details a long list of "valuables," including the rare bird feathers and the capes, cloaks, helmets, *kahili,* and other objects made from them; *lei niho palaoa* ornaments; canoes; cordage; fish nets; stone adzes; fishhooks; barkcloth; mats; and other items. The control and circulation of these material objects, many of which were the productions of craft specialists, constituted a "wealth economy" that had become increasingly important by the Archaic States Period.

An aspect of craft specialization that is particularly well attested in the Hawaiian archaeological record—and which has seen the greatest attention by archaeologists—is adze production (P. L. Cleghorn 1982, 1986; P. C. McCoy 1990, 1999; Williams 1989). The knapping of typical rectangular-sectioned Hawaiian adzes with their near 90-degree angles has been shown through experimental replication to require a high level of skill. Malo (1951, 51) says that adze makers in Hawaiʻi were a "greatly esteemed class."

In addition to the evidence for specialization at the basalt quarries, there is also evidence for craft specialization within individual communities. At Kawela on Molokaʻi, Weisler and Kirch (1982) excavated a terrace situated near the residential complex of the *ahupuaʻa* chief or *konohiki.* This terrace yielded an abundance of fine-grained basalt debitage indicative of adze resharpening and recycling, arguably the workshop of an expert woodworker attached to the nearby elite household. At Nuʻu in Kaupō, Maui, there is evidence for intensive adze production in a small men's house and shrine; a nearby residential site had significant quantities of debitage again suggestive of adze resharpening.

Ethnohistoric documents and museum collections of artifacts associated with *aliʻi* families make it clear that the most sophisticated craft artifacts, such as finely carved wooden bowls and platters, fine mats, and thin, intricately decorated barkcloth (*kapa*) were items that materially signified the exalted status of elites. Similarly, the large, double-hulled canoes used by Hawaiian chiefs for travel and in war required highly specialized experts to hew and construct. The "royal centers" that arose during the Archaic States Period would likely have seen clusters of craft specialists living in close proximity to the ranking *aliʻi,* working to supply the latter with these material goods. Unfortunately, few of these royal centers have been thoroughly investigated, but the salvage excavations conducted by Donald Tuohy (1965) at Hōnaunau, just inland of the main complex defined by the "Great Wall" (see chapter 14), yielded an unprecedented array of adzes (of many sizes), files, abraders, rubbing stones, hammerstones, and stone, bone, and shell detritus from artifact production. A reanalysis of this assemblage might yield new insights into what was likely a concentration of craft specialists residing in close proximity to the *aliʻi* at Hōnaunau.

The apogee of Hawaiian material culture was achieved in the realm of featherwork (Brigham 1899, 1903; Buck 1957; Caldeira et al. eds., 2015). These iconic objects of *aliʻi* status included capes and cloaks (*ʻahu ʻula*), helmets (*mahiole*), sashes (*kāʻei*), standards and wands (*kāhili*), and anthropomorphic images of gods (*akua hulu*), in particular the war god

FIGURE 9.30 Feathered image of the war god Kū, with pearl-shell eyes and mouth ringed with dogs' teeth, collected during the third voyage of Captain James Cook. *(Eigenes Werk, Creative Commons)*

Kū (fig. 9.30; color plate 7). The feathers were obtained from several species of endemic forest birds, especially the *mamo* (*Drepanis pacifica*), *'i'iwi* (*Drepanis coccinea*), and *'ō'ō* (*Moho nobilis*); catching the birds in the high cloud forests was the work of specialists. Bundles of feathers were among the items of tribute demanded by the *ali'i* during the annual procession of the "long god" through each *ahupua'a,* part of the Makahiki rituals (Valeri 1985).

While the production of sophisticated featherwork required great skill, the question of who made these objects has been debated. Hawaiian writers such as Malo and Kamakau are silent on the matter; there are no firsthand ethnohistoric accounts of featherwork making. Jocelyn Linnekin (1988) argued that the feathered garments were made by women, but Adrienne Kaeppler (in Caldeira et al., eds., 2015, 46) disagrees: "In pre-Christian times feathered clothing was made by male priests; the fishnet-knotting technique is associated with men in Hawai'i and throughout Polynesia." That these objects, which carried so much *mana* and were intended to be worn on the bodies of sacred individuals, including those of the *ali'i akua* or divine kings, should have been made by male priests is consistent with what we know about ritualized production in Polynesia.

Almost nothing is known of the history of Hawaiian featherwork prior to European contact. The widespread Polynesian use of feathers in headdresses, for fringing fine mats, or in ritual objects suggests that such practices have a considerable antiquity; some form of featherwork has likely been practiced in Hawai'i since initial settlement. The *mo'olelo* of 'Umi and Līloa (see chapter 5) refers to feathered objects such as cloaks, helmets, and a feathered image of Kū, which would mean that these symbols of *ali'i* status had been developed by the end of the sixteenth century, the close of the Expansion Period. In fact, the sacred sash or *kā'ei* of Līloa, a 3-m-long cordon of *olonā* netting covered in red *'i'iwi* and yellow *'ō'ō* feathers, ornamented with human teeth and fish teeth—handed down in the Hawai'i Island royal line and now in Bishop Museum—has been radiocarbon dated to AD 1402–1447 with 95 percent confidence (Hellmich, in Caldeira et al., eds., 2015, 58n4). With increased competition between *ali'i* lineages during the Archaic States Period, featherwork flourished, becoming a major component of a wealth economy that was grafted on to the older and continuing staple economy based on agricultural production.

It is sobering for the archaeologist to realize that something so unique and culturally significant as featherwork is largely missing from the archaeological record. Were it not for the rich ethnohistoric record describing the use of feathered objects at the time of initial European contact, and for the museum collections of these capes, cloaks, helmets, sashes, and images, we would know nothing of their former existence.

The production of Hawaiian material culture not only indexed social or class distinctions but involved gendered labor distinctions as well. While featherwork may have been the purview of male priests, and adze production and fishhook making were evidently both male activities, women were associated with the weaving of mats and the production of barkcloth (Bayman and Dye 2013, table 5.1; Vacca 2019). Mat weaving and *kapa* making are activities in which both the raw materials and most of the tools are of perishable materials, and thus not often preserved in the archaeological record. At least some of the bone "awls," as well as lithic flakes with evidence of edge wear polish, often found at household sites may well derive from the processing of pandanus leaves. In a methodologically innovative study of household sites at Nu'u, Maui, Kirsten Vacca (2019) investigated the gendered use of space and labor, with a microscale approach that includes the analysis of phytoliths, starch, and other possible indications of plant processing. No doubt future studies of the role of gender in Hawaiian society will necessitate pushing the boundaries of our science even further.

10

THE ARCHAEOLOGY OF EVERYDAY LIFE

In agrarian societies such as that of ancient Hawai'i, most people lived out their lives within a relatively small, circumscribed area. While the *ali'i* traveled about to inspect their lands, or moved at times of war with their armies, the *maka'āinana* generally resided within their *ahupua'a,* which were for the most part economically self-sufficient territories. Extending from the mountains down to the shore and out onto the reef and inshore waters, these *ahupua'a* constituted the landscapes of everyday life. In chapter 7, we reviewed the agricultural and aquacultural facilities that transformed these landscapes into multifaceted systems of production. Interspersed and integrated with the irrigated and dryland fields, and the fishponds, were the dwelling places of the people, their *kauhale*. In this chapter we review the ethnohistory and archaeology of these residential sites, along with other kinds of features that made up the landscapes of everyday life.

Kauhale: The Domestic Unit

The Hawaiian word for house, *hale,* deriving from the older Proto-Polynesian word **fale,* designated any kind of house or structure, typically with a wooden framework and thatched with *pili* grass, *hala* or *kī* leaves, or similar material. *Hale* were differentiated by function, indicated by an adjective suffixed to *hale*. Many *hale* were secular, as in the *hale noa* (*noa,* free from *kapu*) or common sleeping house; others had ritual functions, as with the *hale mana* (*mana,* spiritual power) found on temple platforms (see chapter 11). Hawaiian households separated domestic functions such as sleeping, cooking, or craft activities by maintaining discrete *hale* for each function. A cluster of functionally discrete but spatially aggregated *hale* serving a household group composed a *kauhale,* a group of houses. We call such a *kauhale* as evidenced by archaeological features a "household cluster."

ETHNOHISTORIC ACCOUNTS OF HAWAIIAN *KAUHALE*

The first description of Hawaiian *hale* comes from Captain James Cook's 1778 visit to the Waimea area of Kaua'i Island:

> Their houses are not unlike oblong corn stacks, they are of various sizes from forty
> or fifty feet long and twenty or thirty broad to little huts; they have low walls and

a high roof consi[s]ting of two flat sides inclining to each other, and terminating in a ridge like the thatched houses in England. The framing is of wood, and both walls and roof consi[s]ts of Course dry grass which is very closely put together. . . . The door is so low that a man can hardly get in without going upon his hands and knees, and they have no other light except what may come through the crevices in the wall. . . . The floor is covered with dry hay and upon this they spread Mats to sleep upon. A few gourds and wooden bowls, make up their whole catalogue of household utensils. Their mats are both strong and fine and some are neatly coloured. (Cook, in Beaglehole, ed., 1967, 283)

The expedition's artist, John Webber, augmented Cook's account with a detailed drawing of a Waimea *kauhale* (Beaglehole, ed., 1967, pl. 32), later engraved for publication and reproduced here as figure 10.1.

The French explorer La Pérouse offered a similar description of "four small villages" each made up of 10 to 12 houses, in the vicinity of Keoneʻoʻio Bay on southeast Maui, in 1786:

[The houses] are built and roofed with straw and ressemble those of our poorest peasants, the roofs are coupled, the door is usually situated at the gable end, it is only 3 ½ feet in height and one has to bend to enter—it consists of a small screen which anyhow can open. Their furnishings are merely mats which, like our carpets, make a very clean floor on which these natives sleep. Their only kitchen utensils are gourds of a large size to which they give the desired shape when they are still green; they varnish them and paint various designs on them in black. (in Dunmore, ed., 1994, 89)

FIGURE 10.1 "An Inland View in Atooi" by John Webber, artist on Captain James Cook's third voyage, depicts several *kauhale* near Waimea, Kauaʻi, as seen in 1778. *(From Cook and King 1784)*

Writing in the nineteenth century, Samuel Kamakau and Davida Malo described the household clusters of chiefs and commoners. Kamakau wrote,

> Houses might be large or small. The ruling chiefs, chiefly land holders, land agents, native sons, and prominent people had large establishments, with sheds, men's houses, sleeping sheds, heiau houses, women's eating houses, houses for the storage of provisions, houses for cooking, and many other houses. The establishments of the people [*maka'āinana*] were sometimes large and sometimes small. Each man had several houses—for wife, children, parents, relatives, and retainers. (1976, 96)

Malo remarked on differences between the *kauhale* of "respectable" people and of the common folk. A proper household cluster of a ranking family was described by Malo as follows: "There was a special house for the man to sleep in with his wife and children (*hale noa*), also a number of houses specially devoted to different kinds of work, including one for the wife to do her work in (*hale kua*). There was the *halau*, or canoe house; the *aleo*, a kind of garret or upper story in which to stow things; also the *amana*, consisting of three houses built about a court" (Malo 1951, 122). Malo contrasted this neat and orderly way of life with that of the common folk of "no account," who "cared only for a little shanty, anyway; the fire-place was close to their head, and the *poi* dish conveniently at hand; and so, with but one house, they made shift to get along" (122).

Edward S. C. Handy and Mary Kawena Pukui (1958) described a model household cluster based on their work in rural Ka'ū, Hawai'i, in the early twentieth century. Among the structures included in such a *kauhale*, Handy and Pukui listed (1) the *mua*, or men's house, from which women were excluded and where adult males made daily offerings to the ancestral deities ('*aumākua*); (2) the *hale noa*, or common sleeping house; (3) the *hale pe'a*, or women's menstrual hut; (4) the *hale papa'a*, a storage shed for crops and agricultural implements; (5) the *hālau*, or canoe shed, if the household was situated along the coast; and (6) the *hale kahūmu*, or oven shed, one for the males and one for the female members of the household. It is not clear whether only the *kauhale* of high-ranked persons typically included the full complement of such functionally differentiated houses, although some structures, such as the sleeping and cook houses, were probably present in most if not all household clusters.

Archaeologists in Hawai'i have frequently turned to such ethnohistoric descriptions, and especially to Handy and Pukui's Ka'ū model, when interpreting the archaeological remains of household clusters. There is a danger, however, in assuming that the ethnohistoric record encompasses the full range of variation present in ancient household structures and practices. The archaeological record needs to be evaluated in its own right, as an independent source of information on the patterns of everyday life, and how these changed over time and varied geographically as well as in relation to social status or gender.

The Archaeology of *Kauhale*

Excepting the ubiquitous mounds, terraces, walls, and other features associated with ancient agriculture, the greatest number of Hawaiian archaeological sites are associated with domestic life. Of course, what archaeologists see and record are the stone and earthen foundations of *hale,* devoid of the pole-and-thatch superstructures that once sheltered groups of people working, eating, socializing, and sleeping. Excavating in and around these stone structures, archaeologists recover the detritus of everyday life: scraps of bone and shell from ancient meals, flakes of basalt from resharpening adzes, charred oven stones, and perhaps on rare occasions a treasured object such as a *poi* pounder or tripping club left behind inadvertently. The careful mapping of *kauhale,* coupled with excavation and analysis of the recovered finds, offer glimpses into the mundane yet essential patterns of everyday life.

A distinction is often made by archaeologists in Hawai'i between *temporary* and *permanent* residential sites, particularly in CRM inventory surveys. Realistically, it is usually impossible to determine—without undertaking excavation—whether a particular structure was used only intermittently or as a permanent residence. The criteria proposed by Ross Cordy (1981, 54–71) for distinguishing between permanent and temporary habitation sites (on the basis of size and other surface-survey criteria) are inadequate, and do not reflect the complexity of ancient Hawaiian residential patterns (Kirch 1983b; Weisler and Kirch 1985). The temporary / permanent distinction is in reality a continuum; between the extremes of a short-term fishing camp and a large permanent household complex lie a variety of feature types, such as field shelters occupied repeatedly over a long time span but for only short periods, and sites that were used for an entire season, then abandoned. Paul Rosendahl (1972a), in his study of upland Lapakahi field shelters, distinguished between *temporary, extended,* and *permanent* residence types. The problems of determining duration and intensity of site use are challenging.

One of the important archaeological advances of the late 1960s, and in particular of the Mākaha Valley Project (Green 1980; Green, ed., 1969, 1970), was the recognition of the small *field shelter* as a major category of Hawaiian settlement landscapes. These shelters, temporarily or intermittently (but repeatedly) occupied, were constructed of low walls of heaped or stacked stone; they display a variety of shapes, variously described by archaeologists as "C-shapes," "L-shapes," and "box C-shapes," based on configuration of the stone foundation (fig. 10.2). Large numbers of these shelters have been identified in surveys on all the islands, although they tend to be most frequent in leeward areas and are particularly associated with the dryland field systems.

Nine such shelters were excavated during the Mākaha Valley Project (Green 1980, table 7). The earliest shelter dates from the thirteenth century, while others span the entire later Mākaha sequence (fig. 10.3). Floor area within these shelters is limited, in Mākaha averaging only 8 m^2 (range, 4 to 14 m^2). A defining characteristic of field shelters is the presence of one or more interior hearths or fireplaces, often stone-outlined (fig. 10.4). The Mākaha sites contained some shell and bone midden, as well as a scattering of stone artifacts, including hammerstones, adzes, an *'ulu maika* bowling disc, and flake tools. The Mākaha shelters, dispersed in and among the agricultural terraces, walls, and mounds of the lower valley slopes, are believed to have been occupied on a seasonal basis by commoners who planted and tended the dryland agricultural fields.

In upland Lapakahi in North Kohala, Hawai'i, Rosendahl (1972a) investigated nine residential sites, including several C-shaped field shelters. Two of these, sites 4727 and 4729, were larger and more complex than the Mākaha examples; they were interpreted by Rosendahl

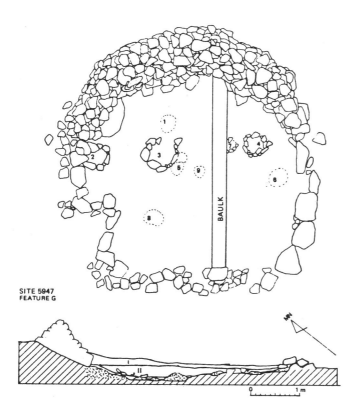

FIGURE 10.2 Plan of a C-shaped shelter at Waikoloa, Hawai'i Island, with several hearths and earth ovens (numbered features) exposed during excavation. *(After Reeve 1983)*

FIGURE 10.3 A small C-shaped shelter in the Mākaha Valley, O'ahu Island. *(Photo courtesy of Bishop Museum Department of Anthropology)*

as "extended use" or "permanent" residential sites. Site 4727 was constructed in a series of phases; it was unique in having a "cupboard" built into the stone wall. Both of these sites contained numerous hearths, firepits, and earth ovens (19 such features in the case of site 4727, and 36 in site 4729), evidence for their repeated use over time. The structures also contained substantial quantities of volcanic-glass flakes and faunal remains. Cupboards, possibly for the storage of sweet potato tubers, are an architectural feature also seen in other areas, as at Kawela on Moloka'i, as illustrated in figure 10.5 (Weisler and Kirch 1985).

The Mākaha and Lapakahi excavations demonstrate variations in size, internal features, cultural contents, and, by inference, use of C- or L-shaped structures. At Kawela, Moloka'i, C-shaped structures were components of larger, permanent residential clusters (Weisler and Kirch 1985). Determining whether a particular structure functioned as a temporary camp, an extended-use habitation, or a component within a permanent *kauhale* requires a range of evidence requiring excavation as well as surface mapping.

FIGURE 10.4 A stone-outlined hearth exposed during the excavation of a C-shaped shelter in the lower Mākaha Valley, O'ahu Island. *(Photo courtesy of Bishop Museum Department of Anthropology)*

Another category of domestic site, also spanning the temporary/permanent use continuum, is that of caves and rockshelters. These sites include lava tubes with collapsed openings (common on Hawai'i Island) as well as overhanging rockshelters on the sides of stream valleys, as in the Anahulu Valley on O'ahu (fig 10.6). Rockshelters vary in size and suitability for occupation. Excavations in these sites, especially during the early years of stratigraphic archaeology in Hawai'i, yielded some of the largest and most important collections of fishing gear and other portable artifacts.

Many rockshelters and lava tubes are found in coastal areas, particularly along the arid coasts of Hawai'i Island, where they were used as temporary fishing camps, utilized repeatedly for short periods. Typical of these are the excavated lava-tube shelters at

FIGURE 10.5 A cupboard feature, with capping stones partially removed, incorporated into the wall of a shelter at Kawela, Moloka'i Island. *(Photo from Oceanic Archaeology Laboratory Archives)*

FIGURE 10.6 A view of Keae rockshelter (site Oa-D6-52) in the Anahulu Valley, Oʻahu Island, after excavation in 1976; a basin-shaped hearth filled with whitish ash is visible in the excavation face. *(Photo by P. V. Kirch)*

ʻAnaehoʻomalu and Kalāhuipuaʻa (Barrera 1971a; Kirch 1979a). Other rockshelters were permanent residences, with internal spatial differentiation of activity areas. This was the case with the large Kuliʻouʻou site (O1) on Oʻahu, to judge from the great variety of domestic artifacts and concentration of faunal remains found within (Emory and Sinoto 1961). The extensive rockshelter complex at Nuʻalolo, Kauaʻi, similarly exhibited a full complement of domestic and craft activities. It is also common to find small rockshelters incorporated within household clusters built upon younger lava flows, as in Manukā on Hawaiʻi Island (M. D. McCoy and Codlin 2016).

A large household cluster, probably an aggregation of several related households at Palauea on Maui (Kirch 1971a), provides a good example of a *kauhale* complex. This site (Ma-B11-2) consists of 13 separate stone structures dispersed along a low ridge not far from the coast. Several larger C-shaped structures contained interior fireplaces, while smaller shelters served as storage sheds. One large structure (Feature 3) was interpreted as a men's house (*mua*). The entire complex constituted "a nucleated settlement of several households, or co-residential domestic groups, each with a dwelling house and storage house, two with a cleared working yard, and all sharing a single *mua,* or men's house" (Kirch 1971a, 84).

In windward regions, habitation sites were frequently constructed on stone-faced, earth-filled terraces situated on lower ridges and spurs. Several inland *kauhale* of this kind in Hālawa Valley, Moloka'i, were excavated by Gil Hendren (1975). One example is site Mo-A1-765, a stone-faced terrace measuring 15 by 18 m, in the *'ili* of Kapana (fig. 10.7). Two separate structures had once stood on the terrace, a dwelling house with a floor paved with river gravel and a smaller cook shed with a stone-lined earth oven. A second earth oven was situated at the rear of the terrace. The presence of two separate ovens conforms with ethnohistoric accounts of separate male and female cooking areas. A stone-filled platform later constructed on top of the terrace is likely to be a nineteenth-century burial.

The age of features making up an archaeological landscape cannot be determined until excavations are undertaken and radiocarbon dates obtained from stratigraphic contexts. Tom Dye (2010b) outlines a methodology for such stratigraphic excavation, with a case study of residential features at Kaiholena, Hawai'i Island. As Dye asserts, the subsurface stratigraphy must be integrated with the surface stone architecture, in order to derive accurate construction and use sequences. Bayesian modeling of radiocarbon dates from such sites can be useful in refining the chronology of stone structures, including episodes of rebuilding.

Excavation within residential sites reveals both internal features, such as hearths, earth ovens, pits, postholes, or pavements, as well as portable artifacts; both kinds of evidence are important in determining the functions of individual structures. The presence of earth ovens, for example, points to the use of a structure as a cookhouse; smaller, slab-lined hearths are often found within the main dwelling house (*hale noa*) or within men's houses (*mua*). The most common artifacts found in residential sites are flakes and cores ("lithics") of basalt and volcanic glass. Basalt flakes result from adze production or resharpening, as well as from making other kinds of tools, such as scrapers or awls. Ground or polished surfaces on flakes reveal that these came from adzes, either during use or as a result of rejuvenation and resharpening (Olszewski 2007). Other stone artifacts sometimes uncovered during excavations of residential sites include whetstones, abraders, lamps, pestles, hammerstones, *'ulu*

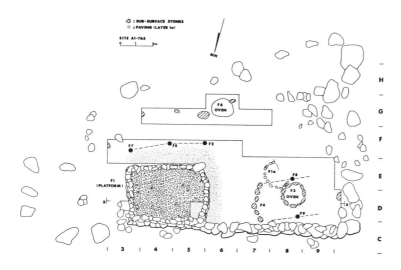

FIGURE 10.7 Plan of site Mo-A1-765 in Hālawa Valley, Moloka'i Island, with a stone-faced terrace supporting a dwelling house and a cookhouse with earth oven. *(After Hendren 1975)*

maika, and *poi* pounders. Artifacts of bone and shell, including fishhooks and ornaments, may be present in sites in arid regions, where preservation conditions are favorable. Faunal materials in residential sites are discussed below.

Most analysis of materials recovered from excavations in residential sites in Hawai'i has been undertaken at the "macro" level of portable artifacts and faunal remains. There is, however, much potential for obtaining additional insights into site use and function through a "micro" level approach. The extraction and identification of microscopic pollen grains, starch grains, and opal phytoliths (silica bodies found in plant cells) from household contexts can indicate the processing of plant materials at these sites (Coil 2003, 2004; Horrocks and Rechtman 2009; Vacca 2019). The micromorphology of cultural sediments in residential sites is another method that has yet to be fully explored in Hawaiian archaeology; Kirch et al. (2004) examined the micromorphology of cultural deposits in Kaupikiawa rockshelter at Kalaupapa, Moloka'i.

In a comprehensive attempt to employ these microlevel techniques, Kirsten Vacca (2019) analyzed variation within a series of household clusters at Nu'u, Maui. Sediment analysis, microartifact and plant microfossil analysis, and soil micromorphology were all applied, along with more traditional approaches, such as portable artifact and faunal analysis. Integration of macro- and microlevel data allowed for more nuanced interpretations of the functions of individual features than would have been possible by relying exclusively on the macrolevel evidence.

Kauhale: Status, Rank, and Gender

Ethnohistoric accounts of Hawaiian *kauhale,* as summarized above, allude to significant differences in the lifestyles of the *ali'i* and the *maka'āinana,* differences that should be evident as well in the archaeological record. In rare cases, specific sites are known to have been associated with particular chiefs, such as the Lonoikamakahiki residence at Kahalu'u, Kona, where Kirch (1973a) investigated what was arguably the *mua* or men's house of this large complex. Three monumental structures on Maui—Haleki'i, Pi'ilanihale, and Pōpō'iwi—are all identified as *luakini heiau* (see chapter 11), yet Kolb's investigations of these sites indicated that all three likely also functioned as royal residences (Kolb 1991, 1999). Other royal residences, such as that at Waipi'o, Hawai'i, have yet to be archaeologically studied.

Aside from the royal centers occupied by the highest ranks of *ali'i,* it is to be expected that the status differences between grades of chiefs, and even among the *maka'āinana* themselves, should be reflected in residential architecture and in the cultural contents of *kauhale.* In their study of household clusters and domestic modes of production in the *ahupua'a* of Makiloa and Kālala, in Kohala District, Hawai'i, Julie Field et al. (2010) showed that one residential complex (site MKI-56), situated near the boundary between the two *ahupua'a* in a strategic position overlooking Kamilo Bay, stands out as an elite residence, probably the *kauhale* of either an *ali'i-'ai-ahupua'a* or of the *konohiki.* According to Field et al.,

> The position of an elite residence at this important *ahupua'a* boundary line, as well as the abundance of artifacts, marine midden, and domestic animal

fauna suggests that this particular household participated in the collection of tribute from Makiloa and Kālala *ahupuaʻa*. This residential complex also exhibits unusually elaborated architecture for the Makiloa and Kālala survey sample, as it includes multiple internal divisions within a single large structure, an attached shrine with branch coral, and a possible canoe shed. (82)

Expanded excavations at site MKI-56 yielded evidence for craft specialization, in the manufacture of fishing gear and other items (J. Kahn and Kirch, unpublished data). A plan of the elaborate MKI-56 residence, showing the attached men's house or shrine, is provided in figure 10.8.

In their study of the settlement landscape of Kawela, Molokaʻi Island, Weisler and Kirch (1985) identified two *kauhale* as being associated with high-status households, probably those of the *ahupuaʻa* chief and of the *konohiki*. They argue that the identification of particular household clusters as high-status residences needs to be based on a diverse range of evidence, including the topographic setting of the cluster, the number of structural components in a cluster, whether a separate ritual feature can be identified, high frequencies of status foods such as pig and dog bone, a high density and range of formal artifacts, and evidence for craft specialization. Applying these criteria, Weisler and Kirch write,

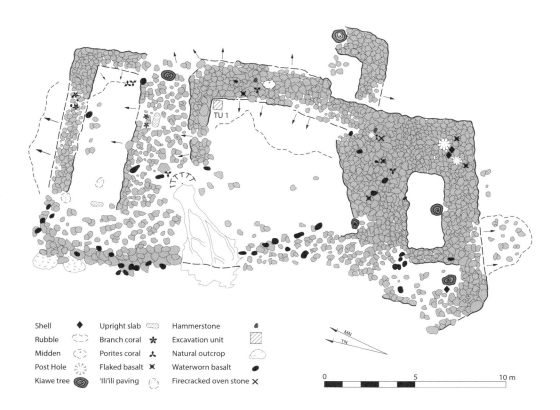

FIGURE 10.8 Plan of site MKI-56, a high-status residence at Makiloa, Hawaiʻi Island. *(Plan by P. V. Kirch)*

Two complexes, in particular, are interpreted as residences of prominent social groups, presumably households which centered around a lesser chief, or *konohiki*, the land manager of a chief. These complexes are more extensive and architecturally complex than other residential sites in the study area. More importantly, only these two residential complexes incorporate rectangular, fully-enclosed and high-walled temples (*heiau*). It is also relevant to note that these two sites command prominent topographic settings, with views of the south Moloka'i coast and its fishponds, the agricultural lands of Kawela Gulch, and beyond to the islands of Lana'i, Maui, and Kaho'olawe. (1985, 147–148)

The settlement landscape of Kawela is discussed in further detail in chapter 12.

A final example of a *kauhale* complex associated with a particular status role is site KIP-117 in the uplands of Kahikinui District, Maui (Kirch et al. 2010). This walled enclosure situated atop a large, stone-faced terrace (fig. 10.9) occupies a prominent ridge surrounded by a cluster of temple sites. The size, substantial architecture, and ritual setting of this *kauhale* suggested that it was the house of a priest, an interpretation strengthened by the results of excavation. Portable artifacts included a small adze likely used for fine carving work, as well as a cache of 67 black and 96 white coral waterworn pebbles not unlike those used in the *kōnane* game, but in this case possibly used in divination (Kamakau 1964, 95; Malo 1951, 207–208). A unique find was a lava stalactite procured from a lava tube in a volcanically active area. The faunal remains recovered during excavation were also of particular interest:

> The individual who occupied KIP-117 also had access to a wide range of status foods, including not only pig and dog, but choice fish and shellfish, especially the black-footed *'opihi*. The pig remains especially are consistent with a cut of meat known to have been given to priests. Also unusual is the range of forest birds represented in the faunal assemblage—these may have had more to do with acquiring the bird's colorful plumage (the colours having particular associations with various deities in the Hawaiian pantheon) than as food items. (Kirch et al. 2010, 159)

The recovery of *gendered* activities in the patterns of everyday life has become a goal of archaeological inquiry in many parts of the world. Given the rich ethnohistoric record for gender roles in traditional Hawai'i, particularly the *'ai kapu* system of gender-restricted cooking and eating, Hawai'i seems an ideal location to pursue such research. Ethnohistoric sources associate men and women with different kinds of activities (Bayman and Dye 2013, table 5.1; Vacca 2019, table 4.6). Male activities included building and thatching houses, fishing and making fishnets and fishhooks, building canoes and carving wooden bowls, and pounding taro into *poi*. Female activities included barkcloth manufacture and mat plaiting, gathering shellfish and seaweed, collecting salt, and nursing children. On the older, westerly islands, agriculture was said to be a male activity, but on Maui and Hawai'i women worked in the fields alongside their menfolk (Kamakau 1961, 239). Food was prepared and cooked by both men and women, in separate cookhouses. Certain foods as well were *kapu* to women, including pork, sea turtle, coconuts, bananas, and certain red fish (Vacca 2019, table 4.4).

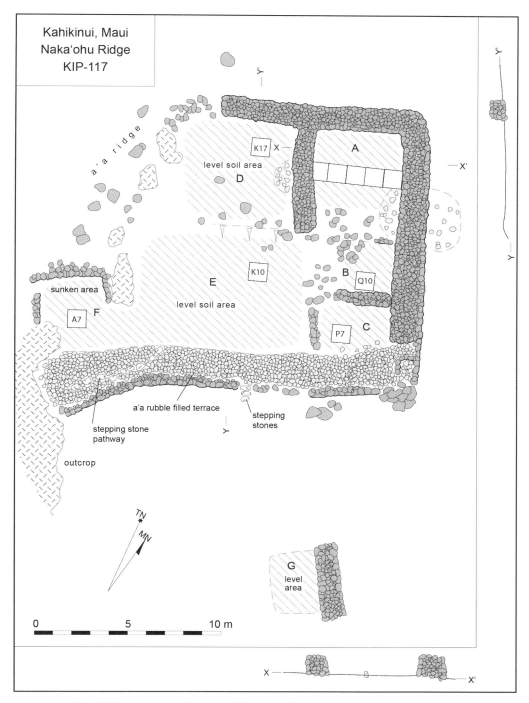

FIGURE 10.9 Plan of site KIP-117, a priest's dwelling house in the uplands of Kahikinui, Maui Island. *(Plan by P. V. Kirch)*

While this ethnohistoric record is rich in gender associations for particular activities, finding unambiguous signals of gender in the archaeological record based solely on collections of artifacts can be challenging. In part this is because certain male-associated activities, such as adze production and fishhook manufacture, are more apt to leave a material signal in the form of lithic assemblages and tools and detritus from working bone and shell. In contrast, the tools and materials used in making barkcloth and in mat weaving are almost entirely of perishable materials such as bark, wood, leaves, bamboo, and fiber that are preserved only in the most favorable conditions. It is partly for this reason that Vacca (2019) implemented an approach emphasizing the recovery of microscopic remains (where plant materials may be more evident) in her study of household sites at Nuʻu, Maui.

Archaeologists have been more successful in identifying gendered spaces. According to the ethnohistoric model, the *ʻai kapu* system of gendered cooking and eating required that men and women cook their food in separate earth ovens (*imu*), and eat in separate *hale*. Men took their meals in the *mua,* while the women, girls, and prepubescent boys ate in the *hale ʻāina* (Handy and Pukui 1958, 9). Excavations at several household clusters in Kahikinui, Maui, have documented the presence of dual *imu* and cook sheds, as well as the presence of dual hearths within what appear to have been the *hale noa* or common dwelling house, as seen in figure 10.10 (van Gilder and Kirch 1997). This pattern of dual hearths, which had not previously been noted in Hawaiian house sites, may indicate that when cooked food was reheated this was done in separate hearths for men and women. This suggests a variation of *ʻai kapu* practice, in which gendered eating took place even within the *hale noa*.

FIGURE 10.10 View of site KIP-752, a residential terrace in the Kīpapa area of Kahikinui, Maui Island, after excavation. Note the two stone-lined hearths next to each other at the far end of the terrace. *(Photo by P. V. Kirch)*

Resource Use and Domestic Consumption: The Contributions of Zooarchaeology and Archaeobotany

"Midden analysis," or the identification and study of faunal remains such as fish, bird, or mammal bone, mollusk shells, and—where taphonomic conditions are favorable—plant remains, has a long tradition in Hawaiian archaeology. Although faunal remains do occur in other contexts, such as *heiau*, most zooarchaeological and archaeobotanical analyses in Hawai'i have focused on residential sites, hence our inclusion of this topic in the present chapter. Tables reporting the results of quantitative midden analyses regularly appear in both research and CRM reports; we make no attempt to synthesize all of these data. Rather, we highlight a few studies that are representative of the range of zooarchaeological and archaeobotanical work in Hawai'i.

Kirch (1982c) argued that an ecological and comparative approach to marine exploitation in ancient Hawai'i was essential to move beyond the typological studies of fishing gear that had previously dominated the field. To illustrate this approach, he analyzed faunal assemblages from three sites, each situated in a different ecological setting: (1) the Hālawa dune site on Moloka'i; (2) the Hāwea Point midden site on western Maui; and (3) a rockshelter (Ha-E1-355) at Kalāhuipua'a on Hawai'i. The Hālawa site lies at the mouth of a valley with extensive freshwater output and virtually no reef development; the Hāwea Point site is on an exposed rocky headland; and the Kalāhuipua'a rockshelter lies adjacent to a complex of anchialine fishponds. Differences in faunal assemblages, as well as in fishing gear, at these sites are closely correlated with these ecological contrasts. In an early use of the "ecological niche" concept, Kirch also applied a quantitative measure of "niche width" finding that Kalāhuipua'a had "the greatest niche diversity, presumably a function of the greater inshore marine resources available at that locale" (1982c, 471).

Jim Bayman and Tom Dye (2013, 58–65, table 4.2) compared vertebrate faunal assemblages from 23 sites located in Kona and Kohala Districts of leeward Hawai'i Island, grouping the sites into (1) coastal sites, (2) sites situated within upland agricultural fields, and (3) sites located within the high forest and alpine zones. Faunal remains were quantified by major zoological class (fish, bird, mammal, rat), with the relative abundance of each class indicated graphically (2013, fig. 4.8). Not surprisingly, fish bones dominate in the coastal sites; inshore and benthic taxa are the most prevalent, with pelagic fishes only rarely represented. Although some of the coastal sites are located near fishponds, bones from fish raised in ponds (such as mullet and milkfish) have rarely been identified in faunal assemblages (but see Weisler 1993). Sites situated within the upland agricultural field systems "typically yield a more diverse faunal assemblage in which pigs and dogs play a prominent role in addition to fish" (Bayman and Dye 2013, 63). This presumably reflects the feeding of pigs and dogs on agricultural produce, and husbanding of these animals near the fields. In the high elevation sites located in the forested and alpine zones, "the nature of the faunal assemblages changes radically," with the assemblages "dominated by bird bone to the virtual exclusion of other kinds of bone" (64). Most of the bird bones are from petrels or the *nēnē* goose, which were likely captured from their nesting sites in this upland region (Moniz 1997; Moniz-Nakamura 1999).

Rockshelter Midden Deposits

Rockshelters or lava-tube sites often contain dense concentrations of both faunal and floral remains, due to the confined space and relatively good preservation conditions. Many of these sites were occupied over long time periods, with stratified deposits that allow for analysis of temporal patterns. The first quantitative analysis of a rockshelter deposit was that made by Kenneth Emory and Yosihiko Sinoto (1961, 15–21, table 1) of two excavation units within the Kuli'ou'ou (O1) site on O'ahu (see chapter 6). They quantified the weights of candlenut, shell, mammal bone, crustacea, fish bone, and bird bone according to the 6-inch levels in which the deposit was excavated, also breaking down the shell content by mollusk family (fig. 12). Among the temporal trends revealed was a sharp decrease from the earliest levels in the amount of seabird bones, and a significant increase of marine mollusks in the upper levels. Although they did not quantify the macroscopic plant remains in the site, they noted the presence of coconut shell, gourd, bamboo, sugarcane, pandanus leaves, 'awa (*Piper methysticum*) stems, and "many candlenuts" (21).

Lava-tube occupation sites at Kalāhuipua'a, an "oasis" of anchialine fishponds on the arid coast of South Kohala, Hawai'i Island, provided an opportunity for quantitative analysis of faunal remains indicative of marine exploitation patterns (Kirch 1979a). Fauna from eight sites was analyzed, along with samples from three surface midden deposits. While Bishop Museum excavation procedures at the time called for the use of 0.25-inch mesh screens, fine-screening of selected sediment samples was used to estimate the amount of smaller-sized material that was not retained by the larger mesh (Kirch 1979a, table 10). By weight, mollusks comprised more than 90 percent of the faunal materials in these lava-tube shelter deposits, with five genera dominating, although many more species were present. The high frequency of small cowries (*Cypraea caputserpentis*) and *pipipi* (*Nerita* spp.) reflects gathering along the rocky shoreline, while *hīhīwai* (*Theodoxus* spp.) and two kinds of bivalves (*Isognomon* sp. and *Brachiodontes* sp.) were harvested from the brackish-water ponds. A total of 409 fishbones were identified to family or genus. Most of the bones came from smaller reef fishes, including parrotfish, pufferfish, triggerfish, and wrasses that were probably caught by spearing, angling, and netting (Kirch 1979a, 136). Larger fish such as snappers and jacks may have been taken by angling or by trolling. Temporal trends included a decrease in the frequency of wrasses and an increase in the frequency of parrotfish over time.

The extremely arid conditions at Kalāhuipua'a favored the preservation of plant materials in the lava-tube occupations. These were identified by ethnobotanist Douglas Yen (Kirch 1979a, table 32), and included coconut, gourd, 'awa, hala, 'ilima, and kī.

Aki Goto (1984, 1986) analyzed faunal assemblages from coastal sites at Wai'ahukini, near South Point, Hawai'i. Goto compared vertebrate assemblages obtained by ¼- versus ⅛-inch mesh screens (see also Gordon 1993). In addition to differences in the number and frequency of fish taxa recovered in the different mesh sizes, Goto's analysis of the sizes of lower pharyngeal plates of *Thalassoma* fish reveals a strong bias toward larger bones when using the ¼-inch mesh (1986, fig 8.3). Thus while most of the fish caught at Wai'ahukini were quite small, this would not be evident based on a sample derived only from using ¼-inch mesh. Among the most frequently occurring fish families in the Wai'ahukini sites are Holocentridae, Labridae, Scaridae, and Acanthuridae (1986, tables 8.10 to 8.15). Among the marine mollusks gathered along the rocky shoreline, small cowries (*Cypraea caputserpentis*) were by far the most abundant.

Ken Longenecker et al. (2014) applied ancient DNA sequencing methods to identify three of the five Hawaiian parrotfish (subfamily Scarinae) in the faunal remains from Wai'ahukini. Consistently large examples of Spectacled Parrotfish (*Chlorurus perspicillatus*) and Ember Parrotfish (*Scarus rubroviolaceus*), the largest of the Hawaiian scarines, are estimated to have been around 47 cm in length when they were caught. Regal Parrotfish (*Scarus dubius*) were rarer and smaller, caught at around 23 cm in length, but were still within the size range of mature females of the species. These findings indicate that all of the fish were taken after they had the chance to reproduce, indicating that people "practiced sustainable fishing techniques" (Kahn, Lundblad, et al. 2016, 200).

Three rockshelters in the Anahulu Valley, O'ahu, provide a contrastive data set to the Kalāhuipua'a or Wai'ahukini sites, as the Anahulu sites are situated in an inland location 4–5 km from the coast, occupied by groups exploiting forest resources and cultivating swidden gardens (Kirch, ed., 1989). In these sites, the cultural sediments were screened through nested 0.25- and 0.12-inch mesh. Out of 401 NISP-identified vertebrate fauna, the most frequent were the bones of domestic dog and pig (Kirch and Collins 1989). Fish bones were present, but in much lower numbers than in the Kalāhuipua'a coastal sites. Of particular note was the range of bird taxa present, not only the domestic fowl (*Gallus gallus*) but also five species of Procellariidae seabirds (petrels and shearwaters), along with several species of forest birds, including the *elepaio,* a species of honeyeater, and several honeycreepers (*Chaetoptila* sp. and *Psittirostra* sp.). The invertebrate fauna included 17 species of marine gastropods, nine species of marine bivalves, and seven species of sea urchins, all gathered in the coastal zone and carried to the inland rockshelters.

Terrestrial gastropods recovered by fine-sieving of the Anahulu rockshelter deposits included a wide range of native taxa in the Achatinellidae, Amastridae, Pupillidae, and other families, as well as the Polynesian-introduced garden snail *Lamellaxis gracilis* (Kirch 1989). Changing frequencies of these land snails reflect the anthropogenic transformation of the vegetation in the middle Anahulu Valley, from the mid-fifteenth century up to the postcontact period. The snail assemblage in the early deposits in Kuolulo rockshelter are indicative of closed canopy native forest, which later gave way to more open conditions, presumably as a result of forest clearance and shifting cultivation (Kirch 1989, 81).

Melinda S. Allen (1989) used flotation of sediment samples from the Anahulu rockshelters to recover carbonized seeds, the majority of which were from the native plant *Chenopodium oahuense,* occurring as a fallow weed in agricultural plots but not cultivated or eaten. Wood charcoal from the Kuolulo shelter was identified by Gail Murakami (1989), providing some indication of the forest composition in the mid–Anahulu Valley; charcoal from Polynesian-introduced breadfruit (*Artocarpus altilis*), and the Malay apple or 'ōhi'a-'ai (*Eugenia malaccensis*) indicates that these trees were being cultivated in the valley.

Sharyn O'Day (2001) conducted a fine-grained zooarchaeological analysis of the cultural deposit in a small rockshelter in the Kīpapa area of Kahikinui, Maui, dating to the Archaic States Period. Sediments were screened through both ¼-inch and ⅛-inch mesh. Not surprisingly, the finer-mesh screen yielded significantly greater numbers of small animal bones, from rats, lizards, birds, and small fish, as well as large quantities of sea urchin remains that passed through the larger mesh (2001, table 7). O'Day suggests that this rockshelter—situated adjacent to a small *kauhale* complex—served as the cooking area or *hale kahūmu* for the household. This interpretation is supported by the quantity of ash and charcoal in the deposit, derived from oven rake-outs, and by the presence of an earth oven that was filled with "numerous red ash and charcoal lenses" and with fire-cracked rocks.

Julie Field, Michael Graves, and others (Field and Graves, eds., 2015) reanalyzed faunal materials excavated by Bishop Museum at the Nu'alolo rockshelter on Kaua'i in the early 1960s (see chapter 6). A complicating factor in this case is that the sampling procedures (including screen size) used in the original excavation are not always evident in the available field records. Nonetheless, studies of the fish, bird, and turtle bones provided significant data on the use of these animal resources over time, even offering implications for contemporary conservation biology (Morrison and Esh, in Field and Graves, eds., 2015).

One example of how archaeology can inform on contemporary ecology centers on the prized *'opihi* (*Cellana* spp.) shellfish. Richard Pearson et al. (1974) examined *pipipi* (*Nerita* spp.) and *'opihi* from Kaupikiawa rockshelter (site 50-60-03-312) at Kalaupapa, Moloka'i, to see whether there were changes in the average size of individuals over time. Contrary their expectations, they found that shellfish increased in size over time, suggesting "a lessening of the pressure on the shell[fish] supply during the time period of the upper levels" (Pearson et al. 1974, 48). Years later, Mark D. McCoy (2006, 2008a) conducted excavations at other sites around Kalaupapa—including an open-air shell midden located on the Nihoa landshelf—and found that average sizes of *'opihi* from deposits dating to the centuries just prior to European contact were small, a reflection of intense harvesting and a high local population density. However, when the human population at Kalaupapa declined in the postcontact era, average *'opihi* sizes increased significantly. Today, thanks to conservation efforts—and the fact that *'opihi* taking is restricted to Kalaupapa residents—average sizes are larger than they have been in 350 years.

Also drawing on archaeological work on Moloka'i, Rogers and Weisler (2020, 2021) examined the exploitation and cultural significance of *'opihi*. The prized limpets are found at both habitation and ritual (shrine) sites, but at the shrines the shells were significantly larger than those in the domestic middens. They also found that the frequency of the three Hawaiian species of limpet in west Moloka'i archaeological sites did not conform to predictions based on optimal foraging theory models. Whereas these models predicted that *Cellana exarata* would be most prevalent, *C. sandwicensis* was in fact the most commonly harvested species, despite being more dangerous to obtain. "The preference for *C. sandwicensis* may be explained by a favoured taste and texture, which is the case among modern *'opihi* gatherers and consumers in Hawai'i. Alternatively, prehistoric harvest of *C. sandwicensis* may have facilitated the display of risk-taking behavior among men, as a social indicator of prowess" (Rogers and Weisler 2021, 1339).

Faunal Analysis of Open Site Middens

In contrast with rockshelter or lava-tube sites, faunal remains in open sites are usually less densely concentrated; preservation of bone and shell ranges from quite good in arid, leeward regions to very poor in the windward valleys or even in the upland zones of leeward regions. The calcium carbonate of shell dissolves rapidly in damp soils with humic acids; bone is likewise subject to chemical and biological weathering and degradation. These taphonomic conditions limit the potential for faunal analysis in many open sites.

Sand dunes, however, provide excellent conditions for preserving shell and bone, even in areas of relatively high rainfall. The faunal assemblage of the stratified Hālawa dune site (Mo-A1-3) on Moloka'i Island was analyzed by Kirch (1975a), who found that the bones of pig and dog were quite common, becoming increasingly frequent in the upper levels of the dune (1975a, tables 16, 17, and 24). The increase in pig and dog, relative to fish bone, is thought to reflect increased production of the valley's agricultural system over time. Bones of the Pacific rat (*Rattus exulans*) were also found in the site. The most frequent fish taxa present were parrotfish (*Scarus* and *Calotomus* spp.), followed by wrasses (Labridae). Among the shellfish remains, the most abundant was the 'opihi (*Cellana exarata*), followed by *pipipi* (*Nerita picea*) and a small drupe (*Drupa ricinus*); all of these occur on the boulder beaches around the bay. Also present were the shells of the freshwater *hīhīwai* (*Neritina cariosa*), now extirpated from Hālawa Stream but formerly abundant.

Faunal assemblages from the stone structures of *kauhale* offer opportunities to test hypotheses regarding feature function as well as status differences between households. Kirch and O'Day (2003) compared faunal assemblages from four household clusters in Kahikinui, Maui, in order to examine whether households of different social status exhibited differential access to prestige or "luxury" foods. In precontact Hawai'i, as elsewhere in Polynesia, the diet was based on staple starch ('*ai*) such as *poi* or sweet potatoes. A meal was ideally augmented with *i'a*, literally "fish," but a term that also referred to any kind of flesh food or relish that accompanied the basic '*ai*. The Hawaiian proverb *ka i'a uahi nui o ka 'āina*, "the many smoky fish of the land," refers to any kind of meat that has been cooked in the earth oven, taking on a smoky flavor. In an ecologically marginal regional such as Kahikinui, which lacks reefs and where sea cliffs made shellfish gathering limited and dangerous, access to *i'a* was limited, whether of domestic pig, dog, or chicken, or of fish or shellfish from the ocean. Kirch and O'Day compared fauna from two *kauhale* believed to represent low-status commoners with two *kauhale* inhabited by higher-status households, including one occupied by a priest. Quantities of dog and pig bone were approximately the same between all households, but the higher-status *kauhale* had more bird and more fish remains (fig. 10.11). Lower-status *kauhale*, in contrast, had far more shellfish remains, suggesting that they depended mostly on shoreline gathering for their *i'a*.

A particularly interesting—and perhaps controversial—finding of the Kirch and O'Day faunal analysis was the presence of significant numbers of bones of the small Pacific rat, especially in the lower-status *kauhale*. As Kirch and O'Day comment,

> Rats accounted for over three times as much of the fauna in commoner deposits. This bone is often fragmentary, burned and covered in carbonized material. If

commoners were consuming rats, as the archaeological evidence strongly indicates, then it is likely that elites were not consuming them, perhaps as a show of status or taste, and / or simply because elites obtained sufficient protein from larger terrestrial mammals such as pigs, dogs and pelagic fish. (2003, 491)

Ethnohistoric sources refer to the hunting of rats with small bows and arrows as a chiefly sport (Malo 1951, 233), but there is no reference to eating rat flesh. However, we know that the Pacific rat was eaten in other Polynesian islands, such as Mangaia and New Zealand. It seems plausible that in a marginal land such as Kahikinui, where *i'a* was scarce, people might well have turned to consuming the roasted bodies of these little creatures. Hunting pressure on the rat populations could also have had a beneficial effect in keeping their numbers down, thereby reducing rat damage to the sweet potato crop.

Field et al. (2016) conducted an extensive study of faunal remains from residential sites in leeward Kohala, examining trends in marine foraging and fishing, based on identification of more than 158,000 specimens of fish bone and invertebrates from 57 precontact residential features, located both along the coast and in the upland agricultural field system. Although individual features were typically single-component occupations, in aggregate the samples span a period of 500 years, allowing for an analysis of temporal trends, with sites divided into three precontact periods (plus a few sites extending into the postcontact period). Twenty fish taxa were identified, the most common being parrotfish (Scaridae), wrasses (Labridae), filefish (Monacanthidae), and triggerfish (Balidtidae), all common inshore reef fish. Among the shellfish, nerites (*Nertia picea*), small cowries (*Cypraea caputserpentis*), and *Drupa* were the most common, reflecting collecting along the rocky shores. Comparison of the sizes of fish bone elements between precontact and modern reference specimens suggest that over the 500-year period there was considerable pressure on fish populations, as the modern samples are significantly larger (Field et al. 2016, fig. 3). The

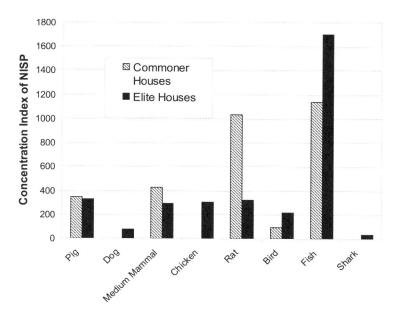

FIGURE 10.11 Frequencies of vertebrate faunal remains in commoner and elite household sites in Kahikinui, Maui Island. *(After Kirch and O'Day 2003)*

small size of fish being taken in precontact times suggests a constant degree of "resource depression," not surprising given that the leeward Kohala inshore ecosystem has only incipient reefs that could not support a large marine biomass. Regarding long-term temporal trends of marine exploitation in leeward Kohala, Field et al. write,

> The amount of marine prey harvested increased over time, a trajectory that matches the trends for human population growth in the region (measured through the establishment of new residential sites) and for agricultural intensification over time, with a peak for both population and intensive farming in the final precontact period, ca. AD 1650–1800. The one notable difference between the coast and the upland residences is the importation of larger-bodied fish, mollusks, and echinoderms into the field system residences. We conclude that the timing of these imports coincides with the development of *ahupuaʻa* as integrated economic units, in which households exchanged or transported foods and other goods between the coast and field system. (2016, 304)

Networks of Communication: Trails

Lacking draft animals, carts, or wheeled vehicles of any kind, the Hawaiians moved heavy loads from point to point along the coasts in single- or double-hulled canoes; communication overland was by means of a large network of trails. Ranking chiefs used runners to carry messages and materials back and forth over their dominions. Hauling of loads on overland trails was facilitated by the use of carrying poles, some of which have been found stashed away in dry caves, as at Kalāhuipuaʻa (Kirch 1979a).

Trails—where not obliterated by modern tracts or roads—formed an important component of settlement landscapes, linking individual communities. Along the leeward coasts of Hawaiʻi Island and in the Kahikinui District of Maui, ancient trails are readily discernible; some are still in use today, by fishermen, hunters, and campers. Where trails passed over rough *ʻaʻā* lava terrain it was common to set down stepping-stones of smooth waterworn cobbles (fig. 10.12) or of flat lava slabs. White coral pebbles, which reflect even partial moonlight, were sometimes dropped along the trailside to guide travelers moving about at night. In other areas, trails crossing *ʻaʻā* flows are marked simply by a worn depression where the impact of countless passing feet has crushed the clinker to a pebble-sized bed. Similarly, trails over *pāhoehoe* lava are often easily traced as they break down the smooth, glassy surface. In North Kohala, trails are more elaborate, consisting of parallel stone alignments spaced about one meter apart, running on *mauka-makai* axes through the dryland field system.

Russ Apple (1965), who studied trails in the Kona District of Hawaiʻi Island, classified precontact and early postcontact trails into four major types. Type A trails are the single-file ancient paths described above. After horses arrived in the islands between AD 1820 and 1840, new Type B trails began to be constructed, modifying existing Type A trails through the addition of kerbstones and of causeways over low spots (fig. 10.13). These gave

FIGURE 10.12 A stepping-stone trail of smooth, waterworn cobbles laid across a rough ʻaʻā lava flow. *(Photo courtesy Bishop Museum Department of Anthropology)*

way to Type C trails, two horses wide and built along straight lines between major points, cutting off lesser coastal settlements. The "Māmalahoa Highway" crossing the Kanikū lava flow between Kalāhuipuaʻa and ʻAnaehoʻomalu is an excellent example of a Type C trail. Some Type C trails were built by corvée labor under the direction of the island governors during the early part of the nineteenth century. This was the case with a Type C trail that runs through Honuaʻula and Kahikinui Districts on Maui, constructed by convict labor in the 1820s and 1830s under the direction of Governor Hoapili. Finally, with the introduction of wheeled vehicles such as ox carts and wagons, Type C trails were modified, widened, and realigned to create Type D trails.

Trails that connected communities along the coast were especially affected by the creation of historic and modern roads. It is, however, in some cases possible to infer the path of earlier routes. Peter Mills (2002b) conducted a survey of coastal Kona with an eye toward

FIGURE 10.13 A trail of Apple's "Type B," constructed in the early nineteenth century to accommodate horses, at 'Anaeho'omalu, Hawai'i Island. *(Photo by Therese Babineau)*

documenting trails, noting that the presence of waterworn stones—a feature of earlier footpaths—were common on or alongside roads that had been modified for horse traffic.

In the North Kohala region of Hawai'i, and especially within Lapakahi *ahupua'a*, trails not only served as communication networks across social boundaries but also marked social boundaries (Cordy and Kaschko 1980; Kaschko 1973; see also Rosendahl 1972a). Michael Kaschko found that trails, usually defined by parallel stone alignments, connected the upland agricultural field zone with the coastal settlements. More importantly, these trails coincided with known boundaries between major land sections, especially *ahupua'a* and *'ili* boundaries. Kirch (1984) noted that the branching patterns of trails through fields could be used to create a relative chronology of social boundaries and agricultural development in Lapakahi. This observation was subsequently expanded to other sections of Kohala's leeward fields (Field, Ladefoged, Sharp, and Kirch 2011; Ladefoged, Graves, and McCoy 2003; Ladefoged and Graves 2008b; M. D. McCoy 2000).

Inscribing the Land: Petroglyphs

Unevenly distributed and present only in some settlement areas—and not especially common in any case—petroglyph sites have long captured the attention and imagination of archaeologists as well as the general public. In their portrayal of men and women, animals, spirits, and events, petroglyphs remind us that these material traces on the landscape were the creations of people with a rich cultural and aesthetic background. Cox and Stasack (1970, 1998), who authored the first definitive study of Hawaiian petroglyphs, enumerated 135 sites on all the islands, with an estimated total of more than 24,000 individual glyph units (1970, 7). Since their study was completed, a number of additional sites have been recorded, such as the large group of petroglyphs on cliff faces at Ahupū, Kahoʻolawe; several groups on boulders and cliffs at Kawela, Molokaʻi (Weisler and Kirch 1982); within a household compound in Manukā, Hawaiʻi (M. D. McCoy and Codlin 2015); and a number of small petroglyph clusters distributed through Kahikinui District on Maui (Millerstrom and Kirch 2002, 2004). The largest sites have no doubt now all been recorded, but additional discoveries of small groups of petroglyphs continue to be made.

Regarding the geographic distribution of petroglyph sites, Halley Cox and Edward Stasack wrote, "The occurrence of petroglyphs is almost entirely limited to the dry sides of the islands and generally to open country near the shore, the dry leeward areas being preferred for habitation by the Hawaiians. The sites are seldom within the small village centers but are on or near the trails between habitation sites" (Cox and Stasack 1970, 7).

About half of all known sites, including the largest complexes, are situated on Hawaiʻi Island, where relatively flat expanses of young *pāhoehoe* lava provide excellent terrain for petroglyphs (fig. 10.14). Among these prominent petroglyph fields are those at Puakō (site Ha-E3-1), ʻAnaehoʻomalu (Ha-E1-7), and Puʻuloa (Ha-HV-225). Although the most extensive sites are on *pāhoehoe* flats, petroglyphs are found in a variety of other topographic settings. On Hawaiʻi Island, petroglyphs were commonly pecked through the glassy surfaces that line the insides of lava tubes. A common location, especially on Lānaʻi and Molokaʻi, is on groups of large outcropping boulders (see fig. 10.15). Vertical cliff faces, as at Olowalu on Maui (site Ma-D2-2) and Nuʻuanu on Oʻahu (Oa-A5-1), also offered good surfaces for rock art, including pictographs, rare in Hawaiʻi. Less common sites are shoreline shelves of limestone or beach rock, as at the Keoneloa Beach site on Kauaʻi (Ka-B2-1).

Petroglyphs were made using four different techniques (Cox and Stasack 1970, 38). Using a stone tool with a sharp point, figures could be made by pecking or incising into the rock surface. With a blunt tool, such as a river cobble, petroglyphs were made by bruising or abrading the rock panel. With the introduction of iron tools after European contact, petroglyphs were more easily made; some glyphs depict European introductions such as horses or sailing ships. After the introduction of writing by the Protestant missionaries, some petroglyphs depict efforts at learning the new alphabet and writing names in Hawaiian (fig. 10.16).

Hawaiian petroglyph motifs include human figures, animals, and objects, either singly or sometimes in associated groups or panels. Anthropomorphic figures are most common and range from simple rectilinear stick figures to triangular-bodied figures to forms that display musculature. Some human figures hold or manipulate objects (clubs, paddles,

FIGURE 10.14 A portion of the extensive petroglyph field at Puakō, Hawai'i Island, with figures pecked into the surface of a *pāhoehoe* lava flow. *(Photo by Therese Babineau)*

FIGURE 10.15 Petroglyphs pecked on a group of boulders at Kawela, Moloka'i Island. *(Photo by P. V. Kirch)*

fishhooks, headdresses, etc.), while others are associated in action (e.g., the marchers at Puakō, Hawai'i). Other human figures display distinct birds' heads or wings and may be manifestations of a widespread East Polynesian bird-man concept (Barrow 1967). Dogs are commonly portrayed, turtles less often. Among the artifacts seen in petroglyph groups, the typical crab-claw sail of Hawaiian canoes is not infrequent. Simple geometric motifs, especially circles and concentric circles, are also common.

Millerstrom and Kirch (2004) recorded 17 previously unknown petroglyph or pictograph sites in Kahikinui District on Maui, containing a total of 168 glyphs. Unlike previous studies that tended to view Hawaiian petroglyphs as divorced from their larger archaeological context, Millerstrom and Kirch interpret this corpus in terms of a landscape-level settlement analysis. The Kahikinui petroglyphs display a limited range of motifs, with certain styles of anthropomorphs and zoomorphs (especially dogs) dominating (fig. 10.17).

FIGURE 10.16 Petroglyphs continued to be made after the introduction of writing and the Hawaiian alphabet in the early 1820s. *(Photo courtesy of Bishop Museum Department of Anthropology)*

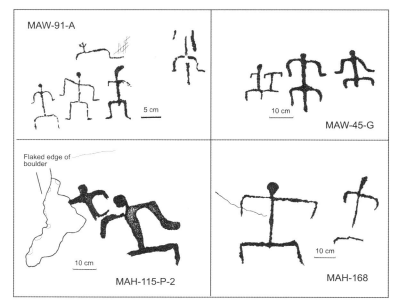

FIGURE 10.17 Examples of petroglyph groups in Kahikinui, Maui Island. *(After Millerstrom and Kirch 2004)*

There are also petroglyphs dating to the early post-European contact period, characterized by Roman lettering reflecting early missionary efforts at literacy. On the landscape, petroglyphs are primarily associated either with an early historic-period trail, or with rockshelters and cliff faces where there is evidence for freshwater springs or seeps. Fresh water was a precious resource in arid Kahikinui, and the petroglyphs may have served as territorial markers, or signs of individual ownership or rights of access to water. Three rockshelter sites with petroglyphs date to the late precontact era, specifically the sixteenth to eighteenth centuries.

Along with petroglyphs, *papamū* must be mentioned. These rectangular grids of spaced dots were pecked into flat lava surfaces or flat-topped boulders as game boards for playing *kōnane* (Buck 1957). Among the waterworn boulders used to pave the top of Puʻukoholā Heiau—famous for having been transported across the island from Pololū Valley—is one that had at one time had been used as a *papamū* (M. D. McCoy 2014, fig. 4).

11

THE ARCHAEOLOGY OF RITUAL, POWER, AND DEATH

During the first half of the twentieth century archaeologists in Hawai'i concentrated their efforts on the many stone foundations of temples and shrines—*heiau*—found in a sometimes bewildering variety of forms, sizes, and locations throughout the islands. Since the late 1960s, a shift to the investigation of residential and agricultural sites led to a neglect of *heiau* as topics of systematic study. Relatively few *heiau* sites have been excavated or studied for their architectural construction sequences. Furthermore, the place of *heiau* in larger settlement patterns has received less attention than agricultural and habitation sites. Yet *heiau* are among the most significant structural elements of ancient Hawaiian landscapes; their formal variation, construction sequences, and relationships to other settlement pattern components are essential topics in Hawaiian cultural history.

Heiau: Places of Prayer, Sacrifice, and Observation

The term *heiau* encompasses all kinds and sizes of temples and shrines, from single upright stones (*pōhaku o Kāne*) to the massive temples of human sacrifice known as *luakini*. Valerio Valeri (1985) suggests that the word *heiau* has its etymological origins in the term *hai*, "to sacrifice"; in older documents, *haiau* is sometimes given as a variant spelling of *heiau*. Thus, a *heiau* in essence can be any place where sacrifices or offerings were made; indeed, the concept of sacrifice is fundamental in Hawaiian religious practice (Handy 1927). Consider, for example, the words of Samuel Kamakau: "There were many heiaus made famous because of the shrine of the grease (*hinu*) of burnt offerings from Hawaii to Kauai; they were offered by the hundreds and thousands (*he lau, he kini, he lehu*). The soil became fertile and saturated with slime from the grease of the heavenly chiefs and from the burnt offerings. It is impossible to count the hundreds and thousands of years of sacrificing" (Kamakau 1976, 145).

People in old Hawai'i imbued natural places with enormous spiritual and historical significance. Certain boulders, for example, are associated with the birthing of chiefs, as at Kūkaniloko on O'ahu. Such unmodified natural features can be difficult for archaeologists to recognize as sites, unless there is specific ethnohistoric information regarding them. And so, while our focus in this chapter is on the built ritual landscape, and on activities that we can detect through archaeological methods, we recognize that our understanding of cultural landscapes in Hawai'i will always have some limitations.

Hawaiian temples and shrines are part of a widespread Eastern Polynesian tradition of temple construction, with roots that can be traced to Ancestral Polynesian Society (Kirch and Green 2001). In most of Eastern Polynesia temples are called *marae* (*me'ae* in the Marquesas), and all of them, including the Hawaiian *heiau*, share certain architectural features. Structurally, Eastern Polynesian temples consist of a court or plaza, usually defined by a terrace, a paved area, or a walled enclosure. At one end of this court is the altar, often a raised platform with representations of ancestral deities and gods. In the Society Islands and the Tuamotus, the gods and deified ancestors are represented by upright slabs of stone or coral; in Easter Island these were elaborated into giant stone statues. In Hawai'i, gods (*akua*) were represented by carved wooden images, which on the larger *luakini* temples were set in semicircular arrangements surrounding the offering platform (*lele*). Many of these basic features are present in the sketch of a *heiau* near Waimea, on Kaua'i Island, made by John Webber during Captain Cook's visit in 1778 (fig. 11.1), the earliest depiction of a Hawaiian temple.

The earliest Hawaiian temples may have been closer in form to the simpler *marae* found in the Society Islands (Emory 1933), the Tuamotus (Emory 1934a, 1947), and on the deserted Equatorial Islands between Hawai'i and the Societies (Emory 1934b). The temples recorded by Kenneth Emory (1928) on Mokumanamana (Necker) Island, and termed *marae* by him, are virtually indistinguishable from the simple *marae* forms in these southeastern Polynesian islands. Examples of *marae*-type temples have also been found in isolated

FIGURE 11.1 Interior of a *heiau* near Waimea, on Kaua'i Island, as drawn by John Webber, artist on Captain James Cook's third voyage in 1778. Among the features evident are the enclosing wall, stone altar, wooden uprights representing deities, oracle tower, and offering stand. *(From Cook and King 1784)*

locations in the main Hawaiian Islands, as in the arrangement of uprights recorded by Emory at Hale-o-Lono on Lānaʻi (1924, pl. V, b), the numerous shrines reported by Patrick C. McCoy (1982; McCoy and Nees 2010, 2014) on the slopes of Mauna Kea, and a simple alignment of uprights at Pālehua on Oʻahu (Swift et al. 2019). Clearly, however, not all of these simple shrines are early; the Pālehua site has been dated to the late precontact era.

According to oral traditions, Hawaiian religion was significantly altered by the arrival of an influential priest, Pāʻao, from Kahiki, around the thirteenth or fourteenth century. Pāʻao brought with him the concept of human sacrifice, constructing the first *luakini*-class *heiau*. Among the temples built by Pāʻao were Wahaʻula in Puna and Moʻokini in Kohala on Hawaiʻi Island. How much historical validity should be accorded these traditions is uncertain, although they are probably rooted in real historical events. It is likely, however, that most of the unique features of Hawaiian religion and temple construction were developed *locally,* in isolation from the rest of Polynesia. As Hawaiian society evolved over the centuries, and as the power of chiefs and priests grew along with burgeoning populations, new rituals were developed to legitimate the political and religious system. One key to unraveling the development of Hawaiian temple ritual lies in the detailed architectural study, excavation, and dating of *heiau*.

Heiau as Known Ethnohistorically

Valerio Valeri (1985) opines that the Hawaiians had two *heiau* classification systems that have not been clearly distinguished, resulting in some confusion. One system was based on function, with the two major classes of *heiau hoʻoulu,* or temples for fertility, growth, and production, and *heiau kaua,* temples of war. Valeri believes that crosscutting this was an architectural typology that included the classes *koʻa, pōhaku o Kāne, unu, waihau,* and *luakini*. The functional classification could be combined with the architectural to produce a wide array of subtypes, such as *unu hoʻoulu ʻai* (a kind of agricultural temple) or *unu poʻokanaka* (a kind of war temple where human sacrifices were made).

The simplest kind of *heiau* is the *pōhaku o Kāne,* consisting of a single upright, often an elongated, phallic stone set into the landscape at some propitious locality. As indicated by the name, these uprights were dedicated to the male procreator deity Kāne. Figure 11.2 illustrates one example of an upright from Kaʻū, Hawaiʻi, with several small coral heads placed around the stone as offerings.

Shrines where offerings were made daily to Lono and to ancestral deities (*ʻaumākua*) were a part of every household. These were frequently incorporated within the men's house or *mua,* as noted by Kamakau: "The *heiau ipu-o-Lono* constantly maintained by the populace was the *hale mua,* the men's eating house, which every household had" (1976, 133). The *ipu* was a gourd container, in which offerings of food and fish were placed. The correspondence of shrines (represented by upright stones and offerings of coral heads) with household clusters was apparent in the settlement pattern of Kawela, Molokaʻi (Weisler and Kirch 1985).

The other common type of shrine is the *koʻa,* where fishermen made offerings to assure bountiful catches of fish and other marine creatures. (The polysemic word *koʻa* also means "coral," as well as fishing grounds situated offshore.) *Koʻa* shrines are found in a wide range of configurations but usually are characterized by a small court, either a pavement or a

FIGURE 11.2 An upright, waterworn stone (*pōhaku o Kāne*) set in a lava flow and surrounded by offerings of branch coral heads. *(Photo courtesy of Bishop Museum Department of Anthropology)*

walled enclosure (often constructed against a large natural boulder or outcrop). Frequently there is an upright waterworn stone, representing the deity Kū'ula, before which offerings were placed (fig. 11.3). *Ko'a* are concentrated along coastlines, often in prominent places such as headlands or promontories with good ocean views, although some *ko'a* are found inland, next to streams, as in Hālawa, Moloka'i. Coastal *ko'a* were associated with particular fishing grounds (also called *ko'a*) offshore, and the shrines sometimes provided visual markers to assist fishermen in locating these fishing spots.

A large group of midsized temples included many functional subtypes (such as *māpele, waihau ipu o Lono, hale o Lono, unu o Lono,* and *heiau ho'oulu 'ai*), all directed to the gods of fertility (especially Lono and Kāne), intended to assure agricultural abundance. Such temples were constructed by prominent persons, the chiefs of *ahupua'a* land divisions, and the priests of Lono, while rituals there were attended by the general populace. Such temples are represented archaeologically by a range of structures, including walled enclosures, stepped terraces, and combinations thereof (see *heiau* classification below). A number of low stepped terraces studied by Ed Ladd (1970) in the lower Mākaha Valley, O'ahu, fall into this category, as do a series of medium-sized temples distributed throughout the interior of Hālawa Valley on Moloka'i (Kirch and Kelly, eds., 1975; Stokes 1909a), such as Kapana Heiau (color plate 8). At Kawela, a medium-sized temple situated just within the eastern border of the *ahupua'a* is believed to have been such a *hale o Lono* (fig. 11.4).

The most complex and largest of all temples were those termed *luakini* or *heiau po'okānaka*, where human sacrifices were offered by the ruling paramount for success in war. These temples were dedicated primarily to Kū, the god of war, although Lono and Kāne were not entirely absent from these "state" temples, and agricultural rituals were also performed there (Valeri 1985). *Luakini* could be constructed and dedicated only by a paramount chief (*ali'i nui*); dedication of such a temple by any other chief was considered an act of rebellion

FIGURE 11.3 The interior of site AUW-11, a *ko'a* enclosure at Auwahi, Maui Island, with upright Kū'ula stone and branch coral offerings. *(Photo by P. V. Kirch)*

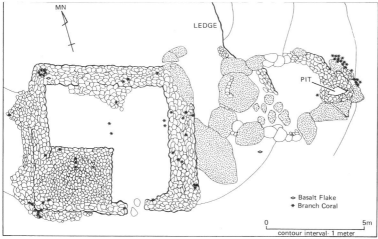

FIGURE 11.4 Plan of a *hale o Lono* temple site at Kawela, Moloka'i Island. The small platform likely supported the *'anu'u* tower. *(After Weisler and Kirch 1985)*

against the ruling polity. *Luakini* ceremonies were lengthy and arduous, requiring not only human victims but also large quantities of pigs, barkcloth, and other offerings (Malo 1951; Kamakau 1976).

The layout of a *luakini* temple is shown in figure 11.5. Among the major features were the *'anu'u* tower, where the priests received inspiration, the semicircular arrangement of wooden images surrounding the *lele* or offering platform, and a number of thatched houses with special functions (drum house, oven house, etc.). Peter Buck (1957) describes temple furnishings and images.

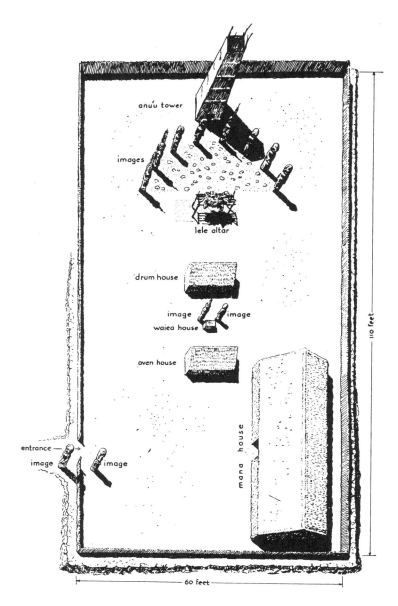

FIGURE 11.5 Layout of a *luakini* temple, based on ethnohistoric accounts. *(Drawing by Paul Rockwood, in 'Ī'ī 1959)*

The largest *luakini* temples, such as 'Ili'ili'ōpae on Moloka'i, Pu'ukoholā on Hawai'i, and Pi'ilanihale and Lo'alo'a on Maui, are truly impressive constructions (see chapters 14 and 15). Such temples reflect the power of the late prehistoric and early historic Hawaiian paramount rulers, and their ability to command the labor necessary to raise such monuments.

The Archaeology of *Heiau*

Heiau sites began to attract attention in the late nineteenth and early twentieth centuries. Abraham Fornander (1878–1885) mentions various *heiau* in connection with the *mo'olelo* pertaining to the chiefly families; Thomas Thrum (1906, 1909) compiled lists of *heiau* along with information obtained from Hawaiian informants. The first archaeological survey of *heiau* structures was by John F. G. Stokes, who in 1906 at the behest of William

T. Brigham, Bishop Museum's director, mapped the *heiau* ruins of Hawai'i Island. Stokes recorded more than 100 temple ruins on Hawai'i, preparing detailed plan maps of more than 40 structures (Stokes 1991). This was followed in 1909 by a survey of temple foundations on Moloka'i Island (Flexner et al. 2017; Stokes 1909a).

During the 1920s and 1930s, Bishop Museum organized archaeological surveys of the main Hawaiian Islands, mostly by young researchers from mainland universities. Kenneth P. Emory surveyed shrines in Haleakalā Crater, Maui, followed by a survey of Lāna'i Island (including a number of *heiau*), and then of the remote islets of Nihoa and Mokumanamana with their intriguing "*marae*" (Emory 1921, 1924, 1928). Between 1928 and 1937, archaeological field surveys of Kaua'i (Bennett 1931), Maui (Walker 1930), O'ahu and Kaho'olawe (McAllister 1933a, 1933b), Hawai'i (Hudson 1931), and Moloka'i (Phelps 1937) were completed. The main emphasis in all of these surveys was *heiau*, with archaeologists guided to sites based on Thrum's lists, and by local informants. There was little effort to locate smaller sites not already known to informants. Investigations were limited to mapping and description of surface remains; no excavations were undertaken within *heiau*. These surveys resulted in the compilation of information on approximately 816 temple sites (Valeri 1985, table 5), including ethnographic details that might otherwise have been lost.

The first attempt to excavate in *heiau* foundations was made by Ed Ladd at the 'Āle'ale'a (fig. 11.6) and Hale o Keawe temple sites at Hōnaunau on Hawai'i Island in the 1960s (Ladd 1969a, 1969b). Ladd showed that these structures were built in a succession of stages that could be architecturally and stratigraphically distinguished. Ladd's excavation of Kāne'ākī Heiau in Mākaha Valley, O'ahu (fig. 11.7), demonstrated how some *heiau* were constructed over long time periods (Ladd 1973). By disassembling Kāne'ākī Heiau, Ladd

FIGURE 11.6 'Āle'ale'a temple platform at Hōnaunau, Hawai'i Island. *(Photo by Therese Babineau)*

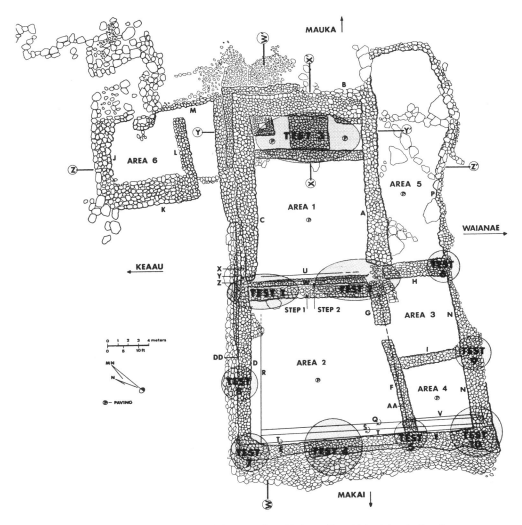

FIGURE 11.7 Plan of Kāneʻaki Heiau, a *luakini* temple in Mākaha Valley, Oʻahu Island, showing areas excavated by Ed Ladd. *(After Ladd 1970)*

showed how this temple, which had functioned as a *luakini* at the time of European contact, had been constructed in a series of six definable stages (fig. 11.8). Construction began in the fifteenth century, as a relatively simple double terrace (Stages 1a, 1b), which Roger Green (1980, 75) argues was a Lono-class *heiau* constructed by a local chief. Over the next one to two centuries, the temple was enlarged and elaborated with a major change occurring about AD 1650, when the addition of a large court upslope (Stage 6) increased the temple size from about 400 m^2 to 1,010 m^2. It was presumably at this time that the temple was rededicated to Kū as a *luakini,* an event that could have been carried out only by one of the Oʻahu paramount chiefs. This rebuilding of Kāneʻakī in the mid-seventeenth century may thus signal a major political event, the incorporation of Mākaha Valley into an island-wide polity.

Michael Kolb investigated 108 temple sites on Maui Island, excavating at eight structures (Kolb 1991, 1992, 1994a, 1994b, 1999). Kolb's research strategy was based on a

RITUAL, POWER, DEATH • 253

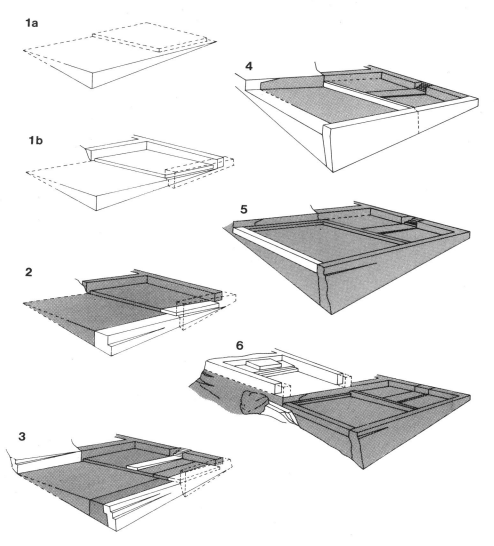

FIGURE 11.8 Stages of construction of Kāneʻaki Heiau in Mākaha Valley, Oʻahu Island. *(After Ladd 1970)*

"processual" theoretical paradigm in which *heiau* were seen as materializations of chiefly power. Kolb excavated at both smaller and large *heiau*, including the *luakini* temples of Loʻaloʻa and Pōpōʻiwi in Kaupō District, and of Piʻilanihale in Hāna District. Stratigraphic information and radiocarbon dates were used to propose construction sequences. Kolb extended his Maui *heiau* research in the mid-1990s to sites in Kahikinui District; unfortunately, only a preliminary report (Kolb and Radewagen 1997) and a listing of radiocarbon dates (Kolb 2006) is available for this latter project.

Recent research on *heiau* includes Kirch's and Ruggles' survey and analysis of 78 *heiau* in the districts of Kahikinui and Kaupō in southeastern Maui (Kirch 2004; Kirch and Ruggles 2019; Ruggles 2007). Kirch and Sharp applied ^{230}Thorium dating of branch coral offerings from *heiau* structures in Kahikinui (Kirch and Sharp 2005; Kirch, Mertz-Kraus, and

Sharp 2015) to refine the chronology of temple building in the region (see below). Other studies of *heiau* have focused on temple distribution across Kalaupapa, Moloka'i (Kirch, ed., 2002; M. D. McCoy 2006, 2008b) and within the leeward field system of Kohala, Hawai'i (Mulrooney and Ladefoged 2005; M. D. McCoy, Ladefoged, Graves, and Stephens 2011; Phillips et al. 2015), on architectural details of Pu'ukoholā Heiau (M. D. McCoy 2014; Mulrooney et al. 2005; Stephens 2016) and Hikiau Heiau (M. D. McCoy 2018), and on the construction sequence of Maunawila Heiau on O'ahu (Thurman 2014, 2015). New research on ritual in liminal locations outside of densely settled areas includes work on the shrines of Mauna Kea (P. C. McCoy 1999; P. C. McCoy et al. 2009; P. C. McCoy et al. 2012), and on the remote northwestern islands of Papahānaumokuākea (Kikiloi 2012), as well as at an upland O'ahu shrine likely used during Makahiki rituals (Gill et al. 2015; Swift et al. 2019).

Despite early efforts to survey religious sites we do not have a complete accounting of *heiau*. Although archaeologists sometimes encounter previously unknown sites that are likely *heiau*, unfortunately, there is no uniformly accepted set of criteria for deciding whether a site was indeed a *heiau*. According to Kehau Cachola-Abad, "As important as such archeological decisions are, few agreed upon criterion, processes, and standards have been established within the discipline" (1996, 11). Differences of interpretation regarding possible *heiau* sites have led to some controversies, such as that surrounding the putative *hale o Papa* in Hālawa Valley, O'ahu, which was situated within the original alignment of the H3 highway (Kawelu 2015, 53; see chapter 1). A further complication arises because, in our view, not all monumental architecture need have been religious in function; some large structures are likely to have been chiefly residential sites, or in some cases, platforms (*kahua*) for hula performance, as for example with site KIP-80 in Kahikinui, Maui (see Kirch and Ruggles 2019, 219–222).

Heiau Form, Classification, and Size

Heiau vary greatly in size and morphology, posing challenges to formal classification. Stokes (1991, 21) wrote of Hawai'i Island *heiau* that "based on the character of their foundations, the heiau would seem to fall into two classes—the platform and the walled enclosure," but he qualified that statement by adding that "there were many intermediate forms and combinations of the two." J. Gilbert McAllister noted that "classifying the heiaus remaining on Oahu into types is an arbitrary and unsatisfactory procedure. Not only are there too few of these structures, but no two heiaus, furthermore, are alike" (1933a, 9). Nonetheless, McAllister opined that the island's temples could be "classified generally" as walled, terraced, or terraced-and-walled structures.

Wendell Bennett proposed a formal classification of the *heiau* of Kaua'i Island, based on the morphology of the stone foundations of 122 sites that he recorded (1931, 30–35):
  I. Natural sites
  II. Small heiau
    A. Open platforms
    B. Walled enclosures
    C. Terraced platforms
  III. Large heiau

A. Platforms
    1. On level ground or terraced against a slope
    2. Crowning the top of a hill or rise
    3. Two or more terraced divisions
B. Walled enclosures
    1. Square and rectangular
    2. Divisioned enclosures
    3. Compound enclosures
C. Terraced heiau
    1. Two terrace types
    2. Three terrace types
    3. Four terrace types
D. Round heiau
E. Unclassified heiau
    1. L-shaped
    2. Community houses
    3. Large structures

Bennett's classification would be considered a taxonomy, even though it was seemingly derived by "grouping" like structures together rather than by systematic delineation of sets of ideational attributes. The difference between "small" and "large" *heiau* was defined with a cutoff of "less than 50 feet on the longest side" for small *heiau* (Bennett 1931, 31), a rather arbitrary distinction.

Kolb (1991, 1992, 1994a) compiled data for 108 *heiau* on Maui Island. Building upon the distinctions in Bennett's scheme between enclosures, terraces, and platforms, Kolb proposed a set of eight "Maui types" (Kolb 1991, fig. 4.8). Kolb's classification of Maui *heiau*, with the percentage of sites in each major category, is as follows:

Enclosure *heiau* (42%)
  Simple enclosure
  Notched enclosure
Terraced *heiau* (37%)
  Simple terrace
  Multiple terrace
  Notched terrace
  Walled terrace
Platform *heiau* (21%)
  Simple platform
  Notched platform

Within the largest group of enclosure type *heiau*, the "notched enclosure" predominates, with 39 examples (36% of the total). Kolb notes that whereas platform type *heiau* are evenly distributed across Maui Island, the terraced and enclosure forms are concentrated in particular regions (1991, 118–123). Terraced *heiau* are more common in the windward districts, including Hāna, Kaupō, and Koʻolau, whereas enclosures are concentrated in the arid, leeward regions of Honuaʻula, Kahikinui, and Kula.

FIGURE 11.9 View of site ALE-140, a typical notched enclosure type *heiau* in Kahikinui, Maui Island. (Photo by P. V. Kirch)

In a survey of 78 *heiau* in the *moku* of Kahikinui and Kaupō, Maui, Kirch and Ruggles (2019) divided the structures into five main types, with a sixth "catchall" category. The most frequent type, with 24 examples (31%), is the *notched enclosure,* a term first coined by Winslow Walker (1930). These structures consist of a square or rectangle from which one corner has been removed (the "notch"), so that a six-sided enclosure results. Presumably, it was not the notch itself that mattered but rather that two adjacent rooms or chambers were created; these spaces are often separated by a low wall, or by a change in floor level. The smaller room is typically higher and often contains branch coral or waterworn stone offerings. A good example of such a notched *heiau* is site ALE-140 in Kahikinui (fig. 11.9). *Square or U-shaped enclosures* are represented by 13 sites in Kahikinui and Kaupō. The third type is the *elongated double-court enclosure,* with 10 sites in this category, represented by site KIP-1 as seen in figure 11.10. *Platform or terraced heiau* make up the fourth category, with 14 sites, an example of which is site NAK-30 (fig. 11.11). The fifth type consists of small fishing shrines (*koʻa*) or agricultural shrines; the *koʻa* are all located near the coast and are marked by the presence of abundant coral heads and branch corals as offerings. A final sixth category, with seven sites, consists of unusual or unique structures that do not readily fit into any of the other types.

Heiau vary not only in architectural form but also in size. Kirch and Ruggles (2019, 44) report that the smallest shrine in the southeast Maui region covers a mere 4 m², while the largest *luakini* temple (Pōpōʻiwi) covers 7,500 m². The rank-size distribution of *heiau* studied by Kirch and Ruggles is graphically displayed on a logarithmic scale in figure 11.12; the majority of temples range between about 60 and 900 m². Most of the temples with areas greater

FIGURE 11.10 Aerial photo of site KIP-1, an example of an elongated double-court type of *heiau*, in Kīpapa, Kahikinui, Maui Island. *(Photo by P. V. Kirch)*

FIGURE 11.11 View of site NAK-30, a small platform type *heiau* in Kahikinui, Maui Island. Note the two uprights at either side of the platform court. *(Photo by P. V. Kirch)*

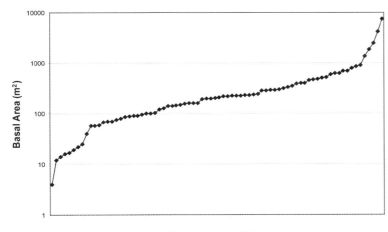

FIGURE 11.12 The rank-size distribution of *heiau* in Kahikinui and Kaupō Districts of Maui Island. *(After Kirch and Ruggles 2019)*

TABLE 11.1. Some major *luakini heiau*

ISLAND	DISTRICT	HEIAU NAME	ASSOCIATED ALI'I	AREA (M²)
Kaua'i	Wailua	Malae		8,650
	Wailua	Poli'ahu		3,000
O'ahu	Ko'olaupoko	Ulupō		3,000
	Waialua	Pu'u o Mahuka		6,500
Moloka'i	Kona	'Ili'ili'ōpae		3,500
	Ko'olau	Mana	Alapa'inui	1,000
Maui	Wailuku	Pīhana	Pi'ilani	4,500
	Hāna	Pi'ilanihale	Pi'ilani	12,120
	Kaupō	Pōpō'iwi	Kekaulike	7,500
	Kaupō	Lo'alo'a	Kekaulike	4,200
	Kaupō	Kou		2,500
Hawai'i	Puna	Waha'ula	Pā'ao	900
	Kona	'Āle'ale'a		730
	Kona	Ahu'ena		270
	Kohala	Pu'ukoholā	Kamehameha I	2,500
	Kohala	Mo'okini	Pā'ao	3,700

than 1,000 m² are believed to have been associated with ranking *ali'i*, such as Kekaulike, who reigned over Maui in the early eighteenth century and is known to have dedicated both Pōpō'iwi and Lo'alo'a *heiau*.

The largest *heiau* are those of *luakini* type. Table 11.1 lists some of the most prominent of these temples, along with estimates of their area in square meters. Area is only one measure of a temple's size; cubic volume of stone incorporated in the structure may more accurately reflect the labor invested in temple construction, but this is more challenging to calculate as the depth of stone fill is not always evident.

Even with these efforts to classify *heiau* based on their layout, orientation, and location, there are some structures and architectural elements that can be understood only in the context of regional history. An example is Nā Imu Kālua Ua Heiau on Molokaʻi, sometimes called "The Rain Heiau." Oral history tells us that stones were carefully laid out by Pauulea in small compartments with the intention of capturing rain and "cooking" it so "she always had fair weather to dry her tapa" (Rice 1923, 109). There is, to our knowledge, no other *heiau* with this particular architectural design or purpose. Interestingly, another seemingly one-of-a-kind site, Ahu a ʻUmi Heiau on the high plateau near the center of Hawaiʻi Island, has a somewhat smaller twin recently discovered during survey on Maui (Dega 2011; Perzinski and Dega 2011). Another architectural detail that appears to connect these rival islands is that the corners of certain Maui *heiau* have the appearance of canoe prows distinctively—perhaps even menacingly—pointed at Hawaiʻi Island (Kirch and Ruggles 2019, 43–44).

Heiau Chronology

Due to the limited number of *heiau* excavations, relatively few sites have been dated using radiocarbon or other methods; the exception is Maui Island, for which we at present have the best chronology of *heiau* construction. Kolb (1991, 367–371; 1992; 1994a) obtained radiocarbon dates from seven *heiau* on Maui; none of the sites he studied dated to earlier than AD 1235–1374, causing him to remark that the initial phases of *heiau* construction were not represented. The earliest phases present, dating between ca. AD 1300 and 1500, were primarily of terrace form (although there was one "stacked enclosure"). These early terraces were stratigraphically buried under later rebuilding phases consisting in four instances of platforms, and in two instances of core-filled enclosures (Kolb 1992, fig. 8). Kolb concluded that "in general, terraced *heiau* appear to be chronologically older than enclosure *heiau*, and probably older than platform *heiau*" (1991, 367). Kolb argued that the greatest period of *heiau* building took place during what he called the "Consolidation Period," roughly coinciding with the fifteenth century AD (Kolb 1994a, fig. 6). However, his interpretation depended heavily upon the evidence from a small test pit at Piʻilanihale Heiau in Hāna District (Kirch 2010, 233–234). Removing the bias created by that limited sample, the greatest period of *heiau* building would have been in Kolb's "Unification Period" (ca. AD 1500–1650) and the following "Annexation Period" (AD 1650 to contact).

Major advances in our understanding of Maui temple chronology have been made in recent years through intensive study of *heiau* in the Kahikinui and Kaupō Districts (Baer 2015, 2016; Kirch and Sharp 2005; Kirch and Ruggles 2019; Kirch et al. 2015; Kolb 2006). The Kahikinui and Kaupō *heiau* have been dated by two different methods. The first is radiocarbon dating of carbonized wood or other plant material; 159 radiocarbon dates have been obtained from Kahikinui and Kaupō *heiau*. The second method, ^{230}Th (also called U/Th, or U-series) dating, is limited to specimens of coral (see chapter 3). Observing that branch corals of the species *Pocillopora meandrina* frequently occurred in Kahikinui *heiau*, where they had been placed as offerings, Kirch and Sharp (2005) pioneered this method of dating Hawaiian temples. They later expanded the sample of coral dates (Kirch, Mertz-Kraus, and Sharp 2015), with a total of 46 ^{230}Th dates now available from Kahikinui and Kaupō temple or shrines. The ^{230}Th method is not only more precise than radiocarbon dating, but ^{230}Th dates do not suffer from the complexities of radiocarbon calibration.

PLATE 1. The Nāpali coast of Kaua'i Island shows the effects of five million years of erosion, with knife-edge ridges and deep valleys. *(Photo by P. V. Kirch)*

PLATE 2. An irrigated pondfield or *loʻi*, recently planted in taro, in the Waipiʻo Valley, Hawaiʻi Island. *(Photo by P. V. Kirch)*

PLATE 3. View of a portion of the Leeward Kohala Field System as seen from Puʻu Kehena in the late afternoon, when the sun's rays illuminate the grid of ancient field embankments and trails. (*Photo by P. V. Kirch*)

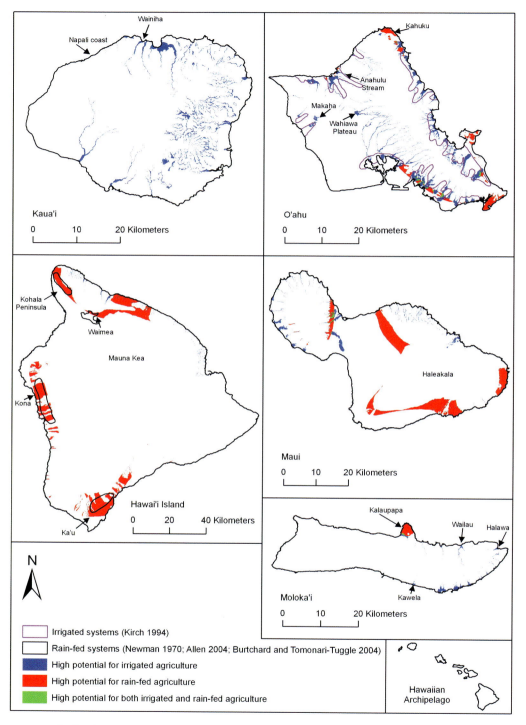

PLATE 4. Distribution of areas of high potential for irrigated and intensive dryland agroecosystems, based on GIS modeling. *(From Kirch, ed., 2010)*

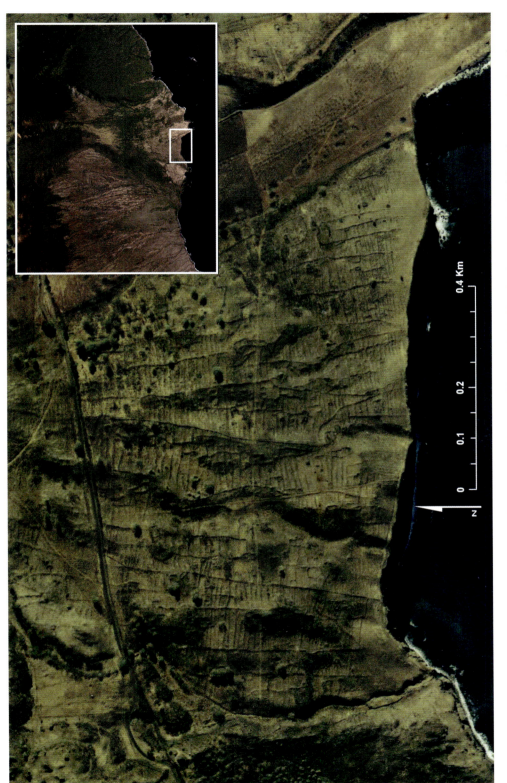

PLATE 5. Aerial photograph of a portion of the Kaupō field system on Maui Island, with the grid of field embankments and walls delineating narrow land sections (probably 'ili) clearly visible. (*Photo map by Alex Baer, Oceanic Archaeology Laboratory*)

PLATE 6. Close-up view of the surface of the Nuʻu adze quarry in Kaupō, Maui, littered with basalt flake debitage and preforms. The gridded unit is 50 × 50 cm. *(Photo by P. V. Kirch)*

PLATE 7. A Hawaiian chief, wearing a feathered cloak and feathered helmet, as drawn by the artist Jacques Arago in 1819. *(From Louis de Freycinet, 1824, Voyage autour de monde, Paris, Imprimerie Royale)*

PLATE 8. Kapana Heiau in Hālawa Valley, Moloka'i, an example of a mid-sized agricultural temple. *(Drone photo by P. V. Kirch)*

PLATE 9. Stone-faced agricultural terraces, formerly irrigated from Makaʻeleʻele Stream, in the Kapana area of Hālawa Valley, Molokaʻi Island. (*Drone photo by P. V. Kirch*)

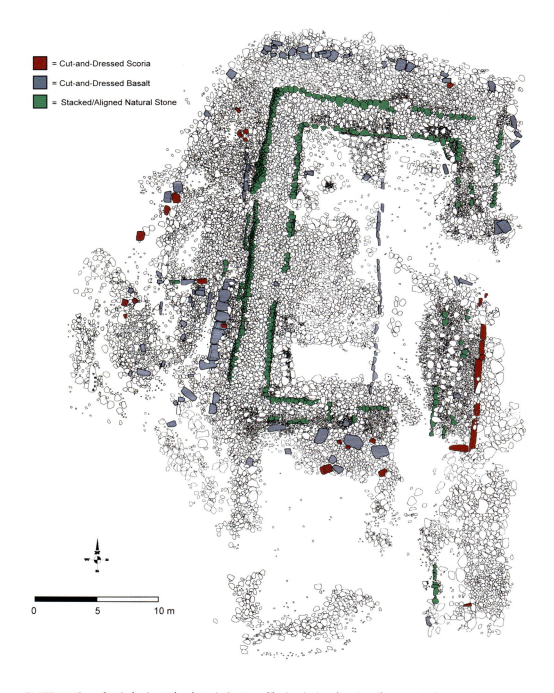

PLATE 10. Plan of Kukuipahu Heiau in Kohala, Hawai'i Island, showing the alignments of cut-and-dressed basalt and of red scoria dating to an earlier phase of the structure, as well as the later stacked-stone walls. *(Map by Alan Carpenter)*

PLATE 11. The main facade of Piʻilanihale Heiau in Hāna, Maui Island, rises in a succession of impressive terraces. *(Photo by P. V. Kirch)*

PLATE 12. The *pānānā* at Hanamauloa, Kahikinui, Maui Island, is oriented so that the constellation Southern Cross is visible in the structure's center notch. *(Photo courtesy of Chad Babayan)*

PLATE 13. Hōkūkano Heiau consists of two massive stone terraces sitting astride a ridge, commanding a view over the south Moloka'i coastline. (*Drone photo by P. V. Kirch*)

PLATE 14. 'Ili'ili'ōpae Heiau at Mapulehu, Moloka'i Island, is a massive terraced platform at the base of a ridge; it is the largest temple site on the island. (*Drone photo by P. V. Kirch*)

PLATE 15. The sunrise illuminates the narrow, barren ridgeline of Mokumanamana Island. *(Photo by Mara Mulrooney)*

PLATE 16. The steep topography of Nihoa Island is dotted with stone-faced terraces and other vestiges of former Polynesian occupation. (*Photo by Mara Mulrooney*)

Kolb (2006) reported 24 radiocarbon dates from 19 *heiau* in southeast Maui. Unfortunately, his charcoal samples were not botanically identified or screened for possible old wood with "inbuilt" age; additionally, Kolb's radiocarbon dates were not corrected for isotopic fractionation through measurement of their $\delta^{13}C$ values. This is an issue because many native Hawaiian dryland forest plants deviate in their $\delta^{13}C$ values; if not corrected the reported age may be significantly younger than the true date of the sample. Furthermore, some of Kolb's samples came from "basal" contexts that probably reflect initial land use such as forest clearance for agriculture rather than actual *heiau* construction or use. Keeping these caveats in mind, Kolb's radiocarbon corpus broadly suggests that temple construction in Kahikinui commenced between the fifteenth and sixteenth centuries.

A different set of 35 radiocarbon dates was obtained by Kirch and Alex Baer from 23 sites in Kahikinui and Kaupō, all on botanically identified, short-lived taxa, and corrected for isotopic fractionation; all dates are directly associated with *heiau* construction or use. These radiocarbon dates are plotted in figure 11.13. One early date (AA-38689) comes from a small *pōhaku o Kāne* shrine in the Kīpapa uplands (site KIP-1317). As Kirch suggests (2015, 82–83), this simple shrine may reflect a phase of exploration of Kahikinui soon after the arrival of people in the islands, because radiocarbon dates from Kahikinui habitation sites indicate that permanent occupation of the district did not begin until the early fifteenth century (Kirch 2014, 80–82, fig. 18). An early date (AA-102213) from Baer's excavation at site KAU-999 in Kaupō is considerably older than two other radiocarbon dates from the same structure (AA-102214, -102215), and is rejected as a valid date for the *heiau* itself. The other 33 radiocarbon dates plotted in figure 11.13 exhibit a consistent pattern. An initial set of six dates indicate that the region's *heiau* began to be constructed in the mid- to late fifteenth century; another seven dates span the late fifteenth through sixteenth centuries. The 20 youngest samples document continued *heiau* construction or use in the mid-seventeenth up through the early eighteenth centuries. Although the calibrated age ranges of some dates extend into the nineteenth century, we know that *heiau* use did not continue more than a few years beyond the overthrow of the *kapu* system in 1819. In total, all of the radiocarbon dates from Kahikinui and Kaupō temples indicate that construction began no earlier than the late fifteenth century, with *heiau* use continuing until the abolishment of the temple system in late 1819.

The 46 ^{230}Th dates on corals from 26 *heiau* in Kahikinui (plus Kou Heiau in Kaupō) add more precision to the chronology of *heiau* construction in the region, attesting to a major phase of temple construction beginning in the second half of the sixteenth century and continuing through the seventeenth century (fig. 11.14). The higher precision of the ^{230}Th dates places initial temple construction about a century later than the time frame indicated by the radiocarbon dates. Given that the corals seem to have been placed in and on the sites as dedicatory offerings at the time of construction, they may more accurately reflect the true onset of temple building in southeast Maui. Moreover, both the ^{230}Th coral and the radiocarbon chronologies are consistent with Kirch and Sharp's hypothesis (2005) that a rapid phase of temple building was initiated under the rule of the Maui Island kings Piʻilani, Kiha-a-Piʻilani, and Kamalālāwalu. On the basis of the royal genealogies, the reigns of these rulers spanned the period from approximately AD 1570 to 1610 (Kirch 2010, table 3.1), during which time they

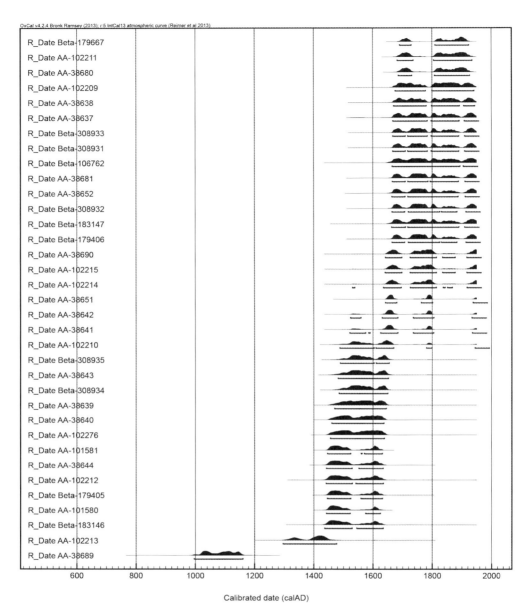

FIGURE 11.13 Oxcal plot of AMS radiocarbon dates from *heiau* sites in Kahikinui and Kaupō, Maui Island. *(After Kirch and Ruggles 2019)*

consolidated several independent chiefdoms into a single, island-wide polity. During this process of archaic state formation, establishment of a hierarchical system of temples would have provided a means for control over agricultural production through a network of *heiau hoʻoulu ʻai* or fertility temples, and would have facilitated the collection of tribute (*hoʻokupu*) provided by the inhabitants of each *ahupuaʻa* during the annual Makahiki rites.

Based on his initial work on Maui *heiau*, Kolb (1991, 1992) argued that there was a progression from early terraced forms to later platform type structures. Kirch, Mertz-Kraus, and Sharp (2015, table 2) used the ^{230}Th chronology of Kahikinui *heiau* to test

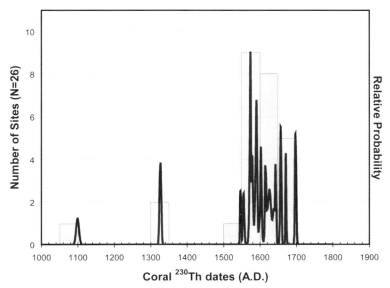

FIGURE 11.14 Temporal distribution of ^{230}Th dates on branch corals from 26 *heiau* sites in Kahikinui and Kaupō, Maui Island. *(After Kirch, Mertz-Kraus, and Sharp 2015)*

whether different forms of temple showed changes over time. Their evidence indicates that the most common form of Kahikinui temple, the notched enclosure, occurs throughout the sequence; the same is true of square enclosures. Two examples of elongated, double-court *heiau* that were dated with ^{230}Th samples are both relatively early; however, other examples of the elongated, double-court type in Nuʻu were dated by radiocarbon to a much later time period. Thus, the elongated, double-court form has a long history. On present evidence, all of the main types of *heiau* in southeast Maui were in use from the sixteenth through the eighteenth centuries; there is no clear-cut temporal succession of *heiau* architectural forms in the region.

Studies of *heiau* on other islands have also failed to detect a temporal succession of structural forms (Kikiloi 2012; M. D. McCoy 2006; M. D. McCoy, Ladefoged, Graves, and Stephens 2011; Swift et al 2019). M. D. McCoy, Ladefoged, Graves, and Stephens (2011) offer a possible explanation for this diversity in architecture, over space and time, based on an examination of structures interpreted as small *heiau* dotted across the leeward Kohala Field System. Some were undoubtedly created for the worship of Lono, but others may have been elaborately built structures such as men's houses (*mua*). After radiocarbon dating these structures, and analyzing different stylistic elements, they noted that architects were constantly experimenting with ways to create and maintain religious authority. This included at times incorporating novel elements—such as courtyards and notches—as well as increasing the size of *heiau,* but not abandoning existing styles of construction. Such a mix of innovation and conservatism can be seen in religious architectural traditions in other parts of the world.

Heiau Orientations

John Stokes, in the first formal survey of *heiau* on Hawaiʻi Island, commented that he "could find no evidence in the foundations of orientation to cardinal points" (1991, 36). At the same time, Stokes noted that some of the temples "did lie almost true north-south or east-west." Most archaeologists subsequently paid little or no attention to *heiau* orientations. However, when Kirch (2004) analyzed the orientations of a sample of *heiau* in Kahikinui, Maui, he discovered a nonrandom distribution, with almost all temple sites falling into one of three orientation clusters, centered on the north, east-northeast, and east. This led Kirch and Ruggles (2019) to focus on orientations and viewsheds in their expanded study of 78 *heiau* across Kahikinui and Kaupō District. Fully 62 out of 66 *heiau* for which orientation could be unambiguously determined fall into one of these three orientation groups.

Kirch (2004) and Kirch and Ruggles (2019) argue that, based on ethnohistorically documented characteristics of the major Hawaiian gods, it is possible to associate each of the three main orientations with a particular *akua*. Kū, known primarily as a war god but also as the patron deity of canoe builders and of fishermen (in his manifestation as Kūʻula), was associated with high mountains, and had directional attributes of "high, east, and right" (Valeri 1985, 15, table 1). The procreator god Kāne was the deity of irrigated (taro) agriculture, with directional associations of "right, east, and north." Kāne was associated with the rising sun, and the eastern sky was known as the flaming path of Kāne (*ke alaula a Kāne*) (Johnson, Mahelona, and Ruggles 2015, 180). The most northerly path of the sun across the sky was known as "the black shining road of Kāne" (2015, 30). Lono, deity of dryland agriculture, to whom the sweet potato was sacred, had directional attributes of "high, leeward." Lono was closely linked to the acronychal rising of the star cluster Pleiades (Makaliʻi), the observation of which determined the onset of the Makahiki season.

Given these ethnohistorically attested directional associations of the main Hawaiian deities, the three main orientation clusters observed in the archaeological data from southeastern Maui can plausibly be linked to the hierarchy of gods. The most obvious association is between the east-oriented temples and Kāne. From these east-oriented *heiau* the priests of Kāne could have observed the progression of the sun throughout the year. Indeed, many of the Kahikinui temples enjoy superb viewsheds toward the east, where the "great Sun of Kāne" rises dramatically over the peninsula of Kaupō. The east-northeast cluster of *heiau* are oriented toward the acronychal rising of the Pleiades, crucial to the onset of the Makahiki season, Lono's season. Kirch and Ruggles argue that these east-northeast-oriented *heiau* were *hale o Lono,* temples dedicated to Lono. Finally, the north-oriented cluster of temples also face the great soaring height of Haleakalā, either its high summit or one of the prominent, reddish-colored cinder cones (*puʻu*) that stand out along the mountain's skyline. Four of the elongated, double-court type *heiau,* as well as many of the largest temples, have this northerly orientation. These were likely dedicated to, or associated with, Kū, the deity linked to the high mountains, to the sky, and to forests. In the *kuaʻāina* districts of Kahikinui and Kaupō, the worship of Kū may have focused primarily on some of his secondary attributes, such as canoe building, adze making, and sorcery.

Limited but systematic evaluation of *heiau* orientation outside of Maui tentatively confirms the expectation of the three main orientation directions of east, northeast, and north (M. D. McCoy 2006; Ruggles 1999). On the eastern coast of the Kalaupapa Peninsula near Makaliʻi Point is a *heiau* (site 50-60-03-2270) that is positioned so as to observe the equinoctial sunrise over an offshore islet but also oriented toward a second islet slightly to the north where both the acronychal rising of Pleiades (Makaliʻi) and the summer solstice would rise over the islet. Using these two landmarks one could mark not only the start of the Makahiki but also the sun's progression from spring equinox in March, to summer solstice in June, and then a return to fall equinox in September, when the sunrise would be blocked by the sea cliffs of Molokaʻi.

Multiple Functions of *Heiau*

Heiau are generally thought of as places of prayer (*pule*) and of sacrifice (*hai*) to the gods. The varied rites and ceremonies that took place at *heiau* were extensively described by nineteenth-century authors such as Davida Malo (1950) and Samuel Kamakau (1976), and were expertly analyzed by Valerio Valeri (1985). There is reason to believe, however, that the functions of *heiau* extended beyond those of religious observance and ritual. Excavations in a number of *heiau* in Kahikinui and Kaupō produced evidence for male craft activities, including adze production or reworking, and fishhook manufacturing (Kirch and Ruggles 2019, 71–74). These excavations also suggested that a range of foods were consumed within the temple confines, beyond what would simply be expected from the remains of offerings. Both Malo (1951, 32–33) and Kamakau (1976, 18) refer to four *kapu* periods within each lunar month, totaling nine days, during which men sequestered themselves in *heiau*, apart from their womenfolk. Given the archaeological indications of craft production, it seems that rather than simply witnessing rituals conducted by *kāhuna* during these *kapu* periods, the assembled men used this time to make and repair objects important to their daily lives. They also cooked and ate together, sharing information and passing down traditions while assembled in these sacred spaces.

Another function of *heiau*—one that we believe has been largely overlooked by archaeologists in the past—is as places for observation, particularly of the heavens and of significant astronomical phenomena (fig. 11.15). This was the conclusion of Kirch and Ruggles based on their extensive study of 78 *heiau* in southeastern Maui:

> What has been so striking to us, as we have surveyed *heiau* over several field seasons, is the ways in which temples were so carefully sited and positioned to take advantage of particular viewsheds, often commanding sweeping views of mountain crests, distant headlands, and looming cinder cones. There can be little doubt that the places where *heiau* were built were carefully selected. . . . *Heiau* were typically situated so as to be observing platforms or stations, using the fixed configuration of the landscape (whether in the near, intermediate, or far distance) to index the regular movements of the sun, the Pleiades, or other asterisms. . . . The annual progression of the sun from solstice to solstice, or the rising of Makaliʻi, could be readily tracked against the sloping profiles of the Lualaʻilua cinder cones or other prominent topographical features. Our fieldwork has convinced us that *heiau* were positioned where they are precisely to take advantage of such viewsheds and skyscapes, and that these temples functioned as much as observatories as places of ritual activity. (2019, 132)

FIGURE 11.15 The eastern horizon as viewed from site WF-AUW-403, a small east-facing, notched *heiau* in Auwahi, Maui Island. The Luala'ilua Hills provide convenient landscape markers for observing the solstices (solid lines), rising of Makali'i (dashed line), and the equinox (dashed and dotted line). *(After Kirch and Ruggles 2019)*

Landscapes of Power: The Royal Centers

Although Hawai'i lacked true urban centers—as in some archaic states elsewhere in the world—the ruling *ali'i* on each island resided within royal compounds situated in certain desirable locations, attended to by retainers and protected by their warrior guard. These royal centers included not only the palatial houses of the *ali'i nui* (his *mua, hale noa,* storehouses) but also houses for his wives, his high priest, other ranking *ali'i* who attended the king, craftspersons (such as the priests who made the precious feathered garments), and so forth. Canoe houses (*halau*) held the large, double-hulled canoes used by the king. Also in close proximity were the state temples, including a *luakini* or temple dedicated to Kū, as well as the king's own *hale o Lono,* where the important rites of the Makahiki were enacted. These royal centers thus combined both secular and sacred structures. The entire complex was off limits to the commoners, who were forbidden to trespass beyond the markers known as *pulo'ulo'u,* upright staffs topped by a ball of white barkcloth that demarcated the boundaries of the *kapu* zone.

John Papa 'Ī'ī (1959) provides a firsthand account of the royal centers occupied by King Kamehameha I in the first two decades of the nineteenth century, first at Honolulu (from 1804 until 1812) and then at Kamakahonu in Kailua, Kona, after the king's return to Hawai'i Island and until his death in 1819. The royal center at Honolulu (to the east of Nu'uanu Stream) included not only Kamehameha's own household compound but also *kauhale* for the king's wives, for the major chiefs, and for the principal warriors (fig. 11.16). Also included within the complex were a *hale o Lono,* two *maika* fields for playing the bowling game, and a gun-drilling ground (this being after the adoption of firearms). Of particular note was the *loku,* "a place where men and women of every kind gathered in the evenings to enjoy themselves" (1959, 63). "Some of the amusements indulged in there were hula dances, chants, the recitation of narratives in chant form, and the telling of legends" (64). Unfortunately, nothing remains today of this royal center, now covered over by the core of downtown Honolulu.

Kamehameha's royal center at Kamakahonu was less extensive than that at Honolulu, but by then the aged king had retired from the affairs of state. The Kamakahonu compound, fronting Kailua Bay and with a good canoe landing, was surrounded on the inland side by a stone wall ('Ī'ī 1959, 117–121). There were three *kī*-leaf-thatched houses, including a

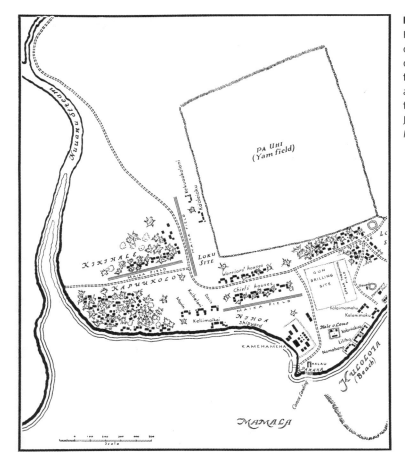

FIGURE 11.16 Map of Kamehameha's royal center at Honolulu, during the period from 1805 to 1812, as reconstructed from the account of John Papa ʻĪʻī. (After Rockwood, in ʻĪʻī 1959)

men's house (*mua*), sleeping house (*hale moe*), and separate eating house (*hale ʻāina*) for Kaʻahumanu, Kamehameha's favorite wife. Ahuʻena Heiau stood on the point overlooking the cove. Outside of the main compound wall were storehouses and work sheds (*halau*), some for the production of *kapa* (121). ʻĪʻī's description of the storehouses is of particular interest:

> In the storehouses were piled bundles of surplus *paʻu* [skirts], malos, and tapa sheets. These had been given to the chiefs as *makahiki* taxes that were presented to the gods when they made a circuit of the island every twelfth month. Because the profit received from these taxes on the land was so large, combined with the king's personal shares from his other lands, goods were piled in great heaps. If one looked into the storehouses, one saw small, large, extra large, and medium-sized bundles and wooden bowls filled with hard poi. There were separate bundles for women and for men. Consequently, separate storehouses were provided for the food to be eaten by each sex. (121)

Most of the royal center of Kamakahonu was destroyed when the King Kamehameha Hotel was constructed in 1960, although the foundations of Ahuʻena Heiau were spared, and the temple was later reconstructed.

On Kauaʻi Island, the main royal center at Wailua was the seat of the island's ranking chiefs at least from the time of the Late Voyaging Period. It was here that Moʻikeha dwelt, and where he greeted his son Laʻamaikahiki after Kila fetched him from Kahiki (Fornander 1878–1885). Housing and resort development at Wailua have obscured much of what must formerly have existed, but a cluster of important *heiau,* including Hikinaakalā, Mana, Poliʻahu, Holoholokū, and Kukui, surround Wailua Bay (Kirch 1996, 16–19).

On Oʻahu, royal centers in precontact times were located at Waikīkī (renown for both its surf and its coconut groves), and at Līhue, a place on the island's central plateau near the sacred birthing stones of Kūkaniloko. While Kūkaniloko remains intact, the *heiau* and other structures that were surely present at Līhue were destroyed by pineapple cultivation in the early twentieth century. Any vestige of the royal center at Waikīkī, including Papaʻenaʻena Heiau, where the last human sacrifices to Kū were offered up by Kamehameha I in 1804 (ʻĪʻī 1959, 33), were tragically paved over decades ago.

On Maui Island, portions of at least three royal centers still exist. The most ancient of these is at Wailuku, where Halekiʻi and Pīhana Heiau occupy a prominent location overlooking ʻĪao Stream. These adjacent monumental structures were investigated by Kolb (1991), who dated the initial construction of Pīhana to AD 1260–1400, the Late Voyaging Period. Following an expansion of Pīhana between AD 1410 and 1640, the structure became a chiefly residence; the terrace of Halekiʻi was also constructed at this time. During the early Archaic States Period, Kiha-a-Piʻilani consolidated the Maui kingdom and moved the royal seat to Hāna District. Piʻilanihale, the largest monumental structure in the Hawaiian Islands, served as both a royal residence and *luakini heiau* (Kolb 1999). In the early eighteenth century, Kekaulike moved the royal court to Kaupō, where he dedicated both Loʻaloʻa and Pōpōʻiwi Heiau (Kamakau 1961, 66). Based on his excavations, Kolb (1991) argued that Pōpōʻiwi, like Piʻilanihale, served as both a residential complex and a *luakini* temple.

On Hawaiʻi Island, the most ancient royal center was situated on the low sand dunes at the mouth of Waipiʻo Valley. The royal residence, Kahaunokamaʻahala, is associated in tradition with Līloa and his son ʻUmi, who ruled from the end of the Expansion and into the Archaic States Periods. A sacred bathing pool, Mōkapu, and a taro pondfield called Kahiki-mai-aea were located adjacent to the residence. Nearby was Pakaʻalana Heiau, both a *luakini* and a *puʻuhonua* (Cordy 2000a, 197, fig. 7-1). A small thatched house, the Hale o Līloa, served as a mausoleum holding the bones of Līloa; this was still in existence in 1823 when the Rev. William Ellis toured Hawaiʻi (Ellis 1963, 260). Another *heiau,* Honuaʻula, was also situated on the dune. The vestiges of the Waipiʻo royal center may still be intact, covered over by the shifting sand dunes, but have never been thoroughly investigated (the land is the property of Bishop Museum).

The most extensive royal center on Hawaiʻi Island—and the most thoroughly investigated archaeologically—is that at Hōnaunau. This complex of residences sprawling over 70 ha of the coastal plain had nested within it a royal compound with several *hōlua* sleds on the slopes above (fig. 11.17). As in Waipiʻo, the Hōnaunau complex incorporated a *puʻuhonua* and also a royal mausoleum, the Hale o Keawe. We describe the Hōnaunau complex in greater detail in chapter 14.

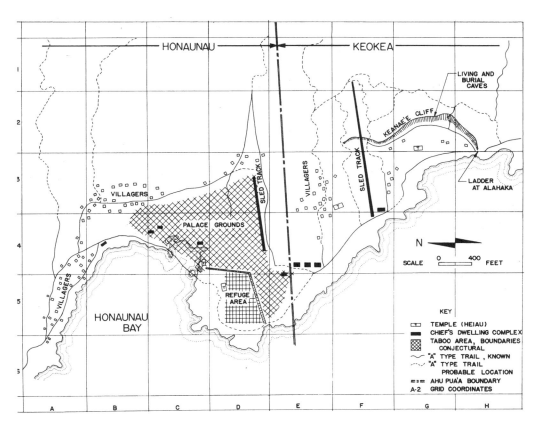

FIGURE 11.17 Map of the royal center at Hōnaunau, Hawai'i Island; note the two *hōlua* sled tracks. (After Apple 1965)

Hōlua Slides

Malo remarked that "sliding down the hill on the *hōlua* sled was a sport greatly in vogue among chiefs and people" (1951, 224). Buck called *hōlua* sledding an "aristocratic game," which "called for a highly specialized sled and carefully constructed runways" (1957, 379). Although some commoners may have practiced *hōlua* sledding, most of the known runways or *hōlua* slides are located near the royal centers, suggesting that the sport was mainly enjoyed by the *ali'i*. All but the smallest islands have documented *hōlua*. About half of the known tracks are located on Hawai'i, with the next most frequent being on Moloka'i.

Hōlua slides were often constructed by stacking two parallel rock faces about 2 m apart and filling the space between with rubble, to create an elevated runway that traversed a slope. According to Malo, "Then earth was put on and beaten hard; lastly the whole was layered with grass, and this was the track for the holua sled to run on" (1951, 224). Other tracks in less stony environments appear to have been dug out, or worn down, into the sides of hills, sometimes with stone platforms at the top to mark the start. Archaeologically documented *hōlua* slides range in length from about 50 m up to 400 m. A famous slide at Keauhou, Kona, was originally 900 m in length. History credits Kamehameha I with constructing it in 1814 to commemorate the birth of his second son Kauikeaouli, the future Kamehameha III. However, given its size, it would not be surprising if this was an expansion or reconstruction of an existing track. Speculation by some archaeologists that the slide once continued to the coastline is unlikely given the terrain, and would make it the only *hōlua* to end with a water landing.

At present, only two studies of the construction of *hōlua* sled tracks, one on Maui (Dixon et al. 1998), the other on Moloka'i (M. D. McCoy 2006, 2008b), have yielded good chronometric data. In each case, the features date to the Archaic States Period, but more research is necessary on the history of *hōlua* (see M. D. McCoy 2018).

Fortifications and *Pu'uhonua*

Although warfare was endemic in late precontact Hawaiian society, the use of fortifications was not as developed as in some other Polynesian societies (such as in New Zealand or on Rapa Island). A few simple forts have been recorded, however. The best known is that at the Nu'uanu *pali* on O'ahu, where artificial cuts in the steep ridge served to protect that fortress. Two other fortifications on O'ahu are situated atop the peaks of Mauna Kapu and Palikea in the Wai'anae mountains. The principal ridges leading to these peaks are cut with artificial fosses, as at Nu'uanu. One such fosse or defensive trench on the south side of Palikea

FIGURE 11.18 A cache of slingstones on a defensive terrace at Kawela, Moloka'i Island. *(Photo by P. V. Kirch)*

cuts across the ridge for a length of 7 m, with a width of 4 m and depth of 4 m. Wendell Bennett (1931, 54–55) describes two ridgetop fortifications on Kaua'i, one of which was "last used on the occasion of Kamehameha's threatened invasion in 1804." Emory (1924, 75) describes and illustrates a fortified ridge at Ho'okio, near the top of Maunalei Gulch, on Lāna'i.

At Kawela, on Moloka'i, the main gulch forks a short distance inland, isolating a steep, knife-edge ridge that served as a fortified stronghold. At various points along this ridge small stone terraces and platforms were constructed as fighting stages; caches of slingstones were noted there, as seen in figure 11.18 (Kirch 2012, 240–241; Weisler and Kirch 1985). As a further means of protection against invasion and attack, the Kawela people also constructed and consecrated a *pu'uhonua* or temple of refuge on the plateau atop the fortified ridge.

Refuge caves were another kind of site associated with warfare; these are known mainly from Hawai'i Island. An especially good example is "Cave 900," which was investigated during the second phase of the Queen Ka'ahumanu Highway salvage archaeology program (Rosendahl 1973, 63–73). This large lava tube, situated inland of Kīholo, had its entrance blocked by tons of lava rock, with only a narrow passageway through which people could pass single file, allowing the cave to be readily defended. The interior floor was divided into

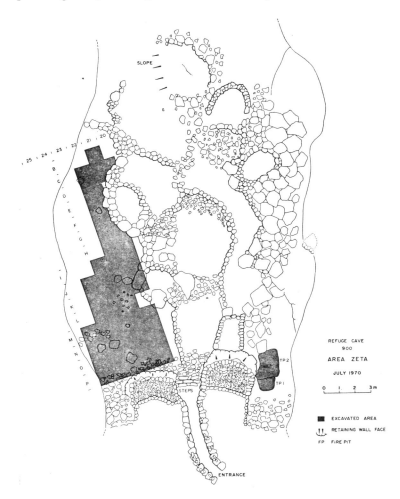

FIGURE 11.19 Plan of site 900, a refuge cave inland of Kīholo, Hawai'i Island. Note the narrow, stone-walled passageway leading into the cave. *(After Rosendahl 1973)*

RITUAL, POWER, DEATH • 271

a series of what appear to be individual living spaces (fig. 11.19). Excavations within the cave yielded 1,742 artifacts, indicating that the site was used for extended periods of time.

The concept of *puʻuhonua* or asylum was closely linked both to warfare and to the *kapu* system. Samuel Kamakau explained *puʻuhonua* in the following words: "A place to which one could escape and be saved from being taken captive or from being put to death was called a *puʻuhonua*—a place of refuge. The king was called a *puʻuhonua* because a person about to die could run to him and be saved; so also were called his queen (*ka Moʻiwahine*) and his god. They were sacrosanct, and therefore their lands were sacrosanct, and were *ʻaina puʻuhonua,* lands of refuge. Some fortifications (*puʻu kaua*) were *puʻuhonua,* when they were close to those about to be captured in battle" (1964, 17).

There were numerous *puʻuhonua* distributed across all of the islands; Marion Kelly (1957) provides an annotated list of known places of refuge. By far the most famous *puʻuhonua* was that at Hōnaunau on Hawaiʻi Island, now a National Historical Park. The "Great Wall" that defines the refuge area is among the largest structures ever built on the island.

The Archeology of Death: Burial Practices in Ancient Hawaiʻi

The ancient Hawaiians disposed of their dead in a variety of environments. Burial procedures differed depending upon the social status of the deceased, along with other factors. Hawaiians frequently buried their dead in sand dunes, under stone monuments and cairns, under house floors, in *heiau* platforms, in lava tubes and caves, and in various other contexts. Burials are frequently encountered during land modification and construction activities, and archaeologists are called in to deal with such "inadvertent" discoveries. Burials differ from other kinds of archaeological remains, for these *iwi kūpuna* are the revered remains of deceased ancestors. The excavation and study of *iwi kūpuna,* whether purposeful or inadvertent, thus raise unique ethical questions.

Before the 1990s, archaeologists across the Americas and in Hawaiʻi often excavated human remains with little consultation with descendant communities; today archaeologists in Hawaiʻi make every effort to avoid disturbing *iwi kūpuna*. The frequent disturbance of Hawaiian burials at construction sites, however, is often prominently featured in the media, which can lead to the misimpression that excavating burial sites is one of the archaeologist's primary occupations. The question of how to treat such burials, once exposed or disturbed, has engendered considerable debate.

From the 1930s until the passage of the Native American Graves Protection and Repatriation Act (NAGPRA) in 1990, archaeologists in Hawaiʻi at times excavated burial sites, or studied burials encountered during the course of excavation of habitation sites, providing information on mortuary practices, and on the demography of precontact communities. Subsequent to the passage of NAGPRA, and to the revision of Hawaiʻi state laws protecting burials, *iwi kūpuna* are no longer excavated for research purposes. Burials, however, continue to be inadvertently uncovered, especially in the course of construction projects. When encountered inadvertently, *iwi kūpuna* must be reported to the State Historic Preservation Office and to the appropriate island burial council, who decide on the disposition of the remains (i.e., reburial in place or in another location). In the event that island burial councils in consultation with lineal descendants decide to relocate *iwi kūpuna,* archaeologists are relied upon to carefully disinter the remains. Kānaka Maoli attorneys Baldauf and Akutagawa (2013) discuss the cultural and legal framework for Hawaiian burial sites and their protection.

Most people are unaware of the information that can be gained through careful—and respectful—study of ancient interments (Halliwell 2017). The study of ancient burials can yield valuable insights into ancient mortuary practices, as well as information on health and demography, but these investigations must be balanced against descendant community concerns for self-determination over the treatment of their ancestors. The information gained from studying burials can also be essential in determining whether a set of skeletal remains is of a precontact Kanaka Maoli person or possibly a postcontact burial of a person of a different ethnicity (or sometimes even a murder victim).

There are two main approaches to the analysis of burials and skeletal remains. The first, commonly referred to as "mortuary analysis," focuses on the cultural and social aspects of the disposal of the dead. Each society treats its deceased members in distinctive ways; individuals within the same society may be treated in quite different ways, depending upon their status in life and the social position of their living relatives. By carefully recording and analyzing the details of burial practice (such as whether the burial is primary or secondary, extended or flexed, with or without grave goods, and so on), archaeologists are able to make inferences about the social context and cultural beliefs associated with internment of the dead. The second approach to burial analysis focuses on the skeletal remains themselves, requiring a physical anthropologist or osteologist who has had professional training in the identification and study of the human skeleton. By observing skeletal remains, it is possible to determine such features of the deceased as stature, age, sex, and genetic traits. The health of an individual can be assessed, and many pathologies leave clear traces in bone. Such study can lead to an "osteobiography" of the deceased individual. Further, if a *population* of burials is recovered, as in sand dune sites or burial caves, it is possible to reconstruct many of the demographic features of the group as a whole, such as life expectancy and mortality rates. Tamara Halliwell, a Kanaka Maoli physical anthropologist, argues that the "osteobiographies of the iwi kūpuna which are inscribed in their bones," and that are interpreted through careful and respectful study, "add another layer of importance and sacredness to learning from the iwi kūpuna" (2017, 33).

What was learned of traditional burial practices during the period that archaeological study of *iwi kūpuna* was permitted prior to contemporary regulations informs us regarding important aspects of ancient cultural practice. For these reasons, we include the following discussion of ancient mortuary behavior and practices; respecting current Kānaka Maoli perspectives, however, we have omitted any photos or illustrations of *iwi kūpuna.*

The death of a person in ancient Hawaiʻi was marked by ceremonies and displays of mourning. Close relatives and neighbors would assemble at the house of the deceased to wail dirges and weep; "chants eulogizing the deceased were recited" (Buck 1957, 565). Relatives might display their grief by cutting their hair or disfiguring their bodies. The death of a kinsman or of a chief might be marked by knocking out a front incisor; crania and mandibles with incisors removed during life are not infrequent in burial sites. After the initial mourning, the body might be disposed of in one of several different ways. Both Buck (1957, 565–580) and Robert Bowen (1961) discuss funerary practices extensively.

Cremation Burial

The use of cremation was referred to by nineteenth-century writers (e.g., Malo 1951, 20, 57), who suggested that this practice was reserved for the bodies of *kapu* breakers. "The body was apparently burned over an open fire until reduced to ashes and charred bones" (Bowen 1961, 77). An archaeological case of cremation is known from the Waimea-Kawaihae Road corridor on Hawai'i Island, where Roland Reeve (1983) excavated the charred skeletal remains of a single individual beneath a simple stone mound. Another probable cremation was discovered during the archaeological survey of Kaho'olawe Island (W. Barrera, pers. comm., 1979). Toni Han and Sara Collins reported a cremation burial from the large Keōpū site in Kona, Hawai'i (Han et al. 1986, 85–88).

Burial Caves

One of the most common types of interment was the placement of bodies in lava tubes, rockshelters, or niches in steep cliffs. Such burials may be single, or in groups of several score or more, the latter evidently representing extended family or *'ohana* sepulchers. Skeletal preservation in burial caves is often excellent, given the protection from moisture and the elements. Artifacts sometimes interred with the dead ranged from tapa cloth and pandanus mats to food bowls and wooden canoe hulls.

An example of a relatively simple niche burial, high in the cliff face of Waimea Valley, O'ahu, was illustrated by McAllister (1933a, pl. 9A). A more elaborate cave burial is exemplified by site Ha-E2-56 at Kalāhuipua'a on Hawai'i Island (Kirch 1979a, 61–67, figs. 24–29, table 4). This large lava tube situated a short distance inland of the fishponds and habitation sites served as a communal burial place for members of an extended family. The cave contains 30 individuals, mostly adults of both sexes. A few of the burials were placed in canoe hulls that had been cut into two pieces. Other burials were situated in depressions in the lava rock floor along the eastern wall of the cave. After detailed recording and an osteological study in situ (Kam 1979), the Kalāhuipua'a burial cave was sealed and designated as part of a historic preserve.

Whereas the Kalāhuipua'a burial cave and similar sites at 'Anaeho'omalu (Barrera 1971a) and elsewhere in west Hawai'i (J. N. J. Cleghorn 1987) were used largely by the commoner class, some burial caves were reserved for use by the *ali'i*. Forbes Cave, a lava tube near Kawaihae in Kohala, contained the remains of a number of *iwi* wrapped in *kapa*. Placed in one of the chambers with *'iwi* were several remarkable objects, including sculptured wooden images (Brigham 1906). Brigham's plan of the cave site is reproduced in figure 11.20. Forbes Cave became the center of a highly contentious NAGPRA case (Kawelu 2015, 60–62), which has yet to be resolved. At issue, in part, is whether the carved images were *moepu*, or funerary objects placed with the *iwi* at the time of burial, or whether these items were hidden later, at the time of the overturning of the *kapu* system (the *'ai noa*) in 1819, in order to safeguard the objects. Irving Jenkins (2017) contends that Forbes Cave was the tomb of the high chief Keōuakūahuula, who was slain at Kawaihae and offered as a sacrifice on the *luakini* of Pu'ukoholā in 1789, but the evidence for this is questionable.

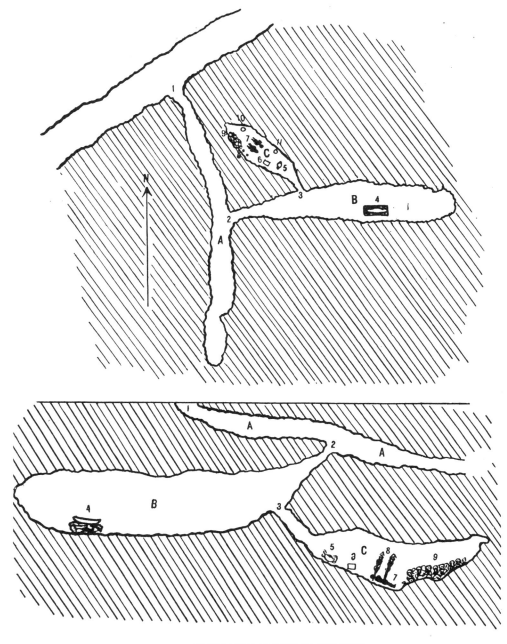

SKETCH PLAN OF PART OF THE CAVE.

1. Opening to cave from gulch.
2. Branch opening to B, closed with rocks.
3. Branch opening to C, closed with rocks.
4. Canoe with skeleton, feet to east.
5. Wooden bowl with carved figure.
6. Papamu or konane board.
7. Two human figures, heads to east.
8. Two aumakuas leaning against wall.
9. Skulls and bones rolled in kapa.
10. Ipu aina with human teeth.
11. Large gourd containing skeleton of infant.

FIGURE 11.20 Plan of Forbes Cave, Kawaihae, Hawai'i Island, prepared by William T. Brigham, showing the location of objects hidden within the burial cave. *(After Brigham 1906)*

Burials in Sand and Earth

The most common and widespread method of interment was burial in sand dunes or in the earth. Nearly all of the large sand dunes around the islands contain precontact burials, such as the famous dunes at Mōkapu on Oʻahu (see chapter 17), at Moʻomomi on west Molokaʻi, and at Honokahua on Maui. Regarding burial in sand dunes, Bowen wrote,

> The high concentrations of burials in sand environments, particularly where dunes exist, indicate that these areas were set aside for the dead and may have been used for long periods of time. Dunes were waste areas incapable of food production and were usually some distance from residences. Digging was easy and preservation of bone material was generally excellent. (1974, 129–130)

The burials themselves take a variety of forms, ranging from secondary bundle burials consisting of only a cranium and long bones to primary flexed burials (the most common position) to fully extended burials (rare). "Grave goods" or portable artifacts associated with such sand dune or earth burials accompany some but by no means all of the burials.

Mōkapu Peninsula on windward Oʻahu was a major burial ground, with extensive sand dunes fronting the shoreline between Pali Kilo (in Heʻeia *ahupuaʻa*) and Ulupau Crater (in Kāneʻohe *ahupuaʻa*). In 1938, the discovery of a unique bone-and-shell bracelet along with eight skulls was reported to Bishop Museum, prompting Kenneth Emory to "make an exploratory excavation" at Mōkapu (Bowen 1974, 132). This exploratory work led to a major excavation between October 1938 and January 1940, with Emory being assisted by Gordon T. Bowles, professor of physical anthropology at the University of Hawaiʻi. This excavation was never fully reported, although Collins, Han, and Armstrong (1993) summarize the work based on the field notes available in Bishop Museum archives. After Mōkapu Peninsula was converted to a Marine Corps military base during World War II, further discovery of human remains led to a second excavation by Bowen in 1957 (Bowen 1974, 133). The two excavations, along with various other inadvertent discoveries of *iwi* eroding from the dunes, resulted in a collection of 1,125 burials, although when this was reanalyzed under NAGPRA, at least 1,582 individuals proved to be represented (Collins, Han, and Armstrong 1993, 135, table 6). The Mōkapu *iwi kūpuna* in 1993 became the object of a NAGPRA action involving multiple claimants; the entire collection is presently awaiting reburial at Mōkapu.

According to Bowen (1974, 139), of the Mōkapu burials excavated in 1957, the majority were tightly flexed; the next most frequent position was semiextended, with fully extended and "sitting upright in a tightly flexed position" also represented. No particular orientation was observed. An immature pig was associated with one female burial, while "the skeletons of domestic or wild fowl were found with [the bones of] four women" (143). The skeletons of fish accompanied the burials of four females and one male. Relatively few artifacts were associated with the Mōkapu burials, but Bowen reports a "significant and elaborate artifact," a bracelet of 33 worked dog's teeth found "around the flexed child's right wrist" (144).

The large Keōpū burial site (Ha-D8-30) in North Kona, Hawaiʻi, was excavated by Han et al. (1986) as part of the realignment of Kuakini Highway. It was initially thought that stone cairns found during surface survey represented a few dozen "forgotten" historic-era graves (xii). By the end of the project the remains of 355 individuals had been uncovered. Radiocarbon dates indicate that individuals began to be interred at Keōpū as early as the Late Voyaging Period; use of the burial ground continued into the postcontact period. The majority of precontact individuals were buried in primary, flexed positions (78%), although semiflexed, extended, and semiextended positions were also represented. Some burials had traces of matting, *kapa,* and cordage, evidently from bundles containing the skeletal remains. A few burials were associated with portable artifacts. These included one older woman with a *lei niho palaoa* neck ornament of rock oyster shell (88, figs. 51–52), presumably indicative of chiefly status. Another woman had two *Terebra* shells on her chest; these had perhaps been strung and worn as ornaments (90, fig. 53). The burial of a male 35 to 40 years old was accompanied by a large cache of fishing gear, including hooks, stone sinkers, and tools used for fishhook manufacture (94–95, figs. 57–63). Collins summarized the history of the Keōpū burial ground as follows:

> The burials of Site D8-30 reflect the social and economic changes seen in other archaeological sites of the Kailua-Kona region. In the beginning, commoners are laid to rest, perhaps with favorite sea foods or an *akua* stone. By late prehistoric times, this *maka'āinana* lineage is a mirror of Hawaiian society in general, with specialized craftsmen (the fisherman, Burial J24-1), an *ali'i maka'āinana* (Burial K23-1), and an outcast or *kapu*-breaker (the cremation, Burial H24-3). (Collins, in Han et al. 1986, 258–259)

After completion of the Keōpū study, the *iwi kūpuna* were reinterred in a stone burial vault at Hualālai Memorial Park in Kona.

The last and one of the most extensive excavations ever undertaken of a sand dune ossuary was at Honokahua on West Maui, in 1987–1988 in conjunction with the planned construction of a Ritz-Carlton hotel. As described by Kawelu (2015, 54–58), the project became highly contentious; eventually, the 867 primary burials, along with 133 individuals in "secondary contexts," were reinterred and the hotel project relocated (see chapter 1). Theresa Donham (1989, 2000) documents the burials and their context in detail, providing a wealth of information on ancient Hawaiian mortuary practices. Curiously, the ratio of males to females at Honokahua was strongly skewed, with almost twice as many females as males (359 females, 175 males, and 330 subadults for which sex was not determined). Flexed burials overwhelmingly dominated (71%), with semiflexed, extended, and semi-extended burial positions also being present. There were seven instances of a primary articulated burial together with a bundle burial of disarticulated bones, representing individuals who were interred with the bones of kinfolk who had predeceased them (Donham 2000, 6.20). While the average depth of burial pits was about 1.5 m, some pits extended as deep as 4 m beneath the dune surface. There were a number of animal burials, some directly associated with human burials, including eleven dogs, three pigs, and eight fowls. Thirty burials showed traces of red ochre (*'alaea*) on or around them (7.77).

Many individuals at Honokahua were interred with items of personal adornment, including pendants of various types, necklaces, and anklets or bracelets. Of particular interest are 16 instances of *lei niho palaoa* (see also chapter 9), a symbol of *aliʻi* status. None of the Honokahua *lei niho palaoa* is actually of whale tooth, however; rather eight are made of bone, six of shell (type not specified), and two of calcite. Notably, of the ten *lei niho palaoa* found in direct association with primary burials, eight were with children; one adult male and one adult female also had these symbols of rank. Some individuals were also buried with fishing gear, as at the Keopū burial ground.

The chronology of the burials at Honokahua was addressed by radiocarbon dating of 31 samples of "charred wood, nut shell [*kukui*], ash, and carbonized organic materials" (Donham 2000, 5.13), although not by any direct dating of the human skeletal remains themselves. Unfortunately, the charcoal samples were not identified to species, leaving open the possibility of inbuilt age (see chapter 3). Of the 31 samples, 25 returned actual dates, ranging from as old as cal AD 636–783 (Beta-30860) up to the postcontact, historic period. This earliest date, however, is likely to have been from old wood, as is the case with three other samples predating AD 1200. The burial ground probably began to be used in the Late Voyaging Period, with its use intensifying in the Expansion and Archaic States Periods.

In 1993, construction associated with a realignment of Kālia Road at Fort DeRussy in Waikīkī, Oʻahu Island, led to the discovery of a mass burial ("Burial Area 6") containing the skeletal remains of at least 21 individuals who had been interred simultaneously in a large pit (Carlson, Collins, and Cleghorn 1994). The individuals appeared on osteological evidence to be males, ranging in age from the late teens to adult (table 3-2). Significantly, 12 individuals showed signs of perimortem trauma, of the kind that would result from "blows and cuts to the bone," or blunt-force trauma (49). The investigators concluded that this unique mass burial contained "the remains of Hawaiian warriors who died in one of the battles of the interisland wars of conquest which occurred during the reign of King Kamehameha I" (70). However, radiocarbon dates obtained on charcoal in the burial pit have an age range from ca. AD 1440 up to the early contact era (table 3-1), raising the possibility that the defeated warriors might alternatively have been associated with the unsuccessful raid on Oʻahu by Maui king Kauhi-a-Kama in the Archaic States Period. According of the *moʻolelo* of this event, Kauhi-a-Kama himself was slain in this battle (Fornander 1878–1885, 2:208).

Monument Burials

Burials were sometimes marked on the surface by stone terraces, mounds, or platforms. A large number of such monument burials were excavated by Donald Tuohy (1965) in the "parking lot" area just inland of the Great Wall at Hōnaunau on Hawaiʻi. The burial itself was generally placed below the monument, often in a crevice in the *pāhoehoe* lava. Other monument burials were recorded by Jeff Clark and Kirch (1983) in the Kawaihae area (see also J. N. J. Cleghorn 1987).

Some clusters of monument burials are reputedly associated with battles. In the center of Kalaupapa Peninsula, 60 stone terraces and cairns cover the surface of a small hill called Makapulapai; these monuments are far from the cemeteries that date to the era of the leprosarium (M. D. McCoy 2006, 2008b). An account of a pitched battle "at the sandbar at

Kalaupapa," relayed by Fornander (Fornander 1916–1917, 416–420, cited in Summers 1971, 16–17), describes an attack led by the Oʻahu king Kualiʻi who came to Molokaʻi to support the Kona chiefs. In that battle Kualiʻi fends off two attempts to capture his canoe by using an unusual weapon, an adze. A petroglyph of a figure holding a raised adze is located at the summit of Makapulapai suggesting this is where those who fell during that attack were laid to rest.

Monument burial became especially common in the historic period, with the construction of stone-walled crypts in large burial monuments. In Kanaio *ahupuaʻa* on Maui Island, several hundred stone platforms and terraces situated within swales or depressions in a massive *ʻaʻā* lava flow appear to be burial monuments; at least some of these date to the postcontact period.

House Burial

The disposal of the dead beneath house floors is an ancient practice in Polynesia, one that is archaeologically attested in Hawaiʻi as well, although the practice was not widespread. The early Bellows dune site (O18) on windward Oʻahu contained a number of burials, most of which were positioned under the gravel pavements of pole-and-thatched structures (see chapter 6). In Hālawa Valley on Molokaʻi, two inland house sites and one habitation rockshelter excavated by Gil Hendren (1975) contained burials within shallow pits directly beneath the house floors. In one case, the house appeared to have been abandoned immediately after the interment, which was placed in a pit dug through the central hearth. (The Hālawa burials were all left in place and covered back over after excavation.)

During the postcontact period there was a return to the practice of burial at house sites, although rather than directly within the house, in this case burial was in pits covered by stone mounds or platforms next to the house or within house enclosures (*pā hale*). This practice is well documented in the case of nineteenth-century house sites in the Anahulu Valley, Oʻahu (Kirch and Sahlins 1992, 2:177–178). Stone cairns, such as the crypts that drew the attention of archaeologists at Keōpū, are commonly found on surveys as add-ons to the stone foundations of house sites and other structures. The postcontact period saw a huge increase in the mortality rate due to introduced diseases, and during this time many people moved to the port cities for work. And so it is likely that many abandoned house sites in the rural areas were transformed into family burial plots.

Heiau Burial and Royal Mausoleums

Temple sites were also burial places, for high-ranking chiefs on the one hand, and for sacrificial victims on the other. Ethnohistoric sources indicate that the bodies of human sacrifices were interred in the temple platform itself, a practice confirmed by Ladd (1969b, 1973) during his excavations in Āleʻaleʻa at Hōnaunau, Hawaiʻi, and at Kāneʻakī in Mākaha Valley, Oʻahu. Temples were also, however, the mausoleums of high chiefs, the most famous being the Hale-o-Keawe at Hōnaunau (fig. 11.21), where the remains of the deified chiefs descending from Keawe were kept and revered (see chapter 14). It was evidently to this temple as well that the remains of Captain James Cook were brought after his death at

FIGURE 11.21 The Hale o Keawe at Hōnaunau, Hawai'i Island, was a sepulchral temple where the bones of Hawai'i Island rulers were deposited. The fence, images, and thatched house were reconstructed by the National Park Service based on early historic drawings and descriptions. *(Photo by Therese Babineau)*

Kealakekua. Another famous mausoleum was the Hale o Līloa in Waipi'o Valley, Hawai'i. Chiefly remains kept within such mausoleums were at times encased in special woven caskets (*kā'ai*) of anthropomorphic shape (illustrated by Buck 1957, 575).

In sum, the disposal of the dead in ancient Hawai'i involved a range of practices. Some of the variation probably reflects local geographic conditions, such as the availability of suitable lava tubes or sand dunes. Much of burial practice, however, also reflects the social position of the deceased individuals—whether they were *ali'i*, members of commoner families, or *kapu* breakers. The kind of interment, the presence and type of associated artifacts or other offerings, association with other individuals, and other such variables provide important clues for reconstructing the social fabric of ancient Hawai'i (e.g., Tainter 1973, 1976; Tainter and Cordy 1977).

12

FROM *UKA* TO *KAI*
Five Settlement Landscapes

The ways in which *kauhale,* trails, agricultural fields, fishponds, temples, burials, petroglyphs, and other features were integrated to form entire settlement landscapes varied across the archipelago. Some differences were responses to local topography and resources; local variation in cultural practices also played a role. In this chapter we explore some of the variation in settlement landscapes, drawing upon five case studies that range across windward and leeward valleys on Moloka'i (Hālawa) and O'ahu (Mākaha), and three leeward regions on Moloka'i (Kawela), Maui (Kahikinui), and Hawai'i (Lapakahi in leeward Kohala). All of these cases draw upon large-scale surveys and settlement pattern studies of one or sometimes more *ahupua'a,* combined with excavations in *kauhale* clusters, agricultural sites, and temples.

In a classic article on "land matters in Hawai'i," Curtis J. Lyons who worked as a land surveyor for the Hawaiian Government Survey in the late nineteenth century wrote the following: "The Ahupuaa ran from the sea to the mountain, theoretically. That is to say the central idea of the Hawaiian division of land was emphatically central, or rather radial. Hawaiian life vibrated from *uka,* mountain, whence came wood, kapa, for clothing, *olonā,* for fish-line, ti-leaf for wrapping paper, *ie* for ratan lashing, wild birds for food, to the *kai;* sea, whence came *ia,* fish, and connected therewith. *Mauka* and *makai* are therefore fundamental ideas to the native of an island" (Lyons 1903, 24).

The case studies that follow highlight the similarities and differences in the way that settlement landscapes were organized within the overarching *ahupua'a* concept.

Mākaha Valley, O'ahu

Mākaha exemplifies a leeward valley on one of the geologically older islands. Bishop Museum's Mākaha Valley Historical Project, directed by Roger Green from 1968 to 1970, was one of the first in Hawai'i to employ a settlement-pattern approach; project results were published in five volumes (Green 1980; Green, ed., 1969, 1970; Ladd 1973; Ladd and Yen 1972). The valley is the third largest *ahupua'a* within Wai'anae *moku* (Lualualei and Wai'anae are larger); during the early historic period Mākaha was under the control of high chief Boki, governor of O'ahu.

Mākaha slices into the leeward side of the Wai'anae Mountains for 7 km in an easterly direction, its headwaters falling away steeply from the peak of Ka'ala, O'ahu's highest mountain. The valley is readily subdivided into two major divisions, termed the "upper" and "lower" valleys (fig. 12.1). The lower valley is fairly wide (about 3 km at the coast) with gentle colluvial slopes of stony clay. Rainfall on the coast is only about 500 mm annually but increases inland to about 1,000 mm at the interface of the lower and the upper valleys. The Mākaha Stream flows only intermittently in the lower valley, so that cultivation there was largely dependent upon rainfall and intermittent, seasonal runoff from side gulches over the colluvial slopes.

The upper valley, which begins where Kāne'ākī Heiau is situated, is much narrower than the lower valley, with steep spur ridges breaking up the landscape. Rainfall ranges from 1,000 to 2,000 mm annually (at the base of Ka'ala). Mākaha Stream flows permanently in the upper valley, making taro irrigation feasible on narrow alluvial flats bordering the stream.

The environmental contrasts between upper and lower valleys profoundly influenced Mākaha's settlement patterns. Coastal settlement was limited, largely due to low rainfall and the unsuitable nature of the coastal zone for agriculture. The colluvial slopes of the lower valley below Kāne'ākī Heiau—heavily cultivated using a variety of

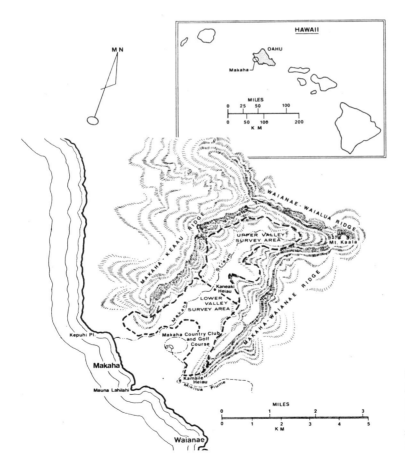

FIGURE 12.1 Map of Mākaha Valley, O'ahu Island, showing the lower and upper valley sectors. *(After Green, ed., 1969)*

dry-field methods—were a focus of permanent housing and agricultural temples. Settlement in the narrower upper valley was strung out along the stream flats and focused on small taro irrigation systems. Green elaborates the distinctions between upper and lower valley settlement patterns:

> The lower valley . . . includes all the culturally well-utilized, gently sloping, dry or *kula* lands, up to the point where the valley narrows and becomes well-watered by rainfall. Only a small part of these lands was capable of being irrigated from the Mākaha Stream. . . . In the upper valley, in contrast, use was made primarily of a low-lying, narrow, lineal zone along the Mākaha Stream, the one exception being along the branch of the only permanent side stream, where limited use was made of the valley sides above the main stream. (Green 1980, 46)

Much attention was devoted during the Mākaha Project to investigating the settlement patterns of the broad, arc-shaped, lower-valley zone seaward of Kāneʻākī Heiau, where the colluvial slopes received sufficient rainfall for dryland cultivation. Intensive survey in "Zone 1" revealed numerous small field shelters, some of which were excavated (Green, ed., 1969, 1970). A portion of Zone 1 with agricultural and residential features is shown in figure 12.2. The major structural features found in Zone 1, in decreasing order of abundance, are: mounds, residential features (especially field shelters), clearings, terraces, walls, and platforms. Regarding the agricultural mounds, Robert Hommon wrote, "The subzone is a gently sloping area of reddish alluvial soil which had been cleared of stones at some period or periods in the past. Most of these stones were tossed onto or built into the dozens of mounds we see today. . . . Some are very rough and informal and look as though they accumulated simply as repositories for stones cleared from the area to simplify the planting; others, however, were carefully built into regular, relatively perpendicular-sided structures" (Hommon 1969a, 45). Most of the clearings and terraces appear to have had agricultural functions as well.

The inland part of the lower valley was the main center of permanent habitation, with rectangular walled enclosures serving as major residential sites. Certain larger, and less common, rectangular enclosures were special-function sites, in many cases presumably men's houses (*mua*). As might be predicted for an intensively cultivated area, there are also a number of agricultural temples (*heiau hoʻouluʻai*); several of these stepped terraces were investigated by Ed Ladd (1970). Kāneʻākī Heiau, which in its earlier stages resembled these stepped temples and was probably an agricultural temple, was later enlarged and expanded to become a *luakini* (fig. 12.3; see chapter 11). According to Ladd's reconstruction, in this final stage the temple's orientation was shifted about 90 degrees; the new orientation of Kāneʻākī was toward the peak of Kaʻala, but also close to the rising position of Makaliʻi, the star cluster whose acronychal rising determined the timing of the Makahiki season. Kāneʻākī commands a central position at the junction of upper and lower valleys, with a sweeping view over the lower valley.

In the upper valley, inland of Kāneʻākī Heiau, the settlement landscape changes dramatically. The valley narrows and the broad colluvial slopes of the lower valley give way to

FIGURE 12.2 Map of a portion of the lower Mākaha Valley, Oʻahu Island, with a range of dryland agricultural features interspersed with residential sites. *(After Hommon 1969a)*

FIGURE 12.3 Kāneʻaki Heiau in Mākaha Valley, Oʻahu Island, was converted to a *luakini heiau* in its final construction stage. The thatched buildings and image are reconstructions based on ethnohistoric accounts. *(Photo by Therese Babineau)*

steeper ridges alternating with side gulches. Most of the sites are concentrated on small, alluvial terraces bordering the stream. As Hommon (1969c, 88–89) observes, in place of the abundant stone mounds that characterize the lower valley agricultural landscape, the upper valley landscape is dominated by stone-faced terraces; many of these were small taro pondfields irrigated either from the main stream or from small tributary streams. One of the upper valley irrigation systems was studied by Douglas Yen et al. (1972), as described in chapter 7.

In sum, Mākaha represents a leeward valley with environmental constraints that mitigated against agricultural development and permanent residence along the coast. In the middle and interior reaches of the valley, however, the fertile colluvial slopes were intensively farmed, as were the narrow alluvial flats of the upper valley. The main zone of permanent residence corresponded with the area of greatest agricultural production, with household clusters, men's houses, and agricultural temples distributed in an arc-shaped zone. Overlooking and symbolically dominating this scene was Kāneʻākī Heiau, ritual seat of a paramount chief who had risen to power a few centuries prior to European contact and who integrated the entire Waiʻanae District.

Hālawa Valley, Molokaʻi

Hālawa Valley on eastern Molokaʻi Island is representative of a windward valley with extensive taro irrigation. Though smaller than Mākaha, Hālawa Valley is richly endowed with natural resources—including a large permanent stream, broad alluvial floodplains, fertile colluvial slopes, and a deep bay—all of which supported one of the densest concentrations of population anywhere in the islands (fig. 12.4). The sheltered bay allowed for canoe landings even in rough weather, a luxury not afforded the other windward valleys of Molokaʻi, where boulder beaches permit landings only in the calm summer months. In the nineteenth century, Hālawa was famed for its production of irrigated taro, much of which supplied the whaling fleet at Lāhaina on Maui (Bates 1854, 277). The valley's great agricultural productivity would have been a prize for any ruling chief who could gain control of the region; indeed, Molokaʻi was several times the scene of conquests from Oʻahu and Maui. During the Great Māhele, Hālawa *ahupuaʻa* was awarded to the high chiefess Victoria Kamāmalu.

Hālawa was settled by the end of the Foundation Period (see chapter 6). By the Late Voyaging Period, the valley's population was expanding inland, possibly with small irrigation systems developed adjacent to side-valley streams, as in Puaʻalaulau and Kapana, two of the valley's *ʻili*. The settlement pattern described below is, however, that which existed in final centuries immediately prior to European contact, after the large alluvial-plain irrigation systems were in place and the valley's population was at its height.

Extensive taro irrigation systems dominated Hālawa's settlement pattern (see fig. 7.4). The lower valley alluvial floodplains were cloaked in large rectangular pondfields watered by long irrigation ditches, while the narrow alluvial flats farther inland were similarly terraced with stone-faced fields. Small irrigated terraces could be found even farther inland, extending to the bases of the large waterfalls that cascade down from the valley's rim. Ringing this ▲-shaped core of irrigated fields (wide at the valley mouth and

FIGURE 12.4 Hālawa Valley, at the eastern end of Molokaʻi Island, offered ideal conditions for extensive taro irrigation, including a permanent stream, alluvial floodplain, and broad colluvial slopes. *(Photo by P. V. Kirch)*

paralleling the stream inland), on the gentle colluvial slopes was the zone of residential sites, dryland gardens, and temples.

Archival records from the Māhele in 1848–1854, along with early twentieth-century maps by Bishop Estate surveyors Wall and Podmore, allow us to see how this settlement pattern integrated with the hierarchical system of traditional land units. The *ahupua'a* itself encompassed not only the main valley but also the long streams feeding Mo'o'ula (or Moa'ula) and Hīpuapua waterfalls, extending far back into the east Moloka'i Mountains. Part of Hālawa *ahupua'a* even extended into the valley of Wailau; the windward landshelves of Hāka'a'ano and Kikipua were also included within the lands of Hālawa (these landshelves had small settlements on them, see chapter 16). The main valley was subdivided into 32 *'ili,* each running from the stream up to the steep cliffs rimming the valley; in this manner both irrigated taro fields (where present) as well as higher, colluvial slopes with dryland gardening features (designated as *kula* lands in the Māhele claims) were included in each land section. Each *'ili* was occupied by one or more households that held smaller land units referred to as *mo'o*. Sandwiched in between the commoner claims within the irrigation complexes were the *kō'ele* pondfields controlled by the valley's *konohiki* (often the larger fields).

The Hālawa Valley Project from 1969 to 1970 (Kirch and Kelly, eds., 1975) mapped and excavated selected features in two study areas, the *'ili* of Kaio and Kapana. The larger of these areas, Kapana (fig. 12.5), is representative of the interior settlement landscape throughout much of Hālawa Valley. The Kapana settlement pattern, analyzed by Paul Rosendahl (in Kirch and Kelly, eds., 1975), is dominated by agricultural features and by permanent residential sites, with several temples and shrines also present. Renewed archaeological studies in Kapana and other parts of Hālawa were initiated by Patrick Kirch and Jillian Swift in 2020; their project has as its main objective determining how the valley's complex agricultural system developed over time (Kirch, Swift, and Lincoln 2020, 2022).

Irrigated pondfields in the western part of Kapana include a set of large fields (complex 6) irrigated by a canal from the main Hālawa Stream, and a set of smaller, steeply terraced fields (complex 7) watered from the tributary Maka'ele'ele Stream (fig. 12.6). A view of the complex 7 terraces is shown in color plate 9. East of Maka'ele'ele Stream the gentle colluvium is corrugated with low swales and intervening stony ridges; the swales were terraced for cultivation but were not permanently irrigated. The ridges, in contrast, were the main focus of permanent residential sites, interspersed among smaller agricultural clearings. The entire colluvial slope was a zone of intensive dryland cultivation, with house sites and agricultural temples dispersed among the plantings.

In Kapana, as through much of Hālawa Valley, residential sites are commonly stone-faced, earth-filled terraces or platforms. Several inland household clusters were excavated by Gil Hendren (1975). In the Kaio area, site Mo-A1-769, dating to the mid-sixteenth century, consists of a rectangular stone-edged terrace built up against several large boulders. The house floor had been paved with fine gravel (*'ili'ili*), while a stone-outlined hearth provided light and heat. Artifacts recovered during excavation included basalt flakes and a grindstone, as well as a beautifully crafted tripping club (see fig. 9.28). A notable feature was a subfloor burial of an adult male; the house was abandoned after the death and interment of this individual.

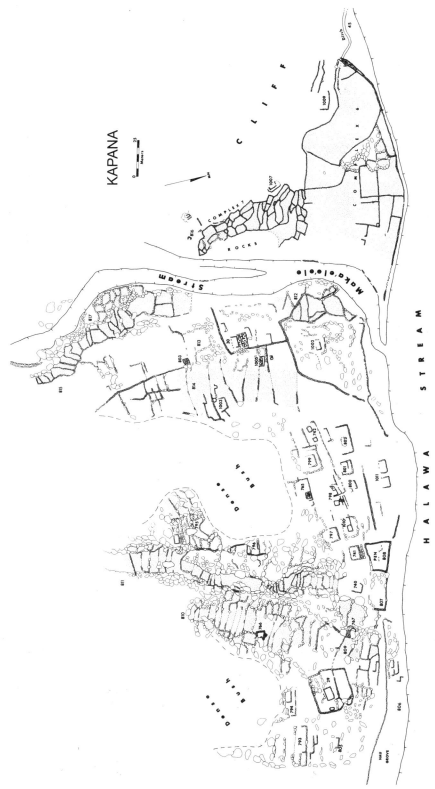

FIGURE 12.5 Map of the *'ili* of Kapana in the interior of Hālawa Valley, Moloka'i Island. *(After Kirch and Kelly 1975)*

FIGURE 12.6 Stone-faced terraces of a side-stream irrigation system in Kapana, Hālawa Valley. At the upper right excavations are ongoing in a habitation terrace overlooking the irrigation system. (Photo by P. V. Kirch)

Subfloor burial within houses was not a common practice in precontact Hawai'i, but in Hālawa it seems that this ancestral Polynesian method of interring the dead was retained.

A short distance from site 769, across a small gully, is another terrace (Site Mo-A1-1001), excavated by Tom Riley. It functioned as a cook shed, the defining feature being a large earth oven (*imu*) filled with fire-cracked cooking stones. This site also contained two subfloor burials, of an adult and a juvenile. Riley regarded the unexcavated terrace immediately upslope from this cookhouse as the main dwelling house, so that the two structures together formed a household cluster or *kauhale*. The burials in sites -769 and -1001 were left in place and covered back over, where they remain today.

Kapana has two medium-sized temples; both are stepped terraces (sites Mo-A1-29 and -30), not unlike those studied by Ladd in Mākaha (see color plate 8). These were agricultural temples, and may also have functioned as men's houses. Two small putative shrines, consisting of enclosures built up against large outcrops, are also present in Kapana.

Reconnaissance survey of other portions of Hālawa Valley suggests that the patterns exhibited in Kapana are representative. John F. G. Stokes (1909a) recorded 13 medium-sized *heiau*, fairly evenly distributed along the valley slopes and generally following the stepped-terrace plan. There is also a *ko'a* or fishing shrine near the coast, with a small enclosure built up against a large natural boulder; another *ko'a* was situated inland, next to Hālawa Stream, associated with catching freshwater *'o'opu* fish. While these temples were probably the domain of local household groups occupying particular *'ili* or sections of the valley, Hālawa also boasts two larger *heiau*, reflective of the larger political structure within which Hālawa *ahupua'a* was embedded. These are Mana Heiau, a large stone platform with multiple-stepped terrace facings on the north slope of the valley, and Pāpā Heiau, a complex structure with several platforms, terraces, and enclosing walls situated in Hālawa Iki Gulch. According to traditions collected by Stokes (1909a), Mana Heiau was built (or perhaps rededicated) by the Hawai'i Island chief Alapa'inui following his conquest of Moloka'i; it functioned as a *luakini* temple where human sacrifices were offered to Kū. Stokes (1909a) thought that Pāpā Heiau may have been a "college" for the training of priests. Like Kāne'ākī in Mākaha, Mana and Pāpā *heiau* are situated on the higher slopes, with panoramic views over the taro fields and out to sea. The choice of such settings for major temples was symbolic of the power and status of the paramount chief who alone had the authority to construct and dedicate such monuments.

Kawela and Makakupaiʻa Iki, Molokaʻi

The environmental contrasts between Hālawa and Kawela could not be more striking. Situated along the arid, leeward south Molokaʻi coast, Kawela and adjacent Makakupaiʻa Iki *ahupuaʻa* straddle moderately dissected flow slopes, with narrow gulches and box canyons extending inland from the coastal plain (fig. 12.7). Only Kawela Gulch is large enough to support an intermittently flowing stream (which may have flowed permanently during precontact times). The steep slopes between the gulches exhibit only shallow, rocky soils. The greatest constraint to agricultural development is the low rainfall, only about 325 mm annually, well below the threshold for dryland cultivation of sweet potatoes. However, the broad reef flat offshore offered an ideal setting for the construction of large fishponds, attracting permanent settlement in the late Expansion to Archaic States Periods.

An archaeological survey of 7.7 km^2 in Kawela and Makakupaiʻa Iki *ahupuaʻa* by Bishop Museum in 1980–1981 recorded 499 archaeological features (Weisler and Kirch 1982, 1985). Many features were excavated, providing a well-controlled data set for settlement pattern analysis. An advantage of Kawela for settlement-pattern studies is the late chronology of occupation. Fifteen radiocarbon dates indicate that most of the area's archaeological features date from one to two centuries prior to European contact. Thus, the settlement pattern is for all intents and purposes contemporaneous. At the time that the archaeological survey was conducted, the landscape had suffered only minimally from historical period ranching. Subsequently, however, a housing subdivision changed the landscape radically (the Kawela Plantation development). The Kawela and Makakupaiʻa Iki settlement pattern is illustrated in figure 12.8.

FIGURE 12.7 Kawela Gulch, in leeward Molokaʻi Island, divides into two narrow box canyons. The steep ridge between the canyons was fortified. *(Photo by P. V. Kirch)*

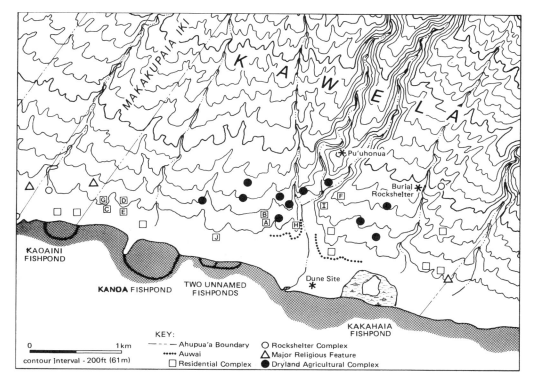

FIGURE 12.8 The settlement pattern of Kawela and Makakupai'a *ahupua'a* in south central Moloka'i Island. *(After Weisler and Kirch 1985)*

In this arid environment, agriculture focused primarily on the alluvial floodplain at the mouth of Kawela Gulch. Two irrigation ditches directed intermittent floodwaters from Kawela Stream out onto the fertile alluvium, which, unlike Hālawa, was not terraced for taro cultivation but was farmed using a furrow technique. Land claims from the Māhele of 1848–1854 document that the floodplain was divided into narrow, parallel strips of land cultivated in sweet potatoes. Irrigated taro at Kawela was restricted to several small terrace sets higher up in the interior of Kawela Gulch (just below the major stream fork), where there was sufficient streamflow to water the small pondfields. Taro was also grown along the swampy margin of Kakahai'a Pond, where springs provided a source of fresh water. Although Kawela lacked extensive areas of dryland cultivation, a few small dryland field complexes were situated on the slopes surrounding Kawela Gulch. These may have been used only for short periods, perhaps during wet years when a higher-than-average winter rainfall permitted a crop of sweet potatoes, gourds, or other dryland crops.

Five large fishponds were strung out along the coastline. Four of these are of *loko kuapā* type, with stone walls constructed out onto the shallow reef flat, while Kakahai'a Pond is a *pu'uone* or "inland" pond situated behind a sand berm. These ponds could have produced between about 14,000 and 23,000 kilograms of fish per year, while the extensive reef was a source of additional fish caught through netting, spearing, and angling. The Kawela inhabitants may have dried excess fish harvested from the ponds and the reef, trading these along with evaporated sea salt for taro or other agricultural products from the windward valleys.

Notably, the Māhele records indicate that a *lele* or detached section of Kawela *ahupua'a* extended over the Moloka'i mountains into the interior of Pelekunu Valley; access to this wet environment was necessary in order to grow the *olonā* plant that provided the fiber with which to make fishing lines and nets.

The distribution of residential sites at Kawela is shown in figure 12.8. Residential complexes are situated atop low ridges, just above the coastal plain, with seaward views and exposure to the cooling trade winds. Each complex centers around a primary residence, usually the largest structure and frequently including both a slab-lined hearth and one or more cupboards built into the stone walls. These main structures are surrounded by ancillary shelters or structures, each of which had a particular function such as storage, cooking, or craft production. Minor horticultural features, such as earthen terraces and stone-clearance mounds, are sometimes part of household clusters at Kawela.

A typical household cluster at Kawela is residential complex F. Here the primary structure is a leveled earthen terrace bordered on the northeast by an L-shaped wall. An upright stone set

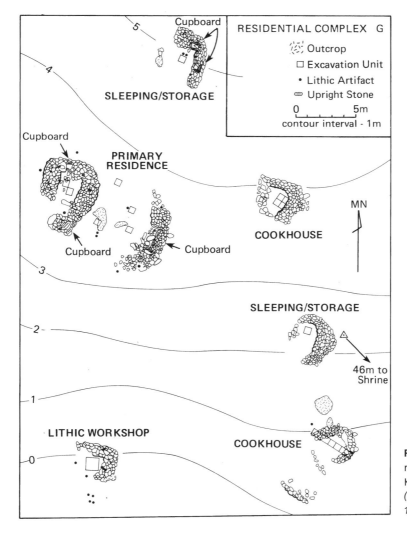

FIGURE 12.9 Map of residential complex G at Kawela, Moloka'i Island. *(After Weisler and Kirch 1985)*

in the corner of this wall is almost certainly a god-stone, representing ʻaumākua deities, suggesting that this primary residence also functioned as a men's house. Upslope is a C-shaped shelter built against a large outcrop, which excavation revealed to have been a cookhouse. Downslope of the primary residence is a large area littered with basalt flakes and containing a grindstone, indicating use as a production area for stone tools. Several meters to the west is another small C-shape, which due to its isolation from the main complex may have served as the hale peʻa, or house where women of the household sequestered themselves during their menstrual periods.

Another household cluster is Kawela residential complex G (fig. 12.9), where the primary residence is a compound structure incorporating three well-built cupboards. Surrounding this are five ancillary structures, C- and L-shaped. Excavations indicated that two of these shelters functioned as cook sheds, two as storage or sleeping areas, and the fifth as a lithic workshop or craft specialization area. Not shown in the plan, and located 46 m to the southeast, is a household shrine.

Residential complexes F and G (as well as others not described here) were probably occupied by commoner households, but three other complexes in the Kawela area were associated with higher-ranking households of konohiki or aliʻi. An analysis of household clusters at Kawela indicates that status differences between residential complexes are reflected by: (1) the number of structures in a complex; (2) the presence/absence of formal temples; (3) the presence/absence of burial platforms; (4) the relative frequency of pig and dog bone (as status foods); (5) the density and range of formal artifacts; (6) the presence/absence of nonlocal stone tools and flakes; (7) the relative density of faunal remains; and (8) the topographic setting and proximity to critical resources (Weisler and Kirch 1985).

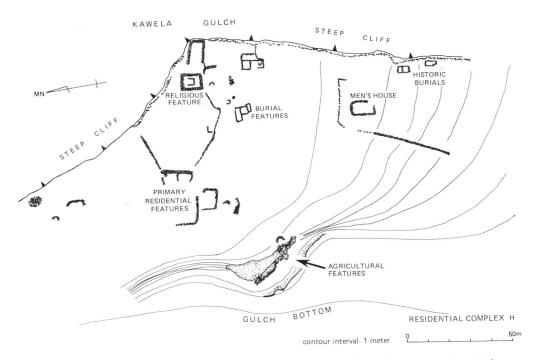

FIGURE 12.10 Map of residential complex H at Kawela, Molokaʻi Island. *(After Weisler and Kirch 1985)*

The largest residential complex in Kawela *ahupuaʻa*, and probably that occupied by the *ahupuaʻa* chief or his *konohiki*, lies astride a low ridge on the western side of Kawela Gulch, with a commanding view of the irrigated lands below (residential complex H, shown in fig. 12.10). Approaching the complex from the coastal plain, one first encounters a rectangular, low stone enclosure, probably the *mua* or men's house. This is symbolically separated from the residential area of the high-status occupants by a low stone wall, which may have signaled that the space above the wall (*mauka*) was *kapu* (fig. 12.11). The main part of the residential complex consists of a group of primary residential features to the west, and a high-walled, formal temple and associated outlying structures to the east. Two substantial cupboards were incorporated into the stone windbreak wall of Feature M, while the leveled floor to the west was further delineated into several activity spaces. Two low stone walls connect Feature M to the walled temple and again probably served to designate

FIGURE 12.11 An alignment of upright slabs at residential complex H at Kawela, Molokaʻi Island, may have demarcated a *kapu* zone. *(Photo from Oceanic Archaeology Laboratory Archives)*

FIGURE 12.12 Aerial view of a high-status residential complex at Kawela, Molokaʻi Island. To the right are the main habitation terraces; the walled enclosure on the left is a small *heiau* or men's house attached to the dwelling site. *(Photo from Oceanic Archaeology Laboratory Archives)*

a *kapu* zone between the chief's dwelling and his private temple. A small residential feature south of the temple was not excavated but may have been the dwelling of a priest associated with the temple.

Religious structures at Kawela include a variety of household shrines. The two residential sites occupied by high-ranking households each have formal walled temples (fig. 12.12). Separate temples are also found just inside the eastern borders of the several *ahupua'a;* these were interpreted as *hale o Lono,* agricultural temples used in connection with the annual Makahiki harvest rites.

The largest stone structure within Kawela *ahupua'a* is situated on the narrow plateau created by the deep east and west forks of Kawela Gulch, accessed by climbing up the steep ridge between the forks. According to oral traditions, this is a *pu'uhonua* or place of refuge that was used during the famous wars between the Kona and Ko'olau Districts of Moloka'i. The structure consists of two adjacent enclosures, one open to the south, the other fully enclosed.

At Kawela as elsewhere, the land was also inscribed in places with petroglyphs. Some occur on isolated boulder outcrops, and it is difficult to comprehend their significance. Others occur in clusters on a cliff face just above one of the *'auwai* or irrigation channels that fed intermittent stream water to the Kawela floodplain. As in Kahikinui (see below), these may have been a way of marking individual rights to the precious water flow.

Kahikinui, Maui

Our fourth settlement landscape encompasses Kahikinui, an entire *moku* on the southeastern slopes of Halekalā volcano, whose summit at 3,055 m elevation looms over east Maui. The *moku,* one of six traditional districts making up east Maui, covers 121.5 km^2. The name Kahikinui translates as "Great Tahiti," presumably named after Tahiti Nui, the larger half of the island of Tahiti, which resembles Maui in being a double volcano. Kahikinui was a classic *kua'āina* or back country (literally "back of the land"), rarely visited by the chiefs; consequently, it barely figures in the traditional histories.

Lying in the rain shadow of Haleakalā, Kahikinui is arid, especially in its lower elevations. But rainfall in the higher elevations above 600 m is sufficient to grow sweet potatoes; as one rises higher up the mountain slopes this rainfall is augmented by fog drip precipitation from the cloud inversion layer that regularly forms at midday, captured by the dryland forest. The geologically youthful terrain, especially in the western part of the *moku,* consists mostly of *'a'ā* lava flows of between 3,000 and 130,000 years old, part of the Hāna volcanic series (fig. 12.13). The eastern part of Kahikinui has a slightly older substrate, of the Kula volcanic series, dating to about 225,000 years ago, giving sufficient time for a few narrow gulches to have been incised into the landscape. But these flow only when occasional southerly *kona* storms drench the land. Otherwise, there is no surface water, although there were probably small seeps or springs in places (Stock, Coil, and Kirch 2003). This lava landscape posed serious challenges to Hawaiian farmers.

The marine environment of Kahikinui is equally challenging. Most of the coastline consists of sea cliffs anywhere from a few meters up to 50 m high, limiting access for gathering shellfish or seaweed. Small canoes could be launched from a few coves here and

FIGURE 12.13
Kahikinui District on southeastern Maui Island encompasses the broad leeward slope of Haleakalā, a *kua'āina* or "backcountry" landscape. *(Photo by P. V. Kirch)*

there; the only bay where large canoes might be hauled ashore is at Auwahi, where a concentration of large sites indicates that this was the location of the *konohiki* residence.

Winslow Walker (1930) rode through Kahikinui on horseback in 1929, recording a few of the district's *heiau,* but modern archaeological research did not begin until 1966, when Bishop Museum sent a team under the direction of Peter Chapman (including Kirch, then a young student) to conduct a settlement-pattern survey (see chapter 1). Although more than 500 sites were recorded, and a few excavated (Chapman and Kirch 1979), the 1966 survey was not completed or published. In 1995, Kirch reinitiated archaeological research in Kahikinui, carrying out survey and extensive excavations over the next two decades (Kirch 2014; Kirch, ed., 1997). Additional work was conducted by Dixon, Conte, et al. (1997a, 1999, 2002) in an area designated for a Hawaiian Home Lands rural subdivision, and by Shapiro et al. (2011) in Auwahi *ahupua'a* where a wind-energy farm was developed. In all, 25.2 km² of the *moku* have been intensively surveyed, and 3,058 archaeological features recorded, making Kahikinui one of the most exhaustively researched regions in the islands, even though large parts of the *moku* still remain to be surveyed (fig. 12.14).

Prince Lot, to whom most of Kahikinui was awarded during the Great Māhele, traded the *moku* with the Hawaiian government for other, more desirable lands. Consequently, the boundaries of the district's *ahupua'a* were never surveyed. We know that Auwahi on the west had the status of an *ahupua'a* (for this was separately awarded to Princess Ruth). Likewise Alena and Kīpapa appear on early maps and were probably also *ahupua'a*. Given the lack of natural features such as stream drainages with which to delineate *ahupua'a,* these were probably arbitrary divisions running from the coast to the uplands.

The land section of Kīpapa, near the middle of the district and situated on the younger Hāna series lava flows, has been intensively surveyed, offering a good idea of the overall settlement landscape of Kahikinui. In close proximity to the rugged, barren

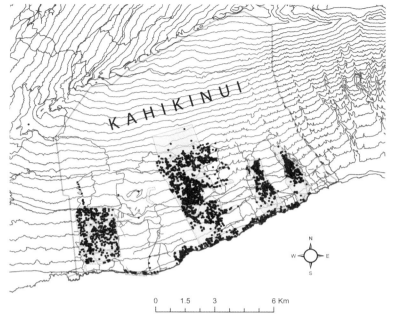

FIGURE 12.14 Map of Kahikinui District on Maui Island, showing areas of archaeological survey (shaded areas) and recorded sites (black dots). Areas not shaded have yet to be surveyed for sites. *(Map by P. V. Kirch)*

coast are a number of walled enclosures, closely following the kerbstone-lined trail that was constructed with convict labor under the direction of Maui governor Hoapili in the 1830s. Excavations in these enclosures revealed that they all date to the nineteenth century. Only a few small structures, some fishing shrines (*koʻa*), and a few coastal *heiau* date to the precontact period; indeed, it appears that the coastal zone was largely uninhabited during precontact times, visited only periodically when the weather permitted fishing or shellfish gathering.

For the most part, the population in Kīpapa and elsewhere in Kahikinui resided in the uplands, above about 600 m in elevation and up to about 900 m, a zone in which rainfall was sufficient to grow sweet potatoes. Kirch et al. (2004, 2005) showed that above 900 m, rain and fog-drip precipitation have leached out much of the nutrient content of the young soils. Thus, the population focused its activities within the "sweet spot" between 600 and 900 m above sea level, where there was sufficient rain to grow crops and the soil nutrients were abundant. In this zone running across the slope of Haleakalā, they "farmed the rock" of these young lava lands.

The farming itself was focused on natural swales or basins formed by the massive *ʻaʻā* lava flows. These swales provide protection from the incessant winds sweeping across Kahikinui, serve as traps for aeolian sediment, and hold moisture longer than the surrounding ridges. Some of the larger swales, as with that *mauka* of Puʻu Hōkū Kano cinder cone, were gridded out in small field systems, with regularly spaced field boundaries (Kirch et al. 2013). Others, such as site KIP-1400, are dotted in dozens of small planting mounds (fig. 12.15). There is little doubt that in this *ʻāina maloʻo* the sweet potato was the dominant crop (Coil and Kirch 2005), although there is some evidence of efforts to divert occasional floodwaters to small-scale fields for growing taro. Carbonized remains of sweet potato tubers were found at a number of the residential sites (Coil and Kirch

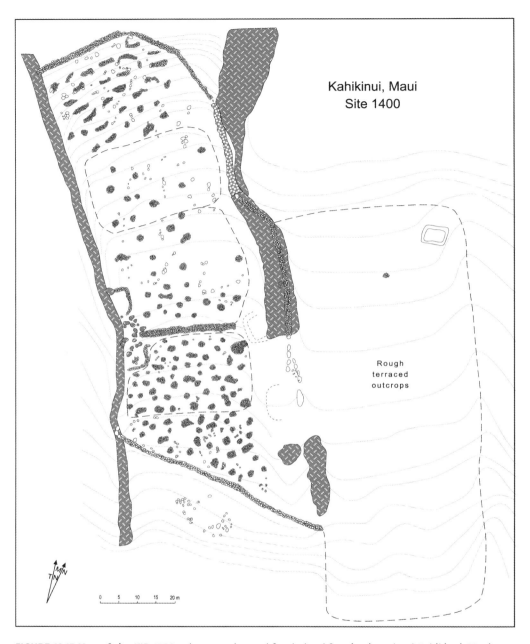

FIGURE 12.15 Map of site KIP-1400, a large swale used for dryland farming in upland Kahikinui, Maui Island. The floor of the swale is covered in numerous stone mounds, and a stone embankment divides the swale into two sections. *(Map by P. V. Kirch)*

2005; Kirch 2014, fig. 23). A stone-lined, semisubterranean pit found at one site may have been used to store seed tubers until they were ready to plant (Kirch 2014, fig. 32).

While planting was concentrated in the swales, the surrounding low ridges or promontories were the setting for *kauhale* that dotted the upland landscape. Two such upland household complexes were excavated by Cindy Van Gilder (2001, 2005), and others were investigated by Kirch (2014). While there is considerable variation in the Kīpapa household sites, there is also an underlying pattern. The structures making up a *kauhale* are typically arrayed along a gently sloping ridge line, with the highest structure in a group usually bearing evidence such as the presence of pig bone and of lithic working, of having served as the *mua*, or men's house. In one of these *mua* a small niche with two waterworn stones presumably served as the household shrine. There is usually a substantial structure, usually consisting of a thick wall about 1 m high and up to 10 or 12 m long, adjoining a low terrace on the leeward (west) side. This thick wall served as a windbreak (the pervasive winds coming from the east), probably anchoring a sloping, thatched roof sheltering the protected terrace. In two such *hale noa* there were dual stone-lined hearths, suggesting that a variant of the *'ai kapu* or separate cooking of food was practiced within the common dwelling (see chapter 10). Other smaller structures within these complexes were cookhouses with earth ovens, or storage houses.

Kua'āina folks though they may have been, the Kahikinui people did not neglect their gods. Numerous *heiau* are distributed across the *moku*, ranging from small *ko'a* and agricultural shrines up to substantial temples (fig. 12.16). The temple system in Kahikinui is one of the best studied anywhere in the islands, due to the intensive research of Kirch and Ruggles (2019), as summarized in chapter 11. Most of the upland *heiau* appear to be *ho'oulu'ai*, agricultural temples, although in architectural form they range from notched enclosures, to square and open U-shaped enclosures, to elongated double-court forms. Of particular note is a complex of temples clustered together on a prominent ridge in the Naka'ohu area (fig. 12.17). Four temples, each of a different type, are arrayed along the ridgeline (sites 404, 75, 115, and 77), along with an oven house (site 76) for cooking offerings. To the west of the temples is the house of a priest (site 117) and what appears to be an assembly area (sites 118 and 119). The entire complex forms a kind of "acropolis" in which each temple was probably dedicated to a different god.

FIGURE 12.16 Aerial view of site KIP-1010 in the uplands of Kahikini, Maui Island. These two adjacent notched *heiau* are together the largest temple site in the district. *(Photo by P. V. Kirch)*

FIGURE 12.17 Map of the *heiau* complex in upland Naka'ohu, Kahiknui, Maui Island. *(Map by P. V. Kirch)*

As noted in chapter 10, the Kahikinui inhabitants inscribed the land with numerous petroglyphs. Most of these are anthropomorphs, although some dog figures and other motifs are present. As Millerstrom and Kirch (2004) argue, the association of many of the petroglyph clusters with ephemeral stream channels suggests that family groups may have been marking or claiming these vital water resources.

Lapakahi, Hawai'i

Lapakahi, just south of the old port of Māhukona, is one of many narrow *ahupua'a* that bisect the steep slopes of North Kohala. It is a typical wedge-shaped *ahupua'a*, about 1.3 km wide at the coast and 7 km deep. The *ahupua'a* was the focus of a University of Hawai'i project, initiated by Richard Pearson and Roger Green in 1968, one of the first in the islands to take an entire *ahupua'a* as the unit of archaeological study. Lapakahi and other land units in this region crosscut three distinct settlement zones. Along the coast and for a short distance inland is a relatively dense settlement zone, with numerous habitation sites and burial features. At Lapakahi, the most substantial of these features form a nucleated hamlet around Koaiʻe inlet. Inland of this coastal strip, the next 1 to 2 km are relatively barren, largely because this lowland zone has insufficient rainfall to support agriculture. Between about 2 and 4 km inland is the intensive zone of agricultural features known as the leeward Kohala Field System, dominated by a reticulate grid of field boundaries (see chapter 7). Interspersed among these fields are minor agricultural features as well as residential sites, largely C-shaped shelters of various forms and dimensions.

During the several seasons of the Lapakahi Project, the entire *ahupuaʻa* was mapped using aerial photography (Newman, n.d.), the coastal strip and selected upland sections were mapped on the ground, and excavations were carried out in both coastal and upland settlement zones, making Lapakahi one of the archaeologically best-known leeward areas in the islands (Pearson, ed., 1968; Rosendahl 1972a, 1994; Tuggle and Griffin, eds., 1973).

David Tuggle and P. Bion Griffin (1973, 61–64) outlined a cultural sequence for Lapakahi, with a chronology based on both radiocarbon and hydration-rind dates. The first use of the area was in the Late Voyaging Period about AD 1300, with a small settlement on the coast at Koaiʻe, seemingly focused on marine exploitation (fig. 12.18). Between about AD 1450 and 1500 two major events occurred. First was the expansion of settlement into the upland agricultural zone, and initial development of the pattern of dryland field cropping. Second was the construction of a major boundary wall (called the "Great Wall" in the Lapakahi reports) and of several substantial platforms in Koaiʻe hamlet. Tuggle and Griffin interpreted these events in sociopolitical terms: "The platform complex, the Great Wall as a symbolic boundary, the amount of labor involved in the construction of the Great Wall and the agricultural exploitation of the upland region all argue for a consolidation of Lapakahi as a distinct social and political unit around AD 1500" (1973, 63). Throughout the sixteenth and seventeenth centuries, settlement continued to expand along the coast from the Koaiʻe hamlet, while the upland field system was gradually intensified. According to Tuggle and Griffin, "It is probable that increasing population

FIGURE 12.18 View of a portion of Koaiʻe village site at Lapakahi, Hawaiʻi Island. The sites are clustered around a small inlet on the coast. *(Photo by Therese Babineau)*

and the production demands of a stratified social system forced continual expansion of the subsistence system" (63). The Lapakahi settlement landscape did not persist long after European contact, however; following rapid contraction of agricultural production, the area was largely abandoned by AD 1825.

Lapakahi settlement patterns can be divided into three major zones. First is a narrow band of sites, concentrated within the first 100 to 200 m inland of the shoreline. These include permanent residential sites, burial platforms, fishing shrines, canoe houses, and other structures. There is a particularly dense concentration of sites at Koaiʻe Inlet, near the middle of the *ahupuaʻa* coastline. At Koaiʻe, a large wall and several substantial platforms have been interpreted as the residential complex of one or more high-ranking households, presumably those of the chief or *konohiki* of Lapakahi. The second settlement zone is a largely barren tract, beginning just inland of the coastal strip and continuing for about 2.5 km inland. Virtually the only archaeological features in this barren zone (where rainfall is not sufficient for agriculture) are several trails that lead from the coast to the agricultural fields in the uplands. The third zone consists of the extensive dryland fields, described in chapter 7. Field embankments divide the landscape into a grid of elongate, rectangular units, dominating the upland zone (fig. 12.19). The zone is furthermore subdivided into narrow, parallel strips by seven trails, and each of these strips probably constituted a separate *ʻili*, or subdivision of the *ahupuaʻa*. A variety of minor agricultural features, water-catchment devices, animal pens and enclosures, and C- and L-shaped residential features are dispersed throughout the upland agricultural zone. Paul Rosendahl's excavations in several residential features suggested repeated, seasonal use (fig. 12.20).

In his detailed survey of two of the narrow *ʻili* segments of the upland zone, Rosendahl (1972a) discovered two religious features, one in each *ʻili*, that appear to have been agricultural temples or men's houses, comparable to the temples seen in Kapana, Hālawa, and to the stepped-terrace temples of Mākaha.

On the coast, Tuggle and Griffin (eds., 1973, 22) were conservative in their classification of features as temples, only reporting two *heiau*, one just north of Koaiʻe (site 50-10-04-4682), and the other to the south (site 50-10-04-4117). They describe site 50-10-04-4682 as a "massive platform" (18 × 7.5 m), about 400 m from the hamlet, constructed with large boulders on the edge of a gully with a downslope face that is up to 2 m high (Tuggle and Griffin 1973, 16). Several possible postholes, presumably the former locations of carved images, were observed. Site -4117 is oriented to the northeast (60°) and thus may have been dedicated to Lono.

Recently, high-resolution drone imagery recorded architecture over the entirety of Lapakahi State Park, a region that spans well beyond the Koaiʻe hamlet, and was accomplished in just a few days (M. D. McCoy, Ladefoged, and Casana 2020). Most of the architectural details that appear on the plane table maps made during the Lapakahi Project are visible in this imagery. Remote sensing is, however, not a substitute for ground survey. In 2019, a GPS field resurvey of Lapakahi was initiated to create a rich and scalable database (Johnson and McCoy 2020). The results will allow Koaiʻe Inlet to be placed in the broader context of coastal settlement. Accounting for the variety in size and distribution of households is fundamental to addressing two critical aspects of settlement: population size and social inequality.

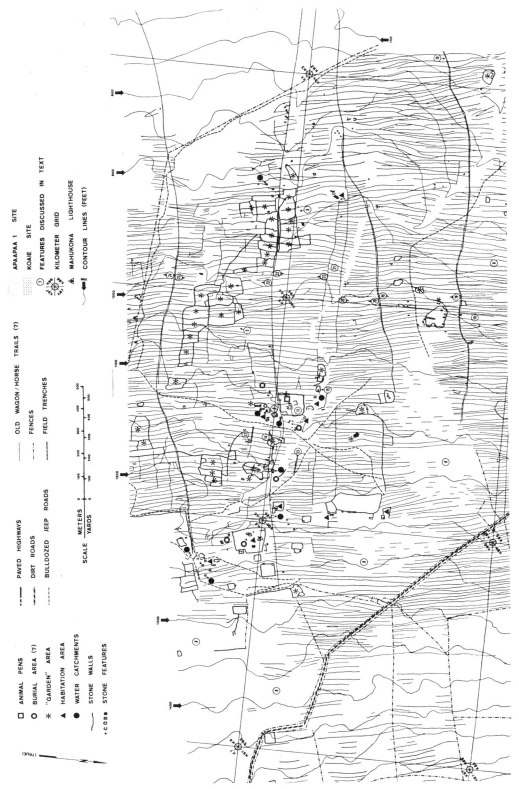

FIGURE 12.19 Map of a portion of the upland field system in Lapakahi *ahupua'a*, Hawai'i Island, showing the grid of field embankments, trails, residential features, and other sites. *(After Newman, n.d.)*

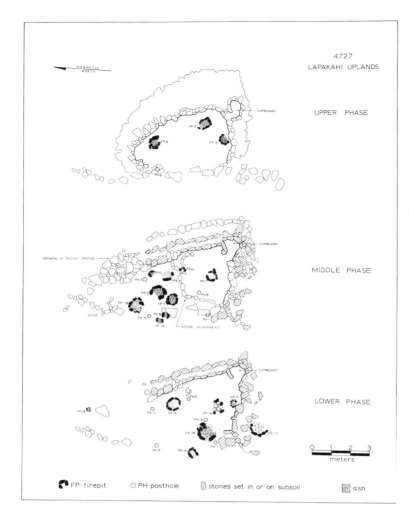

FIGURE 12.20 Plan showing three phases in the use of site 4727, a field shelter in the uplands of Lapakahi, Hawai'i Island. Excavation of the shelter revealed a complex history of repeated use, indicated by multiple fireplaces (FP) and postholes (PH). *(After Rosendahl 1972a)*

Redating of the coastal Lapakahi settlement using contemporary AMS radiocarbon methods and Bayesian calibration using samples from the legacy collections of the original Lapakahi Project may help resolve the chronology of the windward to leeward expansion on Hawai'i Island. It has been proposed that as population increased settlements expanded "laterally along the shoreline" out of core areas with each generation reaping the rewards of staking a claim on unoccupied lands, but also taking on more and more risk than previous generations faced (Hommon 2013, 226). For Hawai'i Island, Pololū Valley fits our expectations for early settlement (ca. AD 1200), with ample rainfall suitable for irrigated agriculture. Between AD 1300 and 1400, irrigated farming commenced in the windward gulches of Kohala, along with the earliest farming on the leeward slopes.

The best previous studies of settlement expansion, which have controlled for chronology and markers of permanent settlement, have occurred in either windward or leeward environments, but not in the transition zone between these environments. Lapakahi sits just on the leeward side of the windward to leeward transition in Kohala. Dates from the Lapakahi Project support the hypothesis that for generations people gradually took on slightly greater risks—occupying Lapakahi around AD 1300, and later down the coast—until there were no more unoccupied lands. This is plausible, but there are alternatives. It is possible, for example, that there were early failed attempts to settle these lands that predate the full expansion into leeward environments. It is also possible that, rather than an incremental increase in risk, people actively avoided these areas until something changed in their risk-reward calculations and within a few generations all unoccupied lands were settled. Developing a well-dated chronology for archaeological sites at the transition from windward to leeward environments would provide evidence with which to accept or reject these hypotheses.

The five settlement landscapes described above illustrate some—though by no means all—of the variation to be found across the Hawaiian archipelago. Much of this variation can be ascribed to regional differences in environment, reflective of the environmental diversity that is so notable in the islands. Dryland field systems on geologically younger leeward slopes, pondfield irrigation and colluvial slope farming in the valleys of the older islands, fishponds along shores protected by fringing reefs: these were all adaptive responses to the constraints and opportunities posed by varied natural landscapes. Other differences in settlement patterns may be due to local social or cultural variation in the communities that ranged from Hawai'i to Kaua'i, such as differences in the layout of *heiau* foundations. Hawaiian culture was not entirely uniform across the archipelago, as we know from variations in material culture. Yet broad similarities are also evident, including the organization of settlement according to the hierarchy of *moku, ahupua'a, 'ili*, and smaller land units. The comparative study of settlement landscapes offers many insights into life in ancient Hawai'i.

13

TRANSFORMATIONS
The Archaeology of Culture Contact and Colonialism

By 1795, the year in which Kamehameha conquered the opposing armies of Oʻahu and Maui at the renowned battle of Nuʻuanu Pali, Hawaiian culture was firmly in the grip of forces that would inexorably alter the fabric of life in the islands. Northwest Coast fur traders were calling regularly in the islands for food and "refreshments." In a few years, the sandalwood trade would turn Hawaiʻi into a major port of call for Western entrepreneurs. Chiefs and commoners alike avidly sought all manner of foreign dress and goods to the extent that they could acquire such exotic items.

Many aspects of the old cultural order lingered on through the first two decades of the nineteenth century, but the death of Kamehameha in 1819 marked the passing of an era. The *kapu* system was abolished when Kamehameha's widow Kaʻahumanu induced the young king Liholiho (Kamehameha II) to partake of a meal together with a number of the chiefly women. In the following year, 1820, the first company of American Protestant missionaries arrived on the brig *Thaddeus*. A Hawaiian orthography was soon prepared, the Bible translated, laws passed and printed; the Hawaiian people avidly embraced reading and writing. By midcentury, the fledgling kingdom undertook the single most significant inducement to cultural change, the Great Māhele or division of lands between the king, chiefs, and government, establishing land ownership on a Western-style, fee-simple basis. From this momentous act, an entire restructuring of the ancient social, economic, and political order followed.

We end the Archaic States Period of our cultural sequence for Hawaiʻi at the year 1795, with Kamehameha's consolidation of political power. By this time the islands' written record becomes substantial, largely due to the accounts and logs of ship captains and explorers. After the development of a Hawaiian orthography in the early 1820s, the volume of historical documents increases exponentially. Given these abundant records, synthesized in many carefully researched and scholarly works, one may ask what archaeology has to contribute to an understanding of postcontact Hawaiian history? The answer is a great deal, for several reasons. Although historical archaeology has not received as much emphasis in Hawaiʻi as the archaeology of the precontact periods, the field has much potential to add to our knowledge of the last two centuries of Hawaiian history, a period of transformation and restructuring of Hawaiian culture in response to foreign intrusion, and of the creation of the multiethnic society of modern Hawai'i.

James Deetz, a pioneer of historical archaeology in North America, defined the field as the study of "cultural remains of literate societies that were capable of recording their own history" (1977, 5). While literate societies do leave written accounts of themselves, such documents reflect only a fraction of what people in these societies actually did, what they believed about their world, and how they regarded and interacted with their neighbors. Many people in literate societies were in fact unable to write, and even among those who did record events, a great deal was passed over as inconsequential, irrelevant, uninteresting—or perhaps too scandalous—or for some other reason was not recorded. But most of these people left material traces of one sort or another, remains that are amenable to the methods of archaeological discovery and analysis and that can help to fill in gaps in the documentary sources. In short, we cannot learn all that we want to know about Hawaiian history from documentary records alone. As Deetz wrote, "In spite of the richness and diversity of the historical record, there are things we want to know that are not to be discovered from it. Simple people doing simple things, the normal, everyday routine of life and how these people thought about it, are not the kinds of things anyone thought worthy of recording" (8).

Historical archaeology in Hawai'i can help to clarify the dramatic changes in the life of indigenous Hawaiians, particularly during the early and middle years of the nineteenth century. Most orthodox Hawaiian history has been written either from the viewpoint of the *ali'i*—the high chiefs and Hawaiian monarchs who quickly adopted foreign ways and attitudes—or from the viewpoint of the increasingly dominant foreigners, whether missionaries, traders, whalers, or sugar planters. Hawaiian history is usually presented as a pageant of royal successions, judicial acts, business ventures, and the like, promulgated by a handful of native and foreign elites. Less often are questions asked concerning the great majority of the Hawaiian people, the farmers and fishermen residing far away from Kailua, Lahaina, and Honolulu. How did they respond to the changes that shaped and molded their daily lives? What role did they play in this historical pageant? Archaeological study of the remains left by these people offers an opportunity to write a more "populist" view of Hawaiian history, a view from bottom up rather than from the eyes and pens of the literate elite. Without attempting a comprehensive review of historical archaeological work in Hawai'i (such as numerous CRM reports that deal with postcontact sites and cultural deposits in Honolulu and other urbanized areas), in this chapter we summarize a few key studies that demonstrate the potential of archaeological research on the postcontact period.

From Stone to Steel: Changes in Material Culture

From the moment of first contact with the British ships of Cook's third expedition, the Hawaiians eagerly sought to acquire Western material goods. Although no natural deposits of iron ore exist in the islands, Cook's expedition observed that the Hawaiians already had a knowledge of iron (Stokes 1931). They had most likely encountered occasional iron objects such as nails and fittings that were attached to driftwood arriving on the islands' beaches, the remains of Japanese or Korean or perhaps even Spanish shipwrecks in the North Pacific.

(Claims have been made for a pre-Cook Spanish discovery of Hawai'i, but no firm evidence for this has ever been put forward [Stokes 1932, 597].) During their stay at Kealakekua Bay, Cook and his crew traded considerable iron to the Hawaiians; Cook himself is reputed to have been stabbed with one of his own iron daggers (or a bayonet) during the fatal skirmish on the rocks at Ka'awaloa.

In 1786, the advent of the Northwest Coast–Canton fur trade, with Hawai'i as a provisioning stop, brought an increasing succession of small trading vessels to the islands, and with them increased opportunities for both chiefs and commoners to obtain foreign goods (Kirch and Sahlins 1992, 1:37–45). The chiefs more than anything wanted guns, powder, and other armament, such as small cannon, which would give them an advantage in the interisland wars of conquest that were raging at the time. After Kamehameha's reconquest of O'ahu in 1804, however, and especially after the onset of the sandalwood trade beginning in 1812, the range of items sought by the Hawaiians expanded greatly. The *ali'i*, in particular, leveraged the sandalwood trade to engage in a "political economy of grandeur" in which the chiefs competed with each other in the acquisition and display of all manner of exotic luxury goods (Sahlins 1990). As Marshall Sahlins writes,

> The *ali'i* turned to an unrestrained competition among themselves in conspicuous accumulation and consumption, using the sandalwood resources they now detained. In this they had the full collaboration of a growing number of resident traders, agents of Boston firms. Urged on by the complementary competition among the merchants, the chiefs decked themselves out in every shape and form of Polynesian flash that could be devised from the deluxe exports of China and New England. (Kirch and Sahlins, 1992, 1:57)

Lacking the same means as the chiefs, the commoners were slower to acquire Western goods, but some kinds of objects, such as glass beads (often traded by visiting sailors in exchange for sex) and iron adze blades, were highly sought after by the *maka'āinana*. By the mid-nineteenth century, many traditional artifacts, such as stone adzes, were already becoming rare. Jim Bayman (2003; Bayman and Dye 2013, 101–104) discusses the transition from stone to iron adzes over the course of the first few decades of the nineteenth century. Stone adzes were already rare in Honolulu by 1825 but continued to be used in certain rural areas such as Waimea, Hawai'i, as late as 1847 (Bayman and Dye 2013, 103). William T. Brigham (1902, 408, 415) dates the last use of the traditional stone adze to around 1864.

In the Anahulu Valley, Kirch traced the movement of Western goods into a rural O'ahu community from the early contact period through the later nineteenth century in artifact assemblages from a series of rockshelters and terraced habitation sites (Kirch and Sahlins 1992, 2:179–182). In the sites of the early postcontact period, the main foreign items present are glass beads, gun flints, fragments of bottle glass (often flaked), and miscellaneous pieces of iron. Sites dating to the 1820s and 1830s contain a wider range of objects, including ceramics, a diversity of bottles, iron nails as well as other metal objects, items of personal adornment, and clothing (such as buttons and buckles). These later sites also contain fragments of slate, derived from the slate tablets distributed by the missionaries in the local schools where reading and writing was taught. Habitation sites of the post-Māhele period, such as those of the old Anahulu residents Kainiki and Kamakea, "now incorporated in their construction iron nails as well as glass windows and doors with iron hinges and locks" (2:181–182). These families possessed "a variety of plates and dishes, bottles and jars of various shapes and contents, Western-style clothing, saddle gear, iron cooking pots, axes, razors, scissors, marbles, even cologne from Paris" (2:182).

Similar trends in the replacement of traditional Hawaiian material culture with Western artifacts are evidenced in other rural areas. Summer Moore (2020a, 2020b) analyzed artifacts of foreign origin excavated from the upper levels of the Nuʻalolo rockshelter on Kauaʻi Island (see chapter 6). As in the Anahulu Valley, at Nuʻalolo "the earliest foreign artefacts were non-essential household goods such as glass beads and other small sundry items," obtained by trade with ships' crews either directly "or through intermediaries via local trade networks" (2020b, 225). More recent levels display a greater diversity of foreign goods, but in this rural area "residents of these house sites continued to use foreign goods in minimal numbers for nearly a century" after first contact (227). James Flexner et al. (2018) examined foreign artifacts recovered from excavations in a series of primarily coastal habitation sites in leeward Kohala, Hawaiʻi Island. Three broad periods of foreign artifact assimilation into these household sites are evidenced: "One representing early moments of culture contact during which foreign trade was dominated by elites and some imported objects may have been used in ritual contexts; a transitional phase where commoners began incorporating foreign objects into daily life more regularly but largely maintained traditional ways; and a third phase of consumer practices when foreign consumer goods became basically ubiquitous in Hawaiʻi" (34).

The Transformation of Rural Landscapes

The changes that swept through Hawaiian society following the arrival of Europeans and the engagement of Hawaiʻi with the "World System" are often best represented in the rural, hinterland, or *kuaʻāina* regions, because these have been least affected by later developments of the twentieth and twenty-first centuries. The Anahulu Valley Project grew out of a long-term ethnohistorical and anthropological study of the early history of the Hawaiian Kingdom (Kirch and Sahlins 1992). Initiated by Sahlins with collaboration from Dorothy Barrère and Marion Kelly, this study drew upon the extensive historical documents of the early nineteenth century, including the records of the Hawaiian government, and on documents pertaining to the Māhele (the records of the Board of Commissioners to Quiet Land Titles; see Chinen 1958). These documents contained a wealth of previously untapped information that, when interpreted anthropologically, permit a reconstruction of the social and economic organization of Hawaiian life in the early decades of the nineteenth century. Among the areas with especially rich documentation is Waialua *moku* of Oʻahu, including the *ahupuaʻa* of Kawailoa and its central geographic feature, the Anahulu Valley.

The lands of Waialua, including Kawailoa, were given by Kamehameha (following his conquest of Oʻahu) to the high chief Keʻeaumoku, and thence to Kaʻahumanu, the famous *kuhina nui* or "regent" of the early Hawaiian Kingdom. These lands subsequently passed to Kīnaʻu (Kaʻahumanu II), and then to Victoria Kamāmalu during the Māhele (Kirch and Sahlins 1992, vol. 1, fig. 2.2). Rich in irrigated taro and fishponds, Waialua provided much of the material support for the ruling chiefs who formed the early Hawaiian government. The Protestant missionary John S. Emerson established a station at the mouth of the Anahulu Valley (in what is now Haleʻiwa town) in 1832; the records of that enterprise (correspondence, journals, church records of marriages, births, deaths, baptisms, etc.) add greatly to our knowledge of historical events in Waialua. Emerson was a staunch advocate of the commoners, and in 1848 helped to assure that the *makaʻāinana* made well-documented claims on their cultivated lands and house lots. Thus, the Māhele records for Anahulu (claims, testimony, awards, and surveys) are particularly rich, permitting a detailed reconstruction of economic production and land rights that can be cartographically tied to specific archaeological sites (fig. 13.1).

An initial survey (Kirch 1979b) revealed that the Anahulu Valley exhibited an intact archaeological landscape, with many house platforms and irrigation systems that could be directly correlated with Māhele era land claims. With support from a National Science Foundation grant to Bishop Museum, in 1982 a 7-km-long segment of the middle and upper valley was intensively studied. Investigation of the numerous irrigation systems that had been the subject of Māhele claims provided information on their construction sequences, estimates of yield and potential surplus, and allocation of water, elucidating details that could not be obtained from the historical records. Habitation sites formerly occupied by commoners of various social status were mapped and excavated (fig. 13.2), yielding examples of the changing mix of indigenous and foreign material culture. The house site excavations revealed how patterns of house construction and use of space changed over the course of the early to mid-nineteenth century. Excavations were also carried out at four rockshelters, adding a precontact dimension to the valley's sequence. The results of the Anahulu Valley Project were reported in two companion volumes by Kirch and Sahlins (1992), a publication awarded the Staley Prize in anthropology for its unique collaboration between ethnohistory and archaeology.

The middle and upper reaches of the Anahulu Valley exhibit signs of human land use as early as the Expansion Period (fifteenth century), but this region remained a hinterland throughout the precontact era, until Kamehameha's conquest of Oʻahu in 1795. Rockshelter excavations (Kirch, ed., 1989) indicate that the interior valley was used for shifting cultivation and forest exploitation at a low level of intensity. Following Kamehameha's conquest and the reapportionment of the Waialua lands to Keʻeaumoku, the settlement pattern and land use in the middle and upper Anahulu Valley changed dramatically. Early in the nineteenth century, probably immediately following the reoccupation of Oʻahu by Kamehameha's troops in 1804, the middle valley was permanently settled by a number of households. Residential sites were constructed on the colluvial slopes, while the alluvial flats were terraced for taro cultivation. This phase of agricultural intensification can be correlated with the historically documented period of agricultural development on Oʻahu during Kamehameha's residence (1804–1812).

Between about 1810 and 1829, the Hawaiian chiefs focused their political economy on the exploitation of sandalwood, with traders incessantly plying the route between

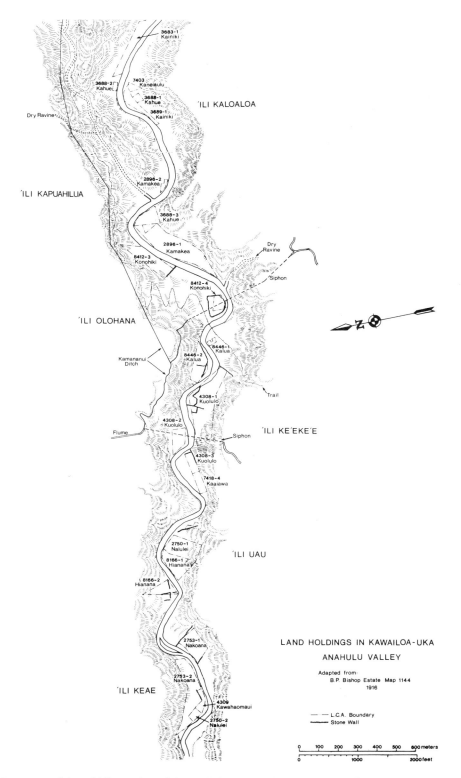

FIGURE 13.1 Map of the middle portion of the Anahulu Valley, Oʻahu Island, showing the locations of Māhele-era land claims distributed across several ʻili land sections. *(Map by P. V. Kirch)*

FIGURE 13.2 The foundations of Kalua's house site (Oa-D6-38) in the Anahulu Valley, O'ahu Island, after excavation. Kalua was a resident of the middle valley and Māhele claimant. *(Photo by P. V. Kirch)*

Hawai'i and Canton. In the Anahulu Valley, this period is reflected by a disintensification of the middle valley production system, evidenced by the abandonment of several residential complexes that had been established after Kamehameha's conquest. Waialua was a major scene of sandalwood cutting in the interior forests, with the commoner population bearing the brunt of the labor required for these commercial activities, working at times for weeks in the mountains, neglecting their taro fields and other gardens.

When the sandalwood trade collapsed abruptly in 1829, the chiefs—having accumulated a substantial debt—returned to their earlier economic strategy of provisioning visiting ships, in this case to the rapidly increasing number of whalers that wintered in the islands. These increased demands for agricultural production (e.g., for *wauke* bark to use as caulking material in ships' hulls) again find their reflections in the ethnohistoric and archaeological records of the Anahulu Valley. The Māhele land claims indicate that several new cultivators were given lands in the valley by the *konohiki* in the early 1830s, often in areas abandoned during the preceding sandalwood phase. The archaeological evidence from both residential sites and irrigation systems confirms this renewed intensification of production. In 'Ili Kaloaloa, stratigraphic evidence confirms a restructuring of the irrigation system, with rearrangement of the main canal to accommodate the newly emplaced cultivators. The 1830s and 1840s witnessed the arrival of the Protestant mission and increased arrival of foreign material culture and ideas.

The division of lands between 1848 and 1854, and the shift to a cash taxation system (from one based on labor), drastically altered the Hawaiian social and economic system. The hierarchical relationships between chiefs and commoners, so closely tied to the system of land rights, rapidly disintegrated; *maka'āinana* cultivators were forced increasingly into the market economy in order to meet tax demands and other obligations. This decay of the old social and economic order is reflected in the gradual abandonment of the Anahulu Valley landscape throughout the later years of the nineteenth century. By about 1890, the last households were gone, the irrigation fields given over to weeds, and the *kuleana* titles sold to the expanding sugar plantations eager to obtain clear title to the valley's water rights.

Elsewhere on Oʻahu, archaeological excavations at three historic-period sites, conducted by Dorothy Riconda (1972), constituted one aspect of the Mākaha Valley Historical Project (Green 1980). In the Mākaha Project, a main objective was to discriminate historic-period sites from those of the precontact era, to assist in the reconstruction of the indigenous settlement pattern. The three sites investigated included the residence of the Waianae Company plantation manager (which yielded such artifacts as Lokelani-style ceramics from Staffordshire, popular in late nineteenth-century Hawaiʻi), a stone-walled house that may have been occupied by an Asian immigrant family, and another late nineteenth-century residence that could not be identified with regard to occupants. Although the ethnohistoric record for Mākaha is not as rich as that for Anahulu, further historical archaeology in the valley could provide an interesting and parallel sequence of historical transformation.

Pia-Kristina Anderson (2001) combined ethnohistorical documentary research with archaeological survey to investigate nineteenth- and early twentieth-century household settlement patterns in the Hālawa Valley, Molokaʻi. The traditional pattern of *ʻili* running from the stream up to the higher colluvial slopes became codified through the Māhele land claims, although the *heiau* that had been the ritual foci of these *ʻili* were now abandoned, replaced by Congregational and Catholic churches near the valley mouth. Although she did not excavate, Anderson mapped many of the historic-period house platforms and identified the surface assemblages of postcontact artifacts associated with these sites. A high percentage of ceramic bowls on these sites was interpreted by Anderson as indicative of "the continued centrality of *poi* in the Hawaiian diet" (301).

Other research focusing on the historic period has contributed to understanding of life on Molokaʻi Island during the Hawaiian Kingdom (Flexner 2010, 2011a, 2011b, 2012). When the Gold Rush hit California in 1849, the shortage of provisions in San Francisco led enterprising ships' captains to sail to Hawaiʻi in search of cargoes of sweet potatoes to feed the hungry miners. Research stemming from a CRM project involving realignment of the small airport runway at Kalaupapa gave a detailed picture of an 1840–1850s farmstead and associated gardens that supplied ships bound for California (Goodwin 1994; Ladefoged 1990). In 1866, the peninsula was designated by the kingdom as a quarantined settlement for those afflicted with leprosy, or Hansen's disease. Flexner (2010) studied the remains of the initial settlement of those forcibly exiled to Molokaʻi, at Kalawao on the eastern side of the peninsula (occupied from 1866 to 1900, when it was moved to the west side). He interpreted material evidence from the household rubbish of people diagnosed with Hansen's disease as supporting the notion that in spite of their forced imprisonment, the patients formed a familiar social organization not unlike other contemporary Hawaiian villages. Flexner also discusses how sites of religious ritual first created in the precontact era were treated by people living in Kalawao in the late nineteenth century (Flexner 2010, 2012; Flexner and McCoy 2016). Flexner found, for example, that while the traditional religious system had been abolished for nearly 50 years prior to the first patients' arrival, *heiau* sites did not have the dense scatters of historic-era artifacts found elsewhere throughout the settlement, suggestive of some combination of avoidance and/or cleaning. Nonetheless, the stone foundations of a *heiau* in Kalawao appear to have been robbed of all but its largest

FIGURE 13.3 Aerial view of the small hamlet of Uliuli in Kahikinui, Maui, where the last Native Hawaiian residents of the district attempted to resist the depredations of rancher Manuel Pico's marauding cattle at the end of the nineteenth century. *(Photo by P. V. Kirch)*

stones for the construction of the church and / or churchyard wall built by the Belgian priest Saint Damien de Veuster; but Flexner also notes that another *heiau* not far away was left untouched (Flexner and McCoy 2016).

Kirch's research in Kahikinui District of southeast Maui provides another case study of postcontact changes in a rural landscape (Kirch 2014, 213–257), in this instance one traditionally dominated by dryland sweet potato cultivation. The first material signs of contact with the Western world are small numbers of glass beads, chert flints or "strike-a-lights," iron or copper nails, and a few scraps of iron hoop (items commonly traded during the first decades of the nineteenth century) that appear in *kauhale* sites alongside traditional artifacts. In the 1820s, Maui's governor Hoapili ordered the construction of a horse trail (Apple's Type B, see chapter 10) along the southeast Maui coastline, in turn encouraging the construction of new residential sites adjacent to this trail (previously, habitation had been almost exclusively in the uplands). A stone-walled schoolhouse was also built near the trail, probably following the edict of Ka'ahumanu in 1824 that the people should all study the new *palapala,* or writing introduced by the Protestant missionaries.

Although Kahikinui witnessed significant depopulation (probably due as much to out-migration as to mortality), some families held on into the later part of the nineteenth century. Most of these had adopted the Catholic faith, with a small upland village now concentrated near the stone-walled chapel named St. Ynez church. At least one of these, possibly the local church leader Simeon Kaoao, built his house within a *heiau* in the Kīpapa uplands, doubtless as a demonstration of his faith in the new god (Kirch 2014, 229–241).

The end of traditional Hawaiian farming in the Kahikinui uplands came rapidly after 1876, when Portuguese rancher Manuel Pico obtained a lease from the Hawaiian government on the *moku* of Kahikinui. The stone remains of a windmill platform, water pump, and cattle trough built by Pico adjacent to the small hamlet of Uliuli are silent testimony to the 250 head of cattle he was running over these lands by 1887 (fig. 13.3). In 1929, Winslow Walker, during his survey of southeast Maui archaeological sites, was told that the last Hawaiians had finally abandoned the little settlement at Uliuli around 1895 (Kirch 2014, 242).

The Archaeology of Colonialism

While much of the archaeological record of the postcontact period in Hawai'i is focused on the rural hinterlands, such as the Anahulu Valley or Kahikinui, Maui, some sites relate directly to major political events that were central to the history of colonialism in the islands. Beginning in 1798, John Young, one of Kamehameha's first European advisors, took up residence at Kawaihae; between 1802 and 1812 he held the position of governor of Hawai'i Island. After first living close to the shore, Young built a permanent homestead on the slopes above Pu'ukoholā Heiau where he lived with his high-born Kānaka Maoli wives and children. In 1978, excavations were conducted at this homestead, aimed at recovering material to confirm that it was in fact the residence of the Young family. Not surprisingly, a large amount of imported material was recovered, as well as a substantial assemblage of food remains. Paul Rosendahl and Laura Carter (1988) also report the recovery of a whale tooth pendent (*lei niho palaoa*) and of worked whale tooth pieces. It is not clear to whom in the household this symbol of high rank belonged.

Further research on the John Young homestead has provided more detail on the household layout and midden composition (Durst 2002). Research has focused on resolving John Young's own description of his home, and the descriptions of visitors, with the foundations that remain in the upper portion of the homestead. Young wrote in his diary (1798–1799), "Have begun four buildings. My house the cook house and storage room the house for the children and tahus and near the small temple a house for storage." There is some debate over how many individual buildings he is referring to, but most agree that this description is referring to the upper portion of his property, with the reference to "the small heiau" referring to one of the temples in the main complex downslope (*makai*) of his homestead. It is presumed his high-born wives resided in the lower portion of the estate which has unfortunately been affected by modern construction.

Rosendahl and Carter (1988) assigned each building foundation an archaeological identifier making a distinction between plastered "structures" (S1, S2, etc.) and unplastered "features" (F1, F2, etc.) built in the traditional Hawaiian style of nonmasonry stonework. The largest building (Structure 1) is interpreted as the main house, where in his later years Young resided on his own (ca. 1830). One visitor described it as "adorned with old rusty muskets, swords, bayonets, and cartridge boxes" (Laura Judd cited in Durst 2002). There are some references to later occupants of the house, but we presume that the compound was largely abandoned not long after Young retired to Honolulu. Near the main house is another well-built plaster building (Structure 2). Structure 2 was thoroughly investigated including

72 m² of excavations inside and around it; based on the richness of artifacts excavated the building north of the main house is interpreted as the storehouse. Other portions of the compound are more difficult to interpret. Feature 3 appears to be the cookhouse on the side of the compound with the children's house, a terraced area that may correspond to an area for shade (*malu*) (Feature 2) in front of the main house.

The artifacts recovered from John Young's compound have mainly been used to confirm the identity of the site based on the age of the imported goods discarded there, and to a lesser degree as reflecting status and *kapu*. As Kamehameha's advisor, and the husband of high-born women, it stands to reason that Young would have been treated in the same way as a high chief. Durst (2002) notes that the small excavations in the main house uncovered bones of *ulua* (*Caranx* sp.), a fish reserved for elite men. Young (1798–1799) reports Kamehameha I as having dined at Young's home, another sign that this compound was regarded as the home of a high-ranking elite.

In Honolulu, several CRM projects associated with urban renewal efforts have opened a window on life in the fledgling town that arose just east of the Nuʻuanu River after Kamehameha I established his royal center there in 1804, following his reconquest of Oʻahu (see chapter 11). Conrad Goodwin et al. (1996) investigated a city block bounded by Maunakea, King, and Smith Streets, and Nimitz Highway. Historical documents indicate that this block incorporated the property occupied by Don Francisco de Paula Marin, an advisor to King Kamehameha I and influential figure in early Honolulu. Marin built a stone house here, and his descendants occupied the property until about 1860. Excavations revealed a number of trash pits, cooking hearths, and other features associated with the Marin household, as well as a small burial ground; the deceased were interred in wooden coffins and were most likely members of Marin's family. Artifacts associated with the period when the Marin family occupied the site include traditional Hawaiian items as well as imported goods from Europe, North America, and Asia. Much of the block was later occupied by the Honolulu Iron Works, which produced machinery for the rapidly expanding sugar plantation industry of the later nineteenth and early twentieth centuries. Goodwin et al. (1996) investigated most of another block bounded by King, Maunakea, Hotel, and Kekaulike Streets in Honolulu's Chinatown. More than 100 subsurface features were exposed, most of them associated with residences from the early years of Western contact and from the first 50 years of Chinese immigration. This was followed by more extensive work on the block, reported by Conrad Goodwin and Jane Allen (2005), who describe the excavation of deposits associated with several house sites dating to the Māhele period of the mid-nineteenth century, as well as the partial remains of a blacksmith's shop.

A Bishop Museum team investigated the site of the Harbor Court redevelopment project, at the intersection of Queen Street and Nimitz Highway, originally part of the small village of Kou (Lebo, ed., 1997). Early commercial interests known to have been located in this area include Skinner's Auction House, the Hudson Bay Company, and the office of the US Consulate. Excavations recovered large quantities of imported artifacts, including Chinese porcelain and stoneware, English creamware, whiteware, and yellowware, and a wide range of bottles, among other items, indicative of the range of products being imported to the Hawaiian Kingdom during the nineteenth century.

James McIntosh et al. (2006) report on the investigation of a block at the corner of Smith and Beretania Streets, where a city parking lot was being developed. Backhoe trenches revealed a complex subsurface stratigraphy, with abundant historic period structural remains and artifacts. Excavations exposed trash pits, cooking features, and structural foundations, while the artifacts indicated that most of the material dated to the period from 1850 to 1900. However, there was also some indication of a precontact deposit.

Several studies have been carried out in and around the grounds of 'Iolani Palace in Honolulu, constructed by King David Kalākaua in 1882. Michael Seelye (1968) excavated trenches in an effort to define the foundations of the royal bungalow, Hale Akala, which had once stood near the palace. Rosendahl (1971) located the bed for the old carriage road beneath the present asphalt driveway. Margaret Luscomb and Roland Reeve (1976) monitored a large number of trenches dug for electrical conduits across the palace grounds, discovering among other finds the entrance to the original palace cesspool. These and other projects have provided a large collection of historic-period artifacts, which, when fully studied, may reveal new aspects of everyday life among Hawai'i's later monarchs.

A brief but fascinating phase in the islands' early contact history began with the wreck of the Russian ship *Bering* at Waimea, Kaua'i on January 31, 1815, and confiscation of her cargo by the island's high chief, Kaumuali'i. Georg Scheffer was subsequently dispatched by the Russian government to recover the cargo, and in 1816 found Kaumuali'i to be a willing ally if the Russians would support Kaumuali'i in his long-standing opposition to Kamehameha (Mills 2002a; Molodin and Mills 2021). Scheffer helped Kaumuali'i build a European-style fort commanding the entrance to Waimea Bay, named Fort Elizabeth in Russian documents, and Pāpū Pā'ula'ula in the first written Hawaiian documents from the

FIGURE 13.4 A portion of the interior wall of Fort Elizabeth at Waimea, Kaua'i Island, with stone steps leading up to a canon emplacement. *(Photo by Therese Babineau)*

Māhele (fig. 13.4). When Kaumualiʻi realized that Scheffer lacked the backing of the Russian military and could not provide promised ships, he expelled Scheffer in May 1817.

Patrick C. McCoy (1972) carried out the first detailed survey of the site and preliminary test excavations. This was followed some years later by Peter Mills' resurvey and excavations (Mills 2002a), combined with a detailed historical analysis of documents pertaining to the fort. Rather than seeing the ruins of the fort solely as a testament to a brief, failed colonial interlude, Mills interprets the structure as part of a longer history of indigenous agency. The stone-walled enclosure, although in plan view clearly a European fortification, was built by Hawaiian laborers on the site of a preexisting *heiau,* and was called by the Hawaiians Pā ʻulaʻula o Hipo ("the Red Enclosure of Hipo"). Mills argues that Pā ʻulaʻula was a hybrid monument, a "nineteenth-century amalgam of Hawaiian and European monumental architecture or, more specifically, a combination of structural elements from a Hawaiian heiau and a European fort; the former was imbued with ritual, the latter with military strategy, and both with social control" (115). Although Russian involvement with the structure was short-lived, Pā ʻulaʻula continued to be used by Kaumualiʻi and others for decades to come, in a variety of ways, as Mills documents.

In Lahaina on Maui, the Fredericksens (1965) were able to locate, through excavation, the foundations of the brick "palace" constructed for Kamehameha I between 1798 and 1802, mentioned in several early historical accounts. Paul Cleghorn (1975) excavated around the Seamen's Hospital building in Lahaina, exposing the foundations of an earlier structure, recovering a large collection of historical artifacts chronicling a lengthy and changing sequence of occupation and use of the site area.

Historical archaeology has not received nearly the same degree of attention in Hawaiʻi as that of the precontact era, but the efforts carried out to date leave no doubt as to the potential for archaeology to contribute to our understanding of the tremendous historical changes that shaped island communities. Through the "small things forgotten," as James Deetz so elegantly phrased it, "a different appreciation for what life is today, and was in the past, can be achieved" (1977, 161).

14

THE ARCHAEOLOGY OF HAWAI'I ISLAND

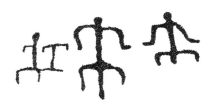

To early Polynesian settlers arriving from their ancestral homeland in central Eastern Polynesia, Hawai'i Island must have seemed a landscape imaginable only in dreams. The island's massive shield volcanoes rise gently at first, then steeply push through the clouds to the snow-capped summits of Mauna Kea, "White Mountain," and Mauna Loa, "Long Mountain." Verdant *'ōhi'a* and *koa* rain forests cloak the windward slopes, while the leeward landscape features waterless, parched lava flows; freezing snowstorms assail mountain peaks, contrasting with the searing heat of volcanic eruptions. The snow and the lava were both phenomena new to Polynesian colonizers coming from the Marquesas or Tahiti.

Five volcanoes merge to form Hawai'i Island, with a land mass greater than all of the other islands combined (fig. 14.1). As the geologically youngest island, Hawai'i exhibits the least eroded and dissected landforms. The only sizable valleys are confined to the windward side of the Kohala Mountains, the oldest part of the island, while narrow gulches slice into the Hāmākua District slopes. The entire western side, from Ka Lae (South Point) to 'Upolu Point, lacks a single permanently flowing stream, limiting the kinds of agriculture that could be practiced. Such constraints, nonetheless, did not thwart the growth of large populations nor the development of centers of political power. When Captain James Cook arrived at Kealakekua late in 1778, Hawai'i Island was the setting for one of the archipelago's most powerful kingdoms.

In this chapter, we summarize Hawai'i Island's archaeology across three broad regions: East Hawai'i, including the *moku* of Hāmākua, Hilo, and Puna; South Hawai'i, home to Ka'ū *moku;* and West Hawai'i, an area of intense interest to archaeologists and location of Kohala and Kona *moku*.

East Hawai'i: Hāmākua and Hilo

Two major geographic features—Waipi'o Valley and Mauna Kea—dominate Hāmākua District, reflecting two environmental extremes: the island's largest windward valley with intensive irrigation, and a desert alpine summit that tested people's physical endurance to obtain its fine-grained adze stone.

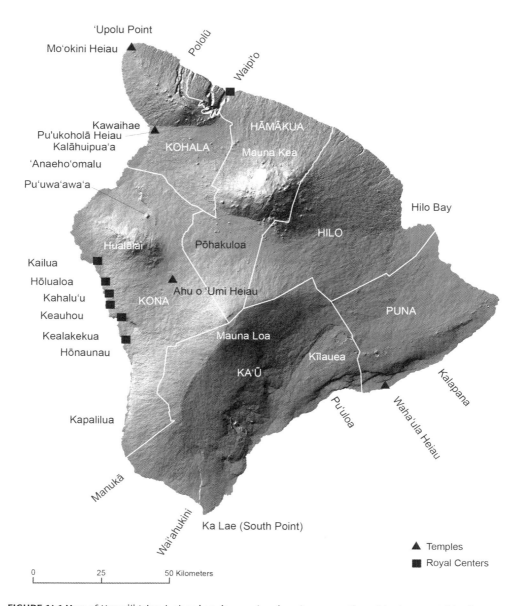

FIGURE 14.1 Map of Hawai'i Island, showing sites and major places mentioned in the text. White lines indicate the boundaries of the traditional districts. *(Map by M. D. McCoy)*

Towering sea cliffs dominate the northern Hāmākua coastline, punctuated by several valleys from Waipi'o north to Pololū. Endowed with permanent streams and alluvial land for irrigated farming, these valleys attracted the island's earliest settlers; oral traditions speak of the island's first chiefs residing here. Archaeological surveys have revealed sites in virtually every valley and on landshelves along this coast, as attested for example by Peter Mills' survey of Laupāhoehoe Nui, where a range of domestic, agricultural, and religious features are situated within the 1.2 km coastal section (Mills 2003). For Waimanu Valley, immediately north of Waipi'o, Shun and Schiltz (1991) report that although the 1946 tsunami likely destroyed features near the coastline, including Haleiwa Heiau recorded by John F. G. Stokes, the valley nonetheless exhibits a high density of features. Their survey included small test excavations with radiocarbon dates suggesting a chronology similar to Pololū Valley, with settlement earliest at the coast and increasing use of the interior portions of the valley.

As a former royal center and earliest seat of the Hawai'i Island rulers, Waipi'o Valley features prominently in the island's history. Kahaunokama'ahala, the royal residence at the valley's mouth, straddled the inland side of a black sand beach ridge, next to the *luakini* temple of Paka'alana; another large *luakini,* Honua'ula, was situated slightly farther to the west (Cordy 2000a, 197–200, fig. 7–1). These sites, entombed within the sand dunes, have yet to be thoroughly investigated. Reconnaissance surveys, limited test excavations, and summaries of historic records have been commissioned by Bishop Museum (P. L. Cleghorn 1983; Cleghorn and Rogers-Jourdane 1983; Dockall, Leidemann, and Olszewski 2001; Lebo et al. 1999; Lennstrom and Olszewski 2001; Olszewski, ed., 2000). Radiocarbon dates suggest that irrigated fields—mapped by aerial LiDAR by Jones, Ladefoged, and Asner (2015)—were in place by cal AD 1400–1640 (Beta-70074), with side valley fields constructed after cal AD 1660–1960 (Beta-70071) (Cordy et al. 2005; see also Jones, Ladefoged, and Asner 2015).

Moving south from Waipi'o, the Hāmākua landscape is one of broad tablelands dissected by more than 40 gulches between Waipi'o and the boundary with North Hilo at Ka'ula Gulch. Head and Goodfellow (1991) surveyed much of this area with an eye toward documenting the now defunct Hamakua Sugar Company, with its mills, farm roads, plantation settlements, and irrigation system. Mills et al. (2013) examined Keanakolu in the Humu'ula region, with evidence of historic *paniolo* (cowboy) life, including corrals, huts, camps, lava tubes used as shelters, a homestead, a ranger station used in the 1930s, and a log cabin dating back to AD 1876 (site 50-10-15-7462).

At the base of Mauna Kea, at 2,700 m above sea level, complexes of caves, shelters, and other features point to the use of this upland zone (Bayman et al. 2004). At Pu'u Kalepeamoa (site 50-10-23-10312), Patrick C. McCoy (1985) recorded five lithic scatters and two shrines. While the site was likely integrated with the main adze quarry higher on the mountain, this location was used for the manufacture of octopus lure sinkers (P. C. McCoy 1991). Situated well above the regularly used upland habitation zone, the area was used by hunting parties and as an outpost when summiting Mauna Kea.

Between 3,355 and 3,780 m on the barren alpine flanks of Mauna Kea lies the extensive ritual landscape and basalt adze quarry where tens of thousands of stone adzes were roughed out over a period of several centuries (see chapter 9). The main quarry, covering an area of more than 19.4 km^2, was the subject of an intensive study by P. C. McCoy (1977; McCoy and Nees 2010) and Paul Cleghorn (1982, 1986). The quarry incorporates 195 features, including extraction areas where large blocks were loosened and roughly reduced, workshops, open-air shelters, shrines, overhang shelters, and rockshelters. Two rockshelters used by the adze makers, Ua'u (site 50-10-23-16205) and Ko'oko'olau (site 50-10-23-16216), were excavated, yielding thousands of basalt flakes and broken adze preforms, along with the remains of plant and animal foods brought by people to sustain themselves while at the quarry (M. S. Allen 1981; P. C. McCoy 1990). Virtually the entire summit area has now been intensively surveyed (P. C. McCoy and Nees 2010), revealing more than 200 shrines (fig. 14.2; P. C. McCoy 1999; P. C. McCoy et al. 2009). While radiocarbon dates indicate visits to these shrines beginning as early as cal AD 1100–1200 (P. C. McCoy 1990, fig. 4), three ^{230}Th series dates document coral offerings deposited at the shrines between cal AD 1350–1450. The earliest date is on unmodified coral found within a shelter (cal AD 1327–1383, site 50-10-23-28637, no lab identification, P. C. McCoy et al. 2012). Another date comes from a branch coral found near a shelter but presumed to have come from a nearby shrine (cal AD 1385–1411, site 50-10-23-16205, Sample 1, P. C. McCoy et al. 2009). The third sample was collected in place on a shrine (cal AD 1437–1443, site 50-10-23-16206, Sample 2, P. C. McCoy et al. 2009). The extensive distribution of shrines over the summit regions of Mauna Kea supports recent claims by Kānaka Maoli that the mountain is sacred.

The discovery of an artifact made of Puʻu Waʻawaʻa volcanic glass in rockshelter deposits at the Mauna Kea quarry (P. C. McCoy et al. 2015) points to visitors coming from west Hawaiʻi (M. D. McCoy, Mills, et al. 2011). Mills and Lundblad (2014) note that sites in east Hawaiʻi and South Kohala contain a high abundance of Mauna Kea basalt debitage, suggesting that they may represent locations where adze blanks were finished. This pattern of finishing adzes is distinct from that resulting from the resharpening of adzes. It is likely that there were also visitors from further afield, but clearly the industrial scale of the quarry was unique to Hawaiʻi Island. Patrick C. McCoy (1999) has argued that the high frequency of shrines, along with evidence of temporary shelters for people overnighting on the mountain, and Paul Cleghorn's (1986) discovery of discrete areas of debitage created by experts (e.g., with little waste) and novices (e.g., with more waste than necessary), indicate that Mauna Kea was a place where people were transformed to *kāhuna* (experts) in adze making.

The saddle region between Mauna Kea and Mauna Loa exhibits evidence for extensive bird hunting (Athens and Kaschko 1989; Athens, Kaschko, and James 1991) as well as quarrying lithic raw material (Williams 2004). Much of the information on this zone comes from CRM work funded by the federal government as part of military exercises at Pōhakuloa

FIGURE 14.2 A simple shrine of upright slabs near the Mauna Kea adze quarry. *(Photo courtesy Bishop Museum Department of Anthropology)*

Training Area (PTA) (Godby and Carson 2004). A CRM inventory survey of some 6,000 acres of the PTA documented 1,506 archaeological features, including "mounds, cairns, terraces, walls, enclosures, hearths, clearings, pavements, platforms, wood caches, a cupboard, lithic scatters, a lithic quarry, and excavated pits" (Filimoehala and Morrison 2020, iii). Many of these features appear to be associated with hunting of petrel birds that nested in these upland regions. Radiocarbon dates indicate regular activities in this area beginning around AD 1400. The saddle region served as a crossroads for communication between windward and leeward sides of the island, for there are traces of former trails, and several lava tubes were used as campsites. One large shelter contained quantities of wooden adze chips, and a wooden adze handle.

On the interior slope of Hualālai, facing the saddle and situated on a barren ash plain, lies the famous temple of Ahu a 'Umi, first mapped by the US Exploring Expedition (fig. 14.3). According to tradition, the temple was constructed to commemorate 'Umi's unification of the island, with the people of each *moku* commanded to carry stones for its construction. If we exclude the V-shaped wall that was likely built by ranchers in the historic era, the site has three components: (1) a main enclosure with thick, low walls (22.8 × 17.4 m); (2) a smaller enclosure immediately west of the main enclosure with a notch on its western corner; and (3) eight large cairns (*ahu*) that encircle the main structure. Each *ahu* is designated with letters A to H (clockwise, beginning with the "A" cairn at 22°). Da Silva and Johnson (1982) noted that from inside the main enclosure one could sight to a number of significant asterisms. For example, from a position in the northern half of the main enclosure, the largest *ahu* ("B," located at 65°), the rising of the Pleiades, and sunrise at the summer solstice are all visible.

The landscape of Hilo District was heavily disturbed by the sugar plantations of the nineteenth and twentieth centuries, resulting in the destruction of countless archaeological sites. Small-scale surveys in and around Hilo have reported that evidence of the precontact settlement pattern was largely obliterated due to historic clearing for agriculture. Reported radiocarbon dates for the Hilo Bay area (cal AD 1298–1626, Beta-68570, site -19431) (Maly, Walker, and Rosendahl 1994) do not predate the Late Voyaging Period. McEldowney (1979) defined five settlement zones for Hilo: a coastal settlement zone where habitation was concentrated, an upland agricultural zone (300–460 m), a lower forest zone (460–760 m) for wood houses / canoes, rain forest (760–1680 m), and a montane zone (+1680 m). More recent research along the contemporary Saddle Road has documented montane trails that no doubt connected to the network of the island's interior roads (Rasmussen and O'Day 2004).

South Hawai'i: Puna and Ka'ū

Puna District, more than any other *moku,* has been continually transformed by lava flows emanating from the East Rift Zone of Kīlauea. Geologist Don Swanson suggests that Puna was radically transformed due to an intense period of volcanism between cal AD 1410 and 1470, the 'Aiā'au eruption. 'Aiā'au flows covered an estimated 430 km^2, ending with the formation of the Kīlauea caldera around AD 1500. Swanson (2008) argues that this period of eruptions became encoded in Hawaiian oral traditions concerning the volcano deity Pele and her sister Hi'iaka'aikapoliopele, whose name is usually shortened to Hi'iaka. Specifically, he

FIGURE 14.3 Plan of Ahu a 'Umi, a temple situated on the interior plateau of Hawai'i Island, drawn by the US Exploring Expedition in 1841. *(Drawn by T. R. Peale, engraved by F. Humphrys. From Wilkes 1845)*

sees stories of Pele's destruction of her sister's precious *'ōhi'a* forest as a reference to the fifteenth-century eruptions, interpreting references in traditions to 'Aiā'au as an early volcano god who was overshadowed by Pele. Certainly, the covering by lava of an area larger than the island of Lāna'i within the lifetime of a single individual would have would seared this event into the collective memory of the Hawaiian people.

In the 1980s, eruptions from the East Rift Zone fostered a new kind of salvage fieldwork: volcano archaeology. Continual episodes of new flows, along with expansions of the Hawai'i Volcanoes National Park's boundaries, have kept archaeologists busy protecting sites and mitigating damage. Not knowing where and when the next flow will occur, cultural resource managers took a proactive approach conducting surveys and limited excavations in anticipation of new flows, at times even excavating sites as active flows threaten to engulf them. Ladefoged, Somers, and Lane-Hamasaki (1987) surveyed the park's then eastern boundary at Kalapana, in a leeward sector of Puna (see also Ladefoged 1991). Ladefoged's team surveyed 467 hectares, in response to applications by Native Hawaiians for access to homestead lands. This project recorded all surface architecture over a large continuous area, classifying the features in formal and functional terms. Eight settlements were identified, including 26 complexes, which were in turn divided into 15,213 unique features. The most commonplace features were those used for agriculture (51% of features were mounds; 28% natural or modified planting features); from this the authors estimated that agricultural activity was concentrated within about 1 km from the coast.

Handy and Handy (1972, 542) opined regarding Puna, "Only in recent time that volcanic eruption has destroyed much of its best land. Unquestionably lava flows in historic times have covered more good gardening land here than in any other district." Salvage survey and excavation in Paliuli in the mid-1990s, *mauka* of the earlier Kalapana survey, revealed that mound planting continued further upslope only to drop off above 180 m (Tuggle and Tomonari-Tuggle 2008). Tuggle and Tomonari-Tuggle remark on the spatial pattern of agriculture in this part of the island, noting the unexpected "intensity of agriculture and habitation on the pali bluffs that are well removed from the coast" (Hilina Pali [upper elevation ca. 690 m] and Hōlei Pali [ca. 335 m] being the most prominent). They observe that clusters of agricultural features "are an unusual configuration, resulting from the ways in which micro-environmental zones occur in this faulted terrain" (Tuggle and Tomonari-Tuggle 2008, 150).

Temple sites abound in leeward Puna. Ladefoged et al. (1987) report 12 *heiau* with a distinct size hierarchy; the two largest *heiau* had footprints of 1,709 and 924 m^2, with the next tier ranging in size from 345 down to 70 m^2. Smaller structures in the 50–18 m^2 size range were interpreted as *ko'a*, with the smallest shrine only 8.3 m^2 in area. The most famous ritual site in Puna District is Waha'ula Heiau, according to Hawaiian tradition one of the first two *luakini heiau* (war temples) built by the Tahitian priest Pā'ao during the Late Voyaging Period, possibly as early as the late AD 1200s (Carter and Somers 1990). Waha'ula was also the last temple to be rededicated by Kamehameha I in 1817 prior to the end of the *'ai kapu* just two years later. Along with Mo'okini Heiau, also attributed to Pā'ao, Waha'ula is essentially the "type site" for *luakini heiau*. Stokes (1991) mapped the temple and constructed a scale model that still stands in Bishop Museum's Hawaiian Hall. Later maps were made by Kekahuna (1951) and by Masse et al. (1991). Tragically, Waha'ula Heiau was entirely consumed by a lava flow in 1997 (fig. 14.4).

Another significant ritual site in Puna is the small lava hillock at Pu'uloa (fig. 14.5), with one of the densest concentration of rock art in Hawai'i (Cox 1974; Cox and Stasack 1998).

FIGURE 14.4 Waha'ula Heiau in Puna District, Hawai'i Island, was reputedly built by the Tahitian priest Pā'ao. Seen here in 1993, the site was later completely covered over by lava. *(Photo by Therese Babineau)*

FIGURE 14.5 Petroglyphs at Pu'uloa, Hawai'i Island. *(Photo by Therese Babineau)*

The abundance of circular cupules (*piko*), which Beckwith (n.d.) suggests were places for the umbilical cord to be placed, indicates a persistent importance of this location, possibly going back to the Expansion Period (Dorn 1996).

Radiocarbon dates for Puna do not predate the Late Voyaging Period (cal AD 1188–1387, Beta-33643, reported for Ka'ili'ili [Carter and Somers 1990]). Kennedy et al. (1991, 50) raise the possibility that radiocarbon dates from sites in this volcanically active landscape might have been affected by proximity to fumaroles or vents with gaseous emissions that "alters dates from samples up to 5.3 km from vents active during the time of the plant's growth." However, this purported effect has yet to be systematically studied in archaeological contexts.

The postcontact archaeological record for Puna shares patterns with the neighboring windward communities. Historical records describe how the uplands were scoured for sandalwood, and how land was later successively transformed to farm coffee, sugar, and, at Kea'au, macadamia nuts. Ladefoged (1991) used Kalapana survey data to identify a shift from traditional multistructure *kauhale* to single-structure dwellings in Hawai'i.

Ka'ū District has long been a focus of archaeological research. As in adjacent Puna, eruptions from Kīlauea as well as Mauna Loa have shaped the natural landform and influenced the course of historical events. Three areas in Ka'ū are of particular interest: (1) the boundary with Puna near Kapapala; (2) the island's southern tip, Ka Lae (South Point), which holds a special place in the development of Hawaiian archaeology (see chapter 1); and (3) the western border with South Kona at Kahuku and Manukā, where intensive survey has revealed a remarkable density of features even in the absence of land suitable for agriculture. As the island's largest district, Ka'ū may have at times encompassed western Puna in what Cordy (2000a) refers to as "Greater Ka'ū."

Ka'ū *moku* has been affected by lava flows from Kilauea's East Rift Zone flowing over the large *ahupua'a* of Kapapala, and in the west from Mauna Loa's Southwest Rift Zone at Kahuku. Between these *ahupua'a,* with their extensive barren inland areas, are 60 km of coastline that was divided into at least 25 *ahupua'a,* each of which stretched inland about 15 km to encompass the resource-rich uplands (Kelly 1980). This upland zone is distinctive from other windward ecozones in that it is on young geological flows not old enough to have been dissected. As with leeward upland gardening areas, such as in Kona, the upper elevation boundary is set by the cloud inversion zone, also known as the great inland desert. But since it is a windward environment, the east-facing Ka'ū coastline has considerable soil development, except where there have been recent lava flows.

In the eastern portion of Ka'ū, Cleghorn (1980) mapped and tested a lava-tube site (50-HV-383) in the uplands above Hilina Pali (fig. 14.6). The smooth, glassy walls of the tube were extensively covered with petroglyphs, including scenes of cockfighting and a typical array of human figures. By dating a midden deposit that had built up over some of the glyphs, Cleghorn was able to determine that the petroglyphs were no younger than about AD 1600 (Cleghorn and Cox 1976). Other research in Kā'u includes surveys of the Wailau-Nīnole area (Barrera and Hommon 1972), and of Wai'ōhinu (Kelly and Crozier 1972), as well as a study of a large lava tube refuge cave, Lua Nunu o Kamakalepo (site H12; Bonk 1969).

To the west of Kilauea Crater a layer of hardened ash from the violent 1790 eruption of Halema'uma'u has preserved over 1,700 human footprints (fig. 14.7). This explosive eruption and subsequent thick ash fall were later recalled by local people as Keonekelelei, or "the falling sands." First brought to public attention in 1919 by a geologist working at the Hawaii Volcanoes Observatory, over the years most people have drawn the conclusion that these footprints were left by the army of Keōua, Kamehameha I's rival. Traditional

FIGURE 14.6 A cache of wooden barkcloth (*kapa*) beaters discovered in a lava-tube shelter cave at Hilina Pali, Hawai'i Island. *(Photo courtesy Bishop Museum Department of Anthropology)*

accounts (e.g., Kamakau 1961, 152) point to Keōua's troops having been caught in the eruption, inflicting heavy casualties and leading to the downfall of Keōua's bid for control of Hawai'i Island. The Footprints Area has been recognized as an archaeological site for many years and was nominated to the National Register of Historic Places in 1974 (site 50-10-61-5505).

New research, however, suggests these tracks may not have been left behind by a fleeing army (Moniz-Nakamura 2003), or at least that there are multiple events cemented into the ash. A systematic evaluation of several hundred footprints suggests that many, if not most, of the tracks were left by women and children crisscrossing the wet ash. This in itself does not negate the interpretation that these footprints represent a fleeing army, since ethnohistoric evidence suggests that women and children followed traveling armies. Travelers left behind more than their footprints; hundreds of other features have been recorded in the immediate area, including shelters and volcanic-glass quarries, one of which appears to have been used during a lull in the eruptions only to be covered over a second time. The spacing between many footprints show people at a walking pace, rather than running, further supporting the notion that these prints were made by regular travel through the Ka'ū desert.

The 'Umi Caverns *kīpuka,* a 40-acre pocket of older lava with a massive lava tube situated at about 2,300 m along the Southwest Rift Zone of Mauna Loa, was surveyed by Tomonari-Tuggle (2019). There are numerous enclosures and other features in the *kīpuka,*

FIGURE 14.7 Human footprints in volcanic ash near Kilauea volcano, Hawai'i Island. *(Photo by Therese Babineau)*

but most notable is Feature KS-01, "a long, narrow platform with seven uprights, which along with three other features (KS-11, KS-89, and KS-93), form a courtyard complex that is similar to shrines identified on Mauna Kea and the saddle area of Hawai'i Island, Haleakalā on Maui, and on Mokumanamana (Necker Island) in the Northwestern Hawaiian Islands" (iii).

Ka Lae, near the center of Ka'ū District, was the scene of intensive work by Bishop Museum's Kenneth Emory and colleagues during the pioneering days of archaeological excavation in the early 1950s; their excavations at the H1 and H2 sites have been described in chapters 1 and 6. The H1 and H2 sites, along with nearby H8, provided the basis for Emory and Sinoto's fishhook chronology (Emory, Bonk, and Sinoto 1959). Wallace and Wallace (1964) excavated another sand dune midden (site H24) at Pinao Bay, not far from Pu'u Ali'i. Moniz-Nakamura (1999) drew upon data from Ka Lae, along with deposits at site O1 on O'ahu, to argue that early sites in the Hawaiian Islands reflect a particularly intense focus on seabird hunting. However, redating based on samples in good contexts suggests that this practice continued much later in time than previously thought.

Ka Lae was famous for its pelagic fishing grounds offshore. Distinctive archaeological features to be seen along the low cliffs near the point are a number of mooring holes carved into the lava rock, used to secure the fishing canoes (fig. 14.8).

FIGURE 14.8 Artificial hole pecked through lava rock at Ka Lae, Hawai'i, used to moor fishing canoes. *(Photo by Therese Babineau)*

Lying in the lee of the great fault cliff called Pali o Kūlani is Wai'ahukini, a dense cluster of sites, including stone structures and lava-tube rockshelters (including site H8), investigated by Bishop Museum archaeologists over a number of years. In the early 1970s, Yosihiko H. Sinoto directed a large-scale investigation of Wai'ahukini, mapping and recording about 125 sites and excavating four important rockshelters with stratified deposits (Sinoto and Kelly 1975). The excavations produced more than 4,600 artifacts, mostly fishing gear and the tools used to manufacture the hooks (fig. 14.9).

Reanalysis of the Wai'ahukini collections have established dates for key sites, including H8, or Wai'ahukini rockshelter (site 50-10-76-10847) (Mulrooney et al. 2014), and two other shelters, Ha-B22-248 (site 50-10-76-20218) and Ha-B22-64 (site 50-10-76-20034) (Kahn, Lundblad, et al. 2016). Wai'ahukini rockshelter was the only shelter used during the Late Voyaging Period (cal AD 1315–1430, Beta-377382*, H8); other shelters yielded dates no earlier than the Expansion Period (cal AD 1489–1654, Beta-290196*, Ha-B22-64), and the Archaic States Period (cal AD 1680–1938, Beta-290197*, Ha-B22-248).

Geochemical analysis of basalt and volcanic-glass artifacts from the South Point sites reveal that the area was surprisingly well connected with other parts of the island and beyond. More than 40 percent of the basalt artifacts (123 artifacts out of 287) came from the Mauna Kea quarries, with a small proportion (2%) coming from as far away as Kaua'i Island. Few examples of volcanic glass have been recovered, never more than about 12 percent of artifacts in a given level (Lundblad et al. 2013), but their size and form are consistent with direct access to the Pu'u Wa'awa'a source (see also DiVito et al. 2020; M. D. McCoy, Mills, et al. 2011; Putzi et al. 2015). It is difficult to determine whether these long-distance connections were round-trip journeys that originated from Ka'ū, or if they are a material signal of occasional visits by Kona chiefs who favored the Ka Lae fishing grounds.

In late precontact and early historic times, Wai'ahukini was periodically occupied by the ruling chiefs of Ka'ū and Kona, who enjoyed the pelagic fish readily caught in the deep waters offshore. Kalani'ōpu'u, the ruling paramount who greeted Captain Cook at Kealakekua, resided from time to time at Wai'ahukini, and died there in January 1772 (Kamakau 1961, 110). Sinoto mapped a group of large stone residential structures, some of which are

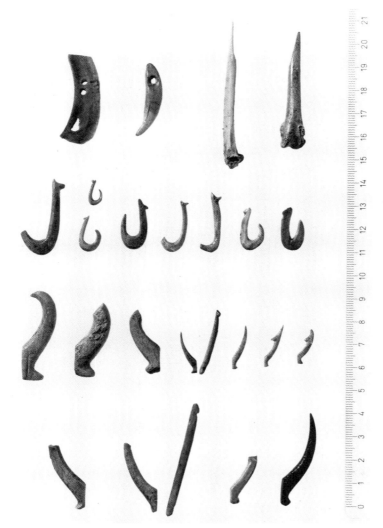

FIGURE 14.9 Artifacts excavated from sites at Wai'ahukini, Hawai'i Island. *Top row:* pig-tusk ornament, dog-tooth pendant, bone picks. *Second row:* one-piece bone fishhooks. *Third and fourth rows:* two-piece bone fishhook points and shanks. *(Photo courtesy Bishop Museum Department of Anthropology)*

likely to have been the residence of Kalani'ōpu'u and his entourage. This "chief's complex" (site Ha-B22-140, site 50-10-76-20110), illustrated in figure 14.10, is an excellent example of residential architecture associated with ruling elites.

Kahuku *ahupua'a,* northwest from Wai'ahukini, has a rugged coastline with bare lava fields inland. Initial surveys of this region found only scattered sites, mostly fishing camps clustered around canoe landings or brackish pools where drinking water could be obtained. However, the apparent bareness of the landscape is at odds with the richness of the archaeology. In 1965 two rockshelters, part of a small fishing settlement at Kahakahakea near Pōhue Bay, were excavated by Lloyd Soehren (1966). Site H66 is a small lava bubble with only about 10 m² of floor area, and a ceiling so low that one can barely sit upright in the main part of the shelter. Nevertheless, excavation produced 1,454 catalogued artifacts (not including volcanic-glass flakes), of which 203 were fishhooks. This density of artifacts (1,817/m³) is probably the highest ever recorded for a Hawaiian archaeological site. Site H65, not far away, is more

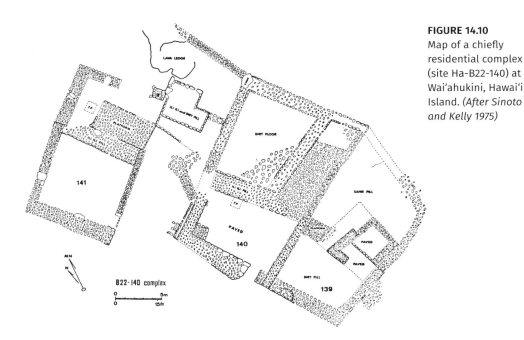

FIGURE 14.10
Map of a chiefly residential complex (site Ha-B22-140) at Wai'ahukini, Hawai'i Island. *(After Sinoto and Kelly 1975)*

spacious, with several stone architectural modifications and a stratified cultural deposit up to 60 cm deep. This site yielded 729 artifacts, mostly fishhooks (90 specimens) and the tools and detritus associated with their manufacture. The sites at Kahakahakea are not limited to these rockshelters, with a variety of small stone shelters and paved areas concentrated inland of the small beach, where canoes could have landed through the surf.

Two large CRM projects have been undertaken in the coastal portions of Kahuku. Haun and Walker (1987) recorded 298 sites consisting of 1,144 features stretching from Kahakahakea past Pōhue Bay and ending at Humuhumu Point, the border with Manukā *ahupua'a*. Based on historic-era accounts they argue that the main settlement zone was upland, above 460 m, where rainfall was higher and the land better suited to agriculture, with the coast uninhabited except for fishing and stone procurement for *pāhoehoe* abraders. More than 1,600 "extraction pits" for these abraders have been recorded near the coast. In contrast, a coastal survey by Lebo, Komori, and T. S. Dye (2011) described Pōhue Bay and Kahakahakea as the main villages in the region, due to their good canoe landings, along with several smaller coastal communities. A series of radiocarbon dates suggest the earliest occupation dates to the Late Voyaging Period (cal AD 1312–1444, Beta-231398*, site 50-10-73-28940).

Most of the extensive Ka'ū dryland agricultural field system—portions of which can be detected on satellite imagery—remains undescribed and in need of study. A radiocarbon date on charcoal recovered from agricultural deposits at Ka'ōpapa suggests that fields were established as early as the Expansion Period (cal AD 1446–1634, Beta-471145*, Ka'ōpapa *kīpuka*) (Quintus and Lincoln 2018).

M. S. Allen and McAnany (1994) undertook a *mauka-makai* assessment of the Ka'ū landscape in the *ahupua'a* of Manukā, chosing the Ka'ū District because it was the childhood home of Mary Kawena Pukui, who in collaboration with anthropologist Edward Handy defined the classic *'ohana* model of settlement and subsistence (Handy and Pukui 1958) that has influenced much archaeological interpretation (e.g., Newman 1969; Tuggle and Griffin, eds., 1973). This "traditional" model, although based on Pukui's experience in the early twentieth century, describes how people living at the coast passed goods such as salt and dried fish to those dwelling in the uplands, receiving taro and other agricultural products in exchange.

Allen and McAnany (1994) found that while there is a high density of residential sites at the coast, particularly within older *kīpuka* such as Malua (site 50-10-71-2153), the uplands showed little evidence of gardening and only a few structures dating to the historic era, contradicting the expectation of extensive upland households. The authors suggest that low household mobility may have been necessary in the historic period to assure rights to land, and under those conditions, permanent settlement in the uplands and coast of Manukā with exchange between them seems likely. They argue that the introduction of horses and mules facilitated regular movement between the coast and uplands during the postcontact period and during the time of Pukui's youth. The Manukā results do not necessarily negate the *'ohana* model but highlight the importance of considering postcontact changes to the lifestyles documented by early twentieth-century anthropologists as "traditional."

In 2012, M. D. McCoy and Codlin resurveyed the coast at Manukā Bay, creating a database of architecture in order to evaluate another classic ethnohistoric model: the *kauhale* (McCoy and Codlin 2016). It is well established that people built their *kauhale* according to rules proscribed under the *kapu* system. But archaeologists have also recorded significant variation in the arrangement and configuration of households, suggesting that *kapu* was more relaxed in some households, or interpreted differently. To test this hypothesis, McCoy and Codlin (2016) recorded a ritual complex and five intact household clusters along the coast. The households varied widely in their sizes; some were about the same size as a new home built today in the United States, others no larger than a trailer home. Each household showed efforts to follow the rules of *kapu* as observed in domestic context, without regard to the apparent rank of the families who occupied them, and without regard to distance from the ritual complex.

West Hawai'i: Kona and Kohala

Kona *moku* encompasses many closely spaced *ahupua'a* framed on the south by lava flows from Mauna Loa, and on the north by an extensive barren zone consisting of recent flows from Mauna Loa and Hualālai. Kona is notable for the high density of royal centers, including well-known examples at Kailua, Hōlualoa, Kahalu'u, Keauhou, Kealakekua, and Hōnaunau.

The southern portion of South Kona extends from the boundary with Ka'ū at Manukā, past the fishing village of Miloli'i, and ends south of Honokua at Kauhako Bay, the location of Ho'okena Beach Park. This 42 km stretch of coastline includes more than 26 *ahupua'a*, with some *ahupua'a* being numbered subdivisions of originally larger territories (e.g., 'Opihihale 1, 'Opihihale 2). This region is sometimes referred to as Kapalilua in reference to the cliffs (*pali*) that dominate the region. The Kapalilua region contains dense concentrations of archaeological sites, including pre- and postcontact-era features. Rosendahl (1983) conducted a large reconnaissance survey in Kapua followed by intensive survey, recording 297 sites made up of

951 individual features (Haun and Walker 1988). The distribution of sites is not uniform, with a higher density of features associated with collapsed lava tubes, isolated patches of older flows (*kīpuka*), and with more and larger sites along the coast. To the north of Miloli'i, there is a cluster of house platforms, a stone-lined well, a *hōlua* slide, and, nearby, a particularly spacious rockshelter opening into the front of a steep 'a'a lava flow. This rockshelter, site H110 in Bishop Museum system, was partially excavated by Soehren (Soehren 1966). A 14-m-long trench excavated across the width of the rockshelter, just inside the overhang, revealed a well-stratified deposit of five layers, up to 80 cm deep. The excavations yielded 555 artifacts, most of them related to fishing activities, including a series of knobbed two-piece fishhook points.

Evidence for agricultural activity within the Kapalilua region does not strictly follow the typical site distribution for the Kona Field System but rather emphasizes discrete aspects of the landform, especially *kīpuka*, the coast, and collapsed lava-tube systems. Studies in the lower half of the *ahupua'a* of 'Opihihale 1 and 2 report boundary and *kuaiwi* walls, as are found in the Kona Field System (McGerty and Spear 1996). More research will be necessary to document the transition from the core of the Kona Field System to its outer margins as in 'Opihihale.

The patchier arrangement of settlement found in the Kapalilua region could reflect a lower population density, or alternatively a landscape where people had adapted to locations with opportunities for farming and fishing. The region was not an isolated rural area, as virtually every large study of the region has reported extensive trails, documenting an extensive communication network.

The question of settlement density raises chronological issues with respect to the region's structures and shelters. Landrum, Schiltz, and Drolet (1992) note the presence of "temporary shelters" down to 130 m elevation in 'Opihihale 2. Located at about 183 m, site -23350 includes three paved terraces sized 56 m^2, 16.25 m^2, and 4 m^2. A single 1 × 1 m unit was placed in the center of each terrace; radiocarbon dates put the earliest use of the site in the Expansion Period. The authors note that the configuration may fit Cordy's (1981) model of a single permanent household, but they advance an alternative interpretation as a "temporary yet recurrent habitation," based partly on a "limited amount of habitation debris" (Landrum, Schiltz, and Drolet 1992, 20). The material recovered from floor deposits included shellfish, fish bone, charcoal, and lithics. The lack of domestic animals such as pig or dog, and presence of shellfish, is a pattern to be expected at a temporary shelter but also in the permanent residences of lower-ranked individuals.

North of Kapalilua lies a densely settled 15 km section bounded by Hōnaunau Bay to the south and Kealakekua Bay to the north. North of Kauhako Bay, there were eleven *ahupua'a* and two royal centers: Hōnaunau and Kealakekua. Here the first remains of the Kona Field System are encountered inland of Hōnaunau Bay (see Horrocks and Rechtman 2009). Three decades of intensive survey and excavations have documented the planting zones associated with intensive agriculture (see chapter 7). Most archaeological reports describe these zones beginning with coastal habitation giving way to the *kula* zone, or, as it is sometimes known, the barren zone (0–150 m). This gives way to the *kalu'ulu* zone, where breadfruit trees dominated, running along the lower-elevation edge of the Kona fields (150–300 m). Cordy (1995, 7) notes that archaeologists have had difficulty identifying the *kalu'ulu* zone based on field survey (but see Lincoln and Ladefoged 2014). Above the *kalu'ulu* zone there is the *'apa'a* zone (300–750 m), the heart of the Kona Field System, where sweet potatoes, dryland taro, and other crops were grown intensively. The *'apa'a* zone eventually gives way to the *'ama'u* zone (600–900 m), the forested uplands. Named for the *'ama'u* fern (*Sadleria cyatheoides*), the zone was a source of wood and bananas. Much of the *'ama'u* zone was part of the broad Kahuku *ahupua'a;* this currently is part of the Kīpāhoehoe Natural Area Reserve that encompasses the upper reaches of Mauna Loa and extends into the Ka'ū desert.

One of the archipelago's most significant archaeological complexes is the *pu'uhonua* at Hōnaunau, or "City of Refuge," along with its associated structures (fig. 14.11). Hōnaunau sits on an irregular tongue of *pāhoehoe* lava protruding into the ocean and defining a small bay on the north. The *pu'uhonua* proper is defined by a massive stone wall—the Great Wall—running roughly north-south and east-west, one of the largest stone constructions in Hawai'i (fig. 14.12). Enclosed within these high stone walls was the sanctuary into which *kapu* breakers could flee and seek protection.

The Hōnaunau complex was more than a *pu'uhonua,* however, for it was a royal center that incorporated several prominent temples within the Great Wall complex, as well as residences for *ali'i* and their retainers outside the walls. One of the *heiau* (known as the "old *heiau*") consists of a great heap of stone rubble, destroyed by several tsunami. Nearby is 'Āle'ale'a Heiau, a massive rectangular platform. Most important of all was the Hale o Keawe, a small but highly sacred mortuary temple situated at the northern end of the Great

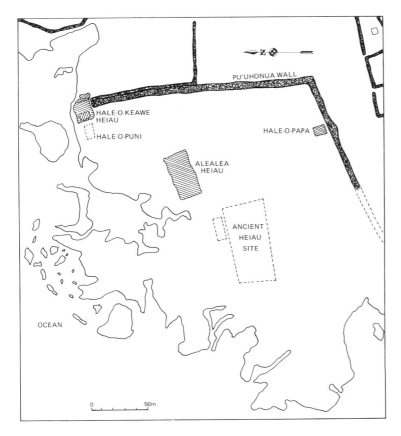

FIGURE 14.11 Map of the *pu'uhonua* and *heiau* complex at Hōnaunau, Hawai'i Island, showing the location of the major temple structures. (Map by P. V. Kirch)

Wall (fig. 14.13). This structure, well described and illustrated by early travelers such as William Ellis (1963), housed the bones of the island's paramount chiefs, some contained in wicker caskets woven in anthropomorphic shapes, and known as *kāʻai* (Buck 1957, 575). This royal sepulcher lent Hōnaunau its great sanctity.

John F. G. Stokes mapped, excavated, and restored several structures at Hōnaunau in 1919. In 1957, at the request of the National Park Service, a Bishop Museum team prepared a two-volume study of the area's natural and cultural history, incorporating the unpublished work of Stokes, along with ethnohistoric studies by Dorothy Barrère and Marion Kelly (Emory et al. 1957). Subsequently, and largely under the aegis of the National Park Service, a variety of excavations and restorations have been carried out, including work on the Great Wall (Ladd 1969c), the ʻĀleʻaleʻa Heiau platform (Ladd 1969b), the Hale o Keawe (Ladd 1969a), sites in the entry road corridor (Ladd 1967), and burials and midden sites immediately outside the Great Wall (Soehren 1962; Tuohy 1965). The considerable body of data pertaining to the development of this major political and religious center has yet to be fully synthesized.

Few radiocarbon dates have been obtained from the principal structures at Hōnaunau, and a series from the ʻĀleʻaleʻa Heiau (Ladd 1969b) gave conflicting results. Oral traditions

FIGURE 14.12 The "Great Wall" at Hōnaunau as seen from the interior of the *puʻuhonua* enclosure, with the stone platform of the *hale o Papa* temple in the foreground. *(Photo by Therese Babineau)*

FIGURE 14.13 The Hale o Keawe mortuary temple is situated at the western end of the "Great Wall" at Hōnaunau. The thatched house, fence, and images were reconstructed by the National Park Service based on early historic descriptions and drawings. *(Photo by Therese Babineau)*

compiled by Barrère (in Emory et al. 1957) thus provide the best basis for a chronology of the complex. Barrère speculates that the *puʻuhonua* may have been founded by the paramount chief ʻEhu-kai-malino. ʻUmi, who unified the entire island, probably reaffirmed the *puʻuhonua* of ʻEhu-kai-malino. The first clear reference to the site occurs with the paramountcy of Keawe-ku-i-ke-kāʻai, four generations after ʻUmi, who is said to have constructed ʻĀleʻaleʻa Heiau and possibly the Great Wall. The Hale-o-Keawe was constructed slightly later, for Keawe-i-kekahi-aliʻi-o-ka-moku.

Ladd's excavations at ʻĀleʻaleʻa Heiau revealed that the temple platform had been built in seven phases, each expanding the size of the temple. This suggests that Keawe-ku-i-ke-kāʻai was not the only one to have built ʻĀleʻaleʻa Heiau, although he probably added the final construction stage. Most likely, ʻĀleʻaleʻa Heiau was in use for nearly two centuries, being successively expanded at the accession of each paramount. With the construction of the Hale-o-Keawe by Keawe-i-kekahi-aliʻi-o-ka-moku, ʻĀleʻaleʻa Heiau was abandoned.

The Great Wall was excavated and stabilized by Stokes, and later by Ladd (1969c). The wall is a massive construction, with an average height of about 3.7 m, width of 5.2 m, and total length of 304.8 m, giving a volume of about 5,864 m^3. In both the Great Wall and in ʻĀleʻaleʻa Heiau, a clever masonry technique called *pao* was used, in which the interior is built up in a sort of column-and-lintel fashion. The resulting honeycomb effect, requiring less rock, is not visible behind the solid exterior facades.

Recent work around Hōnaunau has included limited excavations in coastal deposits, providing a chronology for human activity (Athens, Ward, and Blinn 2007; Athens, Rieth, and Dye 2014; Rieth 2007, 2011). The accumulation of deposits in Kaloko Pond (fig. 14.14) began in the Foundation Period (cal AD 974–1159, Wk-15982*, Layer V), with signs of human activity here through the Late Voyaging Period (cal AD 1288–1405, Beta-212800*, Layer V). The presence of *Pritchardia* palm (in Layer V), and palm casts in *pāhoehoe* flows point to an environment little affected by people until around AD 1450, when cultural deposits began to accumulate elsewhere at Hōnaunau (Rieth 2007, 2011). The first layer with clear signs of activity nearby (Layer IV), including pig and dog bone, predates the construction of the fishpond. A concentration of *Melanoides tuberculata* snail shells (Layer III), a type of brackish-water mollusk that feeds on detritus and algae, and other indicators of a marine environment, mark the transition to fish farming in Koloko Pond. Apple and Macdonald (1966) point to archaeological evidence for rapid coastal subsidence in historic times.

The National Park Service extended the park's boundary to include a historic fishing village at Ki'ilae, south of the royal complex (Rechtman et al. 2001). In the area above the village, Horrocks and Rechtman (2009) used paleoethnobotanical methods to identify crops grown in the Kona Field System. They recovered phytoliths of sweet potato and banana, but evidence of breadfruit was lacking, even though the elevation of the features examined puts them within the breadfruit zone.

A few kilometers north of Hōnaunau, Kealakekua Bay and the village sites of Nāpo'opo'o and Ka'awaloa were the setting for the arrival of HMS *Resolution* and HMS *Discovery* on January 17, 1779, under the command of Captain James Cook (fig. 14.15). Cook was received as the returning god Lono on the temple platform of Hikiau Heiau, and at Ka'awaloa he met his death on a *pāhoehoe* flat at the water's edge. The area is famed for the abrupt cliffs

FIGURE 14.14 Stone-lined fishpond at Hōnaunau, Hawai'i Island. *(Photo by Therese Babineau)*

FIGURE 14.15 The war canoes of Hawai'i Island king Kalani'ōpu'u at Kealakekua Bay, Hawai'i Island, as depicted by John Webber, artist with Captain James Cook in 1778. *(From Cook and King 1784)*

or Pali Kapu of Keōua, containing numerous burial caves. Hommon (1969b) surveyed part of the Ka'awaloa settlement, noted as the residence of the paramount chief Kalani'ōpu'u, whom Cook attempted to take hostage (see also Hommon 2014).

The temple platform of Hikiau Heiau is a state historic monument, but there has been little modern archaeological work in the Kealakekua environs until recently. The ritual precinct surrounding Hikiau Heiau, like 'Āle'ale'a Heiau, was marked by a monumental Great Wall, first mapped by Stokes. A recent drone-based LiDAR survey revealed that this wall was originally at least as large, and likely slightly larger, than the wall at Hōnaunau (M. D. McCoy et al. 2021). Excavations under Kealakekua's Great Wall exposed an occupation layer dated to cal AD 1440–1620 (Wk-48686), a finding that matches current estimates for coastal occupation at Hōnaunau. Further excavations of cultural deposits postdating the wall place its construction at cal AD 1640–1800 (Wk-48688).

The site of Puhina o Lono (site 50-10-48-3734) is believed to be the location where Captain Cook's body was taken after he was killed at Kealakekua Bay. Flexner and McCoy (2016, 316) present a case for the small but well-built structure having been used in the preparation of the bodies of high chiefs for burial.

Detailed studies of the upland Kona Field System have been carried out at the Amy Greenwell Ethnobotanical Garden in upland Kealakekua (M. S. Allen, ed., 2001). Research by Bishop Museum established a chronology of land use beginning with early land clearance, subsequent terrace and field wall (*kuaiwi*) construction, and stone mound gardening, followed in the postcontact era by coffee farming. The study documented the presence of small waterworn stones on mounds and in walls that may be indicative of garden ritual (Kirch 2001; see also Schilt 1984). The upland *heiau* of Pa'ikapahu is situated a short distance downslope from the Amy Greenwell Garden (Stokes 1991, 95, fig. 43).

Attempts to develop a chronology for the Kona Field System (M. S. Allen, ed., 2001; Burtchard 1996; Schilt 1984; Tomonari-Tuggle 2006), arguably the largest continuous site complex in the archipelago covering 163 km^2, have met with a few stumbling blocks. The hypothesis that there was a sequence from terraces to more formal field walls has not been borne out by research. Radiocarbon dates from the Amy Greenwell Garden hint at activity as early as the Foundation Period, while excavations not far downslope at Captain Cook Ranch pushed the entire Kona Field System sequence much later in time, suggesting that "a rethinking of the regional chronology may be necessary" (Tomonari-Tuggle 2006, iii).

Although there continue to be few reliable dates for the development of the Kona Field System, M. D. McCoy et al. (2017) have resolved some key changes after new excavations in the Amy Greenwell Garden, confirming reports of fire as early as AD 1000, although this may be attributable to volcanism, since a continuous record of anthropogenic fires does not occur until cal AD 1430–1485 (Beta-420384*). McCoy et al. (2017) report the earliest direct date on an introduced economic plant in the Kona Field System, paper mulberry (*Broussoneta papyrifera*), dating to cal AD 1485–1650 (Beta-420387*).

The controversial Hōkūli'a development, north of Kealakekua Bay, is estimated to have cost more than one billion dollars. In the early 1990s, a venture named 1250 Oceanside Partners commissioned intensive surveys of the land north of Kealakekua Bay, beginning with a section adjacent to Ka'awaloa (Hammatt et al. 1995), eventually focusing on a ca. 4-km-long section of the coast where a luxury real estate development was planned to cover about 625 ha (Tomonari-Tuggle and Tuggle 1999, 2008). The development plans included a coastal access road, a shoreline park, golf course, and 730 "farm-styled estates" on agricultural zoned land; such residential plots have been called "fake farms" by critics of the project (Callies 2010, 9). From the beginning of these surveys, it was clear that the high density of archaeological remains first described by Hommon (1969b) continued north along the coast; as the steep land behind the coastal zone changed to a gentler grade, the landscape merged with the lower-elevation distribution of the Kona Field System (Kailihiwa 2015). Eight *ahupua'a* were slated for development, with at least a dozen *heiau,* household sites, a range of garden features and shelters, a section of the historic-era Kuakini Wall, and one refuge cave.

In the 2000s, the Hōkūli'a development became a flashpoint in the struggle to protect *iwi kūpuna* (human remains) and cultural sites (Kawelu 2015, 63–65). Ahead of major construction, written management plans recommended preserving sites and known burials. But in practice there were inadequate efforts to avoid and protect burials and to alleviate environmental concerns. After numerous burials were exposed by bulldozing, resulting in a community outcry, the developers were sued by a number of parties. A settlement in 2006 required the construction of 168 affordable homes, the completion of an access road to relieve traffic, and new limitations to construction and expanded site preservation. At Hōkūli'a today there is a golf course and access road, but the development was not completed as planned; in 2013 the developers filed for bankruptcy. Several areas were set aside to preserve agricultural features, coastal sites, and sections of the Ala Loa.

Moving north from Hōkūli'a up to Kailua Bay, there have been hundreds of CRM archaeological projects in North Kona. Just north of the boundary separating South Kona from North Kona, there is a short 3 km stretch of coastline between the Hōkūli'a Golf Course and the

Kona Country Club where the original Ala Loa ("Long Road"), also known as the Old Government Beach Road, cuts across 12 *ahupua'a*. In 1998, Peter Mills surveyed this corridor as part of a University of Hawai'i, Hilo, field school (Mills 2002b; Mills and Irani 2000). Mills recorded 17 new sites as well as updated maps, including named *heiau*. The Ala Loa trail varies along its course, with curbstone lining in sections, and waterworn stones used in some places but not others, suggesting that different portions of the trail date to different time periods.

A *hōlua* slide located above Keauhou Bay built in 1814 to commemorate the birth of Kamehameha's youngest son Kauikeaouli was likely about 1 km long when completed. This was easily the longest *hōlua* in the Hawaiian Islands, and in fact, the steep, long track is so massive that it fits within the technical specifications of an Olympic bobsled track (see M. D. McCoy 2018). The Keauhou *hōlua*, despite being in good condition, is difficult to see today because it is entirely enclosed within a golf course. Another significant site in Kona is the location of the "Battle of Kuamo'o," which occurred after the 1819 breaking of the *'ai kapu* by Liholiho, provoking Kekuaokalani and other "rebel chiefs" to take up arms against the better outfitted warriors of Liholiho. The graves of warriors from both sides were buried in subtle small stone terraces that are today marked by a plaque.

Keauhou *ahupua'a* exhibits a dense archaeological landscape reflecting the area's rich history, including several named coastal *heiau* (Barrera 1971b; Emory, McCoy, and Barrère 1971; Stokes 1991), along with the imposing residence of the high chief Lonoikamakahiki. Kirch (1973a) excavated the stone foundations of what he interpreted as a men's house (*mua*) (Ha-D4-51), constructed in a series of four phases, adjacent to the Lonoikamakahiki residence. Hammatt and Folk (1980b) surveyed a large area along the shore at Kahalu'u, documenting 70 sites.

North of Keauhou is Kahalu'u *ahupua'a*, home to another royal center, several *heiau*, a dense settlement, remnants of the Kona Field System, and refuge caves. The twin temples of Hāpaiali'i and Ke'ekū (Stokes 1991, 71–79, figs. 21–30), constructed on a *pāhoehoe* shelf that is inundated at high tide, have been restored under the aegis of Kamehameha Schools. Hāpaiali'i is a large, elevated platform oriented along cardinal directions, whereas Ke'ekū is an imposing enclosure with massive walls. According to Stokes (1991, 73), Hāpaiali'i is much older than Ke'ekū, the latter having been built by the Hawai'i Island king Lonoikamakahiki following his victory over Maui king Kamalālāwalu.

Excavations in the early 1980s at the Kahalu'u Habitation Cave (site 50-10-37-7702, not to be confused with 'Ōhi'a Cave, site -7962; Tomonari-Tuggle 1994), yielded over 12,000 artifacts from a well-stratified deposit (Rosendahl 1981). Subsequent analyses of the collections by Peter Mills and his students at the University of Hawai'i, Hilo, focused on sourcing the lithic material with XRF analysis, and on and defining the site's chronology, confirming that the site was used intensively after AD 1650 (Mills et al. 2011). Adzes made from basalt sources occurring outside of Kona accounted for most of the artifacts tested; these nonlocal adzes were purposefully made in both large and small sizes, although there was some reworking of larger broken tools to fashion them into rejuvenated small adzes.

Intensive CRM surveys and excavations at Hōlualoa Bay, close to the heart of Kailua-Kona, have documented a high concentration of sites on and near Kamoa Point, the location of a royal center associated with a series of paramount chiefs, including Keākealaniwahine, who traditions relate as one of only two women to have reigned as *ali'i nui*. Henry

Kehahuna's 1950s map of the area known as Keolonāhihi complex (site 50-10-37-2059), and the nearby residence of Keākealaniwahine, has helped raise awareness of the importance of preserving this region. McCoy et al. (2022) used LiDAR to define the major extant archaeological features of the Hōlualoa royal center.

Hammatt, Borthwick, and Chiogioji's (1990) discovery of 285 features in a 0.26 km² section just *mauka* of Kamoa Point, including 100 structures interpreted as parts of habitations, provides evidence for a substantial community supporting the royal court. Site density decreases sharply upslope and away from the royal center but nonetheless remains high, with intensive surveys across Hōlualoa reporting 1,105 features over 1.6 km² (Haun 2001, table 3); these included 241 habitation features and the characteristic *kuaiwi* walls of the Kona Field System. Hōlualoa 4 *ahupua'a* is registered as an "archaeological district" (site 50-10-37-23661), and includes Keolonāhihi State Historical Park.

Previously known as Kaiakeakua Bay, Kailua Bay boasts what is probably Kona's most famous royal center, Kamakahonu, where Kamehameha I resided in old age and died in 1819. During the tumultuous period following Kamehameha's death, it was in Kailua that Kamehameha's favored wife Ka'ahumanu proclaimed herself to be the first Kuhina Nui, or "Regent," encouraging the young king Liholiho (Kamehameha II) to break the *'ai kapu*, bringing an end to the ancient religion and *kapu* system. Ka'ahumanu's brother, John Adams Kuakini, governed the island from his base at Kailua from the 1820s through his death in 1844. The first company of American Protestant missionaries arrived at Kailua Bay on April 4, 1820; later the first Catholic ceremony was held here in 1840. Kuakini oversaw the construction of Hulihe'e Palace and adjacent Protestant church, Moku'aikaua, and donated the land where St. Michael's Catholic Church was built in 1846. Moku'aikaua is said to have incorporated cut-and-dressed stone slabs from an earlier *heiau* site.

'Ahu'ena Heiau (50-Ha-D9-1, or 50-10-27-3839), at Kamakahonu on the north end of Kailua Bay, holds an iconic place in Hawai'i Island's history (Stokes 1991, 43–47). With traditions that go back to Līloa, the *heiau* was rededicated by Kamehameha I, and was sketched by Louis Choris during the visit of the Russian ship *Rurick* in 1816–1817. In 1823, Ellis reported that the site's foundation had been converted by Governor Kuakini into a fort. Indeed, given the temple's location so close to the events of 1819, it may have been one of the first *heiau* destroyed after the abolition of the *'ai kapu*. In the 1970s, the foundations of 'Ahu'ena Heiau were reconstructed by David Roy, with archaeological supervision by Bishop Museum (fig. 14.16), as part of the grounds of the King Kamehameha I Hotel (Vernon 1975).

Henry Kekahuna endeavored to map the landscape of Kailua Bay in the 1950s, with his map showing myriad structures in addition to 'Ahu'ena Heiau (Bishop Museum Archives SP 201861). Two *heiau* that no longer exist are Pā o 'Umi Heiau and 'Opunui Heiau. Kekahuna and Theodore Kelsey (1954) describe these temples as having been dismantled and their stones used for a number of construction projects by Governor Kuakini. In 1835, for example, "hewn stones" from Pā o 'Umi Heiau—a reference to stone cut and dressed for architecture—were reported to have been used in the construction of Moku'aikaua Church (Fornander 1878–1885, 2:101). However, the *heiau* were not completely destroyed. and as recently as the 1980s some of their foundations remained, but when archaeologists returned in 2000 they found nearly all surface architecture had been bulldozed (Rechtman and Dougherty 2000).

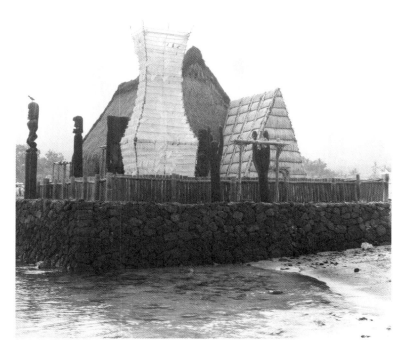

FIGURE 14.16 Ahu'ena Heiau at Kamakahonu, Hawai'i Island, sits on an artificial stone platform on the shore of Kailua Bay. The temple superstructures were reconstructed based on early historic accounts. *(Photo by Therese Babineau)*

Kennedy and Brady (1997, 652) argue that a large lava tube in Kailua was used as a refuge built for "chiefs and their entourages." Another lava tube, site 50-10-44-5060, first described by Schilt (1984) during her study carried out prior to the construction of Kuakini Highway, was one of the most significant encountered. The amount of constructed architecture within the lava tube is remarkable, as is the massive 10 × 5 m defensive wall built to seal the entry. The labor expended in building defenses, and the discovery of a *lei niho palaoa* in the cave, suggest the presence of chiefly individuals.

Nearer to the coast, Loubser and Rechtman (2006) interpret a stone platform (6 × 3 m) in terms of a rare find: two wooden *kapa* beaters (site 50-10-37-22426). The first was an intact four-sided *i'e kuku* beater found 50 cm below the surface of the platform, and the second, a fragment found another 25 cm below that. The beaters were recovered along with cowrie shells on the eastern end of the platform away from where food refuse was found. The authors suggest these tools were stored within the platform and may indicate an area designated for barkcloth production. Each beater was made from *kauwila* wood (*Colubrina oppositifolia*); a radiocarbon date indicates that these artifacts may be of postcontact age (cal AD 1668–1947, Beta-154225*), although the absence of introduced materials such as manufactured glass, metal, or ceramics here or in excavations of a nearby platform (site 50-10-37-22427) suggest that the beaters may date to the Archaic States Period.

North of Kailua, evidence of settlement becomes sparse, reflecting the increased aridity and barren lava flows emanating from Hualālai. At Honokahau Bay and Kaloko Point, however, several fishponds provided a focus of attraction; these are surrounded by a large number of habitation sites, petroglyphs, and the substantial *heiau* of Pu'uoina and Maka'ōpio (Cluff 1969; Emory and Soehren 1961). Maka'ōpio Heiau is noteworthy for the large cut-and-dressed upright slabs incorporated into its face, a rare feature of Hawaiian stonework (fig. 14.17).

FIGURE 14.17 Makaʻōpio Heiau at Honōkahau, Hawaiʻi Island, incorporates several large, cut-and-dressed stone slabs. *(Photo by Therese Babineau)*

Cordy's survey along this northern portion of the North Kona coast (1981) was an influential effort to interpret surface domestic architecture in terms of use duration. Cordy classified architecture in terms of temporary, recurrent, or permanent habitation, basing these classes primarily on feature size and topographic setting, but also using variables such as the number of internal and associated features.

Throughout the Honokohau region lava tubes were used as refuges, with examples reported from virtually every survey in the area. While it is often presumed that the use of lava tubes as refuges reflects an increase in competition in the Archaic States Period (Kolb and Dixon 2002), we have little detailed information on the chronology or variability in use of these shelters.

Moving north from Honokohau, the land becomes too barren, dry, and rocky to support agriculture, hence population density was correspondingly low. The boundary between Kona and Kohala *moku* is at Puʻu Anahulu; the southern part of Kohala incorporates several large *ahupuaʻa*, including Waikoloa and Puakō. The large size of these *ahupuaʻa* reflects their sparse resource base, contrasting with the narrow, densely packed *ahupuaʻa* of Kona, with the highly productive Kona Field System. Kohala *moku* encompasses the northwest-trending Kohala mountain range, the geologically oldest part of the island. Much of the work in this region has been discussed in previous chapters, hence we summarize this research only briefly below.

The "oasis" of ʻAnaehoʻomalu, with its sandy bay offering a sheltered canoe landing and large fishpond, stand out among the barren *ʻaʻā* and *pāhoehoe* lava fields of south Kohala. Barrera (1971a, 1972) surveyed ʻAnaehoʻomalu in the late 1960s prior to resort development, excavating in lava-tube shelters and open sites. During the Archaic States Period, ʻAnaehoʻomalu had a reasonably large and permanent settlement, focused on marine exploitation. Of particular note at ʻAnaehoʻomalu is a large petroglyph field with more than 9,000 glyphs, one of the most extensive petroglyph complexes in the islands (fig. 14.18).

FIGURE 14.18 Petroglyhs on *pāhoehoe* lava at ʻAnaehoʻomalu, Hawaiʻi Island. *(After Barrera 1971a)*

North of the Kanikū ʻaʻā lava flow lies another fishpond "oasis," Kalāhuipuaʻa, studied by Kirch (1979a). An intensive survey revealed 179 sites, including 47 shelter caves, several of these with substantial stratified deposits. Excavations in 10 lava-tube shelter caves (fig. 14.19) yielded an important collection of 12,030 artifacts. One lava-tube shelter, site Ha-E1-355, had initially been occupied as a fishing camp prior to becoming permanently occupied. A large communal burial cave was situated inland of the fishponds, and included canoe burials. After an osteological study of the skeletal remains was conducted, the cave was sealed intact, following appropriate cultural protocol (see chapter 11). The arid climate at Kalāhuipuaʻa preserved a number of wooden artifacts in several of the shelters, including a canoe paddle, carrying poles, a canoe spreader, and a cache of 16 large wooden fishhooks, some certainly intended for taking sharks (fig. 14.20).

Just north of Kalāhuipuaʻa, at Puakō, is site Ha-E3-1, with more than 3,000 petroglyphs (Bishop Museum 1964; Cox and Stasack 1970, 85, fig. 100). Especially notable is a line of 29 marching stick figures, flanked by three slightly larger figures on one side, and one vastly larger figure on the other. These have been interpreted as a portrayal of an army or group of warriors on the march, accompanied by their chiefs, represented by the larger figures.

In the early 1970s, the construction of Queen Kaʻahumanu Highway, connecting Kawaihae and Kailua, and paralleling the South Kohala and North Kona coastline about 0.5 to 2.0 km inland, provided an opportunity to sample archaeological sites in this arid region inland of the major settlements of ʻAnaehoʻomalu, Kalāhuipuaʻa, Kīholo, and Makalawena. Ching (1971) directed an initial survey of the highway corridor, while Rosendahl (1972b, 1973) oversaw subsequent salvage excavations. In Lālāmilo, inland of Puakō and Hāpuna Bays, several small cultural complexes were discovered that utilized alluvial basins, watered by seasonal rains, to produce a crop of sweet potatoes or other dryland crops. One

FIGURE 14.19 A lava-tube rockshelter at Kalāhuipua'a, Hawai'i Island. The interior of the shelter was used as a dwelling for groups exploiting the nearby fishponds. (Photo by P. V. Kirch)

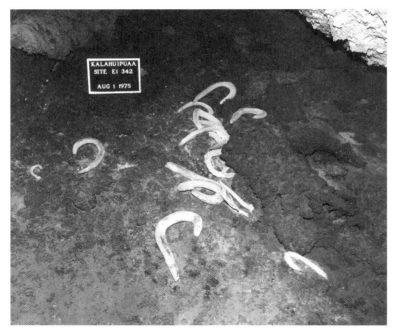

FIGURE 14.20 A cache of large wooden fishhooks for catching sharks, found in the interior of a lava-tube rockshelter at Kalāhuipua'a, Hawai'i Island. (Photo by P. V. Kirch)

large water-diversion wall directed the intermittent flow of a small gulch out onto the adjacent soil basins, a clever innovation in this arid landscape.

Inland of 'Anaeho'omalu as well as at Kalāhuipua'a, hundreds of depressions abraded in the smooth *pāhoehoe* lava indicate where pieces of scoriaceous lava were roughed out into blocks to serve as abrading tools for fishhook and other artifact manufacture (fig. 14.21). The preparation of such lava abraders may have been a major industry of this arid region, for the number of abrader preparation areas seems to be far in excess of what would be required for local use. Alternatively, these depressions may have resulted from a major effort to construct canoes ahead of a planned invasion of a neighboring island—such as the Peleleu fleet built by Kamehameha while in Hilo in 1800–1804 (Jensen 2001, 30; Major 2008, 52).

During the second phase of the Queen Ka'ahumanu Highway salvage program, Rosendahl (1973, 68–73) excavated in a large refuge cave inland of Kīholo. The entrance to

FIGURE 14.21 Basin-shaped depressions in scoriaceous lava inland of 'Anaeho'omalu, Hawai'i Island, resulted from the manufacture of lava abraders. *(Photo courtesy Bishop Museum Department of Anthropology)*

this spacious lava tube, Cave 900, had been blocked by tons of lava rock, leaving only a narrow passageway through which people had to enter single file, at the mercy of those defending the shelter from within.

Kawaihae, with its sheltered natural harbor, was an important calling point for early European voyagers and traders. From 1790 to 1794, Kawaihae was the primary residence of Kamehameha I as he regrouped and prepared his forces for the invasion of Maui, Moloka'i, and O'ahu. On a prominent natural rise above the harbor, Kamehameha I constructed (or possibly rebuilt and expanded) the massive *luakini* war temple of Pu'ukoholā (Cluff et al. 1969). In 1791, Kamehameha offered up the body of his archrival and cousin Keōua to the war god Kūkā'ilimoku, on the altar of Pu'ukoholā. The temple has been reconstructed and stabilized by the National Park Service, which maintains the site as a historical monument (fig. 14.22).

FIGURE 14.22 Pu'ukoholā Heiau at Kawaihae, Hawai'i Island, was constructed by Kamehameha I. *(Photo by Therese Babineau)*

The most recent reconstruction occurred following a 2006 earthquake and involved teams of stonemasons working over several months (Johnson et al. 2013).

There are few archaeological sites, artifacts, or deposits that date to the brief window of time between Captain Cook's visit in 1788–1789 and the establishment of a new pan-archipelago Kingdom of Hawaii in 1810. One of the best known is the Kawaihae home of John Young, a British sailor who was taken captive and then became an advisor to Kamehameha I. After first living close to the shore, Young built a permanent homestead on the slopes above Puʻukoholā Heiau, where he would live with his high-born Kānaka Maoli wives and children (see chapter 13).

Inland of Kawaihae, on the wide saddle between Mauna Kea and the Kohala Mountains, is the Waimea area, where soils are more developed and fertile, and rainfall is adequate for cropping of sweet potatoes and, with supplementary irrigation from streams in the Kohala Mountains, of taro. Like Kona, in late precontact times the Waimea area was a region of extensive agricultural fields. A proposed realignment of the highway connecting Kawaihae to the town of Waimea presented an opportunity for studying a transect extending from the arid coast, up the gentle slope, to the fertile plains at an elevation of 870 m above sea level. Initial survey of the road corridor by Barrera and Kelly (1974) revealed dense concentrations of sites in the uplands. Subsequent survey and excavations by a Bishop Museum team, directed by Jeff Clark and Kirch (eds., 1983), focused on extensive evidence for agriculture and on the reconstruction of the local environment, using a variety of specialist techniques. At the same time, Clark (1981), using aerial photography and ground survey, carried out an intensive survey of the core of the agricultural field area at Lālāmilo. These studies showed that the present town of Waimea was at the center of a large and intensively cultivated field system, which was in operation by at least the seventeenth century, based on radiocarbon dates, and probably earlier. Traversing this field complex was an intricate, reticulated irrigation system, feeding water from two streams out across the fertile slopes.

Excavations at Kawaihae revealed early use of the coast not only for intermittent fishing trips but probably permanent settlement as well as early as the Late Voyaging Period. At site 50-10-05-24053, Carson (2006, 86) reports radiocarbon dates that "indicate an early to middle pre-contact age for Layer VII, within the range of AD 1250 to 1410." While the earliest of these dates is on pearl shell (*Isognomon* sp.) (cal AD 1250–1520, Wk-16335), and thus subject to an unknown degree of correction for old marine carbon, this is overlain by deposits definitively dated to the 1400s, putting the date for Layer VII in the fifteenth century AD. Layer VII contained a range of faunal remains, including turtle and seabirds, but more importantly pig, chicken, and dog; also present were a worked dog tooth, as well as flaked volcanic glass and basalt. Two rockshelters located near Keanuʻiʻomanō Stream were radiocarbon dated, to cal AD 1175–1305 (Beta-135829*) in the case of site 50-10-05-14761, and even earlier in the Foundation Period, cal AD 1015–1280 (Beta-135827*) in the case of site 50-10-05-14750 (Robins, Eble, and Anderson 2000; Schiltz 1994).

Kohala—the geologically oldest part of Hawaiʻi Island—stands out with its more developed soils and—along the windward side—stream-cut gulches and valleys (fig. 14.23). Leeward North Kohala generally lacks stream dissection, but its higher-elevation slopes were the focus of intensive dryland agriculture, while the coastline, punctuated with small bays and patch reefs, provided opportunities for fishing and shellfish gathering. Not

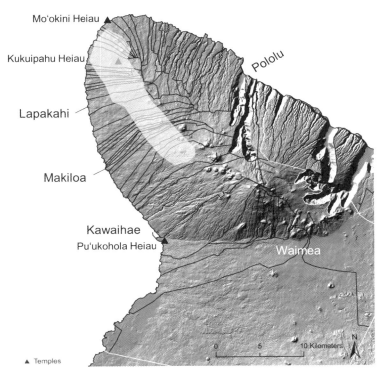

FIGURE 14.23 Map of Kohala peninsula, Hawai'i Island, showing the location of key sites and locations. The shaded area indicates the extent of the leeward Kohala Field System. (Map by M. D. McCoy)

surprisingly, Hawaiian traditions refer to Kohala as one of the first regions of the island to have been occupied (Fornander 1916–1920).

Archaeological research in leeward north Kohala was initiated by the University of Hawai'i at Mānoa's Lapakahi field school in the late 1960s and early 1970s (Griffin et al. 1971; Pearson, ed., 1968; Rosendahl 1972a; Tuggle and Griffin, eds., 1973). Just south of the old port of Māhukona, Lapakahi is one of many narrow *ahupua'a* that bisect the leeward slopes of North Kohala. The settlement landscape of Lapakahi has been described in detail in chapter 12.

Large sections of leeward Kohala remained unoccupied until the Expansion and Archaic States Periods. Dating of habitations in this region did not uncover any signs of people living permanently along the coast or in the uplands prior to AD 1400 (Field, Ladefoged, Sharp, and Kirch 2011). It is, however, possible that low-intensity gardening, or shifting cultivation, in the leeward Kohala Field System could have predated the establishment of permanent communities. A direct date on carbonized sweet potato of cal AD 1290–1430 (Beta-208143*)—some of the earliest evidence of sweet potato dispersal into Polynesia—is suggestive of an initial phase of shifting cultivation in the Kohala uplands at the end of the Late Voyaging Period, a phase that remains poorly documented (Ladefoged, Graves, and Coil 2005).

Windward Kohala is marked by a succession of deeply incised, youthful valleys, providing a remarkable amount of land for irrigated taro (M. D. McCoy, Asner, and Graves 2011). H. D. Tuggle of the University of Hawai'i investigated Pololū and Honokāne valleys from 1972 to 1974 (Tuggle and Tomonari-Tuggle 1980). The earliest secure dates from Hawai'i Island come from a redating of samples from the Pololū Valley dune site (site 50-10-03-4802), placing the start of occupation in the Late Voyaging Period (cal AD 1184–1284, Wk-19311*; Field and Graves 2008).

Renewed research in both leeward and windward Kohala has fleshed out the sequence of agricultural development (see chapter 7), showing how settlement shifted in this part of the island. We suspect, based on the early dates from Pololū Valley (Field and Graves 2008; Rieth et al. 2011) and Hālawa Gulch (M. D. McCoy et al. 2013), that the first generations of settlers favored the windward valleys. Over time, populations expanded to the leeward coast, perhaps first near Lapakahi, and then gradually south toward Kawaihae. Studies of house sites across leeward Kohala confirm that the riskiest lands for farming were avoided until after AD 1650, when the populations of *ahupua'a* such as Makiloa doubled at a time when population growth had already peaked in the more productive, central part of the field system, represented by Kaiholena *ahupua'a* (Field, Ladefoged, and Kirch 2011).

As populations expanded along the leeward coast, residential sites were also being established among the upland fields. Food remains from contemporaneous coastal and upland house sites of the early Expansion Period exhibit different patterns. The upland houses generally lack marine foods, while on the coast, the remains of pig and chicken are absent. After AD 1520, however, shellfish and fish bones are common in upland sites (although still less abundant than in coastal sites), while the bones of domestic animals appear in the coastal house sites. The reciprocal *mauka-makai,* upland-coastal resource loop is a strong signal marking the beginning of communities organized under the *ahupua'a* system.

Architecture in leeward Kohala provides an opportunity to see how smaller religious sites fit into the larger settlement pattern. At Kamilo Bay, the boundary of Makiloa and Kālala, not far from a high-ranked house site (MKI-56), is an unusual U-shaped enclosure (site KAL-1, 24 × 17 m) with thick walls, *'ili'ili* paving, and small depressions with branch coral offerings along the back wall that appear to have once held wooden images. A date of AD 1603 ± 12 from a coral offering, along with dates from charcoal collected under the *heiau* foundation of AD 1400–1630, place the site in the Archaic States Period. This finding, along with studies of a similar-sized coastal *heiau* (site PHH-13), point to local-scaled investments during this period.

Smaller *heiau* in the upland fields appear to have demarcated the boundaries that designated who had the rights over surplus production. The earliest *heiau* were spaced far from one another; then after AD 1520, many new *heiau* were built (McCoy, Ladefoged, Graves, and Stephens 2011). These remained modestly sized until after AD 1650, when not only did the average size of *heiau* increase—the largest in the same size range as coastal *heiau*—but they were built with a greater command of the local viewsheds (Phillips et al. 2015; see also Mulrooney and Ladefoged 2005). There is a remarkable amount of architectural variation, including the distinctive notched-style *heiau* documented elsewhere in the archipelago, which in Kohala dates to the Archaic States Period; this may reflect the influence of priestly cults that extended beyond the boundaries of single island kingdoms.

One of the challenges to reconstructing the ritual landscape of the leeward Kohala Field System is the difficulty in distinguishing structures that were *heiau* as opposed to large house sites or other important structures. For example, site MKI-130, initially thought to be a *heiau* was later revised to more likely being a men's house (*mua*) due to its size and style of construction (Ladefoged, Somers, and Lane-Hamasaki 2020).

One unique structure lying within the leeward Kohala Field System is located in Kukuipahu *ahupua'a* (site 50-10-02-4135). The structure, a rectangular terrace, has a number of features that set it apart, including large cut-and-dressed red scoria blocks and raised-relief petroglyphs of turtles and anthropomorphic figures (color plate 10; fig. 14.24). Kirch et al. mapped the site, noting several phases of construction:

> (1) an initial phase of construction of the terrace utilizing cut-and-dressed basalt slabs to face the terrace along its south, west, and north sides, and with an east facade of red scoria blocks; (2) an episode when the original stonework was to a large extent purposefully dismantled, leaving only portions of the original facade intact; (3) a rebuilding phase during which a rectangular enclosure with thick walls of natural boulders and cobbles was constructed on top of the ruins of the original terrace. (Kirch et al. 2020, 49)

The original terrace, with a footprint of 580 m², would have been similar in layout to the *heiau* that have been recorded on Mokumanamana (Emory 1928) and on Mauna Kea (McCoy and Nees 2014), although on a much larger scale. The site's orientation was intentionally toward the east, within a few degrees of the equinoctial sunrise. While we lack good ethnohistoric information on this site, its placement and orientation could indicate dedication to the god Kāne. Test excavations in 2022 by Kirch and colleagues yielded several radiocarbon dates indicating construction of the original terrace during the sixteenth century AD.

The largest of Kohala's *heiau* by volume of building material—larger than either of the dual temples of Pu'ukoholā Heiau and Mailekini Heiau at Kawaihae—is Mo'okini Heiau near 'Upolu Point (fig. 14.25). Stokes (1991, 173–178) estimated the size of the Mo'okini enclosure as 85 × 43 m, with thick walls almost 6 m high in places. It is attributed to the Tahitian voyaging priest Pā'ao and therefore stands as the type site for *luakini heiau*. There are references in oral history to a royal center having been somewhere in the region. Sadly, while sugarcane farming spared this monument, all other architecture around, except for

FIGURE 14.24 Large boulder at Kukuipahu Heiau, Hawai'i Island, with raised relief carvings of human figures and turtles. *(Photo by Alan Carpenter)*

FIGURE 14.25 Interior of Moʻokini Heiau near ʻUpolu Point, Hawaiʻi Island, attributed to the Tahitian priest Pāʻao. *(Photo by Therese Babineau)*

an enclosure marking the birthplace of Kamehameha I, has been pushed into spoil piles of stone on the margins of fields. There are some sources that indicate that, as at Puʻukoholā, some construction stones were sourced from Pololū Valley. If this was the case, then it may have served as the inspiration for Kamehameha's ambitious temple to the war god.

The largest *heiau* in Kohala when judged by its footprint is located on the edge of the windward sea cliffs above Kapanaia Bay, called Kapālama Heiau (site 50-Ha-F24-3). It is a low platform, paved in places with large waterworn stones, spanning an area equal to two football fields (106 × 96 m). Stokes (1991, 179, fig. 93) was impressed with the site but was unable to collect much oral history regarding it. He suggested based on the name that it was "a locality where the young women of chiefly rank were guarded before uniting with a male chief for the purpose of securing a young chief of the highest *kapu*" (Stokes 1991, 179–180). Today, the site is thickly covered in ironwood trees planted as windbreaks that present a preservation issue. The effects of erosion are on dramatic display just a few kilometers to the south at Kuapalaha Heiau overlooking Kēōkea Bay, which has a 20 m hole in its center where the sea cliffs have given way.

A few kilometers to the north of Kapālama Heiau, Hale o Kāʻili Heiau is an important site in the rise to power of Kamehameha (site 50-10-02-2332; Stokes 1991, 181). The *heiau* is modest, just 40 × 20 m, but stands out as for its use of earthen berms in its main enclosure. Hale o Kāʻili Heiau is notable as having been the storehouse for the many highly coveted *kiʻi* or temple images captured by Kamehameha I during his wars of conquest; the translation of *kāʻili* is "to snatch, grab, take by force, seize, abduct, usurp." We note that in Kona, at the royal center of Keolonāhihi, there is another Hale o Kāʻili that may have served the same purpose for one of the previous island rulers.

15

THE ARCHAEOLOGY OF MAUI, LĀNA'I, AND KAHO'OLAWE ISLANDS

Maui, with a land area of 1,885 km², was an important center of political development in the late precontact and early historic eras, the seat of powerful kings such as Kahekili, archrival of Kamehameha I. Geologically, Maui consists of two separate shield volcanoes that coalesced to form a broad saddle or isthmus (fig. 15.1). Geologically older West Maui, more weathered and dissected, exhibits deep amphitheater valleys penetrating its 1,215 m high summit from both windward and leeward sides. Permanent streams emanating from Waihe'e, Wai'ehu, Wailuku, and Waikapū valleys along the windward side of West Maui (the Nā Wai Ehā region) provided irrigation water for extensive taro pondfields. The arid isthmus was evidently little used until the development of large-scale plantation agriculture in the late nineteenth century, when streams on windward East Maui were diverted to water the sugarcane fields (the streams of Nā Wai Ehā were similarly diverted for plantation agriculture). East Maui, still considered geologically dormant, rather than extinct—the Haleakalā rift last erupted in AD 1790—constitutes the larger part of the island and mostly lacks large valleys. Its broad slopes, however, especially in the Hāna and Kahikinui regions, were densely settled. East Maui rises to an elevation of 2,727 m along the rim of Haleakalā Crater and, like Mauna Kea and Mauna Loa on Hawai'i, has a true alpine zone.

In spite of its size and sociopolitical importance, Maui has been less intensively studied than some of the other islands. Kenneth Emory's 1920 survey of Haleakalā Crater was the first archaeological project on Maui (Emory 1921). In 1929, Winslow Walker (1930) carried out a general survey for Bishop Museum, but his work was judged to be of uneven quality and was never published. Maui was largely bypassed during the Museum's Hawaiian Archaeological Program of the 1950s, when Emory and colleagues sought out artifact-rich sites. The pace of research picked up during the 1960s, with reconnaissance surveys by Lloyd Soehren (1963) in parts of East Maui, including Haleakalā Crater; work by Richard Pearson (1970) at Wai'ānapanapa; and a pioneering settlement-pattern survey combined with stratigraphic excavations by Peter Chapman for Bishop Museum in Kahikinui in southeast Maui

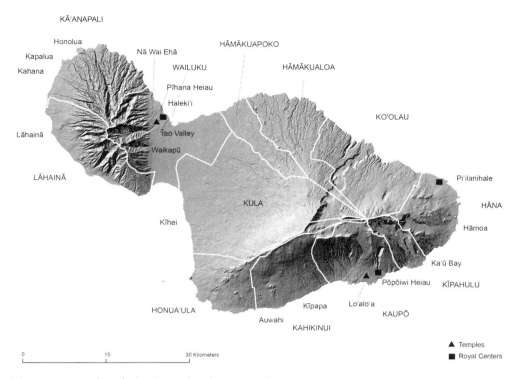

FIGURE 15.1 Map of Maui Island, showing sites and major places mentioned in the text. White lines indicate the boundaries of the traditional districts. *(Map by M. D. McCoy)*

(Chapman and Kirch 1979). Elspeth Sterling, an amateur archaeologist who worked initially with Emory, compiled an extensive dossier titled *Sites of Maui,* published posthumously by Bishop Museum (E. P. Sterling 1998); this remains a valuable guide to the known *heiau* and traditional sites of the island.

Beginning in the early 1970s, urban and resort development in the Kīhei and Mākena region, and at Kāʻanapali and Kapalua on West Maui, generated numerous CRM survey and salvage excavation projects. An extensive research project was initiated by Patrick Kirch and colleagues in Kahikinui and Kaupō Districts, beginning in 1995 and continuing for nearly two decades (Kirch 2014). Large-scale CRM projects on Maui have proliferated during the past few decades as urban and resort development has continued, along with the emergence of other development-based projects, including large renewable energy projects in various areas of Maui. As with Hawaiʻi Island, our knowledge of Maui archaeology is mostly confined to the leeward regions.

West Maui

On West Maui, most archaeological work has been conducted in connection with resort or housing developments along the coast. Excavations in Lāhainā, for example, revealed that what is today Maluʻuluolele Park was between 1837 and 1845 Mokuʻula islet, the royal residence of Kamehameha III. Klieger (1998) excavated fill to expose and map the buried remains of the former islet situated within an artificial pond from the time when Lāhainā was the capital of the Hawaiian Kingdom. The deposits contained different types of imported materials—glass, ceramics, and metals—that appear to be deposited without any sign of reuse, as is commonly found at contemporary sites. To Bayman (2010), this suggested a disposal pattern that may have been exclusive to the upper classes given the high cost of imports in the early 1840s.

South of Lāhainā, at Oluwalu, petroglyphs were inscribed on a vertical rock face known as Puʻu Kilea (site Ma-D2-2). As seen in figure 15.2, the glyphs include not only numerous anthropomorphs but also a particularly good example of a sailing canoe with "crab-claw" mat sail.

Between Lāhainā and Kapalua, historic-era ranching followed by sugarcane and pineapple plantation agriculture on the tablelands and industrial activities along the coast largely obliterated the traditional settlement pattern. In Kahana, for example, Walker (1930) reported the locations of *heiau* that in his time had already been destroyed (sites 12, 13, 14). Handy and Handy (1972) describe taro grown in gulches, while limited surveys have reported agricultural features in Kahana (Walker and Rosendahl 1985). A number of coastal

FIGURE 15.2 Petroglyphs at Olowalu, Maui Island. *(Photo by Therese Babineau)*

settlements and burials have been encountered in the course of modern developments along the coast in this region.

In the Honolua area, about 20 km from Lāhainā, Kirch (1973b) excavated at a small fishing camp (site Ma-D13-1) at Hāwea Point. The coastal midden deposit at Hāwea Point was noteworthy for its high density of burned candlenut shells; several large earth ovens were exposed. Kirch argued that the fishermen who used this site brought the *kukui* nuts from their permanent residence sites in one of the nearby valleys, roasted them at the camp, and prepared the *'inamona* concoction, which combines fish, seaweed, and *kukui*-nut kernels, to be taken back to home sites for consumption (Kirch 1982c).

West Maui is the location of a controversial site in the history of Hawaiian archaeology: the Honokahua burial site (50-50-01-1342) in the Honolua area. Between 1986 and 1989, more than 1,000 burials were exhumed from a sand dune cemetery that covered an area larger than two football fields (see chapter 11). Radiocarbon dating, although not conducted using modern controls for old wood, suggests use from the Foundation Period through to the recent past (Donham 1989, 2000).

The greatest concentration of population on West Maui in ancient times was in the *moku* of Wailuku, encompassing the famous Nā Wai Ehā or "The Four Waters" (Coulter 1931, 22, fig. 8; Handy and Handy 1972, 496–498). These four valleys, each with a permanent stream watering extensive irrigated pondfields, are, from the north proceeding southward, Waiheʻe, Waiʻehu, Wailuku, and Waikapū. Handy and Handy claim that this region "in ancient times was the largest continuous area of wet-taro cultivation in the islands" (1972, 496).

At Waiheʻe, coastal sand dunes containing midden deposits and burials protected Kapoho fishpond. A test excavation by Clark and Balicki (1987) revealed five cultural layers with fire hearths and an earth oven. Unidentified charcoal from the deepest layer yielded a radiocarbon age of cal AD 1029–1265 (Beta-24524), suggesting that occupation here began in the Foundation Period, not surprising given the region's rich marine and terrestrial resources. This earliest date is further supported by dates of cal AD 1042–1282 (Beta-54324) and AD 1041–1386 (Beta-54322) obtained from test pits excavated during CRM projects associated with a proposed golf course at Waiheʻe (Jensen and Boudreau 1992, table 2). Surface finds of artifacts eroding out of the dunes included pearl-shell fishhooks of putative early types. Recent examination of the eroding sand dune face at Waiheʻe by Kirch showed that upper deposits containing cultural materials overlay an older, slightly lithified dune with abundant remains of the extinct terrestrial crab *Geograpsus severnsi*, a pincer of which was radiocarbon dated to cal AD 381–426 (UCIAMS-216112*). This terrestrial crab became extinct across the island chain after Polynesian arrival.

Sand dunes at Waiʻehu (site 50-50-04-4731) also show signs of settlement as early as the Late Voyaging Period (Fredericksen and Fredericksen 2002). Located just outside the town of Kahului, excavations along a long (ca. 820 m), narrow (10–12 m) section of coastal Waiʻehu exposed more than 300 features, including "post holes, hearths, refuse pits, and other pits," as well as 16 human burials, and what appears to be a pig burial (Fredericksen and Fredericksen 2002, i). The earliest dates come from unidentified charcoal uncovered more than 1 m below the ground from a hearth or pit (Area B, BTF 11.1, cal AD 1195–1310, Beta-129854) and from a thin cultural layer (Area F, Layer IIIc, F3F, cal AD 1200–1310, Beta-145221).

FIGURE 15.3 The main terrace of Haleki'i Heiau, Maui Island, with stone walls demarcating probable residential features of the royal household. *(Photo by Therese Babineau)*

The entire Nā Wai Ehā region was a major seat of power during the Expansion through Archaic States Periods, a royal center occupied by Pi'ilani and periodically thereafter by his descendants. This royal seat is evidenced near the coast in Wailuku with a pair of massive structures—Haleki'i and Pīhana Heiau (site 50-04-592), both perched on an ancient lithified sand dune on the banks of 'Īao Stream. Pīhana Heiau, attributed to the chief Ki'ihewa in the time of Maui *ali'i nui* Kaka'e (approximately AD 1540; Hommon 2014, 249; E. P. Sterling 1998, 75), is a *luakini heiau* with a footprint of approximately 4,000 m². Haleki'i, which was originally interpreted as a *heiau,* is roughly the same size, at about 3,930 m² (Kolb [1991, 142] overestimated the size of Haleki'i at 5,633 m², an error repeated by Hommon [2014, 249]); this was reputedly built by Kiha-a-Pi'ilani, probably around AD 1620. Excavations at both structures by Michael Kolb (1991, 1994a, 1997) yielded radiocarbon dates suggesting that these were initially constructed between AD 1450 and 1650. Based on the faunal remains recovered, Kolb (1991, 301) interpreted Haleki'i as a residential structure rather than a *heiau.* This interpretation corresponds well with the architecture at Haleki'i, which suggests a series of houses (a *kauhale* group) situated atop a massive terrace (fig. 15.3). Our interpretation is that Haleki'i was the royal residence of Pi'ilani and others of his line, while Pīhana was the *luakini heiau.*

East Maui

East Maui had substantial populations concentrated in upland Kula, along the northern Hāmākua coast, and in Hāna and Kaupō Districts in the east and southeast (Coulter 1931, fig.8). The great mass of Haleakalā creates a pronounced rain shadow effect, with high rainfall along the windward (north) coast, and to a lesser extent in Hāna and Kaupō, leaving

Kahikinui and Honua'ula Districts to the lee side of the mountain quite arid. In spite of this aridity, these drylands exhibit extensive evidence of ancient Hawaiian occupation.

On the western flanks of Haleakalā, in the upcountry of Makawao in the north and Keōkea in the south, surveys and excavations have revealed evidence of settlement despite disturbance by sugarcane farming. In Makawao, near Hāli'imaile, McGerty and Spear (2006) described agricultural terraces in gulches—settings that were too steeply sloped for industrial sugarcane farming—as well as petroglyphs. In Pukalani, southwest of Makawao town, Kennedy (1990) reports a date of cal AD 1515–1955 (Beta-42173) for a *heiau* (site 50-50-05-2701) that he believed to be Mo'omuku Heiau (Walker's site 224) (see also Kennedy 1991). A surprisingly early date from a *kukui* nutshell (cal AD 1034–1381, Beta-42172*) points to activity in this portion of Kula prior to the Expansion Period.

Upland Kula, between about 400 and 800 m elevation, was a zone of intensive dryland cultivation; remnant portions of field system embankments and walls can be identified on aerial photos, although the zone has never been fully investigated. Kolb (1994b) studied a small portion of this zone in Keōkea, noting numerous agricultural *heiau* and one *luakini* (419, fig. 2). His excavations at one of the smaller *heiau,* Molohai (site 50-50-10-1037), produced a radiocarbon date associated with agricultural activity predating the temple of cal AD 1057–1375 (Beta-40644), confirming the findings in Makawao that farmers were cultivating these fertile slopes from an early time. Initial construction at Molohai dates to AD 1400–1633 (Beta-43010), during the Expansion Period. The site was initially a "small ritual shrine" but was then rebuilt as a community temple between cal AD 1470 and 1820 (Beta-43011), in the form of a classic Maui notched enclosure.

A study by Dega et al. (2004, 219) suggests a shift in "consumptive practices" in Keōkea. They note that the majority of pig remains were recovered in deposits dated to the Late Voyaging and Expansion Periods. In contrast, dog bones do not appear until the Archaic States Period, with the earliest bracketed to cal AD 1630–1820, a time when pig bone was rarely deposited. A study in nearby Waiohuli by Dunn et al. (1999, 100) reports intensified agriculture at this time.

The imposing crater of Haleakalā—traditional scene of the demigod Maui's snaring of the Sun—seems an unlikely locality in which to find archaeological sites, yet the crater floor is dotted with ancient cairns, platforms, and terraces; several small caves and rockshelters also show evidence of human use. Emory (1921) surveyed the crater, recording 58 terraces and platforms, nine groups of open stone shelters, and "several hundred" cairns, as well as a "section of an ancient paved road." None of these sites appears to have been used for permanent or even extended habitation but were interpreted as having religious or ceremonial functions. Upon excavation, several of the terraces and cairns proved to contain burials. There is evidence, however, that the crater was also visited to hunt birds, especially the dark-rumped petrel (*Pterodroma sandwichensis*). On the crater floor, Emory collected 101 natural, waterworn slingstones, which were most likely used in bird hunting.

Another reason that people made the long trek into the crater through the Kaupō and Ko'olau gaps, far above the coast and uplands where people spent most of their daily lives, is the fine-grained basalt of the Haleakalā adze quarry. The quarry is located on a portion of a "1.2 km long intrusive basalt mass . . . [and] is the only major basalt adze quarry on the island of Maui" (Mintmier, Mills, and Lundblad 2012, 618). The complex is spread over 2 km^2 and includes a steep outcrop of fine-grained basalt, a large lithic scatter, and at least two rockshelters. The geochemical signature of this source has been established through 255 lithic samples assayed by energy-dispersive X-ray fluorescence analysis (Mintmier, Mills, and Lundblad 2012). The earliest direct radiocarbon date on the quarry has a range of cal AD 1280–1410 (Carson and Mintmier 2007, 233).

The north coast of East Maui—the districts of Hāmākuapoko, Hāmākualoa, and Koʻolau—encompasses a string of narrow valleys, most of which supported communities that cultivated small taro irrigation complexes. At Keʻanae, a peninsula formed by late eruption in the Haleakalā Crater that flowed out through Koʻolau Gap, a more extensive irrigation complex continues to be farmed to this day (Linnekin 1985). Unfortunately, the archaeology of this windward Maui region remains woefully underresearched. Along some 50 km of coastline, there have been only a few dozen projects, none covering more than a modest area. In Hāmākualoa, for example, excavations in and around an irrigated pondfield in West Hanawana by Perzinski et al. (2002) suggest farming as early as the Foundation Period (AD 990–1200). Most others have documented irrigated farming from the Expansion Period onward (Chun and Dillon 2010, 18–25).

Unfortunately, many *heiau* in northeastern Maui have been heavily affected. Out of the 23 *heiau* described by Walker (1930) in Hāmākualoa (sites 59 to 81)—which represent only well-known sites rather than a complete inventory—at least 18 have been reported as damaged or destroyed (E. P. Sterling 1998).

Hawaiian oral traditions leave no doubt that Hāna District was a well-populated region with political significance even by the time of the famous conflict between Lono-a-Piʻilani and Kiha-a-Piʻilani, for the latter went there to seek the support of Hāna *aliʻi* Hoʻolaemakua. After the defeat of the Maui forces at the fortress of Kaʻuiki, Kiha-a-Piʻilani moved the royal seat to Hāna, constructing the single largest monumental structure in the Hawaiian Islands, Piʻilanihale Heiau (Cordy 1970). Covering 12,126 m^2, Piʻilanihale is an impressive architectural feat, with a main facade of six terraces rising 13.4 m above the lower ground level (figs. 15.4, 15.5; color plate 11). It is the largest stone construction in the islands in terms of the area of its footprint. The name means "House of Piʻilani" and it is regarded "as the royal abode of the great Piilani family of Maui chiefs, who flourished in the 16th century" (E. P. Sterling 1998, 123, quoting Walker [1930]). There are reasons to believe that the complex, which includes multiple enclosures and features, functioned as a combined royal residence and temple. East and west wings flank the main terrace, probably serving as residential wards (Kolb 1999, fig. 5). Kolb obtained seven radiocarbon dates from small excavation units dispersed over this immense structure, but the lack of continuous trenches and stratigraphic sections makes it difficult to relate the dates to the structural components of this complex. Two early dates predating AD 1500 demonstrate some cultural activity on the site (cal AD 1165–1493, Beta-40635; cal AD 1297–1474, Beta-40360) but probably do not correspond to the major construction phases. The onset of significant building activity more likely began between AD 1500 and 1650 (cal 1452–1954, Beta-40362; cal AD 1459–1954, Beta-40634; cal AD 1515–1951, Beta-40361; cal AD 1520–1569, Beta-40363); use of the complex continued through the Archaic States Period (cal AD 1657–1955, Beta-40636).

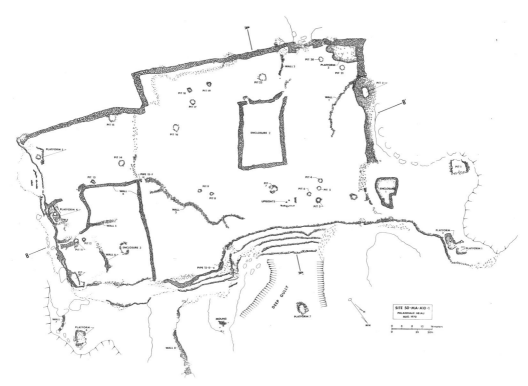

FIGURE 15.4 Map of Pi'ilanihale Heiau, Maui Island. *(After Cordy 1970)*

FIGURE 15.5 The main facade of Pi'ilanihale Heiau, Maui Island. *(Photo by Therese Babineau)*

Young, nutrient-rich lava flows blanketing the Hāna region, combined with ample rainfall, provided ideal conditions for intensive dryland farming. Handy and Handy note that "a great deal of upland taro was grown there, as well as bananas, yams, *wauke,* and *olona,*" and that Hāna was also "famous for its *'awa*" (1972, 502). A dryland field system may have extended over much of the region, but extensive sugarcane plantations developed since the 1860s, followed by ranching, largely obliterated any traces of this.

A feature prominent in Hawaiian traditions is Ka'uiki Hill, a steep-sided cinder cone situated at the south end of Hāna Bay. On more than one occasion, Ka'uiki was used as a fortress redoubt, including by Ho'olaemakua, who was defeated by the forces of 'Umi and Kiha-a-Pi'ilani. At Hāmoa, south of Hāna Bay, Kolb and colleagues surveyed 21 ha, recording 74 features between Hāmoa beach and Pu'u Keāka'amanu (Kolb, ed., 1993). Features included agricultural fields, walls, terraces, mounds, mulch pits, and a set of religious sites recorded as the Hāmoa complex (site 50-50-13-1484), including Pakiokio Heiau (site 121), Kaluanui Heiau (site 120), and Hale o Lono Heiau (site 123). Reported radiocarbon dates go back as far as the Late Voyaging Period, suggesting that Hale o Lono Heiau was in use by the Expansion Period, with Kaluanui Heiau built during the Archaic States Period (Kolb, ed., 1993, table 4).

Reconnaissance survey of ca. 80 ha in the lower reaches of Kīpahulu Valley in the 1970s helped establish the Kīpahulu Historical District (site 50-50-17-299), covering 33 km^2 stretching from the coast up to 500 m above sea level (Rosendahl 1976). Dye, Carson, and Tomonari-Tuggle (2002) relocated features along the coast near Ka'ū Bay, placing test excavations strategically to recover deposits that pre- and postdate the construction of architecture. At one site that Soehren (1963) had suggested was a fishing shrine (site 50-50-17-1088), a shallow 5–10-cm-thick cultural layer was found under foundation stones. A coconut leaf midrib from that layer returned a date of cal AD 1161–1384 (Beta-150615*), suggesting Late Voyaging Period occupation near Ka'ū Bay (Dye, Carson, and Tomonari-Tuggle 2002). In contrast, a well-built habitation site (site 50-50-17-1089) that included an enclosure with thick core-filled walls and branch coral on a small platform was likely built after AD 1625 (cal AD 1420–1620, Beta-150620*). Further studies of coastal residences in the area suggest that most date to the Archaic States Period (Carson and Reeve 2008, table 62), perhaps indicating a dense population when the island's royal center was, for a time, only 9 km distant at Kaupō.

The *moku* of Kaupō, extending from the *ahupua'a* of Nākula in the west to Kālepa Gulch in the east, consists of a broad fan of young lava and mudflows that originated in late-stage volcanic eruptions in Haleakalā Crater and spewed out via the deep valley known as Kaupō Gap. The high nutrient content of these flows, combined with sufficient rainfall, created ideal conditions for sweet potato and dryland taro cultivation. Portions of an extensive dryland field system were mapped by Kirch et al. (2009), while the soil properties of the system were investigated by Baer et al. (2015). Kirch and colleagues conducted survey and selected excavations throughout the *ahupua'a* of Nu'u, including the investigation of a small adze quarry (Kahn et al. 2009; Vacca 2019). Baer (2015, 2016) extended this survey into the central and eastern parts of Kaupō, obtaining a large series of AMS radiocarbon dates from *heiau* and house sites throughout the *moku* as well. These dates indicate permanent settlement in Kaupō beginning in the early Expansion Period, with intensification of agricultural production and the construction or rebuilding of many *heiau* in the Archaic States Period.

During the early eighteenth century, Kaupō became for a time the island's royal center, with two large *luakini heiau* being rebuilt and dedicated by Kekaulike, the island's *aliʻi nui*. Loʻaloʻa Heiau, with a basal area of 4,100 m², is an impressive rectangular platform with terraces rising to a height of 7 m along its eastern facade (Kamakau 1961, 66; Kirch and Ruggles 2019, 319–326; Kolb 1991, 168). Kolb radiocarbon dated eight charcoal samples from Loʻaloʻa (Kolb 1991, 235–240). An older cluster of four dates suggests initial construction of the temple in the sixteenth century, as a rectangular platform (Kolb 1991, 239, fig. 6.7). A major expansion phase occurred in the eighteenth century (documented by four radiocarbon dates), which included the "addition of the massive rock terraces of the east platform" (239), probably undertaken during the reign of Kekaulike, as suggested by the oral traditions. Kirch and Ruggles (2019, 325–326) determined that Loʻaloʻa is oriented within less than one degree to the acronychal rising of the Pleiades (Makaliʻi), suggesting an association with the god Lono. Pōpōʻiwi, a second large temple not far from Loʻaloʻa was also dedicated by Kekaulike. Kolb (1991) thought that like Piʻilanihale, Pōpōʻiwi functioned both as a *luakini* temple and a royal residence. A third large *heiau* lies near the western edge of Kaupō, at Kou, but is not mentioned in the *moʻolelo* (Kirch and Ruggles 2019, 326–331).

Kahikinui, to the west of Kaupō and fully in the rain shadow of Haleakalā, is a large, arid *moku* that—because of its marginality—has escaped modern development, thus offering a virtually intact archaeological landscape. In 1966, Bishop Museum's pioneering settlement pattern survey under the direction of Peter Chapman mapped a portion of the *moku* in the central area of Kīpapa, recording about 450 sites. In 1996, Kirch, who was a member of the 1966 field team, recommenced research in the region (Kirch 2014; Kirch, ed., 1997). This grew into a nearly two-decades-long effort including not only surface survey of some 25 km² and the recording of more than 3,000 archaeological features but also extensive excavations in household, agricultural, and ritual sites. Three University of California, Berkeley, doctoral dissertations were completed on aspects of this project (Coil 2004; Holm 2006; Van Gilder 2005). Among the topics addressed by the Kahikinui project were dryland agricultural practices (Coil and Kirch 2005; Kirch et al. 2004, 2005; Vitousek et al. 2004), household organization (Kirch et al. 2010; Van Gilder 2001; Van Gilder and Kirch 1997), high-precision ^{230}Th dating of ritual sites (Kirch and Sharp 2005; Kirch et al. 2015), water resources (Stock, Coil, and Kirch 2003), faunal remains and subsistence (Jones and Kirch 2007; Kirch and O'Day 2003), and rock art (Millerstrom and Kirch 2002, 2004). Kirch (2014) synthesized the results of the Kahikinui project in *Kuaʻāina Kahiko,* written for a general audience. The settlement pattern of Kahikinui is discussed in chapter 12.

Also in Kahikinui, Boyd Dixon and colleagues conducted a multiyear CRM project in the Kīpapa uplands for the Department of Hawaiian Home Lands, adding significant information on site distributions and agricultural practices (Dixon et al. 1997a, 1999, 2002). Kolb investigated Kahikinui *heiau,* although his findings have not been fully published (Kolb and Radewagen 1997; Kolb 2006). Finally, in Auwahi, an *ahupuaʻa* on the western edge of Kahikinui owned by Ulupalakua Ranch, development of a wind energy project led to an extensive CRM survey and some excavations (Shapiro et al. 2011), as well as a detailed study of intensive swale farming at Puʻu Hoku Kano (Kirch et al. 2013).

FIGURE 15.6 The *pānānā* at Hanamauloa, Kahikinui, Maui Island. *(Photo by P. V. Kirch)*

A unique site located below the Luala'ilua Hills in Kahikinui is the *pānānā* or "sighting wall" at Hanamauloa (fig. 15.6; color plate 12). This well-constructed, freestanding wall has a notch oriented to an *ahu* or cairn on the coast nearby. As Kirch, Ruggles, and Sharp (2013) demonstrated, the notch and *ahu* align to the vertical limb of the Southern Cross, which in Hawaiian star lore points the way to Kahiki, the ancestral homeland. A coral date suggests that the *pānānā* was in use in the fifteenth century; it may have been associated with the famous voyaging chief La'amaikahiki. Also noteworthy is Keahuamanono Heiau, a small structure situated at 2,567 m altitude on the rim of Haleakalā, overlooking both the crater and Kaupō and Kahikinui Districts, a likely place of "celestial and political observation" (Nelson and Vacca 2021, 14).

The large *ahupua'a* of Kanaio formed a buffer zone between Kahikinui and Honua'ula Districts. In the barren *'a'ā* lava *makai* of Pu'u Pīmoe, scores of small platforms and terraces indicate an extensive burial ground, possibly from the early postcontact period (Eblé and Cleghorn 1995).

Development along the Mākena and Kīhei coast in Honua'ula District has made this one of the most intensely studied regions anywhere in the Hawaiian Islands, with several hundred CRM reports documenting a densely settled region known for important fishing grounds and productive lands used for dryland agriculture. Mā'alaea Bay in Kīhei has been the focus of paleoenvironmental coring aimed at determining when people began living and farming in this part of the island. Most of these efforts have focused on Keālia Pond (Athens et al. 1996; Pau, MacDonald, and Gillespie 2012; Pepalis and Kolb 2002). The most recent coring uncovered "a large charcoal peak" around AD 1140 marking the earliest human activity (Pau, MacDonald, and Gillespie 2012, 753). At Kalepolepo fishpond, Pepalis and Kolb (2002, 39) excavated small concentrations of shell midden that they interpret as "either fishpond or agricultural use," with occupation of the coast beginning around AD 1400. Age determinations on 17 other fishponds, mostly on Oʻahu, put the onset of aquaculture in the Hawaiian Islands in the Late Voyaging Period around AD 1300, so it would be unsurprising if Kalepolepo came into use early in the Expansion Period. Pollen records from Keālia Pond point to a drop in the deposition of charcoal from AD 1520 to the time of European contact (Pau, MacDonald, and Gillespie 2012). It is possible that as fixed field farming became more common there were fewer fires for clearing. Recent surveys further inland from the coast have documented intensive dryland farming that utilized stone mounds, terraces, and modified outcrops (Mulrooney et al. 2021; Perzinski et al. 2015).

Another addition to Māʻalaea Bay around AD 1600 was a small pond at Kīhei called Kōʻieʻie (also known as Kalepolepo) (Athens and Ward 2007), which is said to have been constructed under the orders of the Hawaiʻi Island leader ʻUmi-a-Līloa, along with reconstruction of its three neighboring ponds (Donham 2002, 7-8).

Recent research in Kīhei points to another connection to ʻUmi-a-Līloa. Perzinski and Dega (2011) conducted a survey 1.75 km inland from the bay, finding a small *heiau* (site 50-10-10-6786) that has a remarkably similar layout to the much larger Ahu a ʻUmi located in the center of Hawaiʻi Island (see also Dega 2011). Each site has a central enclosure, eight encircling *ahu,* and a second smaller structure nearby. The central feature of the Maui *heiau* is a notched enclosure (9.6 × 5.8 m), about 15 times smaller than its Hawaiʻi Island counterpart. Excavations by Perzinski and Dega (2011) revealed unmodified coral and marine shell within the central enclosure consistent with ritual use; they suggest that the secondary structure was used as a shelter. Radiocarbon dates from hearths date to the Late Expansion Period (AD 1450–1650), suggesting that the "heiau may be associated with Umi-a-Liloa . . . built as a tribute for his help in uniting Maui under Kiha-a-Piʻilani" (Perzinski and Dega 2011, 25). This is a plausible interpretation, especially as the central enclosure's notch is in the southeast corner in the direction of Kōʻieʻie fishpond; more precise dates would help eliminate other possible explanations for the similarities between the two *heiau*.

The Palauea Cultural Preserve is an 8.4 ha parcel deeded to the Office of Hawaiian Affairs in partnership with the University of Hawaiʻi, Maui. Kirch (1971a) carried out an initial study of Palauea, describing several clusters of small C-shaped shelters arrayed along a low ridge, representing three or four *kauhale*. At the seaward end of the ridge a larger structure was interpreted as a *mua* or men's house, which served as a ritual area and a focus for male craft activities. In a small swale below the men's house are a medium-sized *heiau* and a small fishing shrine. Along a low platform or altar on the inland side of the shrine are a row of large coral heads; the wooden handle of a shark's tooth knife (fig. 15.7) was found buried under rubble in this shrine. Subsequent survey and excavations in other *ahupuaʻa* to the west and east of Palauea have provided evidence of similar residential clusters.

FIGURE 15.7 Wooden handle for a shark-tooth knife, excavated from a fishing shrine at Palauea, Maui Island. *(Photo by P. V. Kirch)*

Lānaʻi Island

One of the smaller islands (361 km²), Lānaʻi, along with Molokaʻi and Kahoʻolawe, forms a cluster of central islands dominated by Maui (fig. 15.8). As Emory observed, "These four islands are so grouped as to form between them a partly enclosed and sheltered sea over which the native canoes freely plied" (1924, 4). Not surprisingly, in the Archaic States Period, Lānaʻi was tributary to the more powerful Maui chiefs. In Emory's view, "Everything seems to characterize Lānaʻi as an out district of Maui: much more sparsely populated, poorer in every aspect of culture, but with the political and religious system of Maui entirely superposed" (1924, 123).

Lying in Maui's rain shadow, and with a maximum elevation of only 1,027 m, Lānaʻi, like its neighbor Kahoʻolawe, suffers from limited rainfall. Although the island has a windward coast, with a few narrow valleys and gulches, there are no permanent streams; the entire island falls within the leeward component of the archipelago's climatic continuum. The central plateau and mountain crest receive about 890 mm of rainfall annually; these regions were originally cloaked in dryland native forest, denuded by grazing in the postcontact era. In the lower elevations, rainfall decreases, and in many areas is as low as 305 mm, insufficient for even sweet potato agriculture. The conditions are so poor that a computer model of likely places that intensive agriculture could have been practiced failed to

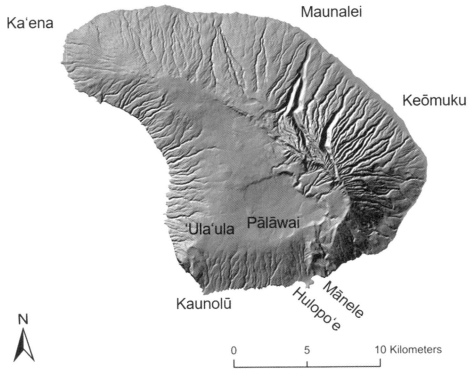

FIGURE 15.8 Map of Lānaʻi Island, showing sites and major places mentioned in the text. *(Map by M. D. McCoy)*

delineate a single suitable location on the island (Ladefoged et al. 2009). This despite evidence for limited irrigated planting in gulches at Maunalei (Madeus et al. 2005), and reports that sweet potato farming was widespread.

Historic-period developments on the island were restricted to ranching and a pineapple plantation that covered the central Pālāwai Basin. While any archaeological sites that formerly existed in the basin have been destroyed, the extensive lower slopes and coastal regions are largely undisturbed, and the preservation of archaeological remains is excellent (Hommon 1974). Nevertheless, Lānaʻi is archaeologically the most neglected of the main islands, except for Niʻihau.

Our knowledge of the island's precontact history comes principally from Emory's pioneering study over seven months in 1921–1922 (Emory 1924). Although Emory was a pace-setting researcher, like other surveys of this era, his work on Lānaʻi suffered from the absence of stratigraphic excavations and dating. In the 1950s, Hector Munro (a Lānaʻi resident and amateur ornithologist) excavated at ʻUlaʻula Cave (site L1), but without modern standards of recording or control. Later excavations were conducted ahead of the development of the Four Seasons Hotel (Kaschko and Athens 1987; Tomonari-Tuggle, Tuggle, and Athens 2000), and by a University of Hawaiʻi, Mānoa, field school that produced some of the only radiocarbon dates for the island—dates that helped archaeologists reject early volcanic-glass dating techniques (Graves and Ladefoged 1991). However, few dates are on identified wood, and there are no high-quality Foundation Period dates reported from the island (Athens, Rieth, and Dye 2014).

Emory's survey of habitation sites on Lānaʻi was unusually complete for its time. He recorded 489 residential structures, generally house terraces and platforms (fig. 15.9), estimating that the actual total might be as high as 630 (Emory 1924, 50). These sites are unevenly distributed, with large gaps along the coasts where there are steep sea cliffs, especially along the southern and western coasts. In other places, settlement was heavily concentrated in certain areas, as at Kaunolū. Water was a critical problem; Emory describes

FIGURE 15.9 Perspective sketch of a Lānaʻi house site with interior fireplace. *(After Emory 1924)*

FIGURE 15.10 Halulu Heiau at Kaunolū, Lāna'i Island. *(Photo by Therese Babineau)*

a number of ingenious methods for obtaining drinking water, including the excavation of shallow wells and the collection of dew from shrubbery.

Lāna'i has 11 recorded *heiau,* two in the center of the island and the rest along the coastal regions, where smaller *heiau* and *ko'a* have been noted (Emory 1924, fig. 4). The largest and most imposing is Halulu Heiau at Kaunolū, situated on the gulch rim (fig. 15.10). Indeed, all of the *heiau* "are on prominences commanding a view over valley, village, and ocean, and face either a valley or the ocean" (Emory 1924, 62). A particularly noteworthy site, located on the northeast coast, is a linear arrangement of nine upright stone slabs that, although lacking a formally defined court, are otherwise similar to the Mokumanamana ritual sites, and to certain shrines on Mauna Kea on Hawai'i Island.

The Kaunolū complex (site 50-40-98-25), or "village," is doubtless the most significant archaeological complex on Lāna'i (fig. 15.11). The concentrated settlement around a small, sheltered bay and intermittent stream gulch, first mapped by Emory, includes substantial residential complexes as well as Halulu Heiau (Emory 1924, pl. II). In the time of Kamehameha I, Halulu was a *pu'uhonua,* but archaeologists have speculated about other uses of the site. Halulu is also the name of a legendary bird that devours people. It may be significant that a number of petroglyphs depicting "bird-men" are to be seen near Halulu Heiau (fig. 15.12). Beckwith (1970, 496) suggested the *heiau* may have been a *luakini* given that its name is suggestive of sacrifice; others have suggested it may have been a *hale o Lono* type of temple (Dixon et al. 1995; Dixon and Major 2011).

A Bishop Museum archaeological team returned to Kaunolū in the late 1980s ahead of opening the area to visitors (Dixon et al. 1995). They recorded surface architecture in great detail to work out how the village may have grown and changed—changes that may be linked to the same political forces felt elsewhere in the Archaic States Period. They suggested that the larger residences (Sectors VI and VIII) might have housed the highest ranked chief of the island and "other elite members of the community," a claim supported by references to visits to Kaunolū by Kamehameha I and his rival, Maui *ali'i nui* Kahekili (Dixon et al. 1995, 247). They further speculate that differences between the layout and architectural styles of

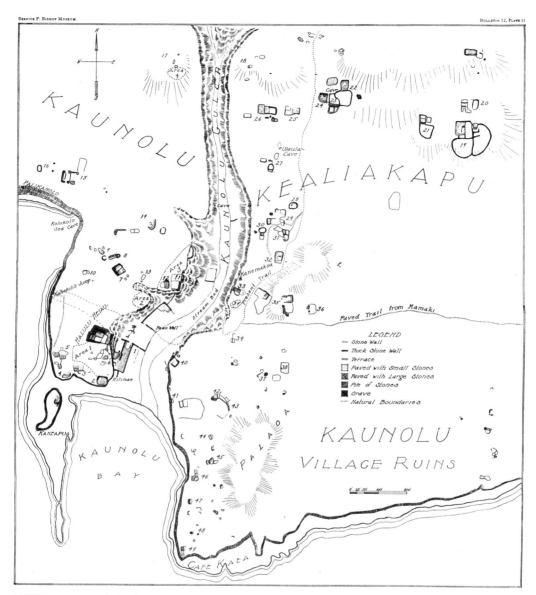

FIGURE 15.11 Map of the site complex at Kaunolū, Lānaʻi Island, made by Kenneth P. Emory in 1924. *(After Emory 1924)*

households might reflect a shift in how *kapu* was observed as Lānaʻi came under the rule of Maui. However, the only site excavated at Kaunolū remains that of ʻUlaʻula Cave, which produced a small but significant assemblage of fishing gear (fig. 15.13) but no absolute dates or clues to help determine how the settlement evolved over time.

Extensive archaeological research at Hulopoʻe and Mānele bays, 6 km to the northeast, gives a clearer picture of the history of settlement along the southern shore of Lānaʻi (Kaschko and Athens 1987; Tomonari-Tuggle, Tuggle, and Athens 2000). At Hulopoʻe Bay, the main settlement (site 50-40-85) consisted of 60 features that were recorded as a series of adjacent clusters. Slightly inland, isolated lithic scatters suggest informal quarrying.

FIGURE 15.12 Bird-men petroglyphs near Halulu Heiau at Kaunolū, Lāna'i Island, photographed by Kenneth P. Emory in 1924. *(Photo courtesy Bishop Museum Library and Archives)*

A short distance away at Mānele Bay several coastal sites were recorded, including a *heiau* (site 157DD). While there was a great deal of activity here in the historic era—this being the location of the first Mormon mission in 1854—in the late precontact era it "could well have been a locale for some of the island's high-ranking chiefs" (107). Dates from these investigations suggest that during the Expansion Period the coastline was home to "small transitory occupation" consisting of "open camps" and simple shelters; a few dates indicate visits going back to the Foundation Period (83–85). At this stage, the closest permanent settlements would have been either down the coast or in the uplands. More permanent habitation concentrated at the coastline occurred only at Hulopo'e and Mānele bays during the Archaic States Period.

Lāna'i may have experienced interisland warfare in some of the same ways, and perhaps for some of the same reasons, as its neighbors. In the uplands near the center of the island, there is a rare example of a fortified ridgeline suggesting at least a response to episodes of violence. Oral histories refer to Lāna'i chiefs and warriors in the annals of battles elsewhere in the islands, as well as plans for revolt against Maui rule. A Lāna'i chief, Haloalena, enlisted the king of O'ahu, Kuali'i, in a revolt against Maui only to have the king pull his support before the revolt could occur (Fornander 1916–1920, 4:426).

An important contribution of Emory's 1924 study was his detailed description and analysis of petroglyphs. He not only provided the first systematic typology for petroglyph forms but also addressed the questions of the age and meaning of the glyphs. This research was extended by Cox

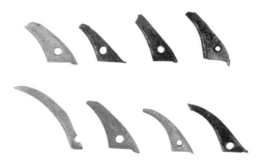

FIGURE 15.13 Bone trolling-lure points excavated from Lāna'i sites. *(Photo by P. V. Kirch)*

and Stasack (1970), who reported 23 petroglyph sites with 760 image units, and later by intensive documentation by Lee (1988). At Kaunolū alone Lee and her team located and recorded 309 individual petroglyphs. She noted many images associated with Halulu Heiau, but also occurring in isolation across the complex, including bird or bird-man symbolism consistent with the name of the *heiau* (G. Lee 1988, 10).

Lānaʻi remains insufficiently researched. We suspect that its history, as Emory suggested, in some ways follows that of other *kuaʻāina* or "back country" districts on Maui. But the island's unique trajectory before it became subjugated by its larger neighbors holds great potential to tell us about the regional diversity in culture and society in the Hawaiian Islands.

Kahoʻolawe Island

Kahoʻolawe, the eroded remnant of a single shield volcano encompassing 116 km², is the smallest of the eight main islands (fig. 15.14). Its summit, at Luamakika, rises just 450 m above sea level, and this low altitude, combined with the island's position in the lee of Maui (11 km to the north), account for the island's extreme aridity. In outline Kahoʻolawe is roughly triangular, with steep sea cliffs (up to 245 m high) along its eastern and southern coasts. From Luamakika, near the eastern end, the central plateau slopes gradually toward the west. Gulches, cut by streams that flow only after occasional heavy rains, radiate outward from the central plateau along the north and west coasts. Several places along the coast at the mouths of gulches, such as Hakioawa, Ahupū, Honokoa, and Lae o Kealaikahiki, were foci of ancient settlement.

J. Gilbert McAllister, who surveyed Kahoʻolawe in 1931, characterized the island as "waterless, barren, and desolate," and wondered whether "environmental influences" had been "so potent as to necessitate a special adaptation" of Hawaiian culture (1933b, 3). The island was only sparsely or intermittently inhabited at the time of Captain Cook's 1779 expedition, which, in sailing past the western end, did not observe any habitations or evidence of cultivation. Lieutenant James King of Cook's expedition described the island as "very desolate," commenting that "it has no wood on it, seems a sandy poor soil, & is altogether a poor Island" (Beaglehole 1967, 583, 1218). Captain George Vancouver, in 1792, was told that Kahoʻolawe had

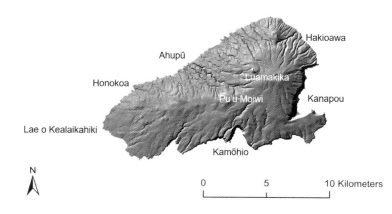

FIGURE 15.14 Map of Kahoʻolawe Island, showing sites and major places mentioned in the text. *(Map by M. D. McCoy)*

formerly been "fruitful and populous" (1801, 301) before it was abandoned. Some years later, Otto von Kotzebue saw campfires along the shore as he passed by at night (1821, 318), while Lieutenant Charles Wilkes in 1841 confirmed that the island was inhabited by a small group of fishermen, as well as being used as a penal colony (1845, 245).

Botanical surveys hint that the island formerly supported a dryland forest or scrub parkland; the reconstruction of this former vegetation is a paleoenvironmental problem that archaeological studies have addressed (Graves and Murakami 1993; Hommon 1982). A particularly important discovery was a skeletal fragment of the native Hawaiian goose or *nēnē* (*Branta sandwicensis*) from one of the fireplaces. Along with similar finds of *nēnē* on Molokaʻi and Oʻahu, this Kahoʻolawe discovery indicates that *nēnē* were once widely distributed throughout the lowlands of most, if not all, of the major islands. In the historic period, the goose was known only from Hawaiʻi Island, with reports of sightings on Maui.

Kahoʻolawe has a long but intermittent history of archaeological research, with the first stratigraphic excavation ever undertaken in the islands at Kamōhio Bay, by John F. G. Stokes in 1913. In 1931, McAllister conducted a weeklong field survey, recording 50 sites and making a surface collection of artifacts. McAllister (1933b) combined his materials with Stokes' earlier survey notes and excavation results in a summary of the island's archaeology. McAllister opined that "there are undoubtedly some isolated sites which were not seen, but as the most habitable parts of the island were examined, it is probable that the material which was missed will not prove to be significant" (3–4). Just how much was missed did not become evident until 1976, when an intensive archaeological survey was initiated for the United States Navy. The survey, taking four years to complete, revealed more than 10 times the number recorded by McAllister: 544 sites incorporating 2,337 discrete features (Barrera 1984; Hommon 1980a, 1980b). The 1976–1980 survey concentrated almost entirely on surface evidence, with only a few test pits placed at selected sites.

A chronology for human occupation of Kahoʻolawe is based on almost 100 radiocarbon dates (obtained in the 1980s) on unidentified wood charcoal, volcanic-glass dates, and the use of paleomagnetic dating (Rosendahl et al. 1987). These data indicate early use of the island's interior between AD 1250 and 1500, and more extensive distribution of sites across the island by AD 1400–1500, with a steady population from AD 1500 onward.

One of the highest concentrations of sites is at Hakioawa Bay, on the northeast coast facing Maui, where two gulches with intermittent streams converge at a large beach suitable for canoe landings. This settlement complex includes 182 individual features—house terraces and platforms, two *heiau*, smaller shrines, midden deposits, lithic activity areas, petroglyphs, and burials.

Upslope from Hakioawa, on the interior central ridge of the island, is the largest concentration of features discovered on survey and given the generic designation as "temporary" habitation. Hommon (1980b) suggested that these uplands could have been gardened in particularly wet years or seasons. There is no direct evidence in the uplands for sweet potato (*Ipomoea batatas*), but charred tubers have been recovered at coastal sites (M. S. Allen 1992; Graves and Murakami 1993, 18).

Charcoal fragments have revealed woody plants not known to exist on the island today that may have been "relatively plentiful during the period of pre-contact human occupation" (Hommon 1982, 146); the most common plant represented in hearth deposits is the shrub ʻakoko (*Chamaesyce* spp.) (Graves and Murakami 1993). The former dryland forest probably included *lama* (*Diospyros sandwicensis*), *naio* (*Myoporum sandwicense*), and ʻaʻaliʻi (*Dodonaea viscosa*), as well as several other woody plants whose charcoal has been recovered from firepits. The island seems a poor environment for arboriculture. Only a single coastal site had an example of ʻulu (*Artocarpus altilis*), and the wood was probably transported to the island (Graves and Murakami 1993, 15).

Concentrations of features along the mouths of gulches on the northwest coast were directly downslope of the possible upland gardening zone. The island's western half is likewise ringed by settlements, although at a lower density. The upland basalt quarry at Puʻu Moiwi (fig. 15.15) appears to have been in use since the Late Voyaging Period (P. C. McCoy, Makanani, and Sinoto 1993).

FIGURE 15.15 Preforms, reject cores, and flakes litter the surface at the Puʻu Moiwi adze quarry, Kahoʻolawe Island. *(Photo courtesy Paul Cleghorn)*

P. C. McCoy, Makanani, and Sinoto (1993) speculate that groups residing at Ahupū and Hakioawa shared the Puʻu Moiwi quarry. The western half of the quarry, accessed by people living at Ahupū, has "individual shrines, a higher frequency of untanged adzes and generally larger adzes," whereas the eastern half, closer to Hakioawa, has more smaller and tanged adzes (149). A shrine complex at the summit of Puʻu Moiwi, it is suggested, was shared by both groups. P. C. McCoy, Makanani, and Sinoto (1993) also make the distinction between the quarry proper near the raw material source and outlier sites that have some evidence for adze manufacture on the north and east slopes of Puʻu Moiwi. Outlying sites could be related to "the process of the adze makers removing the *kapu* of their specialist status and becoming 'common' (*noa*) or free again" (P. C. McCoy 1999; P. C. McCoy, Makanani, and Sinoto 1993, 149).

A total of six *heiau* have been reported as well as 65 shrines, including many in the uplands among the basalt quarry and others within the dense patches of shelters, but most sites of religious ritual are in coastal locations. At Kamōhio Bay, located on the precipitous south coast, is the rockshelter with terraces and a fishing shrine excavated by Stokes in 1913 and described by McAllister (1933b, 13–20). The floor of this spacious rockshelter had been modified with a series of stone-faced terraces that contained well-stratified archaeological deposits; the shelter functioned as a habitation for fishermen and yielded much fishing gear and the tools used in fishhook manufacture. Being dry and protected, the deposits yielded many normally perishable items, including a number of bundled *hoʻokupu,* or offerings.

16

THE ARCHAEOLOGY OF MOLOKAʻI ISLAND

Molokaʻi-Nui-a-Hina, "Great Molokaʻi of [the Moon goddess] Hina," stretches 63 km along a nearly east-west axis, occupying a central position in the archipelago (fig. 16.1). To the east, Maui looms a mere 17 km away across a relatively calm channel, while Oʻahu lies 45 km to the west, separated by the more challenging Kaiwi Channel. According to the island's *moʻolelo,* the independent Kamauaua dynasty ruled Molokaʻi in the late fourteenth century (Fornander 1916–1920; Summers 1971). But in the Archaic States Period, Molokaʻi came successively under the sway of conquering chiefs from Maui and Oʻahu, who coveted the island's rich taro lands, fishponds, and adze quarries. Always a land of *kāhuna,* Molokaʻi turned famously to the arts of sorcery for protection. Lanikaula, perhaps the most famous of the *kaula* seers or oracles, dwelt in the *kukui* grove that bears his name, overlooking Hālawa Valley. The Kālaipāhoa, or poison gods, were carved from the wood of three kinds of trees—*kauila* (*Alphitonia ponderosa*), *nīoi* (*Eugenia* sp.), and *ʻohe* (*Reynoldsia sandwicesis*)—from the summit of Maunaloa in Kaluakoʻi. While elsewhere these trees were used for everyday purposes, this grove was inhabited by the deities Kāne-i-kaulana-ʻula, Ka-huila-o-ka-lani, and Kapo. The priests who wielded the power of the poison gods were deeply feared as *kāhuna ʻanāʻanā,* the "praying to death" priests (Kamakau 1964). To this day, Molokaʻi is noted as a land of *pule ʻoʻo,* "powerful prayer" (Graham 2018).

Geologically, Molokaʻi was formed by the coalescence of the younger and higher East Molokaʻi volcano (ca. 1.5 million years old), whose deeply eroded summit reaches a height of 1,244 m at Kamakou, and the much lower and less eroded West Molokaʻi volcano (ca. 1.8 million years old), whose Maunaloa summit is only 421 m high. A late-stage volcanic rejuvenation (ca. 300,000 years ago) formed the Kalaupapa Peninsula, jutting northward from the island's windward coast, formed of lava flows from the Kauhakō Crater. The windward (Koʻolau District) side of East Molokaʻi—lashed by the moisture-laden tradewinds—has been sculpted by stream erosion into four deep amphitheater-headed valleys, from east to west Hālawa, Wailau, Pelekunu, and Waikolu. The permanent streams of these valleys

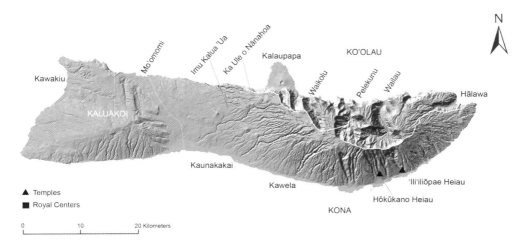

FIGURE 16.1 Map of Moloka'i Island, showing sites and major places mentioned in the text. White lines indicate the boundaries of the traditional districts. *(Map by M. D. McCoy)*

fed stone-lined canals that irrigated extensive taro pondfields. The southeastern slopes (the Kona District) have narrower, less deeply carved valleys, becoming progressively drier as one moves from east to west, so that the more westerly gulches (such as Kawela and Kaunakakai) have only intermittent streamflow. The archipelago's most extensive fringing reef wraps around the entire southern coastline, over a kilometer wide in many places. This broad, protected reef offered an ideal environment in which to build large fishponds, of which Moloka'i boasts at least 73. Arid West Moloka'i, lying in a rain shadow created by the high East Moloka'i mountains, has little potential to support horticulture. This region, known as Kaluako'i ("The Adze Pit") was noted for its basalt quarries and shore fisheries. More than on perhaps any other island, the geology and ecology of Moloka'i shaped its settlement patterns and lifeways (Graham 2018).

Moloka'i has had a long but uneven history of archaeological research. The island's *heiau* were the focus of an early survey by John F. G. Stokes (1909a), who obtained ethnographic details relating to the functions and histories of particular temples from Hawaiian *kūpuna*. Other early work included a reconnaissance of West Moloka'i by Gerard Fowke (1922), and a rather spotty island-wide Bishop Museum survey in 1937 by Southwick Phelps (1937), who focused on adaptations to the island's pronounced ecological contrasts. Catherine Summers compiled the results of these pioneering surveys along with fieldwork of her own in *Moloka'i: A Site Survey* (1971), which remains a foundational resource.

Stratigraphic excavation on Moloka'i began in 1952 with William Bonk's (1954) work at nine sites in Kaluako'i, part of Bishop Museum's Hawaiian Archaeological Program (see chapter 1). The 1969–1970 Hālawa Valley Project applied the then-pioneering settlement-pattern approach along with extensive excavation of the coastal dune site (Kirch and Kelly, eds., 1975). Most subsequent archaeological work on the island has been CRM-related, with a few exceptions, such as the work at Kalaupapa Peninsula by Patrick Kirch (ed., 2004) and his students Mark D. McCoy (2005, 2006, 2008a, 2008b; M. D. McCoy and Hartshorn 2007) and James Flexner (2010, 2011a, 2011b, 2012; Flexner and McCoy 2016; Flexner and

Morgan 2013), research in Kaluakoʻi by Marshall Weisler (2011; Weisler et al. 2006; Weisler et al. 2015; Rogers and Weisler 2020; Weisler and Walter 2002), and by Windy McElroy (2007, 2012; McElroy and Eminger 2011) in Wailau Valley, and renewed research in Hālawa by Kirch, Jillian Swift, and Noa Lincoln (2020, 2022).

Kona District

Molokaʻi was renowned for the many fishponds built out onto the broad reef flat of the southern shore. Some of the island's estimated 73 ponds have areas as large as 20 ha; together the island's fishponds represented over one-third of the total area devoted to aquaculture in the archipelago (fig. 16.2). According to traditional sources, these ponds were built under the aegis of ruling chiefs, for whom they were a significant source of wealth and power. Along with the fishponds, the rich black earth—the *lepo pōpolo*—of the narrow southeast coastal plain provided fertile ground for taro grown in raised beds and irrigated by springs (Handy 1940, 101). With these rich resources, it is not surprising that the greatest population density on Molokaʻi was concentrated "along the eastern third of the south coast" (Coulter 1931, 20).

The importance of the Kona District is evidenced by several clusters of large *heiau*, including 10 out of the island's 13 known *luakini* class war temples (Kirch 1990b). One major cluster of temples is situated in the *ahupuaʻa* of ʻOhiʻa; another cluster lies further east at Manawai. Kaluakapiʻioho Heiau at Manawai, which was according to tradition the residence of a *kahuna kilokilo* named Kapiʻioho (Summers 1971, 115–116), exhibits a remarkable stonework facade rising 11 m high (fig. 16.3). Pakuʻi Heiau, on the ridge to the east of Manawai Valley, is associated in tradition with the Maui *aliʻi* Kiha-a-Piʻilani, who made it his fortress abode during his struggle with his half-brother for the Maui kingship. Downslope on the same ridge is Hōkūkano Heiau, a large double-court structure (color plate 13). Even more impressive is ʻIliʻiliʻōpae Heiau at Mapulehu (color plate 14), a massive stone platform with terraced facades covering an area of about 4,000 m², making it one of the largest *heiau* known anywhere in the archipelago. An archaeoastronomical survey of ʻIliʻiliʻōpae by Kirch and Ruggles showed that the temple platform is precisely oriented to the rising position of the star cluster Makaliʻi (Pleiades).

FIGURE 16.2 Kanoa fishpond at Kawela is typical of the many *loko kuapā* type fishponds situated on the broad reef flat along the southern Molokaʻi Island coastline. *(Photo from Oceanic Archaeology Lab Archives)*

The Foundation and Late Voyaging Periods in Kona District are as yet little understood. A paleoecological study of coastal wetlands near ʻŌhiʻapilo Pond by Denham et al. (1999) revealed proxy evidence for early settlement. At 5 m below the modern ground surface, the core revealed a transition from pristine, endemic dry-mesic forest to a human-modified landscape. The lowest level produced evidence of a lowland forest dominated by *Pritchardia* (*loulu*) palms, similar to the situation on Oʻahu. The ʻŌhiʻapilo Pond core indicates a simultaneous decline in tree and shrub pollen, accompanied by a rise in *Cibotium* ferns, along with the first occurrence of charcoal from land clearing at the start of the Late Voyaging Period (54). Early occupation and use of coastal Kalamaʻula is further documented by Foundation Period radiocarbon dates from deposits nearby (sites 50-60-03-800 and -1753); unfortunately, strong contextual association between these dates and specific human activities is lacking (Bush et al. 2001; Weisler 1989a).

Athens (1985) reported evidence of use of inland Kalamaʻula by around AD 1200. Use of the landscape from an early date was further supported by two surveys by Weisler documenting thirteenth-century deposits, including a midden not far from the inland town of Kualapuʻu (Weisler 1989a), as well as a dryland field system (47 ha in extent) inland of Kaunakakai (Weisler 1989b).

Secure evidence for the construction of fishponds begins with the Expansion Period. The construction of ʻŌhiʻapilo Pond, for example, dates to around AD 1450. Fishponds, however, can be difficult to date securely as they were constructed in a dynamic inshore environment and thus are prone to damage and rebuilding. Today local community efforts are aimed at continuing to maintain the integrity of these remarkable structures.

At Kawela, near the western end of the southern zone of fishponds and concentrated precontact habitation, development in 1980 of an extensive residential subdivision triggered an archaeological survey by Bishop Museum, with 499 archaeological features recorded across the adjacent *ahupuaʻa* of Kawela and Makakupaiʻa Iki (Weisler and Kirch 1982, 1985). The sites

FIGURE 16.3 The eastern facade of Kaluakapiʻioho Heiau as photographed by John F. G. Stokes in 1909. *(Photo courtesy Bishop Museum Library and Archives)*

FIGURE 16.4 A terraced platform shrine at Kawela, Moloka'i Island. *(Photo from Oceanic Archaeology Lab Archives)*

were most densely clustered around Kawela Gulch, where Māhele records showed that the floodplain was intensively cultivated in sweet potatoes. The archaeological survey revealed traces of *'auwai,* along with small pondfield irrigation terraces in the interior portions of the valley. Large residential complexes were situated on the bluffs overlooking the valley. Smaller house sites were located on the lower ridge spurs overlooking the coastal plain and fishponds.

Extensive excavations were carried out at Kawela by Weisler and Kirch in 79 features. Excavations at a sand dune midden adjacent to Kawela Stream revealed evidence of initial occupation in the sixteenth century. The majority of stone structures distributed across the Kawela landscape—including house sites, shrines (fig. 16.4), and dryland agricultural features—were radiocarbon dated to the eighteenth century, just prior to European contact. The settlement landscape of Kawela is further described in chapter 12.

Along the southern coast, between Kawela and Kalama'ula, other research has extended our understanding of the regional settlement pattern (Hommon and Ahlo 1983; McElroy, Eminger, and Donham 2005; Tuggle 1993). Tuggle (1993) measured the permanence and rank of different households by examining site formation processes, labor investment, and relative concentrations of midden, finding fewer permanent or high-ranking households and ritual sites than in nearby Kawela. Weisler (1989b) describes 12 ha of dryland fields that he called the Kaunakakai Field System (sites -886 and -888h) located inland of Kaunakakai at 40 to 70 m above sea level. Radiocarbon dating places the construction of the fields in the Late Voyaging Period, around AD 1280, with use extending into late precontact times. Dye (1998) documented a petroglyph panel (site 50-60-06-1660) east of 'Ōhi'apilo Pond associated with deposits that included "a pig tooth perforated for use in a *kupe'e niho 'ilio*," a type of anklet worn by male dancers (Buck 1957, 553; Dye 1998, fig. 11); the site dates to the Expansion Period.

Ko'olau District

Four great valleys extending from Hālawa in the east to Waikolu in the west punctuate the dramatic sea cliffs of windward Moloka'i. With the exception of Hālawa Valley, the Ko'olau District is accessible only by boat (and then typically only during the summer months) or over a few treacherous trails that traverse the north shore *pali,* including the

Wailau Trail from Mapulehu over the central mountain. Despite this relative inaccessibility, Koʻolau *moku* has been the focus of important studies in Hālawa, Wailau, and Waikolu valleys, along with the Kalaupapa Peninsula.

The earliest residents of Koʻolau probably resided near the shore, as represented in the deepest levels of the Hālawa Dune site, which indicate occupation by the end of the Late Voyaging Period (Kirch and McCoy 2007). The Hālawa Valley Project, which began with reconnaissance by Kirch in the mid-1960s followed by a two-year effort in 1969–1970, was the first to apply a settlement-pattern approach to a wet windward valley dominated by taro irrigation (Kirch and Kelley, eds., 1975). Kirch's excavations in the Hālawa dune site (site Mo-A1-3), described in chapter 6, yielded evidence of round-ended house structures, along with fishhooks, adzes, and other artifacts typical of the earlier time periods in Hawaiʻi.

There was a heavy emphasis on marine resources during the early phase of occupation in Hālawa Valley, although no evidence for turtles or extirpated birds. Over time, greater emphasis came to be placed on terrestrial foods, represented in the dune site's faunal remains of domestic pig and dog. By the Expansion Period, after AD 1400, Hālawa's farmers had expanded their irrigated fields inland, with habitation sites situated on inland ridges. A notable feature of the later habitation sites was continuation of the old Polynesian practice of burials within houses, something rarely seen elsewhere in Hawaiʻi. By the Archaic States Period, major irrigation works covered the valley floor, while the higher colluvial slopes were extensively modified with dryland terraces for mixed-crop gardening and arboriculture (Kurashima and Kirch 2011). Fourteen *heiau*, primarily agricultural temples (*heiau hoʻoulu ʻai*), were distributed around the valley, and one larger temple (Mana Heiau) was a *luakini*. Anderson (2001) investigated the postcontact settlement landscape of Hālawa Valley, incorporating documentary evidence from the Māhele (see chapter 13).

Investigations elsewhere in the Koʻolau valleys provide a picture of life in the pre-European contact era. Early settlers cultivated pondfields on coastal flats at the valley mouths as well as in other prime locations inland (Kirch, ed., 2002; McElroy 2007, table 6.2). At the mouth of Waikolu Valley, Kirch et al. (2002, 46) obtained charcoal from a buried pondfield horizon dating to AD 1200–1290, demonstrating that irrigation systems were in place by the Late Voyaging Period.

McElroy's (2007, 2012) research in Wailau Valley provides the most detailed chronology of irrigated agricultural development on the island. McElroy completed a reconnaissance survey of over 10 percent of the 9.36 km² valley bottom, intensively mapped 13 ha, and dug 66 excavation units at key locations in order to reconstruct the chronology of Wailau's pondfields. This work demonstrated that nearly all "highly productive" irrigated fields within a kilometer of the coast in Wailau Valley were first farmed in the Late Voyaging Period before AD 1400. Smaller, less productive fields continued to be built right up to the historic period. By the beginning of the Archaic States Period, nearly all available farmland was in irrigated production; indeed, out of the radiocarbon dates reported, only a third date to after AD 1600 (McElroy 2012).

Along the northern coast between Hālawa and Wailau valleys three "landshelves" jut out at the base of the towering cliffs (from east to west, Puahaunui, Hākaʻaʻano, and Kikipua), each offering a few acres of relatively level land that could be occupied. Although access is difficult, as their coastlines consist of boulder beaches exposed to the winter swells, each of these landshelves exhibits archaeological features, mostly recorded by Stokes (1909a). Kirch swam in to Kikipua in 1993, briefly exploring the extensive ruins of Heleku Heiau (see Summers 1971, 173–174). Stokes was of the opinion that Heleku Heiau may have been a college for the training of priests.

Kalaupapa, a relatively level peninsula jutting northward from the island's windward coast, was formed by a late-stage volcanic rejuvenation about 300,000 years ago. Due to its young geological age, the Kalaupapa soils are quite fertile, attracting early settlers. Kalaupapa Peninsula is home to a large dryland field system (M. D. McCoy 2005). The first signs of anthropogenic burning appear in the lowest levels of a lava-tube shelter first excavated by Richard Pearson in the late 1960s, Kaupikiawa Cave (Pearson et al. 1974). Initial dating suggested activity as early as the Foundation Period (Weisler 1989a), but reexcavation and more detailed analysis point to the accumulation of charcoal, from mainly aboral taxa, in the Late Voyaging Period, around AD 1300–1400 (Kirch et al. 2004), a time when irrigated agriculture in the windward valleys had already been established.

By the transition to the Archaic States Period, multiple lines of evidence point to the Kalaupapa Peninsula having been transformed from a forested lowland to a broad, continuous field system of windbreaks built to shelter low-growing crops, primarily sweet potato. While this method was effective, the long-term effect of farming was to redeposit soils from exposed fields enriching downwind soils (McCoy and Hartshorn 2007).

M. D. McCoy's (2006) research in the three *ahupuaʻa* that subdivided Kalaupapa Peninsula showed other notable changes during the Archaic States Period. Prior to AD 1650, the majority of people lived in the small valleys of Waikolu and Waiʻaleia, and on colluvial slopes at the base of the *pali*; this is understandable given the peninsula's exposure to the incessant tradewinds. At some point in the Archaic States Period, however, there was a shift of settlement onto the peninsula itself. This evidence includes dates from four house sites, two rockshelters, an enclosure, a possible shrine, and a site interpreted as a men's house (*mua*). Other evidence suggests that this shift was due not to an increase in the local population but rather a reorganization of settlement not unlike the shift to people living in more marginal environments across the islands.

Kalaupapa also exhibits several well-preserved ritual sites that indicate a shift in the relationship between these rural, isolated communities and the rest of the island. The *heiau* and shrines dating to the Expansion Period appear to have been placed to take advantage of the naturally dramatic landscape, such as Kauhakō crater and the views afforded by the steep rise in elevation at the base of the *pali*. Later, in the Archaic States Period, *heiau* were positioned across the entire landscape, also using local landform and viewshed to great advantage. Notable sites dated by radiocarbon and/or tradition to near the end of the Archaic States Period include a temple (site 50-60-03-2270) oriented to mark the acronychal rising of Makaliʻi over Mōkapu Islet, and of the equinox rising over ʻŌkala Islet. Another *heiau* (site 50-60-03-2295) lies just east of an *ahupuaʻa* boundary, and a *hōlua* sled track is situated on the south-facing slopes of the crater (site 50-60-03-293). The burial hill at Makapulapai (site 50-60-03-1928) consists of more than 60 cairns and a petroglyph possibly depicting Kualiʻi, the king of Oʻahu, holding the weapon that oral tradition tells us he used to kill scores of warriors in a battle at Kalaupapa. These remarkable features suggest that it was during the Archaic States Period that Kalaupapa became fully integrated into "a larger tribute and wealth-creation system coordinated through the annual *makahiki* procession" (M. D. McCoy 2008b, 273).

The landshelf of Nihoa lies to the west of the Kalaupapa Peninsula. Although level land on Nihoa is very limited, Kirch's (2002) survey of the land shelf recorded signs of agriculture, permanent habitation, and ritual, including "a complex site, constructed on the inland side of the large boulder concentration in the middle portion of the land shelf, and consisting of several adjacent stone-faced terraces, freestanding walls, and large uprights" (Kirch, ed., 2002, 74–75). This site (50-60-03-2110, also known as NI-6 in Kirch [2002], and site J in M. D. McCoy [2005]), was test excavated by M. D. McCoy (2005) who found a thick marine shell midden dated to the Archaic States Period (AD 1682–1950, Beta-192674*) (M. D. McCoy 2008a). Another site (NI-10) consists of a series of terraces leading up to a precipice, overhanging which is a large boulder with a shape resembling a shark (fig. 16.5). The natural isolation of landshelves, and the potential for intact deposits preserved under land slips, makes them a high priority in future research since they will be among the first locations to be affected by sea level rise.

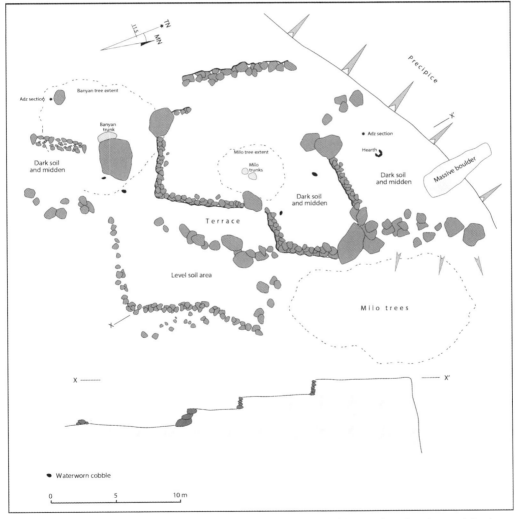

FIGURE 16.5 Plan of site NI-6 at Nihoa, Moloka'i Island. The large boulder overhanging the precipice has the shape of a shark. *(Plan by P. V. Kirch)*

Above the cliffs overlooking Kalaupapa at an elevation of about 500 m above sea level is the famed Ka Ule o Nānāhoa, a large boulder that may have been partially modified to enhance its phallic qualities (fig. 16.6). Summers (1971, 28) describes the site along with a nearby set of female stones. To the west, in Naʻiwa, is the peculiar stone structure known as Nā Imu Kalua ʻUa, or "Ovens for Cooking the Rain" (fig. 16.7), consisting of a grid of squares formed by elongate cobbles set on edge. The Naʻiwa uplands were evidently also the scene

FIGURE 16.6 Ka Ule o Nānāhoa at Palaʻau, Molokaʻi Island. *(Photo by Therese Babineau)*

FIGURE 16.7 Nā Imu Kalua ʻUa at Naʻiwa, Molokaʻi Island, as photographed by John F. G. Stokes in 1909. (Curved lines are cracks in the original glass plate negative.) *(Photo courtesy Bishop Museum Library and Archives)*

of annual Makahiki rites on Moloka'i, as suggested by the presence there of two *hōlua* slides and a *kahua maika* or field for *'ulumaika* bowling (Summers 1971, 80–81).

Kaluako'i

Kaluako'i, consisting of the western third of Moloka'i, was thinly populated, owing to its aridity and older, heavily leached soils that were not conducive to intensive agriculture. There was some limited sweet potato farming on the higher slopes of Maunaloa, but for the most part settlements were confined to small fishing hamlets along the coastline. Bonk (1954) excavated several rockshelters, along with two house sites and one sand dune midden in Kaluako'i (see chapter 1). At Mo'omomi rockshelter (site Mo. 1) about 37 m^2 were excavated, revealing a stratigraphic sequence with three main layers and a depth of about 1 m (fig. 16.8), and yielding one-piece fishhooks and octopus fishing gear (fig. 16.9). Based on his excavations, Bonk (1954, 139) concluded that the western part of Moloka'i, "was a decidedly marginal land. . . . Fishing and the quest for adze stone brought people into the area, and fighting probably sent refugees into it, but temporarily."

Marine resources have always been important in sustaining people on Moloka'i. Weisler (1989a, 127) notes the "first evidence for exploitation of marine resources . . . and land birds" dates to cal AD 1176–1296, based on a sample from Kawa'aloa Bay (site 02-21) from a "pit feature containing predominately fish bone, with much lesser amounts of turtle and birdbone," along with bones of the endemic Hawaiian goose (*Branta sandvicensis*), which was likely associated with a nearby rockshelter (139–140). Both the Hawaiian goose and sea turtle drop out of the faunal assemblages dating later than AD 1450; the most recent example of turtle exploitation on Moloka'i was found in a deposit dated by ^{230}Th to AD 1417 ± 3 (site -I8A; Weisler et al. 2006, 279).

Evidence from surveys and excavations at Kawākiu Bay speak to the importance of fishing in West Moloka'i. On both sides of Kawākiu Bay are extensive midden deposits, as well as several stone structures probably representing a permanent community (Hammatt

FIGURE 16.8 Rockshelter site Mo. 1 at Kawa'aloa Bay, Moloka'i Island, during excavations by Bishop Museum. *(Photo courtesy Bishop Museum Department of Anthropology)*

FIGURE 16.9 Bone fishhooks from site Mo. 1 at Kawaʻaloa Bay, Molokaʻi. *(Photo by P. V. Kirch)*

1979a). Excavations in a well-built stone enclosure that was probably a men's house that may also have served as a *koʻa* (site 50-60-01-38) revealed a two-phase sequence of occupation. The deposits within the enclosure, partially excavated by Hammatt (1979a), yielded a wide range of tools and detritus associated with the manufacture of fishhooks, as well as 61 complete and fragmentary hooks. Weisler and Walter (2002) reanalyzed this collection of fishing gear. Most of the hooks are barbed with inwardly curved rotating points, as opposed to the upward point found on jabbing fishhooks. Weisler and Walter argue that "rotating fishhooks in general, and barbed hooks specifically, are an adaptation to . . . offshore benthic fishing, and in shallower inshore water where seeing the prey and feeling it strike the bait are unlikely" (53). These are precisely the conditions of West Molokaʻi and help explain why these types of hook show up in such large numbers. Octopus fishing was also important along the Kaluakoʻi inshore waters; Major (2000) documented a unique site in central Kaluakoʻi—a location where hematite was used to manufacture breadloaf-type sinkers used on octopus-lure rigs (see chapter 9).

Aside from fishing, quarrying of adze rock was the main focus of human activity on arid West Molokaʻi (Dixon and Major 1992; Dixon et al. 1994; Dye, Weisler, and Riford 1985; Major 2000). At least five separate quarry sites have been identified, at Kapālauoʻa, Mānalo Gulch, Kaʻeo Hill, Maunaloa, and ʻAmikopala (Summers 1971; Weisler 2011). In addition to the quarries, surveys have revealed associated ritual sites and shelters, as well as limited evidence of dryland farming.

Proposed development in the 1990s prompted a CRM investigation by Bishop Museum archaeologists of a large portion of the southwestern sector of West Molokaʻi, covering 2,540 ha; 197 sites were recorded (34 previous sites, 163 new sites) encompassing 596 features (Dixon and Major 1992; Dixon et al. 1994). In contrast to Bonk's earlier assessment, Dixon and Major (1992) discovered what they interpreted as permanent settlements centered on small gulches and bays. Subsistence was heavily reliant on fishing, as described by Weisler and Walter (2002). But there were also small fishponds, and agriculture was "pursued on a household level with little attempt at surplus production by communities" (Dixon and Major 1992, 339–340). The minimal investment in ritual architecture in this marginal and sparsely populated landscape contrasts with the large *heiau* seen in the densely populated regions of eastern Moloka'i. This suggests a lower-status community of people derived from an "excess population [that moved] into Southwest Moloka'i during the late pre-Contact period" acting as "a release valve, allowing more time, space, and resources for east end chiefly development" (Dixon and Major 1992, 344). This hypothesis was further supported by the discovery of intensively occupied ridges between quarries inland near the center of Kalauko'i (Major 2000).

Dixon et al. (1994, 13) suggest that West Molokai went through a period of "superabundant production" of adzes, indicated by an increase in the density of flaked basalt in the quarries (such as site 50-Mo-B6-185) after AD 1400, which they link to agricultural intensification (Dixon et al. 1994, 1). Archaeobotanical evidence of the use of Mountain Apple wood (*Syzygium malaccense*) in the construction of domestic structures "as early as AD 1520" suggests it "may have been transported up to 20 km from its present range" (Weisler and Murakami 1991, 284), further underlining the interconnectedness of the island's regions. We should, however, be cautious of jumping to the conclusion that goods flowed freely from one end of the island to the other. New research has shown that people living on the island's eastern end rarely used tools produced from West Moloka'i quarries. The largest basalt artifact sourcing study on Moloka'i—which included nearly 1,600 artifacts from Hālawa Valley—found that the vast majority of raw material was locally sourced on the eastern half of the island (Mills et al. 2018). The source of the majority of basalt flakes in the Hālawa dune site was recently traced to a previously unknown quarry in Honoko'i Bay, close to Hālawa Valley.

17

THE ARCHAEOLOGY OF O'AHU ISLAND

O'ahu, though much smaller in size than Hawai'i or Maui, was a major population center and the locus of early settlements, presumably due to the island's many fertile valleys along with its developed reef ecosystems. The island has been the focus of important archaeological studies; more sites have been excavated and dated here than on any other island except Hawai'i. However, O'ahu has also suffered a greater loss of archaeological sites than anywhere else in the islands, due to extensive plantation agriculture, land "grubbing" for pasture improvement, the activities of the US military (at Pearl Harbor, Mōkapu, and elsewhere), and, in recent decades, the island's sprawling urbanism. Nevertheless, sections of O'ahu still hold rich concentrations of archaeological sites and much potential for future research.

O'ahu was formed by two separate volcanoes, one making up the Ko'olau mountain range, the other the Wai'anae range, with the intervening Schofield Plateau, an area of coalescing lava flows (fig. 17.1). The windward side of the Ko'olau range is characterized by amphitheater-headed valleys and alluvial plains traversed by permanent streams. This region, divided between the *moku* of Ko'olauloa and Ko'olaupoko, was one of the first to be settled following Polynesian discovery of the archipelago and was later a center of population growth fueled by extensive taro irrigation. On the leeward side, the Kona District encompasses the broad plain of Honolulu, backed by several large and inviting valleys, including Mānoa and Nu'uanu. Though drier than the windward coast, the Kona region was also suitable to irrigation and supported a large population. 'Ewa District includes the Pearl Harbor area, with numerous fishponds and fish traps, as well as the arid 'Ewa Plain made up of exposed reef limestone that formed during a period of higher sea level during the Pleistocene. Wai'anae District, including Nānākuli, Lualualei, Wai'anae, and Mākaha valleys, generally lacks permanent streams, although rainfall was sufficient for extensive cultivation of crops such as yams and sweet potatoes; some irrigation could be practiced in the interior valley reaches. Waialua District, in the northwest, is intermediate along the windward-leeward continuum, with fertile though narrow coastal plains, well watered from narrow gulches penetrating the Koʻolau Range. The higher saddle region between the two mountain ranges was apparently not much used by the Hawaiians, although trails traversed the area, and a sacred site—the temple of Kūkaniloko—is situated there (McAllister 1933a, 134–137). This saddle region is also associated in Hawaiian traditions with a tribe of cannibals, the Halemano king and his people (Kirch and Sahlins 1992, 1:24).

Thomas Thrum (1906) and John F. G. Stokes (1909b) conducted the first archaeological studies on Oʻahu, on *heiau* and the walled fish traps of Pearl Harbor. The first attempt at an island-wide survey was by J. Gilbert McAllister (1933a) who, in the style of his day, concentrated mainly on *heiau,* and on artifacts recovered from surface collections, recording 384 sites. Elspeth Sterling and Catherine Summers (1978) integrated McAllister's data with more recent findings, and with a compilation of oral traditions and other early accounts. When Kenneth P. Emory initiated stratigraphic excavations in 1950, Kuliʻouʻou rockshelter on southeast Oʻahu (site O1) was his first site; several other rockshelters were excavated soon after (Emory and Sinoto 1961). Important research projects on Oʻahu have included the Mākaha Valley Historical Project (Green 1980; Green, ed., 1969, 1970; Ladd 1973; Ladd and Yen 1972) and the Anahulu Valley Project (Kirch and Sahlins 1992). In recent decades, virtually all work carried out on Oʻahu has been CRM archaeology related to the rapid pace of land development, including the extensive survey and excavations associated with the construction of the H3 highway (see chapter 1).

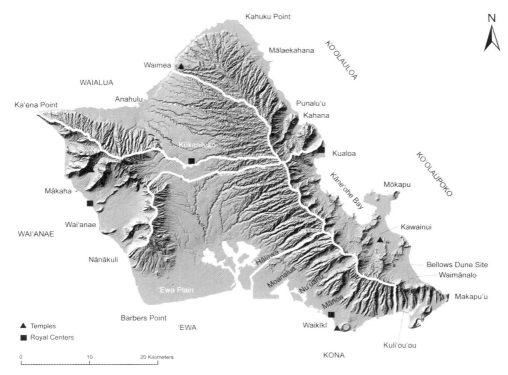

FIGURE 17.1 Map of Oʻahu Island, showing sites and major places mentioned in the text. White lines indicate the boundaries of the traditional districts. *(Map by M. D. McCoy)*

Koʻolaupoko District

The O18 or Bellow's dune site at Waimānalo, with the earliest dates known from a habitation site in the archipelago, is discussed in chapter 6. Dye (2010a; Dye and Sholin 2013) compiled radiocarbon dates and charcoal identified to taxa from more than two dozen archaeological contexts in Waimānalo in an attempt to identify subtle changes in society. For the Expansion Period, Dye found a shift to low-quality local cooking stones, as people "grew tired of selecting and transporting high-quality cooking stones to the [Waimānalo] plain and instead gathered low-quality cooking stones from the closest source, hauling down new stones each time they anticipated cooking on the plain." He argues that the reason for this move was that people "found that they could no longer keep their high-quality cooking stones from being stolen" (Dye 2010a, 733–734). To be clear, Dye is not suggesting this was an era of lawlessness but rather a shift in property rights, specifically, the "long-term decline in the importance of rights of person and a concomitant increase of rights of property associated with the demise of lineage organization and the development of social stratification" (727). He sees these shifts in everyday life as having affected not just the gathering of cooking stones but also of firewood. Up until the Archaic States Period, tree species account for more than half of identified charcoal by weight, suggesting no limits on where makaʻāinana could gather firewood. During the centuries immediately prior to European contact, however, firewood from trees became scarce.

Aside from Bellows Air Force Station, little systematic archaeological work has been carried out in Waimānalo. Archaeological studies report evidence of historic-era sugar production, and there are isolated sites, such as Pueo Heiau (site 50-80-15-1031), which at 76 m by 40 m is the largest known heiau in Waimānalo (site 381 in McAllister 1933a, listed as an unnamed heiau). At the southeastern end of Oʻahu is Makapuʻu, the site of an ancient fishing village recorded by McAllister (1933a). Rounding the cape, a fishermen's camp site at Kaloko Point (near what is popularly called "Queen's Beach") was test-excavated by Wallace (Wallace, Wallace, and Meeker, ms.), yielding a number of fishhooks, coral abraders, and other objects. The site was not dated.

Located behind the present town of Kailua, Kawainui Marsh was once an extensive loko puʻuone or inland fishpond. Investigations along the margins of the marsh revealed evidence of occupation in the later precontact period (Allen-Wheeler 1981a, 1981b; Athens 1983b). The landscape of Kawainui Marsh has witnessed major changes over the past 1,500 years. Stratigraphic borings and other geomorphological studies by Chris Kraft (pers. comm.) and J. Allen-Wheeler (1981a) demonstrated that Kawainui was originally open to the sea; the beach accretion barrier of sand dunes upon which Kailua town is now situated did not yet exist (fig. 17.2). The inner margins of the bay were sandy beaches; the gentle slopes rising up from these beaches would have been ideal locations for settlement sites and for establishing gardens. Only later did the sand barrier build up, turning Kawainui into a brackish lagoon that was later used as a fishpond (Kelly and Clark 1980).

In 1980, J. Clark (Kelly and Clark 1980) of Bishop Museum investigated archaeological features along the inland margins of Kawainui Marsh. Test excavations at two sites (Oa-G6-32 and -33) revealed buried cultural deposits; three radiocarbon dates suggested

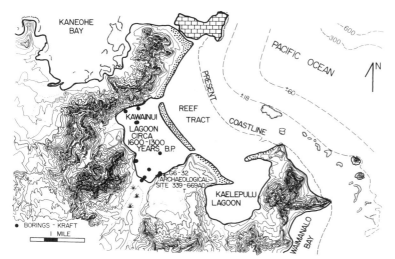

FIGURE 17.2 Paleogeographic map of the Kawainui and Kaelepulu area, windward Oʻahu Island, showing the probable shoreline and coastal configuration prior to the first arrival of Polynesian settlers. *(Map by Chris Kraft)*

that human activity along the shores of the former bay began as early as the fifth century. The dated charcoal, however, was not identified to species, hence these dates almost certainly have some inbuilt age. Nonetheless, they hint at the presence of early sites along the Kawainui Marsh shores. In the case of site Oa-G6-32, the buried charcoal deposits and stone-wall features may reflect agricultural activity. At site Oa-G6-33, a few stone artifacts (seven basalt flakes, a basalt grinder, one adze flake, and three volcanic-glass flakes) suggest other activities. Renewed research around the Kawainui Marsh would be desirable.

On the south side of Kaiwainui Marsh and commanding a view over the former fishpond is Ulupō Heiau, one of the largest *luakini* temples on Oʻahu (fig. 17.3). The stone foundation consists of a square, terraced platform rising nearly 10 m above the platform's base. Not much is known of its history; Thrum was told that it was constructed by the Menehune, which is the case with a number of *heiau* on both Oʻahu and Kauaʻi.

A limited excavation in the 2-km-long sand dune upon which Kailua town is built, near the edge of Kawainui Marsh, revealed a buried midden deposit (site Oa-G6-40) (Athens 1983c). This site, producing among other artifacts an early style of pearl-shell fishhook, was situated upon an existing house lot within the urban area, demonstrating that urban development does not always obliterate archaeological sites.

Excavations on a section of the inland accretionary berm separating Kawainui Marsh from Kailua yielded more evidence of everyday life, including pearl-shell fishhook fragments. Rieth and Duarte (2016, iv) used Bayesian modeling of dates from Kawainui Marsh (10 dates on unidentified charcoal) and Kailua (14 dates on identified charcoal) to argue that the start of cultural activities on the Kailua berm occurred between cal AD 1222–1403 and cal AD 1308–1389. This adds weight to the likelihood that this portion of the island was settled in the Foundation Period and saw a rise of population during the Late Voyaging Period.

A paleoenvironmental core located in Maunawili Valley, not far from the Koʻolau *pali*, points to AD 1200 as "a crucial moment in the history of upper Maunawili valley, and perhaps all of windward Oʻahu" (Athens and Ward 1997, 48). At this location, after AD 1200 "the native forest community quickly declines and Polynesian-introduced plant species

FIGURE 17.3 Ulupō Heiau consists of a massive stone platform overlooking adjacent Kawainui Marsh. *(Photo by Therese Babineau)*

become more common" (48). This indirect evidence for agricultural expansion and intensification is consistent with the results of studies by Jane Allen in Maunawili Valley (Jane Allen et al. 2002) and upland Kāneʻohe (Jane Allen, ed., 1987) (see also Jane Allen 1991).

In Maunawili Valley, Jane Allen et al. (2002) conducted one of the most extensive studies of a windward valley, recording over 600 features grouped into 29 site complexes. Agricultural terraces ranged across the full spectrum of irrigated agriculture, with most terraces organized into Type II or III irrigation systems (Kirch 1977); dryland fields were also present. Although radiocarbon dating was limited and conducted without identification of dated wood charcoal, several important trends are evident. First, results confirm that upland valleys, not just coastal regions, were farmed prior to AD 1200, after which introduced plants become more common in the Maunawili paleoenvironmental core. Second, stone terrace facings became more standardized during the Late Voyaging Period (AD 1200–1400). Jane Allen (1991, 25) notes that construction of facings with five to six stone courses "typically began with a basal course of large, tabular boulders inserted securely, long axis into the slope, in lozenge fashion. Upper courses of carefully sized and carefully fitted small boulders and cobbles were stacked against the slope, with a 70–75° batter angle, for maximum stability." Finally, after AD 1400–1500, Kukapoki Heiau (site 50-80-15-374) was built overlooking Maunawili Stream. This modest-sized structure (20 × 16 m) comprises a stone-faced terrace supporting a core-filled wall. Excavations exposed terrace fill with a date (Layer III, AD 1298–1633, HRC-1050), suggesting that the *heiau* was built around the fourteenth century. Jane Allen et al. (2002) point out that while it is the most substantial religious structure in the valley, the temple does not conform to a *luakini heiau*. Rather, the size and northeast orientation of Kukapoki Heiau is consistent with a *hale o Lono;* given its apparent date of construction, the *heiau* may have been associated with the transition to the *ahupuaʻa* land tenure system.

In upland Kāneʻohe, Jane Allen's (1987) work spanned five *ʻili* but focused mainly on Luluku and Punaluʻu Mauka; this project was carried out as part of Bishop Museum's H3 highway CRM project (see chapter 1). Trenches excavated across low agricultural terraces, even those with just a single course of stone visible on the surface, exposed a surprisingly complex stratigraphy, due to the influx of colluvial soils and gravel burying earlier stages of clearing and gardening. In Punaluʻu Mauka, at site 50-80-10-1887, for example, Trench 1 (Features 7 through 10) exposed pondfield deposits (Layer VIII) buried more than 1 m below the surface. While the charcoal within the deepest layer was not dated, it was capped by colluvium, and then by another later garden deposit with charcoal dated to the Late Voyaging Period (cal AD 1250–1430, Beta-12559, Layer VI). Still later garden deposits were dated to the Expansion Period (cal AD 1415–1675, Beta-16264, Layer IIIb).

Radiocarbon dating within the windward section of the H3 highway corridor continued after Jane Allen's (1987) initial study. Excavations and dating of site -1887 reported by Leidemann et al. (2004) failed to replicate earlier dates; they instead argue that AD 1250–1400 was the peak period for cultivation in the upland fields in Punaluʻu Mauka. Dates from this period include nonagricultural deposits (cal AD 1281–1420, Beta-62637, from firepits on a ridge above the terraces; Leidemann et al. 2004). At lower elevations in Kāneʻohe (about 100 m above sea level), 36 out of 49 sites recorded were radiocarbon dated (with 69 dates), providing a picture of changing use in a small area of about 90 ha (Leidemann 2003; Leidemann et al. 2003). The earliest signs of people, after rejecting an anomalously early date (cal AD 668–998, Beta-34009, site -2204), are features indicating occasional use during the Foundation and Late Voyaging Periods, including an earth oven dated to cal AD 1004–1287 (Beta-34016, site -2207). Beginning around AD 1300–1400, more regular use of the area is evidenced, continuing through to the postcontact era.

A significant controversy arose during the construction of the H3 highway regarding the site of Kukuiokāne Heiau. McAllister reported that Kukuiokāne Heiau was located "at the foot of the ridge above the banana fields" in Luluku (McAllister 1933a, 177). It was by all accounts both an important and a substantial site, albeit one that by the 1930s had been severely affected by plantation agriculture. McAllister (177) observed, "The ploughed-up remains indicate heavy walls and several terraces. It is impossible to obtain dimensions."

Jane Allen's (1987) initial survey in upland Luluku (in Haʻikū Valley) did not report any signs of Kukuiokāne Heiau. She recorded many other sites, including site 50-80-10-1888, which included three large terraces—one (Feature 2) covering about 600 m² with stone facings about 1.75 m high—and other associated features. Although in poor condition these terraces were unlike pondfield terraces recorded elsewhere. The stone terrace facades were "markedly diagonal" (95) in profile, and trenching did not reveal typical pondfield deposits. Allen concluded that the terraces constituted a rain-fed agricultural complex adjacent to an *ʻili* boundary marked by a substantial stone wall (site 50-80-10-1889).

What followed damaged the reputation of Bishop Museum for years to come (for more context, see Kawelu 2007, 90; 2015). After the initial reporting of site -1888, descendants of former landowners, along with historians, cultural practitioners, and archaeologists not involved with the original survey contested Allen's interpretation of the terraces, raising the possibility that site -1888 was in fact the remnants of Kukuiokāne Heiau. Bishop

Museum archaeologists returned to the area, cleared more vegetation, mapping, and excavated newly discovered features grouped into two additional sites (site -2038, -2076), immediately south of site -1888. In the early 1990s, at the museum's recommendation, the entire complex was buried under a massive earth deposit, ostensibly as a means of preservation, allowing highway construction to proceed. Due to numerous staff turnovers at Bishop Museum, a final report on the efforts to detect Kukuiokāne Heiau was not completed until two decades after the initial report (Leidemann et al. 2007). Bishop Museum's archaeological report on Kukuiokāne Heiau contends that the information collected was "insufficient" to identify the *heiau* (Leidemann et al. 2007, 371), but not all archaeologists involved agree. Williams (1989, 18; 1991) excavated a rectangular structure (20 × 18 m) recorded at site -2038 (Feature 20), recovering branch coral and pig bone fragments, both signals of ritual activity. However, it is not clear if this structure was part of Kukuiokāne Heiau, or an unrelated site. In the end, the museum's failure to address the claims that the terrace complex was the remains of Kukuiokāne Heiau led to a greater recognition of the inherent difficulties of identifying religious sites (Cachola-Abad 1996), and of the importance of community input to archaeological work (Kawelu 2007, 2015).

Other H3 highway investigations revealed that while the base of the *pali* in Kāne'ohe was certainly utilized, it was not a locus of dense habitation, intensive agriculture, or large formal religious structures. One possible explanation is that this was an area devoted to arboriculture. Archaeobotanical analysis of plant matter from 44 sites identified the remains of *'ulu* (breadfruit) in seven sites. Leidemann and Hartzell (2003, 638) note the possibility that increased land use around AD 1400 could be "explained in part by people either coming to the uplands specifically to transplant *'ulu* or making regular trips . . . for harvesting." Archaeobotanical analysis also recovered evidence of sweet potato, gourd, *'awa*, coconut, *hala*, and *kukui*.

Interior portions of Kāne'ohe Valley were intensively surveyed in the mid-1970s (Rosendahl, ed., 1976), revealing residential clusters and agricultural sites, including terrace complexes used for taro irrigation. One site (Oa-G5-37) drew particular attention during the initial survey: an elongate earthen mound, about 18 by 6 m, flat-topped with sloping sides, was test-excavated and appeared to be a habitation site. Since raised earthen mounds as foundations for house sites were unknown in Hawai'i (although they are a common feature of Western Polynesian archaeology, especially in Samoa), the site appeared to warrant detailed excavation, since it would be destroyed by a dam to be built by the Army Corps of Engineers. Rosendahl excavated the mound, revealing two occupation layers, dating to the fourteenth and sixteenth centuries. As Rosendahl demonstrated, however, the mound had resulted from fairly recent down-cutting of the surrounding terrain, rather than from construction of an earthen foundation for residential purposes.

In southern Kāne'ohe Bay, He'eia fishpond (site 50-80-10-327), of the classic *loko kuapā* type, has a massive, arc-shaped wall extending out onto the reef flat more than 1,500 m long, with four watch-houses to look over the *makahā* or sluice gates (fig. 17.4). Across from He'eia, framing the eastern side of Kāne'ohe Bay, and from a distance resembling a gigantic humped reptile rising from the sea, Mōkapu Peninsula was the site of the largest precontact burial ground known in the Hawaiian Islands (see chapter 11).

FIGURE 17.4 Heʻeia fishpond in Kāneʻohe Bay, Oʻahu Island. *(Photo by Therese Babineau)*

On the side of ʻIolekaʻa Stream, an upland tributary of Heʻeia Stream, is a large terrace (80 × 62 m) in the likely location of Kaualaukī Heiau (McAllister 1933a, 172). A trench was excavated by Stride and Hammatt (1995); however, this yielded a modern date. More research is necessary to determine if this is the *heiau* described by McAllister.

In northern Kāneʻohe Bay, surveys and excavations have documented many well-preserved sites and deposits across the Koʻolaupoko District. In Waikāne, examples of *loʻi*, habitation terraces, and *heiau* were first noted by McAllister (1933a). Waiāhole has the most intact adze quarry in windward Oʻahu. Modest in scale compared to other quarries in the islands, the Waiāhole quarry has been described as "adze quality boulder and cobble outcrops and talus mixed with flake debitage and rejected tools . . . along with several small, isolated ridge-top flake scatters" (Dye, Weisler, and Riford 1985, 67). Evidence of quarrying can be found in two primary locations, sites 50-Oa-G2-7 and 50-Oa-G2-8, which together would be about the area of a football field. Examination of flaked debitage suggests that craftsmen were mostly producing untanged, rectangular, or trapezoidal section adzes, and, rarely, reverse triangular section adzes. At least two other windward locations were likely used as quarries—the small offshore island of Mokulua, and the outcrops in Kailua—but these are poorly described and may have been inadvertently destroyed.

At Kualoa, at the far northern end of Kāneʻohe Bay, not only do we find the large fishponds at Moʻili, but nearby, archaeologists using high resolution satellite imagery, LiDAR, and images from UAV flights have mapped additional fishpond walls in the bay (Sailors and Honda 2014). Much of the coastal plain at Kualoa, including the land immediately east of Moʻili fishpond, formed only within the past 1,000 years while people were living along the shores of Kāneʻohe Bay. Carson and Athens (2006, 2007) report a "firepit with dense midden" dated to cal AD 1040–1280 (Beta-28136*) that would have been on the shoreline in the Foundation Period but today is about 850 m inland (Carson and Athens 2006, 59). These are among the oldest well-dated cultural deposits in the islands.

Excavations in the 1970s and 1980s revealed cultural deposits across the area of Kualoa Regional Park (summarized in Gunness 1993). In a waterlogged swale, wooden artifacts were preserved, including a *kapa* beater. Excavations also revealed a large earth oven,

FIGURE 17.5 Pig burial and earth oven revealed during excavation at Kualoʻa, Oʻahu Island. *(Photo by Jo Lynn Gunness)*

adjacent to the articulated skeleton of a pig, probably used as an offering (fig. 17.5). The pig offering may have marked the boundary between Hakipuʻu and Kualoa *ahupuaʻa;* we do not know when this offering was made, as it was not dated.

Koʻolauloa District

Kualoa Point is the boundary between Koʻolauloa and Koʻolaupoko *moku*. The first valley of Koʻolauloa, Kaʻaʻawa, lacks a permanently flowing stream, while the next valley, Kahana, is deeply embayed with a permanent stream and fertile alluvial floor and colluvial slopes. Kahana was surveyed in 1971 (Hommon and Barrera 1971), and excavations were carried out in 1972 (Hommon and Bevacqua 1973). Stone structures are located on the colluvial slopes at various places; several small irrigation systems for taro cultivation were mapped in the western portion of the valley. Most of the sites date to a late period in the Hawaiian sequence, but one sand dune locality (site 1546) along the eastern shore of Kahana Bay (adjacent to Huilua fishpond) probably dates to the Foundation Period (fig. 17.6). The early deposits are just a remnant of what may originally have been a more extensive site, as activities associated with the construction and maintenance of the adjacent fishpond have greatly disturbed the early strata. The archaeological excavations, limited to a 5 m² area, revealed a complex stratigraphy with at least seven distinct layers. Charcoal from a small hearth in the deep Layer V yielded an eighth-century date; however, the wood was not identified, so this likely reflects some inbuilt age (Isotopes, Incorporated, date reported as AD 675–845, HRC-233; recalibration using InCal13 places the date range as AD 668–992). The other materials present were a few basalt flakes, an *ʻulu maika* gaming stone, and faunal remains including a pig incisor and an albatross radius. The site appeared to have been only temporarily occupied, perhaps as a fishermen's camp.

Punaluʻu Valley, northwest of Kahana, was heavily disturbed both by sugarcane cultivation and by US military activities during World War II. Nonetheless, a number of archaeological sites remain intact on the higher colluvial slopes, including two notched *heiau* enclosures and a dryland agricultural field system that have been the subject of a recent University of Hawaiʻi archaeological field school (Morrison et al. 2022). Morrison et al. report that "initial vegetation clearing of the area may have occurred as early as the late thirteenth to early fifteenth centuries AD. As early as the fifteenth century, some stands of economic trees were growing, which may have coincided with initial placement of boundary walls along some portions of the slopes. Major expansion of the surface agricultural infrastructure along the landscape occurred through the sixteenth and eighteenth centuries AD" (1).

FIGURE 17.6 Excavation in progress at the Kahana Valley sand dune site, Oʻahu Island. A circular firepit feature is visible in the trench on the right. *(Photo courtesy Bishop Museum Department of Anthropology)*

There are a number of other well-preserved sites in Koʻolauloa. Maunawila Heiau (site -287) was the focus of an MA research project as the site was being acquired by the Hawaiʻi Island Land Trust to be protected and used for education (Thurman 2014, 2015). The locality was in use during the Late Voyaging Period (cal AD 1270 to 1390, Beta-345655*), followed by construction of the *heiau* proper in the Expansion Period (cal AD 1421–1616, Beta-345657*). Today the *heiau* is being stewarded by the local community.

Kahuku, located at the transition from the windward coast to the north shore, has seen extensive grubbing for agriculture and other modern land use that would at first seem to make it an unlikely location to find intact cultural deposits. But, over the past 30 years, more than two dozen projects in and around Kahuku have shown that archaeological remains are common even in places that have been transformed. After hundreds of auger holes, trenches, and test units, we now have an idea of how settlements evolved in the Kahuku area. Haun, Berrigan, and Henry (2011) summarize 85 radiocarbon dates from cultural deposits in the area between Kawela Bay and Kahuku Point, which includes modern Kahuku town, and Punahoʻolapa Marsh. In the Foundation Period they note "use of the area east of Punahoʻolapa Marsh, along with settlements in the sand dunes east and west of Kahuku Point and around Kawela Bay" (71). At Kuilima Point, a site encountered during development produced a date of cal AD 920–1045 (Beta-38668; site -6417, Profile 4, Layer V, HF-1) (Corbin 2003; Sullivan 1990). The Late Voyaging Period appears to have been a time of intensified settlement in those locations, with the earliest dates from deposits found east of Kawela Bay. After AD 1400, there was expansion "west and southwest of Punahoʻolapa Marsh, as well as southwest of Kahuku Point" (Haun et al. 2011, 71). During the Archaic States Period, represented by about a third of the dates, communities continued to focus on the coast and around the marsh.

Waialua District

The Anahulu Valley within Kawailoa *ahupuaʻa* was the focus of a major archaeological study by Kirch and anthropologist Marshall Sahlins (Kirch 1979b; Kirch and Sahlins 1992). The archaeological work concentrated on a section of the Anahulu Valley 3–4 km from the coast (fig. 17.7), where four rockshelters, eight open habitation sites, and several irrigation complexes were surveyed and excavated. The rockshelters were used as early as the fourteenth century, but the permanent residence sites and irrigation systems were not constructed until after the conquest of Oʻahu by Kamehameha in 1795 (fig. 17.8). The Anahulu study is more extensively discussed in chapter 13.

Later work in the upper Anahulu Valley revealed additional sites about 11 km from the coast, within the US Army's Kawailoa Training Area. Dega and McGerty (1998, 2002) mapped, excavated, and radiocarbon dated an irrigated agricultural complex (site -5612), dryland farms, as well as a series of house sites. As in the lower elevations, farming by irrigation near the stream began in the Expansion Period (AD 1400–1600) followed soon after by rain-fed fields on the colluvial slopes (Dega and Kirch 2002). In upland Kawailoa excavations at six house sites confirmed that settlement stretched far inland from early in the Expansion Period and continued through to the Archaic States Period. But, unlike in the lower-elevation section, none of the house sites showed continued occupation into the postcontact era.

Athens, Ward, and Blinn (1995) cored ʻUkoʻa Pond, located near the mouth of the Anahulu Valley, in order to obtain paleoenvironmental evidence of landscape change. The team found signs of human presence—specifically, lowland forest decline—occurring by

FIGURE 17.7 View of the middle sector of the Anahulu Valley, Oʻahu Island. Habitation sites and irrigation complexes were situated on the small stream flats in the valley bottom. *(Photo by P. V. Kirch)*

FIGURE 17.8 A large rockshelter in the Anahulu Valley, Oʻahu Island, during excavations in 1982. *(Photo by P. V. Kirch)*

AD 950 and perhaps as early as AD 800. However, the earliest direct evidence for cultural deposits and architecture date to the Expansion Period.

Waialua District has been the setting for a series of archaeological field schools by the University of Hawaiʻi at Mānoa. Lima et al. (2019) describe work on Kupopolo Heiau that combined education, outreach, and a community-centered approach to archaeology. The full results of excavations on a habitation site at ʻUkoʻa have yet to be published (Carroll et al. 2016).

Further west, on the narrow Waialua Plain, some sites remain relatively untouched despite modern farming. McGerty and Spear (2009) report on excavations across two habitation sites. The first, site -5483, is located near one of five named *heiau* in the area, Kawailoa Heiau (site -191), and may have been a residence of the temple's *kahuna*. Cultural deposits, radiocarbon dated on identified plant charcoal, mainly date to the Expansion and Archaic States Periods. But at the bottom of one test unit the team found a layer of charcoal from native taxa along with Polynesian-introduced *kukui* dated to ca. AD 1200–1300.

Another habitation complex on the Waialua Plain, site -416, covers 9,100 m² and comprises 21 different features that, like the earliest house sites in upper Kawailoa, date to the start of the Expansion Period. On the western half of the complex, one structure stands out for its elaborate architecture, small paved area, and the presence of branch coral (Feature 8), suggesting a ritual function. Given its location within a habitation complex, and size (ca. 16 m long), it may have been a men's house (*mua*). A total of 15 test units, trenches, and shovel probes were dug across the complex. The features near the *mua* were notable for the high concentration of lithics recovered as well as remains of pigs; pig bones were absent in the rest of the site. To McGerty and Spear (2009), this suggested that the household complex was built and used according to the gender separations dictated by the *kapu* system.

Commanding the ridge on the north side of Waimea Valley is Puʻuomahuka Heiau, associated with the capture and sacrificial offering of the commander of HMS *Daedalus* of

FIGURE 17.9 View over the upper court of Puʻuomahuka Heiau, Oʻahu Island. *(Photo by Therese Babineau)*

Vancouver's expedition, along with the ship's astronomer and a sailor, in 1792. The supply ship had tarried behind the main fleet; putting in to Waimea Bay to take on water, the three men were set upon by Kahekili's feared *pahupū* warriors as they explored the valley. The temple foundation is monumental in scale, 175 m long and 51 m wide, with two main courts (fig. 17.9). The upper court is paved with fine gravel from Waimea Stream, while the walls incorporate sandstone slabs from the coast.

Waiʻanae District

There is little evidence for human activity in the leeward district of Waiʻanae prior to the Expansion Period. One notable exception is a quarry located in Nānākuli Valley where Weisler et al. (2013) report a ^{230}Th date on coral of AD 1234 ± 6. The Mākaha Valley Historical Project reported dates from two inland C-shaped shelters from the Late Voyaging Period (AD 1200–1400), but the valley's sequence has yet to be confirmed with modern chronometric techniques.

The leeward coastal valleys, collectively known as Waiʻanae Kai, are connected to an interior valley, Waiʻanae ʻUka, via the Kolekole Pass. Waiʻanae ʻUka is the setting for several notable events in Hawaiian traditional history, as well as the location of the birthing stones of Kūkaniloko (see chapter 5). This inland area may have been targeted for settlement slightly earlier than the rest of the district (Green 1980, 72). Kūkaniloko itself consists of a cluster of natural boulders appearing to rise up out of the reddish earth of the island's central plateau. Many famous chiefs were said to have been born here, including Māʻilikūkahi and Kakuhihewa. Nearby was the *heiau* of Hoʻolono-pahu, now destroyed, where the newborn chief was taken to have his navel cord cut, after which the *pahu* drum was sounded to announce the royal birth. Archaeological research in this interior portion of the island has focused on agricultural features, with excavations yielding several dates from pondfields in the Late Voyaging Period as well as a permanent habitation site (site -5439, cal AD 1290–1450, Beta-94476) (Robins and Spear 2002).

It is possible that due to its aridity, much of the Waiʻanae coast remained underpopulated during the Foundation and Late Voyaging Periods, becoming an attractive location for settlement only once more ecologically favorable districts had been densely settled. However, even sites dated to the Expansion Period are rare in Waiʻanae District. In the largest valley in leeward Oʻahu, Lualualei, the only indication of Expansion Period use is a thin charcoal deposit found in a shovel probe (site 50-80-08-1760) (Haun et al. 1991). The few habitations and dryland agricultural features in the smaller Mākua Valley have returned dates in the Archaic States Period (Dagher and Spear 2013). More intensive excavation and dating here, on the order of what has been done in the leeward Kohala coast on Hawaiʻi Island, would help determine if there were internal shifts in population after permanent settlements were established.

Two settlement-pattern studies in Waiʻanae District—one in Mākaha Valley (Green 1980; Green, ed., 1969, 1970; Ladd 1973; Ladd and Yen 1972), and the other in Lualualei Valley (Dixon, Gosser, and Williams 2008)—have addressed site distribution. Mākaha Valley was intensively studied from 1968 to 1970 by Bishop Museum (see chapter 12). Most of the research effort in Mākaha was directed to the lower valley slopes, which had been extensively modified for intensive dryland agriculture, probably emphasizing sweet potatoes and yams as the main crops (Kirch 1977). Throughout these lower valley garden areas are a large number of small field shelters, usually of the C- or L-shaped type, which were occupied intermittently.

Roger Green (1980) summarized Mākaha's cultural sequence, including its position in relation to the other Waiʻanae valleys, arguing that leeward areas were targeted after the populations of the windward coasts had begun to increase. The earliest dated sites in the valley, temporary field shelters associated with the extensive dryland cultivation complexes, were in place by the thirteenth century. During the fifteenth to sixteenth centuries, several changes occurred in the valley's population, subsistence base, and social organization. The inland parts of the valley were permanently settled for the first time, while irrigation systems for taro cultivation were constructed in the upper valley, where streamflow was adequate. The initial construction of Kāneʻākī Heiau, as an agricultural temple during the fifteenth century, was an important event, for it indicated "the presence in the valley of a ranking chief able to build his own Lono-type heiau, and the means for achieving a surplus of goods for his own use by intensifying the valley's productive capacity" (Green 1980, 75).

In the final precontact phase of Mākaha's development, beginning about AD 1650, the valley was integrated into the fabric of the large-scale political systems that characterized Hawaiʻi at European contact. As Green writes,

> There is now evidence both of permanent housing in the form of ordinary rectangular dwellings, and of an increasing number of religious buildings in the form of stepped stone platforms, shrines, and other specialized structures, some of them men's houses. They suggest that the processes of social segmentation and stratification among the elite, known elsewhere in Hawaiʻi, were underway within the Makaha Valley, and would have continued, had they not been overwhelmed by the consequences of European contact. (Green 1980, 76–77)

During this final phase of development, Kāneʻākī Heiau was rebuilt and its size more than doubled, converting it to a *luakini*-class temple of human sacrifice, dedicated to the war god Kū. Such an event could have been undertaken only by a paramount chief. During this period, a main irrigation ditch was constructed down into the dry lower valley, permitting the chiefs to further intensify the valley's productive capacity.

Surveys across Lualualei, a broad valley partly formed by an extinct caldera, provide an in-depth picture of the distribution of one particular kind of site: the *mua*, or men's house (Dixon, Gosser, and Williams 2008). Ethnohistoric accounts describe the role of the *mua,* as well as some details about its style of construction, and position within a household complex (*kauhale*) (see chapter 10). The challenge for archaeologists is to identify examples of men's houses and try to determine how these may have operated in practice.

The *kauhale* that dotted the interior of Lualualei Valley represent a palimpsest with hundreds of examples of well-intact standing stone architecture. Dixon, Gosser, and Williams (2008) singled out 10 complexes that, based on their size, were likely to have been the residences of *konohiki,* the local land managers. In total, 34 test units (50 × 50 cm) were excavated, in what were interpreted as either *hale noa* or *mua*. At six out of eight putative *mua,* excavations confirmed the presence of corals used as offerings, lithic working, and food remains that included pig bone as well as *ʻulua* fish (*Caranx ignobilis*), foods traditionally reserved for men. Dixon, Gosser, and Williams note that while we would expect rituals, and thus offerings, in a men's house, as well as *kapu* foods, the presence of lithics, while often assumed to indicate male activity, is by no means exclusive to a single gender (Gero 1997). All of the sites were dated to post–AD 1650, with limited evidence for the early historic-era trade goods suggesting some continued use after contact.

The spatial distribution of the Lualualei men's houses, and the size of the structures themselves, suggested to Dixon, Gosser, and Williams (2008) that they played an intermediate political role. The *konohiki* residences, with their *mua* and often a small *heiau* nearby, are dispersed far apart from one another across the back of the valley. A series of spatial clusters were identified, each with a local elite residence and about 35 other residences, presumably the houses of those overseen by the *konohiki.* Other temples, such as Nioiula Heiau, do not conform to the spatial pattern in that they are larger and not bound to a particular cluster. With these larger temples, the interpretation is that these would have been locations where larger-scale political action was organized.

ʻEwa District

Even by leeward standards, ʻEwa District is a hot, parched landscape. The extensive coastal plain, including Kalaeloa (Barbers Point), is made up of an emerged Pleistocene reef, rough and broken in places by deep sinkholes, typical of karst topography. Scattered over the plain are small habitation clusters, many perhaps temporary in nature, including stone enclosures and C-shaped shelters, as well as ovens and low mounds of discarded limestone oven stones. The rock used in these structures consists of limestone slabs, many of which are set upright, giving the sites a distinctive architectural style. Tuggle (1997, 16) has gone so far as to characterize the ʻEwa Plain as home to "gardening families living at the edge of survival."

Some of the most significant finds at Kalaeloa have come from not these open structures, however, but instead from the numerous sinkholes in the karst limestone. Paleoenvironmental studies at Ordy Pond and elsewhere "indicate that settlement was initiated in the AD 1000–1250 range, with rapid expansion dating from AD 1250 to 1400, and a general plateau of occupation from AD 1400 to the time of abandonment" (Tuggle 1997, 16). While there is good evidence for transformation of the native forest and effects on the local bird population, there are few direct signs of bird hunting in the cultural deposits. This does not mean that there was no direct predation, but does suggest that other factors, such as the introduction of the Pacific rat, may be responsible for the ecological shifts witnessed during the Foundation Period.

While important sites of religious ritual are reported to have been destroyed, including Pu'uokapolei Heiau, there are intact fishing shrines and *heiau* across 'Ewa, as in the upper elevations of the district at the Pālehua complex (Gill et al. 2015; Swift et al. 2019). The Pālehua complex, located in the uplands of Honouliuli *ahupua'a,* comprises a main enclosure (40 × 38 m) oriented toward the northeast and defined by a wall of one-to-three courses of relatively uniform sized boulders. A small shrine with six upright stones is located 25 m to the northwest. Excavations and radiocarbon dating place the construction of the main enclosure between cal AD 1504 and 1648. The alignment of the main enclosure walls with the acronychal rising of Makali'i (Pleiades) suggests that the site may have been used during the Archaic States Period (AD 1600–1800) for ceremonies marking the annual Makahiki. The small shrine of upright stones at Pālehua shows that simple shrines of this type, similar to those on Mauna Kea and remote Mokumanamana, continued to be created and used into the late precontact period.

Hālawa Valley has received much attention from archaeologists as a result of the H3 highway project. Early investigations on the leeward side of the H3 road corridor focused on the south branch of Hālawa (Ayres 1970; Crozier 1972, 1974). Crozier (1972, 1974) excavated an extensive walled habitation complex (site Oa-B1-30), with radiocarbon dates indicating occupation from the thirteenth to seventeenth centuries. This complex, which was interpreted as a chief's residence, is one of the few permanent habitation structures that have been extensively excavated, revealing a pattern of separate activity areas for dwelling and cooking. The dwelling house appears to have had rounded ends (similar to the early structures at the Hālawa dune site on Moloka'i); the excavations yielded basalt adzes with triangular cross sections. A small rockshelter overlooking the Moanalua Stream (site O15, 50-80-15-2908) was excavated by the University of Hawai'i in 1980; it displays a notable decrease in bird remains and increase in the concentration of shellfish over time (Thomas 1995).

Between 1987 and 1993, Bishop Museum archaeologists worked along a 6 km section of the narrow North Hālawa Valley, the proposed route of the H3 highway, excavating 770 test units, 326 stratigraphic trenches, and 300 shovel probes (Hartzell 2003). They found more than 1,000 agricultural terraces lining the sides of the Hālawa Stream, interspersed with perhaps 30 household clusters concentrated at 10 sites in the lower and middle elevations, in addition to more informal "temporary" structures and rockshelters. The uppermost elevations were mainly used for gardening.

Putative ritual sites along the leeward side of the H3 highway corridor began to be noted in the 1970s with the restoration of two small structures interpreted as either "agricultural shrines" or "family temples" (fig. 17.10) in South Hālawa Valley (Crozier 1972, 7). By 1992, following the controversy over Kukuiokāne Heiau on the windward side of the H3 corridor (see above), Bishop Museum was accused of suppressing information regarding two important sites within the North Hālawa Valley: a *luakini heiau* and a putative *hale o Papa* designated for women. Structures at several sites within North Hālawa Valley appear to have been used for religious ritual (Hartzell et al. 2003). The archaeologists suggested that these features were for household ritual, either family shrines or men's houses (*mua*). At site 50-80-10-2010, while there was no clear sign of a *luakini heiau*, there is evidence for the presence of priests or other ritual specialists. At an oval-shaped terrace (Feature 75, 78 m^2), dated to the Expansion Period (AD 1400–1600), a "basalt bowl with a carved zoomorphic image" was recovered, likely an effigy bowl (Hartzell et al. 2003, 329). According to Curtis (1995, 24) only nine such effigy bowls are known from Hawai'i; this specimen is the only one ever to have been "found in a controlled archaeological context." At a rectangular enclosure (site -2010, Feature 4, 189 m^2), dated to the Archaic States Period (AD 1600–1800), a small stone vessel was found; it is suggested that the cup was used in ceremonies (*kuni kapuahi 'anā'anā*). In addition, when a small paved platform (Feature 65, 48 m^2) with suspected fallen upright stones was excavated, branch coral was uncovered.

For the archaeologists working on the H3 project, the absence of a *luakini heiau* at site -2010 invalidated the idea that there was a *hale o Papa* within the North Hālawa Valley at site

FIGURE 17.10 A stone-walled *heiau* enclosure in the Hālawa Valley, O'ahu Island. *(Photo courtesy Bishop Museum Department of Anthropology)*

50-80-10-2137. However, they noted two enclosures at site -2137 that they suspected were used for religious ritual. One is a large enclosure (Feature 53, 340 m^2)—the feature proposed to have been a *hale o Papa*—notable for "an unusually high number of boulders set on edge" (Hartzell et al. 2003, 330). Excavations indicate it may have been regularly cleaned since it lacked habitation debris. Feature 53 is oriented to true north on one side (the east wall) and to the northwest (west wall, and adjacent features) on the other long axis. The other enclosure (Feature 36, 290 m^2), is oriented to the northwest and has a boulder on the northwest corner with eight petroglyphs.

Investigations from the later part of the H3 project provided important evidence relating to traditional food practices in North Hālawa Valley (Hartzell et al. 2003, 225–258). The most common vertebrate remains found were fragmentary medium mammal, pig, and dog. Signs of burning, consistent with open-fire roasting, were noted on many bones, except for those of pig. The team cautiously suggested that pig, or some cuts of pig, may have been cooked by other methods, such as in *imu* (earth ovens). Earth ovens found throughout the valley rarely contained faunal remains, instead yielding mostly charcoal and stone backfilled into the oven after use. The consumption of fish and other marine foods was also fairly ubiquitous, with fish remains found at 27 sites, or in about half of the house sites and rockshelters excavated. This is unsurprising given the natural abundance of marine and lagoon resources at Puʻuloa (Pearl Harbor) at the *makai* end of Hālawa *ahupuaʻa,* about 5 km distant. What was surprising was the lack of evidence for the most common fish raised in fishponds despite the presence of major fishponds at Puʻuloa. The distribution of fauna more generally was extremely uneven. Just three sites account for the majority of all faunal remains recovered. The team offered several possible explanations, mainly taphonomic processes affecting the preservation of bone.

Langenwalter and Meeker (2015) summarized the cultural sequence and deposits at the O16 rockshelter site (50-Oa-B01-020) in North Hālawa Valley. A direct radiocarbon date on a dog's tooth from the beginning of the Expansion Period (Beta-354010) is consistent with other evidence of increased use of rockshelters as settlement spread across the island. A companion article on the faunal remains identified several bird taxa that are either extinct or extirpated from Oʻahu (Langenwalter and James 2015). The Hawaiian Petrel, absent from other sites in the valley, may have been hunted near the rockshelter, a montane environment that could have acted as a natural refuge for what remained of a much more expansive territory across ʻEwa.

Kona District

Waikīkī, today one of the most urbanized sectors of the island, was formerly a royal center. Construction projects in Waikīkī, and elsewhere across parts of urbanized Honolulu, have unearthed burials, midden deposits, a major complex of irrigated taro fields, and fishponds. A number of fishponds also extended along the coast between Koko Head and Diamond Head; some of these were filled in for housing developments (such as Wailupe Circle) but are readily visible from the air.

In Nuʻuanu Valley is a well-known group of petroglyphs, while at the head of the valley, on a ridge leading to the peak of Kōnāhuanui, are two artificial cuts or fosses that served

FIGURE 17.11 Artificial fosses cut into a ridge at Nu'uanu Pali served as defensive fortifications. *(Photo by Therese Babineau)*

as fortifications (fig. 17.11). This fort may have been the actual scene of the famous battle of Nu'uanu in 1795, when Kamehameha defeated the O'ahu forces.

Another leeward valley that has been intensively surveyed—also showing evidence of precontact habitation and agriculture extending for some distance inland—is Moanalua (Denison and Forman 1971). A boulder with unique relief carvings (fig. 17.12) in Bishop Museum originally came from Moanalua Valley.

There are few visible remains of the dense settlements and fields that once blanketed Mānoa Valley, the largest valley in what is now urban Honolulu. Oral traditions describe a string of at least eight *heiau* across the valley, including Hipawai Heiau, a large temple that McAllister (1933a, 78) refers to as "*po'okanaka* class." Only two surviving temples are known to archaeologists in Mānoa: Kawapopo Heiau (site 50-80-14-3986) (Luscomb 1975) and Kūka'ō'ō Heiau (site 50-80-14-64) (Cleghorn and Anderson 1993; Tomonari-Tuggle 1998). Kūka'ō'ō Heiau is situated on the estate of Charles Montague Cooke, Jr., whose descendants endowed the Mānoa Heritage Center, of which the *heiau* is now a part. Kūka'ō'ō Heiau is a modest-sized structure comprising a stone

FIGURE 17.12 A boulder with rare raised-relief carvings, originally from Moanalua Valley, O'ahu Island, now in Bishop Museum. *(Photo courtesy Bishop Museum Library and Archives)*

terrace supporting a freestanding enclosure (14 × 12.5 m). The terrace's impressive oblique face on its northeast side, and the orientation of the enclosure toward the northeast, suggest it may have been associated with the Makahiki. There are a number of accounts of the *heiau,* with the most notable being that it had been won by the legendary King Kuali'i, who defeated its Menehune builders and chased them from the valley (McAllister 1933a, 79). Two excavations on nearby terraces produced two dates on scattered charcoal associated with artifacts to the Archaic States Period (AD 1600–1800), the era of Kuali'i (Cleghorn and Anderson 1992).

In the early 1950s, Emory excavated in four rockshelters in the Maunalua Bay area: Kuli'ou'ou rockshelter, site O1; Makani'olu rockshelter, O2; Kawēkiu rockshelter, O4; and along the beach in Hanauma Bay, an overhang rockshelter, O3 (Emory and Sinoto 1961). The rockshelters yielded a wide range of artifacts, including such rare items as the wooden handle of a shark-tooth knife (from O1) and several tattooing needles from Makani'olu rockshelter (fig. 93), of a type previously unknown to Hawaiian scholars. The Kuli'ou'ou site is discussed in more detail in chapter 6.

18

THE ARCHAEOLOGY OF KAUA'I AND NI'IHAU ISLANDS

Nearly circular in outline, with a land area of 1,432 km², Kaua'i is the fourth largest of the main Hawaiian Islands (fig. 18.1). Its central massif rises to 1,598 m at Wai'ale'ale, where annual rainfall in excess of 11,650 mm has led to the popular attribution of the mountain peak as the "wettest spot on earth." The oldest of the main Hawaiian Islands, Kaua'i is topographically dissected and weathered, with broad alluvial plains and deep valleys with permanent streams that made it an attractive locality for settlement by agricultural Polynesians.

Traditionally, the island was divided into six districts, as is the case on most of the islands, although more recent maps often show only five districts (merging the *moku* of Kona and Mānā). Spectacular razor-edged ridges and precipitous cliffs rimming deep, narrow valleys characterize the Nāpali region; the largest valley here is Kalalau. Along the north is Hale'ea District, where the fertile valleys of Wainiha, Lumaha'i, and Hanalei were a focus of irrigated taro agriculture. Ko'olau District occupied the northeastern bulge, while Puna District incorporated the large Wailua and Hulē'ia drainages. The large, relatively arid Kona District takes up most of the leeward side of the island, including Hanapēpē Valley and spectacular Waimea Canyon. Mānā is a small *moku* on the far west side, with several smaller gulches and a broad coastal plain.

Archaeological coverage of Kaua'i has been somewhat uneven. Thomas Thrum (1906) recorded a number of *heiau*, but the first extensive study of the island's archaeology was by Wendell C. Bennett (1931) for Bishop Museum. As was typical of Hawaiian archaeology in the 1920s, Bennett focused on the larger *heiau* sites, with limited notes on house sites and agricultural terracing, along with typological analyses of surface-collected stone artifacts; the possibility of excavation was not seriously entertained. Nevertheless, Bennett's survey data on *heiau* are valuable, especially since many of these sites were subsequently altered or destroyed.

In the 1950s, during the Hawaiian Archaeological Program, Kenneth P. Emory conducted excavations at a large rockshelter, Hā'ele'ele in the Kona District (Bishop Museum

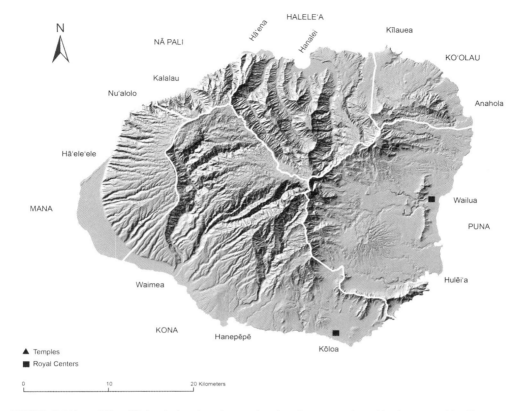

FIGURE 18.1 Map of Kaua'i Island, showing sites and major places mentioned in the text. White lines indicate the boundaries of the traditional districts. *(Map by M. D. McCoy)*

site K1). Unfortunately, much of the deposit there had already been pillaged by pot hunters. Radiocarbon dates from site K1 suggested that the shelter may have been occupied as early as the eleventh century. In the early 1960s, Bishop Museum spent several field seasons excavating at the Nu'alolo rockshelter in Nāpali District; this deeply stratified site is discussed in chapter 6. With a few exceptions, such as Timothy Earle's (1978) study of the Halele'a District irrigation systems, and David Burney's investigations at the Makauwahi Cave complex (Burney 2010; Burney et al. 2001), most archaeological work on Kaua'i in recent decades has been CRM inventory or mitigation driven.

Nāpali District

The Nāpali coastline comprises a string of coastal settlements and irrigated complexes in hanging valleys carved into the stark sea cliffs. Moving clockwise from the west some of the main valleys are Miloli'i, Nu'alolo Kai, Nu'alolo 'Āina, and Honopū, followed by the deep valley of Kalalau, and then Hanakoa and Hanakāpī'ai in the east. There may be no place in the islands, except perhaps the northern coast of Moloka'i, with such a pristine archaeological record. Bennett (1931) identified the Nāpali valleys as a prime location for intensive archaeological study. From 1958 to 1964, Emory and Soehren excavated at the

Nuʻalolo Kai rockshelter (sites K3, K4, and K5), where a high overhanging cliff provided natural shelter from the elements, and a series of stone-faced house terraces had been constructed at the cliff base (see chapter 6).

Although Kahn et al. (2016) regard the Nāpali region as an example of a "hinterland" it would be a mistake to think that people were disconnected from their neighbors elsewhere on the island. A study sourcing more than 800 basalt artifacts from Nuʻalolo Kai shows that the earliest deposits include artifacts from three geochemical groups dispersed across the island (Mills et al. 2010). The first permanent settlers, through to the most recent to use stone adzes, continued to obtain most of their adze material from elsewhere on the island; stone from the Nāpali region never comprised more than 17 percent of the analyzed assemblages. While no basalt tools seem to have been imported from other islands, two stone mirrors from Nuʻalolo are geochemical outliers whose sources are unknown, and may even be external to the Hawaiian Islands.

Miloliʻi, while not far from Nuʻalolo Kai, was home to a community that in many ways kept to themselves. Research by Kahn, Kawelu, et al. (2016) found that locally sourced basalt was consistently preferred; after European contact it appears that people resisted the trend to adopt wooden over thatched houses. They also note a lack of material signals of elites—such as *lei niho palaoa* or stone mirrors—and describe the burial of an immature pig in the stone foundation that originally supported the grass house now on permanent display at Bishop Museum (site 50-30-01-7620). Places such as Miloliʻi that resisted cultural change have been likened to cultural *kīpuka,* conservative rural areas that were surrounded by communities that adopted new practices and thus have an important role in cultural revival (Heinz 2019).

Limited surveys and excavations in other Nāpali valleys have revealed the region's archaeological potential. Yent and Ota (1983), for example, found examples of pearl-shell fishhook manufacture in a rockshelter (site KAL-4) in Kahana Valley. Survey by Tomonari-Tuggle (1979) documented Nāpali's many irrigation systems, such as that in Nuʻalolo Āina, a hanging valley situated next to the Nuʻalolo Kai sites.

Haleleʻa District

Haleleʻa, the "the house of delight," has been the focus of much archaeological work on Kauaʻi (Carson 2005b). At the western edge of Haleleʻa, on the border with Nāpali District, lies Hāʻena, the scene of archaeological study beginning in the late 1970s (Griffin et al. 1977; Hammatt, Bordner, and Tomonari-Tuggle 1978). Earle (1978) mapped the large irrigation complexes that lie just inland of a large sand dune fronted by Kēʻē Beach (see also Major 2001). Excavations by Griffin, Hammatt, and others revealed that these dunes incorporate well-stratified occupation deposits, with many superimposed cultural strata. Several early artifact types were recovered in excavations by Griffin (1984), and by Hammatt, Bordner, and Tomonari-Tuggle (1978), including porpoise-tooth pendants and incipiently knobbed two-piece fishhooks. Hammatt, Bordner, and Tomonari-Tuggle (1978, 168) outlined an initial sequence for the Kēʻē Beach site, with a first phase consisting of a "transient marine-oriented 'fishing settlement.'" By AD 1200 there was a "population increase with a broader resource base," driving settlement to expand inland. The 1400s witnessed "the development of intensified irrigation agriculture in inland areas with a continued use of the littoral environment," a pattern that continued up until the historic period.

Kēʻē is also the location of one of the most renowned sites for *hula* performance, Ke-ahu-a-Laka, or "altar of Laka," goddess of the *hula*. The stone-faced earthen terrace has as its backdrop a sheer cliff, which no doubt not only adds to the dramatic setting but also helped to resonate the drum beats and chanting (fig. 18.2).

Carson (1998, 2004) challenged the notion that coastal settlement proceeded from temporary to increasingly permanent in Hāʻena. Just 5 km from Kēʻē, the Wainiha Beach site has been the subject of more than 400 m² of excavations by various investigators, although most of those were by machine trenching that yielded little information. In 1998, Carson (1998) directed hand excavations of a 16 m² area that exposed multiple occupation layers. The top three layers date to the postcontact period and were separated from the lower three cultural layers by a tsunami or hurricane deposit. The deepest deposit, Layer VII, included five post molds, an oven, and a small pavement 114 cm by 56 cm, and 60 cm thick, composed of coral, waterworn shell, and pebbles. The oven yielded a date with a wide error range spanning the Foundation and Late Voyaging Periods. Other dates from the layer above (cal AD 1290–1470, Beta-119830), in which there were more ephemeral signs of human activity, confirm that it must predate the Expansion Period. Thus, while the precise size or composition of the house, or village, at Wainiha remains unknown, the area was a focus of early settlement and then abandoned as people spread across the valley in the Expansion Period.

FIGURE 18.2 The *kahua* or platform for *hula* performance at Keʻe, Hāʻena, Kauaʻi Island. *(Photo by Therese Babineau)*

In 1971–1972, Earle (1978) studied traditional taro irrigation in Halele'a District, including a survey of extant remains of irrigated complexes awarded during the Māhele of the mid-nineteenth century. Earle's research, a part of Marshall Sahlins' larger study of early Hawaiian society and economy (Sahlins 1971), evaluated several theories concerning irrigation and its relationship with Polynesian social and political development. While Earle's study documents the surface remains of irrigation complexes as known from the nineteenth-century Māhele land claims, he did not excavate or date these irrigation systems; the sequence of development of these large irrigation systems remains unknown.

More extensive excavations in the Hanalei Valley, and in other areas of the Halele'a District, will be necessary before a chronology of agricultural development in this region can be advanced. Carson (2005c), summarizing radiocarbon dates from a number of studies including pondfields (Athens 1983a; Schilt 1980; Calis 2001), notes evidence for coastal settlement in the Late Voyaging Period as well as "a firepit feature in an inland setting in Hanalei" dated to cal AD 1205 to 1315 (Beta-87546; Kaschko 1996). The nature of inland activities preceding the large-scale irrigation complex dating to the Expansion Period remains unexplored. The archaeological potential of Hā'ena, with both stratified beach deposits and extensive irrigation landscapes inland, may yet reveal much about the development of Hawaiian society in this part of Kaua'i.

Ko'olau and Puna Districts

From Kilauea Point in the north to Anahola in the south, the small district of Ko'olau has had sporadic studies along the coastline (see Carson 2005d, 2005e). Historic plantation agriculture left behind a "plow zone" of topsoil where artifacts and features have been churned up. Using a trenching method, Hammatt and Folk (1996) discovered cultural deposits in Kilauea radiocarbon dated to the Expansion Period. In Anahola, Dixon, Curtis, and Hodgins (2005) report on Expansion Period features also found by trenching. Along with evidence of domestic activities represented by several patches of midden and a cooking hearth, they found "small irregular shaped pits" interpreted as a "household garden in the dune sands" (84). The midden included a range of fish, shellfish, and animal domesticates for a house situated near the coast, but "no evidence of species raised in fishponds," suggesting that either a nearby fishpond postdates the abandonment of the house, "or its residents were not privy to this surplus" (101).

The coast of Puna, from Kapa'a to just past Līhue, was especially important in the history of Kaua'i. At the mouth of the Wailua River lay the seat of Kaua'i power, marked by sites similar to those at other royal centers. These include the Hauloa "City of Refuge" and a string of named *heiau,* Malae Heiau, Kukui Heiau, Hikinaakalā Heiau, Ka Lae o ka Manu Heiau, and Poli'ahu Heiau (fig. 18.3). These sites are maintained by the State Parks Division and are among the best examples of monumental architecture in the islands.

The story of Mo'ikeha, one of the best known of the island's rulers, begins with his arrival at Wailua with his entourage. Mo'ikeha had come from Kahiki (Tahiti), made several stops in the islands, and then soon after his arrival on Kaua'i married two daughters of the *ali'i nui,* Ho'oipoikamalanai and Hinau'u. While oral history puts Mo'ikeha's final resting place in

FIGURE 18.3 View of a portion of the main court of Poli'ahu Heiau at Wailua, Kaua'i Island. *(Photo by Therese Babineau)*

the cliffs of Hā'ena, the burials of other individuals have been inadvertently uncovered during the course of development at Wailua. Shideler (2010) notes an "unusual artifact assemblage" among some burials in Waipouli, "including a shell grater, a number of tattoo needles, a cache of sling stones, high-status ornaments and an effigy bowl." Carved stone effigy bowls are rare in the Hawaiian Islands (Curtis 1995), and may be a link back to the Late Voyaging Period.

Near the summit of Wa'iale'ale, at the Alaka'i Swamp, several of the island's districts meet, and here is situated Ka'awakō Shrine near Lake Wai'ale'ale. Thrum (1906, 66) described it as "a small rectangular structure about five by seven feet and two feet high," dedicated to Kāne. He goes on to say, "To this day [in 1906] you must throw on it the most valuable things you have with you—money, food, tools, or whatnot—to propitiate the gods of the mist lest they envelop you and you lose your way in that tangle of woods and gulches and level plateaus of the interior of Kauai." Hammatt and Shideler (2008) revisited the shrine, more than a century after Thrum, noting a dense concentration of coral offerings, testament to the antiquity of this practice.

Kona and Mānā Districts

Along the coast at Kōloa, where Puna meets the arid Kona District, A. Sinoto (1975) and Hammatt, Bordner, and Tomonari-Tuggle et al. (1978) reported a dense site concentration displaying a unique pattern of settlement. Hammatt's survey of 460 acres revealed the presence of 583 sites, including 175 stone enclosures and 108 stone house platforms. These were integrated with an extensive agricultural field complex incorporating both irrigated and dryland field cultivation features. Drawing water from the Waikomo Stream, "an extensive system of highly developed *'auwai* fed the upslope ends of the wet field systems at Kōloa." These ditches "branch off throughout the project area in a generally dendritic pattern subdividing downslope to feed separate field complexes" (Hammatt, Bordner, and Tomonari-Tuggle 1978, 44). Subsequent CRM archaeology has found that the "preponderance of dates is from the AD 1400 to 1650 period, and shows that the area was intensified later by in-filling, rather than outward expansion, from east to west" (Simonson et al. 2009, 329).

Makauwahi Cave, a large sinkhole in limestone karst of Pleistocene age located in Māhā'ulepū, has a deep sedimentary sequence due to the in-washing of materials from the surrounding landscape over thousands of years. Excavation and sifting through 200 m³ of sediment recovered from both cores and block excavations provided a remarkable record of the environment prior to, and after, the arrival of Polynesians (Burney et al. 2001). The first clear signs of people date to the Foundation Period and include a rat bone dated to cal AD 1039–1241 (NZA-10058; Burney et al. 2001), as well as "a small rise in charcoal detected at 381 cm," dated to cal AD 1000–1170 (Beta-164910; Burney and Kikuchi 2006). A tsunami or other major marine event in the Expansion Period eliminated any chance to look at change in life over the last thousand years. However, the excellent depositional environment preserved "ornaments, cordage, gourds, and worked wood" (Burney and Kikuchi 2006, 227). Burney and Kikuchi (2006) report that 60 out of 80 fishhooks recovered are made of pearl shell. Food remains include all the Polynesian introduced domesticates as well as a single example of bitter yam (*Dioscorea bulbifera*). Fish remains include mullet (*Mugil cephalus*), but the investigators note that mullet bones were also deposited naturally in the cave because of a connection to the sinkhole.

In the 1950s, Henry Kekahuna visited Kōloa and mapped what he called "a genuinely authentic Hawaiian Village" at Kāhua O Kānei'olouma (Kekahuna 1959). One of the focal points among the areas divided by thick stone walls is an open performance area ringed by stone bleachers. In addition to the arena are a range of different types of stone foundations of buildings as well as fishponds and irrigated fields. Since 2010 the site has been under the care of Hui Mālama O Kāneiolouma, a nonprofit dedicated to the site's care and restoration.

FIGURE 18.4 A portion of Kīkīaola, an irrigation canal sometimes known as the "Menehune Ditch," showing the cut-and-dressed stonework. *(Photo by Therese Babineau)*

The Kōloa fields are not the only evidence of the ingenuity of water engineering in old Kaua'i. In Waimea, not far from where the Waimea River meets the bay, is the famous Kīkīaola aqueduct, sometimes called the "Menehune Ditch" (Bennett 1931, 105–107), a pre-contact irrigation canal lined with carefully fitted, cut-and-dressed stone slabs (fig. 18.4); this canal has been commented on in historical accounts going back to 1792 (Vancouver 1801, 461). The best-preserved section is a 60-m-long facing of finely shaped and dressed stone; dressed stone is extremely rare in the Hawaiian Islands, reported elsewhere only on temple sites. Waimea Bay was the setting of Captain Cook's first landing in the islands, and where King Kaumuali'i allowed the Russian-American Company to build a fort in 1817 (see chapter 13). Mills (2005, 47), in his discussion of the island's canyonlands, has made the case that the aqueduct that watered the taro fields around Waimea and the fort are linked, since "both of these sites are connected through the development of a complex hierarchical society in Waimea, and there would be no Russian Fort without Menehune Ditch."

At the far southwestern end of the island is the Pacific Missile Range Facility, where more than 25 projects have documented the Nohili site (50-30-05-1829 / 1830), a "dune habitation" dated to the fourteenth century (Knecht and Rieth 2016, 19). Further north along the coast is Polihale Heiau, marking where souls of the deceased cross over to Pō, the afterworld.

Ni'ihau Island and the Islets of Lehua and Ka'ula

The privately owned island of Ni'ihau, in the lee of Kaua'i, remains a blank spot on the archaeological map. John F. G. Stokes briefly visited Ni'ihau in 1912, recording four *heiau* and a small fishing shrine (Bennett 1931, 153–154). William K. Kikuchi (1987) made a brief visit to inspect two proposed helicopter landing sites, finding no surface architecture within the small study areas. We are not aware of any other archaeological studies of Ni'ihau.

There are a number of questions that archaeologists would like to answer about Ni'ihau. Like other smaller islands located in the lee of larger islands, including Kaho'olawe and Lāna'i, we would expect that the precontact community on Ni'ihau was linked with that of Kauaʻi. It is also plausible that Niʻihau enjoyed a degree of autonomy and independence, like Lānaʻi, but at other times functioned as a rural district of its larger neighbor. Research on even smaller offshore islands located around Niʻihau points to a number of interesting possibilities, including early visitation as well as direct connections with remote islands to the northwest.

Two steep, rugged crescent-shaped islets near Niʻihau have been investigated by archaeologists: Lehua and Kaʻula. Lehua is a remnant of an extinct cinder cone, located just 1 km off of Niʻihau's north coast. It holds a special place in the cultural landscape, for its highest point is called the "altar of the sun," Kaunuokalā. Niʻihau's "souls' leap" is on Lehua. Also, as on Mokumanamana, 32 *ahu* or shrines with upright stones were built along the island's ridgeline, some which have coral offerings on the surface (Carpenter and Yent 2008). One of the larger *ahu* (site 50-99-01-01, Feature 23), 3 m by 2.5 m by 80 cm high, was excavated. No cultural material was found, and the structure appears to have been constructed directly on the island's natural tuff. There is reason to believe, however, that this small island was being visited for ceremonies early in the Expansion Period. Kekuewa Kikiloi (2012) reports two corals from surface collections dated to AD 1470 ± 7 and AD 1478 ± 6. We cannot say if these offerings were left in separate events or if they resulted from the same visit; however, if the latter, then this would have been between AD 1472 and 1484.

The tiny islet of Lehua may have been visited long before the Expansion Period. Excavations at a cluster of small platforms, *ahu,* and stone alignments on the south coast (site 50-99-01-02), uncovered a buried hearth that contained a fragment of *hao* charcoal (*Rauvolfia sandwicensis*) dated to the Foundation Period (cal AD 1050–1270, Beta-195943*), as well as a second sample of *hoʻawa* (*Pittosporum* sp.), a small native tree, dating to the Late Voyaging Period (cal AD 1270–1390, Beta-244884*). Carpenter and Yent (2008, 105), reluctant to interpret these results as indicative of early activity in such a marginal environment, offer a number of alternative hypotheses, including the possibility that the dated wood was old driftwood, and that the hearth itself could have been used at a much later time.

Tiny Kaʻula islet, located further to the southwest, 40 km from Niʻihau, was briefly visited by Hommon (1976b), who noted a shelter cave, and a ridgetop "largely natural terraced platform." There were no signs of agriculture, which would have required terracing the steep slopes, artifacts, or the ridgetop *ahu* found on other small islands. This is not to say that Kaʻula had no place in the cultural landscape but that it played a different role than Lehua (see Kikiloi 2012, 61).

19

THE ARCHAEOLOGY OF NIHOA AND MOKUMANAMANA ISLANDS

Sailing northwest past Kaua'i and Ni'ihau, the Hawaiian island chain changes dramatically. The distances between islands grow larger while the size of islands shrinks dramatically, with only basalt pinnacles, coral atolls, and sand cays, remnants of islands that once emerged from the Hawaiian "hot spot" and have been shifted by the relentless conveyor belt of the Pacific Plate to their current position northwest of the main archipelago. When Europeans first explored this region, today called Papahānaumokuākea, they found no residents. But the two small volcanic islands closest to the main Hawaiian Islands, Nihoa and Mokumanamana (the latter also known as Necker Island), exhibit extensive—and to some extent enigmatic—evidence of occupation in precontact times. Scholars have speculated about what drew people to these remote outposts, how they relate to the history of long-distance voyaging, and why they were abandoned by the time of European contact.

Geography and Natural Resources

A mere remnant of a once-larger island, Nihoa has a land area of only 63 ha, attaining a maximum elevation of 272 m above sea level. Sea cliffs plunge sheer to the ocean on three sides; the island slopes steeply to the south, with five small valleys (fig. 19.1). Aside from the limited land area, the constraints on human settlement are ponderous. Annual rainfall is estimated at between 500 and 750 mm, barely adequate for the cultivation of sweet potatoes and gourds, but insufficient for taro and many other Polynesian crops. Since the narrow watercourses flow only after heavy rains, drinking water must be obtained from three small seeps, all of which are tinged with seabird guano. There is no fringing reef to protect the island or to provide a source of reef fish and shellfish, nor is there a beach where canoes could be hauled ashore. Landing must be done onto the rocky shelf, and then only in fair weather.

Nihoa's vegetation is limited to a mere 25 species, including an endemic *loulu* palm, *Pritchardia remota*. Found only on Nihoa, this large palm could have provided a source of

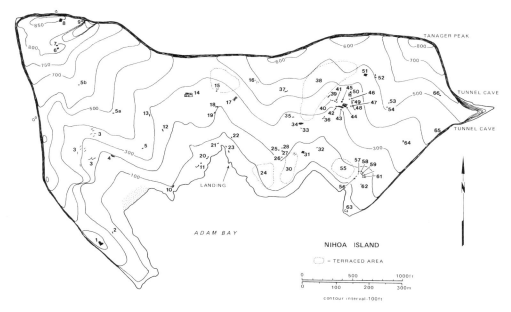

FIGURE 19.1 Map of Nihoa Island, showing the location of archaeological sites. *(Map by Eric Komori, after Emory 1928)*

timber and of thatching material for Polynesian occupants. The remainder of the vegetation consists of low shrubs and grasses, such as *Chenopodium, Solanum,* and *Sida.* About 18 species of seabirds roost on Nihoa, including terns, shearwaters, petrels, and boobies; these could have provided a source of protein for a human population. There are as well two endemic species of passerine, the Nihoa finch (*Telespyza ultima*) and the Nihoa millerbird (*Acrocephalus familiaris kingi*). Additional marine resources would have been inshore fishes, the monk seal, and sea turtles.

Another 248 km to the west lies the even more diminutive Mokumanamana, a sharply rising ridge of volcanic rock with a land area of just 16 ha (fig. 19.2; color plate 15). The constraints to human occupation on Mokumanamana are such that it is doubtful that the island ever supported a permanent population. Clearly, however, it was repeatedly visited by early Polynesians.

Sources of drinking water on Mokumanamana are limited to two small seeps, again heavily tainted with guano. The sparse vegetation clinging to the steep rocky slopes is restricted to just 13 species of low shrubs and grasses; Mokumanamana lacks the larger palms of Nihoa. The islet is a major seabird nesting site. With nearly vertical cliffs rising directly from the ocean, and lacking a protective reef, landings on Mokumanamana are even more difficult and risky than on Nihoa; it is impossible to beach a canoe.

Mokumanamana is the furthest western point in the Hawaiian chain with evidence of precontact human activities. There are, nonetheless, an additional eight groups of atolls to the northwest: French Frigate Shoals, Gardner Pinnacles, Maro Reef, Kauō (Laysan Island), Lisianski, Pearl and Hermes Reef, Midway Atoll, and Kure Atoll. People may have visited these islands, and evidence may yet be uncovered for such visits. Paleoenvironmental coring on Kauō recovered evidence of coconut, however it is unclear when during the past 5,000 years the palm arrived. The Pacific rat has been reported on Kure Atoll, but not on Nihoa or Mokumanamana.

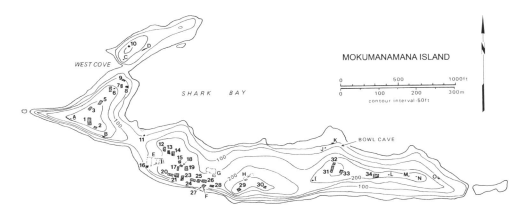

FIGURE 19.2 Map of Mokumanamana or Necker Island, showing the location of archaeological sites. *(Map by Eric Komori after Emory 1928)*

Archaeological Sites

Archaeological research on Nihoa and Mokumanamana began with Bishop Museum's Tanager Expedition in the 1920s, over several visits by natural scientists to the islands. The archaeological remains were described by Kenneth P. Emory (1928), based on his own fieldwork combined with the notes of other scientists. The expedition also produced valuable accounts of the geology and vegetation of the leeward islands (Christophersen and Caum 1931; Palmer 1927). These reports, along with more recent natural history studies, provide a baseline for assessing the natural resources of the islands, including the constraints for human habitation.

Nihoa is mantled with archaeological sites suggestive of a formerly dense population (color plate 16). Emory recorded 66 sites, and his survey—limited to what could be accomplished in five days of fieldwork—was not exhaustive; his work has been supplemented by more recent research (P. L. Cleghorn 1988; Kikiloi 2012). The sites fall into three major categories: (1) religious structures; (2) habitation sites, including terraces and bluff shelters; and (3) agricultural terracing.

The religious structures—14 *heiau* and four smaller shrines—stand out from other sites on the island by the presence of upright dikestone prisms, and of coral heads. Most of these sites are stone-faced, earth-filled terraces, constructed on the steep valley slopes. The dikestones are frequently arranged in rows and probably represented deities, as similar uprights do throughout Eastern Polynesian religious sites (fig. 19.3). Placing coral heads as offerings is a practice known in the main Hawaiian Islands.

Other stone-faced terraces on Nihoa lack the distinctive uprights and coral heads, and given the household implements and tools scattered over their surfaces, have been interpreted as dwelling sites (fig. 19.4). A number of "bluff shelters" (the term Emory used for rockshelters) display evidence of occupation; several of these were crudely excavated by members of the Tanager Expedition, unfortunately without stratigraphic controls.

Emory observed that "the gentler slopes of Nihoa are entirely stepped with cultivation terraces" (1928, 11); he estimated that about 5 ha were terraced in this fashion (fig. 19.5). A resurvey of the island by ethnobotanist Douglas Yen in 1969 suggested that Emory may

FIGURE 19.3 View of Nihoa site 50, a well-constructed set of stone-faced terraces with dikestone uprights. *(Courtesy of Bishop Museum Library and Archives)*

FIGURE 19.4 View of Nihoa site 43, a stone-faced habitation terrace. The palms at the rear of the terrace are the endemic species *Pritchardia remota*. *(Courtesy of Bishop Museum Library and Archives)*

have underestimated the area in agricultural terracing (Yen 1969). Yen described the small, crude agricultural terracing as looking like a series of "fish scales" in plan view. These terraces were not irrigated, and served primarily to retain soil and provide a level planting surface.

Emory estimated the island's precontact population size using two methods. Noting that there are 15 bluff shelters and 25 to 35 house terraces, and assuming an average household size of five persons, Emory calculated the maximum population at 170 to 220, assuming the contemporaneous occupation of all habitation sites. Emory's second estimate was based on the island's agricultural potential. He assumed an annual yield of 4 tons of sweet potatoes per acre per year, calculating that the island's 5 ha of agricultural terraces might yield approximately 48 tons per year. This could support a population of 100 persons, each consuming about 1,000 pounds of tubers per year. Revisiting this calculation based on more accurate productivity estimates used by Ladefoged et al. (2009), then the island's gardens, at full agricultural production, would have supported only about 40 residents.

The diminutive Polynesian high island of Anuta in the southwestern Pacific (Yen and Gordon 1973) is comparable in size to Nihoa, with a land area of only 40 ha. Anuta supports

FIGURE 19.5 An area of agricultural terracing on Nihoa Island, cleared of vegetation by Emory during the Tanager Expedition. *(Courtesy of Bishop Museum Library and Archives)*

a permanent population of about 160 persons. However, it is considerably more fertile than Nihoa and receives more rainfall, so that a greater range of crops is possible (including taro, yams, and breadfruit). Comparing the resource bases of the two islands, it is hard to imagine that Nihoa ever supported a permanent population of more than 100 persons.

Mokumanamana, much smaller and more inhospitable, nevertheless has more than 60 archaeological sites crowding the central ridge crest (see fig. 19.2). It was sighted in November 1786 by the French explorer J. G. de la Pérouse, who bestowed the name of France's minister of finance on the remote pinnacle. Nearly a century later, an expedition to Mokumanamana on the steamer *Iwalani* was organized by the Hawaiian government to formally annex the island. Landing on Sunday morning, May 27, 1894, the annexation party climbed the island's central ridge. Arriving at the summit, they were surprised to find the remains of an ancient temple, upon which were resting a number of well-made male anthropomorphic figures, unique in shape and features (fig. 19.6). These were collected by the annexation party and returned to Honolulu, where they were "set up and placed on exhibition in the windows of the Golden Rule Bazaar" (Emory 1928, 55–56). The images were later deposited in Bishop Museum; two others collected by crew members of HMS *Champion* in September 1894 are in the British Museum.

Emory's account of Mokumanamana (1928), based on the Tanager Expedition findings, noted three site types, including religious structures (34 examples), terraces (25 sites), and bluff shelters (8 sites). By far the most significant are the temples or shrines, which Emory called "*marae*" due to their similarity to structures in central Eastern Polynesia known by this name. The 34 religious structures are consistent in plan and architectural style and, as shown in figure 19.7, consist of a low, narrow, rectangular platform adjoining a paved rectangular court or terrace. Arrayed along the rear of the platform are a series of upright stone slabs, while other slabs are positioned at certain points on the court.

FIGURE 19.6 Stone images from Mokumanamana Island. *(Courtesy of Bishop Museum Library and Archives)*

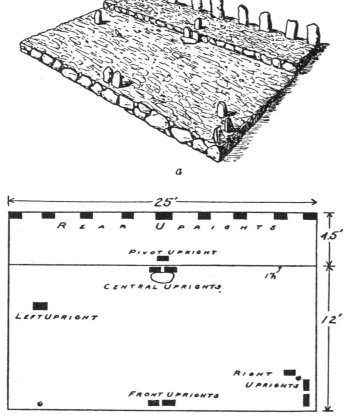

FIGURE 19.7 Sketch and plan map of Mokumanamana site 13, a religious structure closely resembling an Eastern Polynesian *marae*. *(After Emory 1928)*

One structure, near the summit of Flagpole Hill, is more elaborate than the others; this was apparently the original location of the stone images. Site 13 has a low wall on three sides, and the court is paved with waterworn beach pebbles. Emory's plan of the site is shown in figure 19.7. An interesting feature is a small slab-lined compartment in front of the uprights, as in many Society Islands and Tuamotuan *marae*.

Emory also recorded 25 small earthen terraces scattered over the island. None of these revealed any evidence of permanent habitation, nor did they apparently serve a religious function. It is possible that they are agricultural terraces, although the soil is shallow. Eight "bluff shelters" were also recorded, but only one of these, dubbed Bowl Cave, contained substantial evidence of occupation.

Modern surveys of Nihoa and Mokumanamana were directed by Kekuewa Kikiloi as part of his dissertation research (Kikiloi 2012; see also P. L. Cleghorn 1988). This new research has been critical to creating a precise digital map of the island's features that can be used to avoid further disturbing the archaeological landscape while also caring for the island's ecology, especially the seabird population.

Artifacts

The artifacts collected by Emory and other members of the Tanager Expedition on Nihoa included hammerstones, grindstones, adzes, fishhooks, and octopus lures, as well as perishable materials such as cordage, and a tiller made from breadfruit wood. Adzes from these two islands are unlike the typical tanged, quadrangular form of Hawaiian adze but are nearly identical to a well-polished, incipiently tanged adze excavated from the Hālawa dune site on Molokaʻi (fig. 19.8). The single bone fishhook recovered by Emory is similar to types from several early Hawaiian sites. Of particular note are 25 whole or incomplete stone vessels, the most common form being a "jar" form with nearly vertical sides. In shape, these well-made vessels are reminiscent of a late type of ceramics known as Polynesian plainware, and they may reflect a continuity of tradition.

On Mokumanamana, the Tanager Expedition's excavations at Bowl Cave yielded stone bowl fragments, a unique stone "bird-snaring perch," nine stone adzes, a chisel, a hammerstone, three sinkers, and a stone awl. The adzes and bowls are virtually identical to those from Nihoa.

FIGURE 19.8 Stone adzes and a sinker collected on Nihoa and Mokumanamana Islands during the Tanager Expedition. *(Courtesy of Bishop Museum Library and Archives)*

The 10 stone images (there were formerly three others, which have been lost) are all of a highly uniform, anthropomorphic style (see fig. 19.6). Made of vesicular basalt, the images are male, with round faces and thin, wide mouths, protruding eyes, and ears. As Emory noted, they are reminiscent of Marquesan stone images, quite different in style from the classic Hawaiian anthropomorphic figures in stone or wood.

Studies of the geochemical composition of a range of different kinds of stone artifacts from Nihoa and Mokumanamana (Kikiloi 2012; Lebo and Johnson 2007) show that the majority (97%) were made from local stone available on the islands. The six nonlocal artifacts that have been identified are most likely from Kaua'i Island.

Chronology

In 1955, a team of amateur archaeologists was dispatched by Emory to obtain charcoal from Nihoa for dating. Unfortunately, no detailed records were kept of their limited excavations, but charcoal was obtained from a terrace fronting one of the bluff shelters. Portions of the same sample were dated twice, by two different laboratories, with widely differing results. The Michigan Laboratory returned a date in the Late Voyaging or Expansion Period (M-480), while the Gakushuin Laboratory returned a date in the Foundation Period (GaK-754). These dates overlap at two standard deviations, and while it is possible that both are statistically correct, the large standard errors and lack of good stratigraphic context make the dates of little use in tying down the age of the island's archaeological remains.

Kikiloi's (2012) research established the first robust chronology for the islands using radiocarbon dates on identified plant charcoal, and ^{230}Th dates on coral offerings, mainly from Nihoa Island. Based on these dates, the earliest visitors did not arrive until around AD 1400–1500, the early Expansion Period. Dates from this century include a coral offering on Mokumanamana as well as radiocarbon dates from that island's shelter cave. It is possible that Nihoa began supporting a year-round settlement at this stage. Coral offerings were made repeatedly on Nihoa between AD 1500 and 1600, peaking around AD 1550, with the last date in AD 1606. The earliest date on Mokumanamana site 13, the religious structure where carved stone images were recovered, is in the Archaic States Period. Another sample may also date to this era, or could plausibly indicate use of the site in the post-1819 era, cal AD 1696–1918 (OS-95634*).

External versus Internal Explanations

Archaeological theorizing about Nihoa and Mokumanamana has shifted over the years from explanations that reference trends outside of the Hawaiian chain to internal dynamics within the archipelago. Emory (1928, 122) regarded the Mokumanamana sites and artifacts as "a pure sample of the culture prevailing in Hawaii before the thirteenth century." To him, the great distance to the main Hawaiian Islands, the presence of religious architecture and rare stone carvings similar to those in central Eastern Polynesia, and the apparent abandonment of the islands all pointed to an earlier time when there was long-distance voyaging across Polynesia. Kikiloi (2012) argues, through analysis of Hawaiian oral traditions and archaeology, that the foundations of Emory's premises are false. New geochemical sourcing analyses has shown that people made stone artifacts out of local stone, and the rare cases of nonlocal stone appear to derive from Kaua'i, not central Eastern Polynesia. The new radiocarbon and ^{230}Th dates show that it is unlikely that people were visiting these islands in either the Foundation or Late Voyaging Periods. The sites appear to be no older than the early Expansion Period, and in the case of at least one shrine on Mokumanamana may have been built in the Archaic States Period. Further, the synchronic use of both Nihoa and Mokumanamana allows us to reject the idea that religious sites were built by people who were marooned on Mokumanamana (Carlquist 1970, 387).

Why then did people voyage to these remote islands? According to Kikiloi (2012), the answer may lie in the ritual calendar. The sun is at its zenith (when the sun at noon is directly overhead and casts no shadows) over Hawai'i Island in mid-May, providing the first sign of the sun's annual progression toward the solstice. In the north of the archipelago, on Mokumanamana, the summer solstice would occur almost five weeks later, around June 21. Kikiloi (2012, 108) observes that "latitudinal degrees get incrementally smaller as the sun moves more north giving the appearance of slowing down and eventually standing still." Therefore, a priest wishing to recalibrate the lunar calendar to the solar year could observe the summer solstice on Mokumanamana, where the sun was at zenith on the solstice. While such a practice is certainly plausible, it should be noted that ethnographic sources indicate that the Hawaiians traditionally used the acronychal rising of Pleiades for such lunar year recalibration, rather than marking the solstices. However, solar observation to recalibrate the lunar calendar is known from Mangareva in southeastern Polynesia (Kirch 2004b), so a similar practice in Hawai'i is certainly not out of the question.

Kikiloi (2012, vi) argues that "Mokumanamana became the central focus of chiefly elites . . . as a ritual center of power." He suggests that beginning around AD 1400, the islands of Papahānaumokuākea saw pilgrimages that both allowed for calibrating the ritual calendar, something that became the domain of the priestly class, and as a way for chiefs to create and maintain *mana*: "Through commemorative rituals, the west was acknowledged and reaffirmed as the primary pathway of power where elite status, authority and spiritual power originated and was continually legitimized" (Kikiloi 2012, vi). Nihoa, home to a remarkable density of religious structures for such a small island, functioned as a kind of waystation, perhaps maintained by priests.

Why then did people leave? Paul Cleghorn (1988) raises the possibility that at some point Nihoa's seabird colony may have collapsed under pressure from human predation, but more research is necessary to test this hypothesis. Here again, we should look to trends in the broader Hawaiian archipelago. As state religion became institutionalized, the focus of rituals changed. For example, the Makahiki, an annual series of rites linked to the ritual calendar through the rising of Makali'i (Pleiades), may have increased in importance in the Archaic States Period. The ceremonies in Papahānaumokuākea, while enacting a crucial link to the ancestors, would never command the large audiences that were associated with Makahiki on the main islands. Therefore, the effort of maintaining Nihoa as a waystation—which as Kikiloi points out is itself a monumental expense even if the religious architecture itself is modest—may have become too burdensome. If so, this may not be so much a case of abandonment, but a shift to more infrequent visits without the aid of a permanent outpost on Nihoa.

EPILOGUE
The Future of Archaeology in Hawai'i

In the years since the first edition of this book was written, archaeologists have made tremendous strides in advancing our knowledge and understanding of ancient Hawai'i. Both academic and CRM archaeologists have contributed to these gains in knowledge, through the hard work of surveying and excavating sites, and the tedious analysis of fragmentary scraps of evidence that collectively, gradually, yield a portrait of the past. We have a better understanding now of when Polynesian canoes first arrived on Hawaiian shores, of how the early settlers began to transform island landscapes, eventually creating vast, managed agroecosystems across both windward and leeward environments. Demographic trends have emerged from analysis of the thousands of radiocarbon dates now available. Detailed studies of settlement patterns have contributed to a more nuanced appreciation of social organization, of gender, and of class in old Hawai'i. New perspectives have been opened up with regard to the role and function of *heiau* as places of astronomical observation as well as of ritual and prayer. No doubt future work will continue to advance our appreciation of the legacy of *ka po'e kahiko,* the people of old. Yet there are obstacles that stand in the way of future archaeological endeavors.

Four decades ago, archaeology in Hawai'i was in the throes of a transition. For nearly 70 years, archaeological work in the islands had been the purview of a handful of academic scholars, primarily associated with the Bernice Pauahi Bishop Museum, and later with the University of Hawai'i. But the rapidly increasing pace of development unleashed by statehood in 1959, coupled with a spate of new federal and state laws and regulations pertaining to antiquities and historic sites, rapidly influenced the nature of archaeological practice. Private developers as well as state and federal agencies (such as the National Park Service and the US military) needed professional archaeological assistance in order to comply with the new regulatory landscape.

At first Bishop Museum stepped into this void, seeking to combine its long-standing research program in Hawaiian and Polynesian archaeology with the new "contract archaeology." But not only was there more work than a single institution could handle, the emerging opportunities inspired an increasing number of archaeologists to set up for-profit consulting firms. Today, the transition that began in the 1970s has evolved to the point where nearly all archaeological work carried out in Hawai'i is of the CRM variety. Only a few archaeologists (including the authors) work for academic institutions, or carry out research projects solely designed to address and answer new questions about the Hawaiian past. As of April 2021, the State Historic Preservation Division listed 29 permitted archaeological consulting firms (some with multiple investigators and offices on several islands), and just six permitted nonconsulting archaeologists.

As a recent review of archaeological practice in Hawaiʻi observed, CRM has become an "industry," supported by private and governmental contracts worth millions of dollars every year (Kaliʻuokapaʻakai Collective 2021, 29). If we ask whose interests this "CRM industry" serves, the answer would appear to be, first and foremost, those of the developers and agencies who must comply with the regulatory process in order to get their projects approved and permitted, and only secondarily, the interests of those whose cultural heritage is at stake. Perhaps this is the inevitable outcome of an uneasy marriage between an academic discipline and capitalism.

Looking deeper into the current state of CRM-dominated archaeology in Hawaiʻi, it seems that the interests of the Native Hawaiian people—whose cultural history is represented by the archaeological sites and "cultural resources" inventoried in countless pages of reports (seldom summarized or synthesized for public consumption)—are often an afterthought. Moreover, the original intent of much of the federal and state laws and regulations that underpin CRM archaeology—that is, the preservation and perpetuation of history and culture—is frequently circumvented in the process of fostering "development." While some archaeological projects in Hawaiʻi result in the preservation of important sites or cultural landscapes, the impacts of development are often "mitigated" by a few test pits, the reports of which are filed away and forgotten. Kānaka Maoli frequently complain that archaeologists fail to reach out to the communities affected by development projects, to consult and solicit the communities' views and concerns, or to share the results of their surveys and "mitigation" work. While consultation is now mandated by federal and state funded statutes, the effort made to reach out to local communities can fall short of what is necessary.

Cultural resource management is supposed to preserve the archaeological record for future generations. And yet the records of archaeological surveys and excavations in Hawaiʻi, along with the artifacts and other samples resulting from this work, are too often not being curated for the benefit of future generations. There is no statewide repository for archaeological materials, and there are no laws requiring the long-term curation of archaeological collections, which are the property of the owner of record for the lands from which they are recovered. Bishop Museum is officially recognized as the "state museum" but receives no regular budgetary allocation from the legislature to care for its irreplaceable archaeological collections. Meanwhile, many private CRM firms store the collections and records generated by their many consulting projects in garages and public storage lockers. Is this how the legacy of Hawaiian culture should be dealt with? It is well known that there is a "curation crisis" in Hawaiian archaeology, yet there is currently no plan in place to correct the problem. The recent efforts of Kamehameha Schools / Bishop Estate to curate collections from their lands, as well as to inventory and protect sites, is a welcome development.

To be sure, CRM archaeology in Hawaiʻi over the past four decades has enabled the survey and investigation of many areas, and of thousands of sites, that would not otherwise have been studied. And while much CRM work is routine, important advances in our understanding of the Hawaiian past have indeed resulted from CRM projects. The launch in 2020 of the State Historic Preservation Division's HICRIS (Hawaii Cultural Resource Information System) provided a long-overdue framework for making the information contained in the vast CRM literature available to archaeologists working in Hawai'i, as well as to the general public. Hopefully, this will be just the first of many steps that will be taken to safeguard this information and make it available to future generations. The State Historic Preservation Division, if provided with more adequate funding and staffing, could be more proactive regarding the inventory and protection of sites on state as well as private lands, rather than simply solely reactive.

As we bring this second edition of *Feathered Gods and Fishhooks* to a conclusion, a recent report by the Kali'uopapa'akai Collective—a consortium of largely Native Hawaiian archaeologists and colleagues—has called for another transition in archaeological practice in Hawai'i. Poignantly observing that CRM archaeology is "defined from an outside perspective by federal and state legislation, [and] is not aligned with Hawaiian culture, values, and practices," they propose replacing the CRM paradigm with a new approach, one that draws upon Kānaka Maoli cultural perspectives and epistemology (Kali'uokapa'akai Collective 2021, 29). They term this approach Wahi Kūpuna Stewardship (WKS).

Whether WKS or some other paradigm will replace the current CRM model, and whether the current shortcomings of archaeological practice in Hawai'i can be rectified in coming years, is not for us to say. We are students of the past, not predictors of the future. But we do feel that the current status quo is not fully serving the broader interests of the communities in which archaeologists in Hawai'i carry out their work. As currently practiced, archaeology in Hawai'i does not do all that it could to protect important sites and to generate new knowledge of Hawai'i's past, and often fails to share the fruits of its labors broadly with Kānaka Maoli and other stakeholders. In concluding, we return again to the words one of us penned nearly 40 years ago:

> The legacy that we leave to future generations, both to those in Hawai'i and to those outside who also wish to learn and benefit from her past, depends upon the decisions that we make now and in the next few generations . . .
>
> The people of Hawai'i, all who regard knowledge and understanding of the past as a vital part of any civilized society, as well as the Native Hawaiians, must take an active part in assuring that the finite treasures of ancient Hawai'i are not squandered in the next few years. (*Feathered Gods and Fishhooks,* 1st ed., p. 320)

GLOSSARY OF HAWAIIAN TERMS

ahupuaʻa	A territorial land unit, under the control of a subchief (the *aliʻi ʻai ahupuaʻa*). Such units typically ran from the mountains to the sea.
ʻāina	Land.
akua	God, spirit, deity.
aliʻi	Elite, member of the chiefly class.
aliʻi akua	Literally, "god king." An expression reserved for the highest-ranking *aliʻi*, especially those of *piʻo* rank.
aliʻi nui	Literally, "great chief." The highest-ranked chief within a polity; king.
ʻaumakua	Ancestral deities; literally "collective parents."
ʻawa	Kava, *Piper methysticum*, the root of which was used to prepare a psychoactive (but nonalcoholic) beverage consumed in substantial quantity by the elites.
hale o Lono	Temple dedicated to the god Lono (literally, "house of Lono").
heiau	The general term for a Hawaiian ritual place, where sacrifices of any kind were offered to the gods or to ancestral spirits.
heiau hoʻouluʻai	Agricultural temple (literally, "temple to increase food").
hōlua	A competitive sport of the elites, involving riding a narrow two-runner sled down a specially prepared course.
hoʻokupu	Tribute (literally, "to cause to grow or increase").
hula	Various forms of traditional dance.
ʻieʻie	An indigenous climbing shrub of the Pandanus family (*Freycinetia arborea*), the tough fibers of which were used to weave the foundations for feathered garments.
ʻili	A land unit, smaller in size than an *ahupuaʻa*.
ʻili kūpono	A special kind of *ʻili* segment within an *ahupuaʻa*, under the direct control of the king, rather than the *ahupuaʻa* chief, and whose tribute was reserved for the king.
kahuna	Priest. (Plural, *kāhuna*.)
Kanaloa	One of the four major gods of the Hawaiian pantheon.
Kāne	A principal god of the Hawaiian pantheon; the creator god, also deity of flowing waters and irrigation, to whom taro (*kalo*) was sacred.
kapa	Barkcloth.
kapu	Sacred; prohibited; forbidden.

kapu moe	The prostrating taboo, obligatory for the highest-ranked chiefs.
kauā	Member of the lowest social class, sometimes referred to as "outcasts" or "slaves." *Kauā* were suitable for offerings of human sacrifice at the *luakini* temples
kī	The ti plant, *Cordyline fruticosum*.
ko'a	A fishing shrine, dedicated to the god Kū'ula.
kō'ele	An area of pondfields or a garden segment worked by the common people on behalf of the *konohiki* and the chief; the production of the *kō'ele* was reserved for the use of the *konohiki* and *ali'i*.
konohiki	Land manager for an *ahupua'a* land unit, representing the *ali'i 'ai ahupua'a* chief.
Kū	One of the four principal gods of the Hawaiian pantheon; god of war.
kuaiwi	Literally, "backbone." A stone wall or alignment running up and down the slope, demarking divisions within a dryland field system, as in the Kona Field System.
kula	Dryland cultivation areas; in Māhele land claims *kula* lands are typically distinguished from irrigated taro lands (*lo'i*).
lei niho palaoa	A special neck ornament worn by chiefs, consisting of a tongue-shaped pendant suspended by braids of human hair.
lele	The sacrificial altar on a temple.
lo'i	An irrigated pondfield for the cultivation of taro (*Colocasia esculenta*).
loko kuapā	A fishpond formed by constructing a stone wall out onto the reef flat.
Lono	One of the four principal gods of the Hawaiian pantheon; god of dryland agriculture, to whom the sweet potato (*'uala*) was sacred.
lua	A pit, such as the pit for disposing of sacrificial offerings on a temple.
luakini	A state temple dedicated to the god Kū, at which human sacrifice was performed.
Māhele	The division of lands between 1848 and 1854.
maika	A game in which a special bowling stone was rolled along a pitch with two upright sticks at the end.
maka'āinana	Commoner.
Makahiki	A four-month period that commenced with the first visibility of the Pleiades in November; this was the period of tribute collection, sacred to Lono, when war was forbidden.
mana	Supernatural or divine power, efficacy.
moku	A political district.
mo'o	A land unit, smaller in size than an *'ili*.
mo'okū'auhau	Genealogy or pedigree.
mo'olelo	Oral tradition, history.
mua	The men's eating house. The *mua* of a king was where he would hold court with other high-ranking males and advisors.
noa	Free, without *kapu*, the opposite of *kapu*.

pahu	Particular kind of cylindrical drum, with a tympanum of shark's skin, used during *luakini* temple ceremonies.
pūloʻuloʻu	A barkcloth covered ball on a shaft, either carried before the king or set up in front of his residence, as a mark of taboo.
waiwai	Wealth, goods, property (literally, "water" reduplicated).

REFERENCES

Allen, Jane. 1991. The role of agriculture in the evolution of the pre-contact Hawaiian state. *Asian Perspectives* 30:117–132.

———. 1992. Farming in Hawai'i from colonization to contact: Radiocarbon chronology and implications for cultural change. *New Zealand Journal of Archaeology* 14:45–66.

Allen, Jane, ed. 1987. *Five Upland 'Ili: Archaeological and Historical Investigations in the Kāne'ohe Interchange, Interstate Highway H-3, Island of O'ahu*. Department of Anthropology Report 87-1. Honolulu, HI: Bernice P. Bishop Museum.

Allen, Jane, M. F. Riford, P. Brennan, D. Chaffee, L. S. Cummings, C. Kawachi, L. Liu, and G. Murakami, eds. 2002. *Kula and Kahawai: Geoarchaeological and Historical Investigations in Middle Maunawili Valley, Kailua, Ko'olau Poko, O'ahu*. Honolulu, HI: AMEC Earth and Environmental.

Allen, Jim. 1996. The pre-Austronesian settlement of island Melanesia: Implications for Lapita archaeology. In W. H. Goodenough, ed., *Prehistoric Settlement of the Pacific*, pp. 11–27. *Transactions of the American Philosophical Society* 86 (5): 11–27. Philadelphia.

Allen, M. S. 1981. An Analysis of the Mauna Kea Adz Quarry Archaeobotanical Assemblage. Master's thesis, University of Hawai'i at Mānoa.

———. 1983. Analysis of archaeobotanical materials. In J. T. Clark and P. V. Kirch, eds., *Archaeological Investigations of the Mudlane-Waimea-Kawaihae Road Corridor, Island of Hawai'i*, pp. 384–400. Department of Anthropology Report 83-1. Honolulu, HI: Bernice P. Bishop Museum.

———. 1989. Archaeobotanical assemblages from the Anahulu rockshelters. In P. V. Kirch, ed., *Prehistoric Hawaiian Occupation in the Anahulu Valley, O'ahu Island: Excavations in Three Inland Rockshelters*, pp. 83–102. Archaeological Research Facility Contribution No. 47. Berkeley: University of California.

———. 1992. Appendix A: Kaho'olawe archaeobotanical materials. In P. H. Rosendahl, ed., *Kaho'olawe Excavations 1982–83: Data Recovery Project*. Hilo, HI: Paul H. Rosendahl.

———. 1996. Style and function in East Polynesian fish-hooks. *Antiquity* 70:97–116.

———. 2014. Marquesan colonisation chronologies and post-colonisation interaction: Implications for Hawaiian origins and the "Marquesan Homeland" hypothesis. *Journal of Pacific Archaeology* 5:1–17.

Allen, M. S., ed. 2001. *Gardens of Lono: Archaeological Investigations at the Amy B. H. Greenwell Ethnobotanical Garden, Kealakekua, Hawai'i*. Honolulu, HI: Bishop Museum Press.

Allen, M. S., and P. A. McAnany. 1994. Environmental variability and traditional Hawaiian land use patterns: Manuka's cultural islands in seas of lava. *Asian Perspectives* 33:19–56.

Allen, M. S., and A. E. Morrison. 2013. Modelling site formation dynamics: Geoarchaeological, chronometric and statistical approaches to a stratified rockshelter sequence, Polynesia. *Journal of Archaeological Science* 40:4560–4575.

Allen-Wheeler, J. 1981a. Archaeological excavations in Kawainui Marsh, Island of Oʻahu. Unpublished report in Library, Bernice P. Bishop Museum, Honolulu.

———. 1981b. Archaeological reconnaissance survey and test excavations in Kailua, Oʻahu. Unpublished report in Library, Bernice P. Bishop Museum, Honolulu.

Anderson, A. 2001. Towards the sharp end: The form and performance of prehistoric Polynesian voyaging canoes. In C. M. Stevenson, G. Lee, and F. J. Morin, eds., *Pacific 2000: Proceedings of the Fifth International Conference on Easter Island and the Pacific,* pp. 29–36. Los Osos, CA: Easter Island Foundation.

Anderson, A., and Y. Sinoto. 2002. New radiocarbon ages of colonization sites in East Polynesia. *Asian Perspectives* 41:242–257.

Anderson, P-K. B. 2001. Houses of the *Kamaʻaina:* Historical anthropology in a rural Hawaiian valley. PhD diss., University of California, Berkeley.

Apple, R. A. 1965. *Hawaiian Archaeology: Trails.* Bernice P. Bishop Museum Special Publication 53. Honolulu, HI: Bishop Museum Press.

Apple, R. A., and G. A. MacDonald. 1966. The rise of sea level in contemporary times at Honaunau, Kona, Hawaii. *Pacific Science* 20:125–136.

Athens, J. S. 1983a. Prehistoric pondfield agriculture in Hawaiʻi: Archaeological investigations at the Hanalei National Wildlife Refuge, Kauaʻi. Unpublished report in Library, Bernice P. Bishop Museum, Honolulu.

———. 1983b. Archaeological excavations on the Pohākupu-Kukanono slope, Kawainui Marsh, Oʻahu. Unpublished report in Library, Bernice P. Bishop Museum, Honolulu.

———. 1983c. Archaeological excavations at a beach midden deposit, Kailua, Oʻahu: The H.A.R.C. site (50-Oa-G6-40). Unpublished report in Library, Bernice P. Bishop Museum, Honolulu.

———. 1985. Prehistoric investigations at an upland site on the leeward slopes of central Molokaʻi. Unpublished report. Honolulu, HI: International Archaeological Research Institute.

———. 1997. Hawaiian native lowland vegetation in prehistory. In P. V. Kirch and T. L. Hunt, eds., *Historical Ecology in the Pacific Islands: Prehistoric Environmental and Landscape Change,* pp. 248–270. New Haven, CT: Yale University Press.

———. 2002. Paleoenvironmetnal study of Auiki and Ananoho fishponds, Kalihi Kai, Honolulu, Oʻahu. Unpublished report. Honolulu, HI: International Archaeological Research Institute.

———. 2008. Rattus exulans and the catastrophic disappearance of Hawaiʻi's native lowland forest. *Biological Invasions.* doi:10.1007/s10530–008–9402–3.

Athens, J. S., and M. W. Kaschko. 1989. Prehistoric upland bird hunters: Archaeological inventory survey and testing for the MPRC project area and the Bobcat Trail Road, Pohakuloa Training Area, Island of Hawaii. Honolulu, HI: International Archaeological Research Institute.

Athens, J. S., M. W. Kaschko, and H. F. James. 1991. Prehistoric bird hunters: High altitude resource exploitation on Hawaiʻi Island. *Bishop Museum Occasional Papers* 31:63–84. Honolulu, HI: Bishop Museum Press.

Athens, J. S., T. M. Rieth, and T. S. Dye. 2014. A paleoenvironmental and archaeological model-based age estimate for the colonization of Hawaiʻi. *American Antiquity* 79:144–155.

Athens, J. S., M. J. Tomonari-Tuggle, and J. V. Ward. 1996. Archaeological inventory survey and paleoenvironmental coring for kiosks, boardwalk and parking areas, Kealia Pond National Wildlife Refuge, Kihei, Maui, Hawaiʻi. Unpublished report. Honolulu, HI: International Archaeological Research Institute.

Athens, J. S., H. D. Tuggle, J. V. Ward, and D. J. Welch. 2002. Avifaunal extinctions, vegetation change, and Polynesian impacts in prehistoric Hawaiʻi. *Archaeology in Oceania* 37:57–78.

Athens, J. S., and J. V. Ward. 1993. Environmental change and prehistoric Polynesian settlement in Hawai'i. *Asian Perspectives* 32:205–223.

———. 1997. The Maunawili core: Prehistoric inland expansion of settlement and agriculture, O'ahu, Hawai'i. *Hawaiian Archaeology* 6:37–51.

———. 2007. Kō'ie'ie Fishpond, Kīhei, Maui: Chronology and paleoenvironment. Unpublished report. Honolulu, HI: International Archaeological Research Institute.

Athens, J. S., J. V. Ward, and D. W. Blinn. 1995. Paleoenvironmental investigations at 'Uko'a Pond, Kawailoa Ahupua'a, O'ahu, Hawai'i. Unpublished report. Honolulu, HI: International Archaeological Research Institute.

———. 2007. Paleoenvironment of Pu'uhonua o Hōnaunau National Historical Park, South Kona, Hawai'i Island. Unpublished report. Honolulu, HI: International Archaeological Research Institute.

———. 2014. Fishpond cores of Pu'uhonua o Hōnaunau National Historical Park, South Kona, Hawai'i Island. Unpublished report. Honolulu, HI: International Archaeological Research Institute.

Athens, J. S., J. Ward, H. D. Tuggle, and D. J. Welch. 1999. Environment, vegetation change, and early human settlement of the 'Ewa Plain: A cultural resource inventory of Naval Air Station, Barbers Point, O'ahu, Hawai'i. Part 3, Paleoenvironmental investigations. Unpublished report. Honolulu, HI: International Archaeological Research Institute.

Athens, J. S., J. Ward, and S. Wickler. 1992. Late Holocene lowland vegetation, O'ahu, Hawai'i. *New Zealand Journal of Archaeology* 14:9–34.

Avery, C. 2011. Water and power: Agricultural intensification in windward North Kohala, Hawaii Island. Master's thesis, San José State University.

Ayres, W. S. 1970. *Archaeological Survey and Excavations, Kamana-Nui Valley, Moanalua Ahupua'a, South Halawa Valley, Halawa Ahupua'a.* Department of Anthropology Report 70-8. Honolulu, HI: Bernice P. Bishop Museum.

———. 1973. The cultural context of Easter Island religious structures. PhD diss., Tulane University.

Baer, A. 2015. On the cloak of kings: Agriculture, power, and community in Kaupō, Maui. PhD diss., University of California, Berkeley.

———. 2016. Ceremonial architecture and the spatial proscription of community: Location versus form and function in Kaupō, Maui, Hawaiian Islands. *Journal of the Polynesian Society* 125:289–305.

Baer, A., O. Chadwick, and P. V. Kirch. 2015. Soil nutrients and intensive dryland agricultural production in Kaupo, Maui, Hawaiian Islands. *Journal of Archaeological Science: Reports* 3:429–436.

Baldauf, N., and M. Akutagawa. 2013. *Ho'i Hou I Ka Iwikuamo'o: A Legal Primer for the Protection of Iwi Kūpuna in Hawai'i Nei.* Honolulu, HI: Ka Huli Ao Center for Excellence in Native Hawaiian Law, and the Office of Hawaiian Affairs.

Barrau, J. 1965. L'humide et le sec: An essay on ethnobotanical adaptation to contrastive environments in the Indo-Pacific area. *Journal of the Polynesian Society* 74:329–346.

Barrera, W., Jr. 1971a. *Anaehoomalu: A Hawaiian Oasis.* Pacific Anthropological Records 15. Honolulu, HI: Bernice P. Bishop Museum.

———. 1971b. *Archaeological Excavations and Survey at Keauhou, North Kona, Hawaii.* Department of Anthropology Report 71-10. Honolulu, HI: Bernice P. Bishop Museum.

———. 1972. Excavation of a beach midden deposit at Anaehoomalu Bay. Unpublished report in Library, Bernice P. Bishop Museum. Honolulu.

———. 1984. Kaho'olawe archaeology: An overview. *Hawaiian Archaeology* 1:31–43.

Barrera, W., Jr., and R. J. Hommon. 1972. *Salvage Archaeology at Wailau-Ninole, Kaʻu, Island of Hawaii.* Department of Anthropology Report 72-1. Honolulu, HI: Bernice P. Bishop Museum.

Barrera, W., Jr., and M. Kelly. 1974. *Archaeological and Historical Surveys of the Waimea to Kawaihae Road Corridor, Island of Hawaii.* Department of Anthropology Report 74-1. Honolulu, HI: Bernice P. Bishop Museum.

Barrera, W., Jr., and P. V. Kirch. 1973. Basaltic glass artefacts from Hawaii: Their dating and prehistoric uses. *Journal of the Polynesian Society* 82:176–187.

Barrère, D. B. 1975. *Kamehameha in Kona: Two Documentary Studies.* Pacific Anthropological Records 23. Honolulu, HI: Bernice P. Bishop Museum.

Barrow, T. 1967. Material evidence of the bird-man concept in Polynesia. In G. A. Highland et al., eds., *Polynesian Culture History,* pp. 191–214. Bernice P. Bishop Museum Special Publication 56. Honolulu, HI: Bishop Museum Press.

Barton, C. M., J. Bernabeau, J. Aura, E. O. Garcia, S. Schmich, and L. Molina. 2004. Long-term socioecology and contingent landscapes. *Journal of Archaeological Method and Theory* 11:253–291.

Bates, M. 1854. *Sandwich Island Notes, by A Haole.* New York: Harper & Brothers.

Bayman, J. M. 2003. Stone tool economies in post-contact Hawaiʻi. In C. R. Cobb, ed., *Stone Tool Traditions in the Contact Era,* pp. 94–108. Tuscaloosa: University of Alabama Press.

———. 2010. The precarious middle ground: Exchange and the reconfiguration of social identity in the Hawaiian Kingdom. In C. D. Dillian and C. L. White, eds., *Trade and Exchange: Archaeological Studies from History and Prehistory,* pp. 129–148. New York: Springer.

Bayman, J. M., and T. S. Dye. 2013. *Hawaii's Past in a World of Pacific Islands.* Washington, DC: Society for American Archaeology.

Bayman, J. M., and J. J. Moniz-Nakamura. 2001. Craft specialization and adze production on Hawaiʻi Island. *Journal of Field Archaeology* 28:239–252.

Bayman, J. M., J. J. Moniz-Nakamura, T. M. Rieth, and C. K. Paraso. 2004. Stone adze production and resource extraction at Pōhakuloa, Hawaiʻi Island. *Hawaiian Archaeology* 9:83–104.

Beaglehole, J. C., ed. 1967. *The Journals of Captain James Cook on His Voyages of Discovery.* Vol. 3, *The Voyage of the* Resolution *and* Discovery. Cambridge: Cambridge University Press for the Hakluyt Society.

Beckwith, M. W. 1970. *Hawaiian Mythology.* Honolulu: University of Hawaiʻi Press.

———. n.d. Unpublished field notes. Department of Anthropology. Honolulu, HI: Bernice P. Bishop Museum.

Beckwith, M. W., ed. 1932. *Kepelino's Traditions of Hawaii.* Bernice P. Bishop Museum Bulletin 95. Honolulu, HI: Bishop Museum Press.

Bellwood, P. 1996. Hierarchy, founder ideology, and Austronesian expansion. In J. J. Fox and C. Sather, eds., *Origins, Ancestry, and Alliance: Explorations in Austronesian Ethnography,* pp. 18–40. Canberra: Australian National University Press.

———. 2017. *First Islanders: Prehistory and Human Migration in Island Southeast Asia.* Oxford: Wiley Blackwell.

———. 2019. The earthenware pottery from the North Moluccan excavations. In P. Bellwood, ed., *The Spice Islands in Prehistory: Archaeology in the Northern Moluccas, Indonesia*, pp. 81–106. Terra Australis 50. Canberra: Australian National University Press.

Bennett, W. C. 1930. Hawaiian heiaus. PhD diss., Chicago, IL: University of Chicago.

———. 1931. *Archaeology of Kauai.* Bernice P. Bishop Museum Bulletin 80. Honolulu, HI: Bishop Museum Press.

Berger, A. J. 1972. *Hawaiian Birdlife*. Honolulu: University of Hawai'i Press.

Bevacqua, R. F., ed. 1972. *Archaeological Survey of Portions of Waikoloa, South Kohala District, Island of Hawaii*. Department of Anthropology Report 72-4. Honolulu, HI: Bernice P. Bishop Museum.

Binford, L. 1962. Archaeology as anthropology. *American Antiquity* 28:217–225.

Binford, L., and S. Binford, eds. 1968. *New Perspectives in Archaeology*. Chicago, IL: Aldine.

Birdsell, J. B. 1957. Some population problems involving Pleistocene man. *Cold Spring Harbor Symposium on Quantitative Biology* 22:47–69.

Bishop Museum, Department of Anthropology. 1964. Report on the Puako petroglyph field in the proposed State Historic Petroglyph Park, Puako, South Kohala. Unpublished report in Library, Bernice P. Bishop Museum. Honolulu.

Blust, R. A. 1976. Austronesian culture history: Some linguistic inferences and their relations to the archaeological record. *World Archaeology* 8:19–43.

———. 2013. *The Austronesian Languages*. Rev. ed. Asia-Pacific Linguistics, Open Access Monographs A-PL 008. Canberra: Australian National University Press. http://hdl.handle.net/1885/10191.

Bonk, W. J. 1954. Archaeological Excavations on West Molokai. Master's thesis, University of Hawai'i at Mānoa.

———. 1961. Prehistoric man in Hawaii. *Archaeology* 14:88–94.

———. 1969. Lua Nunu o Kamakalepo: A cave of refuge in Ka'u, Hawaii. In R. Pearson, ed., *Archaeology on the Island of Hawaii*, pp. 75–92. Asian and Pacific Archaeology Series No. 3. Honolulu: Social Science Research Institute, University of Hawai'i.

Boserup, E. 1965. *The Conditions of Agricultural Growth: The Economics of Agrarian Change under Population Pressure*. London: Allen and Unwin.

Bowen, R. N. 1961. Hawaiian Disposal of the Dead. Master's thesis, University of Hawai'i at Mānoa.

———. 1974. Mokapu: Its historical and archaeological past. In C. E. Snow, *Early Hawaiians: An Initial Study of Skeletal Remains from Mokapu, Oahu*, pp. 129–148. Lexington: University of Kentucky Press.

Brigham, W. T. 1899. *Hawaiian Feather Work*. Bernice P. Bishop Museum Memoir, vol. 1, part 1. Honolulu, HI: Bishop Museum Press.

———. 1902. *Stone Implements and Stone Work of the Ancient Hawaiians*. Bernice P. Bishop Museum Memoir, vol. 1, part 5. Honolulu, HI: Bishop Museum Press.

———. 1903. *Additional Notes on Hawaiian Feather Work*. Bernice P. Bishop Museum Memoir, vol. 1, part 5. Honolulu, HI: Bishop Museum Press.

———. 1906. *Old Hawaiian Carvings*. Bernice P. Bishop Museum Memoir, vol. 2, part 2. Honolulu, HI: Bishop Museum Press.

———. 1909. *The Volcanoes of Kilauea and Mauna Loa on the Island of Hawaii*. Bernice P. Bishop Museum Memoir, vol. 2, part 4. Honolulu, HI: Bishop Mueum Press.

Bronk-Ramsey, C. 2009. Bayesian analysis of radiocarbon dates. *Radiocarbon* 51:337–360.

Brookfield, H. C. 1972. Intensification and disintensification in Pacific agriculture: A theoretical approach. *Pacific Viewpoint* 13:30–48.

———. 1984. Intensification revisited. *Pacific Viewpoint* 25:15–44.

Brookfield, H. C., and P. M. Blaikie. 1987. *Land, Degradation, and Society*. London: Methuen.

Buck, P. H. (Te Rangi Hiroa). 1938. *Vikings of the Sunrise*. New York: Frederick Stokes.

———. 1957. *Arts and Crafts of Hawaii*. Bernice P. Bishop Museum Special Publication 45. Honolulu, HI: Bishop Museum Press.

Buck, P. H., K. P. Emory, H. D. Skinner, and J. F. G. Stokes. 1930. Terminology for ground stone cutting implements in Polynesia. *Journal of the Polynesian Society* 39:174–180.

Burley, D. V., A. Barton, W. R. Dickinson, S. P. Connaughton, and K. Taché. 2010. Nukuleka as a founder colony for West Polynesian settlement: New insights from recent excavations. *Journal of Pacific Archaeology* 1:128–144.

Burley, D., K. Edinborough, M. Weisler, and J. Zhao. 2015. Bayesian modeling and chronological precision for Polynesian settlement of Tonga. *PLOS ONE* 10 (3): e0120795.

Burney, D. A. 2002. Late Quaternary chronology and stratigraphy of twelve sites on Kauaʻi. *Radiocarbon* 44:13–44.

———. 2010. *Back to the Future in the Caves of Kauaʻi: A Scientist's Adventures in the Dark*. New Haven, CT: Yale University Press.

Burney, D. A., H. F. James, L. P. Burney, S. L. Olson, W. Kikuchi, W. L. Wagner, M. Burney, et al. 2001. Fossil evidence for a diverse biota from Kauaʻi and its transformation since human arrival. *Ecological Monographs* 71:615–641.

Burney, D. A., and W. P. Kikuchi. 2006. A millenium of human activity at Makauwahi Cave, Mahaʻulepu, Kauaʻi. *Human Ecology* 34 (2): 219–247.

Burney, L. P., and D. A. Burney. 2003. Charcoal stratigraphies for Kauaʻi and the timing of human arrival. *Pacific Science* 57:211–226.

Burtchard, G. C. 1996. Population and land-use on the Keauhou Coast, the Mauka Land Inventory Survey, Keauhou, North Kona, Hawaii Island. Unpublished report. Honolulu, HI: International Archaeological Research Institute.

Burtchard, G. C., and M. J. Tomonari-Tuggle. 2004. Agriculture on leeward Hawaiʻi Island: The Waimea agricultural system reconsidered. *Hawaiian Archaeology* 9:50–73.

Bush, A., D. Shildeler, D. F. Borthwick, K. McGuire, M. Heidel, and H. H. Hammatt. 2001. Archaeological data recovery report for Kalamaʻula residence lots, Unit I: Kalamaʻula, Molokaʻi. Unpublished report. Honolulu: Cultural Surveys of Hawaiʻi.

Cachola-Abad, C. K. 1996. The significance of heiau diversity in site evaluations. *Cultural Resource Management* 8:11–16.

———. 2000. The evolution of Hawaiian socio-political complexity: An analysis of Hawaiian oral traditions. PhD diss., University of Hawaiʻi at Mānoa.

Cachola-Abad, C. K., and E. H. Ayau. 1999. *He pane hoʻomalamalama:* Setting the record straight and a second call for partnership. *Hawaiian Archaeology* 7:74–82.

Caldeira, L., C. Hellmich, A. L. Kaeppler, B. L. Kam, and R. G. Rose, eds. 2015. *Royal Hawaiian Featherwork: Nā Hulu Aliʻi*. Honolulu: University of Hawaiʻi Press.

Calis, I. 2001. An archaeological inventory survey of two lots (106 and 107) in the Limahuli National Tropical Botanical Gardens, Hāʻena Ahupuaʻa, Haleleʻa District, Island of Kauaʻi, Hawaiʻi. Unpublished report. Honolulu, HI: Scientific Consultant Services.

Callies, D. L. 2010. *Regulating Paradise: Land Use Controls in Hawaiʻi*. 2nd ed. Honolulu: University of Hawaiʻi Press.

Calugay, C., and W. K. McElroy. 2005. An analysis of coral, basalt, and sea urchin spine abrading tools from Nuʻalolo Kai, Kauaʻi. In M. T. Carson and M. W. Graves, ed., *Na Mea Kahiko o Kauaʻi: Archaeological Studies in Kauaʻi*, pp. 212–235. Society for Hawaiian Archaeology Special Publication 2. Honolulu: Society for Hawaiian Archaeology.

Carlquist, S. 1970. *Hawaii: A Natural History*. New York: Natural History Press.

Carlson, I. K., S. Collins, and P. L. Cleghorn. 1994. Report of human remains found during the realignment of Kālia Road, Fort DeRussy, Waikīkī, Oʻahu. Unpublished report. Honolulu: Biosystems Analysis.

Carpenter, A., and M. Yent. 2008. Archaeological inventory survey: Lehua Island, Waimea District (Niʻihau), County of Kauaʻi. Unpublished report. Honolulu: Hawaiʻi State Parks.

Carroll, H. K., R. Fuentes, C. Ledesma, J. M. Bayman, and T. P. K. Tengan. 2016. End of the year report for the 2016 UH Mānoa North Shore Archaeological Field School at ʻUkoʻa Habitation Site, Kawailoa Ahupuaʻa, Waialua District, Oʻahu Island. Unpublished report. Honolulu: University of Hawaiʻi at Mānoa.

Carson, M. T. 1998. Archaeological data recovery of a portion of state site number 50-30-02-1879 at Lot 44, a residential property, Wainiha, Haleleʻa District, Island of Kauaʻi, Hawaiʻi. Unpublished report. Honolulu, HI: Scientific Consultant Services.

———. 2004. Resolving the enigma of early coastal settlement in the Hawaiian Islands: The stratigraphic sequence of the Wainiha Beach site in Kauaʻi. *Geoarchaeology* 19:99–118.

———. 2005a. A radiocarbon dating synthesis for Kauaʻi. In M. T. Carson and M. W. Graves, eds., *Na Mea Kahiko o Kauaʻi: Archaeological Studies in Kauaʻi,* pp. 11–32. Society for Hawaiian Archaeology Special Publication No. 2. Honolulu: Society for Hawaiian Archaeology.

———. 2005b. Haleleʻa District. In M. T. Carson and M. W. Graves, eds., *Na Mea Kahiko o Kauaʻi: Archaeological Studies in Kauaʻi,* pp. 106–108. Society for Hawaiian Archaeology Special Publication No. 2. Honolulu: Society for Hawaiian Archaeology.

———. 2005c. Haleleʻa agricultural systems reconsidered. In M. T. Carson and M. W. Graves, eds., *Na Mea Kahiko o Kauaʻi: Archaeological Studies in Kauaʻi,* pp. 109–116. Society for Hawaiian Archaeology Special Publication No. 2. Honolulu: Society for Hawaiian Archaeology.

———. 2005d. Puna District. In M. T. Carson and M. W. Graves, eds., *Na Mea Kahiko o Kauaʻi: Archaeological Studies in Kauaʻi,* pp. 62–65. Society for Hawaiian Archaeology Special Publication No. 2. Honolulu: Society for Hawaiian Archaeology.

———. 2005e. Koʻolau District. In M. T. Carson and M. W. Graves, eds., *Na Mea Kahiko o Kauaʻi: Archaeological Studies in Kauaʻi,* pp. 72–73. Society for Hawaiian Archaeology Special Publication No. 2. Honolulu: Society for Hawaiian Archaeology.

———. 2006. Archaeological data collection at sites 50-10-05-24053 and -24055 in the Pelekane Area of Puʻukoholā Heiau National Historic Site, Kawaihae 2 Ahupuaʻa, South Kohala District, Island of Hawaiʻi. Unpublished report. Honolulu, HI: International Archaeological Research Institute.

Carson, M. T., and J. S. Athens. 2006. Archaeological monitoring and data recovery at Kualoa Regional Park, Kualoa Ahupuaʻa, Koʻolaupoko District, Oʻahu Island, Hawaiʻi. Unpublished report. Honolulu, HI: International Archaeological Research Institute.

———. 2007. Integration of coastal geomorphology, mythology, and archaeological evidence at Kualoa Beach, Windward Oʻahu, Hawaiian Islands. *Journal of Coastal and Island Archaeology* 2:24–43.

Carson, M. T., H. Hung, G. Summerhayes, and P. Bellwood. 2013. The pottery trail from Southeast Asia to Remote Oceania. *Journal of Island and Coastal Archaeology* 8:17–36.

Carson, M. T., and M. A. Mintmier. 2006. Radiocarbon chronology of prehistoric campsites in alpine and subalpine zones at Haleakalā, Maui Island, USA. *Radiocarbon* 48:227–236.

———. 2007. Archaeological survey of previously recorded sites in front country areas in the summit district of Haleakalā National Park, Maui Island, Hawaiʻi. Unpublished report. Honolulu, HI: International Archaeological Research Institute.

Carson, M. T., and R. Reeve. 2008. Archeological inventory survey of portions of the Kīpahulu Unit of Haleakalā National Park, Maui Island, State of Hawaiʻi. Unpublished report. Honolulu, HI: International Archaeological Research Institute.

Carter, L. A., and G. F. Somers. 1990. *Here Today, Lava Tomorrow: Archaeological Work in Hawaii Volcanoes National Park, 1987 to 1989.* Honolulu, HI: National Park Service.

Chang, K. C. 1967. *Rethinking Archaeology.* New York: Random House.

Chapman, P. S., and P. V. Kirch. 1979. *Archaeological Excavations at Seven Sites, Southeast Maui, Hawaiian Islands.* Department of Anthropology Report 79-1. Honolulu, HI: Bernice P. Bishop Museum.

Chappel, H. G. 1927. *Jaws and Teeth of Ancient Hawaiians.* Bernice P. Bishop Museum Memoir, vol. 9, part 3. Honolulu, HI: Bishop Museum Press.

Chinen, J. J. 1958. *The Great Mahele: Hawaii's Land Division of 1848.* Honolulu: University of Hawaiʻi Press.

Ching, F. K. W. 1971. *The Archaeology of South Kohala and North Kona: Surface Survey, Kailua-Kawaihae Road corridor.* Hawaii State Archaeological Journal 71-1. Honolulu: Department of Land and Natural Resources, State of Hawaii.

Ching, F. K. W., S. Palama, and C. Stauder, 1974. *The Archaeology of Kona, Kauaʻi: Na Ahupuaʻa Weliweli, Paʻa, Mahaʻulepu, Surface Survey of Coastal Lands.* Hawaiian Archaeological Journal 74-1. Lawaʻi, Kauaʻi: Archaeological Research Center Hawaii.

Chorover, J., and O. A. Chadwick. 2001. The chemistry of pedogenic thresholds. *Geoderma* 100:321–353.

Christensen, C. C. 1983. Analysis of land snails. In J. T. Clark and P. V. Kirch, eds., *Archaeological Investigations of the Mudlane-Waimea-Kawaihae Road Corridor, Island of Hawaiʻi,* pp. 449–471. Department of Anthropology Report 83-1. Honolulu, HI: Bernice P. Bishop Museum.

Christensen, C., and P. V. Kirch. 1986. Non-marine mollusks and ecological change at Barbers Point, Oʻahu, Hawaiʻi. *Bishop Museum Occasional Papers* 26:52–80. Honolulu, HI: Bishop Museum Press.

Christophersen, E., and E. L. Caum. 1931. *Vascular Plants of the Leeward Islands, Hawaii.* Bernice P. Bishop Museum Bulletin 81. Honolulu, HI: Bishop Museum Press.

Chun, A., and D. D. Dillon. 2010. Archaeological inventory survey report for a 3.75-acre lot in Haʻiku, Maui. Unpublished report. Wailuku: Archaeological Services Hawaii, LLC.

Clague, D. A., and G. B. Dalrymple. 1987. The Hawaiian-Emperor volcanic chain. Part 1, Geologic evolution. In R. W. Decker, T. L. Wright, and P. H. Stauffer, eds., *Volcanism in Hawaiʻi,* pp. 5–54. Washington, DC: Government Printing Office.

Clapp, R. B., and E. Kridler. 1977. *The Natural History of Necker Island, Northwestern Hawaiian Islands.* Atoll Research Bulletin 206. Washington, DC: Smithsonian Institution.

Clapp, R. B., E. Kridler, and R. R. Fleet. 1977. *The Natural History of Nihoa Island, Northwestern Hawaiian Islands.* Atoll Research Bulletin 207. Washington, DC: Smithsonian Institution.

Clark, D. T., and J. F. Balicki. 1987. Preliminary research report: The Maui archaeology project of Waiheʻe. Unpublished report. Washington, DC: The Catholic University of America, Department of Anthropology.

Clark, J. T. 1981. Archaeological survey of the proposed Lālāmilo Agricultural Park, South Kohala, Island of Hawaiʻi. Unpublished report in Library, Bernice P. Bishop Museum. Honolulu.

Clark, J. T., and P. V. Kirch, eds. 1983. *Archaeological Investigations of the Mudlane-Waimea Kawaihae Road Corridor, Island of Hawaiʻi: An Interdisciplinary Study of an Environmental Transect.* Department of Anthropology Report 83-1. Honolulu, HI: Bernice P. Bishop Museum.

Clark, R. 1979. Language. In J. Jennings, ed., *The Prehistory of Polynesia,* pp. 249–270. Cambridge, MA: Harvard University Press.

Clarke, A. C., M. K. Burtenshaw, P. A. McLenachan, D. L. Erickson, and D. Penny. 2006. Reconstructing the origins and dispersal of the Polynesian bottle gourd (*Lagenaria siceraria*). *Molecular Biology and Evolution* 23:893–900.

Clarke, D. 1968. *Analytical Archaeology.* London: Methuen.

Clarkson, C., C. Shipton, and M. I. Weisler. 2014. Determining the reduction sequence of Hawaiian quadrangular adzes using 3D approaches: A case study from Molokaʻi. *Journal of Archaeological Science* 49:361–371.

———. 2015. Front, back, and sides: Experimental replication and archaeological analysis of Hawaiian adzes and associated debitage. *Archaeology in Oceania* 50:71–84.

Cleghorn, J. N. J. 1987. Hawaiian burial reconsidered: An archaeological analysis. Unpublished Master's thesis, University of Hawaiʻi at Mānoa.

Cleghorn, P. L. 1975. Phase I archaeological research at the Seamen's Hospital (Site D5-10), Lahaina, Maui. Unpublished report in Library, Bernice P. Bishop Museum. Honolulu.

———. 1980. *The Hilina Pali Petroglyph Cave, Hawaiʻi Island: A Report on Preliminary Archaeological Investigations.* Department of Anthropology Report 80-1. Honolulu, HI: Bernice P. Bishop Museum.

———. 1982. The Mauna Kea Adze Quarry: Technological analyses and experimental tests. PhD diss., University of Hawaiʻi at Mānoa.

———. 1983. Summary report on archaeological investigations in Waipio Valley, Hawaii Island. Unpublished report in Library, Bernice P. Bishop Museum. Honolulu.

———. 1986. Organizational structure at the Mauna Kea Adze Quarry Complex, Hawaiʻi. *Journal of Archaeological Science* 13:375–387.

———. 1988. The settlement and abandonment of two Hawaiian outposts: Nihoa and Necker Islands. *Bishop Museum Occasional Papers* 28:35–49. Honolulu, HI: Bishop Museum Press.

———. 1992. A Hawaiian adze sequence or just different kinds of adzes? *New Zealand Journal of Archaeology* 14:129–149.

Cleghorn, P. L., and L. Anderson. 1992. Archaeological inventory survey in Manoa Valley, Oʻahu (TMK: 2-9-19-36) and Preservation Plan for Kukaoʻo Heiau. Unpublished report prepared for Samuel A. Cooke. Kailua, HI: Paul Cleghorn Consulting.

Cleghorn, P. L., and D. W. Cox. 1976. Phase I archaeological survey of the Hilina Pali Petroglyph Cave (Site HV-383). Unpublished report in Library, Bernice P. Bishop Museum. Honolulu.

Cleghorn, P. L., T. Dye, M. Weisler, and J. Sinton. 1985. A preliminary petrographic study of Hawaiian stone adze quarries. *Journal of the Polynesian Society* 94:235–252.

Cleghorn, P. L., and E. Rogers-Jourdane. 1983. Archaeological and historical research in Waipiʻo Valley, Hamakua District. Hawaiʻi Island. Unpublished report in Library, Bernice P. Bishop Museum. Honolulu.

Cline, M. G., et al. 1955. *Soil Survey of the Territory of Hawaii.* Soil Survey Series 1939, no. 25. Washington, DC: US Department of Agriculture.

Cluff, D. F. 1969. *An Archaeological Survey of the Seaward Portion of Honokohau #1 and #2, North Kona, Hawaii Island.* Department of Anthropology Report 69-5. Honolulu, HI: Bernice P. Bishop Museum.

Cluff, D. F., W. K. Kikuchi, R. A. Apple, and Y. H. Sinoto. 1969. *The Archaeological Surface Survey of Puu Kohola Heiau and Mailekini Heiau, South Kohala, Kawaihae, Hawaii Island.* Hawaii State Archaeological Journal 69-3. Honolulu: Department of Land and Natural Resources, State of Hawaii.

Cobb, J. N. 1902. Commercial Fisheries of the Hawaiian Islands. *U.S. Fish Commission Report for 1901,* pp. 353–499. Washington, DC: Government Printer.

Coil, J. 2003. Design, methods, and initial results for microfossil research in Kahikinui, Maui, Hawaiian Islands. In D. M. Hart and L. A. Wallis, eds., *Phytolith and Starch Research in the Australian-Pacific Asian Regions: The State of the Art,* pp. 55–68. Canberra: Pandanus Books.

———. 2004. "The beauty that was": Archaeological investigations of ancient Hawaiian agriculture and environmental change in Kahikinui, Maui. PhD diss., University of California, Berkeley.

Coil, J., and P. V. Kirch. 2005. An Ipomoean landscape: Archaeology and the sweet potato in Kahikinui, Maui, Hawaiian Islands. In C. Ballard, P. Brown, R. M. Bourke, and T. Harwood, eds., *The Sweet Potato in Oceania: A Reappraisal,* pp. 71–84. Oceania Monograph No. 56. Sydney, Australia: University of Sydney.

Collerson, K. D., and M. I. Weisler. 2007. Stone adze compositions and the extent of ancient Polynesian voyaging and trade. *Science* 317:1907–1911.

Collins, S. 1995. Avifaunal remains from the Kawailoa site, Oʻahu Island (BPBM Site 50-OA-D6-62). *Hawaiian Archaeology* 4:4–16.

Collins, S., T. Han, and L. Armstrong. 1993. Inventory of human skeletal remains from Mokapu Peninsula, Koʻolaupoko District, Kaneʻohe and Heʻeia Ahupuaʻa, Oʻahu Island, Hawaiʻi. Unpublished report prepared for Naval Facilities Engineering Command. Honolulu, HI: Bernice P. Bishop Museum.

Conte, E., and G. Molle. 2014. Reinvestigating a key site for Polynesian prehistory: New results from the Hane dune site, Ua Huka (Marquesas). *Archaeology in Oceania* 49:121–136.

Cook, J., and J. King. 1784. *A Voyage to the Pacific Ocean, Undertaken by the Command of His Majesty for Making Discoveries in the Northern Hemisphere.* London: W. and A. Strahan for G. Nichol.

Corbin, A. B. 2003. Archaeological mitigation, Kuilima Resort Expansion Project. Lands of Kahuku, Kawela, and ʻŌpana, Koʻolauloa District, Island of Oʻahu. Unpublished report. Hilo, HI: Paul H. Rosendahl.

———. 2005. Archaeological data recovery excavations at Site 2005, Feature A and associated cultural deposits, land of Puaʻa 1st, North Kona District Island of Hawaiʻi. Unpublished report. Hilo, HI: Paul H. Rosendahl.

Cordy, R. H. 1970. *Piilanihale Heiau Project, Phase I Site Report.* Department of Anthropology Report 70-9. Honolulu, HI: Bernice P. Bishop Museum.

———. 1974a. Cultural adaptation and evolution in Hawaii: A suggested new sequence. *Journal of the Polynesian Society* 83:180–191.

———. 1974b. Complex rank cultural systems in the Hawaiian Islands: Suggested explanations for their origin. *Archaeology and Physical Anthropology in Oceania* 9:89–109.

———. 1974c. The Tahitian migration to Hawaii ca. 1100–1300 A.D.: An argument against its occurrence. *New Zealand Archaeological Association Newsletter* 17:65–76.

———. 1975. Hawaiian activity sets: Initial results of R-mode multivariate statistical analyses. *New Zealand Archaeological Association Newsletter* 18:59–75.

———. 1981. *A Study of Prehistoric Social Change: The Development of Complex Societies in the Hawaiian Islands.* New York: Academic Press.

———. 1995. Central Kona archaeological settlement patterns. Unpublished report. Honolulu, HI: State Historic Preservation Division.

———. 1996. The rise and fall of the Oʻahu kingdom: A brief overview of Oʻahu's history. In J. Davidson, G. Irwin, F. Leach, A. Pawley, and D. Brown, eds., *Oceanic Culture History: Essays in Honour of Roger Green,* pp. 591–613. Dunedin: New Zealand Journal of Archaeology Special Publication.

———. 1999. Thoughts from the chaotic midst of Hawaiian archaeology. *Hawaiian Archaeology* 7:82–89.

———. 2000a. *Exalted Sits the Chief: The Ancient History of Hawai'i Island*. Honolulu, HI: Mutual Publishing.

———. 2000b. *The Rise and Fall of the O'ahu Kingdom*. Honolulu, HI: Mutual Publishing.

———. 2004. Considering archaeological indicators of the rise of appointed chiefs and the feudal-land system in the Hawaiian Islands. *Hawaiian Archaeology* 9:1–24.

Cordy, R. H., and M. W. Kaschko. 1980. Prehistoric archaeology in the Hawaiian Islands: Land units associated with social groups. *Journal of Field Archaeology* 7:403–416.

Cordy, R. H., E. Komori, and K. Shun. 2005. Archaeological work in Waipi'o Valley, Hāmākua District, Hawai'i Island. *Hawaiian Archaeology* 10:70–95.

Cordy, R. H., J. Tainter, R. Renger, and R. Hitchcock. 1991. *An Ahupua'a Study: The 1971 Archaeological Work at Kaloko Ahupua'a North Kona, Hawai'i: Archaeology at Kaloko-Honokohau National Historical Park*. Tucson, AZ: Western Archeological and Conservation Center.

Cordy, R. H., and H. D. Tuggle. 1976. Bellows, Oahu, Hawaiian Islands: New work and new interpretations. *Archaeology and Physical Anthropology in Oceania* 11:207–235.

Costin, C. L. 1991. Craft specialization: Issues in defining, documenting, and explaining the organization of production. In M. B. Schiffer, ed., *Archaeological Method and Theory*, vol. 3, pp. 1–56. Tucson: University of Arizona Press.

Costin, C. L., and R. P. Wright, eds. 1998. *Craft and Social Identity*. American Anthropological Association, Anthropological Papers 8. Arlington, VA: American Anthropological Assocation.

Coulter, J. W. 1931. *Population and Utilization of Land and Sea in Hawaii, 1853*. Bernice P. Bishop Museum Bulletin 88. Honolulu, HI: Bernice P. Bishop Museum.

Cox, D. W. 1974. Fieldwork report on mapping of Puuloa petroglyph field—Puna Site HA-HV-225. Unpublished report in Library, Bernice P. Bishop Museum. Honolulu.

Cox, J. H., and E. Stasack. 1970. *Hawaiian Petroglyphs*. Bernice P. Bishop Museum Special Publication 60. Honolulu, HI: Bishop Museum Press.

———. 1998. *Hawaiian Petroglyphs*. 2nd ed. Bernice P. Bishop Museum Special Publication 60. Honolulu, HI: Bishop Museum Press.

Crozier, S. N. 1971a. *Archaeological Survey of Kamehameha III Road, North Kona, Island of Hawaii*. Department of Anthropology Report 71-5. Honolulu, HI: Bernice P. Bishop Museum.

———. 1971b. *Archaeological Excavations at Kamehameha III Road, North Kona, Island of Hawaii, Phase II*. Department of Anthropology Report 71-11. Honolulu, HI: Bernice P. Bishop Museum.

———. 1972. A preliminary report on the Phase II, Part 2 survey of H3 Highway corridor in the South Halawa Valley, Oahu. Unpublished report in Library, Bernice P. Bishop Museum. Honolulu.

———. 1974. Precontact archaeological contrasts of three valley systems on Oahu, Hawaii. Master's thesis, University of Victoria, British Columbia.

Curtis, D. B. 1995. *The Hawaiian Carved Stone Image Bowl*. Bishop Museum Bulletins in Anthropology 6. Honolulu, HI: Bishop Museum Press.

Dagher, C. A., and R. L. Spear. 2013. An archaeological inventory survey for the Kamehameha Schools Community Learning Center at Mā'ili, Lualualei Ahupua'a, Wai'anae District, Island of O'ahu, Hawai'i. Unpublished report. Honolulu, HI: Scientific Consultant Services.

Dalton, G. 1960. A note of clarification on economic surplus. *American Anthropologist* 62:483–490.

Danielsson, B. 1967. Kia Ora Keneti. In G. A. Highland et al., eds., *Polynesian Culture History*, pp. 1–36. Bernice P. Bishop Museum Special Publication 56. Honolulu, HI: Bishop Museum Press.

Da Silva, A. M., and R. K. Johnson. 1982. Ahu a 'Umi Heiau: A Native Hawaiian astronomical and directional register. *Annals of the New York Academy of Sciences* 385:313–331.

Davenport, W. H. 1994. *Pi'o: An Enquiry into the Marriage of Brothers and Sisters and Other Close Relatives in Old Hawai'i*. Lanham, MD: University Press of America.

Davis, E. H. 1979. *Abraham Fornander: A Biography*. Honolulu: University of Hawai'i Press.

Dean, J. 1978. Independent dating in archaeological analysis. In M. Schiffer, ed., *Advances in Archaeological Method and Theory*, vol. 1, pp. 223–265. New York: Academic Press.

De Brosses, C. 1756. *Histoire des Navigations aux Terres Australes*. Paris: Durand.

Deetz, J. 1977. *In Small Things Forgotten: The Archaeology of Early American Life*. New York: Anchor Books.

Dega, M. 2011. A Tale of Two Heiau: Maui and Hawai'i Island. Paper presented at 24th Annual Society for Hawaiian Archaeology Conference, University of Hawai'i Maui College, September 30–October 2.

Dega, M., and P. V. Kirch. 2002. A modified culture history of Anahulu Valley, O'ahu, Hawai'i, and its significance for Hawaiian prehistory. *Journal of the Polynesian Society* 111:107–126.

Dega, M. F., and L. McGerty. 1998. Cultural resources inventory survey and limited testing of the Kawailoa Training Area for the preparation of a cultural resource management plan for U.S. Army training ranges and areas, O'ahu Island, Hawai'i. Unpublished report. Honolulu, HI: Scientific Consultant Services.

———. 2002. A cultural resources inventory survey, Phase II, of the U.S. Army Kawailoa Training Area (KLOA), for the U.S. Garrison, Hawai'i, Ecosystem Management Program, O'ahu Island, Hawai'i: Traditional and historic settlement of the Kawailoa Uplands. Unpublished report. Honolulu, HI: Scientific Consultant Services.

Dega, M. F., L. Morawski, and C. Monahan. 2004. The archaeology of Upland Kēōkea: An archaeological data recovery report for the Department of Hawaiian Homelands (DHHL) Kula Residential Lots, Unit 1 of the Kēōkea Subdivision, Kēōkea Ahupua'a, Makawao District, Maui Island, Hawai'i. Unpublished report. Honolulu, HI: Scientific Consultant Services.

DeMarrais, E., L. J. Castillo, and T. Earle. 1996. Ideology, materialization, and power strategies. *Current Anthropology* 37:15–31.

Denham, T. 2011. Early agriculture and plant domestication in New Guinea and Island Southeast Asia. *Current Anthropology* 52 (S4): S3479–S395.

Denham, T., F. J. Eble, B. Winsborough, and J. V. Ward. 1999. Paleoenvironmental and archaeological investigations at 'Ohi'apilo Pond, leeward coast of Moloka'i, Hawai'i. *Hawaiian Archaeology* 7:35–59.

Denham, T., C. B. Ramsey, and J. Specht. 2012. Dating the appearance of Lapita pottery in the Bismarck Archipelago and its dispersal to remote Oceania. *Archaeology in Oceania* 47:39–46.

Denison, D., and A. S. Forman. 1971. *Archaeological Investigations in South Halawa Valley, Ewa District, Island of Oahu, Phase II*. Department of Anthropology Report 71-9. Honolulu, HI: Bernice P. Bishop Museum.

Diaz, H. F., E. R. Wahl, E. Zorita, T. W. Giambelluca, and J. K. Eischeid. 2016. A five-century reconstruction of Hawaiian Islands winter rainfall. *Journal of Climate* 29:5661–5674.

DiNapoli, R. J., and A. E. Morrison. 2017. A spatiotemporal model of risk and uncertainty for Hawaiian dryland agriculture and its implications for *ahupua'a* community formation. *Journal of Archaeological Science: Reports* 15:109–119.

DiVito, N. J., T. S. Dye, K. Elkington, J. L. Gunness, E. Hellebrand, E. Jourdane, S. Lundblad, N. Mello, P. R. Mills, and J. M. Sinton. 2020. Volcanic glass at Kualoa, O'ahu, Hawaiian

Islands: Paired technological and geochemical sourcing analyses of an expedient tool industry. *Journal of Archaeological Science: Reports* 30:102117.

Dixon, B., A. Carpenter, F. Eble, C. Mitchell, and M. Major. 1995. Community growth and heiau construction: Possible evidence of political hegemony at the site of Kaunolu, Lana'i, Hawai'i. *Asian Perspectives* 34:229–256.

Dixon, B., P. J. Conte, V. Curtis, and W. K. Hodgins. 2005. A late pre-contact domestic habitation area and garden in Anahola Ahupua'a, Ko'olau District, Kaua'i. In M. T. Carson and M. W. Graves, eds., *Na Mea Kahiko o Kaua'i: Archaeological Studies in Kaua'i,* pp. 74–105. Society for Hawaiian Archaeology Special Publication No. 2. Honolulu: Society for Hawaiian Archaeology.

Dixon, B., P. J. Conte, V. Nagahara, and W. K. Hodgins. 1997a. Upland forest periphery subsistence and settlement in the Ahupua'a of Kipapa, Nakaohu, and Nakaaha: A preliminary assessment. In P. V. Kirch, ed., *Na Mea Kahiko o Kahikinui: Studies in the Archaeology of Kahikinui, Maui, Hawaiian Islands,* pp. 28–43. Berkeley, CA: Archaeological Research Facility.

———. 1997b. An archaeological inventory survey of the Anahola Subdivision G and G-1, Anahola Ahupua'a, Kawaihau District, Kaua'i. Unpublished report. Honolulu: Department of Hawaiian Home Lands.

———. 1998. A newly discovered *holua* sledding complex in Kahikinui, Maui, and its context. In C. M. Stevenson, G. Lee, and F. J. Morin, eds., *Easter Island in Pacific Context: South Seas Symposium,* pp. 264–270. Los Osos, CA: Easter Island Foundation.

———. 1999. Risk minimization and the traditional *ahupua'a* in Kahikinui, Island of Maui, Hawai'i. *Asian Perspectives* 38:229–254.

———. 2002. Settlement patterns and subsistence strategies in Kahikinui, Maui. *Hawaiian Archaeology* 8:12–32.

Dixon, B., D. Gosser, and S. S. Williams. 2008. Traditional Hawaiian men's houses and their socio-political context in Lualualei, leeward West O'ahu, Hawai'i. *Journal of the Polynesian Society* 117:267–295.

Dixon, B., and M. Major. 1992. Kapukahehu to Pu'uhakina: An archaeological inventory survey of Southwest Moloka'i, Hawaii. Unpublished report in Library, Bernice P. Bishop Museum. Honolulu.

———. 2011. Floodwater farming of ritual offerings at Kaunolū and Māmaki on leeward Lāna'i, Hawai'i. *Hawaiian Archaeology* 12:27–46.

Dixon, B., M. Major, M. Price, A. Carpenter, C. Stine, and B. Longton. 1994. Lithic tool production and dryland planting adaptations to regional agricultural intensification: Preliminary evidence from leeward Moloka'i, Hawai'i. *Bishop Museum Occasional Papers* 39:1–19. Honolulu, HI: Bishop Museum Press.

Dixon, B., D. Soldo, and C. C. Christensen. 1997. Radiocarbon dating land snails and Polynesian land use on the island of Kaua'i, Hawai'i. *Hawaiian Archaeology* 6:52–62.

Dockall, J. E., H. H. Leidemann, and D. I. Olszewski. 2001. Trajectories of change in the nineteenth century: Waipio Valley, Hawaii, and Kalihi-Kapalama, Oahu. Unpublished report in Library, Bernice P. Bishop Museum. Honolulu.

Donham, T. K. 1989. Interim Report—Kapalua Mitigation Program: Data recovery excavations at the Honokahua Burial Site. Unpublished report. Hilo, HI: Paul H. Rosendahl.

———. 2000. Data recovery excavations at the Honokahua Burial Site. Unpublished report prepared for Kapalua Land. Hilo, HI: Paul H. Rosendahl.

———. 2002. Underwater archaeological inventory survey of Kō'ie'ie Fishpond (State and National Register Site No. 50-50-09-1288), Ka'ono'ulu Ahupua'a, Kula District, Kīhei, Maui (TMK: [2]-3-9-01). Unpublished report. Kīhei: Akahele Archaeology.

Donham, T. K., S. T. Goodfellow, and P. H. Rosendahl. 1992. Additional archeological subsurface testing, proposed Waihee Golf Club Project. Unpublished report prepared for Waihee Oceanfront Hawaii. Hilo, HI: Paul H. Rosendahl.

Dorn, R. I. 1996. [Letter report on radiocarbon dates for Puʻuloa Petroglyphs] Letter of July 22, from Dorn, Arizona State University, to Dr. Don Marshall, Peabody Essex Museum. MS on file, Hawaiʻi Volcanoes National Park, Volcano.

Duff, R. 1959. Neolithic adzes of Eastern Polynesia. In J. D. Freeman and W. R. Geddes, eds., *Anthropology in the South Seas,* pp. 121–147. New Plymouth, New Zealand: Thomas Avery and Sons.

Dunmore, J., ed. 1994. *The Journal of Jean-François de Galaup de la Pérouse, 1785–1788.* 2 vols. London: The Hakluyt Society.

Dunn, A., M. T. Carson, M. F. Dega, and R. L. Spear. 1999. Archaeological data recovery of the DHHL Kula Residential Lots, Unit 1 of Waiohuli Subdivision, Waiohuli, Kula, Maui Island, Hawaiʻi. Unpublished report. Honolulu, HI: Scientific Consultant Services.

Durst, M. 2002. A cooperative archaeological excavation project at the John Young Homestead, Puʻukohola National Historic Site, Kawaihae 2, South Kohala, Island of Hawaiʻi. Unpublished report. Honolulu, HI: National Park Service.

Dye, T. S. 1989. Tales of two cultures: Traditional historical and archaeological interpretations of Hawaiian prehistory. *Bishop Museum Occasional Papers* 29:3–22. Honolulu, HI: Bishop Museum Press.

———. 1992. The South Point radiocarbon dates thirty years later. *New Zealand Journal of Archaeology* 14:89–97.

———. 1994. Population trends in Hawaiʻi before 1778. *Hawaiian Journal of History* 28:1–20.

———. 1998. Archaeological inventory survey for the Kūlana, ʻŌiwi Multi-Services Center Project, Kalamaʻula, Kona, Molokaʻi. Unpublished report. Honolulu, HI: International Archaeological Research Institute.

———. 2010a. Social transformation in old Hawaii: A bottom-up approach. *American Antiquity* 75:727–741.

———. 2010b. Traditional Hawaiian surface architecture: Absolute and relative dating. In T. S. Dye, ed., *Research Designs for Hawaiian Archaeology,* pp. 93–156. Society for Hawaiian Archaeology Special Publication 3. Honolulu: Society for Hawaiian Archaeology.

———. 2011a. A model-based age estimate for Polynesian colonization of Hawaiʻi. *Archaeology in Oceania* 46:130–138.

———. 2011b. Contemporary practice of archaeology in Hawaiʻi. *Hawaiian Archaeology* 12:125–142.

———. 2011c. The tempo of change in the leeward Kohala field system, Hawaiʻi Island. *Rapa Nui Journal* 25:21–30.

———. 2014a. Wealth in old Hawaiʻi: Good-year economics and the rise of pristine states. *Archaeology in Oceania* 49:59–85.

———. 2014b. Structure and growth of the leeward Kohala field system: An analysis with directed graphs. *PLOS ONE* 9 (7): e102431.

———. 2015. Dating human dispersal in Remote Oceania: A Bayesian view from Hawaiʻi. *World Archaeology* 47:661–676.

Dye, T. S., ed. 2010. *Research Designs for Hawaiian Archaeology: Agriculture, Architecture, Methodology.* Society for Hawaiian Archaeology Special Publication 3. Honolulu: Society for Hawaiian Archaeology.

Dye, T. S., and J. M. Bayman. 2013. *Hawaii's Past in a World of Pacific Islands.* Washington, DC: Society for American Archaeology Press.

Dye, T. S., M. T. Carson, and M. J. Tomonari-Tuggle. 2002. Archaeological survey of sixty acres of the Kīpahulu Historic District within the Kīpahulu District of Haleakalā National Park, Maui. Unpublished report. Honolulu, HI: International Archaeological Research Institute.

Dye, T. S., and E. Komori. 1992. A pre-censal population history of Hawaii. *New Zealand Journal of Archaeology* 14:113–128.

Dye, T. S., and J. J. Pantaleo. 2010. Age of the O18 Site, Hawai'i. *Archaeology in Oceania* 45:113–119.

Dye, T. S., and C. E. Sholin. 2013. Changing patterns of firewood use on the Waimānalo Plain. *Hawaiian Archaeology* 13:30–68.

Dye, T. S., M. I. Weisler, and M. Riford. 1985. Adze quarries on Moloka'i and O'ahu, Hawaiian Islands. Unpublished report in Library, Bernice P. Bishop Museum. Honolulu.

Earle, T. K. 1977. A reappraisal of redistribution: Complex Hawaiian chiefdoms. In T. Earle and J. Erikson, eds., *Exchange Systems in Prehistory,* pp. 213–229. New York: Academic Press.

———. 1978. *Economic and Social Organization of a Complex Chiefdom: The Halele'a District, Kaua'i, Hawai'i.* Anthropological Papers of the Museum of Anthropology, University of Michigan, no. 63. Ann Arbor.

———. 1980. Prehistoric irrigation in the Hawaiian Islands: An evaluation of evolutionary significance. *Archaeology and Physical Anthropology in Oceania* 15:1–28.

———. 1987. Specialization and the production of wealth: Hawaiian chiefdoms and the Inka empire. In T. K. Earle and E. M. Brumfiel, eds., *Specialization, Exchange, and Complex Societies,* pp. 64–75. Cambridge: Cambridge University Press.

———. 1997. *How Chiefs Come to Power: The Political Economy in Prehistory.* Stanford, CA: Stanford University Press.

———. 2012. Irrigation and primary state formation in Hawai'i. In M. Spriggs, D. Addison, and P. J. Mathews, eds., *Irrigated Taro* (Colocasia esculenta) *in the Indo-Pacific,* pp. 95–114. Senri Ethnological Studies 78. Osaka, Japan.

Earle, T., and M. Spriggs. 2015. Political economy in prehistory: A Marxist approach to Pacific sequences. *Current Anthropology* 56:515–544.

Eblé, F. J., and P. L. Cleghorn. 1995. Report of archaeological reconnaissance survey conducted at the Hawaii National Guard Kanaio Training Area, on the Island of Maui, State of Hawaii. Unpublished report. Kailua, Hawai'i: BioSystems Analysis.

Edmonson, C. H. 1946. *Reef and Shore Fauna of Hawaii.* Bernice P. Bishop Museum Special Publication 22. Honolulu, HI: Bishop Museum Press.

Elbert, S. 1953. Internal relationships of Polynesian languages and dialects. *Southwestern Journal of Anthropology* 9:147–173.

———. 1982. Lexical diffusion in Polynesia and the Marquesan-Hawaiian relationship. *Journal of the Polynesian Society* 91:499–518.

Ellis, W. 1963. *Journal of William Ellis.* Honolulu, HI: Advertiser Publishing. Reprint of 1827 London edition.

Emory, K. P. 1921. An archaeological survey of Haleakala. *Bishop Museum Occasional Papers* 7:237–259. Honolulu, HI: Bishop Museum Press.

———. 1924. *The Island of Lanai: A Survey of Native Culture.* Bernice P. Bishop Museum Bulletin 12. Honolulu, HI: Bishop Museum Press.

———. 1928. *Archaeology of Nihoa and Necker Islands.* Bernice P. Bishop Museum Bulletin 53. Honolulu, HI: Bishop Museum Press.

———. 1933. *Stone Remains in the Society Islands.* Bernice P. Bishop Museum Bulletin 116. Honolulu, HI: Bishop Museum Press.

———. 1934a. *Tuamotuan Stone Structures.* Bernice P. Bishop Museum Bulletin 118. Honolulu, HI: Bishop Museum Press.

———. 1934b. *Archaeology of the Pacific Equatorial Islands.* Bernice P. Bishop Museum Bulletin 123. Honolulu, HI: Bishop Museum Press.

———. 1947. *Tuamotuan Religious Structures and Ceremonies.* Bernice P. Bishop Museum Bulletin 191. Honolulu, HI: Bishop Museum Press.

———. 1968. East Polynesian relationships as revealed through adzes. In I. Yawata and Y. Sinoto, eds., *Prehistoric Culture in Oceania,* pp. 151–169. Honolulu, HI: Bishop Museum Press.

Emory, K. P., W. J. Bonk, and Y. H. Sinoto. 1959. *Hawaiian Archaeology: Fishhooks.* Bernice P. Bishop Museum Special Publication 47. Honolulu, HI: Bishop Museum Press.

———. 1969. *Waiahukini Shelter, Site H8, Ka'u, Hawaii.* Pacific Anthropological Records 7. Honolulu, HI: Bernice P. Bishop Museum.

Emory, K. P., P. C. McCoy, and D. B. Barrère. 1971. *Archaeological Survey: Kahaluu and Keauhou, North Kona, Hawaii.* Department of Anthropology Report 71-4. Honolulu, HI: Bernice P. Bishop Museum.

Emory, K. P., and Y. H. Sinoto. 1961. *Hawaiian Archaeology: Oahu Excavations.* Bernice P. Bishop Museum Special Publication 49. Honolulu, HI: Bishop Museum Press.

———. 1965. Preliminary report on the archaeological excavations in Polynesia. Mimeographed report prepared for the National Science Foundation; copy in Library, Bernice P. Bishop Museum. Honolulu.

———. 1969. *Age of Sites in the South Point Area, Ka'u, Hawaii.* Pacific Anthropological Records 8. Honolulu, HI: Bernice P. Bishop Museum.

Emory, K. P., and L. J. Soehren. 1961. *Archaeological and Historical Survey, Honokahau Area, North Kona, Hawaii.* Department of Anthropology Report 61-1. Honolulu, HI: Bernice P. Bishop Museum.

Emory, K. P., J. F. G. Stokes, D. B. Barrère, and M. A. Kelly. 1957. The natural and cultural history of Honaunau, Kona, Hawaii. Mimeographed report prepared for the National Park Service. 2 vols. Copy in Library, Bernice P. Bishop Museum. Honolulu.

Esh, K. S. 2015. Avifauna from Nu'alolo Kai. In J. S. Field and M. W. Graves, eds., *Abundance and Resilience: Farming and Foraging in Ancient Kaua'i,* pp. 75–106. Honolulu: University of Hawai'i Press.

Estioko-Griffin, A., and G. W. Lovelace. 1980. Patterns of coastal adaptation in the Ahupua'a of Keawa'ula: The archaeology of Site 50-80-03-2802. Unpublished report, Division of Historic Sites, Department of Land and Natural Resources, State of Hawaii. Honolulu.

Field, J. S., and M. W. Graves. 2008. A new chronology for Pololu Valley, Hawai'i Island: Occupational history and agricultural development. *Radiocarbon* 50:205–222.

Field, J. S., and M. W. Graves, eds. 2015. *Abundance and Resilience: Farming and Foraging in Ancient Kauai.* Honolulu: University of Hawai'i Press.

Field, J. S., J. G. Kahn, P. V. Kirch, and T. N. Ladefoged. 2009. Archaeological Survey and Excavations of Makiloa and Kālala Ahupua'a, Kohala, Hawai'i Island. Unpublished report.

Field, J. S., P. V. Kirch, K. Kawelu, and T. N. Ladefoged. 2010. Households and hierarchy: Domestic modes of production in leeward Kohala, Hawai'i Island. *Journal of Island and Coastal Archaeology* 5:52–85.

Field, J. S., T. N. Ladefoged, and P. V. Kirch. 2011. Household expansion linked to agricultural intensification during emergence of Hawaiian archaic states. *Proceedings of the National Academy of Sciences of the United States of America* 108:7327–7332.

Field, J. S., T. N. Ladefoged, W. D. Sharp, and P. V. Kirch. 2011. Residential chronology, household subsistence, and the emergence of socioeconomic territories in leeward Kohala, Hawai'i Island. *Radiocarbon* 53:605–627.

Field, J. S., J. N. Lipphardt, and P. V. Kirch. 2016. Trends in marine foraging in precontact and historic leeward Kohala, Hawai'i Island. *Pacific Science* 70:287–307.

Filimoehala, C. W., and A. E. Morrison. 2020. The bird hunters of Hawai'i Island's Saddle Region: Archaeological inventory survey in Training Area 23, U.S. Army Pōhakuloa Training Area, Hawai'i Island, Hawai'i. Unpublished report. Honolulu, HI: International Archaeology, LLC.

Filimoehala, D., S. Howard, T. Duarte, S. Lundblad, and P. Mills. 2015. Hematite in Hawai'i: Analyzing the distribution of an uncommon lithic tool material. *Hawaiian Archaeology* 14:1–16.

Finney, B. R. 1994. *Voyage of Rediscovery: A Cultural Odyssey through Polynesia*. Berkeley: University of California Press.

———. 1996a. Colonizing an island world. In W. H. Goodenough, ed., *Prehistoric Settlement of the Pacific,* pp. 71–116. Transactions of the American Philosophical Society, vol. 86, part 5. Philadelphia.

———. 1996b. Putting voyaging back into Polynesian prehistory. In J. Davidson, G. Irwin, F. Leach, A. Pawley, and D. Brown, eds., *Oceanic Culture History: Essays in Honour of Roger Green,* pp. 365–376. New Zealand Journal of Archaeology Special Publication. Dunedin: New Zealand Journal of Archaeology.

Finney, B., P. Frost, R. Rhodes, and N. Thompson. 1989. Wait for the west wind. *Journal of the Polynesian Society* 98:261–302.

Flexner, J. L. 2010. Archaeology of the recent past at Kalawao: Landscape, place, and power in a Hawaiian Hansen's disease settlement. PhD diss., University of California, Berkeley.

———. 2011a. Bottles, abandonment, and re-visitation in the Hansen's disease settlement at Kalawao, Moloka'i. *Hawaiian Archaeology* 12:108–124.

———. 2011b. Foreign animals, Hawaiian practices: Zooarchaeology in the Leprosarium at Kalawao, Moloka'i, Hawaii. *Journal of Pacific Archaeology* 2:82–91.

———. 2012. An institution that was a village: Archaeology and social life in the Hansen's disease settlement at Kalawao, Moloka'i, Hawaii. *International Journal of Historical Archaeology* 16:135–163.

Flexner, J. L., J. S. Field, M. D. McCoy, T. N. Ladefoged, and P. V. Kirch. 2018. Foreign material culture from Hawaiian households in Leeward Kohala. *Australian Historical Archaeology* 36:29–37.

Flexner, J. L., and P. V. Kirch. 2016. Field mapping and Polynesian prehistory: A methodological history and thoughts for the future. *Séances de la Société Préhistorique Française* 7:15–30. Paris.

Flexner, J. L., and M. D. McCoy. 2016. After the missionaries: Historical archaeology and sites of traditional religious ritual in the Hawaiian Islands. *Journal of the Polynesian Society* 125:307–332.

Flexner, J. L., and C. Morgan. 2013. The industrious exiles: An analysis of flaked glass tools from the Leprosarium at Kalawao, Moloka'i. In J. J. Card, ed., *The Archaeology of Hybrid Material Culture,* pp. 295–317. Carbondale, IL: Center for Archaeological Investigations.

Flexner, J. L., M. A. Mulrooney, M. D. McCoy, and P. V. Kirch. 2017. Visualizing Hawaiian sacred sites: The archives and J. F. G. Stokes's pioneering archaeological surveys, 1906–1913. *Journal of Pacific Archaeology* 8 (1): 63–76.

Flint, J., A. J. Boyce, J. J. Martinson, and J. B. Clegg. 1989. Population bottlenecks in Polynesia revealed by minisatellites. *Human Genetics* 83:257–263.

Fornander, A. 1878–1885. *An Account of the Polynesian Race: Its Origins and Migrations and the Ancient History of the Hawaiian People.* 3 vols. London: Trubner.

———. 1916–1920. *Fornander Collection of Hawaiian Antiquities and Folk-lore.* T. G. Thrum, ed. Bernice P. Bishop Museum Memoirs, vols. 4, 5, and 6. Honolulu, HI: Bishop Museum Press.

Fosberg, F. R. 1963. The island ecosystem. In F. R. Fosberg, ed., *Man's Place in the Island Ecosystem,* pp. 1–6. Honolulu, HI: Bishop Museum Press.

Fowke, G. 1922. Archaeological investigations. *Bureau of American Ethnology Bulletin* 76:174–195. Washington, DC.

Fredericksen, W., and D. Fredericksen. 1965. Report on the excavation of the "brick palace" of King Kamehameha I at Lahaina, Maui, Hawaii. Unpublished report in Library, Bernice P. Bishop Museum. Honolulu.

Fredericksen, E. M., and D. L. Fredericksen. 2002. Archaeological data recovery report for the Waiʻehu Kou Phase II project area, site 50–50–04–4731, Waiʻehu Ahupuaʻa, Wailuku District, Island of Maui. Unpublished report. Pukalani: Xamanek Researches, LLC.

Friedlaender, J. S., ed. 2007. *Genes, Language, and Culture History in the Southwest Pacific.* Oxford: Oxford University Press.

Frier, B. 2009. Demographics. *The Cambridge Ancient History XI: The High Empire, A.D. 70–192,* pp. 788–789. Cambridge: Cambridge University Press.

Funk, E. 1982. The aboriginal use and domestication of *Touchardia latifolia* Gaud. (Urticaceae) in Hawaii. *Archaeology in Oceania* 17:16–19.

Geertz, C. 1963. *Agricultural Involution: The Processes of Ecological Change in Indonesia.* Berkeley: University of California Press.

Gero, J. 1997. Genderlithics: Women's roles in stone tool production. In J. Gero and M. Conkey, eds., *Engendering Archaeology: Women and Prehistory,* pp. 163–193. Oxford: Blackwell.

Giambelluca, T. W., and T. A. Schroeder. 1998. Climate. In S. P. Juvik and J. O. Juvik, eds., *Atlas of Hawaiʻi.* 3rd ed., pp. 49–59. Honolulu: University of Hawaiʻi Press.

Gifford, E. W. 1951. Archaeological excavations in Fiji. *University of California Anthropological Records* 13:189–288.

Gill, T. M., P. V. Kirch, C. Ruggles, and A. Baer. 2015. Ideology, ceremony, and calendar in pre-contact Hawaiʻi: Astronomical alignment of a stone enclosure on Oʻahu suggests ceremonial use during the Makahiki season. *Journal of the Polynesian Society* 124:243–268.

Godby, W. C., and M. T. Carson. 2004. An overview of the archaeological context of Pohakuloa Training Area in Hawaiʻi Island. *Hawaiian Archaeology* 9:74–82.

Goldman, I. 1970. *Ancient Polynesian Society.* Chicago, IL: University of Chicago Press.

Golson, J. 1997. From horticulture to agriculture in the New Guinea Highlands: A case study of people and their environments. In P. V. Kirch and T. L. Hunt, eds., *Historical Ecology in the Pacific Islands: Prehistoric Environmental and Landscape Change,* pp. 39–50. New Haven, CT: Yale University Press.

Gon, S. M., III, S. L. Tom, and U. Woodside. 2018. ʻAina momona, honua au loli—productive lands, changing world: Using the Hawaiian footprint to inform biocultural restoration and future sustainability in Hawaiʻi. *Sustainability* 10 (3420). doi: 10.3390/su10103420.

Goodwin, C. M. 1994. *A Kalaupapa Sweet Potato Farm: Report on Archaeological Data Recovery Operations, Kalaupapa Airport Improvement Project, Kalaupapa, Molokai, Hawaiʻi.* Honolulu, HI: International Archaeological Research Institute.

Goodwin, C. M., and J. Allen. 2005. *Kikihale to Honolulu: From Village to City.* Honolulu, HI: International Archaeological Research Institute.

Goodwin, C. M., F. Beardsley, S. Wickler, and B. Jones. 1996. *Honoruru to Honolulu: From Village to City.* 2 vols. Honolulu, HI: International Archaeological Research Institute.

Gordon, E. A. 1993. Screen size and differential faunal recovery: A Hawaiian example. *Journal of Field Archaeology* 20:453–460.

Gosline, W. A., and V. E. Brock. 1960. *Handbook of Hawaiian Fishes.* Honolulu: University of Hawai'i Press.

Gosser, D., and B. Dixon. 1998. An organizational analysis of Kaunolu, Lana'i, Hawai'i. In C. M. Stevenson, G. Lee, and F. J. Morin, eds., *Easter Island in Pacific Context: South Seas Symposium,* pp. 253–258. Los Osos, CA: Easter Island Foundation.

Goto, A. 1984. Marine exploitation at South Point, Hawai'i Island. *Hawaiian Archaeology* 1:44–63.

———. 1986. Prehistoric ecology and economy of fishing in Hawaii: An ethnoarchaeological approach. PhD diss., University of Hawai'i at Mānoa.

Graham, W. 2018. *Braided Waters: Environment and Society in Molokai, Hawai'i.* Berkeley: University of California Press.

Graves, M. W., and C. K. Cachola-Abad. 1996. Seriation as a method of chronologically ordering architectural design traits: An example from Hawai'i. *Archaeology in Oceania* 31:19–32.

Graves, M. W., and T. N. Ladefoged. 1991. The disparity between radiocarbon and volcanic glass dates: New evidence from the island of Lana'i. *Archaeology in Oceania* 26:70–77.

Graves, M. W., and W. K. McElroy. 2005. Hawaiian fishhook classification, identification, and analysis, Nu'alolo Kai (Site 50–30–01–196), Kaua'i. In M. T. Carson and M. W. Graves, eds., *Na Mea Kahiko o Kaua'i: Archaeological Studies in Kaua'i,* pp. 188–211. Society for Hawaiian Archaeology Special Publication 2. Honolulu: Society for Hawaiian Archaeology.

Graves, M. W., and G. Murakami. 1993. The identification of charcoal from archaeological assemblages on Kahoolawe: Implications for reconstructing prehistoric vegetation. Unpublished reported prepared for Kaho'olawe Island Conveyance Commission, Consultant Report No. 8. N.p.

Green, R. C. 1966. Linguistic subgrouping within Polynesia: The implications for prehistoric settlement. *Journal of the Polynesian Society* 75:6–38.

———. 1971a. Evidence for the development of the early Polynesian adz kit. *New Zealand Archaeological Association Newsletter* 14:12–44.

———. 1971b. The chronology and age of sites at South Point, Hawaii. *Archaeology and Physical Anthropology in Oceania* 6:170–176.

———. 1977. Polynesian ancestors. In J. Siers, *Taratai: A Pacific Adventure,* pp. 220–239. Wellington, New Zealand: Millwood Press.

———. 1979. Lapita. In J. Jennings, ed., *The Prehistory of Polynesia,* pp. 27–60. Cambridge, MA: Harvard University Press.

———. 1980. *Mākaha before 1880 A.D.* Makaha Valley Historical Project Summary Report No. 5. Pacific Anthropological Records 31. Honolulu, HI: Bernice P. Bishop Museum.

———. 1991. Near and remote Oceania: Disestablishing "Melanesia" in culture history. In A. Pawley, ed., *Man and a Half: Essays in Pacific Anthropology and Ethnobiology in Honour of Ralph Bulmer,* pp. 491–502. Auckland, New Zealand: Polynesian Society.

———. 2005. Sweet potato transfers in Polynesian prehistory. In C. Ballard, P. Brown, R. M. Bourke, and T. Harwood, eds., *The Sweet Potato in Oceania: A Reappraisal,* pp. 43–62. Oceania Monograph 56. Sydney, Australia: University of Sydney.

Green, R. C., ed. 1969. *Makaha Valley Historical Project: Interim Report No. 1.* Pacific Anthropological Records 4. Honolulu, HI: Bernice P. Bishop Museum.

———. 1970. *Makaha Valley Historical Project: Interim Report No. 2.* Pacific Anthropological Records 10. Honolulu, HI: Bernice P. Bishop Museum.

Gregory, H. E., ed. 1921. *Proceedings of the First Pan-Pacific Scientific Conference.* Bernice P. Bishop Museum Special Publication 7. Honolulu, HI: Bishop Museum Press.

Griffin, P. B. 1984. Where Lohiʻau ruled: Excavations at Haʻena, Haleleʻa, Kauaʻi. *Hawaiian Archaeology* 1:1–18.

———. 1999. Hawaiian archaeology: A post-colonial history. *Hawaiian Archaeology* 7:90–96.

Griffin, P. B., R. Bordner, H. H. Hammatt, M. Morgenstein, and C. Stauder. 1977. Preliminary archaeological investigations at Haʻena, Haleleʻa, Kauaʻi Island. Unpublished report. Archaeological Research Center Hawaii. Lawaʻi, Kauaʻi.

Griffin, P. B., and G. W. Lovelace, eds. 1977. *Survey and Salvage—Honoapiʻilani Highway: The Archaeology of Kāʻanapali, Maui.* Archaeological Research Center Hawaii Occasional Papers 77-1. Lawai, Kauaʻi.

Griffin, P. B., T. Riley, P. Rosendahl, and H. D. Tuggle. 1971. Archaeology of Halawa and Lapakahi: Windward valley and leeward slope. *New Zealand Archaeological Association Newsletter* 14:101–112.

Groube, L. M., J. Chappell, J. Muke, and D. Price. 1986. A 40,000 year-old human occupation site at Huon Peninsula, Paupa New Guinea. *Nature* 324:453–455.

Gunness, J. L. 1993. The Kualoa Archaeological Research Project, 1975–1985: A brief overview. *Hawaiian Archaeology* 2:50–71.

Hale, H. 1846. Ethnography and philology. *United States Exploring Expedition.* Vol. 6. Philadelphia, PA: Sherman.

Halliwell, T. K. 2017. Moʻolelo ʻo Nā Iwi Kūpuna: Connecting the past, present, and future of the Nā ʻŌiwimamo. Master's thesis, University of Hawaiʻi at Hilo.

Hammatt, H. H. 1979a. Archaeological excavations: Kawakiu-Nui, Kaluakoʻi, Molokaʻi Island, Hawaii. Unpublished report. Archaeological Research Center Hawaii. Lawaʻi, Kauaʻi.

———. 1979b. Archaeological survey and excavation at the proposed Komohana Kai subdivision, Holualoa, Kona, Hawaii Island. Unpublished report, Archaeological Research Center Hawaii. Lawaʻi, Kauaʻi.

Hammatt, H. H., R. M. Bordner, and M. J. Tomonari-Tuggle. 1978. Archaeological and biological survey of the proposed Kiahuna Golf Village area, Koloa, Kona, Kauaʻi Island, Hawaii. Unpublished report, Archaeological Research Center Hawaii. Lawaʻi, Kauaʻi.

Hammatt, H. H., D. F. Borthwick, and R. Chiogioji. 1990. Archaeological inventory survey of a 64-acre property, Holualoa, Hawaii Island. Unpublished report. Honolulu: Cultural Surveys of Hawaiʻi.

Hammatt, H. H., and W. H. Folk. 1979. Archaeological excavations in the Waioli Mission Hall, Haleleʻa, Kauaʻi. Unpublished report, Archaeological Research Center Hawaii. Lawaʻi, Kauaʻi.

———. 1980a. Archaeological excavations within the proposed Keahole Agricultural Park, Kalaoa Oʻoma, Kona, Hawaii Island. Unpublished report, Archaeological Research Center Hawaii. Lawaʻi, Kauaʻi.

———. 1980b. Archaeological survey, Phase II. Portions of Keauhou-Kona Resort, Keauhou and Kahaluʻu, Kona, Hawaiʻi Island. Honolulu: Cultural Surveys of Hawaiʻi.

———. 1981. Archaeological and paleontological investigation at Kalaeloa (Barbers Point), Honouliuli, ʻEwa, Oʻahu, Federal Study Areas 1a and 1b, and State of Hawaii Optional Area 1. Unpublished report, Archaeological Research Center Hawaii. Lawaʻi, Kauaʻi.

———. 1996. Archaeological inventory survey report at Kahili, Koʻolau, Kauaʻi. Unpublished report. Honolulu: Cultural Surveys of Hawaiʻi.

Hammatt, H. H., and V. W. Meeker. 1979. Archaeological excavations and heiau stabilization at Kahului, Kona, Hawai'i Island. Unpublished report, Archaeological Research Center Hawaii. Lawa'i, Kaua'i.

Hammatt, H. H., and D. Shideler. 2008. Archaeological assessment for the Alaka'i Protective Fence Project Waimea and Wainiha Ahupua'a, Waimea and Hanalei Districts, Island of Kaua'i. Unpublished report. Honolulu: Cultural Surveys of Hawai'i.

Hammatt, H. H., M. J. Tomonari-Tuggle, and C. Streck. 1978. Archaeological investigations at Ha'ena State Park, Halele'a, Kaua'i Island. Phase II: Excavations of beach localities and visitors facilities area. Unpublished report, Archaeological Research Center Hawaii. Lawa'i, Kaua'i.

Hammatt, H. H., P. O. Walsh, J. J. Robins, M. Stride, and T. R. Barr. 1995. Archaeological inventory survey and limited subsurface testing of a 500-acre parcel in the Ahupua'a of Keopuka, District of South Kona Island of Hawai'i. Honolulu: Cultural Surveys of Hawai'i.

Han, T. L., S. L. Collins, S. D. Clark, and A. Garland. 1986. *Moe Kau a Ho'oilo: Hawaiian Mortuary Practices at Keōpū, Kona, Hawai'i*. Anthropology Departmental Report 86-1. Honolulu, HI: Bernice P. Bishop Museum.

Handy, E. S. C. 1927. *Polynesian Religion*. Bernice P. Bishop Museum Bulletin 34. Honolulu, HI: Bishop Museum Press.

———. 1930. The problem of Polynesian origins. *Bishop Museum Occasional Papers* 9:1–27. Honolulu, HI: Bishop Museum Press.

———. 1940. *The Hawaiian Planter*. Vol. 1. Bernice P. Bishop Museum Bulletin 161. Honolulu, HI: Bishop Museum Press.

Handy, E. S. C., and E. G. Handy. 1972. *Native Planters in Old Hawaii: Their Life, Lore, and Environment*. Bernice P. Bishop Museum Bulletin 233. Honolulu, HI: Bishop Museum Press.

Handy, E. S. C., and M. K. Pukui. 1958. *The Polynesian Family System in Ka-'u, Hawai'i*. Wellington, New Zealand: The Polynesian Society.

Hara, K. 2008. From dates to rates: Emergent demographic trends through the analysis of radiocarbon data from Hawai'i Island. Unpublished senior honors thesis, University of California, Berkeley.

Harries, H. C. 1978. The evolution, dissemination and classification of *Cocos nucifera*. Botanical Review 44:265–320.

Hartshorn, A. S., O. A. Chadwick, P. M. Vitousek, and P. V. Kirch. 2006. Prehistoric agricultural depletion of soil nutrients in Hawaii. *Proceedings of the National Academy of Sciences USA* 103:11092–11097.

Hartzell, L. L., S. A. Lebo, H. A. Lennstrom, S. P. McPherron, and D. I. Olszewski. 2003. Imu, adzes, and upland agriculture: Inventory survey archaeology in the North Hālawa Valley, O'ahu. Unpublished report in Library, Bernice P. Bishop Museum. Honolulu.

Hather, J., and P. V. Kirch. 1991. Prehistoric sweet potato (*Ipomoea batatas*) from Mangaia Island, Central Polynesia. *Antiquity* 65:887–893.

Haun, A. 2001. Archaeological assessment and inventory survey Lako Street Extension, Lands of Holualoa 3 and 4, North Kona District, Island of Hawaii. Unpublished report. Kailua-Kona: Haun & Associates.

Haun, A. E., D. M. Berrigan, and D. Henry. 2011. Plan for supplemental archaeological inventory survey, Lands of Kahuku, Punalau, Ulupehupehu, 'Ōi'o, Hanaka'oe, Kawela and 'Ōpana, Ko'olauloa District, Island of Oahu. Unpublished report. Kailua-Kona: Haun & Associates.

Haun, A. E., and A. T. Walker. 1987. Archaeological reconnaissance survey Hawaiian Riviera Resort Project Area Land of Kahuku Kau District, Island of Hawaii. Unpublished report. Kailua-Kona: Haun & Associates.

———. 1988. Archaeological reconnaissance survey, Farms of Kapua Mauka Lands Project Area. Unpublished report. Kailua-Kona: Haun & Associates.

Haun, A., S. Williams, M. Kelly, and M. Major. 1991. An archaeological survey of the Naval Magazine and Naval Communications Area Transmission Facility, Lualualei, Oahu, Hawaii. Unpublished report in Library, Bernice P. Bishop Museum. Honolulu.

Head, J. A., and S. T. Goodfellow. 1991. Archaeological inventory survey Hamakua Sugar Company Waipio Lands. Unpublished report. Hilo, HI: Paul H. Rosendahl.

Heinz, K. 2019. Nā Wahine o nā'ina Kuleana: Assessing the impact of colonization on gender experience in North Kohala, Hawai'i Island. Paper presented at the 84th Annual Society for American Archaeology Meetings, Albuquerque.

Heizer, R. 1950. *A Manual of Archaeological Field Methods: Prepared for Use by the Archaeological Survey and the Department of Anthropology of the University of California at Berkeley.* Berkeley: University of California.

Hendren, G. H. 1975. Excavation of eight inland prehistoric habitation sites. In P. V. Kirch and M. Kelly, eds., *The Prehistory and Ecology of a Windward Hawaiian Valley: Halawa Valley, Molokai,* pp. 117–152. Pacific Anthropological Records 24. Honolulu, HI: Bernice P. Bishop Museum.

Heyerdahl, T. 1952. *American Indians in the Pacific.* London: Allen and Unwin.

Hiroa, Te Rangi: *See* Buck, P. H.

Hoffman, E. S. 1979. Archaeological survey and limited test excavations in Waipā and Lumaha'i valleys, Island of Kauai. Unpublished report in Library, Bernice P. Bishop Museum. Honolulu.

Holm, L. A. 2006. The archaeology and the 'Aina of Mahamenui and Manawainui, Kahikinui, Maui Island. PhD diss., University of California, Berkeley.

Hommon, R. J. 1969a. An interim report on archaeological Zone 1. In R. C. Green, ed., *Makaha Valley Historical Project: Interim Report No. 1,* pp. 41–54. Pacific Anthropological Records 4. Honolulu, HI: Bernice P. Bishop Museum.

———. 1969b. An intensive survey of the northern portion of Kaawaloa, Kona, Hawaii. Mimeographed report in Library, Bernice P. Bishop Museum. Honolulu.

———. 1969c. Preliminary report on the archaeological survey of the upper Makaha Valley. In R. C. Green, ed., *Makaha Valley Historical Project: Interim Report No. 1,* pp. 85–94. Pacific Anthropological Records 4. Honolulu, HI: Bernice P. Bishop Museum.

———. 1970a. Notes on a formal classification of Hawaiian archaeological features. *Hawaii State Archaeological Journal* 70 (2): 44–55. Department of Land and Natural Resources, State of Hawaii.

———. 1970b. Subzone 1c of archaeological Zone 1 in the lower Makaha Valley. In R. Green, ed., *Makaha Valley Historical Project: Interim Report No. 2,* pp. 27–34. Pacific Anthropological Records 10. Honolulu, HI: Bernice P. Bishop Museum.

———. 1974. Comments on the archaeological sites on the island of Lanai. Unpublished Report.

———. 1976a. The formation of primitive states in pre-contact Hawaii. PhD diss., University of Arizona.

———. 1976b. Fieldnotes from Ka'ula Island. Unpublished report.

———. 1980a. Multiple resources nomination form for Kaho'olawe archaeological sites. Washington, DC: National Register of Historic Places.

———. 1980b. Kaho'olawe: Final report on the archaeological survey. Unpublished report prepared for U.S. Navy, Pacific Division. Honolulu: Hawaii Marine Research Inc.

———. 1982. Kaho'olawe archaeological excavations, 1981. Unpublished report, Prepared for U.S. Navy, Pacific Division. Honolulu, HI: Science Management.

———. 1986. Social evolution in ancient Hawai'i. In P. V. Kirch, ed., *Island Societies: Archaeological Approaches to Evolution and Transformation,* pp. 55–68. Cambridge: Cambridge University Press.

———. 2013. *The Ancient Hawaiian State: Origins of a Political Society.* New York: Oxford University Press.

———. 2014. The Kealakekua Region: Salubrious core, political centre. *Journal of Pacific Archaeology* 5:40–50.

Hommon, R. J., and H. Ahlo. 1983. An archaeological survey of selected lands proposed for military training near Kaunakakai, Island of Molokai, Hawaii. Unpublished report. Pearl Harbor: Science Management.

Hommon, R. J., and W. Barrera, Jr. 1971. *Archaeological Survey of Kahana Valley, Koolauloa District, Island of Oahu.* Department of Anthropology Report 71-3. Honolulu, HI: Bernice P. Bishop Museum.

Hommon, R. J., and R. F. Bevacqua, 1973. *Excavations in Kahana Valley, Oahu, 1972.* Department of Anthropology Report 73-2. Honolulu, HI: Bernice P. Bishop Museum.

Horrocks, M., and R. B. Rechtman. 2009. Sweet potato (*Ipomoea batatas*) and banana (*Musa* sp.) microfossils from the Kona Field System, Island of Hawai'i. *Journal of Archaeological Science* 36:1115–1126.

Hosaka, E. Y. 1937. Ecological and floristic studies in Kipapa Gulch, Oahu. *Bishop Museum Occasional Papers* 13:175–232. Honolulu, HI: Bishop Museum Press.

———. 1944. *Sport Fishing in Hawaii.* Honolulu, HI: Bond's.

Howard A. 1967. Polynesian origins and migrations. In G. A. Highland et al., eds., *Polynesian Culture History,* pp. 45–101. Bernice P. Bishop Museum Special Publication 56. Honolulu, HI: Bishop Museum Press.

Hudson, A. E. 1931. Archaeology of Hawaii. Typescript in Library, Bernice P. Bishop Museum. Honolulu.

Hung, H.-C., and M. T. Carson. 2014. Foragers, fishers, and farmers: Origins of the Taiwanese Neolithic. *Antiquity* 88:1115–1131.

Hunt, T. L. 2006. Archaeological stratigraphy and chronology at Nu'alolo Kai, Nā Pali District, Kaua'i. In M. T. Carson and M. W. Graves, ed., *Na Mea Kahiko o Kaua'i: Archaeological Studies in Kaua'i,* pp. 236–258. Society for Hawaiian Archaeology Special Publication 2. Honolulu: Society for Hawaiian Archaeology.

Hurles, M. E., E. Matisoo-Smith, R. D. Gray, and D. Penny. 2003. Untangling Oceanic settlement: The edge of the knowable. *Trends in Ecology and Evolution* 18:531–540.

Hutchinson, G. E. 1978. *An Introduction to Population Biology.* New Haven, CT: Yale University Press.

'Ī'ī, J. P. 1959. *Fragments of Hawaiian History.* Bernice P. Bishop Museum Special Publication 70. Honolulu, HI: Bishop Museum Press.

Ioannidis, A.G., J. Blanco-Portillo, K. Sandoval, et al. 2021. Paths and timings of the peopling of Polynesia inferred from genomic networks. *Nature* 597:522–526. https://doi.org/10.1038/s41586-021-03902-8.

Ioannidis, A. G., J. Blanco-Portillo, K. Sandoval, E. Hagelberg, J. F. Miquel-Poblete, V. Moreno-Mayar, J. E. Rodríguez-Rodríguez et al. 2020. Native American gene flow into Polynesia predating Easter Island settlement. *Nature* 583:572–577.

Irwin, G. 1992. *The Prehistoric Exploration and Colonisation of the Pacific.* Cambridge: Cambridge University Press.

James, H. F., and S. L. Olson. 1983. Flightless birds. *Natural History* 9/83:30–40.

James, H. F., T. W. Stafford, Jr., D. W. Steadman, S. L. Olson, P. S. Martin, H. J. T. Jull, and P. C. McCoy. 1987. Radiocarbon dates on bones of extinct birds from Hawaii. *Proceedings of the National Academy of Sciences U.S.A.* 84:2350–2354.

Jenkins, I. 2017. *Lord of the Haao Rain*. Honolulu, HI: Kalaiopua Publishing.

Jennings, J., ed. 1979. *The Prehistory of Polynesia*. Cambridge, MA: Harvard University Press.

Jensen, P. 2001. Data recovery at Site 21877, Development "Site L," Land of Waikoloa, South Kohala District, Island of Hawaii. Unpublished report. Hilo, HI: Paul H. Rosendahl.

Jensen, P. M., and M. Boudreau. 1992. Additional inventory survey, non-burial findings, Waihee Golf Club. Unpublished report prepared for Waihee Oceanfront Hawaii. Hilo, HI: Paul H. Rosendahl.

Johnson, A., M. Slater, L. Carter Schuster, and J. Naone. 2013. The 2006 Earthquake Project at Puʻukohola Heiau National Historical Site, Hawaiʻi. *APT Bulletin: Journal of Preservation Technology* 44 (2/3): 63–70.

Johnson, A. M., and M. D. McCoy. 2020. Intensive Survey of a Portion of Lapakahi State Historical Park, Lakapahi Hawaii. Unpublished report.

Johnson, R. K., J. K. Mahelona, and C. L. N. Ruggles. 2015. *Nā Inoa Hōkū: Hawaiian and Pacific Star Names*. Rev. ed. Bognor Regis, UK: Ocarina Books.

Jones, B. D., T. N. Ladefoged, and G. Asner. 2015. Tracing the resilience and revitalisation of historic taro production in Waipio Valley, Hawaiʻi. *Journal of the Polynesian Society* 124:83–109.

Jones, S., and P. V. Kirch. 2007. Indigenous Hawaiian fishing practices in Kahikinui, Maui: A zooarchaeological approach. *Hawaiian Archaeology* 11:39–53.

Kagawa-Viviani, A., N. K. Lincoln, S. Quintus, M. P. Lucas, and T. W. Giambelluca. 2018. Spatial patterns of seasonal crop production suggest coordination within and across dryland agricultural systems of Hawaiʻi Island. *Ecology and Society* 23 (3): 20.

Kahn, J. G., and T. S. Dye. 2015. A note on Hawaiian stone axes. *Journal of Pacific Archaeology* 6:18–25.

Kahn, J. G., K. Kawelu, V. Wichman, A. B. Carpenter, S. Moore, and T. Hunt. 2016. Understanding variability in the hinterlands: Settlement and subsistence in Miloliʻi, Kauaʻi, Hawaiian Islands. *Archaeology in Oceania* 51:196–213.

Kahn, J. G., S. P. Lundblad, P. R. Mills, P. Y. Chan, K. Longenecker, and Y. Sinoto. 2016. Settlement chronologies and shifting resource exploitation in Kaʻū District, Hawaiian Islands. *Asian Perspectives* 55:184–207.

Kahn, J. G., P. R. Mills, S. P. Lundblad, J. Holson, and P. V. Kirch. 2009. Tool production at the Nuʻu Quarry, Maui, Hawaiian Islands: Manufacturing sequences and energy dispersive X-ray analyses. *New Zealand Journal of Archaeology* 30:135–165.

Kahn, J. G., T. M. Rieth, P. V. Kirch, J. S. Athens, and G. M. Murakami. 2014. Re-dating of the Kuliʻouʻou Rockshelter, Oʻahu, Hawaiʻi: Location of the first radiocarbon date from the Pacific Islands. *Journal of the Polynesian Society* 123:67–90.

Kahn, J., and Y. H. Sinoto. 2017. Refining the Society Island cultural sequence: Colonization Period and Developmental Period coastal occupation on Moʻorea Island. *Journal of the Polynesian Society* 126:33–60.

Kailihiwa, S. H., III. 2015. Using Maxent to model the distribution of prehistoric agricultural features in a portion of the Hōkūliʻa Subdivision in Kona, Hawaiʻi. Master's thesis, University of Southern California.

Kaliʻuokapaʻakai Collective. 2021. *The Kaliʻuokapaʻakai Collective Report, Re-envisioning Wahi Kūpuna Stewardship in Hawaiʻi*. Honolulu, Hawaiʻi. https://www.kaliuokapaakai.org/kcreport.

Kam, W. 1979. Osteological study of human skeletal remains at Kalāhuipuaʻa. In P. V. Kirch, *Marine Exploitation in Prehistoric Hawaiʻi,* pp. 211–228. Pacific Anthropological Records 29. Honolulu, HI: Bernice P. Bishop Museum.

Kamakau, S. M. 1961. *Ruling Chiefs of Hawaii.* Honolulu, HI: Kamehameha Schools Press.

———. 1964. *Ka Poʻe Kahiko: The People of Old.* Bernice P. Bishop Museum Special Publication 51. Honolulu, HI: Bishop Museum Press.

———. 1976. *Na Hana o Ka Poʻe Kahiko: The Works of the People of Old.* Bernice P. Bishop Museum Special Publication 61. Honolulu, HI: Bishop Museum Press.

———. 1991. *Tales and Traditions of the People of Old. Nā Moʻolelo a ka Poʻe Kahiko.* Translated by M. K. Pukui, and edited by D. B. Barrère. Honolulu, HI: Bishop Museum Press.

Kaschko, M. W. 1973. Functional analysis of the trail system of the Lapakahi area, North Kohala. In H. D. Tuggle and P. B. Griffin, eds., *Lapakahi, Hawaii: Archaeological Studies,* pp. 127–146. Asian and Pacific Archaeology Series No. 5. Honolulu: Social Science Research Institute, University of Hawaiʻi.

———. 1996. An archaeological inventory survey of Phase IV-A of Citizens Utility—Kauai Electric Division's powerline pole removal, replacement, and installation, Island of Kauaʻi. Unpublished report. Honolulu, HI: Scientific Consultant Services.

Kaschko, M. W., and J. S. Athens. 1987. Archaeological inventor survey of the Hulopoe Bay and Manele Bay Areas Island of Lanai, Hawaii. Unpublished report. Honolulu, HI: International Archaeological Research Institute.

Kawelu, K. 2007. A sociopolitical history of Hawaiian archaeology: Kuleana and commitment. PhD diss., University of California, Berkeley.

———. 2015. *Kuleana and Commitment: Working toward a Collaborative Hawaiian Archaeology.* Honolulu: University of Hawaiʻi Press.

Kawelu, K., and D. Pakele. 2014. Community-based research: The next step in Hawaiian archaeology. *Journal of Pacific Archaeology* 5:62–71.

Kay, A. E. 1979. *Hawaiian Marine Shells.* Bernice P. Bishop Museum Special Publication 64. Honolulu, HI: Bishop Museum Press.

Kekahuna, H. 1951. Wahaula Heiau including sketch and dimensions of the sacrificial stone within; Pulama, Puna, Hawaii. Unpublished report in Library, Bernice P. Bishop Museum. Honolulu.

———. 1959. A genuinely authentic Hawaiian village for Kauaʻi. Manuscript on file at Hawaiʻi State Archives.

Kekahuna, H. E. P., and T. Kelsey. 1954. Kamehameha In Kailua. *Hawaii Tribune-Herald.* March 17, p. 4.

Kelly, M. 1957. Annotated list of places of refuge in the Hawaiian Islands. In K. P. Emory, J. F. G. Stokes, D. B. Barrère, and M. A. Kelly, *The Natural and Cultural History of Honaunau, Hawaii,* pp. 113–136. Unpublished report in Library, Bernice P. Bishop Museum. Honolulu.

———. 1975. *Loko Iʻa o Heʻeia: Heʻeia Fishpond.* Department of Anthropology Report 75-2. Honolulu, HI: Bernice P. Bishop Museum.

———. 1980. *Majestic Kaʻū: Moʻolelo of Nine Ahupuaʻa.* Department of Anthropology Report 80-2. Honolulu, HI: Bernice P. Bishop Museum.

———. 1983. *Nā Māla o Kona: Gardens of Kona.* Department of Anthropology Report 83-2. Honolulu, HI: Bernice P. Bishop Museum.

Kelly, M., and J. T. Clark. 1980. *Kawainui Marsh, Oʻahu: Historical and Archaeological Studies.* Department of Anthropology Report 80-3. Honolulu, HI: Bernice P. Bishop Museum.

Kelly, M. and N. Crozier. 1972. *Archaeological Survey and Excavations at Waiohinu Drainage Improvement Project.* Department of Anthropology Report 72-6. Honolulu, HI: Bernice P. Bishop Museum.

Kennedy, J. 1990. Archaeological investigations at a suspected heiau site located near Pukalani, District of Kula, Maui. Unpublished report. Puʻunene, Maui: Archaeological Consultants of Hawaii, LLC.

———. 1991. Archaeological inventory survey and test results for the proposed Pukalani Highlands Property Located at Pukalani, Ahupuaʻa of Kailua, District of Makawao, Island of Maui. Unpublished report. Puʻunene, Maui: Archaeological Consultants of Hawaii, LLC.

Kennedy, J., and J. E. Brady. 1997. Into the netherworld of island Earth: A reevaluation of refuge caves in ancient Hawaiian society. *Geoarchaeology* 12:641–655.

Kennedy, J., P. Brennan, M. A. B. Malgret, E. Gehr, and L. Reitsema. 1991. An inventory survey and subsurface testing at TMK: 1-4-02: 13, 14, 24, 69 & 70 Puna, Island of Hawaii. Unpublished report. Puʻunene, Maui: Archaeological Consultants of Hawaii, LLC.

Kepelino: *See* Beckwith, M. W. 1932.

Khaweerat, S., M. Weisler, J. Zhao, Y. Feng, and K. Yu. 2010. Human-caused stratigraphic mixing of a coastal Hawaiian midden during prehistory: Implications for interpreting cultural deposits. *Geoarchaeology* 25:527–540.

Kikiloi, K. S. T. 2012. Kūkulu Manamana: Ritual power and religious expansion in Hawaiʻi: The ethno-historical and archaeological study of Mokumanamana and Nihoa Islands. PhD diss., University of Hawaiʻi at Mānoa.

Kikuchi, W. K. 1963. Archaeological survey and excavations on the Island of Kauai, Kona District, Hawaiian Islands. Unpublished report in Library, Bernice P. Bishop Museum. Honolulu.

———. 1973. Hawaiian aquacultural systems. PhD diss., University of Arizona.

———. 1976. Prehistoric Hawaiian fishponds. *Science* 193:295–299.

———. 1987. Archaeological surface survey of proposed helicopter landing site: Lehua landing and Keanahaki: Island of Niʻihau. Letter report on file with Hawaiʻi State Historic Preservation Division. Honolulu.

Kirch, P. V. 1971a. Archaeological excavations at Palauea, Southeast Maui, Hawaiian Islands. *Archaeology and Physical Anthropology in Oceania* 6:62–86.

———. 1971b. The Halawa Dune site (Hawaiian Islands): A preliminary report. *Journal of the Polynesian Society* 80:228–236.

———. 1972. Five triangular adzes from Haiku, Maui, Hawaiian Islands. *New Zealand Archaeological Association Newsletter* 15:140–143.

———. 1973a. *Archaeological Excavations at Kahaluʻu, North Kona, Island of Hawaii.* Department of Anthropology Report 73-1. Honolulu, HI: Bernice P. Bishop Museum.

———. 1973b. Archaeological excavations at Site D13–1, Hawea Point, Maui, Hawaiian Islands. Unpublished report in Library, Bernice P. Bishop Museum. Honolulu.

———. 1975a. Excavations at Sites A1-3 and A1-4: Early settlement and ecology in Halawa Valley. In P. V. Kirch and M. Kelly, eds., *Prehistory and Ecology in a Windward Hawaiian Valley: Halawa Valley, Molokai,* pp. 17–70. Pacific Anthropological Records 24. Honolulu, HI: Bernice P. Bishop Museum.

———. 1975b. Halawa Valley in Hawaiian prehistory. In P. V. Kirch and M. Kelly, eds., *Prehistory and Ecology in a Windward Hawaiian Valley: Halawa Valley, Molokai,* pp. 167–184. Pacific Anthropological Records 24. Honolulu, HI: Bernice P. Bishop Museum.

———. 1977. Valley agricultural systems in prehistoric Hawaii: An archaeological consideration. *Asian Perspectives* 20:246–280.

———. 1979a. *Marine Exploitation in Prehistoric Hawai'i: Archaeological Excavations at Kalāhuipua'a, Hawai'i Island.* Pacific Anthropological Records 29. Honolulu, HI: Bernice P. Bishop Museum.

———. 1979b. *Late Prehistoric and Early Historic Settlement-Subsistence Systems in the Anahulu Valley, O'ahu.* Department of Anthropology Report 79-2. Honolulu, HI: Bernice P. Bishop Museum.

———. 1980. Polynesian prehistory: Cultural adaptation in island ecosystems. *American Scientist* 68:39–48.

———. 1982a. The impact of the prehistoric Polynesians on the Hawaiian ecosystem. *Pacific Science* 36:1–14.

———. 1982b. Transported landscapes. *Natural History* 12/82:32–35.

———. 1982c. The ecology of marine exploitation in prehistoric Hawaii. *Human Ecology* 10:455–476.

———. 1983a. Man's role in modifying tropical and subtropical Polynesian ecosystems. *Archaeology in Oceania* 18:26–31.

———. 1983b. Archaeology and the evolution of social complexity: The Hawaiian case. *Reviews in Anthropology* 10:17–28.

———. 1984. *The Evolution of the Polynesian Chiefdoms.* Cambridge: Cambridge University Press.

———. 1985a. *Feathered Gods and Fishhooks: An Introduction to the Archaeology and Prehistory of Hawai'i.* Honolulu: University of Hawai'i Press.

———. 1985b. Intensive agriculture in prehistoric Hawai'i: The wet and the dry. In I. S. Farrington, ed., *Prehistoric Intensive Agriculture in the Tropics,* pp. 435–454. Oxford: B. A. R. International Series 232.

———. 1988. *Niuatoputapu: The Prehistory of a Polynesian Chiefdom.* Thomas Burke Memorial Washington State Museum Monograph No. 5. Seattle: Burke Museum.

———. 1989. Non-marine molluscs from the rockshelter sediments. In P. V. Kirch, ed., *Prehistoric Hawaiian Occupation in the Anahulu Valley, O'ahu Island: Excavations in Three Inland Rockshelters,* pp. 73–82. Archaeological Research Facility Contribution No. 47. Berkeley: University of California.

———. 1990a. Production, intensification, and the early Hawaiian Kingdom. In D. E. Yen and J. M. J. Mummery, eds., *Pacific Production Systems: Approaches to Economic Prehistory,* pp. 190–210. Occasional Papers in Prehistory, no. 18. Canberra: Australian National University Press.

———. 1990b. Monumental architecture and power in Polynesian chiefdoms: A comparison of Tonga and Hawaii. *World Archaeology* 22:206–222.

———. 1992. Kenneth Pike Emory, 1897–1992. *Asian Perspectives* 31:1–8.

———. 1994. *The Wet and the Dry: Irrigation and Agricultural Intensification in Polynesia.* Chicago, IL: University of Chicago Press.

———. 1996. *Legacy of the Landscape: An Illustrated Guide to Hawaiian Archaeological Sites.* Honolulu: University of Hawai'i Press.

———. 1997. *The Lapita Peoples: Ancestors of the Oceanic World.* Oxford: Blackwell.

———. 1999. Hawaiian archaeology: Past, present, and future. *Hawaiian Archaeology* 7:60–73.

———. 2001. Early archaeological excavations, 1978–1982. In M. S. Allen, ed., *Gardens of Lono,* pp. 47–66. Honolulu, HI: Bishop Museum Press.

———. 2004a. Temple sites in Kahikinui, Maui, Hawaiian Islands: Their orientations decoded. *Antiquity* 78 (299): 102–114.

———. 2004b. Solstice observation in Mangareva, French Polynesia: New perspectives from Archaeology. *Archaeoastronomy* 18:1–19.

———. 2007a. Hawaii as a model system for human ecodynamics. *American Anthropologist* 109:8–26.

———. 2007b. Three islands and an archipelago: Reciprocal interactions between humans and island ecosystems in Polynesia. *Earth and Environmental Science Transactions of the Royal Society of Edinburgh* 98:1–15.

———. 2007c. "Like shoals of fish": Archaeology and population in pre-contact Hawai'i. In P. V. Kirch and J.-L. Rallu, eds., *The Growth and Collapse of Pacific Island Societies: Archaeological and Demographic Perspectives*, pp. 52–69. Honolulu: University of Hawai'i Press.

———. 2007d. Paleodemography in Kahikinui, Maui: An archaeological approach. In P. V. Kirch and J.-L. Rallu, eds., *The Growth and Collapse of Pacific Island Societies: Archaeological and Demographic Perspectives*, pp. 90–107. Honolulu: University of Hawai'i Press.

———. 2010. *How Chiefs Became Kings: Divine Kingship and the Rise of Archaic States in Ancient Hawai'i.* Berkeley: University of California Press.

———. 2012. *A Shark Going Inland Is My Chief: The Island Civilization of Ancient Hawai'i.* Berkeley: University of California Press.

———. 2014. *Kua'āina Kahiko: Life and Land in Ancient Kahikinui, Maui.* Honolulu: University of Hawai'i Press.

———. 2015. *Unearthing the Polynesian Past: Adventures and Explorations of an Island Archaeologist.* Honolulu: University of Hawai'i Press.

———. 2017. *On the Road of the Winds: An Archaeological History of the Pacific Islands Before European Contact.* Rev. ed. Berkeley: University of California Press.

Kirch, P. V., ed. 1989. *Prehistoric Hawaiian Occupation in the Anahulu Valley, O'ahu Island: Excavations in Three Inland Rockshelters.* Contributions of the University of California Archaeological Research Facility No. 47. Berkeley.

———. 1997. *Na Mea Kahiko o Kahikinui: Studies in the Archaeology of Kahikinui, Maui,* Oceanic Archaeology Laboratory, Special Publication No. 1, Archaeological Research Facility, University of California, Berkeley.

———. 2002. *From the "Cliffs of Keolewa" to the "Sea of Papaloa": An Archaeological Reconnaissance of Portions of the Kalaupapa National Historical Park, Moloka'i, Hawaiian Islands.* Oceanic Archaeology Laboratory, Special Publication No. 2, Archaeological Research Facility, University of California, Berkeley.

———. 2010. *Roots of Conflict: Soils, Agriculture, and Sociopolitical Complexity in Ancient Hawai'i.* Santa Fe, NM: School for Advanced Research.

———. 2017. *Tangatatau Rockshelter: The Evolution of an Eastern Polynesian Socio-Ecosystem.* Monumenta Archaeologica 40. Los Angeles, CA: Cotsen Institute of Archaeology Press.

———. 2021. *Talepakemalai: Lapita and Its Transformations in the Mussau Islands of Near Oceania.* Monumenta Archaeologica 47. Los Angeles, CA: Cotsen Institute of Archaeology Press.

Kirch, P. V., G. Asner, O. A. Chadwick, J. Field, T. Ladefoged, C. Lee, C. Puleston, S. Tuljapurkar, and P. M. Vitousek. 2012. Building and testing models of long-term agricultural intensification and population dynamics: A case study from the Leeward Kohala Field System, Hawai'i. *Ecological Modeling* 227:18–28.

Kirch, P. V., A. Carpenter, and C. Ruggles. 2019. Kukuipahu: A unique Hawaiian monumental structure utilizing cut-and-dressed stone masonry. *Rapa Nui Journal* 32:37–57.

Kirch, P. V., J. H. Coil, A. S. Hartshorn, M. Jeraj, P. M. Vitousek, and O. A. Chadwick. 2005. Intensive dryland farming on the leeward slopes of Haleakala, Maui, Hawaiian Islands:

Archaeological, archaeobotanical, and geochemical perspectives. *World Archaeology* 37:240–258.

Kirch, P. V., and S. Collins. 1989. Faunal assemblages of the Anahulu rockshelter sites. In P. V. Kirch, ed., *Prehistoric Hawaiian Occupation in the Anahulu Valley, Oʻahu Island: Excavations in Three Inland Rockshelters,* pp. 61–72. Archaeological Research Facility Contribution No. 47. Berkeley: University of California.

Kirch, P. V., E. Conte, W. Sharp, and C. Nickelsen. 2010. The Onemea site (Taravai Island, Mangareva) and the human colonization of Southeastern Polynesia. *Archaeology in Oceania* 45:66–79.

Kirch, P. V., and R. C. Green. 2001. *Hawaiki: Ancestral Polynesia. An Essay in Historical Anthropology.* Cambridge: Cambridge University Press.

Kirch, P. V., A. Hartshorn, O. A. Chadwick, P. M. Vitousek, D. Sherrod, J. Coil, L. Holm, and W. Sharp. 2004. Environment, agriculture, and settlement patterns in a marginal Polynesian landscape. *Proceedings of the National Academy of Sciences, U.S.A.* 101:9936–9941.

Kirch, P. V., J. Holson, and A. Baer. 2009. Intensive dryland agriculture in Kaupō, Maui, Hawaiian Islands. *Asian Perspectives* 48:265–290.

Kirch, P. V., J. Holson, P. Cleghorn, T. Schneider, and O. Chadwick. 2013. Five centuries of dryland farming and floodwater irrigation at Hōkūkano Flat, Auwahi, Maui Island. *Hawaiian Archaeology* 13:69–102.

Kirch, P. V., and M. Kelly, eds. 1975. *Prehistory and Ecology in a Windward Hawaiian Valley: Halawa Valley, Molokai.* Pacific Anthropological Records 24. Department of Anthropology, Bernice P. Bishop Museum.

Kirch, P. V., and D. Lepofsky. 1993. Polynesian irrigation: Archaeological and linguistic evidence for origins and development. *Asian Perspectives* 32:183–204.

Kirch, P. V., and M. D. McCoy. 2007. Reconfiguring the Hawaiian cultural sequence: Results of re-dating the Halawa dune site (Mo-A1–3), Molokaʻi Island. *Journal of the Polynesian Society* 116:385–406.

Kirch, P. V., R. Mertz-Kraus, and W. D. Sharp. 2015. Precise chronology of Polynesian temple construction and use for southeastern Maui, Hawaiian Islands determined by ^{230}Th dating of corals. *Journal of Archaeological Science* 53:166–177.

Kirch, P. V., S. Millerstrom, S. Jones, and M. D. McCoy. 2010. Dwelling among the gods: A late pre-contact priest's house in Kahikinui, Maui, Hawaiian Islands. *Journal of Pacific Archaeology* 1:145–160.

Kirch, P. V., P. R. Mills, S. P. Lundblad, J. Sinton, and J. G. Kahn. 2012. Interpolity exchange of basalt tools facilitated via elite control in Hawaiian archaic states. *Proceedings of the National Academy of Sciences, U.S.A.* 109:1056–1061.

Kirch, P. V., and S. O'Day. 2003. New archaeological insights into food and status: A case study from pre-contact Hawaii. *World Archaeology* 34:484–497.

Kirch, P. V., S. J. O'Day, J. Coil, M. Morgenstein, K. Kawelu, and S. Millerstrom. 2004. The Kaupikiawa Rockshelter, Kalaupapa Peninsula, Molokaʻi: New investigations and reinterpretation of its significance for Hawaiian prehistory. *People and Culture in Oceania* 19:1–27.

Kirch, P. V., and J.-L. Rallu, eds. 2007. *The Growth and Collapse of Pacific Island Societies: Archaeological and Demographic Perspectives.* Honolulu: University of Hawaiʻi Press.

Kirch, P. V., and C. Ruggles. 2019. *Heiau, ʻAina, Lani: The Hawaiian Temple System in Ancient Kahikinui and Kaupō, Maui.* Honolulu: University of Hawaiʻi Press.

Kirch, P. V., C. Ruggles, and W. D. Sharp. 2013. The *Pānānā* or "Sighting Wall" at Hanamauloa, Kahikinui, Maui: Archaeological investigation of a possible navigational monument. *Journal of the Polynesian Society* 122:45–68.

Kirch, P. V., and M. Sahlins. 1992. *Anahulu: The Anthropology of History in the Kingdom of Hawaii*. 2 vols. Chicago, IL: University of Chicago Press.

Kirch, P. V., and W. D. Sharp. 2005. Coral ^{230}Th dating of the imposition of a ritual control hierarchy in precontact Hawaii. *Science* 307:102–104.

Kirch, P. V., J. A. Swift, and N. Lincoln. 2020. Preliminary field report on archaeological survey and test excavations in Pualaulau and Kapana, Hālawa Valley, Moloka'i, July 11–August 17. Report submitted to US National Science Foundation. Honolulu: University of Hawai'i.

———. 2022. Preliminary field report on archaeological survey and test excavations in Hālawa Valley, Moloka'i, December 2020 to July 2021. Report submitted to US National Science Foundation. Honolulu: University of Hawai'i.

Klieger, P. C. 1998. *Moku'ula: Maui's Sacred Island*. Honolulu, HI: Bishop Museum Press.

Knecht, D. P., and T. M. Rieth. 2016. Archaeological monitoring in support of the Power Distribution Upgrades Phase III, Kaua'i Test Facility, Pacific Missile Range Facility, Waimea Ahupua'a, Kona District, Island of Kaua'i. Unpublished report. Honolulu, HI: International Archaeological Research Institute.

Kolb, M. J. 1991. Social power, chiefly authority, and ceremonial architecture in an island polity, Maui, Hawaii. PhD diss., University of California, Los Angeles.

———. 1992. Diachronic design changes in *heiau* temple architecture on the island of Maui, Hawai'i. *Asian Perspectives* 31:9–38.

———. 1994a. Monumentality and the rise of religious authority in precontact Hawai'i. *Current Anthropology* 35:521–548.

———. 1994b. Ritual activity and chiefly economy at an upland religious site on Maui, Hawai'i. *Journal of Field Archaeology* 21:417–436.

———. 1997. Labor mobilization, ethnohistory, and the archaeology of community in Hawai'i. *Journal of Archaeological Method and Theory* 4:265–285.

———. 1999. Monumental grandeur and political efflorescence in pre-contact Hawai'i: Excavations at Pi'ilanihale Heiau, Maui. *Archaeology in Oceania* 34:71–82.

———. 2006. The origins of monumental architecture in ancient Hawai'i. *Current Anthropology* 47:657–665.

Kolb, M. J., ed. 1993. Na Wahi Pana o Hāmoa: A historical and archaeological survey of a windward East Maui Community, Hāna District, Maui. Unpublished report. Honolulu, HI: State Historic Preservation Division.

Kolb, M. J., and B. Dixon. 2002. Landscapes of war: Rules and conventions of conflict in ancient Hawai'i (and elsewhere). *American Antiquity* 67:514–534.

Kolb, M. J., and G. M. Murakami. 1994. Cultural dynamics and the ritual role of woods in pre-contact Hawai'i. *Asian Perspectives* 33:57–78.

Kolb, M. J., and E. Radewagen. 1997. Na Heiau o Kahikinui: The temples of Kahikinui. In P. V. Kirch, ed., *Na Mea Kahiko o Kahikinui: Studies in the Archaeology of Kahikinui, Maui, Hawaiian Islands*, pp. 61–77. Berkeley, CA: Archaeological Research Facility.

Kotzebue, O. von. 1821. *Voyage of Discovery, into the South Seas and to Bering's Straits . . . 1815–1818*. 3 vols. London: Longman, Hurst.

Kurashima, N., L. Fortini, and T. Ticktin. 2019. The potential of indigenous agricultural food production under climate change in Hawai'i. *Nature Sustainability* 2:191–199.

Kurashima, N., and P. V. Kirch. 2011. Geospatial modeling of pre-contact Hawaiian production systems on Moloka'i Island, Hawaiian Islands. *Journal of Archaeological Science* 38:3662–3674.

Krauss, B. 1988. *Keneti: South Seas Adventures of Kenneth Emory.* Honolulu: University of Hawai'i Press.

Ladd, E. J. 1967. Archaeological salvage of the City of Refuge by-pass and entrance roads, Honaunau, Kona, Hawaii. Unpublished report in Library, Bernice P. Bishop Museum. Honolulu.

———. 1969a. Hale-o-Keawe temple site, Honaunau. In R. Pearson, ed., *Archaeology on the Island of Hawaii,* pp. 163–189. Asian and Pacific Archaeology Series No. 3. Honolulu: Social Science Research Institute, University of Hawai'i.

———. 1969b. Alealea temple site, Honaunau: Salvage report. In R. Pearson, ed., *Archaeology on the Island of Hawaii,* pp. 95–130. Asian and Pacific Archaeology Series No. 3. Honolulu: Social Science Research Institute, University of Hawai'i.

———. 1969c. The Great Wall stabilization: Salvage report. In R. Pearson, ed., *Archaeology on the Island of Hawaii,* pp. 133–160. Asian and Pacific Archaeology Series No. 3. Honolulu: Social Science Research Institute, University of Hawai'i.

———. 1970. Test excavations of three stepped platforms. In R. C. Green, ed., *Makaha Valley Historical Project, Interim Report No. 2,* pp. 81–96. Pacific Anthropological Records 10. Honolulu, HI: Bernice P. Bishop Museum.

———. 1973. Kaneaki temple site—an excavation report. In E. Ladd, ed., *Makaha Valley Historical Project: Interim Report No. 4,* pp. 1–30. Pacific Anthropological Records 19. Honolulu, HI: Bernice P. Bishop Museum.

Ladd, E. J., ed. 1973. *Makaha Valley Historical Project: Interim Report No. 4.* Pacific Anthropological Records 19. Honolulu, HI: Bernice P. Bishop Museum.

Ladd, E. J., and D. E. Yen, eds. 1972. *Makaha Valley Historical Project: Interim Report No. 3.* Pacific Anthropological Records 18. Honolulu, HI: Bernice P. Bishop Museum.

Ladefoged, T. N. 1990. A dryland agricultural system at Kalaupapa, Moloka'i: Archaeological inventory survey, Airport Improvement Project. Unpublished report. Honolulu, HI: International Archaeological Research Institute.

———. 1991. Hawaiian architectural transformations during the early historic era. *Asian Perspectives* 30:57–70.

Ladefoged, T. N., and M. W. Graves. 2000. Evolutionary theory and the historical development of dry-land agriculture in North Kohala, Hawai'i. *American Antiquity* 65:423–448.

———. 2007. Modeling agricultural development and demography in Kohala, Hawai'i Island. In P. V. Kirch and J.-L. Rallu, eds., *The Growth and Collapse of Pacific Island Societies: Archaeological and Demographic Perspectives,* pp. 70–89. Honolulu: University of Hawai'i Press.

———. 2008a. Variable development of dryland agriculture in Hawai'i: A fine-grained chronology from the Kohala Field System, Hawai'i Island. *Current Anthropology* 49:771–802.

———. 2008b. The formation of Hawaiian territories. In I. Lilley, ed., *Archaeology of Oceania: Australia and the Pacific Islands,* pp. 259–283. Oxford: Blackwell Publishing.

Ladefoged, T. N., M. W. Graves, and J. H. Coil. 2005. The introduction of sweet potato in Polynesia: Early remains in Hawai'i. *Journal of the Polynesian Society* 114:359–374.

Ladefoged, T. N., M. W. Graves, and R. P. Jennings. 1996. Dryland agricultural expansion and intensification in Kohala, Hawai'i Island. *Antiquity* 70:861–880.

Ladefoged, T. N., M. W. Graves, and M. D. McCoy. 2003. Archaeological evidence for agricultural development in Kohala, Island of Hawai'i. *Journal of Archaeological Science* 30:923–940.

Ladefoged, T. N., P. V. Kirch, S. M. Gon III, O. A. Chadwick, A. S. Hartshorn, and P. M. Vitousek. 2009. Opportunities and constraints for intensive agriculture in the Hawaiian archipelago prior to European contact. *Journal of Archaeological Science* 36:2374–2383.

Ladefoged, T. N., C. T. Lee, and M. W. Graves. 2008. Modeling life expectancy and surplus production of dynamic pre-contact territories in leeward Kohala, Hawai'i. *Journal of Anthropological Archaeology* 27:93–110.

Ladefoged, T. N., M. D. McCoy, G. Asner, P. V. Kirch, C. O. Puleston, O. A. Chadwick, and P. M. Vitousek. 2011. Agricultural potential and actualized development in Hawai'i: An airborne LiDAR survey of the leeward Kohala field system (Hawai'i Island). *Journal of Archaeological Science* 38:3605–3619.

Ladefoged, T. N., M. D. McCoy, and M. W. Graves. 2020. Collective action and political agency in the leeward Kohala hinterlands, Hawai'i Island. *Journal of Pacific Archaeology* 11 (1): 10–20.

Ladefoged, T. N., G. F. Somers, and M. M. Lane-Hamasaki. 1987. *A Settlement Pattern Analysis of a Portion of Hawaiian Volcanoes National Park*. Denver, CO: Western Archeological and Conservation Center Publications in Anthropology No. 44.

Landrum, J., A. Schiltz, and R. Drolet. 1992. Archaeological inventory survey and limited test excavations at specified lands within Opihihali 2 Ahupua'a, South Kona District, Island of Hawai'i. Unpublished report. Honolulu, HI: Ogden Environmental and Energy Services.

Langenwalter, P. E., and H. F. James. 2015. Extinct and extirpated birds and other vertebrates in the faunal assemblage of Hālawa Cave, a rockshelter in North Hālawa Valley, O'ahu, Hawai'i. *Hawaiian Archaeology* 14:65–78.

Langenwalter, P. E., and L. K. Meeker. 2015. Excavation of the Hālawa Cave Rockshelter, North Hālawa Valley, O'ahu, Hawai'i. *Hawaiian Archaeology* 14:47–64.

La Selle, S., B. M. Richmond, B. E. Jaffe, A. R. Nelson, F. R. Griswold, M. E. Arcos, C. Chagué, et al. 2019. Sedimentary evidence of prehistoric distant-source tsunamis in the Hawaiian Islands. *Sedimentology* 67:1249–1273.

Lass, B. 1994. *Hawaiian Adze Production and Distribution: Implications for the Development of Chiefdoms*. Monograph 37, Institute of Archaeology, University of California, Los Angeles.

Lebo, S. A., ed. 1997. Native Hawaiian and Euro-American Culture Change in Early Honolulu. Unpublished report. Honolulu, HI: Bernice P. Bishop Museum.

Lebo, S. A., J. E. Dockall, and D. I. Olszewski. 1999. Life in Waipio Valley, Hawaii: 1880 to 1942. Unpublished report in Library, Bernice P. Bishop Museum. Honolulu.

Lebo, S. A., and K. T. M. Johnson. 2007. Geochemical sourcing of rock specimens and stone artifacts from Nihoa and Necker Islands, Hawai'i. *Journal of Archaeological Science* 34:858–871.

Lebo, S. A., E. K. Komori, and T. S. Dye. 2011. An archaeological inventory survey of the coastal portion of Kahuku Ahupua'a. Unpublished report. Honolulu, HI: T. S. Dye & Colleagues, Archaeologists.

Ledyard, J. 1963. *John Ledyard's Journal of Captain Cook's Last Voyage*. Edited by J. K. Munford. Corvallis: Oregon State University Press.

Lee, C. T., C. Puleston, and S. Tuljapurkar. 2009. Food and prehistory III: Food-dependent demography in variable environments. *Journal of Theoretical Population Biology* 76:179–188.

Lee, C. T., and S. Tuljapurkar. 2010. Quantitative, dynamic models to integrate environment, population, and society. In P. V. Kirch, ed., *Roots of Conflict: Soils, Agriculture, and Sociopolitical Complexity in Ancient Hawai'i*, pp. 111–133. Santa Fe, NM: School for Advanced Research Press.

Lee, C. T., S. Tuljapurkar, and P. M. Vitousek. 2006. Risky business: Temporal and spatial variation in preindustrial dryland agriculture. *Human Ecology* 34:739–763.

Lee, G. 1988. Petroglyphs of Lanai, Hawaii. Unpublished report on file at State Historic Preservation Division, Honolulu.

———. 1998. Function and form: A study of petroglyphs at Puʻuloa, Hawaiʻi. In C. M. Stevenson, G. Lee, and F. J. Morin, eds., *Easter Island in Pacific Context: South Seas Symposium,* pp. 240–245. Los Osos, CA: Island Foundation.

Lee, G., and E. Stasack. 1999. *Spirit of Place: Petroglyphs of Hawaiʻi.* Los Osos, CA: Easter Island Foundation.

Lee, R. D. 1986. Malthus and Boserup: A dynamic synthesis. In D. Coleman and R. S. Schofield, eds., *The State of Population Theory: Forward from Malthus,* pp. 96–103. Oxford: Basil Blackwell.

Leidemann, H. 2003. Site 50-80-10-1890 and Site 50-80-10-1901. In H. Leidemann, L. H. Hartzell, I. P. Gordon, S. A. Lebo, J. E. Dockall, H. A. Lennstrom, S. McPherron, and B. Dolan, eds., Continuity and change in upland Kāneʻohe habitation: Data recovery and monitoring investigations in Luluku, Kapalai, and Punaluʻu Mauka ʻIli, Oʻahu, pp. 35–88, Unpublished report in Library, Bernice P. Bishop Museum. Honolulu.

Leidemann, H., J. Dockall, H. A. Lennstrom, and S. A. Lebo. 2004. Continuity and Change in upland Kāneʻohe agriculture: Data recovery and monitoring investigations at Site 50–80–10–1887, Luluku ʻIli, Oʻahu. Unpublished report in Library, Bernice P. Bishop Museum. Honolulu.

Leidemann, H., L. H. Hartzell, I. P. Gordon, S. A. Lebo, J. E. Dockall, H. A. Lennstrom, S. McPherron, and B. Dolan, eds. 2003. Continuity and change in upland Kāneʻohe habitation: Data recovery and monitoring investigations in Luluku, Kapalai, and Punaluʻu Mauka ʻIli, Oʻahu. Unpublished report in Library, Bernice P. Bishop Museum. Honolulu.

Leidemann, H., S. A. Lebo, H. A. Lennstrom, L. L. Hartzell, S. Williams, J. L. Perry, and T. Jiao. 2007. Final report of H-3 archaeological investigations at Kukuiokāne Sites 50-80-10-1888, -1889, -2038, and -2076 Kāneʻohe, Oʻahu. Unpublished report in Library, Bernice P. Bishop Museum. Honolulu.

Leidemann, H. H., and L. L. Hartzell. 2003. The archaeology of an upland region: An overview of the windward project area. In *Windward Highway Archaeological Investigations: Inventory Survey, Data Recovery, and Monitoring for Interstate Route H-3 in Kāneʻohe, Oahu,* pp. 623–640. Honolulu: Department of Anthropology, Bishop Museum.

Lennstrom, H. A., and D. I. Olszewski. 2001. Heritage resources in Waipio Valley, Hawaii. Unpublished report in Library, Bernice P. Bishop Museum. Honolulu.

Lerner, H. R. L., M. Meyer, H. F. James, M. Hofreiter, and R. C. Fleischer. 2011. Multilocus resolution of phylogeny and timescale in the extant adaptive radiation of Hawaiian honeycreepers. *Current Biology* 21:1838–1844.

Liebherr, J. K., and N. Porch. 2015. Reassembling a lost lowland carabid beetle assemblage (Coleoptera) from Kauai, Hawaiian Islands. *Invertebrate Systematics* 29:191–213.

Lima, C-A. P., M. M. T. Labra, W. K. McElroy, T. P. K. Tengan, and J. M. Bayman. 2019. A pedagogical approach to indigenous community based archaeology in Hawaiʻi: The north shore field school. *Journal of Community Archaeology & Heritage* 6:69–81.

Lincoln, N. K. 2020. Agroforestry form and ecological adaptation in ancient Hawaiʻi: Extent of the pākukui swidden system of Hāmākua, Hawaiʻi Island. *Agricultural Systems* 181:102808.

Lincoln, N. K., O. A. Chadwick, and P. M. Vitousek. 2014. Indicators of soil fertility and opportunities for pre-contact agriculture in Kona, Hawaiʻi. *Ecosphere* 5:1–20.

Lincoln, N. K., and T. N. Ladefoged. 2014. Agroecology of pre-contact Hawaiian dryland farming: The spatial extent, yield, and social impact of Hawaiian breadfruit groves in Kona, Hawaiʻi. *Journal of Archaeological Science* 49:192–202.

Lincoln, N. K., and P. Vitousek. 2015. Nitrogen fixation during decomposition of sugarcane (*Saccharum officinarum*) is an important contribution to nutrient supply in traditional dryland agricultural systems of Hawai'i. *International Journal of Agricultural Sustainability* 14 (2): 214–230.

Linnekin, J. 1985. *Children of the Land: Exchange and Status in a Hawaiian Community.* New Brunswick, NJ: Rutgers University Press.

———. 1988. Who made the feather cloaks? A problem in Hawaiian gender relations. *Journal of the Polynesian Society* 97:265–280.

Longenecker, K., Y. L. Chan, R. J. Toonen, D. B. Carlon, T. L. Hunt, A. M. Friedlander, and E. E. Demartini. 2014. Archaeological evidence of validity of fish populations on unexploited reefs as proxy targets for modern populations. *Conservation Biology* 28:1322–1330.

Loubser, J., and R. B. Rechtman, R. B. 2006. Archaeological data recovery investigations at SIHP Sites 22426 and 22427 Kahului 2nd, North Kona District, Island of Hawai'i. Unpublished report. Hilo, HI: Rechtman Consulting, LLC.

Lundblad, S. P., P. R. Mills, J. Kahn, K. Mulliken, and C. Cauley. 2014. New insights from the Wai'ahukini rockshelter site (H8), Ka'ū District, Hawai'i Island from non-destructive EDXRF geochemistry. *Society for Hawaiian Archaeology Special Publication 4,* pp. 73–84. Honolulu: Society for Hawaiian Archaeology.

Lundblad, S. P., P. R. Mills, M. D. McCoy, J. G. Kahn, K. Mulliken, and D. Kaylor. 2013. Identification of volcanic glass sources inferred from geochemical analysis of artifacts on leeward Hawai'i Island. In G. R. Summerhayes and H. Buckley, eds., *Pacific Archaeology: Documenting the Past 50,000 Years,* pp. 67–75. Dunedin, New Zealand: University of Otago Studies in Archaeology No. 25.

Luscomb, M. L. K. 1975. Report on inspection of heiau at 2626 Anuenue St., Manoa, Oahu. Unpublished report on file in the State Historic Preservation Division, Department of Land and Natural Resources. Honolulu.

Luscomb, M., and R. Reeve. 1976. Archaeological surveillance and salvage during the electrical conduit excavations on the grounds of 'Iolani Palace, Honolulu, O'ahu. Unpublished report in Library, Bernice P. Bishop Museum. Honolulu.

Lyons, C. J. 1903. *A History of the Hawaiian Government Survey with Notes on Land Matters in Hawaii.* Appendices 3 and 4 of the Report of the Surveyor to the Governor of the Territory of Hawaii. Honolulu: Hawaiian Gazette.

MacArthur, R. H., and E. O. Wilson. 1967. *The Theory of Island Biogeography.* Princeton, NJ: Princeton University Press.

Macdonald, G. A., and A. T. Abbott. 1970. *Volcanoes in the Sea: The Geology of Hawaii.* Honolulu: University of Hawai'i Press.

Madeus, J. K., J. E. Dockall, T. Lee-Greig, and H. H. Hammatt. 2005. An archaeological inventory survey of 72.0 acres at Maunalei and Wahane Gulch Maunalei Ahupua'a, Lahaina District, Island of Lāna'i. Unpublished report. Honolulu, HI: Scientific Consultant Services.

Major, M. 1995. The cultural construction of culture reconstruction: An ethnography of Hawai'i archaeologists in the Contract Era. Master's thesis, University of Hawai'i, Mānoa.

———. 2000. Archaeological inventory survey at Kukui Summit, Ahupua'a of Kaluakoi, Moloka'i. Unpublished report. Honolulu: Cultural Landscapes Hawaii.

———. 2001. Archaeological inventory in the Ke'e Wetland Field System, Kaua'i. Unpublished report. Honolulu: Hawai'i Division of State Parks.

———. 2008. Historic preservation plan for Parcel 32, Mauna Lani Resort, Waikaloa Ahupua'a South Kohala District, Hawai'i Island, Hawai'i. Unpublished report. Honolulu, HI: Pacific Consulting Services.

Malo, D. 1951. *Hawaiian Antiquities.* Bernice P. Bishop Museum Special Publication 2. Honolulu, HI: Bishop Museum Press.

Malthus, T. R. 1798. *An Essay on the Principle of Population.* London: J. Johnson.

Maly, K., A. T. Walker, and P. H. Rosendahl. 1994. Archaeological inventory survey, Waiakea Cane Lots Portion of Parcel 6, Land of Waiakea, South Hilo District, Island of Hawaiʻi. Unpublished report. Hilo, HI: Paul H. Rosendahl.

Marck, J. 1996. 2000. *Topics in Polynesian Language and Culture History.* Pacific Linguistics No. 504. Canberra: Australian National University Press.

Martinson, J. J., R. M. Harding, G. Philippon, F. Flye Sainte-Marie, J. Roux, A. J. Boyce, and J. B. Clegg. 1993. Demographic reductions and genetic bottlenecks in humans: Minisatellite allele distributions in Oceania. *Human Genetics* 91:445–450.

Masse, W. B., L. A. Carter, and G. F. Somers. 1991. Wahaʻula *Heiau:* The regional and symbolic context of Hawaiʻi Island's "red mouth" temple. *Asian Perspectives* 30:19–56.

Matisoo-Smith, E., R. M. Roberts, G. J. Irwin, J. S. Allen, D. Penny, and D. M. Lambert. 1998. Patterns of prehistoric human mobility revealed by mitochondrial DNA from the Pacific rat. *Proceedings of the National Academy of Sciences, U.S.A.* 95:15145–15150.

Maunupau, T. K. 1998. *Huakai Makaikai a Kaupo, Maui / A Visit to Kaupō, Maui.* Edited by N. N. K. Losch. Honolulu, HI: Bishop Museum Press.

Mayr, E. 1997. *This Is Biology: The Science of the Living World.* Cambridge, MA: Harvard University Press.

McAllister, J. G. 1933a. *Archaeology of Oahu.* Bernice P. Bishop Museum Bulletin 104. Honolulu, HI: Bishop Museum Press.

———. 1933b. *Archaeology of Kahoolawe.* Bernice P. Bishop Museum Bulletin 115. Honolulu, HI: Bishop Museum Press.

McCoy K. S., I. D. Williams, A. M. Friedlander, H. Ma, L. Teneva, and J. N. Kittinger. 2018. Estimating nearshore coral reef-associated fisheries production from the main Hawaiian Islands. *PLOS ONE* 13 (4): e0195840.

McCoy, M. D. 2005. The development of the Kalaupapa field system, Molokaʻi Island, Hawaiʻi. *Journal of the Polynesian Society* 114:339–358.

———. 2006. Landscape, social memory, and society: An ethnohistoric-archaeological study of three Hawaiian communities. PhD diss., University of California, Berkeley.

———. 2007. A revised late Holocene culture history for Molokaʻi Island, Hawaiʻi. *Radiocarbon* 49:1273–1322.

———. 2008a. Hawaiian limpet harvesting in historical perspective: A review of modern and archaeological data on *Cellana* spp. from the Kalaupapa Peninsula, Molokaʻi Island. *Pacific Science* 62:21–38.

———. 2008b. Life outside the temple: Reconstructing traditional Hawaiian ritual and religion through new studies of ritualized practices. In L. Fogelin, ed., *Religion, Archaeology, and the Material World,* pp. 261–278. Carbondale, IL: Center for Archaeological Investigations.

———. 2011. Geochemical characterization of volcanic glass from Puʻu Waʻawaʻa, Hawaiʻi Island. *Rapa Nui Journal* 25:43–51.

———. 2014. The significance of religious ritual in ancient Hawaiʻi. *Journal of Pacific Archaeology* 5:72–80.

———. 2018. Celebration as a source of power in archaic states: Archaeological and historical evidence for the Makahiki festival in the Hawaiian Islands. *World Archaeology* 50:242–270.

———. 2020a. *Maps for Time Travelers: How Archaeologists Used Technology to Bring Us Closer to the Past.* Oakland: University of CaliforNa Press.

———. 2020b. The Site Problem: A critical review of the site concept in archaeology in the digital age. *Journal of Field Archaeology* 45 (S1): S18–S26.

McCoy, M. D., G. P. Asner, and M. W. Graves. 2011. Airborne lidar survey of irrigated agricultural landscapes: An application of the slope contrast method. *Journal of Archaeological Science* 38:2141–2154.

McCoy, M. D., A. T. Browne Ribeiro, M. W. Graves, O. A. Chadwick, and P. M. Vitousek. 2013. Irrigated taro (*Colocasia esculenta*) farming in North Kohala, Hawai'i: Sedimentology and soil nutrient analyses. *Journal of Archaeological Science* 40:1528–1538.

McCoy, M. D., J. Casana, A. C. Hill, E. Jakoby Laugier, and T. N. Ladefoged. 2022. Mapping ancient architecture via aerial vehicle-acquired Lidar: A case study of Hōlualoa royal centre, Kona District, Hawai'i Island. *Journal of the Polynesian Society* 131:71–92.

McCoy, M. D., J. Casana, A. C. Hill, E. Jakoby Laugier, M. A. Mulrooney, and T. N. Ladefoged. 2021. Unpiloted aerial vehicle acquired Lidar for mapping monumental architecture: A case study from the Hawaiian Islands. *Advances in Archaeological Practice* 9 (2): 160–174.

McCoy, M. D., and M. C. Codlin. 2015. Decoding the rock art of old Hawai'i: A brief report on petroglyphs in Manukā, Ka'ū District, Hawai'i Island. *Hawaiian Archaeology* 14:33–46.

———. 2016. The influence of religious authority in everyday life: A landscape scale study of domestic architecture and religious law in ancient Hawai'i. *World Archaeology* 48 (3): 411–430.

McCoy, M. D., and M. W. Graves. 2010. The role of agricultural innovation on Pacific Islands: A case study from Hawai'i Island. *World Archaeology* 42:90–107.

McCoy, M. D., M. W. Graves, and G. Murakami. 2010. Introduction of Breadfruit (*Artocarpus altilis*) to the Hawaiian Islands. *Economic Botany* 64 (4): 374–381.

McCoy, M. D., and A. S. Hartshorn. 2007. Wind erosion and intensive prehistoric agriculture: A case study from the Kalaupapa field system, Hawai'i. *Geoarchaeology: An International Journal* 22:511–532.

McCoy, M. D., and T. N. Ladefoged. 2009. New developments in the use of spatial technology in archaeology. *Journal of Archaeological Research* 17:263–295.

McCoy, M. D., T. N. Ladefoged, and J. Casana. 2020. Report on the utility of unpiloted aerial vehicle (UAV) archaeological survey in Kealakekua Bay Historical State Park, Keolonāhihi State Historical Park, and Lapakahi State Historical Park, Hawai'i Island. Unpublished report.

McCoy, M. D., T. N. Ladefoged, M. W. Graves, and J. W. Stephens. 2011. Strategies for constructing religious authority in ancient Hawai'i. *Antiquity* 85:927–941.

McCoy, M. D., P. R. Mills, S. Lundblad, T. Rieth, J. G. Kahn, and R. Gard. 2011. A cost surface model of volcanic glass quarrying and exchange in Hawai'i. *Journal of Archaeological Science* 38:2547–2560.

McCoy, M. D., M. Mulrooney, M. Horrocks, H. Cheng, and T. N. Ladefoged. 2017. Evaluating agricultural bet-hedging strategies in the Kona Field System: New high-precision ^{230}Th/U and ^{14}C dates and plant microfossil data from Kealakekua, Hawai'i Island. *Archaeology in Oceania* 52:70–80.

McCoy, P. C. 1972. *Archaeological Research at Fort Elizabeth, Waimea, Kauai, Hawaiian Islands, Phase I*. Department of Anthropology Report 72-7. Honolulu, HI: Bernice P. Bishop Museum.

———. 1976. The Mauna Kea adze quarry complex, Hawaii: A first analysis. *Proceedings of the First Conference in Natural Sciences in Hawaii*, pp. 135–142. Honolulu, HI: National Park Service.

———. 1977. The Mauna Kea adze quarry project: A summary of the 1975 field investigations. *Journal of the Polynesian Society* 86:223–244.

———. 1982. Cultural resources reconnaissance of the Mauna Kea summit region: Report 2. Archaeological reconnaissance survey. Unpublished report in Library, Bernice P. Bishop Museum. Honolulu.

———. 1985. Preliminary archaeological survey of the Puʻu Kalepeamoa Site, Mauna Kea, Hawaiʻi. Unpublished report in Library, Bernice P. Bishop Museum. Honolulu.

———. 1990. Subsistence in a "non" subsistence environment: Factors of production in a Hawaiian alpine desert adze quarry. In D. E. Yen and J. M. J. Mummery, eds., *Pacific Production Systems: Approaches to Economic Prehistory,* pp. 85–119. Occasional Papers in Prehistory No. 18. Canberra: Australian National University Press.

———. 1991. Survey and test excavations of the Puʻu Kalepeamoa Site, Mauna Kea, Hawaiʻi. Unpublished report. Honolulu, HI: Mountain Archaeology Research Corporation.

———. 1999. Neither here nor there: A rites of passage site on the eastern fringes of the Mauna Kea adze quarry, Hawaiʻi. *Hawaiian Archaeology* 7:11–34.

———. 2011. Signs of a divine reality: The materiality of bird cook stones (*pohaku ʻeho*) from the dry interior uplands and mountainous regions of the island of Hawaiʻi. *Hawaiian Archaeology* 12:65–107.

McCoy, P. C., and R. A. Gould. 1977. Alpine archaeology in Hawaii. *Archaeology* 30:234–243.

McCoy, P. C., A. Makanani, and A. Sinoto. 1993. Archaeological investigations of the Puʻu Moiwi Adze Quarry Complex, Kahoʻolawe. Unpublished report prepared for Kahoʻolawe Island Conveyance Commission, Consultant Report No. 14. N.p.

McCoy, P. C., and R. Nees. 2010. Archaeological inventory survey of the Mauna Kea Science Reserve Kaʻohe Ahupuaʻa, Hāmākua District, Island of Hawaiʻi. Unpublished report. Honolulu, HI: Pacific Consulting Services.

———. 2014. A re-examination of Kenneth P. Emory's theory of Necker type *marae* in the summit region of Mauna Kea, Hawaiʻi: Many *marae* or shrines later. *Hawaiian Archaeology, Society for Hawaiian Archaeology Special Publication 4,* pp. 27–50. Honolulu: Society for Hawaiian Archaeology.

McCoy, P. C., R. Nees, M. I. Weisler, and J. Zhao. 2012. ^{230}Thorium dating of toolstone procurement strategies, production scale and ritual practices at the Mauna Kea Adze Quarry complex, Hawaiʻi. *Journal of the Polynesian Society* 121:407–420.

McCoy, P. C., M. I. Weisler, E. J. St. Pierre, R. Bolhar, and Y. Feng. 2015. Geochemistry and technology of basaltic glass artefacts from an embedded source and two high-altitude base camps in the Mauna Kea Adze Quarry Complex, Hawaiʻi. *Journal of Pacific Archaeology* 6:1–20.

McCoy, P. C., M. I. Weisler, J. Zhou, and X. Feng. 2009. ^{230}Th dates for dedicatory corals from a remote alpine desert adze quarry on Mauna Kea, Hawaiʻi. *Antiquity* 83:445–457.

McEldowney, H. 1979. Archaeological and historical literature search and research design, lava flow control study, Hilo, Hawaiʻi. Unpublished report in Library, Bernice P. Bishop Museum. Honolulu.

McElroy, W. K. 2004. Poi pounders of Kauaʻi Island, Hawaiʻi: Variability through time and space. *Hawaiian Archaeology* 9:25–49.

———. 2007. The development of irrigated agriculture in Wailau Valley, Molokaʻi Island, Hawaiʻi. PhD diss., University of Hawaiʻi at Mānoa.

———. 2012. Approaches to dating wetland agricultural features: An example from Wailau Valley, Molokaʻi Island, Hawaiʻi. In M. Spriggs, D. Addison, and P. J. Matthews, eds., *Irrigated Taro* (Colocasia esculenta) *in the Indo-Pacific,* pp. 135–154. Osaka, Japan: Senri Ethnological Studies.

McElroy, W. K., T. S. Dye, and E. H. R. Jourdane. 2006. Archaeological monitoring and investigations during installation of leach fields at Bellows Air Force Station and Hickam Air Force Base, Waimānalo, Koʻolaupoko, and Moanalua, Kona, Oʻahu. Unpublished report submitted to Shaw Environmental. Honolulu, HI: T. S. Dye & Colleagues.

McElroy, W. K., and S. Eminger. 2011. Anatomy of an unfinished loʻi system: The Kuʻele West complex in Wailau Valley, Molokaʻi. *Hawaiian Archaeology* 12:47–64.

McElroy, W., S. Eminger, and T. Donham. 2005. University of Hawaiʻi Molokaʻi Archaeological Training Project 2004–2005: Results Kamalō, Molokaʻi, Hawaiʻi. Unpublished report. Honolulu: Department of Anthropology, University of Hawaiʻi.

McGerty, L., and R. L. Spear. 1996. Archaeological inventory survey of a portion of Opihihali 1 Ahupuaʻa, South Kona, Island of Hawaiʻi. Unpublished report. Honolulu, HI: Scientific Consultant Services.

———. 2006. An archaeological inventory survey report on approximately 817 acres of Land Hāliʻimaile Ahupuaʻa, Makawao District, Maui Island, Hawaiʻi. Unpublished report. Honolulu, HI: Scientific Consultant Services.

———. 2009. Phase II archaeological evaluation of all sites except sites 5487 and 191, Dillingham Military Reservation, Island of Oʻahu, Hawaii. Unpublished report. Honolulu, HI: Scientific Consultant Services.

McIntosh, J. D., J. L. Putzi, C. C. Le Suer, and P. L. Cleghorn. 2006. Archaeological Inventory Survey at "Block 10": The Smith-Beretania Parking Lot, Ahupuaʻa of Honolulu, Kona District, Island of Oʻahu. Unpublished report. Honolulu, HI: Pacific Legacy.

Menzies, A. 1920. *Hawaii Nei 128 Years Ago.* Honolulu, HI: W. F. Wilson.

Meyer, M., T. N. Ladefoged, and P. M. Vitousek. 2007. Soil phosphorus and agricultural development in the Leeward Kohala Field System, Island of Hawaiʻi. *Pacific Science* 61:347–353.

Michels, J. W. 1973. *Dating Methods in Archaeology.* New York: Seminar Press.

Millerstrom, S., and P. V. Kirch. 2002. History on stones: A newly-discovered petroglyph site at Kahikinui, Maui. *Hawaiian Archaeology* 8:3–12.

———. 2004. Petroglyphs of Kahikinui, Maui, Hawaiian Islands: Rock images within a Polynesian settlement landscape. *Proceedings of the Prehistoric Society* 70:107–127.

Mills, P. 2001. Speaking up for the small fish in the big pond: Establishing a mission for the University of Hawaiʻi at Hilo in Hawaiian archaeology. In C. M. Stevenson, G. Lee, and F. J. Moran, eds., *Pacific 2000: Proceedings of the Fifth International Conference on Easter Island and the Pacific,* pp. 151–155. Los Osos, CA: Easter Island Foundation.

———. 2002a. *Hawaii's Russian Adventure: A New Look at Old History.* Honolulu: University of Hawaiʻi Press.

———. 2002b. Social integration and the *ala loa:* Reconsidering the significance of trails in Hawaiian exchange. *Asian Perspectives* 41:148–166.

———. 2003. Laupāhoehoe Nui: Archaeology of a high-risk landscape on Windward Hawaiʻi Island. *Rapa Nui Journal* 17:106–113.

———. 2005. Connecting with Kauaʻi's Canyonlands. In M. T. Carson and M. W. Graves, ed., *Na Mea Kahiko o Kauaʻi: Archaeological Studies in Kauaʻi,* pp. 47–61. Society for Hawaiian Archaeology Special Publication No. 2. Honolulu.

Mills, P. R., and M. Irani. 2000. A walk through history: Pedestrian survey along the Old Government Beach Road, Honalo to Honuaʻino, North Kona, Hawaiʻi. Unpublished report. Hilo: University of Hawaiʻi.

Mills, P., P. Lima, L. Brandt, J. Kahn, P. Kirch, and S. Lundblad. 2018. Paired geochemical and technological analyses of basalt adze debitage at the Hālawa Dune Site, Moloka'i Island, Hawai'i. *Archaeology in Oceania* 53:78–91.

Mills, P. R., and S. P. Lundblad. 2014. Current perspectives on Hawai'i's stone tool economies. *Journal of Pacific Archaeology* 5:30–39.

Mills, P. R., S. P. Lundblad, C. Cauley, D. S. Coleman, J. S. Field, A. L. Hafner, J. G. Kahn, J. M. Sinton, and P. V. Kirch. 2022. Provenance, production, and distribution of basalt and volcanic glass artifacts in Leeward Kohala, Hawai'i Island. *Geoarchaeology* 37:733-749.

Mills, P. R., S. P. Lundblad, J. S. Field, A. B. Carpenter, W. K. McElroy, and P. Rossi. 2010. Geochemical sourcing of basalt artifacts from Kaua'i, Hawaiian Islands. *Journal of Archaeological Science* 37:3385–3393.

Mills, P. R., S. P. Lundblad, K. Hon, J. J. Moniz-Nakamura, E. L. Kahahane, A. Drake-Raue, T. M. Souza, and R. Wei. 2011. Reappraising craft specialization and exchange in pre-contact Hawai'i through non-destructive sourcing of basalt adze debitage. *Journal of Pacific Archaeology* 2:79–92.

Mills, P. R., S. P. Lundblad, J. G. Smith, P. C. McCoy, and S. P. Naleimaile. 2008. Science and sensitivity: A geochemical characterization of the Mauna Kea adze quarry complex. *American Antiquity* 73:743–758.

Mills, P. R., C. L. White, and B. Barna. 2013. The paradox of the paniolo: An archaeological perspective of Hawaiian ranching. *Historical Archaeology* 47:110–132.

Mintmier, M. A. 2007. Adze production on Maui: Analysis of lithic materials from the west rim of Haleakala. *Hawaiian Archaeology* 11:3–17.

Mintmier, M. A., P. R. Mills, and S. P. Lundblad. 2012. Energy-dispersive X-Ray fluorescence analysis of Haleakalā basalt adze quarry materials, Maui, Hawai'i. *Journal of Archaeological Science* 39:615–623.

Molodin, A. V., and P. R. Mills. 2021. Addressing tensions between colonial and post-colonial histories: Modeling Hawaiian Fort Pā'ula'ula/Russian Fort Elizabeth, Kaua'i Island, Hawai'i. *Asian Perspectives* 60:2–31.

Moniz, J. J. 1997. The role of seabirds in Hawaiian subsistence: Implications for interpreting avian extinction and extirpation in Polynesia. *Asian Perspectives* 36:27–50.

Moniz-Nakamura, J. J. 1999. The archaeology of human foraging and bird resources on the Island of Hawai'i: The evolutionary ecology of avian predation, resource intensification, extirpation, and extinction. PhD diss., University of Hawai'i at Mānoa.

———. 2003. Keonehelelei—The Falling Sands: Uncovering the origin of preserved footprints and associated Ka'u desert features. Unpublished report. Hawaii Volcanoes National Park: National Park Service.

Moore, S. 2020a. On the margins of the market: Change and continuity in nineteenth-century Hawaiian household economies on the Nā Pali Coast, Kaua'i Island. *Journal of Pacific Archaeology* 11:27–40.

———. 2020b. Foreign objects in colonial-era Hawaiian sites: Change and continuity in nineteenth-century Nu'alolo Kai, Kaua'i Island. *Journal of the Polynesian Society* 129:193–235.

Morgenstein, M., and T. J. Riley. 1974. Hydration-rind dating of basaltic glass: A new method for archaeological chronologies. *Asian Perspectives* 17:145–159.

Morgenstein, M., and P. Rosendahl 1976. Basaltic glass hydration dating in Hawaiian archaeology. In R. E. Taylor, ed., *Advances in Obsidian Glass Studies,* pp. 141–614. Park Ridge, NJ: Noyes Press.

Morrison, A. E., S. Quintus, T. M. Rieth, C. Filimoehala, T. Duarte, J. Tulchin, A. Dosseto, H. K. Anae, D. Filimoehala, D. Knecht, and F. Dux. 2022. Colluvial slope agriculture in context: An extensive agricultural landscape along the slopes of Punaluʻu Valley, Oʻahu Island, Hawaiʻi. *The Journal of Island and Coastal Archaeology*. doi: 10.1080/15564894.2021.1998936.

Morrison, K. D. 1994. The intensification of production: Archaeological approaches. *Journal of Archaeological Method and Theory* 1:111–160.

Mulrooney, M. A., K. S. Esh, M. D. McCoy, S. H. Bickler, and Y. H. Sinoto. 2014. New dates from old samples: A revised radiocarbon chronology for the Waiʻahukini Rockshelter site (H8), Kaʻu District, Hawaiʻi Island. *Hawaiian Archaeology, Society for Hawaiian Archaeology Special Publication 4*, pp. 17–26. Honolulu: Society for Hawaiian Archaeology.

Mulrooney, M. A., and T. N. Ladefoged. 2005. Hawaiian *heiau* and agricultural production in the Kohala dryland field system. *Journal of the Polynesian Society* 114:45–68.

Mulrooney, M. A., T. N. Ladefoged, R. Gibb, and D. McCurdy. 2005. Eight million points per day: Archaeological implications of laser scanning and three-dimensional modeling of Puʻukohola Heiau. *Hawaiian Archaeology* 10:18–28.

Mulrooney, M. A., K. M. Pacubas, J. McIntosh, and P. L. Cleghorn. 2021. Archaeological inventory survey of the proposed Paeahu Solar Project on ʻUlupalakua Rranch lands in the Ahupuaʻa of Paeahu, District of Makawao, Island of Maui. Unpublished report. Kailua, HI: Pacific Legacy.

Mulrooney, M. A., and J. A. Swift. 2022. *Huli hele nā wahi pana* (seeking out storied places): The contribution of John F. G. Stokes to Hawaiian archaeology. In H. Howes, T. Jones, and M. Spriggs, eds., *Uncovering Pacific Pasts: Histories of Archaeology in Oceania*, pp. 257–270. Canberra: Australian National University Press.

Murakami, G. M. 1983. Analysis of charcoal from archaeological contexts. In J. T. Clark and P. V. Kirch, eds., *Archaeological Investigations in the Mudlane-Waimea-Kawaihae Road Corridor, Island of Hawaiʻi*, pp. 514–526. Department of Anthropology Report 83-1. Honolulu, HI: Bernice P. Bishop Museum.

———. 1989. Identification of charcoal from Kuolulo rockshelter. In P. V. Kirch, ed., *Prehistoric Hawaiian Occupation in the Anahulu Valley, Oʻahu Island: Excavations in Three Inland Rockshelters*, pp. 103–110. Archaeological Research Facility Contribution No. 47. Berkeley: University of California.

Nakuina, E. M. 1894. Ancient Hawaiian water rights and some of the customs pertaining to them. *Thrum's Hawaiian Annual for 1894*, pp. 79–84. Honolulu.

Nāleimaile, S. P., and L. Brandt. 2013. Is Hawaiian archaeology really Hawaiian? A Native Hawaiian perspective. *The SAA Archaeological Record* 13:31–32.

Nelson, R. E. H., and K. M. G. Vacca. 2021. Mapping pre-contact Keahuamanono Heiau in Haleakalā National Park, Maui, Hawaiʻi. *Journal of Field Archaeology*. https://doi.org/10.1080/00934690.2021.1968610.

Newman, T. S. 1969. Cultural adaptations to the island of Hawaii ecosystem. In R. Pearson, ed., *Archaeology on the Island of Hawaii*, pp. 3–14. Asian and Pacific Archaeology Series No. 3. Honolulu: Social Science Research Institute, University of Hawaiʻi.

———. n.d. [1970]. *Hawaiian Fishing and Farming on the Island of Hawaii, A.D. 1778*. Honolulu: Divison of State Parks, Department of Land and Natural Resources, State of Hawaii.

Nunn, P. D., and F. Petchey. 2013. Bayesian re-evaluation of Lapita settlement in Fiji: Radiocarbon analysis of the Lapita occupation at Bourewa and nearby sites on the Rove Peninsula, Viti Levu Island. *Journal of Pacific Archaeology* 4:21–34.

O'Connell, J. F., and J. Allen. 2015. The process, biotic impact, and global implications of the human colonization of Sahul about 47,000 years ago. *Journal of Archaeological Science* 56:73–84.

O'Day, S. J. 2001. Excavations at the Kipapa Rockshelter, Kahikinui, Maui, Hawai'i. *Asian Perspectives* 40:279–304.

O'Leary, O. 2005. Analysis of the Nu'alolo Kai 1/4-inch fishbone assemblage, Nā Pali Coast, Kaua'i. In M. T. Carson and M. W. Graves, ed., *Na Mea Kahiko o Kaua'i: Archaeological Studies in Kaua'i,* pp. 259–274. Society for Hawaiian Archaeology Special Publication 2. Honolulu: Society for Hawaiian Archaeology.

Olson, L. 1983. Hawaiian volcanic glass applied "dating" and "sourcing": Archaeological context. In J. T. Clark and P. V. Kirch, eds., *Archaeological Investigations of the Mudlane-Waimea-Kawaihae Road Corridor,* pp. 325–340. Department of Anthropology Report 83-1. Honolulu, HI: Bernice P. Bishop Museum.

Olson, S. L., and H. F. James, 1982a. Fossil birds from the Hawaiian Islands: Evidence for wholesale extinction by man before Western contact. *Science* 217:633–635.

———. 1982b. Prodromus of the fossil avifauna of the Hawaiian Islands. *Smithsonian Contributions to Zoology* 365:1–59.

———. 1984. The role of Polynesians in the extinction of the avifauna of the Hawaiian Islands. In P. S. Martin and R. L. Klein, eds., *Quaternary Extinctions: A Prehistoric Revolution,* pp. 768–780. Tucson: University of Arizona Press.

Olszewski, D. I. 2007. Interpreting activities in North Halawa Valley, O'ahu: Adze recycling and resharpening. *Hawaiian Archaeology* 11:18–32.

Olszewski, D. I., ed. 2000. The Mahele and later in Waipio Valley, Hawaii. Unpublished report in Library, Bernice P. Bishop Museum. Honolulu.

Orans, M. 1966. Surplus. *Human Organization* 25:24–32.

Palmer, H. S. 1927. *Geology of Kaula, Nihoa, Necker, and Gardner Islands, and French Frigates Shoal.* Bernice P. Bishop Museum Bulletin 35. Honolulu, HI: Bishop Museum Press.

Palmer, M. A., M. Graves, T. N. Ladefoged, O. A. Chadwick, T. K. Duarte, S. Porder, and P. M. Vitousek. 2009. Sources of nutrients to windward agricultural systems in precontact Hawai'i. *Ecological Applications* 19:1444–1453.

Pau, S., G. M. MacDonald, and T. W. Gillespie. 2012. A dynamic history of climate change and human impact on the environment from Keālia Pond, Maui, Hawaiian Islands. *Annals of the Association of American Geographers* 102:748–762.

Pawley, A. K., and M. Pawley. 1994. Early Austronesian terms for canoe parts and seafaring. In *Austronesian Terminologies: Continuity and Change,* ed. A. K. Pawley and M. D. Ross, pp. 329–361. Pacific Linguistics Series C-127. Canberra: Australian National University Press.

Pawley, A. K., and M. Ross. 1993. Austronesian historical linguistics and culture history. *Annual Review of Anthropology* 22:425–459.

Pearson, R. J. 1962. Some bases for ecological inferences about the aboriginal population of the Hanapepe Valley, Kauai. *Journal of the Polynesian Society* 71:379–385.

———. 1970. *The Archaeology of Hana: Preliminary Survey of Waianapanapa State Park.* Hawaii State Archaeological Journal 70–2. Honolulu: Department of Land and Natural Resources, State of Hawai'i.

———. 1995. A brief report on test excavations at the Hawaiian Mission, Honolulu. *Hawaiian Archaeology* 4:27–33.

Pearson, R. J., ed. 1968. *Excavations at Lapakahi: Selected Papers.* Hawaii State Archaeological Journal 69–2. Honolulu: Department of Land and Natural Resources, State of Hawai'i.

———. 1969. *Archaeology on the Island of Hawaii*. Asian and Pacific Archaeology Series No. 3. Honolulu: Social Science Research Institute, University of Hawai'i.

Pearson, R., J. Hirata, L. Potts, and F. Harby. 1974. Test pitting of Cave 1, Kalaupapa Peninsula, Molokai, Hawaii. *New Zealand Archaeological Association Newsletter* 17:44–49.

Pearson, R. J., P. V. Kirch, and M. Pietrusewsky. 1971. An early prehistoric site at Bellows Beach, Waimanalo, Oahu, Hawaiian Islands. *Archaeology and Physical Anthropology in Oceania* 6:204–234.

Pepalis, J., and M. J. Kolb. 2002. Early human activity at a leeward coastal pondfield near Kalepolepo, Maui. *Hawaiian Archaeology* 8:33–41.

Perzinski, D., T. Bushnell, W. Folk, and H. H. Hammatt. 2002. An archaeological inventory survey on an approximately one-acre parcel in West Hanawana Ahupuaa, Makawao District, Island of Maui. Unpublished report. Honolulu, HI: Scientific Consultant Services.

Perzinski, D., and M. Dega. 2011. An archaeological inventory survey of approximately 427-acres in Kihei, Waiohuli and Waiakoa Ahupuaa, Makawao District, Island of Maui, Hawaii. Unpublished report. Honolulu, HI: Scientific Consultant Services.

Perzinski, D., K. Lyman, C. Medieros, H. Rachel, and M. Dega. 2015. Archaeological Inventory Survey of a 670-Acre Parcel in Honua'ula (Formerly Wailea 670), in Palauea, Paeahu, and Keauhou Ahupua'a, Makawao District, Island of Maui, Hawai'i. Unpublished report. Honolulu, HI: Scientific Consultants Services.

Petchey, F. J. 2001. Radiocarbon determinations from the Mulifanua Lapita site, Upolu, Western Samoa. *Radiocarbon* 43:63–68.

Petchey, F., and P. V. Kirch. 2019. The importance of shell: Redating of the To'aga site (Ofu Island, Manu'a) and a revised chronology for the Lapita to Polynesian Plainware transition in Tonga and Sāmoa. *PLOS ONE* 14 (9): e0211990.

Pfeffer, M. T. 1995. Distribution and design of Pacific octopus lures: The Hawaiian octopus lure in regional context. *Hawaiian Archaeology* 4:47–56.

Phelps, S. 1937. A regional study of Molokai. Unpublished manuscript in Library, Bernice P. Bishop Museum. Honolulu.

Phillips, N., T. N. Ladefoged, B. W. McPhee, and G. P. Asner. 2015. Location, location, location: A viewshed analysis of heiau spatial and temporal relationships in leeward Kohala, Hawai'i. *Journal of Pacific Archaeology* 6:21–40.

Piddington, R., ed. 1939. *Essays in Polynesian Ethnology*. By R. W. Williamson (Part 2 by Piddington). Cambridge: Cambridge University Press.

Pietrusewsky, M. 1970. An osteological view of indigenous populations in Oceania. In R. C. Green and M. Kelly, eds., *Studies in Oceanic Culture History,* pp. 1–12. Pacific Anthropological Records 11. Honolulu, HI: Bishop Museum.

———. 1971a. Application of distance statistics to anthroposcopic data and a comparison of results with those obtained by using discrete traits of the skull. *Archaeology and Physical Anthropology in Oceania* 6:21–33.

———. 1971b. *Human Skeletal Remains at Anaehoomalu*. Department of Anthropology Report Series 71-7. Honolulu, HI: Bernice P. Bishop Museum.

———. 1997. Biological origins of Hawaiians: Evidence from skulls. *Man and Culture in Oceania* 13:1–37.

Pietrusewsky, M., M. T. Douglas, and P. A. Kalima. 1990. Human skeletal remains recovered from 'Anaeho'omalu, South Kohala, Hawai'i Island: A second study. Unpublished report. Prepared for Waikoloa Development.

Pietrusewsky, M., M. T. Douglas, P. A. Kalima, and R. M. Ikehara. 1991. Human skeletal and dental remains from the Honokahua Burial Site, Land of Honokahua, Lahaina District, Island of Maui. Unpublished report. Hilo, HI: Paul H. Rosendahl.

Polanyi, K. 1944. *The Great Transformation*. New York: Farrar and Rinehart.

Polanyi, K., C. M. Arensberg, and H. W. Pearson, eds. 1957. *Trade and Market in the Early Empires: Economies in History and Theory*. Glencoe, IL: Free Press.

Porder, S., A. Paytan, and P. M. Vitousek. 2005. Erosion and landscape development affect plant nutrient status in the Hawaiian Islands. *Oecologia* 142:440–449.

Portlock, N. 1789. *A Voyage round the World . . . in 1785–1788*. London: Stockdale.

Powers, H. A., J. C. Ripperton, and Y. B. Goto. 1932. *Survey of the Physical Features That Affect the Agriculture of the Kona District of Hawaii*. Honolulu: Hawaii Agricultural Experiment Station Bulletin 66.

Price-Beggerly, P. 1993. Artifactual landscape: Kahana Valley, Oʻahu, Hawaiʻi. *Hawaiian Archaeology* 2:10–15.

Pukui, M., and S. Elbert. 1957. *Hawaiian-English Dictionary*. Honolulu: University of Hawaiʻi Press.

Puleston, C., S. Tuljapurkar, and B. Winterhalder. 2014. The invisible cliff: Abrupt imposition of Malthusian equilibrium in a natural-ferility, agrarian society. *PLOS ONE* 9 (1): e87541.

Puleston, C. O., and S. Tuljapurkar. 2008. Population and prehistory II: Space-limited human populations in constant environments. *Theoretical Population Biology* 74:147–160.

Putzi, J. L., N. J. DiVito, C. E. Sholin, P. R. Mills, S. Lundblad, B. Camara, and T. S. Dye. 2015. Alternative models of volcanic glass quarrying and exchange in Hawaiʻi. *Journal of Archaeological Science: Reports* 2:341–352.

Quintus, S., J. Huebert, P. V. Kirch, N. K. Lincoln, and J. Maxwell. 2019. Qualities and contributions of agro-forestry practices and novel forests in pre-European Polynesia and the Polynesian Outliers. *Human Ecology* 47:811–825.

Quintus, S., and N. K. Lincoln. 2018. Integrating local and regional in pre-contact Hawaiian agriculture at Kahuku, Hawaiʻi Island. *Environmental Archaeology* 25:53–68.

Randall, J. E. 2010. *Shore Fishes of Hawaiʻi*. Honolulu: University of Hawaiʻi Press.

Rasmussen, C. M., and P. O'Day. 2004. Trails through time: The changing landscape of the Mauna Kea Saddle, Island of Hawaiʻi Saddle Road data recovery investigations. Unpublished report. Honolulu, HI: International Archaeological Research Institute.

Rechtman, R., K. Maly, D. Dougherty, M. Clark, and O. Maly. 2001. Archeological inventory survey of the Kiʻilae Estates Development Area (TMK: 3-8-5-05: 19, 22, 26, 27), Kiʻilae and Kauleolī Ahupuaʻa, South Kona District, Island of Hawaiʻi. Unpublished report. Hilo, HI: Rechtman Consulting, LLC.

Rechtman, R. B., and D. S. Dougherty. 2000. An archaeological inventory survey of TMK: 3-7-5-04: 9 Lanihau 2nd Ahupuaʻa North Kona District Island of Hawaiʻi. Unpublished report. Hilo, HI: Rechtman Consulting, LLC.

Reeve, R. 1983. Archaeological investigations in Section 3. In J. T. Clark and P. V. Kirch, eds., *Archaeological Investigations of the Mudlane-Waimea-Kawaihae Road Corridor, Island of Hawaiʻi*, pp. 181–239. Department of Anthropology Report 83-1. Honolulu, HI: Bernice P. Bishop Museum.

Reinecke, J. 1930. Archaeology of Kona, Hawaii. Unpublished manuscript in Library, Bernice P. Bishop Museum. Honolulu.

Renger, R. C. 1970. *Archaeological Reconnaissance of Coastal Kaloko and Kukio I, North Kona, Hawaii*. Department of Anthropology Report 70-10. Honolulu, HI: Bernice P. Bishop Museum.

Rice, W. H. 1923. *Hawaiian Legends.* Bernice P. Bishop Museum Bulletin 3. Honolulu, HI: Bishop Museum Press.

Rick, J. W. 1987. Dates as data: An examination of the Peruvian preceramic radiocarbon record. *American Antiquity* 52:55–73.

Riconda, D. 1972. Historical archaeology of Makaha Valley. In E. Ladd and D. Yen, eds., *Makaha Valley Historical Project: Interim Report No. 3,* pp. 3–22. Pacific Anthropological Records 18. Honolulu, HI: Bernice P. Bishop Museum.

Rieth, T. M. 2007. Archeological data recovery at Keoneʻele Cove (PUHO-008), Puʻuhonua o Hōnaunau National Historical Park, Hōnaunau Ahupuaʻa, South Kona District, Island of Hawaiʻi. Unpublished report. Honolulu, HI: International Archaeological Research Institute.

———. 2011. Archeological inventory survey of the Paumoa coastal archeological sites (PUHO-006 and PUHO-028), Puʻuhonua o Hōnaunau National Historical Park, Kēōkea Ahupuaʻa, South Kona District, Island of Hawaiʻi. Unpublished report. Honolulu, HI: International Archaeological Research Institute.

Rieth, T. M., and T. Duarte. 2016. Archaeological monitoring and emergency data recovery at the Ka Malanai in Kailua Development, Kailua Ahupuaʻa, Koʻolaupoko District, Island of Oʻahu. Unpublished report. Honolulu, HI: International Archaeological Research Institute.

Rieth, T. M., T. L. Hunt, C. Lipo, and J. M. Wilmshurst. 2011. The 13th century Polynesian colonization of Hawaiʻi Island. *Journal of Archaeological Science* 38:2740–2749.

Rieth, T. M., P. R. Mills, S. P. Lundblad, A. E. Morrison, and A. Johnson. 2013. Variation in lithic sources utilized by late precontact elites in Kona, Hawaiʻi Island. *Hawaiian Archaeology* 13:103–130.

Riley, T. J. 1973. Wet and dry in a Hawaiian valley: The archaeology of an agricultural system. PhD diss., University of Hawaiʻi at Mānoa.

———. 1975. Survey and excavations of the aboriginal agricultural system. In P. V. Kirch and M. Kelly, eds., *Prehistory and Ecology in a Windward Hawaiian Valley: Halawa Valley, Molokai*, pp. 79–116. Pacific Anthropological Records 24. Honolulu, HI: Bernice P. Bishop Museum.

Ripperton, J. C., and E. Y. Hosaka. 1942. *Vegetation Zones of Hawaii.* Hawaii Agricultural Experiment Station Bulletin 89. Honolulu.

Robins, J., F. Eble, and L. Anderson. 2000. Data recovery of archaeological sites in the land of Ouli, District of South Kohala, Hawaiʻi Island, Hawaiʻi. Unpublished report. Hilo, HI: Paul H. Rosendahl.

Robins, J. J., and R. L. Spear. 2002. Cultural resources inventory survey and limited testing, Phase I, of the Schofield Barracks Training Areas for the preparation of a cultural resource management plan for U.S. Army training ranges and areas, Oʻahu Island, Hawaiʻi. Unpublished report. Honolulu, HI: Scientific Consultant Services.

Rock, J. F. 1913. *The Indigenous Trees of the Hawaiian Islands.* Honolulu, HI: Privately published.

Rogers, A. J., and M. I. Weisler. 2020. Assessing the efficacy of genus-level data in archaeomalacology: A case study of the Hawaiian limpet (*Cellana* spp.), Molokaʻi, Hawaiian Islands. *Journal of Island and Coastal Archaeology* 15:28–56.

———. 2021. He i ʻa make ka ʻopihi: Optimal foraging theory, food choice, and the fish of death. *Journal of Archaeological Method and Theory* 28:1314–1347.

Rolett, B. V. 1998. *Hanamiai: Prehistoric Colonization and Cultural Change in the Marquesas Islands (East Polynesia).* Yale University Publications in Anthropology No. 84. New Haven, CT: Department of Anthropology, Yale University.

———. 2002. Voyaging and interaction in ancient East Polynesia. *Asian Perspectives* 41:182–194.
Rose, R. G. 1980. *A Museum to Instruct and Delight: William T. Brigham and the Founding of the Bernice P. Bishop Museum.* Bernice P. Bishop Museum Special Publication 68. Honolulu, HI: Bishop Museum Press.
Rosendahl, P. 1971. A report on the archaeological excavation and exploration of the old carriage road at Iolani Palace. Unpublished report in Library, Bernice P. Bishop Museum. Honolulu.
———. 1972a. Aboriginal agriculture and residence patterns in upland Lapakahi, Island of Hawaii. PhD diss., University of Hawai'i at Mānoa.
———. 1972b. *Archaeological Salvage of the Hapuna-Anaehoomalu Section of the Kailua-Kawaihae Road, Island of Hawaii.* Department of Anthropology Report 72-5. Honolulu, HI: Bernice P. Bishop Museum.
———. 1973. *Archaeological Salvage of the Ke-ahole to Anaehoomalu Section of the Kailua-Kawaihae Road, Island of Hawaii.* Department of Anthropology Report 73-3. Honolulu: HI: Bernice P. Bishop Museum.
———. 1976. Phase I: Preliminary cultural resource inventory, Kipahulu Historic District, Haleakalā National Park, Hana, Maui, Hawaii. Unpublished report prepared for U.S. Department of Interior. Honolulu.
———. 1981. Archaeological salvage excavations at Site 50-10-37-7702, Kahalu'u, North Kona District, Island of Hawaii. Unpublished report prepared for West Hawaii Housing Foundation. Honolulu.
———. 1983. Archaeological reconnaissance survey: Farms of Kapua, South Kona, Island of Hawaii. Unpublished report. Hilo, HI: Paul H. Rosendahl.
———. 1994. Aboriginal Hawaiian structural remains and settlement patterns in the upland agricultural zone at Lapakahi, Island of Hawai'i. *Hawaiian Archaeology* 3:14–70.
Rosendahl, P., ed. 1976. *Archaeological Investigations in Upland Kaneohe.* Department of Anthropology Report 76-1. Honolulu, HI: Bernice P. Bishop Museum.
Rosendahl, P., and D. E. Yen. 1971. Fossil sweet potato remains from Hawaii. *Journal of the Polynesian Society* 80:379–385.
Rosendahl, P. H., and L. A. Carter. 1988. *Excavations of John Young's Homestead, Kawaihae, Hawaii.* Western Archaeological and Conservation Center, Publications in Anthropology No. 47. National Park Service, U.S. Department of the Interior. N.p.
Rosendahl, P. H., A. E. Haun, J. B. Halbig, M. W. Kaschko, and M. S. Allen. 1987. Kaho'olawe excavations, 1982–3 data recovery project, Island of Kaho'olawe, Hawaii. Unpublished report. Hilo, HI: Paul H. Rosendahl.
Roullier, C., L. Benoit, D. B. McKey, and V. Lebot. 2013. Historical collections reveal patterns of sweet potato in Oceania obscured by modern plant movements and recombination. *Proceedings of the National Academy of Sciences, U.S.A.* 110:2205–2210.
Ruggles, C. 1999. Astronomy, oral literature, and landscape in ancient Hawai'i. *Archaeoastronomy: The Journal of Astronomy in Culture* 14:33–86.
Sahlins, M. D. 1958. *Social Stratification in Polynesia.* Seattle: American Ethnological Society.
———. 1971. An interdisciplinary investigation of Hawaiian social morphology and economy in the late prehistoric and early historic periods. Research proposal submitted by Bernice P. Bishop Museum to the National Science Foundation. Honolulu.
———. 1972. *Stone Age Economics.* Chicago, IL: Aldine-Atherton.
———. 1990. The political economy of grandeur in Hawaii from 1810 to 1830. In E. Ohnuki-Tierney, ed., *Culture through Time,* pp. 26–56. Stanford, CA: Stanford University Press.

———. n.d. [1999]. From totemic differences to political society in Polynesia: The Hawaiian invent "The People." Unpublished paper presented at the Valerio Valeri Memorial Symposium, University of Chicago. Copy in author's possession.

Sailors, D., and S. S. Honda. 2014. Remote survey of a near-coastal archaeological alignment at Kualoa, Hawai'i, using Worldview 2 Satellite, LiDAR and UAV imagery. Paper presented at the Asia-Pacific Conference on Underwater Cultural Heritage, Honolulu, Hawai'i.

Sand, C. 2010. *Lapita Calédonien: Archéologie d'un premier peuplement insulaire océanien.* Paris: Société des Océanistes.

Sand, C., and S. Bedford, eds. 2010. *Lapita: Ancêtres ccéaniens / Oceanic Ancestors.* Paris: Musée de Quai Branly.

Schendel, S. A., G. Walker, and A. Kamisugi. 1980. Hawaiian craniofacial morphometrics: Average Mokapuan skull, artificial cranial deformation, and the "rocker" mandible. *American Journal of Physical Anthropology* 52:491–500.

Schilt, A. R. 1980. Archaeological investigations in specified areas of the Hanalei Wildlife Refuge, Hanalei Valley, Kaua'i. Unpublished report in Library, Bernice P. Bishop Museum. Honolulu.

———. 1984. *Subsistence and Conflict in Kona, Hawai'i: An Archaeological Study of the Kuakini Highway Realignment Corridor.* Department of Anthropology Report 84-1. Honolulu, HI: Bernice P. Bishop Museum.

Schiltz, A. J. 1994. Archaeological survey and evaluation, Land of Ouli District of South Kohala, Island of Hawaii, Hawaii. Unpublished report. Honolulu, HI: Ogden Environmental and Energy Services.

Schmitt, R. C. 1971. New estimates of the pre-censal population of Hawaii. *Journal of the Polynesian Society* 80:237–243.

———. 1973. *The Missionary Censuses of Hawaii.* Pacific Anthropological Records 20. Honolulu, HI: Bernice P. Bishop Museum.

Schousboe, R., M. F. Riford, and P. Kirch. 1983. Volcanic-glass flaked stone artifacts. In J. T. Clark and P. V. Kirch, eds., *Archaeological Investigations of the Mudlane-Waimea-Kawaihae Road Corridor, Island of Hawai'i,* pp. 348–370. Department of Anthropology Report 83-1. Honolulu, HI: Bernice P. Bishop Museum.

Sear, D. A., M. S. Allen, J. D. Hassall, Ashley E. Maloney, P. G. Langdon, A. E. Morrison, A. C. G. Henderson, et al. 2020. Human settlement of East Polynesia earlier, incremental, and coincident with prolonged South Pacific drought. *Proceedings of the National Academy of Sciences, U.S.A.* 117 (16): 8813–8819.

Seelye, M. D. 1968. *The Preliminary Archaeology of Hale Akala, the Royal Bungalow.* Hawaii State Archaeological Journal 69–1. Honolulu: Department of Land and Natural Resources, State of Hawai'i.

Shapiro, W., P. L. Cleghorn, P. V. Kirch, L. Holm, E. L. Kahahane, and J. D. McIntosh. 2011. Archaeological inventory survey for the proposed Auwahi Wind Farm, Ahupua'a of Auwahi, District of Kahikinui, Island of Maui, Hawai'i. Unpublished report. Honolulu, HI: Pacific Legacy.

Sharp, A. 1956. *Ancient Voyagers in the Pacific.* Wellington, New Zealand: Polynesian Society.

Shideler, D. 2010. Southern affinities of a ki'i pōhaku effigy bowl from East Kaua'i. Paper presented at the 23rd Annual Society for Hawaiian Archaeology Conference, Kaua'i, October 15–17.

Shun, K., and A. Schiltz. 1991. Archaeological investigations in Waimanu Valley, Hamakua, Hawaii Island, Hawaii. Unpublished report. Honolulu, HI: ERC Environmental and Energy Services.

Simonson. M., A. Hammermeister, R. Runyon, and H. H. Hammatt. 2009. Archaeological data recovery report for a portion of the Eric A. Knudsen Trust Lands Kōloa Ahupuaʻa, Kona District, Island of Kauaʻi. Unpublished report. Honolulu: Cultural Surveys of Hawaiʻi.

Sinoto, A. 1975. Archaeological reconnaissance survey of Knudsen Trust lands at Koloa, Poipu, Kauai. Unpublished report in Library, Bernice P. Bishop Museum. Honolulu.

Sinoto, Y. H. 1962. Chronology of Hawaiian fishhooks. *Journal of the Polynesian Society* 71:162–166.

———. 1966. A tentative prehistoric cultural sequence in the northern Marquesas Islands, French Polynesia. *Journal of the Polynesian Society* 75:287–303.

———. 1967. Artifacts from excavated sites in the Hawaiian, Marquesas, and Society Islands. In G. A. Highland et al., eds., *Polynesian Culture History,* pp. 341–361. Bernice P. Bishop Museum Special Publication 56. Honolulu, HI: Bishop Museum Press.

———. 1970. An archaeologically based assessment of the Marquesas Islands as a dispersal center in East Polynesia. In R. C. Green and M. Kelly, eds., *Studies in Oceanic Culture History,* pp. 105–132. Pacific Anthropological Records 11. Honolulu, HI: Bernice P. Bishop Museum.

———. 1983. An analysis of Polynesian migrations based on the archaeological assessments. *Journal de la Sociéte des Océanistes* 76:57–67.

———. 1991. A revised system for the classification and coding of Hawaiian fishhooks. *Bishop Museum Occasional Papers* 31:85–105. Honolulu, HI: Bishop Museum Press.

———. 1996. Tracing human movement in East Polynesia: A discussion of selected artifact types. In M. Julien, M. Orliac, and C. Orliac, eds., *Mémoire de Pierre, Mémoire d'homme: Tradition et archéologie en Océanie,* pp. 131–152. Paris: Publications de la Sorbonne.

———. 1999. Some comments on "Hawaiian archaeology: Past, present and future." *Hawaiian Archaeology* 7:100–102.

———. n.d.a. Analysis of Hawaiian ornaments and a tentative chronology (preliminary report). Unpublished manuscript in Department of Anthropology, Bernice P. Bishop Museum. Honolulu.

———. n.d.b. Archaeological specimens from the South Point sites H1, H2, and H8 on the Island of Hawaii, Hawaiian Islands. Unpublished manuscript in Department of Anthropology, Bernice P. Bishop Museum. Honolulu.

Sinoto, Y. H., with H. Aramata. 2016. *Curve of the Hook: An Archaeologist in Polynesia. Mānoa.* Special ed. Honolulu: University of Hawaiʻi Press.

Sinoto, Y. H., and M. Kelly. 1975. *Archaeological and Historical Survey of Pakini-Nui and Pakini-Iki Coastal Sites: Waiahukini, Kailikii, and Hawea, Kaʻu, Hawaii.* Department of Anthropology Report 75-1. Honolulu, HI: Bernice P. Bishop Museum.

Skoglund, P., C. Posth, K. Sirak, M. Spriggs, F. Valentin, S. Bedford, G. R. Clark, C. Reepmeyer, F. Petchey, D. Fernandes, et al. 2016. Genomic insights into the peopling of the Southwest Pacific. *Nature* 538:510–513.

Smart, C. 1964. A report of excavations on Site H22, Puako, Hawaii Island. Mimeographed report in Library, Bernice P. Bishop Museum. Honolulu.

———. 1965. An archaeological survey of parts of Hawaii Volcanoes National Park, Hawaii. Unpublished report in Library, Bernice P. Bishop Museum. Honolulu.

Snow, C. E. 1974. *Early Hawaiians: An Initial Study of Skeletal Remains from Mokapu, Oahu.* Lexington: University of Kentucky Press.

Soehren, L. J. 1962. Archaeological excavations at City of Refuge National Historical Park, Honaunau, Kona, Hawaii. Mimeographed report in Library, Bernice P. Bishop Museum. Honolulu.

———. 1963. An archaeological survey of portions of East Maui, Hawaii. Mimeographed report in Library, Bernice P. Bishop Museum. Honolulu.

———. 1966. Hawaii excavations: 1965. Unpublished report in Library, Bernice P. Bishop Museum. Honolulu.

———. n.d. Archaeological excavations at Nualolo, Kauai. Unpublished report in Department of Anthropology Bernice P. Bishop Museum. Honolulu.

Soehren, L. J., and T. S. Newman. 1968. The archaeology of Kealakekua. Mimeographed "special publication" of the Departments of Anthropology, Bernice P. Bishop Museum and University of Hawai'i. Honolulu.

Spear, R. L. 1992. Settlement and expansion in an Hawaiian valley: The archaeological record from North Halawa, O'ahu. *New Zealand Journal of Archaeology* 14:79–88.

Spoehr, A. 1957. *Marianas Prehistory.* Fieldiana: Anthropology 48.

Spooner, B., ed. 1972. *Population Growth: Anthropological Implications.* Cambridge, MA: MIT Press.

Spriggs, M. T. 1989. God's police and damned whores: Images of archaeology in Hawaii. In P. Gathercole and D. Lowenthal, eds., *Politics of the Past,* pp. 118–129. London: Unwin Hyman.

———. 1991. Facing the Nation: Archaeologists and Hawaiians in the era of sovereignty. *Contemporary Pacific* (Fall): 380–392. Honolulu.

Spriggs, M. J. T., and A. Anderson. 1993. Late colonization of East Polynesia. *Antiquity* 67:200–217.

Spriggs, M., and P. V. Kirch. 1992. *'Auwai, kanawai,* and *waiwai:* Irrigation in Kawailoa-Uka. In P. V. Kirch and M. Sahlins, *Anahulu: The Anthropology of History in the Kingdom of Hawaii,* vol. 2, pp. 118–164. Chicago, IL: University of Chicago Press.

Stannard, D. 1989. *Before the Horror: The Population of Hawai'i on the Eve of Western Contact.* Honolulu: Social Science Research Institute, University of Hawai'i.

Steadman, D. W., P. C. Vargas, and C. F. Cristino. 1994. Stratigraphy, chronology, and cultural context of an early faunal assemblage from Easter Island. *Asian Perspectives* 33:79–96.

Stearns, H. T. 1978. *Quaternary Shorelines in the Hawaiian Islands.* Bernice P. Bishop Museum Bulletin 237. Honolulu: Bishop Museum Press.

Stephens, J. W. 2016. Making sense of monumentality: A multisensory archaeological approach to Hawaiian ritual architecture. PhD diss., University of Hawai'i at Mānoa.

Sterling, E. P. 1998. *Sites of Maui.* Honolulu, HI: Bernice P. Bishop Museum.

Sterling, E. P., and C. S. Summers. 1978. *Sites of Oahu.* Honolulu, HI: Bernice P. Bishop Museum.

Stevenson, C. M., and P. Mills. 2013. A chronometric tool for Hawaiian archaeology: The hydration dating of Pu'u Wa'awa'a trachytic glass. *Journal of Archaeological Science* 40:405–415.

Stevenson, J., A. Benson, J. S. Athens, J. Kahn, and P. V. Kirch. 2017. Polynesian colonization and landscape changes on Mo'orea, French Polynesia: The Lake Temae pollen record. *The Holocene* 27:1963–1975.

Stock, J., J. Coil, and P. V. Kirch. 2003. Paleohydrology of arid southeastern Maui, Hawaiian Islands, and its implications for prehistoric human settlement. *Quaternary Research* 59:12–24.

Stokes, J. F. G. 1909a. Heiau of Molokai. Unpublished manuscript in Library, Bernice P. Bishop Museum. Honolulu.

———. 1909b. Walled fish traps of Pearl Harbor. *Bishop Museum Occasional Papers* 4:199–212. Honolulu, HI: Bishop Museum Press.

———. 1921. Fish poisoning in the Hawaiian Islands, with notes on the custom in southern Polynesia. *Bishop Museum Occasional Papers* 7:219–236. Honolulu, HI: Bishop Museum Press.

———. 1931. Iron with the early Hawaiians. *Papers of the Hawaiian Historical Society* 18:6–14.

———. 1932. Spaniards and the sweet potato in Hawaii and Hawaiian-American contacts. *American Anthropologist* 34:594–600.

———. 1933. New bases for Hawaiian chronology. *Hawaiian Historical Society, Forty-First Annual Report,* pp. 23–65. Honolulu.

———. 1991. *Heiau of the Island of Hawaiʻi: A Historic Survey of Native Hawaiian Temple Sites.* Edited by T. Dye. Bishop Museum Bulletins in Anthropology 2. Honolulu, HI: Bishop Museum Press.

Stride, M., and H. H. Hammatt. 1995. Archaeological inventory survey of Heʻeia Kai 272 Reservoir, Heʻeia, Koolaupoko, Oʻahu (TMK 4-6-14: 5). Unpublished report. Honolulu: Cultural Surveys of Hawaiʻi.

Suggs, R. C. 1961. *Archaeology of Nuku Hiva, Marquesas Islands, French Polynesia.* Anthropological Papers of the American Museum of Natural History, vol. 49, part 1. New York.

Sullivan, R. B. 1990. Status reports 1–8, Phase III—archaeological monitoring, archaeological mitigation program, Kawela Bay Mitigation Project, Lands of ʻŌpana, Kawela, Hanakaʻoe, ʻŌiʻo, Ulupehupehu, Punalau, and Kahuku, Koʻolauloa District, Island of Oʻahu. Unpublished report. Hilo, HI: Paul H. Rosendahl.

Summers, C. C. 1964. *Hawaiian Archaeology: Fishponds.* Bernice P. Bishop Museum Special Publication 52. Honolulu, HI: Bishop Museum Press.

———. 1971. *Molokai: A Site Survey.* Pacific Anthropological Records 14. Honolulu, HI: Bernice P. Bishop Museum.

———. 1990. *Hawaiian Cordage.* Pacific Anthropological Records 39. Department of Anthropology, Bernice P. Bishop Museum.

———. 1999. *Material Culture: The J. S. Emerson Collection of Hawaiian Artifacts.* Honolulu, HI: Bishop Museum Press.

Svihla, A. 1957. Dental caries in the Hawaiian dog. *Bishop Museum Occasional Papers* 22:7–13. Honolulu, HI: Bishop Museum Press.

Swanson, David A. 2019. A new estimate for the Hawaiian population for 1778, the year of first European contact. *Hūlili* 11:205–224.

Swanson, Donald A. 2008. Hawaiian oral tradition describes 400 years of volcanic activity at Kīlauea. *Journal of Volcanology and Geothermal Research* 176:427–431.

Swift, J. A., P. V. Kirch, A. Baer, J. Huebert, and T. Gill. 2019. Late pre-contact construction and use of an "archaic" shrine at the Pālehua Complex (Honouliuli District, Oʻahu Island, Hawaiʻi). *Journal of Pacific Archaeology* 10:1–18.

Tainter, J. A. 1973. The social correlates of mortuary patterning at Kaloko, North Kona, Hawaii. *Archaeology and Physical Anthropology in Oceania* 8:1–11.

———. 1976. Spatial organization and social patterning in the Kaloko cemetery, North Kona, Hawaii. *Archaeology and Physical Anthropology in Oceania* 11:91–105.

Tainter, J. A., and R. Cordy. 1977. An archaeological analysis of social ranking and residence groups in prehistoric Hawaii. *World Archaeology* 9:95–112.

Takayama, J., and R. C. Green. 1970. Excavations of three additional field shelters in archaeological Zone 1. In R. Green, ed., *Makaha Valley Historical Project: Interim Report No. 2,* pp. 35–54. Pacific Anthropological Records 10. Honolulu, HI: Bernice P. Bishop Museum.

Taylor, W. 1948. *A Study of Archaeology.* American Anthropological Association Memoir 69. Washington, DC.

Thomas, F. R. 1995. Excavations at Maunalua Cave, Hawaiʻi Kai, Oʻahu. *Hawaiian Archaeology* 4:17–26.

Thompson, C. 2019. *Sea People: The Puzzle of Polynesia.* New York: HarperCollins.

Thrum, T. G. 1906. Heiau and heiau sites throughout the Hawaiian Islands. *The Hawaiian Annual for 1907,* pp. 36–48. Honolulu.

———. 1909. Tales from the temples. *The Hawaiian Annual for 1909,* pp. 44–54. Honolulu.

Thurman, R. M. R. 2014. Archaeological investigations at Maunawila Heiau: Traditional Hawai'i in Hauula's backyard. Master's thesis, University of Hawai'i at Mānoa.

———. 2015. The archaeology of Maunawila Heiau, Hau'ula Ahupua'a, Ko'olauloa District, O'ahu. *Hawaiian Archaeology* 14:17–32.

Titcomb, M. 1952. *The Native Use of Fish in Hawaii.* Polynesian Society Memoir 29. Wellington, New Zealand: The Polynesian Society.

———. 1969. *Dog and Man in the Ancient Pacific, with Special Attention to Hawaii.* Bernice P. Bishop Museum Special Publication 59. Honolulu, HI: Bishop Museum Press.

Tomonari-Tuggle, M. J. 1979. An archaeological reconnaissance survey: Na Pali Coast State Park, Island of Kaua'i. Unpublished report in Department of Land and Natural Resources, State of Hawaii. Honolulu.

———. 1994. A preservation plan for the 'Ohi'a Cave Historic Preserve. Unpublished report. Honolulu, HI: International Archaeological Research Institute.

———. 1998. Kukaoo Heiau: A glimpse at Manoa's past, historical research, and an interpretive master plan. Unpublished report. Honolulu, HI: International Archaeological Research Institute.

———. 2006. Archaeological data recovery investigations of the northern portion of Captain Cook Ranch. Unpublished report. Honolulu, HI: International Archaeological Research Institute.

———. 2019. C-shapes and shrines of the Southwest Rift: Archaeological inventory survey of the 'Umi Caverns Kīpuka, Hawai'i Volcanoes National Park. Unpublished report. Honolulu, HI: International Archaeology, LLC.

Tomonari-Tuggle, M. J., and H. D. Tuggle. 1999. Hokuli'a: An integrated archaeological mitigation plan. Unpublished report. Honolulu, HI: International Archaeological Research Institute.

———. 2008. Preservation plan for non-burial sites at Hōkūli'a, Districts of North and South Kona, Island of Hawai'i. Unpublished report. Honolulu, HI: International Archaeological Research Institute.

Tomonari-Tuggle, M. J., H. D. Tuggle, and J. S. Athens. 2000. Archaeology on a south coast landscape: Hulupo'e Lāna'i, Hawai'i. Unpublished report. Honolulu, HI: International Archaeological Research Institute.

Trask, H.-K. 1993. *From a Native Daughter: Colonialism and Sovereignty in Hawai'i.* Monroe, ME: Common Courage Press.

Tuggle, H. D. 1993. Kamiloloa archaeology: Data recovery and site inventory for a portion of Kamiloloa, Island of Moloka'i, Hawai'i. Unpublished report. Honolulu, HI: International Archaeological Research Institute.

———. 1997. The 'Ewa Plain. *Hawaiian Archaeology* 6:3–36.

Tuggle, H. D., R. Cordy, and M. Child. 1978. Volcanic glass hydration-rind age determination for Bellows Dune, Hawaii. *New Zealand Archaeological Association Newsletter* 21:57–77.

Tuggle, H. D., and P. B. Griffin, eds. 1973. *Lapakahi, Hawaii: Archaeological Studies.* Asian and Pacific Archaeology Series No. 5. Honolulu: Social Science Research Institute, University of Hawai'i.

Tuggle, H. D., and L. Olson. 1978. A review of "hydration dating" of Hawaiian volcanic glass. Unpublished report in Department of Anthropology, University of Hawai'i. Honolulu.

Tuggle, H. D., and M. J. Spriggs. 2000. The age of the Bellows Dune Site O18, Oʻahu, Hawaiʻi and the antiquity of Hawaiian colonization. *Asian Perspectives* 39:165–188.

Tuggle, H. D., and M. J. Tomonari-Tuggle. 1980. Prehistoric agriculture in Kohala, Hawaii. *Journal of Field Archaeology* 7:297–312.

———. 1997. Synthesis of Cultural Resource Studies of the ʻEwa Plain. Unpublished report. Honolulu, HI: International Archaeological Research Institute.

———. 2008. Archeological overview and assessment and research design, Hawaiʻi Volcanoes National Park. Unpublished report. Honolulu, HI: International Archaeological Research Institute.

Tuohy, D. R. 1965. Salvage excavations at City of Refuge National Historical Park, Honaunau, Kona, Hawaii. Unpublished report in Library, Bernice P. Bishop Museum. Honolulu.

Underwood, J. H. 1969. *Human Skeletal Remains from Sand Dune Site (H1), South Point (Ka Lae), Hawaii.* Pacific Anthropological Records 9. Honolulu, HI: Bernice P. Bishop Museum.

Vacca, K. M. G. 2019. A question of design: The investigation of space and structure in Hawaiian Kauhale. PhD diss., University of California, Berkeley.

Valeri, V. 1985. *Kingship and Sacrifice: Ritual and Society in Ancient Hawaii.* Chicago, IL: University of Chicago Press.

Vancouver, G. 1801. *A Voyage of Discovery to the North Pacific Ocean and round the World . . . Performed in the Years 1790–95.* London: G. G. & J. Robinson.

Van der Leeuw, S., and C. L. Redman. 2002. Placing archaeology at the center of socio-natural studies. *American Antiquity* 67:597–605.

Van Gilder, C. L. 2001. Gender and household archaeology in Kahikinui, Maui. In C. M. Stevenson, G. Lee, and F. J. Morin, eds., *Pacific 2000: Proceedings of the Fifth International Conference on Easter Island and the Pacific,* pp. 135–140. Los Osos, CA: Easter Island Foundation.

———. 2005. Families on the land: Archaeology and identity in Kahikinui, Maui. PhD diss., University of California, Berkeley.

Van Gilder, C., and P. V. Kirch. 1997. Household archaeology in Kipapa and Nakaohu, Kahikinui. In P. V. Kirch, ed., *Na Mea Kahiko o Kahikinui: Studies in the Archaeology of Kahikinui, Maui,* pp. 45–60. Oceanic Archaeology Laboratory, Special Publication No. 1. Berkeley: University of California.

Vernon, C. S. 1975. Archaeological excavations and reconstruction of Ahuena Heiau platform and Hale Nana Mahinaai at Kamakahonu, North Kona, Island of Hawaii—progress reports nos. 1 to 23. Uupublished reports in Department of Anthropology, Bernice P. Bishop Museum. Honolulu.

Vitousek, P. M. 2004. *Nutrient Cycling and Limitation: Hawaiʻi as a Model System.* Princeton, NJ: Princeton University Press.

Vitousek, P. M., O. A. Chadwick, G. Hilley, P. V. Kirch, and T. N. Ladefoged. 2010. Erosion, geological history, and indigenous agriculture: A tale of two valleys. *Ecosystems* 13 (2010): 782–793.

Vitousek, P. M., O. A. Chadwick, S. C. Hotchkiss, T. N. Ladefoged, and C. M. Stevenson. 2014. Farming the rock: A biogeochemical perspective on intensive agriculture in Polynesia. *Journal of Pacific Archaeology* 5:51–61.

Vitousek, P. M., T. N. Ladefoged, A. Hartshorn, P. V. Kirch, M. Graves, S. Hotchkiss, S. Tuljapurkar, and O. A. Chadwick. 2004. Soils, agriculture, and society in precontact Hawaiʻi. *Science* 304:1665–1669.

Wagner, W. C., D. R. Herbst, and S. H. Sohmer. 1990. *Manual of the Flowering Plants of Hawai'i.* 2 vols. Bishop Museum Special Publication 83. Honolulu: University of Hawai'i Press and Bishop Museum Press.

Wagner, W. L., and V. A. Funk, eds. 1995. *Hawaiian Biogeography: Evolution on a Hot Spot Archipelago.* Washington, DC: Smithsonian Institution Press.

Walker, A. T., and P. H. Rosendahl. 1985. Testing cultural remains associated with the Kahana desilting basin, Honolua Watershed, Land of Kahana, Lahaina District, County of Maui. Kurtistown, HI: Paul H. Rosendahl.

Walker, W. M. 1930. Archaeology of Maui. Unpublished manuscript in Library, Bernice P. Bishop Museum. Honolulu.

Wallace, W. J., and E. T. Wallace. 1969. *Pinao Bay Site (H24): A Small Prehistoric Fishing Settlement near South Point (Ka Lae), Hawaii.* Pacific Anthropological Records 2. Honolulu, HI: Bernice P. Bishop Museum.

Wallace, W. J., E. T. Wallace, and V. Meeker. MS. [1967]. Excavation of a coastal dwelling site (O17) on the Island of Oahu. Unpublished manuscript in Library, Bernice P. Bishop Museum. Honolulu.

Walworth, M. 2014. Eastern Polynesian: The linguistic evidence revisited. *Oceanic Linguistics* 53:256–272.

Weisler, M. 1983. An archaeological survey and geomorphological reconstructions of the Kakahai'a National Wildlife Refuge, Kawela, Moloka'i, Hawaiian Islands. Unpublished report in Library, Bernice P. Bishop Museum. Honolulu.

———. 1988. Observations and regional significance of an adze preform cache from Kipu, Moloka'i, Hawai'ian Islands. *Archaeology in New Zealand* 31:94–99.

———. 1989a. Chronometric dating and late Holocene prehistory in the Hawaiian Islands: A critical review of radiocarbon dates from Moloka'i island. *Radiocarbon* 31:121–145.

———. 1989b. An intensive archaeological survey of Kipu, Moloka'i. Unpublished report. Berkeley, CA: Archaeological Research and Consulting Services.

———. 1990a. A technological, petrographic, and geochemical analysis of the Kapohaku adze quarry, Lana'i, Hawaiian Islands. *New Zealand Journal of Archaeology* 12:29–50.

———. 1990b. Sources and sourcing of volcanic glass in Hawai'i: Implications for exchange studies. *Archaeology in Oceania* 25:16–23.

———. 1993. The importance of fish otoliths in Pacific Island archaeofaunal analysis. *New Zealand Journal of Archaeology* 15:131–159.

———. 1995. Henderson Island prehistory: Colonization and extinction on a remote Polynesian island. *Biological Journal of the Linnean Society* 56:377–404.

———. 1998. Hard evidence for prehistoric interaction in Polynesia. *Current Anthropology* 39:521–532.

———. 2011. A quarried landscape in the Hawaiian Islands. *World Archaeology* 43:298–317.

Weisler, M. I., K. D. Collerson, Y. X. Feng, J. X. Zhao, and K. F. Yu. 2006. Thorium-230 coral chronology of a late prehistoric Hawaiian chiefdom. *Journal of Archaeological Science* 33:273–282.

Weisler, M. I., S. L. Collins, Y. Feng, J. Zhao, C. Shipton, and X. Wei. 2013. A new major adze quarry from Nānākuli, O'ahu: Implications for interaction studies in Hawai'i. *Journal of Pacific Archaeology* 4:35–57.

Weisler, M. I., and M. Haslam. 2005. Determining the function of Polynesian volcanic glass artifacts: Results of a residue study. *Hawaiian Archaeology* 10:1–17.

Weisler, M., and P. V. Kirch. 1982. The archaeological resources of Kawela, Moloka'i. Unpublished report in Library, Bernice P. Bishop Museum. Honolulu.

———. 1985. The structure of settlement space in a Polynesian chiefdom: Kawela, Molokai, Hawaiian Islands. *New Zealand Journal of Archaeology* 7:129–158.
Weisler, M. I., W. P. Mendes, and Q. Hua. 2015. A prehistoric quarry/habitation site on Moloka'i and a discussion of an anomalous early date on the Polynesian introduced candlenut (kukui, *Aleurites moluccana*). *Journal of Pacific Archaeology* 6:37–57.
Weisler, M. I., and G. M. Murakami. 1991. The use of Mountain Apple (*Syzigium malaccense*) in a prehistoric Hawaiian domestic structure. *Economic Botany* 45:282–285.
Weisler, M. I., and R. Walter. 2002. Late prehistoric fishing adaptations at Kawakiu Nui, West Moloka'i. *Hawaiian Archaeology* 8:42–61.
Whistler, W. A. 2009. *Plants of the Canoe People: An Ethnobotanical Voyage through Polynesia.* Lawa'i, Kaua'i: National Tropical Botanical Garden.
Wilkes, C. 1845. *Narrative of the United States Exploring Expedition.* Vol. 4. Philadelphia, PA: Lea & Blanchard.
Williams, S. S. 1989. A preliminary report of test excavations on sites 50-OA-G5-106 and -G5-110, Luluku Kāne'ohe, Ko'olau Poko, O'ahu. Unpublished report in Library, Bernice P. Bishop Museum. Honolulu.
———. 1991. The sound of one head banging: Kukuiokāne Heiau one year later. Paper presented at the 4th Annual Society for Hawaiian Archaeology Conference, Honolulu, May 25.
———. 1992. Early inland settlement expansion and the effect of geomorphological change on the archaeological record in Kane'ohe, O'ahu. *New Zealand Journal of Archaeology* 14:67–78.
———. 2004. The Pōhakuloa chill glass quarry complex, U.S. Army Pohakuloa Training Area, Hawai'i. *Hawaiian Archaeology* 9:105–118.
Wilson, W. H. 2012. Whence the East Polynesians? Further linguistic evidence for a Northern Outlier source. *Oceanic Linguistics* 51:238–359.
———. 2021. East Polynesian subgrouping and homeland implications within the Northern Outlier–East Polynesian hypothesis. *Oceanic Linguistics* 60:36–71.
Withrow, B. 1991. Prehistoric distribution of stone adzes on Hawai'i Island: Implications for the development of Hawaiian chiefdoms. *Asian Perspectives* 29:235–250.
Wittfogel, K. A. 1957. *Oriental Despotism: A Study of Total Power.* New Haven, CT: Yale University Press.
Wong, C., M. Mulrooney, and S. Moore. 2014. Commentary: Recent approaches to digitizing Hawaiian archaeological collections at Bishop Museum. *Hawaiian Archaeology, Society for Hawaiian Archaeology Special Publication 4,* pp. 85–91. Honolulu: Society for Hawaiian Archaeology.
Wood, J. W. 1998. A theory of preindustrial population dynamics: Demography, economy, and well-being in Malthusian systems. *Current Anthropology* 39:99–135.
Yen, D. E. 1969. Nihoa—1969. Unpublished report. Department of Anthropology. Honolulu, HI: Bernice P. Bishop Museum.
———. 1973. The origins of Oceanic agriculture. *Archaeology and Physical Anthropology in Oceania* 8:68–85.
———. 1974. *The Sweet Potato and Oceania.* Bernice P. Bishop Museum Bulletin 236. Honolulu, HI: Bishop Museum Press.
———. 1991. Polynesian cultigens and cultivars: The questions of origin. In P. A. Cox and S. A. Banack, eds., *Islands, Plants, and Polynesians,* pp. 67–98. Portland, OR: Dioscorides Press.
Yen, D. E., and J. Gordon, eds. 1973. *Anuta: A Polynesian Outlier in the Solomon Islands.* Pacific Anthropological Records 21. Honolulu, HI: Bernice P. Bishop Museum.

Yen, D. E., P. V. Kirch, P. Rosendahl, and T. Riley. 1972. Prehistoric agriculture in the upper valley of Makaha, Oahu. In E. Ladd and D. Yen, eds., *Makaha Valley Historical Project: Interim Report No. 3,* pp. 59–94. Pacific Anthropological Records 18. Honolulu, HI: Bernice P. Bishop Museum.

Yent, M., and J. Ota. 1983. Archaeological investigations: Site KAL-4 rockshelter Kalalau, Na Pali Coast, Kauai. Unpublished report in Hawaiʻi Division of State Parks. Honolulu.

Ziegler, A. C. 2002. *Hawaiian Natural History, Ecology, and Evolution.* Honolulu: University of Hawaiʻi Press.

Ziegler, A. C., F. G. Howarth, and N. B. Simmons. 2016. A second endemic land mammal for the Hawaiian Islands: A new genus and species of fossil bat (Chiroptera: Vespertilionidae). *American Museum Novitates* 3854. New York.

Zimmerman, E. C. 1963. Nature of the land biota. In F. Fosberg, ed., *Man's Place in the Island Ecosystem,* pp. 57–64. Honolulu, HI: Bishop Museum Press.

INDEX

abraders, 4, 39, 62, 72, 82, 91, 120, 132, 139, 189, 199–200, 205, 217, 332, 347, 388

adzes, 190–199; classification of, 91, 94; cone-shell, 139; iron, 308; plano-convex, 128, 133, 134; production, 190, 196–197, 211, 217, 219, 232, 265, 373; quadrangular, 91, 94, 139; quarrying, 36, 49, 94, 96, 139, 194, 321–322, 358, 361, 374, 384, 393, 408; reverse-triangular, 123, 133, 134; XRF analysis of, 25. *See also* craft specialization; quarries

agriculture: archaeology of, 144–145; colluvial slope, 45, 155–156; dryland, 20, 25, 156–168, 348, 363, 399; ethnohistoric accounts of, 142; intensive, 3, 103, 143, 146, 325, 334, 392; intensification of, 184–187; irrigated, 145, 147–154, 291, 304, 380, 390, 406, 409; population and, 183–184; rituals, 112; women and, 230. *See also* arboriculture; dryland field systems; irrigation

Ahu'ena Heiau, Hawai'i, 259, 267, 342, 343

Ahu a 'Umi, 260, 324, 364

Ahupū, Kaho'olawe, 196, 242, 370, 373

ahupua'a: boundaries, 158, 241, 296, 380; communities, 198, 213, 239; population and, 350; segmentation of, 167; system, 3, 5, 97, 98, 99, 102, 111, 160, 281, 350, 390; tribute collection in, 217, 262. See also *konohiki;* land divisions

Alapa'inui, 90, 104–105, 107, 109, 259, 289

'Āle'ale'a Heiau, Hawai'i, 252, 259, 279, 335–337, 339

ali'i. See chiefs

Allen, Jane, 25, 152–153, 316, 390, 391

Allen, Melinda S., 25, 163, 204, 235, 332–333

'Amikopala, Moloka'i, 194, 384

'Anaeho'omalu, Hawai'i, 96, 180, 205, 226, 240, 241, 242, 274, 344, 345, 347

Anahulu Valley, O'ahu, 18, 25, 55, 95, 96, 144, 150, 151, 168, 175, 225, 235, 279, 308–312, 387, 396–397

ancestral Polynesian Culture, 7, 70, 71–73, 91, 97, 98, 102, 114, 247, 289

animal husbandry, 170–171. *See also* domestic animals

Apple, Russ, 239, 241, 314, 338

aquaculture, 4, 97, 103, 171–174, 364, 376. *See also* fishponds

arboriculture, 168–170, 372, 379, 392

archaeology: of agriculture, 144–145; of colonialism, 315–318; community-based, 23–25, 397; curation crisis and, 56, 425; excavation, 53–56; historical, 306–307, 313; oral traditions and, 88–89 422; settlement-pattern, 16–18; stratigraphic, 12–15; survey, 51–53; women in, 25–26. *See also* cultural resource management

archaic states, 87, 100, 167, 266

Archaic States Period, 87–88, 102–104; traditional history of, 104–109

art. *See* featherwork, petroglyphs

Athens, J. Stephen, 19, 41, 42, 80, 81, 377, 393, 396

'aumākua, 5. 6, 222, 248, 293

Austronesian languages, 66–67, 71, 115, 170. *See also* linguistics

awls, 68, 95, 227; bone, 139, 209, 210, 219; stone, 200, 201

bananas, 6, 38, 66, 72, 141, 155, 157, 184, 230, 335, 361

Barbers Point, O'ahu, 400. *See also* Kalaeloa

barkcloth, 4, 9, 103, 130, 132, 142, 189, 209, 212, 217, 219, 230, 232, 250, 328, 343

Barrera, William, 19, 211, 347, 348

Barrère, Dorothy, 14, 25, 88, 309, 336–337

bat, native, 33, 41
Bayesian calibration, 78, 79, 113, 122, 125, 128, 137, 304
Bayman, James, 25, 233, 308, 355
beads, 68, 72, 213, 308, 309, 314
Bellows dune site (O18), Oʻahu, 78, 79, 90, 130–134, 192, 207, 209, 279
Bennett, Wendell C., 12, 127, 144, 255–256, 271, 406, 407
Bernice P. Bishop Museum. *See* Bishop Museum
birds, 33, 34, 36, 37, 41, 42, 53, 56, 72, 103, 119, 127, 211, 218, 230, 235, 244, 281, 323, 348, 358, 383; fossil, 34, 35, 41, 81 379
bird-man concept, 367, 369
Bishop Museum, 8–12, 16, 17, 19, 20, 22, 23, 50, 51, 56, 61, 116, 119, 125, 127, 128, 130, 140, 193, 218, 234, 252, 276, 290, 310, 316, 330, 336, 339, 342, 348, 353, 367, 375, 377, 384, 388, 391, 401, 402, 407, 419, 424, 425. *See also* Tanager Expedition
Bonk, William J., 13, 15, 58, 85, 117, 121, 189, 206, 207, 383
bowls, stone, 209, 421
breadfruit, 44, 67, 72, 91, 93, 94, 142, 154, 155, 162, 168–169, 334, 338, 392, 419, 421. *See also* arboriculture
Brigham, William T., 9, 10, 189, 252, 275, 309
Buck, Sir Peter H. *See* Hiroa, Te Rangi
burials: canoe, 345; cave, 9, 181, 274–275, 339, 345; cremation, 216–217, 229, 274, 277, 293; *heiau,* 279; house, 279; mass, 106, 278; monument, 278–279; pig, 356, 408; sand dune, 180, 276–278. *See also* Forbes Cave; Honokahua burial site; Keōpū burial site; Mōkapu; NAGPRA

canoes, 4, 27, 37, 66, 67, 74, 101, 110, 132, 203, 205, 217, 218, 230, 239, 244, 266, 295, 296, 323, 329, 330, 339, 347, 415
Carson, Mike, 182, 348, 361, 393, 409, 410
caskets, woven, 280, 336
Chapman, Peter S., 16, 189, 296, 353, 362
chicken. *See* fowl
chiefdoms, 85, 87, 103, 112, 113, 174, 262
chiefs: craft specialization and, 4, 103; conquest by, 111; district, 5, 108, 199;
houses of, 228, 266–267; featherwork and, 4, 112–113; genealogies of, 88, 113; *kapu* and, 6; land and, 4, 98, 100, 102 111, 142, 173, 249, 312; ruling, 5, 6, 47, 89, 103, 111, 222, 239, 310, 330, 376; sacred, 98; surplus and, 111, 112, 149; tribute and, 100, 114
Ching, Francis, 19, 345
chisels, 4, 39, 68, 129, 193
classification: of abraders, 199; of artifacts, 189; of fishhooks, 201–204; of *heiau,* 248–249, 255–257, 302; of sites, 47–49. *See also* typology
Cleghorn, Paul, 18, 19, 21, 190, 192, 195–196, 197, 318, 321, 423
club, tripping, 215, 223, 387
coconut grater, 91, 132, 133, 209, 411
colonialism, 315–318
colonization, of Hawaiian Islands, 81, 113, 185
communication: interisland, 27–28, 119; intraisland, 239–241, 323, 334
contract archaeology. *See* cultural resource management
Cook, Captain James, 1–2, 6, 7, 63, 87, 102, 105, 109, 110, 141, 171, 177–178, 218, 221, 247, 279–280, 308, 319, 330, 338–339
coral: abraders, 72, 82, 91, 95, 120, 124, 133, 139, 189, 199–200, 205, 388; dating of, 61–62, 69, 196, 197, 254, 260, 261–262, 322, 422; offerings, 62, 229, 248, 249, 250, 257 350, 361, 364, 397, 412, 415, 417, 422; pendants, 215. *See also* [230]Th dating
cordage, 37, 128, 130, 155, 168, 169, 201, 209, 217, 277, 412, 421. See also *ʻolonā*
Cordy, Ross, 17, 18, 25, 85, 89, 132, 181–182, 223, 327, 334, 344
craft specialization, 4, 215–217, 218, 229, 293
cremation, 216–217, 229, 274, 277, 293. *See also* burial
CRM. *See* cultural resource management
C-shaped shelters, 50, 224, 225, 293
cultural resource management (CRM), 8, 19, 20–23, 24, 26, 53, 55, 56, 144, 180, 182, 200, 205, 223, 233, 307, 313, 316, 322, 340, 341, 354, 356, 362, 363, 375, 384, 387, 391, 407, 412, 424–425

cultural sequences, 85–88, 123, 133, 140, 301, 306, 399, 403
culture history, 12, 17

dating: hydration-rind, 58, 60–61, 301; radiocarbon, 12–13, 15, 26, 57, 59–60, 75, 81, 96, 113, 118–120, 122–124, 128–129, 136, 173, 260; relative, 12, 13, 58, 159, 208; seriation, 12, 13, 58–59, 122, 125, 208–209; uranium-thorium (^{230}Th), 25, 26, 58, 61–62, 196, 197, 260–263, 322, 362, 383, 398, 422, 423
Developmental Period, 86
disease, 2, 178–179, 180–181, 279, 313
disposal of the dead. See burials
Dixon, Boyd, 296, 362, 384, 385, 400, 410
dogs, 4, 33, 72, 91, 95, 98, 134, 140, 170–171, 233, 238, 244, 277. See also domestic animals
dog-tooth ornaments, 95, 139, 213–214, 331
domestic animals, 66, 334, 350. See also dogs; fowl; pigs
domestic implements, 208–211
drills, 133, 201, 205
drought. See hazards, environmental
dryland field systems. See agriculture
dwelling sites. See kauhale
Dye, Tom, 19, 22, 78–79, 81, 160, 171, 182, 193, 227, 233, 338, 361, 378, 388

Earle, Timothy, 18, 110, 112–113, 149, 174–175, 217, 408, 410
earth ovens, 6, 72, 75, 91, 224, 227, 232, 236, 237, 289, 299, 356, 391, 393, 403
Easter Island, 66, 77, 137, 247
economy: political, 26, 111, 112, 113, 168, 175, 310; staple, 103, 112, 174–176, 216, 218; wealth, 103, 176, 199, 215–219
edge-wear analysis, 190, 219
'Ehu-kai-malino, 337
Ellis, William, 171, 268, 336, 342
Emory, Kenneth P.: adze study, 191–192; appointment to Bishop Mueum, 11; fishhook study, 14, 54, 58, 85, 189, 201, 206–207; Haleakalā survey, 11, 252, 353, 358; Kuli'ou'ou excavations, 11, 12–13, 50, 116–120, 234, 387, 405; Lāna'i survey, 11, 197, 248, 365–370; Mōkapu excavation, 12, 23, 276; Nihoa and Mokumanamana surveys, 11, 247, 417–421; Nu'alolo excavations, 15, 127–130, 407–408; Polynesian dispersal theories, 74, 81, 94, 189, 422; radiocarbon dating, 13, 59; South Point excavations, 14, 50, 58, 121–127, 239
environmental change, 41–45
ethics, 179, 272
'Ewa District, O'ahu, 30, 31, 41, 42, 81, 92, 95, 109, 386, 400–403
excavation, methods of, 53–56
exchange, 18, 26, 168, 198, 204, 308, 333
Expansion Period, 86, 87, 94, 95–102, 107, 108, 120, 125, 137, 167, 182, 186–187, 218, 310, 326, 334, 350, 358, 361, 369, 377, 379, 380, 388, 396–397, 402, 409, 414, 422–423
experimental archaeology, 190, 196, 217
extinct fauna. See birds

famine, 166, 184, 187
featherwork, 9, 103, 112, 189, 217–219
Field, Julie, 25, 26, 128, 167, 213, 228, 236, 238, 239
field shelters. See C-shaped shelters
field systems. See agriculture
files. See abraders
fish, 5, 10, 36, 37, 53, 65, 72, 91, 120, 121, 125, 136, 171, 173, 201, 205, 230, 233–235, 237–239, 248, 276, 289, 291, 316, 330, 333, 338, 400, 403
fishhooks: chronology of, 206–208; classification of, 201–205; Foundation Period, 91; Hālawa dune site, 139; manufacture of, 205, 384; Marquesan, 81; Nu'alolo site, 129; seriation of, 13, 58; site H1, 123; site H8, 125; site O1, 119
fishing shrines (ko'a), 10, 49, 205, 215, 216, 257, 289, 297, 302, 361, 364, 373, 401, 413
fish poisoning, 10
fishponds, 3, 49, 96, 97, 103, 108, 112, 171–174, 184, 233, 234, 290, 291, 310, 343, 364, 375, 376, 377, 385, 386, 393, 403, 412
Flexner, James, 309, 313, 314, 339, 375
floods. See hazards, environmental

Forbes Cave, Hawaiʻi, 23, 274, 275
Fornander, Abraham, 7, 9, 12, 88–89, 101, 104, 107, 108, 251, 279
Fort Elizabeth, Kauaʻi, 317–318
fortifications, 270–271, 404
Foundation Period, 87, 89–92, 94, 113, 154, 187, 286, 338, 340, 348, 356, 359, 366, 369, 377, 380, 389, 393, 394, 395, 401, 412, 414, 422
founder effect, 76
Fowke, G., 375
fowl, 4, 91, 98, 134, 170, 171, 235, 276. See also domestic animals

gaming stones. See ʻulumaika
genealogy, 5, 7, 12, 88–89, 92, 93, 97, 109, 173, 261. See also oral traditions
geographic information system (GIS), 24, 26, 44, 45, 53, 146, 155, 164, 178
global positioning system (GPS), 16, 24, 26, 52, 302
Goldman, Irving, 110–111
Graves, Michael, 25, 128, 129, 159, 160, 167, 184, 204, 236
Great Māhele. See Māhele
"Great Wall," Hōnaunau, Hawaiʻi, 217, 272, 278, 335–337
Green, Roger C., 16–17, 25, 65, 72, 73, 85, 114, 191, 253, 281, 283, 300, 399
Gregory, Herbert E., 10–11, 64
Griffin, P. Bion, 16, 85, 301, 302, 408
grindstones, 191, 200, 287, 293, 421

H1 site. See Puʻu Aliʻi sand dune site
H2 site. See Makalai shelter site
H3 Highway project, 21–22, 255, 387, 391–392, 401–403
H8 site. See Waiahukini rockshelter site
H65 site, 331
H66 site, 331
H110 site, 334
Haʻeleʻele rockshelter site, Kauaʻi, 406
Hāʻena, Kauaʻi, 40, 85, 408–409, 410
Haʻikū, Maui, 164, 193
Hakioawa, Kahoʻolawe, 196, 370, 371, 373
halau, 222, 266, 267

Hālawa dune site (Mo-A1-3), Moloka ʻi, 94, 95, 134–140, 192, 197, 198, 199, 200, 207, 214, 233, 237, 379, 385, 401, 421
Hālawa Gulch, Hawaiʻi, 95, 154, 350
Hālawa Valley, Molokaʻi, 17, 32, 39, 78, 85, 108, 135, 144, 149, 150, 155, 184, 227, 249, 279, 236–290, 313, 375, 378
Hālawa Valley, Oʻahu, 21–22, 96, 193, 255, 401–403
Haleakalā, Maui, 11, 29, 36, 40, 94, 101, 197, 252, 264, 297, 329, 353, 357, 358–359, 361, 362, 363
Halekiʻi Heiau, Maui, 228, 268, 357
Haleleʻa District, Kauaʻi, 18, 38, 112, 144, 147, 149, 174, 406, 407, 408–410
Hale-o-Keawe, Hawaiʻi, 105, 252, 268, 279–280, 335–336, 337
hale o Lono, 249, 250, 266, 295, 367, 390
Halulu Heiau, Lānaʻi, 367, 369, 370
Hāmākua District, Hawaiʻi, 319–321
Hammatt, Hal, 19, 341, 342, 384, 393, 408, 410, 412
hammerstones, 72, 139, 190, 200, 211, 217, 223, 227, 421
Hāna, Maui, 38, 101, 103, 105, 106, 107, 157, 164, 254, 256, 260, 268, 295, 353, 357, 359, 361
Hanalei Valley, Kauaʻi, 147, 149, 406, 410
Hanapēpē Valley, Kauaʻi, 144
Handy, Edward S. C., 8, 25, 64, 144, 164, 165, 168, 169, 222, 325, 332, 355, 356, 361
Haun, Alan, 332, 395
Haunauma Bay site (O3), Oʻahu, 405
Hawaiʻi Biocomplexity Project, 25, 145, 146, 158, 160, 161, 165, 166, 184, 185
Hawaii Register of Historic Places, 20, 51
Hawaiian Archaeological Program, 13–14, 120, 189, 353, 375, 406
Hawaiian Kingdom, 8, 18, 309, 313, 316, 355
Hawaiki, 1
Hāwea Point site, Maui, 233, 356
hazards, environmental, 37, 39–40
Heʻeia, Oʻahu, 152, 376, 392, 393
heiau: chronology of, 260–263; classification of, 49, 255–258; ethnohistoric accounts of, 248–251; dating of, 25, 61–62, 254–255, 260–263; excavation of, 246, 252–254;

functions of, 265–266; *heiau hoʻouluʻai*, 5, 155, 170, 283, 299, 379; mapping of, 9–10, 12, 14; meaning, 246; orientations of, 263–265. See also *luakini*; *marae*
hematite, 39, 130, 189, 204, 384
Hikiau Heiau, Hawaiʻi, 51, 255, 338, 339
Hilina Pali, Hawaiʻi, 325, 327, 328, 347
Hilo District, Hawaiʻi, 109, 319–323
historical archaeology, 306–307, 393, 318
Hōkūkano Heiau, Molokaʻi, 376, color plate 13
Hōkūleʻa, 74, 93
Hōkūliʻa, Hawaiʻi, 340
Hōlualoa, Hawaiʻi, 333, 341–342
hōlua slides, 268, 269–270, 334, 341, 380, 383
Hommon, Robert, 17, 19, 47, 95, 86, 89, 91, 110, 113–114, 156, 178, 181, 283, 285, 339, 340, 371, 414
Hōnaunau, Hawaiʻi, 103, 104, 105, 198, 213, 217, 252, 268, 269, 272, 278, 279, 333, 334, 335–338
honeycreepers. See birds
Honokahua burial site, Maui, 22–23, 180, 276, 277–278, 356
Honokāne Valley, Hawaiʻi, 18, 349
Honokōhau, Hawaiʻi, 344
Honolua, Maui, 356
Honolulu, Oʻahu, 31, 170, 173, 266, 267, 307, 308, 315, 316–317, 386, 403, 404
Hoʻolehua, Molokaʻi, 32
household clusters, 96, 222, 226, 228–229, 232, 237, 248, 285, 287, 292–293, 401. See also *kauhale*
houses. See *kauhale*
Hualālai, Hawaiʻi, 36, 39, 162, 198, 277, 323, 333, 343
hula, 6, 21, 171, 255, 266, 409
hydration-rind dating, 58, 60–61, 301. See also volcanic glass

ʻĪʻī, John Papa, 7, 266
ʻili. See land divisions
ʻIliʻiliʻōpae Heiau, Molokaʻi, 251, 259, 376, color plate 14
images: sea-urchin-spine, 216; stone, 11, 420–422; temple, 4, 105, 170, 214, 247, 250, 274, 280, 302, 337, 350, 352
inland expansion, 181
intensification: agricultural, 26, 40, 86, 102, 112–113, 115, 140, 143, 153–154, 160, 166, 174–175, 184–187, 310, 361, 385, 390; cropping cycle, 162; landesque capital, 143, 157; of production, 97, 102, 114, 172, 312; population and, 112
ʻIolani Palace, 317
irrigation: archaeological study of, 144–145; canals (ʻauwai), 39, 47, 144, 145, 150, 164, 190; Hawaiʻi Island, 95, 102, 154, 348; intensification of, 186–187; Kauaʻi Island, 112, 407, 408–410, 413; Maui Island, 102, 359; Molokaʻi Island, 95, 150, 153–154, 286–287, 291, 295, 378, 379; Oʻahu Island, 95, 151–153, 285, 310, 312, 386, 390, 394, 396, 399, 400; political economy of, 174–175; surplus provided by, 112, 175; systems, 149–152; of taro, 38, 142, 175; zones of, 146. See also agriculture; taro

K3, K4 sites. See Nuʻalolo rockshelter sites
Kaʻahumanu, 267, 271, 306, 309, 314, 342
Kaʻawaloa, Hawaiʻi, 308, 338–339, 340
Kahakahakea, Hawaiʻi, 331–332
Kahaluʻu, Hawaiʻi, 61, 162, 198, 228, 333, 341
Kahaluʻu habitation cave, 198, 341
Kahana Valley, Oʻahu, 95, 394–395, 408
Kahekili, 90, 105, 107, 108, 109, 353, 367
Kahiki, 7, 92, 93, 94, 169, 248, 268, 363, 410
Kahikinui, Maui: basalt artifacts in, 198–199; dryland farming in, 96, 97, 146, 157, 165–166; faunal analysis, 235, 237–238; *heiau*, 59, 61–62, 254–255, 257–264, 265; historic period sites, 314–315; *kauhale* sites, 230–232; Kirch's survey of, 24, 51, 53, 314; petroglyphs, 242, 244–245; population, 177, 178, 183–184; settlement patterns, 16, 295–300, 353–354, 362–363; soils, 38, 165–166 ; trails, 239–240
Kahn, J., 25, 76, 119, 193, 197, 408
Kahoʻolawe Island, 3, 6, 10, 12, 27, 28, 32, 35, 51, 53, 56, 85, 93, 94, 96, 101, 103, 196, 216, 230, 242, 252, 274, 370–373, 413
kāhua, 255, 383, 409
Kāhua o Kāneiʻolouma, Kauaʻi, 412

Kailua, Hawaiʻi, 5, 103, 162, 266, 307, 333, 340, 341, 342–343
Kakahaiʻa Fishpond, Molokaʻi, 291
Kalāhuipuaʻa, Hawaiʻi, 36, 48, 96, 180, 181, 199, 201, 205, 209, 211, 226, 233, 234, 235, 239, 340, 345, 346
Kalaniʻōpuʻu, 7, 90, 104, 105, 107, 109, 110, 187, 330, 331, 339
Kalapana, Hawaiʻi, 325, 327
Kalaupapa, Molokaʻi, 38, 42, 44–45, 97, 146, 157, 166, 236, 255, 264, 278, 313, 374, 380
kalo. See taro
Kaloko, Hawaiʻi, 338, 343
Kaloko Point, Oʻahu, 388
Kaluakapiʻioho Heiau, Molokaʻi, 376, 377
Kaluakoʻi, Molokaʻi, 96, 194, 197, 374, 375–376, 383–385
Kamakahonu, Hawaiʻi, 266, 267, 342, 343
Kamakau, Samuel N., 7, 14, 25, 88, 89, 98, 104, 170, 171, 218, 222, 246, 265, 272
Kamalālāwalu, 90, 106, 261, 341
Kamehameha I, 9, 87, 90, 93, 107, 109, 266, 268, 269, 278, 306, 309, 316, 317, 318, 325, 342, 347, 348, 352, 367, 396, 404
Kamehameha II (Liholiho), 306, 342
Kamehamehanui, 90, 104, 107
Kamōhio Bay rockshelter and shrine, Kahoʻolawe, 10, 216, 371, 373
Kāne, 5, 6, 100, 142, 246, 248, 249, 261, 264, 351, 374
Kāneʻākī Heiau, Oʻahu, 17, 252–253, 254, 279, 282, 283, 285, 289, 399–400
Kāneʻohe, Oʻahu, 21, 30, 32, 152, 213, 276, 390, 391–393
Kapālama Heiau, Hawaiʻi, 352
Kapalilua, Hawaiʻi, 333–334
Kapalua, Maui, 22, 354, 355
Kapana, Molokaʻi, 155, 227, 286, 287, 288, 289, 302
Kapana Heiau, Molokaʻi, 249, 289, color plate 8
kapu, 5–6, 26, 91, 120, 170, 220, 230, 232, 261, 265, 272, 274, 277, 280, 294–295, 299, 306, 316, 325, 333, 341, 342, 352, 368, 373, 397, 400
Kaʻū, Hawaiʻi, 2, 8, 33, 38, 97, 103, 105, 121, 157, 164, 222, 327–333

kauhale, 5, 50, 103, 220–232, 236, 237, 266, 289, 298–299, 314, 327, 333, 364, 400
Kaunolū, Lānaʻi, 366–368, 369, 370
Kaupikiawa rockshelter, Molokaʻi, 42–44, 45, 228, 236, 380
Kaupō, Maui, 30, 96, 97, 102, 103, 104, 107, 146, 157, 165, 183–184, 254, 257, 260–262, 264, 268, 354, 361–362
Kawaihae, Hawaiʻi, 23, 164, 274, 278, 315, 345, 347–348, 351
Kawailoa, 309, 396–397. See also Anahulu Valley
Kawainui Marsh, Oʻahu, 36, 80, 194, 388–389, 390
Kawākiu, Molokaʻi, 21, 205, 206, 383
Kawela, Molokaʻi, 50, 51, 96, 103, 107, 170, 216–217, 225, 229–230, 242, 243, 248, 249, 271, 290–295, 377–378
Kawelu, Kathy, 21, 23, 24, 277, 408
Keaʻau, Hawaiʻi, 327
Keae rockshelter site (Oa-D6-52), Oʻahu, 226
Kealakekua, Hawaiʻi, 7, 51, 52, 103, 110, 142, 162, 177, 280, 308, 319, 330, 334, 338–339
Keauhou, Hawaiʻi, 269, 333, 341
Kēʻē Beach Site, Kauaʻi, 408–409. See also Haʻena
Keʻekū Heiau, Hawaiʻi, 341
Kekahuna, Henry, 14, 23, 325, 324, 412
Kelly, Marion, 21, 25, 272, 309, 336, 348
Keōkea, Maui, 358
Keoneloa petroglyph site, Kauaʻi, 242
Keōpū burial site, Hawaiʻi, 274, 276–277, 279
Keōua, 40, 104, 327, 339, 347
Kīhei, Maui, 354, 363–364
Kīholo, Hawaiʻi, 271, 345, 347
Kikuchi, William K., 16, 172, 173, 197, 412, 413
Kīlauea, Hawaiʻi, 29, 40, 213, 323, 327, 329
King, Lt. James, 2, 109, 141, 178, 370
Kīpapa, Maui, 232, 235, 258, 261, 296–297, 299, 314, 262
Kirch, Patrick V.: on agricultural intensification, 159; Anahulu Valley project, 18, 25, 144, 151, 175, 235, 279, 308–312, 387, 396; Bellows dune site excavation, 132–134; coral dating, 61, 254–255, 260, 262–263; cultural sequence for Hawaiian Islands, 86–87; explanation of cultural change, 110, 114–115; Hālawa dune site excavation,

135–140, 207, 237; Hālawa Valley project, 17, 85, 197, 287–290, 375, 379; Hāwea Point, Maui, site, 356; *heiau* study, 257–260, 261–265; Kahikinui, Maui, project, 16, 24, 165, 198, 237–238, 244–245, 300, 314–315, 354, 362; Kalāhuipuaʻa project, 274, 345–346; Kaupō, Maui, survey, 361–362; Kawela, Molokaʻi survey, 20, 350, 217, 223, 229–230, 271, 290–295, 377–378; Kukuipahu, Hawaiʻi, site, 351; Lonoikamakahiki site, 341; on marine exploitation, 233; Palauea site, Maui, 226, 364; *pānānā* site, 363; phylogenetic model of, 72; on population, 182–184, 187; on valley agricultural systems, 155

Kīwalaʻō, 90

koʻa. See fishing shrines

Koaiʻe, Hawaiʻi, 16, 96, 301–302. *See also* Lapakahi

Kohala District, Hawaiʻi, 25, 38, 53, 93, 95, 97, 104, 154, 157, 178, 216, 223, 233, 238, 241, 304, 309, 344–352

Kohala Field System, 59, 86, 97, 103, 144, 158–162, 166–167, 184, 185, 263, 301. *See also* agriculture

Kolb, Michael, 253–254, 256, 260–261, 262, 268, 357, 358, 359, 361, 362

Kōloa, Kauaʻi, 412–413

Kona District, Hawaiʻi, 3, 30, 33, 38, 97, 102, 104, 107, 157, 182–183, 187, 198, 233, 259, 277, 330, 333–334

Kona District, Kauaʻi, 406, 412–413

Kona District, Molokaʻi, 109, 279, 295, 375, 376–378

Kona District, Oʻahu, 92, 109, 386, 403–405

Kona Field System, Hawaiʻi, 20, 162–164, 166, 169, 339–340. *See also* agriculture

kōnane, 47, 230, 245. *See also papamū*

konohiki, 3, 4, 5, 149, 150, 151, 170, 173, 217, 228, 229, 230, 287, 293, 294, 296, 302, 312, 400

Kū, 5, 6, 9, 93, 100, 102, 112, 218, 249, 253, 264, 266, 268, 289, 400

Kualoa, Oʻahu, 213, 393–394

Kūkāʻilimoku, 347

Kūkaniloko Heiau, 98, 99, 108, 246, 268, 387, 398

Kūkaʻōʻō Heiau, Oʻahu, 404

kukui, 59, 79, 91, 143, 169, 278, 356, 358, 374, 392, 397

Kukuiokāne Heiau, Oʻahu, 391–392, 402

Kukuipahu Heiau, Hawaiʻi, 47, 351, color plate 10

Kula, Maui, 32, 38, 101, 102, 187, 256, 357, 358

Kuliʻouʻou rockshelter (site O1), Oʻahu, 12–13, 34, 50, 59, 116–120, 226, 234, 387, 405

Laʻa-mai-Kahiki, 93, 268, 363

Ladd, Ed, 17, 249, 252, 279, 283, 289, 337

Ladefoged, Thegn, 25, 146, 157, 159, 160, 161, 164, 167, 169, 184, 321, 325, 327, 418

Lahaina, Maui, 107, 286, 307, 318, 354, 355

Lālāmilo, Hawaiʻi, 52, 164, 345, 348

lamps, stone, 4, 209, 227

Lānaʻi Island, 3, 6, 11, 28, 101, 146, 242, 248, 252, 271, 365–370

land divisions, 3, 98, 249. *See also ahupuaʻa*

landsnails, 20, 34, 35, 36, 41, 42, 46, 57, 81, 140, 235

land tenure, 174, 177, 390. *See also* Māhele

Lapakahi, Hawaiʻi, 16, 17, 25, 52, 85, 96, 144, 158–159, 223, 241, 300–305, 349

Lapita Cultural Complex, 65, 68–71, 73, 75

Late Voyaging Period, 87, 92–95, 97, 100, 154, 157, 169, 268, 277, 286, 301, 325, 330, 332, 338, 348, 349, 356, 361, 364, 372, 377, 379, 380, 390, 391, 395, 398, 410, 414

lei niho palaoa, 5, 97, 132, 134, 214, 215, 277, 278, 315, 343, 408. *See also* ornaments

LiDAR, 52–53, 161, 321, 339, 342, 393

Līloa, 7, 90, 100, 218, 268, 280, 342

Lincoln, Noa, 162, 164, 169, 376

linguistics, 6, 8, 84, 91, 114

lithic assemblages, 198, 219, 232, 293, 299, 321, 341, 359, 368, 371, 400. *See also* adzes; volcanic glass

Loʻaloʻa Heiau, Maui, 107, 251, 254, 259, 268, 362

loʻi. See irrigation

loko. See fishponds

Lokoea fishpond, Oʻahu, 173

Lono, 5, 6, 102, 112, 142, 170, 248, 249, 253, 263, 264, 302, 338, 359, 362, 399. *See also hale o Lono*

Lono-a-Piʻilani, 101, 102
Lonoikamakahiki, 90, 104, 228, 341
luakini temples, 6, 49, 93, 99, 103, 170, 228, 246, 247, 249–250, 253, 254, 257, 266, 283, 321, 325, 347, 351, 357, 358, 362, 367, 376, 379, 389, 400, 402. See also *heiau*
Lualualei, Oʻahu, 281, 386, 399, 400
Lua Nunu o Kamakalepo Refuge Cave (site H12), 327
Luluku, Oʻahu, 95, 152–153, 391
Lumahaʻi Valley, Kauaʻi, 95, 406
Lundblad, Steve, 25, 125, 198, 213, 322

Māhele, 18, 151, 286–287, 291–292, 296, 306, 309–313, 316, 318, 378–379, 410
Māʻilikūkahi, 90, 98 108, 153, 398
makaʻāinana, 5–6, 88, 91, 98, 101, 112, 114, 220, 222, 228, 277, 308, 310, 312, 388
Mākaha Valley, Oʻahu, 17, 19, 39, 85, 95, 97, 144, 150, 155–156, 162, 223–225, 249, 252–254, 279, 281–286, 289, 302, 313, 386–387, 398–400
Makahiki, 6, 99, 102, 111, 120, 142, 175, 217–218, 255, 262, 264–267, 283, 295, 380, 383, 401, 405, 423
Makakupaʻa Iki, Molokaʻi, 290–295, 377
Makalai shelter site (H2), Hawaiʻi, 125, 206, 329
Makaniʻolu rockshelter site (O2), Oʻahu, 214, 215, 405
Makaʻōpio Heiau, Hawaiʻi, 343, 344
Makapuʻu, Oʻahu, 388
Makauwahi Cave, Kauaʻi, 35, 42, 44, 80, 90, 407, 412
Mākena, Maui, 354, 363–364
Malo, David, 7, 41, 88, 104, 145, 151, 166, 187, 216–218, 222, 230, 265, 269
mana, 5, 73, 91, 205, 218, 220, 423
Mana Heiau, Molokaʻi, 108, 289, 379
Mānalo Gulch, Molokaʻi, 384
Mānoa, Oʻahu, 23–25, 38, 366, 386, 397, 404
Manukā, Hawaiʻi, 226, 242, 327, 332–333
marae, 93, 247, 252, 419–421
Marquesas Islands, 1, 11, 14, 27, 38, 74–78, 81–82, 84, 113, 123, 133, 169, 189, 192–193, 204, 208–209, 247, 319

Mauna Kea, Hawaiʻi, 1, 29, 32, 36, 211, 248, 255, 319, 321–322, 329, 330, 348, 351, 353, 367, 401
Mauna Kea adze quarry site, 18, 39, 94, 96, 125, 190, 192, 194–196, 198
Mauna Loa, Hawaiʻi, 1, 29, 32, 36, 162, 194, 197, 213, 319, 322, 327–328, 333, 335, 353
Maunawila Heiau, Oʻahu, 255, 395
Maunawili, Oʻahu, 80, 95, 152–153, 389–390
McAllister, J. Gilbert, 10, 12, 144, 255, 274, 370–371, 373, 387–388, 391, 393, 404
McCoy, Mark D., 65, 87, 95, 154, 163–164, 212, 236, 263, 320, 333, 340, 349, 354, 365, 370, 375, 380–381, 387, 407
McCoy, Patrick C., 18, 20, 61, 195–196, 211, 248, 318, 321–322, 373
McElroy, Windy, 95, 129, 154, 200, 204, 208–209, 213, 276, 376, 379
"Menehune Ditch" site, Kauaʻi. See Kīkīaola.
men's eating house. See *mua*
Menzies, Archibald, 158
methods, archaeological, 51–57
migrations. See origins; voyaging
milkfish, 4, 173, 233
Mills, Peter, 23, 25, 61, 129, 139, 198, 212, 240, 318, 320–322, 341, 413
mirrors, stone, 129, 213, 408
Moanalua Valley, Oʻahu, 401, 404
Moʻikea, 7, 39, 92–94, 169, 268, 410
Mōkapu, Oʻahu, 12, 23, 180, 268, 276, 380, 386, 392
Mokumanamana Island, 11, 26–28, 62, 139, 247, 252, 329, 351, 367, 401, 414, 415–423
mollusks, 36–37, 48, 56, 65, 72, 91, 97, 134–136, 140, 209, 230, 236–238, 295, 297, 334, 348, 350, 401, 410, 415. See also landsnails; ʻopihi
moku. See land divisions
Moʻokini Heiau, Hawaiʻi, 93, 248, 259, 325, 351, 352
Moʻomomi, Molokaʻi, 194, 276
Moʻomomi rockshelter site (Mo. 1), Molokaʻi, 383
mua, 5, 6, 205, 217, 222, 226–229, 248, 263, 267, 283, 285, 289, 293–294, 299, 302, 341, 350, 364, 380, 384, 397, 399–400, 402
mullet, 4, 173, 233, 412. See also fishponds
Mulrooney, Mara, 25, 26, 124

NAGPRA, 22–23, 122, 130, 132, 272, 274, 276
Nā Imu Kalua ʻUa Heiau, Molokaʻi, 260
Nakaʻohu, Maui, 299–300
Nā Pali, Kauaʻi, 127–129, 198
Nāpoʻopoʻo, Hawaiʻi, 338
Near Oceania, 65–71
Necker Island. *See* Mokumanamana Island
nēnē, 35, 56, 233, 371. *See also* birds
New Guinea, 65–66
Newman, T. Stell, 16, 52, 85, 144, 162, 303
New Zealand (Aotearoa), 2, 25, 59, 63, 65, 75, 77, 238, 270
Nihoa Island, 11, 26, 27, 28, 62, 139, 236, 252, 381, 415–423
Niʻihau Island, 27–28, 32, 166, 194, 248–249, 366, 406–407, 409, 411, 413–415
Nuʻalolo ʻĀina, Kauaʻi, 127, 148, 408
Nuʻalolo rockshelter sites, 14–15, 26, 34, 94, 126–130, 147–148, 198, 200, 204, 208–209, 213, 216, 226, 236, 309, 407–408
Nuʻu, Maui, 194, 197, 217, 219, 228, 232, 263, 361
Nuʻuanu Valley, Oʻahu, 242, 266, 270, 306, 316, 386, 403–404

O18 site. *See* Bellows sand dune site
Oalalauo Heiau, Hawaiʻi, 40
octopus lures, 39, 189, 201, 203–205, 321, 384, 421
ʻōhiʻa, 36, 100, 143, 235, 319, 324
olonā, 155, 169–170, 209, 281, 292
Olowalu, Maui, 242, 355
ʻopihi, 36, 135, 140, 230, 236, 237. *See also* mollusks
oral traditions, 7, 31, 39, 71, 86, 88–89, 92, 98, 104, 115, 173–174, 248, 260, 295, 320, 323, 336, 351–352, 359, 362, 369, 380, 387, 404, 410, 422
origins: Hawaiian, 8, 78–84; Polynesian, 10, 63–84
ornaments, 4–5, 66, 69, 81–82, 103, 124, 132, 139, 189, 213–217, 228, 277, 331, 411–412

Pāʻao, 7, 9, 93, 248, 259, 325–326, 351–352
Palauea, Maui, 200, 226, 364
Pālehua, Oʻahu, 248, 401
pānānā, 363, color plate 12

Pandanus, 1, 4, 34, 72, 142, 209, 219, 234, 274
Papa Heiau, Molokaʻi, 289
papamū, 47, 49, 245
Pearl Harbor, Oʻahu, 21, 172, 386–387, 403
Pearson, Richard J., 16, 78, 130–132, 144, 189, 236, 300, 353, 380
Pele, 29, 40, 92, 323–324
Pelekunu Valley, Molokaʻi, 153, 170, 292, 374
pendants. *See* ornaments
petroglyphs, 10, 49, 63, 171, 195, 242–245, 279, 281, 295, 300, 326–327, 343–345, 351, 355, 358, 367, 369–371, 378, 380, 403
Phelps, Southwick, 375
physical anthropology, 11, 179–180, 273, 276
picks, 130, 209–210, 331
pictographs, 242, 244. *See also* petroglyphs
Pietrusewsky, Michael, 84, 180, 189
pigs: agriculture and, 95, 140, 157, 171, 233, 237, 379; artifacts, use as, 97, 132, 171, 204, 213, 378; burials, 276, 277, 356, 394; food, use as, 4, 66, 72, 140, 170, 229, 230, 237, 238, 293, 297, 358, 403, 408; husbandry of, 103, 134, 170–171; introduction of, 33, 42; surplus and, 175; temple offerings, 6, 170–171, 250; tribute, 9. *See also* domestic animals
Piʻilanihale Heiau, Maui, 101, 106, 228, 251, 259–260, 268, 359–360, 362
Pinao Bay, Hawaiʻi, 329
plant remains, 33, 36, 41–42, 44, 54, 57, 75–76, 78, 80, 146, 159, 169, 185, 211, 219, 228, 232–235, 260, 340, 372, 392, 397, 422
Pōhakuloa, Hawaiʻi, 195, 322–323
pōhaku o Kāne, 49, 246, 248–249, 261
Pōhue Bay, Hawaiʻi, 331–332
poi pounders, 208, 223, 228,
political economy, 111–113, 168, 175, 308, 310
pollen analysis, 20, 34, 41–43, 46, 57, 76, 78, 80–81, 228, 364, 377
Pololū Valley, Hawaiʻi, 18, 39, 94, 155, 194, 245, 304, 320–321, 349, 350, 352
Polynesian: diaspora, 73–78; homeland, 71–73
pondfields. *See* irrigation
Pōpōʻiwi Heiau, Maui, 107, 254, 259, 268, 362
population, 178–187; of Nihoa Island, 418
porpoise-tooth pendants, 91, 123, 132, 134, 408

pottery: Lapita, 68; Polynesian Plain Ware, 72, 421
pounders. *See poi* pounders
Pritchardia palms, 34, 36, 42, 80, 338, 377, 415, 418
Proto-Polynesian language, 67. *See also* linguistics
Puakō, Hawaiʻi, 106, 242–245
Puhina o Lono, Hawaiʻi, 339
Pukui, Mary Kawena, 8, 14, 25, 88, 222, 332
Puna District, Hawaiʻi, 40, 93, 105, 168, 248, 259, 323–333
Puʻu Aliʻi sand dune site (H1), Hawaiʻi, 120–124, 205–206, 329
puʻuhonua, 108, 268, 270–272, 295, 335–337, 367
Puʻukoholā Heiau, Hawaʻi, 164, 251, 259, 274, 315, 347–348, 351–352
Puʻuloa Petroglyph Site, Hawaiʻi, 242, 325–326
Puʻu Mōiwi, Kahoʻolawe, 194, 196, 372–373

quarries, 194–197. *See also* Mauna Kea adze quarry site

radiocarbon dating. *See* dating
rainfall, 4, 30–31, 37–38, 40, 135, 146, 156–158, 161–162, 166–167, 169, 183, 237, 282–283, 290–291, 295, 297, 301–302, 304, 332, 348, 357, 361, 365, 386, 406, 415, 419
rats, 4, 33–34, 41–42, 76, 78, 80–81, 84, 91, 127, 134, 140, 204, 233, 236, 237–238, 401, 412, 416
Reeve, Roland, 211, 274, 317
refuge caves, 271, 327, 340, 347
relief carving, 351, 404
religion, 6, 72, 93, 246–280, 342, 423
Remote Oceania, 64–78
residential features, 220–232. *See also* household clusters; *kauhale*
Riley, Thomas, 17, 144, 153, 289
ring pounders, 208–209. *See also poi* pounders
rockshelters: burial in, 274; domestic use of, 96, 97, 169, 195, 197, 205, 225, 226, 235, 308, 321, 332, 358, 380; excavation of, 14, 54, 235, 310, 330, 331, 383, 387, 396, 403, 405; on Nihoa Island, 417; preservation in, 57. *See also* Kuliʻouʻou rockshelter site; Nuʻalolo rockshelter site; Waiahukini rockshelter site
Rosendahl, Paul, 16–17, 19, 22, 144, 159, 223, 271, 287, 302, 315, 317, 333, 345, 347, 392
royal centers, 5, 26, 47, 89, 103, 217, 228, 266–269, 333, 334, 410
Ruggles, Clive, 254, 257, 264–265, 299, 362, 363, 376
Russians, in Hawaiʻi, 317–318, 342, 413

sacrifice, human, 6, 9, 88, 93, 246, 248–249, 268, 279, 289, 400
Sahlins, Marshall, 18, 25, 110–112, 174–175, 217, 308–310, 396, 410
salt pans, 47
Samoa, 64, 69–77, 111, 392
sandalwood trade, 35, 306, 308, 310, 312, 327
Schilt, A., 25, 162, 343
scrapers, 4, 68, 72, 95, 190, 209–210, 227
sea level, change, 31, 381, 386
sea urchins, 4, 37, 59, 69–72, 82, 91, 95, 120, 122, 124, 133, 139, 189, 199–200, 205, 216, 235–236
seriation, 12–13, 58–59, 122, 125, 208–209. *See also* dating
settlement: of Hawaiʻi, 81–84; of Oceania, 63–81
settlement patterns, 15–18, 20, 24, 26, 31, 50, 52–54, 85–86, 98, 103, 144, 246, 248, 281–283, 286–287, 290–291, 296, 302, 305, 310, 313, 323, 350, 353, 355, 362, 375, 378–379, 399, 424
shark hooks, 201–202, 205, 345–346
shark-tooth knife, 364, 405
shelters. *See* C-shaped shelters
shifting cultivation, 42, 72, 86, 95, 97, 113, 156, 159–160, 166, 169, 187, 235, 310, 349
shrines: agricultural, 157, 257, 299; fishing, 216, 248–249, 257, 297, 302, 401; in Haleakalā Crater, 252; household, 5, 216, 248, 295, 402; on Kahoʻolawe Island, 343; on Lehua Island, 414; on Mauna Kea, 195–196, 248, 255, 321–322; on Mokumanamana Island, 419; on Nihoa Island, 417; at Pālehua, Oʻahu, 401; uprights on, 196. *See also* fishing shrines; *heiau*

sinkers, 39, 68, 82, 128, 130, 139, 189, 201, 203–204, 277, 321, 384, 421
Sinoto, Yoshihiko H., 13–14, 17, 20, 58, 74, 76, 81, 85, 94, 117–119, 122–125, 189, 191, 194, 196, 201, 204–209, 234, 329–330, 373, 412
sites, classification of, 47–51, 255–256
skeletal remains, 23, 84, 122, 179–181, 187, 273–274, 277–278, 345, 371
slingstones, 68, 215, 270–271, 358
Snow, C. E., 180–181
social organization, 17, 72, 86, 216, 313, 399, 424
Society for Hawaiian Archaeology 21, 23
Society Islands, 1, 11, 14, 16, 21, 23, 26, 38, 74–76, 81–82, 84, 93–94, 111, 113, 169, 189, 192, 204, 247, 421
sociopolitical change, 86–87, 89, 98, 100, 114, 166, 174–176, 182, 187, 301, 353
Soehren, Lloyd J., 14–15, 17, 52, 127–128, 130, 162, 189, 201, 331, 334, 353, 361, 407
soils, 25, 31, 37–38, 46, 120, 135, 144, 146, 149, 155, 161–162, 166, 169, 183, 237, 290, 297, 348, 380, 383, 391
Solomon Islands, 65, 84
South America, 77–78, 97, 142, 157
Southeast Asia, 23, 66, 71
South Point, Hawai'i, 13–14, 58, 85, 94, 120, 125, 180, 192, 201, 203–208, 234, 319, 327, 330
Spriggs, Matthew J. T., 75, 78, 144, 151, 175
stirrup pounders, 208–209. See also *poi* pounders
Stokes, John F. G., 9–10, 25, 89, 172, 251–252, 255, 263, 289, 321, 325, 336–337, 339, 341, 351–352, 371, 373, 375, 377, 380, 382, 387, 413
stone structures, 11, 16, 46–52, 58, 223, 226–227, 237, 330, 378, 383, 394
stylistic change, in artifacts, 188. See also seriation
sugarcane, 35, 142, 143, 155, 157, 186
Summers, Catherine C., 14, 25, 172, 190, 194, 209, 375, 382, 387
surplus, 111–112, 114, 167–169, 171, 174–176, 216–217, 267, 310, 350, 385, 399, 410
sweet potato: chiefs and, 101–102; carbonized remains of, 57, 97, 159, 165, 297, 349 371; crop, 4, 97, 142, 146, 155, 157, 169, 184, 238, 297, 314, 380, 383; dating of, 77, 97, 349; dryland field systems and, 38, 97, 102, 142, 157, 164, 166; Lono and, 142, 170, 264; origins of, 77, 142, 157, 349; pigs and, 157, 170–171, 175; Polynesian name for, 77; rainfall and, 31, 37, 38, 166, 361, 365; storage of, 225; varieties of, 142
Swift, Jillian, 25, 135, 287, 376

Tahiti. *See* Society Islands
Tanager Expedition, 417, 419, 421
taro: chiefs and, 102; colluvial slope cultivation, 155; crop, 4, 5, 37, 66, 67, 72, 142; dryland, 32, 46, 144, 268, 285, 375; intensification, 187; irrigated, 17, 18, 32, 33, 38, 87, 92, 100, 141–142, 144, 145, 147–154, 174, 282, 283, 286–287, 291, 310, 349, 353, 355, 356, 359, 379, 386, 392, 394, 399, 403, 406, 410, 413; Kāne and, 142, 264; leaves, use of, 72; *poi*, 208, 230; population and, 184; raised-bed cultivation of, 376; surplus potential, 174–175; varieties, 142. *See also* agriculture; irrigation
tattooing, 4, 68, 214, 215, 405, 411
temples. *See heiau*
Te Rangi Hiroa, 12, 190, 250, 269, 274
terraces, agricultural, 223, 358, 390–391, 401, 418, 421
^{230}Th dating, 25–26, 58, 61, 69, 196–197, 254, 260–263, 322, 362, 383, 398, 422, 423
Thrum, Thomas G., 10, 251–252, 387, 389, 406, 411–412
Tomonari-Tuggle, Myra, 144, 164, 325, 328, 361, 408, 412
Tonga, 11–12, 29, 64, 69, 71, 73, 75, 111, 113
tools. *See* abraders; adzes; chisels; drills; hammerstones; scrapers
trails, 16, 40, 47, 49, 68, 103, 157–161, 165, 239–242, 245, 281, 297, 302–303, 314, 323, 333, 334, 341, 378–379, 387
tribute, 3, 5, 6, 98–100, 102, 111, 175, 216–217, 229, 262, 364, 380
tsunami, 39–40, 135–136, 321, 335, 409
Tuamotu Islands, 11, 64, 76, 94, 137, 247, 421
Tuggle, H. David, 16–17, 78, 85, 132, 144, 301–302, 325, 349, 378, 400

typology, 18, 189, 207, 248, 369. *See also* artifacts; classification

'Uko'a Fishpond, O'ahu, 80, 173, 396
'ulumaika, 94–95, 139, 215, 223, 228, 266, 383, 394
'Umi a Līloa ('Umi), 88, 90, 100–102, 104, 115, 217–218, 268, 337, 361, 364
United States Exploring Expedition. *See* Wilkes Expedition
University of Hawai'i, 12, 16–17, 23–25, 83, 117, 124, 128, 130, 132, 144–145, 158, 197–198, 276, 300, 341, 349, 364, 366, 395, 397, 401, 424
Uwēkahuna Heiau, Hawai'i, 40

Vacca, Kirsten, 219, 228, 232
Valeri, Valerio, 246, 248, 265
Vancouver, George, 2, 370, 398
Vitousek, Peter, 25, 155, 161, 162
volcanic eruptions. *See* hazards
volcanic glass, 25, 39, 58, 60–61, 125, 139, 182, 188, 190, 211–213, 224, 227, 322, 328, 330–331, 348, 366, 371, 389; hydration-rind dating of, 58, 60–61, 301
voyaging, 1, 4, 71, 74, 76–78, 87–89, 91–94, 141, 169, 177, 351, 363, 415, 422

Waha'ula Heiau, Hawai'i, 93, 248, 259, 325–326
wahi kupuna, 24, 26, 426,
Waiahukini, Hawai'i, 14
Waiahukini rockshelter site (H8), Hawai'i, 14, 94, 122, 124–125, 206, 329, 330
Waialua, O'ahu, 92, 150, 170, 173, 184, 259, 309–310, 312, 386, 396–397
Wai'ānapanapa, Maui, 353
Waiehu, Maui, 90
Waihe'e, Maui, 90, 152, 353, 356
Waikīkī, O'ahu, 5, 98, 103, 106, 168, 268, 278, 403
Waikōloa, Hawai'i, 211, 224, 344
Waikolu Valley, Moloka'i, 95, 153–154, 374, 378–379, 380
Wailau-Ninole, Hawai'i, 327

Wailau Valley, Moloka'i, 95, 153–154, 287, 374, 376, 379
Waimānalo, O'ahu, 78–79, 120, 130, 132, 134, 170, 200, 213, 388
Waimea, Hawai'i, 20, 32, 163–164, 166, 190, 211–212, 274, 308, 348, 397
Waimea, Kaua'i, 141, 157, 194, 220–221, 247, 317, 398, 406, 413
Waimea-Kawaihae road corridor, 20, 190, 211–212, 274
Waimea Valley, O'ahu, 274
Wai'ōhinu, Hawai'i, 327
Waipi'o Valley, Hawai'i, 5, 39, 92, 100, 102, 147, 228, 268, 280, 319–321
Walker, Winslow, 257, 296, 315, 353, 355, 358–359
warfare, 4, 31, 86–87, 98–99, 105, 112, 114, 215–216, 270–272, 369
Weisler, Marshall, 20, 50, 61, 76, 190, 197, 205, 211–212, 217, 229, 236, 276, 377–387, 384–385, 398
Wilkes Expedition, 323–324, 371
women: agriculture and, 4, 230; burials, 132, 181, 276, 278; contributions to archaeology, 25; crafts, 217, 219, 230; dogs and, 171; eating taboos, 230, 232; health of, 180; *kapu* system and, 6, 179, 222, 230, 232, 352; menstrual house, 293; rulers, 104, 108; women's temple, 22
wooden artifacts, 4, 5, 9, 72, 94, 103, 107, 128, 141, 172, 190, 192–193, 201–204, 209, 216, 217, 220–221, 230, 247, 250, 267, 274, 316, 323, 328, 343, 345–346, 350, 364, 393, 405

X-ray fluorescence (XRF), 25–26, 125, 129, 198, 212, 341, 359

yams, 38, 42, 72–73, 141–143, 146, 155–157, 361, 386, 399, 412, 419
Yen, Douglas, 20, 77, 144, 171, 234, 285, 417–418
Young, John, 315–316, 348

zooarchaeology, 233–239